A PRACTICAL GUIDE TO ADVANCED NETWORKING

JEFFREY S. BEASLEY AND PIYASAT NILKAEW

Pearson
800 East 96th Street
Indianapolis, Indiana 46240 USA

A PRACTICAL GUIDE TO ADVANCED NETWORKING

Copyright © 2013 by Pearson Education, Inc.

ISBN-13: 978-0-7897-4904-8
ISBN-10: 0-7897-4904-1

The Library of Congress Cataloging-in-Publication Data is on file.

Printed in the United States of America

First Printing: November 2012

Trademarks

Warning and Disclaimer

Bulk Sales

Pearson IT Certification offers excellent discounts on this book when ordered in quantity for bulk purchases or special sales. For more information, please contact

> **U.S. Corporate and Government Sales**
> **1-800-382-3419**
> corpsales@pearsontechgroup.com

For sales outside of the U.S., please contact

> **International Sales**
> international@pearsoned.com

ASSOCIATE PUBLISHER
Dave Dusthimer

EXECUTIVE EDITOR
Brett Bartow

SENIOR DEVELOPMENT EDITOR
Christopher Cleveland

MANAGING EDITOR
Sandra Schroeder

PROJECT EDITOR
Mandie Frank

COPY EDITOR
Sheri Cain

INDEXER
Ken Johnson

PROOFREADERS
Leslie Joseph
Dan Knott

TECHNICAL EDITORS
Iantha Finley Malbon
Wayne Randall

PUBLISHING COORDINATOR
Vanessa Evans

INTERIOR DESIGNER
Gary Adair

COVER DESIGNER
Chuti Prasertsith

COMPOSITOR
Bronkella Publishing

CONTENTS AT A GLANCE

TABLE OF CONTENTS

ABOUT THE AUTHORS

Jeffrey S. Beasley is with the Department of Engineering Technology and Surveying Engineering at New Mexico State University. He has been teaching with the department since 1988 and is the co-author of *Modern Electronic Communication and Electronic Devices and Circuits*, and the author of *Networking*.

Piyasat Nilkaew is a network engineer with 15 years of experience in network management and consulting, and has extensive expertise in deploying and integrating multiprotocol and multivendor data, voice, and video network solutions on limited budgets.

DEDICATIONS

This book is dedicated to my family, Kim, Damon, and Dana. —Jeff Beasley

This book is dedicated to Jeff Harris and Norma Grijalva. Not only have you given me my networking career, but you are also my mentors. You inspire me to think outside the box and motivate me to continue improving my skills. Thank you for giving me the opportunity of a lifetime. I am very grateful. —Piyasat Nilkaew

ACKNOWLEDGMENTS

I am grateful to the many people who have helped with this text. My sincere thanks go to the following technical consultants:

- Danny Bosch and Matthew Peralta for sharing their expertise with optical networks and unshielded twisted-pair cabling, and Don Yates for his help with the initial Net-Challenge Software.
- Abel Sanchez, for his review of the Linux Networking chapter.

I also want to thank my many past and present students for their help with this book:

- David Potts, Jonathan Trejo, and Nate Murillo for their work on the Net-Challenge Software. Josiah Jones, Raul Marquez Jr., Brandon Wise, and Chris Lascano for their help with the Wireshark material. Also, thanks to Wayne Randall and Iantha Finley Malbon for the chapter reviews.

Your efforts are greatly appreciated.

I appreciate the excellent feedback of the following reviewers: Phillip Davis, DelMar College, TX; Thomas D. Edwards, Carteret Community College, NC; William Hessmiller, Editors & Training Associates; Bill Liu, DeVry University, CA; and Timothy Staley, DeVry University, TX.

My thanks to the people at Pearson for making this project possible: Dave Dusthimer, for providing me with the opportunity to work on this book, and Vanessa Evans, for helping make this process enjoyable. Thanks to Brett Bartow, Christopher Cleveland, and all the people at Pearson, and to the many technical editors for their help with editing the manuscript.

Special thanks to our families for their continued support and patience.

—Jeffrey S. Beasley and Piyasat Nilkaew

ABOUT THE TECHNICAL REVIEWERS

Wayne Randall started working in the Information Technology field in 1994 at Franklin Pierce College (now Franklin Pierce University) in Rindge, NH, before becoming a Microsoft Certified Trainer and a consultant at Enterprise Training and Consulting in Nashua, NH.

Wayne acquired his first certification in Windows NT 3.51 in 1994, became an MCSE in NT 4.0 in 1996, was a Certified Enterasys Network Switching Engineer in 2000, and then worked as a networking and systems consultant from 2001 to 2006 before becoming a director of IT for a privately held company. Wayne currently works for Bodycote, PLC, as a network engineer/solutions architect. Bodycote has 170 locations across 27 countries with 43 locations in North America. Wayne has taught for Lincoln Education since 2001 and developed curricula for it since 2011. Mr. Randall holds a BA in American Studies from Franklin Pierce University.

Iantha Finley Malbon's teaching career has spanned 20 years from middle school to collegiate settings and is currently a CIS professor at Virginia Union University. She is also an adjunct professor at ECPI University, having previously served as CIS Department Chair, teaching Cisco routing, networking, and Information Technology courses. She implemented the Cisco Academy for Hanover Schools and was the CCAI for the Academy. She earned her master's degree in Information Systems from Virginia Commonwealth University and bachelor's degree in Technology Education from Virginia Tech. She holds numerous certifications including CCNA, Network+, A+, and Fiber Optic Technician.

WE WANT TO HEAR FROM YOU!

As the reader of this book, you are our most important critic and commentator. We value your opinion and want to know what we're doing right, what we could do better, what areas you'd like to see us publish in, and any other words of wisdom you're willing to pass our way.

As the associate publisher for Pearson IT Certification, I welcome your comments. You can email or write me directly to let me know what you did or didn't like about this book—as well as what we can do to make our books better.

Please note that I cannot help you with technical problems related to the topic of this book. We do have a User Services group, however, where I will forward specific technical questions related to the book.

When you write, please be sure to include this book's title and author as well as your name, email address, and phone number. I will carefully review your comments and share them with the author and editors who worked on the book.

Email: feedback@pearsonitcertification.com

Mail: Dave Dusthimer
        Associate Publisher
        Pearson IT Certification
        800 East 96th Street
        Indianapolis, IN 46240 USA

READER SERVICES

Visit our website and register this book at www.pearsonitcertification.com/register for convenient access to any updates, downloads, or errata that might be available for this book.

INTRODUCTION

This book looks at advanced computer networking. It first guides readers through network infrastructure design. The readers are then introduced to configuring static, RIPv2, OSPF, ISIS, EIGRP routing protocols, techniques for configuring Juniper router, managing the network infrastructure, analyzing network data traffic using Wireshark, network security, IPv6, Linux networking, Internet routing, and Voice over IP. After covering the entire text, readers will have gained a solid knowledge base in advanced computer networks.

In my years of teaching, I have observed that technology students prefer to learn "how to swim" after they have gotten wet and taken in a little water. Then, they are ready for more challenges. Show the students the technology, how it is used, and why, and they will take the applications of the technology to the next level. Allowing them to experiment with the technology helps them to develop a greater understanding. This book does just that.

ORGANIZATION OF THE TEXT

This textbook is adapted from the second edition of *Networking*. This third volume has been revised and reorganized around the needs of advanced networking students. This book assumes that the students have been introduced to the basics of computer networking. Throughout the text, the students are introduced to more advanced computer networking concepts. This involves network infrastructure design, advanced router configuration, network security, analyzing data traffic, Internet routing, and Voice over IP.

Key Pedagogical Features

- Chapter Outline, Key Terms, and Introduction at the beginning of each chapter clearly outline specific goals for the reader. An example of these features is shown in Figure P-1.

Chapter Outline

Chapter Objectives

Introduction: Chapter openers
clearly outline specific goals

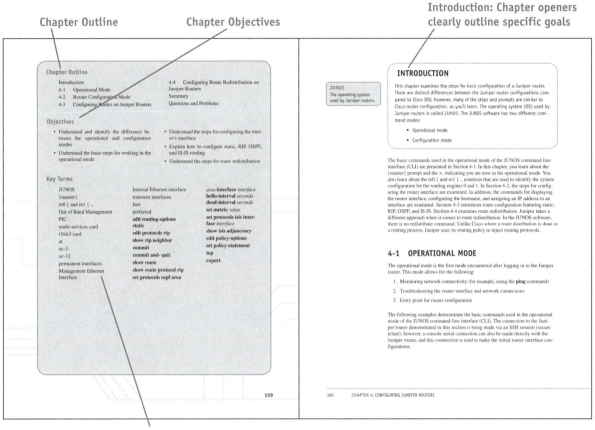

Key Terms for this Chapter

FIGURE P-1

- Net-Challenge Software provides a simulated, hands-on experience in configuring routers and switches. Exercises provided in the text (see Figure P-2) and on the CD challenge readers to undertake certain router/network configuration tasks. The challenges check the students' ability to enter basic networking commands and set up router function, such as configuring the interface (Ethernet and Serial) and routing protocols (that is, static, RIPv2, OSPF, ISIS, EIGRP, BGP, and VLANs). The software has the look and feel of actually being connected to the router's and switch console port.

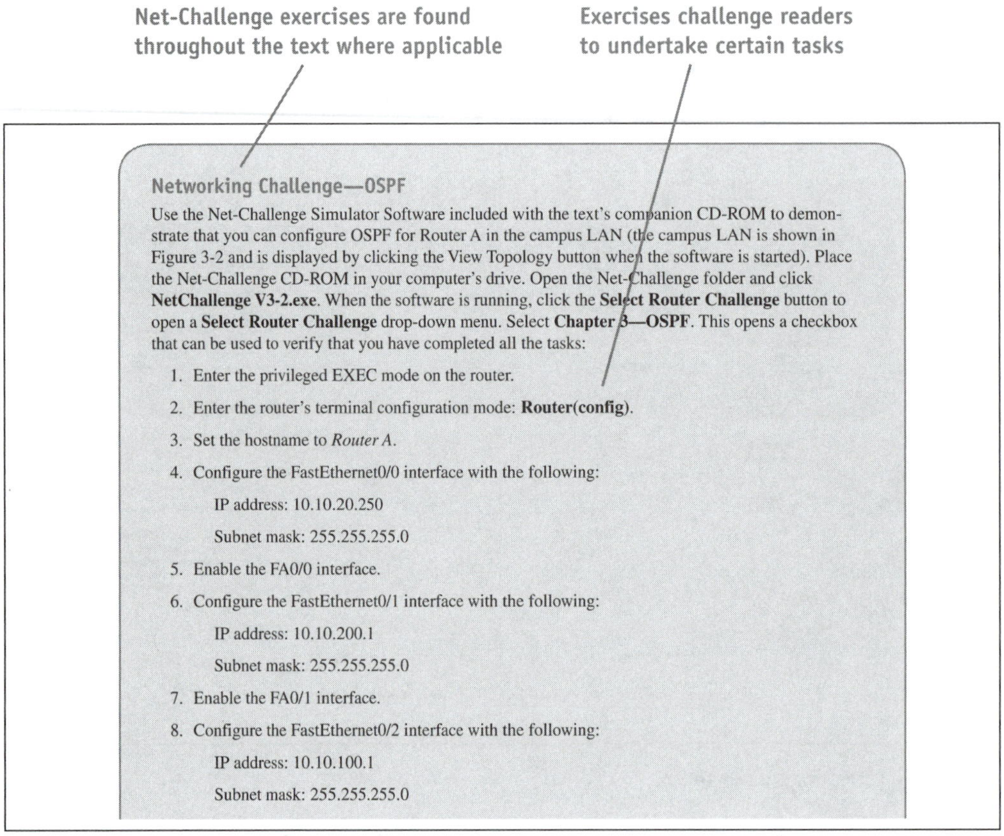

Net-Challenge exercises are found throughout the text where applicable

Exercises challenge readers to undertake certain tasks

Networking Challenge—OSPF

Use the Net-Challenge Simulator Software included with the text's companion CD-ROM to demonstrate that you can configure OSPF for Router A in the campus LAN (the campus LAN is shown in Figure 3-2 and is displayed by clicking the View Topology button when the software is started). Place the Net-Challenge CD-ROM in your computer's drive. Open the Net-Challenge folder and click **NetChallenge V3-2.exe**. When the software is running, click the **Select Router Challenge** button to open a **Select Router Challenge** drop-down menu. Select **Chapter 3—OSPF**. This opens a checkbox that can be used to verify that you have completed all the tasks:

1. Enter the privileged EXEC mode on the router.

2. Enter the router's terminal configuration mode: **Router(config)**.

3. Set the hostname to *Router A*.

4. Configure the FastEthernet0/0 interface with the following:

   IP address: 10.10.20.250

   Subnet mask: 255.255.255.0

5. Enable the FA0/0 interface.

6. Configure the FastEthernet0/1 interface with the following:

   IP address: 10.10.200.1

   Subnet mask: 255.255.255.0

7. Enable the FA0/1 interface.

8. Configure the FastEthernet0/2 interface with the following:

   IP address: 10.10.100.1

   Subnet mask: 255.255.255.0

FIGURE P-2

- The textbook features and introduces how to use the *Wireshark Network Protocol Analyzer*. Examples of using the software to analyze data traffic are included throughout the text, as shown in Figure P-3.

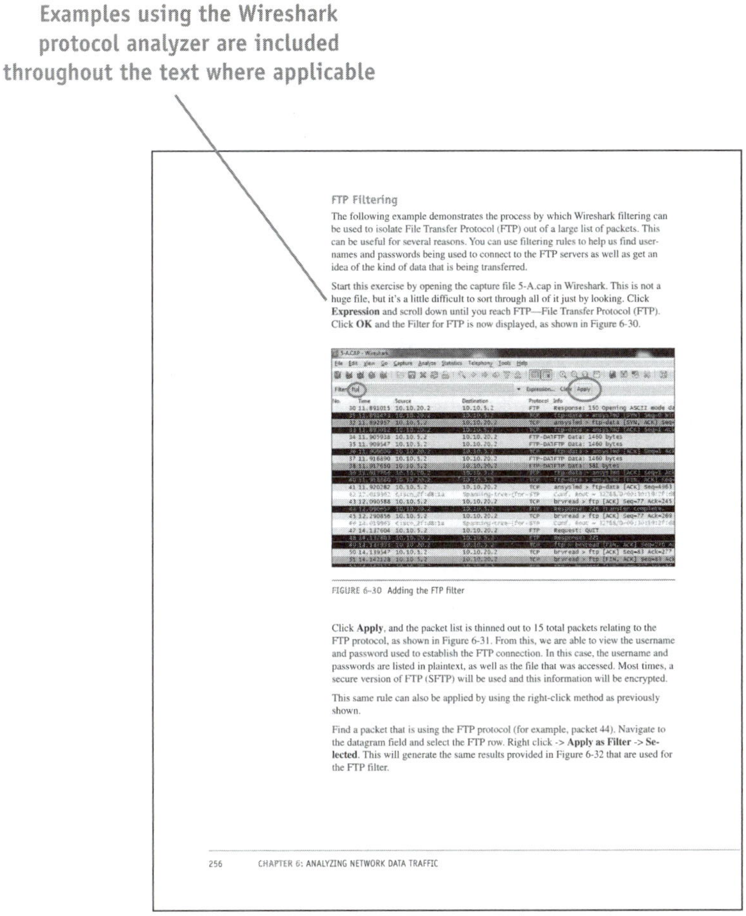

Examples using the Wireshark
protocol analyzer are included
throughout the text where applicable

FTP Filtering

The following example demonstrates the process by which Wireshark filtering can be used to isolate File Transfer Protocol (FTP) out of a large list of packets. This can be useful for several reasons. You can use filtering rules to help us find usernames and passwords being used to connect to the FTP servers as well as get an idea of the kind of data that is being transferred.

Start this exercise by opening the capture file 5-A.cap in Wireshark. This is not a huge file, but it's a little difficult to sort through all of it just by looking. Click **Expression** and scroll down until you reach FTP—File Transfer Protocol (FTP). Click **OK** and the Filter for FTP is now displayed, as shown in Figure 6-30.

FIGURE 6-30 Adding the FTP filter

Click **Apply**, and the packet list is thinned out to 15 total packets relating to the FTP protocol, as shown in Figure 6-31. From this, we are able to view the username and password used to establish the FTP connection. In this case, the username and passwords are listed in plaintext, as well as the file that was accessed. Most times, a secure version of FTP (SFTP) will be used and this information will be encrypted.

This same rule can also be applied by using the right-click method as previously shown.

Find a packet that is using the FTP protocol (for example, packet 44). Navigate to the datagram field and select the FTP row. Right click -> **Apply as Filter** -> **Selected**. This will generate the same results provided in Figure 6-32 that are used for the FTP filter.

FIGURE P-3

- Numerous worked-out examples are included in every chapter to reinforce key concepts and aid in subject mastery, as shown in Figure P-4.

Configuring, analyzing, and troubleshooting sections guide readers through advanced techniques in networking

Screen captures and network topologies guide students through different hands-on activities

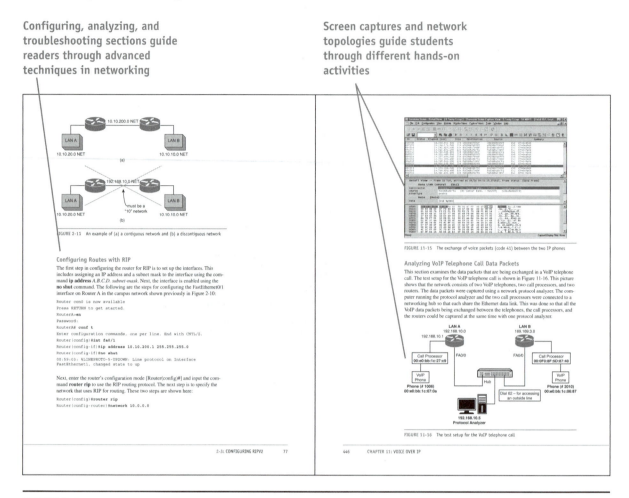

FIGURE P-4

- Key Terms and their definitions are highlighted in the margins to foster inquisitiveness and ensure retention. This is illustrated in Figure P-5.

Key terms are highlighted in the text and defined in the margin

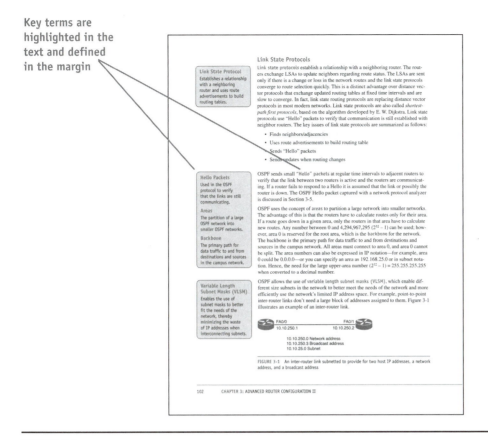

- Extensive Summaries, Questions, and Problems, as well as Critical Thinking Questions, are found at the end of each chapter, as shown in Figure P-6.

Summary of
key concepts

Questions and problems
are organized by section

Critical Thinking questions and problems
further develop analytical skills

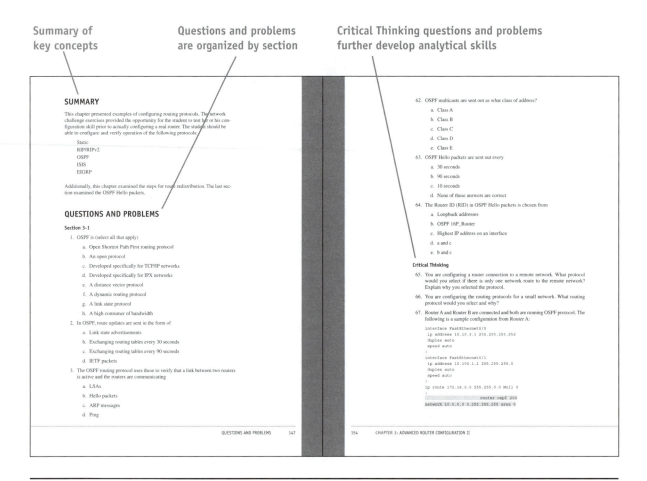

SUMMARY

This chapter presented examples of configuring routing protocols. The network challenge exercises provided the opportunity for the student to test her or his configuration skill prior to actually configuring a real router. The student should be able to configure and verify operation of the following protocols:

Static
RIP/RIPv2
OSPF
ISIS
EIGRP

Additionally, this chapter examined the steps for route redistribution. The last section examined the OSPF Hello packets.

QUESTIONS AND PROBLEMS

Section 3-1

1. OSPF is (select all that apply)
   a. Open Shortest Path First routing protocol
   b. An open protocol
   c. Developed specifically for TCP/IP networks
   d. Developed specifically for IPX networks
   e. A distance vector protocol
   f. A dynamic routing protocol
   g. A link state protocol
   h. A high consumer of bandwidth

2. In OSPF, route updates are sent in the form of
   a. Link state advertisements
   b. Exchanging routing tables every 30 seconds
   c. Exchanging routing tables every 90 seconds
   d. IETF packets

3. The OSPF routing protocol uses these to verify that a link between two routers is active and the routers are communicating
   a. LSAs
   b. Hello packets
   c. ARP messages
   d. Ping

62. OSPF multicasts are sent out as what class of address?
   a. Class A
   b. Class B
   c. Class C
   d. Class D
   e. Class E

63. OSPF Hello packets are sent out every
   a. 30 seconds
   b. 90 seconds
   c. 10 seconds
   d. None of these answers are correct

64. The Router ID (RID) in OSPF Hello packets is chosen from
   a. Loopback addresses
   b. OSPF 16P_Router
   c. Highest IP address on an interface
   d. a and c
   e. b and c

Critical Thinking

65. You are configuring a router connection to a remote network. What protocol would you select if there is only one network route to the remote network? Explain why you selected the protocol.

66. You are configuring the routing protocols for a small network. What routing protocol would you select and why?

67. Router A and Router B are connected and both are running OSPF protocol. The following is a sample configuration from Router A:

```
interface FastEthernet0/0
 ip address 10.10.3.1 255.255.255.252
 duplex auto
 speed auto
!
interface FastEthernet0/1
 ip address 10.100.1.1 255.255.255.0
 duplex auto
 speed auto
!
ip route 172.16.0.0 255.255.0.0 Null 0
!
                          router ospf 200
network 10.0.0.0 0.255.255.255 area 0
```

FIGURE P-6

- An extensive Glossary is found at the end of this book and offers quick, accessible definitions to key terms and acronyms, as well as an exhaustive Index (see Figure P-7).

Complete Glossary of terms and acronyms provide quick reference

Exhaustive Index provides quick reference

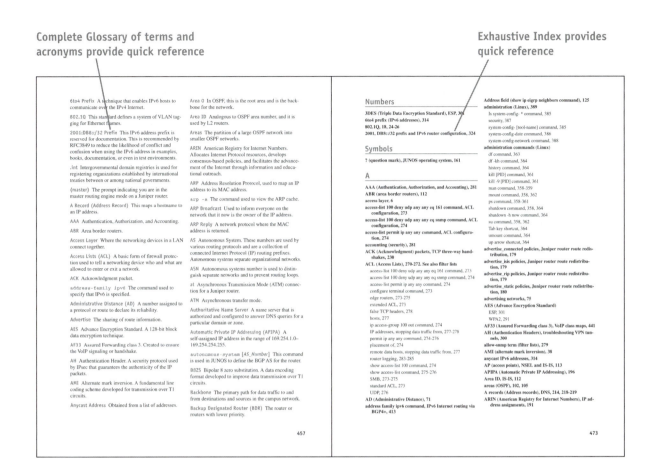

FIGURE P-7

Accompanying CD-ROM

The CD-ROM packaged with the text includes the captured data packets used in the text. It also includes the Net-Challenge Software, which was developed specifically for this text.

Instructor Resources

The Instructor's Manual to accompany *A Practical Guide to Advanced Networking*, (ISBN: 978-0-132-88303-0) provides the entire book in PDF format along with instructor notes for each section within each chapter, recommending key concepts that should be covered in each chapter. Solutions to all Chapter Questions and Problems sections are also included. In addition, the instructor can also access 13 lab and lab-related exercises and a test bank with which to generate quizzes on the material found within the student edition of the book.

1

CHAPTER

NETWORK INFRASTRUCTURE DESIGN

Chapter Outline

Objectives

- Understand the purpose of the three layers of a campus network design
- Understand the issue of data flow and selecting the network media
- Develop techniques for IP allocation and subnet design
- Understand the process of configuring a VLAN
- Understand the issues of configuring the Layer 3 routed network

Key Terms

core

distribution layer

access layer

CIDR

ISP

intranets

NAT

PAT

Overloading

supernet

gateway

broadcast domain

flat network

VLAN (virtual LAN)

port-based VLAN

tag-based VLAN

protocol-based VLAN

VLAN ID

802.1Q

static VLAN

dynamic VLAN

show vlan

vlan database

vlan *vlan_id*

show vlan name *vlan-name*

interface vlan 1

show interface status

trunk port

Inter-Switch Link (ISL)

Switchport mode trunk

switchport trunk encapsulation dot1q

switchport trunk encapsulation isl

switchport trunk allowed vlan *vlan_id*

show interfaces trunk

network address

logical address

router interface

routing table

subnet, NET

multilayer switch (MLS)

wire speed routing

routed network

Layer 3 network

SONET

WAN

terminal monitor (term mon)

terminal no monitor (term no mon)

show ip interface brief (sh ip int br)

no switchport

secondary IP address

InterVLAN routing

router on a stick

SVI

DS

CSU/DSU

AMI

B8ZS

Minimum Ones Density

HDLC

PPP

WIC

VWIC

service-module t1

show controller t1 *slot/ port*

ATM

Virtual Path Connection (VPC)

Virtual Channel Connection (VCC)

SVC

VPI

VCI

INTRODUCTION

The objective of this chapter is to examine the computer networking issues that arise when planning a campus network. The term *campus network* applies to any network that has multiple LANs interconnected. The LANs are typically in multiple buildings that are close to each other and interconnected with switches and routers. This chapter looks at the planning and designs of a simple campus network, including network design, IP subnet assignment, VLAN configuration, and routed network configuration.

The basics of configuring the three layers of a campus LAN (core, distribution, and access) are first examined in Section 1-1. This section also addresses the important issues of data flow and selecting the proper network media. Section 1-2 examines IP allocation and subnet design. Section 1-3 discusses the VLAN network, including a step-by-step process of how to configure a VLAN, which provides an introduction to the basic switch commands and the steps for configuring a static VLAN. Section 1-4 examines the Layer 3 routed network. This section explores the functions of the router and includes configuration examples in different scenarios.

1-1 PHYSICAL NETWORK DESIGN

Most campus networks follow a design that has core, distribution, and access layers. These layers, shown in Figure 1-1, can be spread out into more layers or compacted into fewer, depending on the size of these networks. This three-layer network structure is incorporated in campus networks to improve data handling and routing within the network. The issues of data flow and network media are also examined in this section.

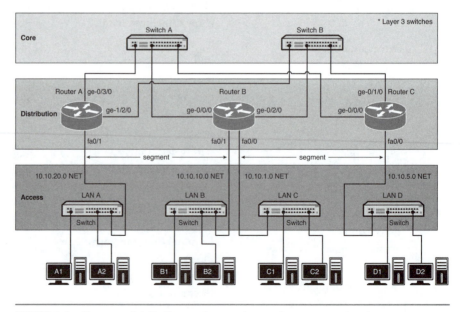

FIGURE 1-1 The core, distribution, and access layers of a campus network

Core

The network core usually contains high-end Layer 3 switches or routers. The **core** is the heart, or backbone, of the network. The major portion of a network's data traffic passes through the core. The core must be able to quickly forward data to other parts of the network. Data congestion should be avoided at the core, if possible. This means that unnecessary route policies should be avoided. An example of a route policy is *traffic filtering,* which limits what traffic can pass from one part of a network to another. Keep in mind that it takes time for a router to examine each data packet, and unnecessary route policies can slow down the network's data traffic.

High-end routers and Layer 3 switches are typically selected for use in the core. Of the two, the Layer 3 switch is the best choice. A Layer 3 switch is essentially a router that uses electronic hardware instead of software to make routing decisions. The advantage of the Layer 3 switch is the speed at which it can make a routing decision and establish a network connection.

Another alternative for networking hardware in the core is a Layer 2 switch. The Layer 2 switch does not make any routing decisions and can quickly make network connection decisions based on the network hardware connected to its ports. The advantage of using the Layer 2 switch in the core is cost. The disadvantage is that the Layer 2 switch does not route data packets; however, high-speed Layer 2 switches are more affordable than high-speed routers and Layer 3 switches.

An important design issue in a campus network and the core is redundancy. *Redundancy* provides for a backup route or network connection in case of a link failure. The core hardware is typically interconnected to all distribution network hardware, as shown in Figure 1-1. The objective is to ensure that data traffic continues for the entire network, even if a core networking device or link fails.

Each layer beyond the core breaks the network into smaller networks with the final result being a group of networks that are capable of handling the amount of traffic generated. The design should thus incorporate some level of redundancy.

> **Core**
> The Backbone of the Network

Distribution Layer

The **distribution layer** in the network is the point where the individual LANs connect to the campus network routers or Layer 3 switches. Routing and filtering policies are more easily implemented at the distribution layer without having a negative impact on the performance of the network data traffic. Also, the speed of the network data connections at the distribution layer is typically slower than at the core. For example, connection speeds at the core should be the highest possible, such as 1 or 10 gigabits, where the data speed connections at the distribution layer could be 100 Mbps or 1 gigabit. Figure 1-1 shows the connections to the access and core layers via the router's Ethernet interfaces.

> **Distribution Layer**
> Point where the individual LANs connect together.

Access Layer

Access Layer

Where the networking devices in a LAN connect together.

The **access layer** is where the networking devices in a LAN connect together. The network hardware used here is typically a Layer 2 switch. Remember, a switch is a better choice because it forwards data packets directly to destination hosts connected to its ports, and network data traffic is not forwarded to all hosts in the network. The exception to this is a broadcast where data packets are sent to all hosts connected to the switch.

NOTE

Hubs are not recommended at all in modern computer networks.

Data Flow

An important networking issue is how data traffic flows in the core, distribution, and access layers of a campus LAN. In reference to Figure 1-1, if computer A1 in LAN A sends data to computer D1 in LAN D, the data is first sent through the switch in LAN A and then to Router A in the distribution layer. Router A then forwards the data to the core switches, Switch A or Switch B. Switch A or Switch B then forwards the data to Router C. The data packet is then sent to the destination host in LAN D.

The following are some questions often asked when setting up a network that implements the core, distribution, and access layers:

- **In what layer are the campus network servers (web, email, DHCP, DNS, and so on) located?** This varies for all campus networks, and there is not a definitive answer. However, most campus network servers are located in the access layer.

- **Why not connect directly from Router A to Router C at the distribution layer?** There are network stability issues when routing large amounts of network data traffic if the networks are fully or even partially meshed together. This means that connecting routers together in the distribution layer should be avoided.

- **Where is the campus backbone located in the layers of a campus network?** The backbone of a campus network carries the bulk of the routed data traffic. Based on this, the backbone of the campus network connects the distribution and the core layer networking devices.

Selecting the Media

The choices for the media used to interconnect networks in a campus network are based on several criteria. The following is a partial list of things to consider:

- Desired data speed
- Distance for connections
- Budget

The desired data speed for the network connection is probably the first consideration given when selecting the network media. Twisted-pair cable works well at 100 Mbps and 1 Gbps and is specified to support data speeds of 10-gigabit data traffic. Fiber-optic cable supports LAN data rates up to 10 Gbps or higher. Wireless networks support data rates up to 200+ Mbps.

The distance consideration limits the choice of media. CAT 6/5e or better have a distance limitation of 100 meters. Fiber-optic cable can be run for many kilometers, depending on the electronics and optical devices used. Wireless LAN connections can also be used to interconnect networks a few kilometers apart.

The available budget is always the final deciding factor when planning the design for a campus LAN. If the budget allows, fiber-optic cable is probably the best overall choice, especially in the high-speed backbone of the campus network. The cost of fiber is continually dropping, making it more competitive with lower-cost network media, such as twisted-pair cable. Also, fiber cable will always be able to carry a greater amount of data traffic and can easily grow with the bandwidth requirements of a network.

Twisted-pair cable is a popular choice for connecting computers in a wired LAN. The twisted-pair technologies support bandwidths suitable for most LANs, and the performance capabilities of twisted-pair cable is always improving.

Wireless LANs are being used to connect networking devices together in LANs where a wired connection is not feasible or mobility is the major concern. For example, a wireless LAN could be used to connect two LANs in a building together. This is a cost-effective choice if there is not a cable duct to run the cable to interconnect the LANs or if the cost of running the cable is too high. Also, wireless connections are playing an important role with mobile users within a LAN. The mobile user can make a network connection without having to use a physical connection or jack. For example, a wireless LAN could be used to enable network users to connect their mobile computers to the campus network.

1-2   IP SUBNET DESIGN

Once the physical infrastructure for a network is in place, the next big step is to plan and allocate IP space for the network. Take time to plan the IP subnet design, because it is not easy to change the IP subnet assignments once they are in place. It is crucial for a network engineer to consider three factors before coming up with the final IP subnet design. These three factors are

1. The assigned IP address range

2. The number of subnetworks needed for the network

3. The size or the number of IP host addresses needed for the network

The final steps in designing the IP subnet is to assign an IP address to the interface that will serve as the gateway out of each subnet.

IP Address Range

The IP address range defines the size of the IP network you can work with. In some cases, a classless interdomain routing (CIDR) block of public IP addresses might be allocated to the network by an ISP. For example, the block of IP address 206.206.156.0/24 could be assigned to the network. This case allocates 256 IP addresses to the 206.206.156.0 network. In another case, a CIDR block of private IP addresses, like 10.10.10.0/24, could be used. In this case, 256 IP addresses are assigned to the 10.10.10.0 network. For established networks with an IP address range already in use, the network engineer generally has to work within the existing IP address assignments. With a brand new network, the engineer has the luxury of creating a network from scratch.

In most network situations, an IP address block will have been previously assigned to the network for Internet use. The public IP addresses are typically obtained from the ISP (Internet service provider). This IP block of addresses could be from Class A, B, or C networks, as shown in Table 1-1.

TABLE 1-1   Address Range for Each Class of Network

Class	Address Range
Class A	0.0.0.0 to 127.255.255.255
Class B	128.0.0.0 to 191.255.255.255
Class C	192.0.0.0 to 223.255.255.255

Today, only public Class C addresses are assigned by ISPs, and most of them are not even a full set of Class C addresses (256 IP addresses). A lot of ISPs partition their allotted IP space into smaller subnets and then, in turn, provide those smaller portions to the customers. The bottom line is the limited number of public IP addresses are now a commodity on the Internet, and it is important to note that there are fees associated with acquiring an IP range from an ISP.

Not many institutions or businesses have the luxury of using public IP addresses inside their network anymore. This is because the growing number of devices being used in a network exceeds the number of public IP addresses assigned to them. The solution is that most networks are using private IP addresses in their internal network. Private addresses are IP addresses set aside for use in private intranets. An intranet is an internal internetwork that provides file and resource sharing. Private addresses are not valid addresses for Internet use, because they have been reserved for internal use and are not routable on the Internet. However, these addresses can be used within a private LAN (intranet) to create the internal IP network.

The private IP addresses must be translated to public IP addresses using techniques like NAT (Network Address Translation) or PAT (Port Address Translation) before being routed over the Internet. For example, computer 1 in the home network (see Figure 1-2) might be trying to establish a connection to an Internet website. The wireless router uses NAT to translate computer 1's private IP address to the public IP address assigned to the router. The router uses a technique called overloading, where NAT translates the home network's private IP addresses to the single public

---

CIDR
Classless Interdomain Routing

ISP
Internet service provider: An organization that provides Internet access for the public.

Intranets
Internetwork that provides file and resource sharing.

NAT
Network Address Translation. A technique used to translate an internal private IP address to a public IP address.

PAT
Port Address Translation. A port number is tracked with the client computer's private address when translating to a public address.

Overloading
Where NAT translates the home network's private IP addresses to a single public IP address.

IP address assigned by the ISP. In addition, the NAT process tracks a port number for the connection. This technique is called Port Address Translation (PAT). The router stores the home network's IP address and port number in a NAT lookup table. The port number differentiates the computer that is establishing a connection to the Internet because the router uses the same public address for all computers. This port number is used when a data packet is returned to the home network. This port number identifies the computer that established the Internet connection, and the router can deliver the data packet back to the correct computer. An example of this conversion is provided in Figure 1-3. This example shows three data connections originating from the home network of 192.168.0.0/24. A single 128.123.246.55 IP address is used for the Internet connection. Port address translation is being used to map the data packet back to the origination source. In this case, the port numbers are 1962, 1970, and 1973.

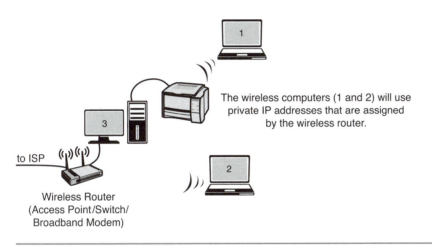

The wireless computers (1 and 2) will use private IP addresses that are assigned by the wireless router.

to ISP

Wireless Router
(Access Point/Switch/
Broadband Modem)

FIGURE 1-2 An example of a home computer connecting to the ISP

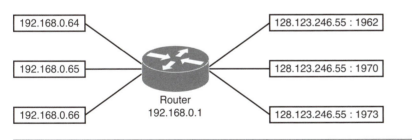

FIGURE 1-3 This example shows the three data connections originating from the home network of 192.168.0.0/24

Determining the Number of Subnetworks Needed for the Network

The use of private IP addresses is a viable technique for creating a large amount of IP addresses for intranet use. Obviously, there is a big difference when designing an IP network for a single network than there is when designing an IP network for multiple networks. When designing an IP network for one single network, things are quite simple. This type of configuration is typically found in the home, small office, or a small business environment where one IP subnet is allocated and only one small router is involved.

For situations requiring multiple networks, each network must be sized accordingly. Therefore, the subnet must be carefully designed. In addition, networks with multiple subnets require a router or multiple routers with multiple routed network interfaces to interconnect the networks. For example, if the network engineer is using private addresses and needs to design for three different networks, one possibility is to assign 10.10.10.0/24 for the first network, 172.16.0.0/24 for the second network, and 192.168.1.0/24 for the third network. Is this a good approach? Technically, this can be done, but it is probably not logically sound. It makes more sense to group these networks within the same big CIDR block. This will make it easier for a network engineer to remember the IP assignments and to manage the subnets. A better design is to assign 10.10.10.0/24 to the first network, 10.10.20.0/24 to the second network, and 10.10.30.0/24 to the third network. All three networks are all in the same "10" network, which makes it easier for the network engineer to track the IP assignments. The term *subnet* and *network* are used interchangeably in multiple network environments. The term subnet usually indicates a bigger network address is partitioned and is assigned to smaller networks or subnets.

Another design factor that the network engineer must address is the network size. Two questions that a good network engineer must ask are

- How many network devices must be accommodated in the network? (Current demand)
- How many network devices must be accommodated in the future? (Future growth)

Simply put, the IP network must be designed to accommodate the current demand, and it must be designed to accommodate future growth. Once the size of a network is determined, a subnet can be assigned. In the case of a single network, the design is not too complicated. For example, if the network needs to be able to accommodate 150 network devices, an entire Class C address, like 192.168.1.0/24, can be assigned to the network. This will handle the current 150 network devices and leave enough room for growth. In this example, 104 additional IP address will be available for future growth.

When allocating IP address blocks, a table like Table 1-2 can be used to provide the CIDR for the most common subnet masks and their corresponding number of available IP addresses.

TABLE 1-2   CIDR—Subnet Mask-IPs Conversion

CIDR	Subnet Mask	IPs
/16	255.255.0.0	65534
/17	255.255.128.0	32768
/18	255.255.192.0	16384

CIDR	Subnet Mask	IPs
/19	255.255.224.0	8192
/20	255.255.240.0	4096
/21	255.255.248.0	2048
/22	255.255.252.0	1024
/23	255.255.254.0	512
/24	255.255.255.0	256
/25	255.255.255.128	128
/26	255.255.255.192	64
/27	255.255.255.224	32
/28	255.255.255.240	16
/29	255.255.255.248	8
/30	255.255.255.252	4
/31	255.255.255.254	2
/32	255.255.255.255	1

Even with a much smaller network, like the home network, where only a handful of network computers and peripherals are present, an entire Class C private address is generally allocated to the home network. In fact, most home routers are preconfigured with a private Class C address within the 192.168.0.0–192.168.0.255 range. This technique is user friendly and easy to use and sets aside private IP addresses for internal network use. This technique virtually guarantees that users will never have to worry about subnetting the CIDR block.

For a bigger network that must handle more than 254 network devices, a supernet can be deployed. A supernet is when two or more classful contiguous networks are grouped together. The technique of supernetting was proposed in 1992 to eliminate the class boundaries and make available the unused IP address space. Supernetting allows multiple networks to be specified by one subnet mask. In other words, the class boundary could be overcome. For example, if the network needs to be able to accommodate 300 network devices, two Class C networks, like 192.168.0.0/24 and 192.168.1.0/24, can be grouped together to form a supernet of 192.168.0.0/23, which can accommodate up to 510 network devices. As shown in Table 1-2, a /23 CIDR provides 512 available IP addresses. However, one IP is reserved for the network address and another one is reserved for the network broadcast address. Therefore, a /23 CIDR yields 512 – 2 = 510 usable host IP addresses.

> **Supernet**
> Two or more classful contiguous networks are grouped together.

Determining the Size or the Number of IP Host Addresses Needed for the Network

The problem with randomly applying CIDR blocks to Class A, B, and C addresses is that there are boundaries in each class, and these boundaries can't be crossed. If a boundary is crossed, the IP address maps to another subnet. For example, if a CIDR block is expanded to include four Class C networks, all four Class C networks need to be specified by the same CIDR subnet mask to avoid crossing boundaries. The following example illustrates this.

Example 1-1

Figure 1-4 shows three different networks with different size requirements. The needed capacity (number of devices) for each network is specified in the figure. Your task is to determine the CIDR block required for each network that will satisfy the number of expected users. You are to use Class C private IP addresses when configuring the CIDR blocks.

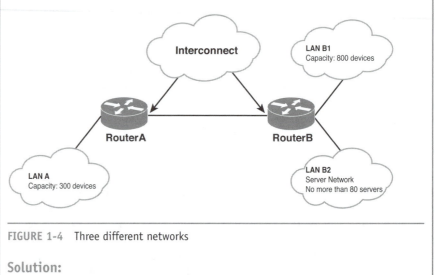

FIGURE 1-4   Three different networks

Solution:

For LAN A, a CIDR block that can handle at least 300 networking devices must be provided. In this case, two contiguous Class C networks of 192.168.0.0/24 and 192.168.1.0/24 can be grouped together to form a 192.168.0.0/23 network. Referring to Table 1-2, a /23 CIDR with a subnet mask of 255.255.254.0 provides 512 IP addresses which more than satisfies the required 300 networking devices.

The next question is to determine what the network address is for LAN A. This can be determined by ANDing the 255.255.254.0 subnet mask with 192.168.0.0 and 192.168.1.0.

192. 168. 0. 0	192. 168. 1. 0
255. 255. 254. 0 (/23)	255. 255. 254. 0 (/23)
192. 168. 0. 0	**192. 168. 0. 0**

This shows that applying the /23 [255.255.254.0] subnet mask to the specified IP address places both in the same 192.168.0.0 network. This also means that this CIDR block does not cross boundaries, because applying the subnet mask to each network address places both in the same 192.168.0.0 network.

For LAN B1, the requirement is that a CIDR block that can handle 800 network devices must be provided. According to Table 1-2, a /22 CIDR yields 1,022 usable host IP addresses and is equivalent to grouping four Class C networks together. Therefore, a /22 CIDR can be used.

The next decision is selecting the group of IP addresses to create the CIDR block and decide where the IP addresses should start. Recall that the 192.168.0.0 and 192.168.1.0 networks are being used to create the LAN A CIDR block. Should LAN B1 start from 192.168.2.0/22, which is the next contiguous space? The answer is no. The 192.168.2.0/22 is still within the boundary of the 192.168.0.0/23 network. Remember, the requirement is that a CIDR block that can handle 800 network devices must be provided and that boundaries cannot be crossed, and the designer must be careful not to overlap the networks when assigning subnets to more than one network. In this case, when the /22 subnet mask (255.255.252.0) is applied to 192.168.2.0, this yields the network 192.168.0.0. The AND operation is shown:

192. 168. 2. 0
255. 255.252. 0 (/22)
192. 168. 0. 0

This happens to be the same network address as when the /23 CIDR subnet mask (255.255.254.0) is applied to any IP within the range of 192.168.0.0-192.168.1.255, as shown:

192. 168.   0. 0   192. 168.   1. 255
255. 255. 254. 0 (/23)   255. 255. 254.   0   (/23)
192. 168.   0. 0   192. 168.   0.   0

There is an overlap between 192.168.0.0/23 and 192.168.2.0/22. Moving to the next contiguous Class C of 192.168.3.0/22, we still find that it's still in the 192.168.0.0:

192.168.3.0
255.255.252.0 (/22)
192.168.0.0 is still in the same subnet.

Based on this information, the next Class C range 192.168.4.0/22 is selected. This yields a nonoverlapping network of 192.168.4.0, so the subnet 192.168.4.0/22 is a valid for this network:

192.168.4.0
255.255.252.0 (/22)
192.168.4.0 is **not** the same subnet; therefore, this is an acceptable CIDR block.

Recall that the CIDR for LANB1 is a /22 and is equivalent to grouping four Class C networks. This means that LANB1 uses the following Class C networks:

192.168.4.0
192.168.5.0
192.168.6.0
192.168.7.0

The IP subnet design gets more complicated when designing multiple networks with different size subnets. This generally means that the subnet mask or the CIDR will not be uniformly assigned to every network. For example, one network might be a /25 network or /22, while another is a /30 network.

The next requirement is that a CIDR block that can handle 800 network devices must be tasked to assign a CIDR block to LAN B2. This LAN is a server network that houses a fixed number of servers. The number is not expected to grow beyond 80 servers. One easy approach is to assign a /24 CIDR to this network.

This means that the next network is 192.168.8.0/24, which is the next nonoverlapping CIDR block after 192.168.4.0/22. The /24 CIDR gives 254 host IP addresses, but only 80 IP addresses are required. Another approach is to size it appropriately. According to Table 1-2, a good CIDR to use is a /25, which allows for 126 host IP addresses. Therefore, a network 192.168.8.0/25 can be used for this network.

Assigning a 192.168.8.0/24 CIDR, which can accommodate 254 hosts, seems like a waste, because the network is expected to be a fixed size, and it will house no more than 80 servers. By assigning a 192.168.8.0/25 CIDR, enough room is left for another contiguous CIDR, 192.168.8.128/25. Obviously, this is a more efficient way of managing the available IP space.

Last but not least is the interconnection shown in Figure 1-4. This is the router-to-router link between Router A and Router B. The interconnection usually gets the least attention, but it exists everywhere in the multiple networks environment. Nonetheless, a CIDR block has to be assigned to it. Because there are always only two interface IP addresses involved plus the network and broadcast address, giving an entire Class C address would definitely be a waste. Typically, a /30 CIDR is used for this type of connection. Therefore, a CIDR block for the interconnection between Router A and Router B can be 192.168.9.0/30. This yields two IP host addresses: one for Router A and one for Router B.

The complete subnet assignment for Example 1-1 and Figure 1-4 is provided in Table 1-3.

TABLE 1-3   Completed Design of Subnets for Figure 1-4

Network	Subnet	CIDR	Subnet Mask
LAN A	192.168.0.0	/23	255.255.254.0
LAN B1	192.168.4.0	/22	255.255.252.0
LAN B2	192.168.8.0	/24 or /25	255.255.255.0 or 255.255.255.128
Interconnect	192.168.9.0	/30	255.255.255.252

IP Assignment

The next task requirement is that a CIDR block that can handle 800 network devices must be required to assign an IP address to each routed interface. This address will become the **gateway** IP address of the subnet. The gateway describes the networking device that enables hosts in a LAN to connect to networks (and hosts) outside the LAN. Figure 1-5 provides an example of the gateway. Every network device within its subnet (LAN) will use this IP address as its gateway to communicate from its local subnet to devices on other subnets. The gateway IP address is preselected and is distributed to a network device by way of manual configuration or dynamic assignment.

> **Gateway**
> Describes the networking device that enables hosts in a LAN to connect to networks (and hosts) outside the LAN.

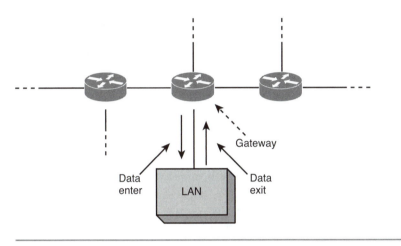

FIGURE 1-5   The gateway for a network

For LAN A in Example 1-1, the IP address 192.168.0.0 is already reserved as the network address, and the IP address 192.168.0.255 is reserved as the broadcast address. This leaves any IP address within the range 192.168.0.1–192.168.0.254 available for use for the gateway address. Choosing the gateway IP address is not an exact science. Generally, the first IP address or the last IP address of the available range is chosen. Whatever convention is chosen, it should apply to the rest of the subnets for the ease of management. Once the gateway IP address is chosen, this IP address is reserved and is not to be used by any other devices in the subnet. Otherwise, an IP conflict will be introduced. The following is an example of how the gateway IP addresses could be assigned to the LANs in Example 1-1.

Network	Gateway
LAN A	192.168.0.1
LAN B1	192.168.4.1
LAN B2	192.168.8.1

1-3 VLAN NETWORK

This section examines the function of using a switch in a VLAN within the campus network. The terminology and steps for implementing VLANs will be presented first. The second part examines basic Cisco switch configuration and provides an introduction to the commands needed for configuring the VLAN. The third part of Section 1-3 demonstrates the commands needed to set up a static VLAN. Next is a discussion on VLAN tagging using 802.1Q. The section concludes with a look at configuring an HP Procurve switch.

LANs are not necessarily restricted in size. A LAN can have 20 computers, 200 computers, or even more. Multiple LANs also can be interconnected to essentially create one large LAN. For example, the first floor of a building could be set up as one LAN, the second floor as another LAN, and the third floor another. The three LANs in the building can be interconnected into essentially one large LAN using switches, with the switches interconnected, as shown in Figure 1-6.

> **Broadcast Domain**
> Any broadcast sent out on the network is seen by all hosts in this domain.

Is it bad to interconnect LANs this way? As long as switches are being used to interconnect the computers, the interconnected LANs have minimal impact on network performance. This is true as long as there are not too many computers in the LAN. The number of computers in the LAN is an issue, because Layer 2 switches do not separate broadcast domains. This means that any broadcast sent out on the network (for example, the broadcast associated with an ARP request) will be sent to all computers in the LAN. Excessive broadcasts are a problem, because each computer must process the broadcast to determine whether it needs to respond; this essentially slows down the computer and the network.

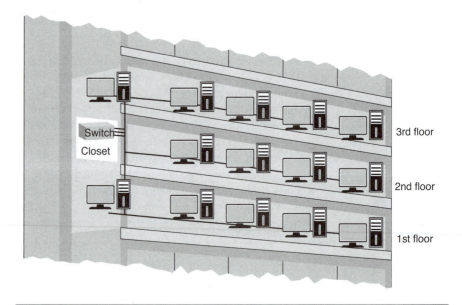

FIGURE 1-6 Three floors of a building interconnected using switches to form one large LAN

A network with multiple LANs interconnected at the Layer 2 level is called a flat network. A flat network is where the LANs share the same broadcast domain. The use of a flat network should be avoided if possible for the simple reason that the network response time is greatly affected. Flat networks can be avoided by the use of virtual LANs (VLAN) or routers. Although both options can be used to separate broadcast domains, they differ in that the VLAN operates at the OSI Layer 2, while routers use Layer 3 networking to accomplish the task. The topic of a virtual VLAN is discussed next.

Flat Network
A network where the LANs share the same broadcast domain.

Virtual LAN (VLAN)

Obviously, if the LANs are not connected, then each LAN is segregated only to a switch. The broadcast domain is contained to that switch; however, this does not scale in a practical network, and it is not cost effective because each LAN requires its own Layer 2 switches. This is where the concept of virtual LAN (VLAN) can help out. A VLAN is a way to have multiple LANs co-exist in the same Layer 2 switch, but their traffic is segregated from each other. Even though they reside on the same physical switch, they behave as if they are on different switches (hence, the term virtual). VLAN compatible switches can communicate to each other and extend the segregation of multiple LANs throughout the entire switched network. A switch can be configured with a VLAN where a group of host computers and servers are configured as if they are in the same LAN, even if they reside across routers in separate LANs. Each VLAN has its own broadcast domain. Hence, traffic from one VLAN cannot pass to another VLAN. The advantage of using VLANs is the network administrator can group computers and servers in the same VLAN based on the organizational group (such as Sales, Engineering) even if they are not on the same physical segment—or even the same building.

VLAN (Virtual LAN)
A group of host computers and servers that are configured as if they are in the same LAN, even if they reside across routers in separate LANs.

There are three types of VLANs: port-based VLANs, tag-based VLANs, and protocol-based VLANs. The port-based VLAN is one where the host computers connected to specific ports on a switch are assigned to a specific VLAN. For example, assume the computers connected to switch ports 2, 3, and 4 are assigned to the Sales VLAN 2, while the computers connected to switch ports 6, 7, and 8 are assigned to the Engineering VLAN 3, as shown in Figure 1-7. The switch will be configured as a port-based VLAN so that the groups of ports [2,3,4] are assigned to the sales VLAN while ports [6,7,8] belong to the Engineering VLAN. The devices assigned to the same VLAN will share broadcasts for that LAN; however, computers that are connected to ports not assigned to the VLAN will not share the broadcasts. For example, the computers in VLAN 2 (Sales) share the same broadcast domain and computers in VLAN 3 (Engineering) share a different broadcast domain.

Port-Based VLAN
Host computers connected to specific ports on a switch are assigned to a specific VLAN.

Tagged-Based VLAN
Used VLAN ID based on 802.1Q.

Protocol-Based VLAN
Connection to ports is based on the protocol being used.

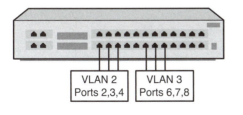

FIGURE 1-7   An example of the grouping for port-based VLANs

In tag-based VLANs, a tag is added to the Ethernet frames. This tag contains the VLAN ID that is used to identify that a frame belongs to a specific VLAN. The addition of the VLAN ID is based on the 802.1Q specification. The 802.1Q standard defines a system of VLAN tagging for Ethernet frames. An advantage of an 802.1Q VLAN is that it helps contain broadcast and multicast data traffic, which helps minimize data congestion and improve throughput. This specification also provides guidelines for a switch port to belong to more than one VLAN. Additionally, the tag-based VLANs can help provide better security by logically isolating and grouping users.

In protocol-based VLANs, the data traffic is connected to specific ports based on the type of protocol being used. The packet is dropped when it enters the switch if the protocol doesn't match any of the VLANs. For example, an IP network could be set up for the Engineering VLAN on ports 6,7,8 and an IPX network for the Sales VLAN on ports 2,3, and 4. The advantage of this is the data traffic for the two networks is separated.

There are two approaches for assigning VLAN membership:

- **Static VLAN:** Basically a port-based VLAN. The assignments are created when ports are assigned to a specific VLAN.
- **Dynamic VLAN:** Ports are assigned to a VLAN based on either the computer's MAC address or the username of the client logged onto the computer. This means that the system has been previously configured with the VLAN assignments for the computer or the username. The advantage of this is the username and/or the computer can move to a different location, but VLAN membership will be retained.

VLAN Configuration

This section demonstrates the steps for configuring a static VLAN. In this example, the ports for VLAN 2 (Sales) and VLAN 3 (Engineering) will be defined. This requires that VLAN memberships be defined for the required ports. The steps and the commands will be demonstrated.

The show vlan command can be used to verify what ports have been defined for the switch. By default, all ports are assigned to VLAN 1. An example using the **show vlan** command is provided next.

```
SwitchA# show vlan
```

```
VLAN Name                         Status      Ports
---- ------------------------- --------- -------------------------
--
1    default                       active      Fa0/1, Fa0/2,
Fa0/3, Fa0/4
                                                          Fa0/5,
Fa0/6, Fa0/7, Fa0/8
                                                          Fa0/9,
Fa0/10
```

This shows that all the FastEthernet interfaces on the switch are currently assigned to VLAN 1, which is a default VLAN. In the next step, two additional VLANs will be created for both Sales and Engineering. The two new VLANs will have the VLAN ID of 2 and 3 respectively, and each VLAN will be assigned a name associated to it. This is accomplished by modifying the VLAN database using the vlan database command, as shown in the next steps.

vlan database
The command used on older Cisco switches to enter the VLAN database.

```
SwitchA#vlan database

SwitchA(vlan)#vlan 2 name Sales
VLAN 2 modified:
    Name: Sales
SwitchA(vlan)#vlan 3 name Engineering
VLAN 3 modified:
    Name: Engineering
```

On newer Cisco switches, users will get the following message that the command **vlan database** is being deprecated:

```
% Warning: It is recommended to configure VLAN from config mode,
  as VLAN database mode is being deprecated. Please consult user
  documentation for configuring VTP/VLAN in config mode.
```

Cisco has moved away from the VLAN database-style command to an IOS global command. Similarly to other IOS global commands, the switch must be in the configuration mode (config)#. However, the concept remains the same that a VLAN must be created for it to be activated and ready for use. The steps for creating the VLAN on newer Cisco switches are as follows:

```
SwitchA# conf t
SwitchA(config)#vlan 2
SwitchA(config-vlan)#name Sales
SwitchA(config-vlan)#vlan 3
SwitchA(config-vlan)#name Engineering
SwitchA(config-vlan)#exit
SwitchA(config)#exit
```

To start configuring a VLAN, one must specify which VLAN needs to be configured using the **vlan** [*vlan_id*] command. If the specific VLAN does not exist, this command will create the VLAN as well. As shown in the preceding example, the command **vlan 2** is entered to configure vlan 2 and then the command name **Sales** is entered to configure the name associated to the VLAN. The similar steps are done for VLAN 3 with the name Engineering.

vlan [*vlan_id*]
The IOS global command used to create VLAN ID.

The rest of the VLAN commands are almost identical in the older switches and newer switches. The next step is used to verify that the new VLANs have been created using the **show vlan** command:

```
Switch#show vlan

VLAN Name                            Status    Ports
---- -------------------------------- --------- --------------------------
--
1    default                         active    Fa0/1, Fa0/2, Fa0/3,
Fa0/4

                                                Fa0/5, Fa0/6,
Fa0/7, Fa0/8

                                                Fa0/9, Fa0/10
2    Sales                           active
3    Engineering              active
```

This shows that both the Sales and Engineering VLANs have been created. In the next steps, ports will be assigned to the newly created VLANs. This requires that the configuration mode be entered and each FastEthernet interface (port) must be assigned to the proper VLAN using the two commands **switchport mode access** and **switchport access vlan** *vlan-id*. An example is presented for FastEthernet interface 0/2 being assigned to VLAN 2 on a Cisco switch:

```
SwitchA#conf t
Enter configuration commands, one per line. End with CNTL/Z.
SwitchA(config)#int fa 0/2
SwitchA(config-if)#switchport mode access
SwitchA(config-if)#switchport access vlan 2
SwitchA(config-if)#end
```

The next step is used to verify that FastEthernet 0/2 has been assigned to the Sales VLAN (VLAN2). This can be verified using the **show vlan brief** command, as shown. This command only displays the interfaces assigned to each VLAN:

```
SwitchA#sh vlan brief

VLAN Name                            Status    Ports
---- ---------------------------- --------- -----------------------
---
1    default                         active    Fa0/1, Fa0/3, Fa0/4,
Fa0/5

                                                Fa0/6, Fa0/7,
Fa0/8, Fa0/9

                                                Fa0/10
2    Sales                           active    Fa0/2
```

The next steps are to assign ports 3 and 4 to the Sales VLAN (VLAN 2) and ports 6,7,8 to Engineering (VLAN 3). Once this is completed, the port assignments can be verified using the **show vlan** command, as shown:

```
SwitchA#show vlan

VLAN Name                         Status    Ports
---- ---------------------------- --------- ------------------------
---
1    default                      active    Fa0/1, Fa0/5,
Fa0/9, Fa0/10

2    Sales                        active    Fa0/2, Fa0/3,
Fa0/4

3    Engineering                  active    Fa0/6, Fa0/7, Fa0/8
```

You can look specifically at the assignments for only one of the VLANs by entering the command **show vlan name** *vlan-name*, where *vlan-name* is the name assigned to the VLAN. Note that the name is case-sensitive. You can also use the number of the VLAN instead of using the command **show vlan id** *vlan-id*. Examples of both are presented:

show vlan name *vlan-name*
The command to look specifically at only one of the VLANs.

```
SwitchA#show vlan name Engineering

VLAN Name                          Status    Ports
---- ------------------------------ --------- --------------------
---
3    Engineering                    active    Fa0/6, Fa0/7,
Fa0/8
```

```
Switch#show vlan id 3

VLAN Name                          Status    Ports
---- ------------------------------ --------- --------------------
---
3    Engineering                    active    Fa0/6, Fa0/7,
Fa0/8
```

On Layer 2 switches, an IP address can be assigned to a VLAN interface. This merely assigns an IP address to a switch, so that a switch can communicate with other network devices on the same VLAN and vice-versa. The IP VLAN interface does not perform any routing functions when running as a layer 2 switch. As a matter of fact, the IP VLAN interface is not required in order for a switch to start forwarding packets and perform its other Layer 2 functions. By default, the interface VLAN 1 is automatically created. The following command sequence demonstrates how to assign the IP address to the VLAN interface:

interface VLAN 1
The default vlan for the switch.

```
SwitchA(config)# interface VLAN 1
SwitchA(config-if)# ip address 192.168.1.1 255.255.255.0
SwitchA(config-if)# no shutdown
```

Note that the IP address is being set for VLAN 1. The interface for the switch is also enabled at this same point using the **no shutdown** command, as shown. In order for the interface VLAN to be up, at least one switch port in the VLAN must

show interface status
Used to verify the status of a switchport.

be up or have a physical link. The status of a switch port can be verified with the command **show interface** or, better yet, with the command **show interface status**. Although the command **show interface** shows detailed information of individual interface one at a time, the command **show interface status** displays the status of all the switch ports including their speed, duplex, and VLAN, as shown. This gives a quick and precise look of the port status of a switch where port density is high.

```
SwitchA#show interface status
```

```
Port     Name    Status       Vlan       Duplex  Speed Type
Fa0/1            connected    1          a-full  a-100
10/100BaseTX
Fa0/2            connected    2          a-full  a-100
10/100BaseTX
Fa0/3            connected    2          a-full  a-100
10/100BaseTX
Fa0/4            connected    2          a-full  a-100
10/100BaseTX
Fa0/5            connected    1          a-full  a-100
10/100BaseTX
Fa0/6            connected    3          a-full  a-100
10/100BaseTX
Fa0/7            connected    3          a-full  a-100
10/100BaseTX
Fa0/8            connected    3          a-full  a-100
10/100BaseTX
Fa0/9            connected    1          a-full  a-100
10/100BaseTX
Fa0/10           connected    1          a-full  a-100
10/100BaseTX
```

The overall configuration of the switch can be viewed using the **show running-config** (**sh run**) command, as shown. (Only a part of the configuration is displayed.)

```
Switch#sh run        -     -
Building configuration...

Current configuration : 1411 bytes
!
version 12.1
no service pad
service timestamps debug uptime
service timestamps log uptime
no service password-encryption
!
hostname Switch
!
ip subnet-zero
!
spanning-tree mode pvst
no spanning-tree optimize bpdu transmission
spanning-tree extend system-id
```

```
!
interface FastEthernet0/1
!-
 interface FastEthernet0/2
 switchport access vlan 2
 switchport mode access
    .      .
    .      .
    .      .
    .      .
interface FastEthernet0/5
!
interface FastEthernet0/6
 switchport access vlan 3
 switchport mode access
!
interface FastEthernet0/9
!
interface FastEthernet0/10
!
!
interface Vlan1
 ip address 192.168.1.1 255.255.255.0
 no ip route-cache
!
ip http server
!
line con 0
line vty 0 15
 login
end
```

The running-configuration for the switch shows that the FastEthernet interfaces have been assigned to the proper VLANs. Additionally, this shows that an IP address has been assigned to the default interface VLAN1.

This portion of the text has demonstrated the steps for creating a static VLAN. Both Sales and Engineering VLANs were created, and specific ports on the switch were assigned to the respective VLANs. Unassigned ports remained as part of the default VLAN 1.

VLAN Tagging

This section explores the concept of VLAN tagging (802.1Q) and demonstrates the steps required for this configuration. The concept of VLAN tagging can be explained using the example network shown in Figure 1-8. In this network, the Sales team is spread out in two different buildings. Therefore, the Sales VLAN network must be available in both buildings. Each building has its own network switch, and both switches are connected via one physical link.

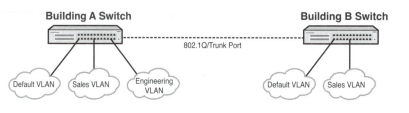

FIGURE 1-8   An example of a scenario with two VLANS spread across two buildings

In a scenario like this, not only is it necessary to have the same Sales VLAN running on both building switches, it is also important to have members of the same VLAN being able to communicate with each other across buildings and to adhere to the same VLAN restrictions. To accomplish this, a technique called VLAN tagging is used. VLAN tagging is a technique deployed on a switch interface to carry Ethernet frames of multiple VLANs. The interface must connect to another switch port, router port, or network device that understands VLAN tagging, and both sides must agree on the VLAN tagging protocol.

The standard protocol for VLAN tagging is IEEE 802.1Q. This standard protocol is widely supported by every switch manufacturer, as well as Cisco. A switch interface or port configured to carry traffic for multiple VLANs is often referred to as a trunk port. The term was made famous by Cisco, and it is used explicitly as the VLAN tagging command in Cisco switches. Note that Cisco has its own proprietary VLAN tagging protocol called Inter-Switch Link (ISL). The big difference between ISL and 802.1Q is how the frame is treated. In ISL, every Ethernet frame is encapsulated within a 26-Byte header containing the VLAN ID and a 4 Byte CRC at the end. This makes the size of an ISL frame bigger than an 802.1Q frame, as discussed next.

To accomplish the VLAN tagging of the Ethernet frames, IEEE 802.1Q simply inserts additional data to the Ethernet frame header, as shown in Figure 1-9. An 802.1Q tag is a 4-Byte tag field that is inserted between the Source Address field and the Ethernet Type/Length field. By inserting an additional 4-Byte field, the Ethernet frame size is increased. Its minimum frame size is now increased from 64 Bytes to 68 Bytes, and its maximum frame size is now increased from 1,518 Bytes to 1,522 Bytes. Figure 1-9 also provides a detailed calculation of the Ethernet frame size. Because of the additional tag field and the increased frame size, it is important that both sides of the link be compatible. Otherwise, the tagged Ethernet frames will not be understood and, therefore, the frames will be dropped by a non-802.1Q-compliant interface.

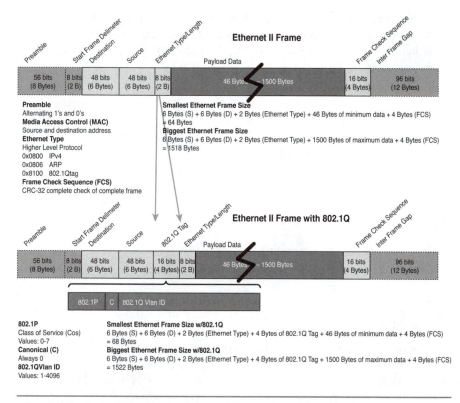

FIGURE 1-9 Typical Ethernet frame versus Ethernet frame with 802.1Q tag

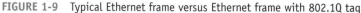

802.1Q Configuration

This section demonstrates the steps for configuring 802.1Q VLAN tagging. The 802.1Q VLAN tagging is configured at the switch interface that interconnects to another network switch. In this case, interface FastEthernet 0/1 of Switch A is selected as a 802.1Q VLAN tagging port or a trunk port. The following demonstrates how to configure an interface as a trunk port on a Cisco switch.

First, the interface is assigned as a trunk port by the command switchport mode trunk. This essentially turns on trunking. The next step is to define the tagging protocol, which is 802.1Q, in this case. The command switchport trunk encapsulation dot1q is used. If ISL is used, the command would be switchport trunk encapsulation isl. The next command, switchport trunk allowed vlan *vlan-id*, is optional, but it is useful in limiting VLANs that can be carried across the link.

```
SwitchA#conf t
Enter configuration commands, one per line. End with CNTL/Z.
SwitchA(config)#int fa 0/1
SwitchA(config-if)#switchport mode trunk
SwitchA(config-if)#switchport trunk encapsulation dot1q
SwitchA(config-if)#switchport trunk allowed vlan 1,2
SwitchA(config-if)#end
```

switchport mode trunk

Turns on trunking.

switchport trunk encapsulation dot1q

This command defines that 802.1Q tagging protocol is being used.

switchport trunk encapsulation isl

This command defines that the tagging protocol is ISL.

switchport trunk allowed vlan *vlan-id*

This command is used to limit the VLANs that can be carried across the link.

By default, all configured VLANs are allowed across the trunk port. In order for VLAN tagging to work properly, it is important to configure the same commands on SwitchB's trunk port. To verify the 802.1Q configuration, the command show interfaces trunk can be used:

```
SwitchA#sh interfaces trunk
Port        Mode                  Encapsulation  Status      Native vlan
Fa0/1       on                    802.1q                     trunking    1


Port        Vlans allowed on trunk
Fa0/1       1,2


Port        Vlans allowed and active in management domain
Fa0/1       1,2


Port        Vlans in spanning tree forwarding state and not pruned
Fa0/1       1,2
```

Networking Challenge: Static VLAN Configuration

Use the Net-Challenge Simulator Software included with the text's companion CD-ROM to demonstrate that you can perform basic switch and static VLAN configuration and set up a trunk connection. Place the CD-ROM in your computer's drive. Open the *Net-Challenge* folder, and click **NetChallengeV3-2. exe**. After the software is running, click the **Select Challenge** button. This opens a Select Challenge drop-down menu. Select the **Chapter 1 - Static VLAN Configuration** challenge to open a checkbox that can be used to verify that you have completed all the tasks. Do the following:

1. Enter the privileged EXEC mode on the switch (password: **Chile**).

2. Enter the switch's configuration mode: **Router(config)**.

3. Set the hostname of the switch to switch-A.

4. Configure the IP address for VLAN 1 interface with the following:

   IP address: 10.10.20.250

   Subnet mask: 255.255.255.0

5. Enable the VLAN 1 interface.

6. Use the command to display the current VLAN settings for the switch.

7. Issue the command that lets you modify the VLAN database.

8. Create a VLAN 2 named Sales.

9. Verify that a new Sales VLAN has been created.

10. Issue the command to enter the fa0/2 interface configuration mode.

11. Enter the sequence of commands that are used to assign interface fa0/2 to the Sales VLAN.

12. Enter the command that enables you to display the interface assigned to each VLAN.

13. Enter the command that enables you to view specifically the assignments for the Sales VLAN.

14. Issue the command that allows you to view the switch's running-configuration.

15. Issue the command to turn on trunking for SwitchA.

16. Issue the command to set trunk encapsulation to 802.1Q.

17. Issue the command that enables VLAN 1 and VLAN 2 to be carried across the link.

Configuring the HP Procurve Switch

This should not come as a surprise to learn that many switch manufacturers follow a similar configuration path as the Cisco switches. A similar Cisco-styled command-line interface (CLI) is deployed by those manufacturers as well. The following is an example of how to configure an HP Procurve switch. The first step is to enter the configuration mode using the command **configure**. Next, the VLAN # is entered using the **vlan 2** command. Finally, the VLAN is assigned a name from the (vlan-2) prompt using the command **name-Sales**:

```
SwitchHP# configure
SwitchHP(config)#vlan 2
SwitchHP(vlan-2)#name Sales
```

The command **show vlan** also exists on the HP switches, but the output result is different than the one produced from Cisco switches. The HP's **show vlan** command does not provide ports with VLAN membership, while the Cisco command does:

```
SwitchHP# show vlan
Status and Counters - VLAN Information

  Maximum VLANs to support : 8
  Primary VLAN : DEFAULT_VLAN
  Management VLAN :

  802.1Q VLAN ID Name            Status        Voice Jumbo
  -------------- ------------ ------------ ----- -----
  1              DEFAULT_VLAN    Port-based    No    No
  2              Sales           Port-based    No    No
```

On a Cisco switch, the VLAN membership is configured at the interface level. On an HP switch, it is configured at the VLAN level, where each VLAN contains its port members. This example shows how a VLAN membership is assigned on an HP switch:

```
SwitchHP# configure
SwitchHP(config)#vlan 2
SwitchHP(vlan-2)#untagged 48
```

In VLAN 2, port 48 is configured as an untagged member. This means that the port is not a tagged VLAN port. It is essentially just a port-based VLAN. It was mentioned earlier that the HP's command **show vlan** does not give much detail. To get more VLAN details, one must specify the VLAN ID. The **show vlan 2** command can be used to verify that port 48 has been assigned to the Sales VLAN (VLAN2):

```
SwitchHP# show vlan  2
  Status and Counters - VLAN Information - Ports - VLAN 2


  802.1Q VLAN ID : 2
  Name : Sales
  Status : Port-based  Voice : No
  Jumbo : No


  Port Information   Mode Unknown     VLAN     Status
  ----------------   ----------------  ----------  ---------
  48                     Untagged                 Learn       Up
```

On HP switches and other switch manufacturers, the command syntax for enabling a port to carry 802.1Q tagged frames is basically the same. On HP switches, there is not a trunk command. The step is to simply assign tagging ability to the switch port by issuing the command **tagged** *port_number.* Because this is a non-Cisco switch, 802.1Q is the only VLAN tagging protocol that can be used. The following command sequence demonstrates how to configure an interface port 24 on an HP switch as a 802.1Q VLAN tagging port:

```
SwitchHP# conf
SwitchHP(config)# vlan  1
SwitchHP(vlan-1)# tagged 24
SwitchHP(vlan-1)# exit
SwitchHP(config)# vlan 2
SwitchHP(vlan-2)# tagged 24
SwitchHP(vlan-2)# exit
```

Unlike Cisco switches where an 802.1Q is configured at the interface level, the tagging configuration is done at the VLAN level on HP switches. Port 24 is designated as tagged port for both VLAN 1 and VLAN 2, which enables it to carry VLAN 1 and VLAN 2 frames. Generally, untagged ports belong to one specific VLAN, while tagged ports can belong to one or more VLANs.

1-4   ROUTED NETWORK

This section examines the Layer 3 network and how data is routed in the network. This section also introduces another Layer 3 device, the multilayer switch. You need to understand the advantages and disadvantages of this device. This section also introduces interVLAN configuration, which enables VLANs to communicate across networks. The section concludes with a look at both serial and ATM configurations. Some network engineers will argue that the serial and ATM technologies are a dying technology and are now considered obsolete. However, being obsolete does not mean they are nonexistent. These technologies are still being used throughout the world, and it is still an important topic.

Router

The router is a powerful networking device used to interconnect LANs. The router is a Layer 3 device in the OSI model, which means the router uses the **network address** (Layer 3 addressing) to make routing decisions regarding forwarding data packets. In the OSI model, the Layer 3, or network, layer responsibilities include handling of the network address. The network address is also called a *logical address,* rather than being a physical address (such as the MAC address, which is embedded into the network interface card [NIC]). The **logical address** describes the IP address location of the network and the address location of the host in the network.

Essentially, the router is configured to know how to route data packets entering or exiting the LAN. This differs from the bridge and the Layer 2 switch, which use the Ethernet address for making decisions regarding forwarding data packets and only know how to forward data to hosts physically connected to their ports.

Routers are used to interconnect LANs in a campus network. Routers can be used to interconnect networks that use the same protocol (for example, Ethernet), or they can be used to interconnect LANs that are using different Layer 2 technologies, such as an Ethernet, ATM, T1, and so on. Routers also make it possible to interconnect to LANs around the country and the world and interconnect to many different networking protocols. The router ports are *bidirectional,* meaning that data can enter and exit the same router port. Often, the router ports are called the **router interface**, which is the physical connection where the router connects to the network.

The network provided in Figure 1-10 is an example of a simple three-router campus network. This configuration enables data packets to be sent and received from any host on the network after the routers in the network have been properly configured. For example, computer A1 in LAN A could be sending data to computer D1 in LAN D. This requires that the IP address for computer D1 is known by the user sending the data from computer A1. The data from computer A1 will first travel to the switch where the data is passed to Router A via the FA0/0 FastEthernet data port. Router A will examine the network address of the data packet and use configured routing instructions stored in the router's routing tables to decide where to forward the data. Router A determines that an available path to Router C is via the FA0/2 FastEthernet port connection. The data is then sent directly to Router C. Router C determines that the data packet should be forwarded to its FA0/0 port to reach computer D1 in LAN D. The data is then sent to D1. Alternatively, Router A could have sent the data to Router C through Router B via Router A's FA0/1 FastEthernet port.

Network Address
Another name for the Layer 3 address.

Logical Address
This describes the IP address location of the network and the address location of the host in the network.

Router Interface
The physical connection where the router connects to the network.

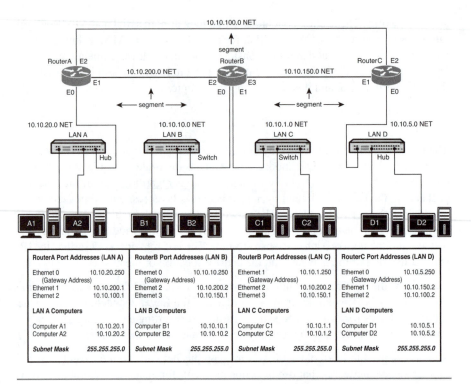

RouterA Port Addresses (LAN A)		RouterB Port Addresses (LAN B)		RouterB Port Addresses (LAN C)		RouterC Port Addresses (LAN D)	
Ethernet 0 (Gateway Address)	10.10.20.250	Ethernet 0 (Gateway Address)	10.10.10.250	Ethernet 1 (Gateway Address)	10.10.1.250	Ethernet 0 (Gateway Address)	10.10.5.250
Ethernet 1	10.10.200.1	Ethernet 2	10.10.200.2	Ethernet 2	10.10.200.2	Ethernet 1	10.10.150.2
Ethernet 2	10.10.100.1	Ethernet 3	10.10.150.1	Ethernet 3	10.10.150.1	Ethernet 2	10.10.100.2
LAN A Computers		**LAN B Computers**		**LAN C Computers**		**LAN D Computers**	
Computer A1	10.10.20.1	Computer B1	10.10.10.1	Computer C1	10.10.1.1	Computer D1	10.10.5.1
Computer A2	10.10.20.2	Computer B2	10.10.10.2	Computer C2	10.10.1.2	Computer D2	10.10.5.2
Subnet Mask	*255.255.255.0*	*Subnet Mask*	*255.255.255.0*	*Subnet Mask*	*255.255.255.0*	*Subnet Mask*	*255.255.255.0*

FIGURE 1-10 The three-router campus LAN

Delivery of the information over the network was made possible by the use of an IP address and routing table. Routing tables keep track of the routes used for forwarding data to its destination. RouterA used its routing table to determine a network data path so computer A1's data could reach computer D1 in LAN D. After the data packet arrived on Router C, an ARP request is issued by Router C to determine the MAC address of computer D1. The MAC address is then used for final delivery of the data to computer D1.

If Router A determines that the network path to Router C is down, Router A can route the data packet to Router C through Router B. After Router B receives the data packet from Router A, it uses its routing tables to determine where to forward the data packet. Router B determines that the data needs to be sent to Router C. Router B will then use its FA0/3 FastEthernet port to forward the data to Router C.

Gateway Address

As previously discussed, the term *gateway* is used to describe the address of the networking device that enables the hosts in a LAN to connect to networks and hosts outside the LAN. For example, the gateway address for all hosts in LAN A will be 10.10.20.250. This address is configured on the host computer, as shown in Figure 1-11. Any IP packets with a destination outside the LAN A network will be sent to this gateway address. Note that the destination network is determined by the subnet mask. In this case, the subnet mask is 255.255.255.0.

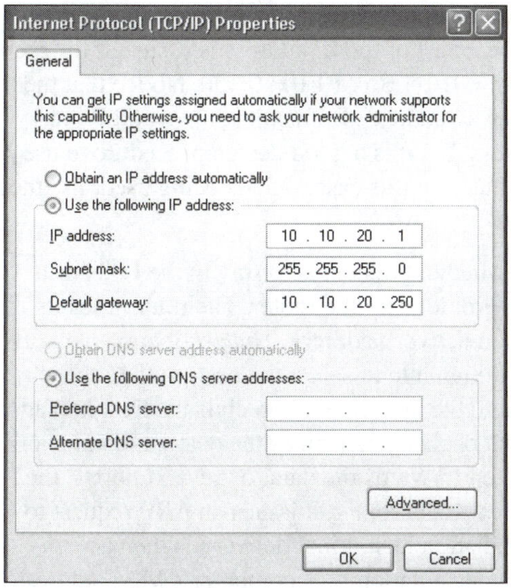

FIGURE 1-11 Network settings configuration for the default gateway

Network Segments

The *network segment* defines the networking link between two LANs. There is a segment associated with each connection of an internetworking device (for example, router-hub, router-switch, router-router). For example, the IP address for the network segment connecting LAN A to the router is 10.10.20.0. All hosts connected to this segment must contain a 10.10.20.x, because a subnet mask of 255.255.255.0 is being used. Subnet masking is fully explained in *Network Essentials* Chapter 6, "TCP/IP."

Routers use the information about the network segments to determine where to forward data packets. For example, referring to Figure 1-10, the network segments that connect to Router A include

    10.10.20.0
    10.10.200.0
    10.10.100.0

The segment is sometimes called the subnet or NET. These terms are associated with a network segment address, such as 10.10.20.0. In this case, the network is called the 10.10.20.0 NET. All hosts in the 10.10.20.0 NET will have a 10.10.20.x IP address. The network addresses are used when configuring the routers and defining which networks are connected to the router.

> **Subnet, NET**
> Other terms for the segment.

According to Figure 1-11, all the computers in LAN A must have a 10.10.20.x address. This is defined by the 255.255.255.0 subnet mask. For example, computer A1 in LAN A will have the assigned IP address of 10.10.20.1 and a gateway address of 10.10.20.250. The computers in LAN B (see Figure 1-10) are located in the

10.10.10.0 network. This means that all the computers in this network must contain a 10.10.10.x IP address. In this case, the *x* part of the IP address is assigned for each host. The gateway address for the hosts in LAN B is 10.10.10.250. Notice that the routers are all using the same .250 gateway address. Remember, any valid IP address can be used for the gateway address, but it is a good design procedure to use the same number for number for all routers. In this case, .250 is being used. In other cases, it could be .1 or .254.

The subnet mask is used to determine whether the data is to stay in the LAN or is to be forwarded to the default gateway provided by the router. The router uses its subnet mask to determine the destination network address. The destination network address is checked with the router's routing table to select the best route to the destination. The data is then forwarded to the next router, which is the next hop address. The next router examines the data packet, determines the destination network address, checks its routing table, and then forwards the data to the next hop. If the destination network is directly connected to the router, it issues an ARP request to determine the MAC address of the destination host. Final delivery is then accomplished by forwarding the data using the destination host computer's MAC address. Routing of the data through the networks is at Layer 3, and the final delivery of data in the network is at Layer 2.

Multilayer Switch

Multilayer Switch (MLS)

Operates at Layer 2, but functions at the higher layers.

Wire Speed Routing

Data packets are processed as fast as they arrive.

So far, the topic of network switches revolves around their Layer 2 functionalities. Today, the scope of operations has changed for switches. Newer switch technologies are available to help further improve the performance of computer networks. This new development started with Layer 3 switches and now there are multilayer switches. The term used to describe these switches that can operate above the OSI Layer 2 is multilayer switches (MLS). An example is a Layer 3 switch. Layer 3 switches still work at Layer 2, but additionally work at the network layer (Layer 3) of the OSI model and use IP addressing for making decisions to route a data packet in the best direction. The major difference is that the packet switching in basic routers is handled by a programmed microprocessor. The multilayer switch uses application specific integrated circuits (ASIC) hardware to handle the packet switching. The advantage of using hardware to handle the packet switching is a significant reduction in processing time (software versus hardware). In fact, the processing time of multilayer switches can be as fast as the input data rate. This is called wire speed routing, where the data packets are processed as fast as they are arriving. Multilayer switches can also work at the upper layers of the OSI model. An example is a Layer 4 switch that processes data packets at the transport layer of the OSI model.

Through this evolution, the line between routers and multilayer switches is getting more and more blurry. Routers were once considered the more intelligent device, but this is no longer true. With new developments, the multilayer switches can do almost everything the routers can. More importantly, most of the Layer 3 switch configuration commands are almost identical to the ones used on the routers. Routers tend to be more expensive when it comes to cost per port. Therefore, most of the traditional designs have a router connecting to a switch or switches to provide more port density. This can be expensive depending on the size of the network. So, there has been a shift toward deploying multilayer switches in the network LAN environment in place of routers. In this case, the routers and switches in Figure 1-10 then could all be replaced with multilayer switches. This also means there will be less network equipment to maintain, which reduces the maintenance cost and makes this a more cost-effective solution. With its greater port density, a multilayer switch can serve more clients than a router could. However, there is a common drawback for most multilayer switches: These devices only support Ethernet. Other Layer 2 technologies, such as ATM, DSL,T1, still depend on routers for making this connection.

Layer 3 Routed Networks

As discussed previously, the hosts are interconnected with a switch or hub. This allows data to be exchanged within the LAN; however, data cannot be routed to other networks. Also, the broadcast domain of one LAN is not isolated from another LAN's broadcast domain. The solution for breaking up the broadcast domains and providing network routing is to incorporate routing hardware into the network design to create a routed network. A routed network uses Layer 3 addressing for selecting routes to forward data packets, so a better name for this network is a Layer 3 network.

> **Routed Network**
> Uses Layer 3 addressing for selecting routes to forward data packets.
>
> **Layer 3 Network**
> Another name for a routed network.

In Layer 3 networks, routers and multilayer switches are used to interconnect the networks and LANs, isolating broadcast domains and enabling hosts from different LANs and networks to exchange data. Data packet delivery is achieved by handing off data to adjacent routers until the packet reaches its final destination. This typically involves passing data packets through many routers and many networks. An example of a Layer 3 network is shown in Figure 1-10. This example has four LANs interconnected using three routers. The IP address for each networking device is listed.

The physical layer interface on the router provides a way to connect the router to other networking devices on the network. For example, the FastEthernet ports on the router are used to connect to other FastEthernet ports on other routers or switches. Gigabit and 10-gigabit Ethernet ports are also available on routers to connect to other high-speed Ethernet ports (the sample network shown in Figure 1-10 includes only FastEthernet ports). Routers also contain other types of interfaces, such as serial interfaces and Synchronous Optical Network (SONET) interfaces. These interfaces were widely used to interconnect the router and the network to other wide-area networks (WAN). For example, connection to WANs requires the use of a serial interface or SONET interface to connect to a communications carrier, such as Sprint, AT&T, Century Link, and so on. The data speeds for the serial communication ports on routers can vary from slow (56 kbps) up to high-speed DS3 data rates (47+ Mbps), and the SONET could range from OC3 (155 Mbps), OC12 (622 Mbps), or even OC192 (9953 Mbps).

> **Synchronous Optical Network (SONET)**
> Used to interconnect the router and the network to other WANs.
>
> **WAN**
> Wide-area network.

Routed Port Configuration

Routers can have Ethernet (10 Mbps), Fast Ethernet (100 Mbps), Gigabit Ethernet (1,000 Mbps), and 10 gigabit (10 GB), Serial, and ATM interfaces. These routers can have multiple interfaces, and the steps for configuring each interface are basically the same. Each interface is assigned a number. For example, a router could have three FastEthernet interfaces identified as

FastEthernet 0/0
FastEthernet 0/1
FastEthernet 0/2

The notation 0/0 indicates the [*interface-card-slot/port*].

On Cisco's routers, a routed port can be configured simply by assigning an IP address to the interface. Once an IP address and its subnet mask are assigned to the interface and the interface is enabled, a Layer 3 network is created. The interface IP address becomes the gateway for that network. To program the interface, the router must be in the configuration mode. The following demonstrates how to configure a router's FastEthernet 0/0 port (FastEthernet 0/0, also listed as fa0/0 and FA0/0) as a routed interface.

```
Router(config)# int fa0/0
Router(config-if)# ip address 10.10.20.250 255.255.255.0
Router(config-if)#no shut
2w0d: %LINEPROTO-5-UPDOWN: Line protocol on Interface FastEthernet0/0,
changed state to up
```

terminal monitor (term mon)

Displays log messages on the remote terminal.

Notice that the router prompts you that the line protocol on interface FastEthernet 0/0 changed state to up. These log messages are always displayed when connecting via the console port. However, they are suppressed when it is a remote terminal session, like Telnet or SSH. To display log messages on the remote terminal, issue the command **terminal monitor** or **term mon** at the router prompt:

```
Router# term mon
```

terminal no monitor (term no mon)

Disables the logging to the terminal.

The log messages can be useful when bringing up a new connection. Sometimes, they can be annoying if the router is logging too many events. To disable the logging to the terminal, the command is **terminal no monitor** or **term no mon**. One would think the command syntax would start with **no**, like typical Cisco command, but it is not so in this case:

```
Router# term no mon
```

show ip interface brief (sh ip int brief)

Verifies the status of the router interfaces.

The command **show ip interface brief (sh ip int brief)** entered at the enable prompt (**Router#**) can be used to verify the status of the router interfaces. The following is an example:

```
Router# sh ip int brief
Interface       IP-Address    OK? Method Status             Protocol
FastEthernet0/0 10.10.20.250  YES manual up                 up
FastEthernet0/1 unassigned    YES manual administratively down
down
FastEthernet0/2 unassigned    YES manual administratively down
down
```

The output shows that the interface FastEthernet0/0 was configured with the IP address and its status is up. Because the FastEthernet0/1 and FastEthernet0/2 were not yet configured, their IP addresses are shown as unassigned and their interfaces are still administratively shut down.

Also, a routed port can be assigned to a multilayer switch. This configuration is simple and the same as configuring a router port. The first step is to convert the native switch port to a router port. This is accomplished by issuing the command **no switchport** on the desired switch interface. Then, the IP address and other configuration can be applied to the interface just like a typical router port:

> **no switchport**
> Converts the native switch port to a router port.

```
SwitchA(config)# interface FastEthernet0/1
SwitchA(config-if)# no switchport
SwitchA(config-if)# ip address 192.168.1.1 255.255.255.0
SwitchA(config-if)# no shutdown
```

One concept that is worth exploring is secondary IP address. The primary address is the IP address that is assigned to the interface. The secondary IP address is a way to support multiple IP addresses per router interface. Hence, it allows multiple Layer 3 networks to reside on the same physical link. Secondary IP addresses can be useful when you want to add more networks without having to disturb the existing network or to use it as a transitional network for network migration. Some people might just want to run multiple logical subnets on one physical subnet. To add a secondary IP address to the interface, the command is **ip address** [*ip_address*] [*subnet_mask*] **secondary**. The keyword **secondary** is used to specify the secondary IP address. The secondary IP address configuration is as follows:

> **Secondary IP Address**
> Allows multiple Layer 3 networks to reside on the same physical link.

```
Router(config)# interface FastEthernet0/0
Router(config-if)# ip address 10.10.20.250 255.255.255.0
Router(config-if)# ip address 172.16.1.1 255.255.255.0 secondary
```

In order to configure the secondary IP address, the primary IP address must exist first. There can be as many secondary IP addresses as needed. The secondary IP address cannot be verified with the **show int** or **show ip int brief** command. The results will only display the primary IP address information.

InterVLAN Routing Configuration

As previously discussed in Section 1-3, "VLAN Network," each VLAN is its own broadcast domain. It cannot forward traffic across its VLAN boundaries. However, it is almost impractical in today's applications for a VLAN not to be able to communicate beyond itself. To enable communications among VLANs, InterVLAN routing is required.

> **InterVLAN routing**
> Enables communications among VLANs.
>
> **router on a stick**
> Eliminates connecting a link from each VLAN to a router port by utilizing a trunk or 802.1Q port.

The most logical solution to route traffic between different VLANs is to introduce or create a Layer 3 routed network between them. One traditional way is to connect each VLAN to a router interface. Then, each router interface is configured as a different Layer 3 network. This enables VLANs to communicate and pass traffic via the Layer 3 IP network. For a few VLANs, this does not present an issue, but for a large number of VLANs, this could create some issues. This means that every VLAN will require a physical connection to a router port. Router ports are expensive, and this design can be costly as the number of VLANs increases and more physical links are required. A more common and popular design is to implement a router on a stick. The router on a stick design eliminates connecting a link from each VLAN to a router port by utilizing a trunk or 802.1Q port. A single trunk port is connected to a router, and it passes the tagged VLAN traffic to the router, as depicted in Figure 1-12.

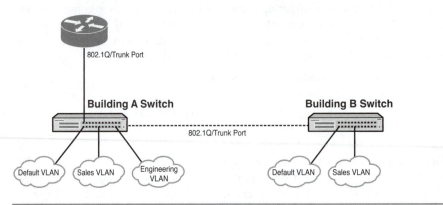

FIGURE 1-12 Router on a stick topology

This design requires that the router must be configured to accept the tagged VLANs. A Layer 3 network is then assigned to each VLAN coming to the router. To accomplish this, subinterfaces are created under the router interface at which the switch trunk port is terminated. The subinterface is a virtual interface, and its notation is a dot followed by the subinterface number. In the example provided, the subinterfaces are listed as FastEthernet0/0.1, 0.2, and 0.3. For the ease of programming, it is recommended to keep the subinterface number the same as the VLAN ID. Recall that the default VLAN is 1, the Sales VLAN is 2, and the Engineering VLAN is 3. The next step is to define the VLAN tagging encapsulation. In this case, it is dot1q, which essentially is 802.1Q. With the encapsulation, the appropriate VLAN ID is specified. Next, the IP address is assigned creating a routed Layer 3 network for a VLAN. The following example demonstrates how to configure a Cisco router for a 802.1Q interVLAN routing:

```
Router(config)#interface FastEthernet0/0
Router(config-if)#no ip address
Router(config-if)#interface FastEthernet0/0.1
Router(config-if)#description Default VLAN
Router(config-subif)#encapsulation dot1Q 1
Router(config-subif)#ip address 172.16.10.1 255.255.255.0

Router(config-subif)#interface FastEthernet0/0.2
Router(config-subif)#description Sales VLAN
Router(config-subif)#encapsulation dot1Q 2
Router(config-subif)#ip address 172.16.20.1 255.255.255.0

Router(config-subif)#interface FastEthernet0/0.3
Router(config-subif)#description Engineering VLAN
Router(config-subif)#encapsulation dot1Q 3
Router(config-subif)#ip address 172.16.30.1 255.255.255.0
```

As mentioned in Section 1-3, an IP address can be assigned to a VLAN interface for management purposes. The IP VLAN interface does not perform any routing functions when running as a Layer 2 switch. However, this concept is changed in multilayer switching. Different virtual interfaces can be created on each of the VLANs. These interfaces are called SVIs (switched virtual interfaces). When an SVI is created and the IP address is assigned, the multilayer switch that has routing enabled can start routing VLANs. Thus, an SVI acts like a virtual router interface. The SVI is another way to route VLANs. SVI's deployment is common in multi-layer switches. The following example demonstrates how to configure an SVI:

```
SwitchA(config)# ip routing
SwitchA(config)# interface VLAN 1
SwitchA(config-if)# ip address 192.168.1.1 255.255.255.0
SwitchA(config-if)# no shutdown

SwitchA(config)# interface VLAN 2
SwitchA(config-if)# ip address 192.168.2.1 255.255.255.0
SwitchA(config-if)# no shutdown
```

The command **ip routing** is entered to ensure the routing is enabled on a multilayer switch. After that, the switched virtual interfaces are created for every VLAN that we want to route. Then, the IP address is assigned to each SVI interface. By default the SVI interface is not enabled, hence the command no shutdown needs to be issued. The preceding example shows the steps on how to enable configuring an SVI for VLAN 1 and VLAN2.

Serial and ATM Port Configuration

As mentioned in the previous section, routers can have different types of interfaces, such as a serial and Asynchronous Transfer Mode (ATM) interfaces. At one time, these interfaces were the standard of WAN connection technologies. Now, they are being replaced by Ethernet WAN based technology. Some network engineers will argue that the serial and ATM technologies are a dying technology and are now considered to be obsolete. However, being obsolete does not mean they are nonexistent. Many of the rural networks in America and around the world still use these technologies for their WAN connection and rely on these technologies to deliver services to people's homes and businesses. Therefore, it is still beneficial to have a basic understanding of these legacy technologies and how they operate. After all, knowledge is always a commodity.

Serial technology provides communications data rates for end users in the form of DS-0 to DS-3 and T1 to T3. The T1/DS-1 and T3/DS-3 designations are actually the same data rates and the terms are used interchangeably. The Bell system *T* carriers were established in the 1960s primarily for transporting digitized telephone conversations. In the early 1980s, the digital signal (DS) subscriber lines became available. Table 1-4 lists the data rates for the T/DS carriers. The DS0 designation is for the base rate of the digital signal lines, basically the data rate of a digitized telephone call. The DS0 channels can be multiplexed together to provide more transmission bandwidth. For example, the T1 line is capable of carrying 24 DS-0 transmissions, which provide the data rate of 1.544 Mbps.

TABLE 1-4   Data Rates for the T and DS Carriers

Designation	Data Rate
DS-0	64 kbps
T1 (DS-1)	1.544 Mbps
T2 (DS-2)	6.312 Mbps
T3 (DS-3)	44.736 Mbps

CSU/DSU

Channel service unit/ data service unit.

AMI

Alternate mark inversion. A fundamental line coding scheme developed for transmission over T1 circuits.

B8ZS

Bipolar 8 zero substitution. A data encoding format developed to improve data transmission over T1 circuits.

Minimum Ones Density

A pulse is intentionally sent in the data stream even if the data being transmitted is a series of all 0s.

HDLC

High-level data link control, a synchronous proprietary protocol.

PPP

Point-to-Point Protocol. A full duplex protocol used for serial interface connections such as that provided by modems.

The communications carrier will require the serial data connection be made through a CSU/DSU (channel service unit/data service unit). The CSU/DSU provides the hardware data interface to the carrier. This includes adding the framing information for maintaining the data flow, storing performance data, and providing line management. The T1 data stream is broken into frames. Each frame consists of 24 voice channels (8 kbps)—8 bits per channel plus one framing bit, for a total of 193 bits. There are two framing techniques used in T1: D4 and ESF. D4, sometimes known as SF (Super Frame), is the original framing technique. Later on, ESF (Extended Super Frame) was introduced as an improvement in data performance over D4 framing.

Along with Framing, T1 requires line coding. The data connection to the communications carrier requires that the proper data encoding format be selected for the CSU/DSU. Data are encoded in such a way that timing information of the binary stream is maintained and the logical 1s and 0s can still be detected. A fundamental coding scheme that was developed for transmission over T1 circuits is alternate mark inversion (AMI). The AMI code provides for alternating voltage level pulses V(+) and V(-) to represent the 1s. With AMI, a long string of 0s can produce a loss of timing and synchronization. This deficiency can be overcome by the transmission of the appropriate start, stop, and synchronizing bits, but this comes at the price of adding overhead bits to the data transmission and consuming a portion of the data communication channel's bandwidth. The bipolar 8 zero substitution (B8ZS) data encoding format was developed to improve data transmission over T1 circuits. T1 circuits require that a minimum ones density level be met so that the timing and synchronization of the data link is maintained. Maintaining a minimum ones density means that a pulse is intentionally sent in the data stream even if the data being transmitted is a series of all 0s. Intentionally inserting the pulses in the data stream helps maintain the timing and synchronization of the data stream. B8ZS is sometimes referred to as clear channel by the Telecommunication engineers. Both framing and line coding are configured at the CSU/DSU. The configuration must match at both ends of the connection. The CSU/DSU could be its own unit or it could be built into the router serial interface. Typically, AMI signaling is paired with D4/SF, while B8ZS signaling uses frames that are grouped into ESF.

Two other serial line protocols commonly used in wide-area networking are high-level data link control (HDLC) and Point-to-Point Protocol (PPP). Both protocols are used by routers to carry data over a serial line connection, typically over direct connections, such as with T1. PPP is used for serial interface connections, such as that provided by modems. PPP is a full duplex protocol and is a subset of the HDLC data encapsulation.

The routers at each end must be configured with the proper data encapsulation. *Data encapsulation* means the data is properly packaged for transport over a serial communications line. The type of encapsulation depends on the hardware being used to make the connection. The command for setting the data encapsulation is **encapsulation (encap)**. The options for the data encapsulation on the router can be viewed by entering **encap ?** at the router's (config-if)# prompt, as demonstrated here:

```
Router(config-if)#encap ?
  atm-dxi      ATM-DXI encapsulation
  frame-relay  Frame Relay networks
  hdlc         Serial HDLC synchronous
  lapb         LAPB (X.25 Level 2)
  ppp          Point-to-Point protocol
  smds         Switched Megabit Data Service (SMDS)
  x25          X.25
```

The following configuration example is from an older Cisco router, which has a serial interface connecting to a CSU/DSU. The steps for setting the data encapsulation to HDLC and PPP on the Serial1/0 interface and configuring the serial interface IP address are shown. The T1 encapsulation on Cisco routers is HDLC by default, if the encapsulation is not specified. The encapsulation can be overwritten by issuing the new encapsulation option. Finally, the interface can be enabled via the command **no shut**.

```
Router# conf t
Router(config)# int s1/0
Router(config-if)#encap hdlc
Router(config-if)#ip address 10.10.128.1 255.255.255.0
Router# conf t
Router(config)# int s1/0
Router(config-if)#encap ppp
Router(config-if)# no shut
2w0d: %LINK-3-UPDOWN: Interface Serial0/0, changed state to up
2w0d: %LINEPROTO-5-UPDOWN: Line protocol on Interface Serial0/0,
changed state to up
```

The status of the serial interfaces can be checked using the **sh ip int brief** command, as demonstrated here:

```
Router# sh ip int brief
Interface       IP-Address     OK?   Method   Status       Protocol
FastEthernet0   10.10.20.250   YES   manual    up           up
FastEthernet0/1 unassigned      YES   manual     administratively
down       down
FastEthernet0/2 unassigned      YES   manual     administratively
down       down
Serial1/0        10.10.128.1    YES   manual    up           up
```

The data encapsulation can be verified by using the **sh int s0/0** command. The last line in this example shows that the encapsulation is PPP:

```
Router#sh int s1/0
Serial0 is up, line protocol is up
Hardware is HD64570
Description: ISP Connection
Internet address is 192.168.1.2/24
MTU 1500 bytes, BW 1544 Kbit, DLY 20000 usec, rely 255/255, load 1/255
Encapsulation PPP, loopback not set, keepalive set (10 sec)
```

The type of network being configured and the equipment being used to make the direct connection determines the selection of the format for data encapsulation. For example, Cisco routers automatically configure the serial interfaces to run HDLC, but the Cisco routers support many data encapsulation formats. The HDLC data encapsulation formats are implemented differently by some vendors, and there are times when some equipment is not interoperable with other equipment even though they both have specified the HDLC encapsulation. In that case, another encapsulation format such as PPP can be used to make the direct connection.

On newer Cisco routers, there is a variety of T1 interface cards available. Most of them fall under these two types. They are either WAN interface cards (**WICs**) that only provide data support or they are Voice/WAN interface cards (**VWICs**) that can provide both voice and data support. These types of cards all have an integrated CSU/DSU, which makes it convenient for setup. In this case, a T1 connection with an RJ45 interface can be directly connected to the card. If the names WIC and VWIC are not confusing enough, the configuration steps for these cards will certainly create some confusion. The configuration steps are presented next.

The first example shows the configuration of a router with a T1 WIC card. The T1 configuration, usually programmed on a CSU/DSU, is now done under a serial interface. The T1 framing, line coding, and clock source are configured via command **service-module t1**. In this case, ESF is selected as the framing technique, and B8ZS is used as the line coding. The clock source line means the clock is provided by the carrier through the T1 line. This is critical for synchronizing the T1 transmission. The timeslot defines the speed of the DS0 channel and the number of DS0 channels being used.

```
Router(config)#interface Serial0/1
Router(config-if)#ip address 10.10.128.1 255.255.255.0
Router(config-if)#service-module t1 timeslots 1-24 speed 64
Router(config-if)#service-module t1 framing ESF
Router(config-if)#service-module t1 linecode B8ZS
Router(config-if)#service-module t1 clock source line
Router(config-if)#encapsulation ppp
```

The second example shows the configuration of a router with a T1 VWIC type card. The framing, line coding, and clock source are now defined under a T1 controller. Next, a corresponding serial interface is created with an IP address and the T1 encapsulation:

```
Router(config)#controller T1 1/0
Router(config-controller)#framing esf
Router(config-controller)#clock source line
Router(config-controller)#linecode b8zs
Router(config-controller)#channel-group 0 timeslots 1-24 speed 64

Router(config-if)#interface Serial1/0:0
Router(config-if)#ip address 10.10.128.1 255.255.255.0
Router(config-if)#encapsulation ppp
```

You can verify the T1 status with the command **show controller T1** *slot/port*. This command displays the T1 status with details that one would find in a CSU/DSU. The output result shows the T1 is up in a good clean state. So far, there are no errors for the last 24 hours:

> **show controller T1**
> *slot/port*
> Verifies the status of the T1 interface.

```
Router#show controller T1 1/0
T1 0/1/0 is up.
  Applique type is Channelized T1
  Cablelength is long 0db
  No alarms detected.
  alarm-trigger is not set
  Soaking time: 3, Clearance time: 10
  AIS State:Clear  LOS State:Clear  LOF State:Clear
  Version info Firmware: 20090408, FPGA: 13, spm_count = 0
  Framing is ESF, Line Code is B8ZS, Clock Source is Line.
  CRC Threshold is 320. Reported from firmware  is 320.
  Data in current interval (195 seconds elapsed):
     0 Line Code Violations, 0 Path Code Violations
     0 Slip Secs, 0 Fr Loss Secs, 0 Line Err Secs, 0 Degraded Mins
     0 Errored Secs, 0 Bursty Err Secs, 0 Severely Err Secs, 0 Unavail
Secs
  Total Data (last 24 hours)
     0 Line Code Violations, 0 Path Code Violations,
     0 Slip Secs, 0 Fr Loss Secs, 0 Line Err Secs, 0 Degraded Mins,
     0 Errored Secs, 0 Bursty Err Secs, 0 Severely Err Secs, 0 Unavail
Secs
```

Asynchronous Transfer Mode (**ATM**) is a cell relay technique designed for voice, data, and video traffic. It uses fixed length data packets called cells. The size of each cell is 53 bytes with 5 bytes being the ATM header. The ATM protocol was designed for use in high-speed multimedia networking, including operation in high-speed data transmission found in SONET's OC-1, OC-3, OC-12, OC-48, and OC-192.

> **ATM**
> Asynchronous transfer mode.

Virtual Path Connection (VPC)
Used to connect the end users.

Virtual Channel Connection (VCC)
Carries the ATM cell from user to user.

Switched Virtual Circuit (SVC)
A dynamic virtual circuit that is established on demand by end devices through the Network-Network Interface signaling method.

ATM is connection oriented, using two different types of connections: a **virtual path connection (VPC)** and a **virtual channel connection (VCC)**. A VCC is used to carry the ATM cell data from user to user. The virtual channels are combined to create a virtual path connection, which is used to connect the end users. Virtual circuits can be configured as permanent virtual connections (PVC) or they can be configured as switched virtual circuits (**SVC**).

Five classes of services are available with ATM, based on the needs of the user. In some applications, users need a constant bit rate for applications such as teleconferencing. In another application, users might need only limited periods of higher bandwidth to handle bursty data traffic. Table 1-5 describes the five ATM service classes.

TABLE 1-5   Five ATM Service Classes

ATM Service Class	Acronym	Description	Typical Use
constant bit-rate	CBR	Cell rate is constant.	Telephone, video-conferencing television
Variable bit-rate/non–real time	VBR-NRT	Cell rate is variable.	Email
Variable bit-rate/real time	VBR-RT	Cell rate is variable but can be constant on demand.	Voice traffic
Available bit-rate	ABR	Users are allowed to specify a minimum cell rate.	File transfers/email
Unspecified bit-rate	UBR		TCP/IP

VPI
Virtual path identifier.

VCI
Virtual channel identifier.

ATM uses an 8-bit virtual path identifier (**VPI**) to identify the virtual circuits used to deliver cells in the ATM network. A 16-bit virtual channel identifier (**VCI**) is used to identify the connection between the two ATM stations. The VPI and VCI numbers are provided by the telco. Together, the numbers are used to create an ATM PVC (permanent virtual circuit) through the ATM cloud, as demonstrated in Figure 1-13.

The VPI/VCI numbers (1/33) shown in Figure 1-13 are for the ATM PVC interface. Router A connects to the ATM cloud via an ATM physical interface on the router. Router B also connects to the ATM cloud via an ATM physical interface on the router. In this example, the name for the physical interface on Router A is ATM 4/0. This is comparable to the E0 name for the router's Ethernet0 interface.

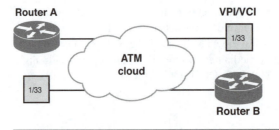

FIGURE 1-13   An example of a connection to an ATM cloud

The following listing is from a router configured to run ATM:

```
Interface ATM 4/0
description net atm (1 2 3 4 5 6 7 8 9)
no ip address
atm scrambling cell-payload atm framing cbitplcp
no atm ilmi-keepalive
```

The first line, **Interface ATM 4/0**, identifies the physical interface being configured (in this case, ATM interface 4). The second line, **description net atm (1 2 3 4 5 6 7 8 9)**, is a description of the ATM connection. The name of the connection is net; it is an ATM connection, and the telco circuit number is 1 2 3 4 5 6 7 8 9. The third line, **no ip address**, indicates that no IP address is specified for the ATM interface. The physical interface on an ATM connection is not assigned an IP address. The two commands **atm scrambling cell-payload** and **atm framing cbitplcp** are entries required to make the connection to the telco interface. Telco specifies the format for these commands. The entry **no atm ilmi-keepalive** is used to disable the generation of keepalive messages.

The next group of commands is used to configure the router's subinterface:

```
interface ATM4/0.33 point-to-point
description PVC to CityB (1 2 3 4 5 4 3 2 1)
ip address 192.168.23.1 255.255.255.0
pvc netB 1/33
vbr-nrt 3000 3000 1 broadcast encapsulation aal5snap
```

The entry interface **ATM 4/0.33 point-to-point** indicates that the VCI number for the subinterface is 33 and it is on the ATM 4 physical interface. It also indicates that this is a point-to-point connection. The second line is for the description of the subinterface. It indicates that this is a PVC for connecting to CityB's network, and the telco circuit number is 1 2 3 4 5 4 3 2 1. The third line specifies the IP address for the subinterface.

The entry **pvc netB 1/33** creates a PVC with a VPI of 1 and a VCI of 33. The entry **vdr-nrt 3000 3000 1** is used to configure the peak, average, and burst options for voice traffic over the PVC. This parameter is typically specified by telco. The output pcr (peak cell rate) is 3,000 kbps and the output scr (sustained cell rate) is 3000 kbps. The **1** indicates an output mbs (maximum burst size) of 1.

The entry **broadcast** enables broadcasts to be forwarded across the ATM PVC. The entry **encapsulation aal5snap** indicates that the ATM adaptation layer 5 is to be used to prepare the data for transmission over ATM. AAL5 encapsulation is typically specified to transport TCP/IP data traffic over ATM.

To display the ATM interfaces, enter the **show atm vc** router command, as demonstrated in the following ouput:

```
router#sh atm vc
Interface  VCD/                          Peak  Avg/Min Burst
           Name VPI VCI Type Encaps SC   Kbps  Kbps    Cells  Sts
2/0.32      1    1   32  PVC  SNAP   UBR  100000                UP
2/0.33      2    1   33  PVC  SNAP   UBR  3000                  UP
2/0.34      6    1   34  PVC  SNAP   CBR  5000                  DOWN
```

The **1/0.32** indicates this is the 1/0 physical interface and the .32 is the PVC. The type is a **PVC** (permanent virtual circuit), the encapsulation is **SNAP** (the Subnetwork Access Protocol), the service class is **UBR**, which is an unspecified bit rate running TCP/IP. The bit rate is **100000** kbps and the status (**Sts**) is **UP**.

The next command shows how to display only a specific ATM virtual channel (VC); the command is **show atm vc interface atm1/0.33**. This command only displays the atm1/0.33 virtual channel. The types of ATM interfaces typically listed are DS3 (44.736 Mbps), OC-3 (155.52 Mbps), OC-12 (622.08 Mbps), and OC-192 (9953.28 Mbps) .

```
router#sh atm vc interface atm1/0.33
VCD/                                            Peak  Avg/Min Burst
Interface   Name      VPI  VCI  Type  Encaps SC Kbps  Kbps    Cells
Sts
1/0.33      2         1    33   PVC   SNAP   UBR 3000
UP
router#
```

The last command examined is used to display information on the interface. The command used is **show controller atm** *slot/port*. In this case, the information on the atm1/0 interface is displayed. Part of the display for the atm1/0 interface is listed:

```
router#sh controller atm1/0
Interface ATM1/0 is up
Hardware is ENHANCED ATM PA Plus - OC3 (155000Kbps)
Framer is PMC PM5346 S/UNI-155-LITE, SAR is LSI ATMIZER II
Firmware rev: X102, Framer rev: 0, ATMIZER II rev: 4
  idb=0x638A43E0, ds=0x638AC000, vc=0x638F76E0
  slot 1, unit 1, subunit 0, fci_type 0x03A9, ticks 226930
  2400 rx buffers: size=512, encap=64, trailer=28, magic=4
Curr Stats:
  VCC count: current=6, peak=6
  AAL2 VCC count: 0
  AAL2 TX no buffer count: 0
```

SUMMARY

The fundamentals of configuring and managing a campus network have been presented in this chapter. This has been an overview of the campus network infrastructure, and you should understand that each of the topics presented in this chapter could easily be expanded to fill an entire textbook(s). What you should understand from this reading is that configuring and managing a campus network is a major task. You should appreciate the fact that configuring and managing a campus type network requires the expertise of many people with many different networking capabilities, as well as understand the following:

- The importance and function of the three layers of a campus network
- The issue of data flow in a network
- Have an understanding of IP allocation and subnet design
- Understand the steps and process for configuring a VLAN
- Understand the issues of configuring the Layer 3 routed network

QUESTIONS AND PROBLEMS

Section 1-1

1. What networking equipment is usually found in the core of a campus network?

2. How are route policies applied in the core?

3. What is the advantage of using a Layer 3 switch in the core of the campus network?

4. Can a Layer 2 switch be used in the core of the campus network? Why or why not?

5. What is the function of the distribution layer in a campus network?

6. Can routing policies be implemented in the distribution layer? Why or why not?

7. What is the purpose of the access layer?

8. The campus network servers are typically located in what layer?

9. Why are routers typically not interconnected at the distribution layer?

10. What is the name for the part of the campus network that carries the bulk of the routed data traffic?

11. List three criteria for selecting the network media. Which is the final decision factor?

12. Which media is the best choice in a campus network?

13. Referring to Figure 1-1 from the beginning of the chapter, discuss how data flows from a computer in LAN B to a computer in LAN D. Assume that Switch A has been configured to be the preferred switch.

Section 1-2

14. What are three factors that should be considered before coming up with the final IP subnet design?

15. What are the address ranges for Class A, B, and C IP addressing?

16. Which public IP address space is now being assigned by the ISPs?

17. What is an Intranet?

18. What is the purpose of NAT and PAT?

19. What is overloading?

20. Which of the following are questions that the network engineer should ask when designing addressing for the IP network? (Select two.)

    a. How many network devices must be accommodated in the network?

    b. What is the cost of applying IP addresses to each network?

    c. How many network devices must be accommodated in the future?

    d. What Layer 3 technology should be used for routing?

21. What is the subnet mask for the following CIDRs and the number of available IP addresses?

/16, /22, /25, /30

22. Most home routers are preconfigured with what private class address, and what is the typical range of IP addresses?

23. What technique is used when a CIDR block greater than 254 IP addresses is required?

24. Is there a problem randomly applying CIDR blocks?

25. A /22 CIDR block is being used for supernetting. What subnet will IP addresses 192.168.80.0 to 192.168.83.0 be in?

26. How is a network address of 192.168.6.0 and a subnet mask of 255.255.254.0 written in CIDR?

27. A CIDR block contains the following subnets with the IP addresses of

192.168.68.0/22

192.168.69.0/22

192.168.70.0/22

192.168.71.0/22

Are there any problems with this group of subnets in the CIDR block? Show your work.

28. Are there any problems if the following four Class C networks are used to create a /22 CIDR block?

192.168.78.0/22

192.168.79.0/22

192.168.80.0/22

192.168.81.0/22

29. Figure 1-14 shows three different networks with different size requirements. The needed capacity (number of devices) for each network is specified in the figure. Your task is to determine the CIDR block required for each network that will satisfy the number of expected users. You are to use Class C private IP addresses when configuring the CIDR blocks. Assign IP addresses and gateway addresses to the networks. The IP addresses should start with 192.168.0.0. Design your network so that the minimum IP address space is consumed.

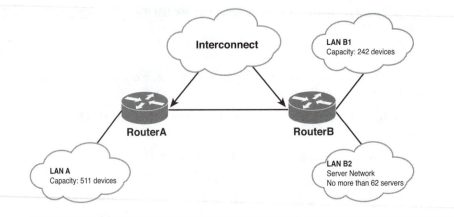

FIGURE 1-14 The networks for problem 29

Section 1-3

30. What is a VLAN?

31. What is a flat network?

32. List the three types of VLANs.

33. What type of VLAN is port-based?

34. Which type of LAN is based on 802.1Q specifications?

35. In what type of VLANs are port assignments created when they are assigned to a specific VLAN?

36. In this VLAN, ports are assigned to a VLAN based on either the computer's MAC address or the username of the client logged onto the computer.

37. The 802.1Q standard defines which of the following?

    a. Defines a system of VLAN tagging for Ethernet frames

    b. Provides specifications for inter router communication

    c. Helps to contain broadcast and multicast data traffic that help to minimize data congestion and improve throughput

    d. Provides guidelines for a switch port to belong to more than one VLAN

    e. All of the above

38. What commands are used to assign the IP address 192.168.20.5 to VLAN1?

    ```
    SwitchA(config-if)#ip address 172.16.32.2 255.255.255.0
    ```

39. What switch command is used to display the interfaces assigned to a VLAN?

40. List the commands used to create VLAN5 and name this VLAN Marketing group.

41. List the commands used to assign FA0/5 to the Marketing-group VLAN (VLAN5). Show the switch prompts.

42. What Cisco IOS command is used to turn on trunking for a Cisco switch?

43. What is SwitchA(config-if)#**switchport trunk encapsulation dot1q** used for?

44. What command is used to enable ISL for trunking on a Cisco switch?

45. What is the Cisco IOS command that is used to limit the VLANs carried across the trunk if only VLANs 2 and 4 are allowed?

46. On an HP ProCurve Switch, what does it mean for a port to be untagged?

47. On an HP ProCurve Switch, what does it mean for a port to be tagged?

48. The following information is input to an HP ProCurve switch:

```
SwitchHP# conf
SwitchHP(config)# vlan  3
SwitchHP(vlan-1)# tagged 15
SwitchHP(vlan-1)# exit
SwitchHP(config)# vlan 5
SwitchHP(vlan-2)# tagged 15
```

What does inputting these commands on the HP switch indicate?

Section 1-4

49. Define Network address and Logical address.

50. What is the purpose of a routing table?

51. What is the purpose of a gateway address?

52. What is a network segment?

53. Define "wire speed" routing.

54. Switches that can operate above the OSI Layer 2 are called what?

55. What is another name for a routed network?

56. What types of interfaces were widely used to interconnect the router and the network to other wide area networks (WAN)?

57. What is the Cisco IOS command for turning on the **display of log messages for the remote terminal?**

58. What does the following information indicate?

```
Interface       IP-Address   OK? Method Status Protocol
FastEthernet0/0 10.10.200.2  YES manual up     down
```

59. What does the following command do?

```
SwitchA(config-if)# no switchport
```

60. What is the purpose of the following command sequence, and why is this done?

```
Router(config)# interface FastEthernet0/0
Router(config-if)# ip address 10.10.20.250 255.255.255.0
Router(config-if)# ip address 172.16.1.1 255.255.255.0 secondary
```

61. Define InterVLAN routing.

62. What does the router on a stick design do?

63. What is the purpose of the switched virtual interfaces?

64. What is the purpose of a CSU/DSU?

65. List the sequence of router commands required to set the data encapsulation to hdlc.

66. List the sequence of router commands required to set the data encapsulation to ppp.

67. List the command used on a router to verify the data encapsulation being used on the serial 0/0 interface.

68. List the command used to set the framing to ESF on the router's serial 0/0 interface.

69. List the command that can be used to verify the T1 status on port 0/0.

70. What is ATM?

71. List the command used to enable ATM on serial interface 3/0.

72. Your supervisor asks you if a Layer 2 switch could be used in the core of the campus network. Prepare a response to your supervisor. Be sure to justify your recommendation.

73. How does a Layer 3 switch differ from a Layer 2 switch?

Critical Thinking

74. Figure 1-15 shows three different networks with different size requirements. The needed capacity (number of devices) for each network is specified in the figure. Your task is to determine the CIDR block required for each network that will satisfy the number of expected users. You are to use Class C private IP addresses when configuring the CIDR blocks. Assign IP addresses and gateway addresses to the networks. The IP addresses should start with 192.168.0.0. Design your network so that the minimum IP address space is consumed.

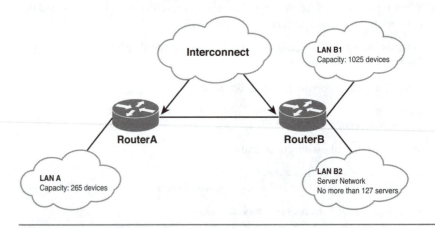

FIGURE 1-15 The networks for problem 74

75. A router has a TI WIC card. Your task is to configure the serial 0/0 interface to satisfy the following requirements. Specify the commands to accomplish this task.

IP address: 192.168.12.3

Subnet mask: 255.255.255.0

Service: DS0 / 24 channels

Framing: ESF

Linecode: B8ZS

Clock source: Line

Encapsulation: ppp

76. A non-Cisco switch configured with two VLANs: 2 and 100. VLAN 2 is a 192.168.10.0/24 network, and VLAN 100 is a 172.16.20.0/24 network. This switch is not 802.1Q compliant. How can we route between these VLANs given that we have a Cisco router with 3 available interfaces: FastEhternet 0/1, 1/0, and 1/1?

77. The following five computers are connected to a switch. Their information is as follows:

	IP Address	Subnet Mask	Gateway	VLAN
Computer1	192.168.1.5	255.255.254.0	192.168.1.1	1
Computer2	192.168.2.5	255.255.254.0	192.168.2.1	1
Computer3	192.168.3.5	255.255.255.0	192.168.3.1	3
Computer4	192.168.4.5	255.255.255.0	192.168.4.1	3
Computer5	192.168.5.5	255.255.255.0	192.168.5.1	5

The switch is connected via its 802.1Q port to a router. The router has the following configuration:

```
!
interface FastEthernet0/0

interface FastEthernet0/0.3
 description VLAN 3
 encapsulation dot1Q 3
 ip address 192.168.3.1 255.255.254.0

interface FastEthernet0/0.5
 description VLAN 5
 encapsulation dot1Q 5
 ip address 192.169.5.1 255.255.255.0
```

Discuss the connectivity among the computers.

78. What is the expected behavior in the following network scenarios?

a. When connecting SwitchA port 2, which is a member of port-based VLAN 10, to Switch B port 24, which is a member of port-based VLAN 5.

b. When connecting SwitchA port 3, which is a member of port-based VLAN 3, to Switch B port 1, which is configured as a 802.1Q trunk port.

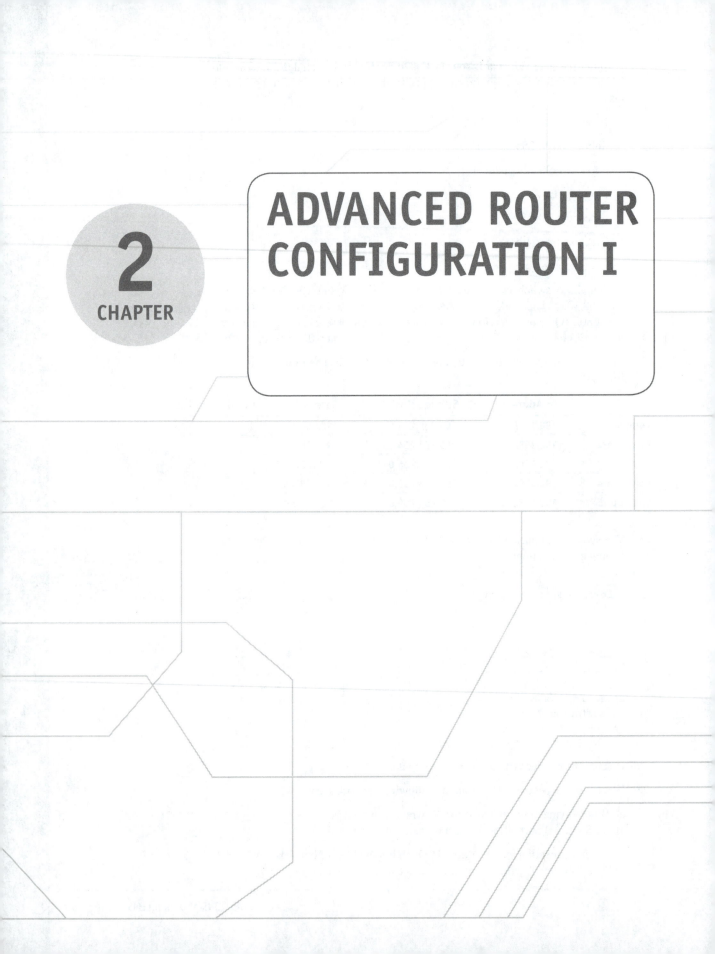

2

CHAPTER

ADVANCED ROUTER CONFIGURATION I

Chapter Outline

Objectives

- Describe the difference between static and dynamic routing protocols
- Describe the difference in distance vector and link state protocols
- Be able to configure a basic setup for static, RIP, and RIPv2 routing protocols
- Understand the relative amount of traffic generated by each protocol
- Understand the purpose of and be able to configure a TFTP sever

Key Terms

routing protocols
static route
netstat -r
route print
loopback
ip route
Variable Length Subnet Masking
show ip route (sh ip route)
routing table code S
routing table code C
gateway of last resort
show ip route static (sh ip route static)
exit interface
null0 interface
show running-config (sh run)

show startup-config (sh start)
copy run start
write memory (wr m)
traceroute *destination-ip-address*
datagrams
tracert *destination-ip-address*
destination unreachable
load balancing
equal-cost load balancing
floating static route
Dynamic Routing Protocols
prefix length
Administrative Distance (AD)
path determination
metric

convergence
Hop Count
reliability
bandwidth
delay
cost
load
ticks
Distance Vector Protocol
Link State Protocol
RIP
routing loops
advertise
class network address
classful addressing
show ip protocol (sh ip protocol)
no auto-summary
TFTP

INTRODUCTION

This chapter introduces the basic concepts of **routing protocols**. Routing protocols provide a standardized format for route management, including route selection, sharing route status with neighbor routers, and calculating alternative routes if the best path route is down. The focus of this chapter is on the use of routing protocols in a campus network environment (in particular static, RIP, and RIPv2).

Static routing protocols are first presented in Section 2-1. This section includes examples of how to configure static routes and view the routes in a routing table. The material includes a discussion of when and where static protocols are used and when and why it is not advantageous to use a static routing protocol. Section 2-2 provides an overview of the concept of dynamic protocols. Dynamic protocols are divided into two categories: distance vector and link state. Section 2-3 provides examples of configuring the distance vector protocols RIP and RIPv2. Chapter 3, "Advanced Router Configuration II," examines configuring link state protocols. It is important to periodically back up the router configuration files configured for a router. A procedure for doing this is by using a Trivial File Transfer Protocol (TFTP) server, as examined in Section 2-4.

Each routing protocol section in this chapter contains a networking challenge that is included with the Net-Challenge Software. These challenges enable you to verify you know the proper commands used to configure each routing protocol.

Routing Protocols
Provide a standardized format for route management.

2-1 CONFIGURING STATIC ROUTING

The objective of this section is to demonstrate how data packets are routed in a network using a static routing protocol. A **static route** is an IP address to which data traffic can be forwarded and has been manually entered into either a router's or computer's routing table. A static route is specified in a PC computer in terms of the computer's default gateway, and routers sometimes use a static route when specifying where the network data traffic is to be forwarded. Examples of specifying the static route(s) for a computer are first examined.

Static Route
A data traffic route that has been manually entered into either a router's or a computer's routing table.

The most common static route used in a host computer is the default gateway. The *default gateway* specifies where the data traffic is to be sent when the destination address for the data is not in the same LAN or is unknown. For example, if your PC is on the 10.10.0.0 network and it wants to send data to 100.100.20.1, the data is sent to the default gateway as specified by the TCP/IP setup on your PC. An example of setting the host computer's default gateway is shown in Figure 2-1 for both (a) Windows and (b) Mac OS X. In this example, the default IP address is 10.10.20.250 with a subnet mask of 255.255.255.0 for the computer in LAN A with the IP address of 10.10.20.1.

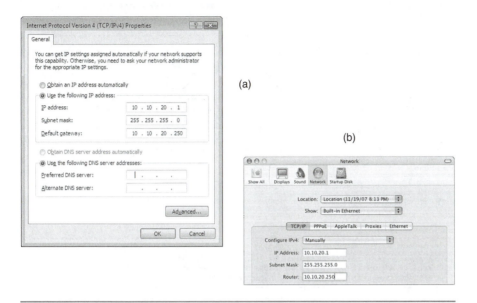

(a)

(b)

FIGURE 2-1 Setting the default gateway address or default static route on the host computer (a) PC and (b) Mac OS X

The routing tables for the host PC computer can be obtained by entering the command **netstat -r** at the PC's command prompt and from the Mac OS X terminal screen. An example is shown in Figure 2-2 (a). The command **route print** can also be used to view the active routes from the host PC, as shown in Figure 2-2 (b).

> **netstat -r**
> The command used to obtain the routing table for a host PC computer.
>
> **route print**
> Produces same displayed result as **netstat -r**.

The default route is specified in the routing table by a 0.0.0.0 network address entry with a subnet mask of 0.0.0.0. The 0.0.0.0 indicates that, if the destination address is unknown and the subnet mask is unknown, then send the data packet to the gateway. The gateway address of 10.10.20.250 is the IP address of the FastEthernet port of the router connected to the LAN. The IP address of 10.10.20.1 is the IP address for the host computer's network interface card (NIC).

The network destination of 10.10.20.0 is returned to the computer's NIC at IP address 10.10.20.1. The gateway for the network destination of 10.10.20.1 is 127.0.0.1, which is a **loopback** to the host computer. A loopback means the data is routed directly back to the source. In this case, the source is the computer's NIC. The loopback can be used to check whether the network interface is working; if it is, pinging IP address 127.0.0.1 will generate a reply.

> **Loopback**
> The data is routed directly back to the source.

```
C:\netstat -r

Route Table
-------------------------------------------------------------------------------
Interface List
0x1 .......................... MS TCP Loopback interface
0x2 ...00 b0 d0 25 bf 48 ...... 3Com 3C920 Integrated Fast Ethernet Controller
3C905C-TX Compatible) - Packet Scheduler Miniport
-------------------------------------------------------------------------------
-------------------------------------------------------------------------------
Active Routes:
Network Destination         Netmask          Gateway        Interface    Metric
        0.0.0.0             0.0.0.0      10.10.20.250      10.10.20.1        20
      10.10.20.0      255.255.255.0        10.10.20.1      10.10.20.1        20
      10.10.20.1    255.255.255.255         127.0.0.1       127.0.0.1        20
  10.255.255.255    255.255.255.255        10.10.20.1      10.10.20.1        20
       127.0.0.0          255.0.0.0         127.0.0.1       127.0.0.1         1
       224.0.0.0          240.0.0.0        10.10.20.1      10.10.20.1        20
 255.255.255.255    255.255.255.255        10.10.20.1      10.10.20.1         1
Default Gateway:          10.10.20.250
-------------------------------------------------------------------------------
Persistent Routes:
  None
```

(a)

```
C:\route print
-------------------------------------------------------------------------------
Interface List
0x1 .......................... MS TCP Loopback interface
0x2 ...00 b0 d0 25 bf 48 ...... 3Com 3C920 Integrated Fast Ethernet Controller
3C905C-TX Compatible) - Packet Scheduler Miniport
-------------------------------------------------------------------------------
-------------------------------------------------------------------------------
Active Routes:
Network Destination         Netmask          Gateway        Interface    Metric
        0.0.0.0             0.0.0.0      10.10.20.250      10.10.20.1        20
      10.10.20.0      255.255.255.0        10.10.20.1      10.10.20.1        20
      10.10.20.1    255.255.255.255         127.0.0.1       127.0.0.1        20
  10.255.255.255    255.255.255.255        10.10.20.1      10.10.20.1        20
       127.0.0.0          255.0.0.0         127.0.0.1       127.0.0.1         1
       224.0.0.0          240.0.0.0        10.10.20.1      10.10.20.1        20
 255.255.255.255    255.255.255.255        10.10.20.1      10.10.20.1         1
Default Gateway:          10.10.20.250
-------------------------------------------------------------------------------
Persistent Routes:
  None
```

(b)

FIGURE 2-2   (a) A host computer's static route listing obtained using the netstat
-r command; (b) a host computer's static route listing obtained using the route print
command

What about setting static routes for a router in a small campus network? First, let's examine how data packets travel from one LAN to another in the three-router campus network shown in Figure 2-3. Specifically, how is information sent from a host computer in LAN A (10.10.20.0 subnet) to a host computer in LAN B (10.10.10.0 subnet)? The data packets must travel from LAN A to the Router A gateway (FA0/0 interface), from Router A to Router B via the 10.10.200.0 subnet, and then to LAN B via the Router B gateway (FA0/0 interface). This requires that a physical communications link be established between the routers and a routing protocol defined for Routers A and B before data packets can be exchanged. The physical connection from the routers to the LAN computers is typically a CAT6/5e UTP or a fiber connection. The physical connection between the routers is typically fiber.

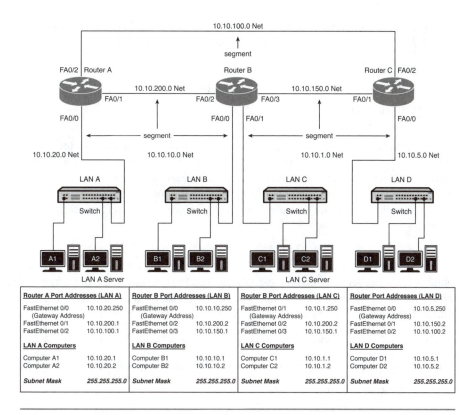

FIGURE 2-3 A three-router campus network

The following is a representation of the Router Port Address and LAN Computer tables shown in Figure 2-3:

Router A Port Addresses (LAN A)		Router B Port Addresses (LAN B)		Router B Port Addresses (LAN C)		Router Port Addresses (LAN D)	
FastEthernet 0/0 (Gateway Address)	10.10.20.250	FastEthernet 0/0 (Gateway Address)	10.10.10.250	FastEthernet 0/1 (Gateway Address)	10.10.1.250	FastEthernet 0/0 (Gateway Address)	10.10.5.250
FastEthernet 0/1	10.10.200.1	FastEthernet 0/2	10.10.200.2	FastEthernet 0/2	10.10.200.2	FastEthernet 0/1	10.10.150.2
FastEthernet 0/2	10.10.100.1	FastEthernet 0/3	10.10.150.1	FastEthernet 0/3	10.10.150.1	FastEthernet 0/2	10.10.100.2
LAN A Computers		**LAN B Computers**		**LAN C Computers**		**LAN D Computers**	
Computer A1	10.10.20.1	Computer B1	10.10.10.1	Computer C1	10.10.1.1	Computer D1	10.10.5.1
Computer A2	10.10.20.2	Computer B2	10.10.10.2	Computer C2	10.10.1.2	Computer D2	10.10.5.2
Subnet Mask	**255.255.255.0**	**Subnet Mask**	**255.255.255.0**	**Subnet Mask**	**255.255.255.0**	**Subnet Mask**	**255.255.255.0**

A simplified network can be used to demonstrate what is required to develop static routes in a multiple-router network. For this example, two routers from the campus network are used. The two routers, Router A and Router B, connect to LANs A and B, as shown in Figure 2-4. This simplified network will be used to describe how data packets travel from LAN A to Router A to Router B to LAN B and what is required to define the static routes.

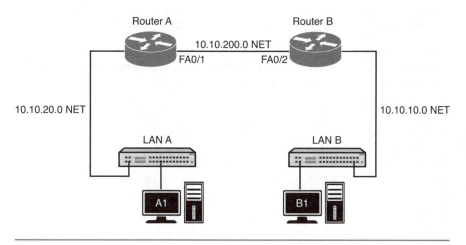

FIGURE 2-4 A simplified two-router network

The data packets pass through three subnets (indicated by *NET*) when traveling from LAN A to LAN B. The IP subnets for each network are as follows:

- **10.10.20.0 NET**: LAN A
- **10.10.200.0 NET**: Router A connection to Router B
- **10.10.10.0 NET**: LAN B

ip route
The router configuration command for manually setting the next hop IP address.

In this network, there are only two routers, with Router A directly connected to Router B. This means that the only route between the routers is via the 10.10.200.0 NET, which is the connection between the FastEthernet interfaces on Routers A and B. The static route information is entered from the router's configure terminal prompt **(config)**# using the **ip route** command. The command structure for **ip route** is

```
Router(config)#ip route destination subnet-mask next-hop
```

where the *destination* is the network's destination IP address (NET), the *subnet mask* is what has been defined for the subnets, and the *next hop* is the IP address of the next router interface in the link. The command for routing the data to the 10.10.10.0 subnet is as follows:

```
RouterA(config)#ip route 10.10.10.0    255.255.255.0    10.10.200.2
```

This results in the following configuration information being entered into Router A:

- Destination subnet IP address: 10.10.10.0
- Subnet mask: 255.255.255.0
- Next hop IP address: 10.10.200.2

The next hop IP address is the IP address of the FastEthernet0/2 interface on RouterB. Now, the router knows how to deliver data packets from host computers in the 10.10.20.0 NET (LAN A) to the destination computers in the 10.10.10.0 NET (LAN B). The next hop IP address is essentially the gateway to LAN B from the Router A's perspective.

Variable Length Subnet Masking
Routes can be configured using different subnet masks.

Each static route can use a different subnet mask. This is called **variable length subnet masking**. For example, one static route could have a subnet mask of 255.255.255.0 and another could have a subnet mask of 255.255.255.252.

show ip route (sh ip route)
The command that displays the routes and the routing address entry into the routing table.

The routing address entry into the routing table can be verified by entering the command **show ip route (sh ip route)** from the router's # prompt. The following example demonstrates output from **show ip route**:

```
RouterA#show ip route
Codes: C connected, S static, I IGRP, R RIP, M mobile, B BGP D EIGRP,
EX EIGRP external, O OSPF, IA OSPF inter area
N1 OSPF NSSA external type 1, N2 OSPF NSSA external type 2
E1 OSPF external type 1, E2 OSPF external type 2, E EGP
i IS-IS, L1 IS-IS level-1, L2 IS-IS level-2, * candidate default
U per-user static route, o ODR T traffic engineered route
Gateway of last resort is not set
10.0.0.0/24 is subnetted, 2 subnets
S 10.10.10.0 [1/0] via 10.10.200.2
C 10.10.200.0 is directly connected, FastEthernet1
```

This shows that a static route (S) has been configured for the 10.10.10.0 network via the 10.10.200.2 next hop address.

What about data traffic flow from the 10.10.10.0 NET (LAN B) back to the 10.10.20.0 NET (LAN A)? Once again, the data packets pass through three subnets (indicated by NET) when traveling from LAN B to LAN A. The IP addresses for each subnet are as follows:

- 10.10.10.0 NET: LAN B
- 10.10.200.0 NET: Router B connection to Router A
- 10.10.20.0 NET: LAN A

In this scenario, LAN B connects directly to Router B and the only route to LAN A from Router B is via the 10.10.200.0 NET, which is the connection between Routers B and A. The destination network IP address is 10.10.20.0. The command input to Router B for routing the data to the 10.10.20.0 subnet is as follows:

```
RouterB(config)#ip route 10.10.20.0 255.255.255.0 10.10.200.1
```

The following information is entered into the router:

- Destination subnet IP address: 10.10.20.0
- Subnet mask: 255.255.255.0
- Next hop IP address: 10.10.200.1

The next hop IP address is the IP address of the FastEthernet0/1 port on RouterA. Now, a static route has been configured on Router B to route data packets from host computers in the 10.10.10.0 NET (LAN B) to destination computers in the 10.10.20.0 NET (LAN A). The entries into Router B's routing table can be confirmed by using the command **sh ip route** at the Router# prompt, as shown:

```
RouterB#sh ip route
Codes: C connected, S static, I IGRP, R RIP, M mobile, B BGP D EIGRP,
EX EIGRP external, O OSPF, IA OSPF inter area
N1 OSPF NSSA external type 1, N2 OSPF NSSA external type 2
E1 OSPF external type 1, E2 OSPF external type 2, E EGP
i IS-IS, L1 IS-IS level-1, L2 IS-IS level-2, * candidate default
U per-user static route, o ODR T traffic engineered route
Gateway of last resort is not set
10.0.0.0/24 is subnetted, 2 subnets
S 10.10.20.0 [1/0] via 10.10.200.1
C 10.10.200.0 is directly connected, FastEthernet0/2
```

The **sh ip route** command lists a table of codes first, followed by the routes. This listing shows a static route (S) 10.10.20.0 via 10.10.200.1, which indicates that a static route to the destination 10.10.20.0 subnet can be reached via the next hop of 10.10.200.1. The C indicates that the 10.10.200.0 network is directly connected to the FastEthernet02 port.

---

routing table code S
The router code for a static route.

routing table code C
The router code for specifying a directly connected network.

This simplified network has only one route; therefore, the entries for the static routes using the **ip route** command are limited but were required for each router. Static routes are sometimes used when configuring the routers for routing in a small network. Static routing is not the best choice, as we will learn, but it can be suitable if the network is small (for example, the two-router network). It can be suitable for situations in which there is only one route to the destination, such as a wide-area network or Internet feed.

What about using static routes in the three-router campus network shown in Figure 2-3? A computer in LAN A (10.10.20.0 NET) sends data to a computer in LAN B (10.10.10.0 NET). This is the same requirement specified in the two-router network example. Once again, a static route must be entered into Router A's routing table telling the router how to forward data to the 10.10.10.0 NET. However, in this example, there are two possible choices for a data packet to travel to the 10.10.10.0 NET from Router A. The IP addresses for the two possible next hops are 10.10.200.2 and 10.10.100.2. The following are the router commands required to configure the routes:

```
RouterA(config)#ip route 10.10.10.0 255.255.255.0 10.10.200.2
RouterA(config)#ip route 10.10.10.0 255.255.255.0 10.10.100.2
```

What about sending information from LAN A to LAN C or to LAN D? This requires four more additional **ip route** entries into the router's routing table, as shown:

```
RouterA(config)#ip route 10.10.1.0 255.255.255.0 10.10.200.2
RouterA(config)#ip route 10.10.1.0 255.255.255.0 10.10.100.2
RouterA(config)#ip route 10.10.5.0 255.255.255.0 10.10.200.2
RouterA(config)#ip route 10.10.5.0 255.255.255.0 10.10.100.2
```

But wait, we aren't done. We must enter return static routes for all the LANs back to LAN A, and then enter the static routes for the other three LANs. For troubleshooting purposes, we want to be able to ping all the Ethernet interfaces on the subnets, so we need to add static IP routes to each subnet (NET). For example, the following are the static IP route entries required for defining a route to the 10.10.150.0 NET:

```
RouterA(config)#ip route 10.10.150.0 255.255.255.0 10.10.200.2
RouterA(config)#ip route 10.10.150.0 255.255.255.0 10.10.100.2
```

This means that many static route entries must be made for the routes in this network to be completely defined. This requires a lot of time and if routes change in the network, new static entries must be made and old static routes must be deleted. The problem with using a static routing protocol in a large network is the amount of maintenance required by the network administrator just to keep the route selections up to date. Assume that the network connection uses five router hops. The entries for the static routes on each router are numerous, and if the routes change, the routing tables in all routers must be manually updated to account for the data path changes.

When static routes are used, the network administrator in essence becomes the routing protocol. In other words, the network administrator is making all the decisions regarding data traffic routing. This requires the administrator to know all network data routes, set up the routes to each subnet, and be constantly aware of any route changes. This is in contrast to dynamic routing protocols that communicate routing information between the routers to determine the best route to use to forward the data packets. The concept of a dynamic routing protocol is introduced in Section 2-2, and in Section 2-3, we examine examples of configuring the dynamic routing protocols RIP and RIPv2.

Gateway of Last Resort

One of the most important applications for using a static route is for configuring the gateway of last resort on a router. The gateway of last resort is the IP address of the router in your network where data packets with unknown routes should be forwarded. The purpose of this is to configure a route for data packets that do not have a destination route configured in the routing table. In this case, a default route can be configured that instructs the router to forward the data packet(s) with an unknown route to another router. The command for doing this is as follows:

```
ip route 0.0.0.0   0.0.0.0   next-hop-address
```

If this static route has not been configured, the router will display the following message when the **show ip route** command is entered:

```
Gateway of last resort is not set
```

This means the router does not know how to route a data packet with a destination IP address that differs from the routes stored in the routing table. A critical concept that one must realize about the gateway of last resort is that it must be directly connected to the router. This means it must be on the same network as the router's interfaces, and it must be reachable immediately by the router on the local subnet. This is not only for the routers; it applies to the default gateway of a host computer as well. Remember that the ARP broadcast is the fundamental method of how network devices communicate. If the gateway address is not on the same local subnet as the router, then the ARP broadcast will not work. Therefore, it will not be possible for a computer to forward a network packet outside the network via the gateway of last resort.

> **Gateway of Last Resort**
> The IP address of the router in your network where data packets with unknown routes should be forwarded.

Configuring Static Routes

The following discussion describes how to configure static routes on a Cisco router. The topology being used is the three-router campus network shown previously in Figure 2-3. This demonstration is for configuring the static routes for Router A only.

The first step is to connect to the router via a console or virtual terminal connection. Next, enter the privileged EXEC mode, as shown:

```
Router con0 is now available Press RETURN to get started!
RouterA>en
RouterA#
```

Next, enter the configure terminal mode on the router [RouterA(config)#] using the **configure terminal** (**conf t**) command. Before configuring the static routes, make sure the interfaces are configured. The FastEthernet0/1 interface is configured with the assigned IP address of 10.10.200.1 and a subnet mask of 255.255.255.0, and the FastEthernet0/2 interface is assigned the 10.10.100.1 IP address and a subnet mask of 255.255.255.0. The **no shut** command is used to enable the FastEthernet interfaces.

```
Router#conf t
Enter configuration commands, one per line. End with CNTL/Z.
Router(config)#int fa0/1
Router(config-if)#ip address 10.10.200.1 255.255.255.0
Router(config-if)#no shut
00:19:07: %LINK-3-UPDOWN: Interface FastEthernet0/1, changed state to
up
Router(config)#int fa0/2
Router(config-if)#ip address 10.10.100.1 255.255.255.0
Router(config-if)#no shut
00:21:05: %LINK-3-UPDOWN: Interface FastEthernet0/2, changed state to
up
```

Notice that the FastEthernet0/1 and FastEthernet0/2 interfaces change state to *up* after the **no shut** command is issued. It is good to verify the interface status using the **show ip interface brief** (**sh ip int brief**) command, as shown:

```
RouterA#sh ip int brief
00:22:18: %SYS-5-CONFIG_I: Configured from console
Interface          IP-Address  OK? Method Status   Protocol
FastEthernet0/1    10.10.200.1 YES manual up       down
FastEthernet0/2    10.10.100.1 YES manual up       down
```

The status for both FastEthernet ports show that they are *up*; however, the line protocol *down* tells us that there is not a physical connection established between the routers. This problem with the "protocol down" is fixed by reestablishing the physical connection between the routers.

The static routes are entered using the **ip route** command after the interfaces are configured. You don't have to enter all routes at once, but all routes must be properly entered for the network to work. The static route command syntax is **ip route** *network-address subnet-mask next-hop-ip-address*. Only the routes to the 10.10.10.0 NET have been listed to shorten the example:

```
RouterA(config)#ip route 10.10.10.0 255.255.255.0 10.10.200.2
RouterA(config)#ip route 10.10.10.0 255.255.255.0 10.10.100.2
```

> **show ip route static (sh ip route static)**
> Limits the routes displayed to only static.

There are two places to verify whether the static routes are properly configured. First, verify that the routes are in the routing table using either the **show ip route** or the **show ip route static** (**sh ip route static**) command. Adding the word *static* after **show ip route** limits the routes displayed to only *static routes*. An important note is that the routes are displayed using the **show ip route** command *only* if the line protocol is *up*.

```
RouterA#sh ip route
Codes: C connected, S static, I IGRP, R RIP, M mobile, B BGP D EIGRP,
EX EIGRP external, O OSPF, IA OSPF inter area
N1 OSPF NSSA external type 1, N2 OSPF NSSA external type 2
E1 OSPF external type 1, E2 OSPF external type 2, E EGP
i IS-IS, L1 IS-IS level-1, L2 IS-IS level-2, * candidate default
U per-user static route, o ODR T traffic engineered route
Gateway of last resort is not set
     10.0.0.0/24 is subnetted, 2 subnets
S       10.10.10.0 [1/0] via 10.10.200.2
                   [1/0] via 10.10.100.2
C       10.10.20.0 is directly connected, FastEthernet0/0
C       10.10.200.0 is directly connected, FastEthernet0/1
C       10.10.100.0 is directly connected, FastEthernet0/2
```

The command for showing only the static routes is as follows:

```
RouterA#sh ip route static
     10.0.0.0/24 is subnetted, 2 subnets
S       10.10.10.0 [1/0] via 10.10.200.2
                   [1/0] via 10.10.100.2
```

A static route is added to the routing table when the next hop address is reachable by the router. If the link to the next hop address is down or the destination IP address cannot be reached, then the static route is automatically removed. An alternate way to configure a static route is to specify an **exit interface** instead of a next hop address. In this case, a router interface will be specified as the outgoing interface that is used to forward packets to the destination network. By using the exit interface, the network specified in the static route command will appear as if it is directly connected to the interface. The following example will alter one of the static routes previously configured in the last example to use the exit interface.

> **exit interface**
> A router interface will be specified as the outgoing interface that is used to forward packets to the destination network.

```
RouterA(config)#no ip route 10.10.10.0 255.255.255.0 10.10.100.2
RouterA(config)#ip route 10.10.10.0 255.255.255.0 FA0/2
```

```
RouterA#sh ip route
Codes: C connected, S static, I IGRP, R RIP, M mobile, B BGP D EIGRP,
EX EIGRP external, O OSPF, IA OSPF inter area
N1 OSPF NSSA external type 1, N2 OSPF NSSA external type 2
E1 OSPF external type 1, E2 OSPF external type 2, E EGP
i IS-IS, L1 IS-IS level-1, L2 IS-IS level-2, * candidate default
U per-user static route, o ODR T traffic engineered route
Gateway of last resort is not set
     10.0.0.0/24 is subnetted, 4 subnets
S       10.10.10.0 [1/0] via 10.10.200.2
                   is directly connected, FastEthernet0/2
C       10.10.20.0 is directly connected, FastEthernet0/0
C       10.10.200.0 is directly connected, FastEthernet0/1
C       10.10.100.0 is directly connected, FastEthernet0/2
```

The **show ip route** command output shows one of the 10.10.10.0 routes has changed to be directly connected via interface FastEthernet0/2, even though the route still remains a type S for static. Because the router assumes the network 10.10.10.0 is now a directly connected interface, every packet destined for an IP address on the 10.10.10.0 network, whether it is valid or not, the router will perform an ARP broadcast on the behalf of the network. This is different than a typical static route, where the only ARP needed is for the next hop IP address. Therefore, using the exit interface option can slow down the data traffic due to the increased number of ARP broadcasts that the router has to perform on the exit interface. The exit interface is used in the point-to-point connection where there is only one possible next hop device and the exit interface must be up in order for the static route to be inserted into the routing table.

The exit interface can be more beneficial when used in conjunction with the next hop address. When using it this way, it is possible to enforce how a static route should properly behave. As previously mentioned, a static route is removed from the routing table when the next hop address is not reachable. What if there is another path to reach the next hop address, but the path is not a desirable one? The network engineer can force the static route to be dependent on an exit interface without putting additional burden on the router.

The **ip route** *network-address subnet-mask exit-interface next-hop-address* command specifies the exit interface through which the next hop address should be found. The static route is installed only if the next hop address is reachable via the specified interface. Also, the router no longer assumes that the destination is directly connected.

Another static route concept that you should be familiar with is the static route to null0. This is a useful technique for network loop prevention. A **null0 interface** is a virtual bit-bucket interface where every packet gets discarded. As we have learned, a router uses its routing table to route packets. If a route is unknown or it is not in the routing table, the data packet is forwarded to its gateway of last resort.

Assume that Router A is connecting to an ISP router and it is advertising the network 10.10.0.0/16 to the ISP, as illustrated in Figure 2-5. Now, the ISP router is sending Router A a packet with destination 10.10.90.5, which is nowhere to be found in Router A's routing table. Router A will forward the same packet back to the ISP router, which will forward the packet back to Router A again. So, the game of network ping-pong has just begun. This network loop will last until the TTL is expired. However, if the network 10.10.0.0/16 is entered as a null0 route on Router A, then the route exists in the routing table. Therefore, Router A will not forward the packet with destination 10.10.90.5 back to the ISP router.

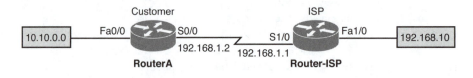

FIGURE 2-5 An example of a connection from a customer router to the ISP router

The static route null 0 command syntax is

```
ip route network-address subnet-mask null 0
```

as demonstrated in the example that follows:

```
RouterA(config)#ip route 10.10.0.0 255.255.0.0 null 0
RouterA#sh ip route
Codes: C connected, S static, I IGRP, R RIP, M mobile, B BGP D EIGRP,
EX EIGRP external, O OSPF, IA OSPF inter area
N1 OSPF NSSA external type 1, N2 OSPF NSSA external type 2
E1 OSPF external type 1, E2 OSPF external type 2, E EGP
i IS-IS, L1 IS-IS level-1, L2 IS-IS level-2, * candidate default
U per-user static route, o ODR T traffic engineered route
Gateway of last resort is 10.10.200.3 to network 0.0.0.0
10.0.0.0/24 is subnetted, 5 subnets
S 10.10.0.0/16 is directly connected, Null 0
S 10.10.10.0/24 [1/0] via 10.10.200.2
                     is directly connected, FastEthernet0/2
C 10.10.200.0/24 is directly connected, FastEthernet0/1
C 10.10.100.0/24 is directly connected, FastEthernet0/2
```

The other place to check the routing configuration is by examining the router's running-configuration file using the command **show running-config (sh run)**, as shown in the output example that follows. The command displays the current configuration of the router, but it does not show what is currently saved in the router's nonvolatile memory (NVRAM). The command **show startup-config (sh start)** displays the router's configuration saved in NVRAM.

> **show running-config (sh run)**
> The command that displays the router's running-configuration.
>
> **show startup-config (sh start)**
> The command that displays the router's startup-configuration.

```
RouterA#sh run
Using 519 out of 32762 bytes
!
version 12.0
service timestamps debug uptime service timestamps log uptime no
service password-encryption
!
hostname Router
!
!
ip subnet-zero
!
interface FastEthernet0/1
ip address 10.10.200.1 255.255.255.0
 no ip directed-broadcast no keepalive
!
interface FastEthernet0/2
 ip address 10.10.100.1 255.255.255.0
 no ip directed-broadcast no keepalive
!
ip classless
ip route 10.10.10.0 255.255.255.0 10.10.200.2
ip route 10.10.10.0 255.255.255.0 10.10.100.2
```

```
!
line con 0
transport input none line aux 0
line vty 0 4
!
end
```

It is important that you save your configuration changes to the router as you go. Save changes to the router configuration by using the **copy running-configuration startup-configuration** command (**copy run start**) or **write memory (wr m)**, as shown:

```
RouterA#copy run start
RouterA#wr m
```

Once your network is set up, you can use the **traceroute** *destination-ip-address* command to discover the routes the data packets (**datagrams**) actually take when traveling from the source to the destination. The command is issued from the Privileged EXEC mode on a router, as shown:

```
R1#traceroute destination-ip-address
```

Referring to the three-router campus network shown in Figure 2-6, the **traceroute** command is issued from RouterA to the FastEthernet 0/0 interface on RouterB. The destination IP address is 10.10.10.250. The result of the **traceroute** is shown next.

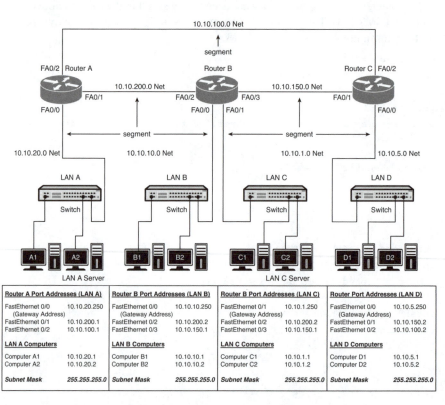

Router A Port Addresses (LAN A)		Router B Port Addresses (LAN B)		Router B Port Addresses (LAN C)		Router Port Addresses (LAN D)	
FastEthernet 0/0 (Gateway Address)	10.10.20.250	FastEthernet 0/0 (Gateway Address)	10.10.10.250	FastEthernet 0/1 (Gateway Address)	10.10.1.250	FastEthernet 0/0 (Gateway Address)	10.10.5.250
FastEthernet 0/1	10.10.200.1	FastEthernet 0/2	10.10.200.2	FastEthernet 0/2	10.10.200.2	FastEthernet 0/1	10.10.150.2
FastEthernet 0/2	10.10.100.1	FastEthernet 0/3	10.10.150.1	FastEthernet 0/3	10.10.150.1	FastEthernet 0/2	10.10.100.2
LAN A Computers		**LAN B Computers**		**LAN C Computers**		**LAN D Computers**	
Computer A1	10.10.20.1	Computer B1	10.10.10.1	Computer C1	10.10.1.1	Computer D1	10.10.5.1
Computer A2	10.10.20.2	Computer B2	10.10.10.2	Computer C2	10.10.1.2	Computer D2	10.10.5.2
Subnet Mask	*255.255.255.0*	*Subnet Mask*	*255.255.255.0*	*Subnet Mask*	*255.255.255.0*	*Subnet Mask*	*255.255.255.0*

FIGURE 2-6   A three-router campus network

```
R1#traceroute 10.10.10.250
Type escape sequence to abort.
Tracing the route to 10.10.10.250
1    10.10.10.250              8msec     8msec     9msec
R1#
```

The result shows that the data packets travel trough one router to arrive at the destination. What happens to the results from a traceroute if the destination is changed to the FastEthernet 0/0 interface on Router C in Figure 2-3? In this case, the data packets must travel through two routers to arrive at the destination, as shown:

```
R1#traceroute 10.10.5.250
Type escape sequence to abort.
Tracing the route to 10.10.10.250
1    10.10.10.250        8msec      8msec       9msec
2    10.10.5.250         8msec      10msec      10msec
R1#
```

Notice that in this case, the datagrams pass through two routers indicated by 1 and 2 and there are three times listed. These three times represent the three datagrams that are sent when the **traceroute** command is issued. The times listed for "1" are the times it took for the datagrams to hit the first router. The datagrams timeout as soon as they arrive at the first router. The times it took for the datagrams to hit the second router are listed in "2".

You can also trace packets from the PC by using the tracert *destination-ip-address* command. An example is provided. Once again using the three-router campus network shown in Figure 2-6, the **traceroute** command is issued from computer A1 to the FastEthernet 0/0 interface on Router B.

tracert *destination-ip-address*
The command used to trace packets on a PC.

```
C:\>tracert 10.10.10.250
Tracing route to 10.10.10.250 over a maximum of 30 hops:

1    9ms     5ms     9ms     10.10.20.250
2    17ms    12ms    14ms    10.10.10.250

Trace complete.
```

In this case, the data packets travel from the PC through the FA0/0 interface on Router A and arrive at the FA0/0 interface on Router B passing through two routers. In some cases, a "time exceeded" error message is displayed indicating that the TTL (Time to Live) for the datagram has been exceeded and the packet has been discarded. In the case that the TTL timer expires before a response is received, a * is displayed. An example is provided for a trace route issued from Router A to the FastEthernert 0/0 interface on Router C for the LAN shown in Figure 2-6. In this case, a datagram expired before being delivered to the destination of 10.10.5.250. Reasons for this happening could be traffic congestion or a momentary loss of connectivity.

```
Router1#traceroute 10.10.5.250

Type escape sequence to abort.
Tracing the route to 34.0.0.4
   1 10.10.200.2   4 msec 4 msec 4 msec
   2 10.10.5.250   16 msec *   16 msec
```

destination unreachable

This error is displayed indicating that the destination node received the packet and discarded it because it could not deliver the packet.

Load Balancing

Technique used to equally distribute data traffic on a per-packet basis.

Equal-Cost Load Balancing

A way to distribute traffic equally among multiple paths.

Cost Paths

A cost it takes to route traffic along the path from the source to the destination.

Another situation occurs when a "destination unreachable" error is displayed, indicating that the destination node received the packet and discarded it because it could not deliver the packet.

Load Balancing and Redundancy

This section examines the technique used to configure load balancing on a network that is configured for static routing. Load balancing is a technique used to equally distribute data traffic on a per-packet basis. Static routes support equal-cost load balancing, which is a way to distribute traffic equally among multiple paths. On Cisco routers, load balancing is automatic if several equal cost paths to a destination exist on multiple interfaces. Cost path is used by a routing protocol to calculate the cost along the path to route from the source to the destination. The cost path calculation is different depending on a routing protocol. Some routing protocol use the bandwidth, some use hop count along the path. This concept will be discussed throughout this and the next chapter.

To configure load balancing using static routing, one simply needs to create multiple static routes for more than one interface. As a matter of fact, the static route configuration examples of Router A to 10.10.10.0 network shown throughout this section already demonstrate the load balancing technique. Two independent static routes for the network 10.10.10.0 were configured. The result of the **show ip route** command also confirms that the 10.10.10.0 network can be reached on two paths: one is via 10.10.100.2 and another is via 10.10.200.2.

Not only can these paths be used for load balancing, they can be used to increase the redundancy and reliability of the network. When a network failure happens on one path, the other path will act as a backup path and assume the sole responsibility of routing traffic to the destination. This situation could happen if the next hop address is unreachable, which causes its static route to be removed from the routing table.

floating static route

Static backup route.

If load balancing is not required, static routing can offer redundancy via a backup route. A backup route (secondary route) is used when the primary route or preferred route fails. Sometimes, a static backup route is referred to as a floating static route. It the route is less preferred than other routes in the routing table, the route does not appear in the routing table until the more preferred route fails. The Administrative Distance (AD) is the number used to determine the preferability of the static routes. The AD ranges from 0–255, where the lower the AD number, the more preferred the route. By default, a static route already has the lower AD of 1. To create a floating route, you must assign a higher AD number. The concept of Administrative Distance (AD) will be discussed more in Section 2-2, "Dynamic Routing Protocols." The following example demonstrates how to assign a floating static route to Router A.

```
RouterA(config)#ip route 10.10.10.0 255.255.255.0 10.10.200.2
RouterA(config)#ip route 10.10.10.0 255.255.255.0 10.10.100.2 250


RouterA#sh ip route
Codes: C connected, S static, I IGRP, R RIP, M mobile, B BGP D EIGRP,
EX EIGRP external, O OSPF, IA OSPF inter area
```

```
N1 OSPF NSSA external type 1, N2 OSPF NSSA external type 2
E1 OSPF external type 1, E2 OSPF external type 2, E EGP
i IS-IS, L1 IS-IS level-1, L2 IS-IS level-2, * candidate default
U per-user static route, o ODR T traffic engineered route
Gateway of last resort is not set
10.0.0.0/24 is subnetted, 4 subnets
S 10.10.10.0 [1/0] via 10.10.200.2
C 10.10.20.0 is directly connected, FastEthernet0/0
C 10.10.200.0 is directly connected, FastEthernet0/1
C 10.10.100.0 is directly connected, FastEthernet0/2
```

Notice that an administrative distance of 250 is specified on the route with the next hop address of 10.10.100.2. This forces this route to be less desirable than the route with the next hop address of 10.10.200.2. Remember, a static route already has the lower AD of 1. The output from **show ip route** shows that only the more preferred static route is in the routing table. The floating static route via 10.10.100.2 is no longer in the table.

Table 2-1 provides a summary of the commands used when configuring the static routes.

TABLE 2-1   Summary of Commands Used to Configure the Static Routing Protocol

Command	Use
ip route	Specifies the destination IP address, the subnet mask, and the next hop IP address
show ip route	Displays the IP routes listed in the routing table
show ip route static	Displays only the static IP routes listed in the routing table
show running-configuration	Displays the router's running-configuration
show startup-configuration	Displays the router's saved configuration in NVRAM
write memory	Copies the current router changes to memory (NVRAM)
copy run start	Copies the current router changes to memory (NVRAM)
traceroute *destination-IP*	Used on a router to run a trace to a specified destination IP address
tracert *destination-IP*	Used on a PC to run a trace to a specified destination IP address

Networking Challenge—Static Routes

Use the Network Challenge Software included with the text's companion CD-ROM to demonstrate that you can configure static routes for a router. Place the CD-ROM in your computer's drive. Open the Net-Challenge folder and double click the *Net-Challenge V3-2.exe* file. Select the Chapter 7—Static Routes challenge. Use the software to demonstrate that you can complete the following tasks.

This challenge requires you to configure the static routes for Router A:

1. Click the Router A select button and press Return to get started.

2. Configure the default gateway address for computerA1 in LAN A (10.10.20.250). To do so, click the computer A1 icon in LAN A to bring up the TCP/IP Properties menu. Click OK on the menu, and press Enter to see the check.

3. Configure the IP addresses for the FastEthernet0/0 and FastEthernet0/1 ports. *Note:* Click the Router A symbol in the topology to display the IP addresses and subnet mask for the router.

4. Use the **no shut** command to enable both FastEthernet ports.

5. Use the **show ip int brief** command to view the current interface status.

6. Use the **ip route** command to configure two routes to the 10.10.10.0 subnet (NET). *Note:* Click the RouterB and RouterC symbols in the network topology to display the IP addresses for the router interfaces. (Use a 255.255.255.0 subnet mask.)

7. Use the **show ip route** command to view whether the routes are entered into the router's routing table.

8. Use the **show run** command to verify whether the static routes are listed in the router's running-configuration.

9. Use the proper command to set the FA 0/0 for Router A as the exit interface.

10. Use the proper command to incorporate null 0 features to prevent network loops to the 10.10.5.0 network.

2-2   DYNAMIC ROUTING PROTOCOLS

The concept of configuring a network using a static routing protocol was presented in this chapter's introduction. It became obvious that the time required for entering and maintaining the static routes was a problem. Therefore, a static routing protocol is of limited use for campus-wide network routing, but is essential when configuring the default route (gateway of last resort) on routers. However, static routes are used in situations such as configuring small networks with a limited number of routes.

Dynamic Routing Protocols

The routing table is dynamically updated to account for loss or changes in routes or changes in data traffic.

This section introduces an improvement over static routing through the use of dynamic routing protocols. Dynamic routing protocols enable the router's routing tables to be dynamically updated to account for a loss or a change in routes or changes in data traffic. The routers update their routing tables using information obtained from adjacent routers. The following list defines the features of dynamic routing protocols:

- What information is exchanged between routers
- When updated routing information is exchanged
- Steps for reacting to changes in the network
- Criteria for establishing the best route selection

The routing protocol is responsible for managing the exchange of routing information between the routers, and the choice of protocol defines how the routing information is exchanged and used.

A router could be running more than one routing protocol. This is sometimes necessary when a router is connecting to another router with a different routing protocol. A router could be learning about the same particular network from different routing protocols at the same time or the same network could be advertised with multiple paths. These are just some of the complications. Nonetheless, the router will learn network routes from its neighbor and install the best route in its routing table or routing information base (RIB). This will be used to allow the router to make a decision as to which is the best route to forward packets to a particular network. To determine the best route to a destination, a router considers three elements. These are listed in the order used to select the best route:

1. Prefix length

2. Administative Distance

3. Metric

The **prefix length** is the number of bits used to identify the network. The longer the prefix length means the route is more specific. For example, the network 10.10.10.0/24 has a longer prefix length than the network 10.10.0.0/16. Therefore, the network 10.10.10.0/24 is said to be a more specific route. The router will always prefer a more specific route no matter what routing protocol is being used.

If you have the same route to a destination configured with static route and the RIP routing protocol, the preferred route is with static route. This preference is accomplished with a parameter called **Administrative Distance (AD)**. The AD is a number assigned to a protocol or a route to declare its reliability. The lower the AD number, the better the protocol or route. Each routing protocol has a default administrative distance.

A router uses the administrative distance to resolve which routing protocol is chosen when there are conflicts. For example, a router might learn a route to a 10.0.0.0 network using RIP. The same router might also learn of a route to the 10.0.0.0 network using a static route. RIP has an administrative distance of 120 and static has an administrative distance of 1. Static has the lower administrative distance number; therefore, the router will select the static route. Table 2-2 provides a summary of administrative distances for selected routing protocols.

> **Prefix Length**
> The number of bits used to identify the network.
>
> **Administrative Distance (AD)**
> A number assigned to a protocol or route to declare its reliability.

TABLE 2-2   Administrative Distances and Routing Protocols

Protocol	Administrative Distance
Connected	0
Static route	1
eBGP	20
EIGRP	90
OSPF	110
IS-IS	115
RIP	120

The metric is a numerical parameter that allows a router to choose the best path within a routing protocol. So, the metric can be used to determine the best path when a single routing protocol advertises multiple paths to the same network. A metric is sometime referred to as "distance" or "cost" depending on the routing protocol. A metric is one of the four key issues associated with dynamic routing protocols. The four key issues are path determination, metric, convergence, and load balancing. These issues are defined in Table 2-3.

TABLE 2-3   Four Key Issues in Dynamic Routing Protocols

Item	Issue	Purpose
1	Path determination	A procedure in the protocol that is used to determine the best route.
2	Metric	A numeric measure assigned to routes for ranking the routes best to worst; the smaller the number, the better.
3	Convergence	This happens when a router obtains a clear view of the routes in a network. The time it takes for the router to obtain a clear view is called the convergence time.
4	Load balancing	A procedure in the protocol that enables routers to use any of the multiple data paths available from multiple routers to reach the destination.

Examples of route metrics are as follows:

- Hop count: The number of routers the data packet must pass through to reach the destination network.

- Reliability: A measure of the reliability of the link, typically in terms of the amount of errors.

- Bandwidth: Having to do with the data capacity of the networking link; a Fast-Ethernet 100 Mbps link has greater data capacity than a 10 Mbps Ethernet link.

- **Delay:** The time it takes for a data packet to travel from source to destination.
- **Cost:** A value typically assigned by the network administrator that takes into account bandwidth and expense.
- **Load:** Having to do with the network activity on a link or router.
- **Ticks:** The measured delay time in terms of clock ticks, where each tick is approximately 55 milliseconds (1/18 second).

There are two types of dynamic routing protocols: distance vector and link state. These protocols are briefly introduced in this section. The procedures for configuring a router to use a dynamic routing protocol is examined in Section 2-3. The procedures for configuring link state protocols is discussed in Chapter 3.

Distance Vector Protocols

A **distance vector protocol** is a routing algorithm that periodically sends the entire routing table to its neighboring or adjacent router. When the neighboring router receives the table, it assigns a distance vector number to each route. The distance vector number is typically specified by some metric, such as hop count.

In a distance vector protocol, the router first determines its neighbors or adjacent routers. All the connected routes will have a distance or hop count of 0, as illustrated in Figure 2-7. Routers use the hop count metric to determine the best route to forward a data packet. Figure 2-8 provides an example of determining the hop count to a destination subnet.

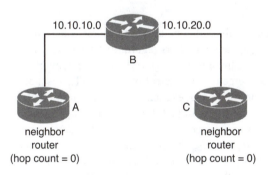

FIGURE 2-7 An example of router neighbors (hop count = 0)

Table 2-4 lists the hop count from Router A to the 10.10.200.0, 10.10.150.0, and 10.10.50.0 subnets.

TABLE 2-4   Hop Counts from Router A to Subnets

From	To	Hop Count
Router A	10.10.200.0	0
Router A	10.10.150.0	1
Router A	10.10.50.0	2

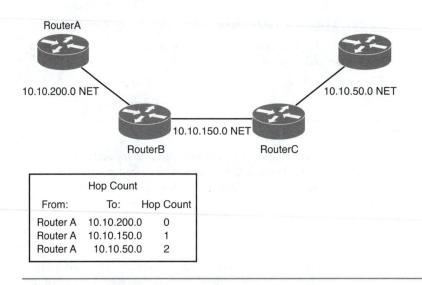

FIGURE 2-8   An example of determining the router hops

In a distance vector protocol, each router determines its neighbors, builds its list of neighboring routers, and sends its routing table to its neighbors. The neighboring routers update their routing table based on the received information. When complete, each router's routing table provides a list of known routes within the network.

Link State Protocols

Link state protocols establish a relationship with a neighboring router. The routers exchange link state advertisements to update neighbors regarding route status. The link state advertisements are sent only if there is a change or loss in the network routes and the link state protocols converge to route selection quickly. This is a distinct advantage over distance vector protocols that exchange updated routing tables at fixed time intervals and are slow to converge. In fact, link state routing protocols are replacing distance vector protocols in most computer networks. Link state protocols are also called *shortest-path first protocols*, based on the algorithm developed by E. W. Dijkstra. An example of a link state protocol is Open Shortest Path First (OSPF), examined in more detail in Chapter 3. Link state protocols use Hello packets to verify that communication is still established with neighbor routers. The key issues of link state protocols are as follows:

- Finds neighbors/adjacencies
- Uses route advertisements to build routing table
- Sends Hello packets
- Sends updates when routing changes

2-3 CONFIGURING RIPV2

Routing Information Protocol (RIP) is a dynamic routing protocol, meaning the routers periodically exchange routes. RIP is classified as a distance vector protocol using router hop count as the metric. RIP permits a maximum of 15 hops to prevent routing loops. Routing loops occur when a router forwards packets back to the router that sent them, as graphically shown in Figure 2-9. RIP and other distance vector routing protocols send the entire routing table to neighbor routers at regular time intervals. Sometimes, the routing tables can be quite large and the transfer can consume network bandwidth. This is of great concern in networks with limited bandwidth because the periodic exchange can lead to slowdowns in data traffic. The default time interval for RIP for exchanging routing tables is 30 seconds. This results in slow route convergence, and if there are multiple routers sharing RIP routes, there will be even longer convergence time.

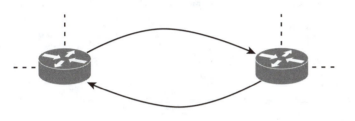

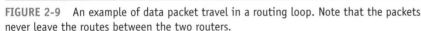

FIGURE 2-9 An example of data packet travel in a routing loop. Note that the packets never leave the routes between the two routers.

The RIP routing protocol is enabled on the router by entering the command **router rip** at the Router(config)# prompt. Next, network statements are required to declare what networks will be advertised by the RIP routing protocol. To advertise the network means the routing table containing the network is shared with its neighbors. The **network** command requires the use of a class network address (Class A, Class B, Class C) after the **network** command. This is called classful addressing. A class network address or classful address is the network portion of the address for the particular class of the network. For example, LAN A in our campus network is on the 10.10.20.0 NET, as shown in Figure 2-10. This is a class A network, and the network portion of the address is 10.0.0.0. The structure of the network command is **network** *[network-address]*, where the *network address* is the network where RIP is to be advertised; therefore, the command in RIP will be **network 10.0.0.0**.

The following discussion explains how to initialize RIP and how to set the networks attached to the router for RIP routing. After these commands are entered, any interfaces that are part of the 10.0.0.0 network will run the RIP routing protocol. Note that subnets or subnet masks are not specified in the RIP network command because the class network address is used and all IP addresses in the network (for example, 10.0.0.0) are enabled to use RIP.

```
Router(config)#router rip
Router(config-router)#network 10.0.0.0
```

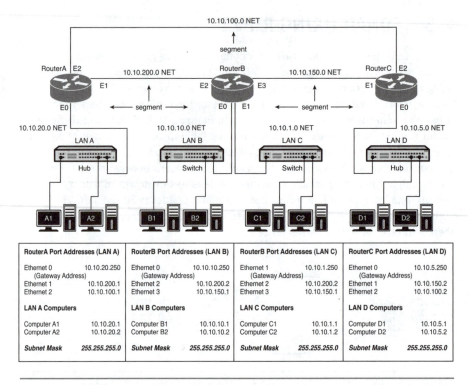

10.10.100.0 NET

segment

RouterA E2   10.10.200.0 NET   RouterB   10.10.150.0 NET   RouterC E2
         E1   E2   E3   E1
    E0   ← segment →   E0 E1   ← segment →   E0

10.10.20.0 NET   10.10.10.0 NET   10.10.1.0 NET   10.10.5.0 NET

LAN A   Hub   LAN B   Switch   LAN C   Switch   LAN D   Hub

A1   A2   B1   B2   C1   C2   D1   D2

RouterA Port Addresses (LAN A)		RouterB Port Addresses (LAN B)		RouterB Port Addresses (LAN C)		RouterC Port Addresses (LAN D)	
Ethernet 0	10.10.20.250	Ethernet 0	10.10.10.250	Ethernet 1	10.10.1.250	Ethernet 0	10.10.5.250
(Gateway Address)		(Gateway Address)		(Gateway Address)		(Gateway Address)	
Ethernet 1	10.10.200.1	Ethernet 2	10.10.200.2	Ethernet 2	10.10.200.2	Ethernet 1	10.10.150.2
Ethernet 2	10.10.100.1	Ethernet 3	10.10.150.1	Ethernet 3	10.10.150.1	Ethernet 2	10.10.100.2
LAN A Computers		**LAN B Computers**		**LAN C Computers**		**LAN D Computers**	
Computer A1	10.10.20.1	Computer B1	10.10.10.1	Computer C1	10.10.1.1	Computer D1	10.10.5.1
Computer A2	10.10.20.2	Computer B2	10.10.10.2	Computer C2	10.10.1.2	Computer D2	10.10.5.2
Subnet Mask	***255.255.255.0***	***Subnet Mask***	***255.255.255.0***	***Subnet Mask***	***255.255.255.0***	***Subnet Mask***	***255.255.255.0***

FIGURE 2-10   LAN A in the campus network

RIP can be used only in *contiguous* networks, meaning the networks and routes must have the same class network address. This means the router addresses for the network connecting the routers must be the same class as the LAN connected to the router. This is shown in Figure 2-11 (a) and (b). LAN A and B have a 10.#.#.# address (also called a *10 network* address). The network address connecting the two routers must also be a "10" network address. The IP address for the network connecting the two routers in Figure 2-11 (a) is 10.10.200.0. This is a "10" network address. The network shown in Figure 2-11 (b) uses the IP address of 192.168.10.0 for the network connecting the two routers. An address of 192.168.10.0 is in the 192.168.10.0 network. This is not part of the 10.0.0.0 network; therefore, the 192.168.10.0 address is not suitable for use in RIP.

RIP is a relatively simple routing protocol to configure. However, RIP is good only for very small networks that have a limited staff size for managing the network and is not suited for networks that need fast convergence. RIP is a standard protocol, not a proprietary protocol, meaning that the use of the protocol is not limited to certain equipment manufacturers.

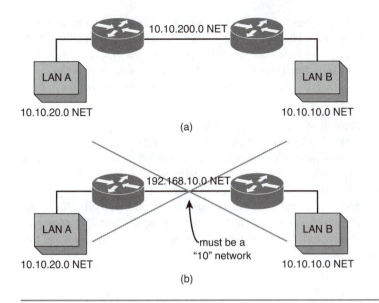

LAN A

10.10.20.0 NET

LAN B

10.10.10.0 NET

(a)

192.168.10.0 NET

LAN A

10.10.20.0 NET

must be a
"10" network

LAN B

10.10.10.0 NET

(b)

FIGURE 2-11   An example of (a) a contiguous network and (b) a discontiguous network

Configuring Routes with RIP

The first step in configuring the router for RIP is to set up the interfaces. This includes assigning an IP address and a subnet mask to the interface using the command **ip address** *A.B.C.D. subnet-mask*. Next, the interface is enabled using the **no shut** command. The following are the steps for configuring the FastEthernet0/1 interface on Router A in the campus network shown previously in Figure 2-10:

```
Router con0 is now available
Press RETURN to get started.
RouterA>en
Password:
RouterA# conf t
Enter configuration commands, one per line. End with CNTL/Z.
Router(config)#int fa0/1
Router(config-if)#ip address 10.10.200.1 255.255.255.0
Router(config-if)#no shut
00:59:03: %LINEPROTO-5-UPDOWN: Line protocol on Interface
FastEthernet1, changed state to up
```

Next, enter the router's configuration mode [Router(config)#] and input the command **router rip** to use the RIP routing protocol. The next step is to specify the network that uses RIP for routing. These two steps are shown here:

```
Router(config)#router rip
Router(config-router)#network 10.0.0.0
```

The command **router rip** enables the RIP routing protocol, and the command **network 10.0.0.0** instructs the router to use RIP on the "10" network. Remember, RIP requires the use of a class network address (for example, 10.0.0.0). Notice that the **router rip** command places the router in the (config-router) mode, as shown in the prompt. This indicates that the router is in the state for specifying the networks using RIP.

It's a good idea to periodically check that the router interfaces are properly configured. The command **show ip interface brief** (**sh ip int brief**) is used to check the interfaces. This is an important troubleshooting command when looking for reasons why the router is not working. Use this command to check to see if the IP address has been assigned to the interface and to check the status and protocol settings. In this case, the FastEthernet0/1 port has been assigned the IP address 10.10.200.1, the status is *up*, and the protocol is *up*. The FastEthernet 0/0 and 0/2 ports for RouterA have not been configured, as shown, and the status is administratively down and the protocol is down:

```
Router#sh ip int brief
Interface          IP-Address     OK? Method  Status
-Protocol
FastEthernet0/0    unassigned     YES manual  administratively down  down
FastEthernet0/1    10.10.200.1    YES manual  up                     up
FastEthernet0/2    unassigned     YES unset   administratively down  down
```

> **show ip protocol (sh ip protocol)**
> Displays the routing protocol running on the router.

The command **show ip protocol** (**sh ip protocol**) is used to display the routing protocols running on the router, as shown. This command will display protocol information only after the routing protocol has been enabled and the network addresses are specified. Notice that there are no values specified for the FastEthernet0/0 and FastEthernet0/2 ports. Neither of these interfaces has been configured. The **show ip protocol** command also shows that router updates are being sent every 30 seconds and indicates that the next update is due in 5 seconds.

```
RouterA#sh ip protocol
Routing Protocol is "rip"
Sending updates every 30 seconds, next due in 5 seconds
Invalid after 180 seconds, hold down 180, flushed after 240
Outgoing update filter list for all interfaces is Incoming update
filter list for all interfaces is Redistributing: rip
Default version control: send version 1, receive any version
Interface         Send Recv Key-chain
FastEthernet0/0    0    0    0
FastEthernet0/1    1    1    2
FastEthernet0/2    0    0    0
Routing for Networks:
10.0.0.0
Routing Information Sources:
Gateway Distance Last Update
10.10.200.1 120 00:00:14
Distance: (default is 120)
```

The routes configured for the router can be displayed using the **show ip route** (**sh ip route**) command, as shown. In this example, the FastEthernet0/0 and FastEthernet0/2 ports for Router A have been configured and are displayed:

```
Router#sh ip route
Codes: C - connected, S - static, I - IGRP, R - RIP, M - mobile, B -
BGP D - EIGRP, EX - EIGRP external, O - OSPF, IA - OSPF inter area
N1 - OSPF NSSA external type 1, N2 - OSPF NSSA external type 2
E1 - OSPF external type 1, E2 - OSPF external type 2, E - EGP
I - IS-IS, L1 - IS-IS level-1, L2 - IS-IS level-2, * candidate default
U - per-user static route, o - ODR T - traffic engineered route
Gateway of last resort is not set
10.0.0.0/24 is subnetted, 1 subnets
C 10.10.20.0 is directly connected, FastEthernet0/0
C 10.10.200.0 is directly connected, FastEthernet0/1
C 10.10.100.0 is directly connected, FastEthernet0/2
```

This shows the connected (C) networks but RIP (R) is not enabled for any networks. Why? At this point, RIP has been enabled only on Router A in the campus network. Router B and Router C also need to have RIP enabled. Use the commands **router rip** and **network** to enable RIP on Router B. RIP was next configured on Router B and the updated routing table for Router A is provided:

```
Router#sh ip route
Codes: C - connected, S - static, I - IGRP, R - RIP, M - mobile, B -
BGP D - EIGRP, EX - EIGRP external, O - OSPF, IA - OSPF inter area
N1 - OSPF NSSA external type 1, N2 - OSPF NSSA external type 2
E1 - OSPF external type 1, E2 - OSPF external type 2, E - EGP
I - IS-IS, L1 - IS-IS level-1, L2 - IS-IS level-2, * candidate default
U - per-user static route, o - ODR T - traffic engineered route
Gateway of last resort is not set
10.0.0.0/24 is subnetted, 5 subnets
R 10.10.1.0 [120/1] via 10.10.200.2, 00:00:05, FastEthernet0/1
R 10.10.10.0 [120/1] via 10.10.200.2, 00:00:05, FastEthernet0/1
C 10.10.20.0 is directly connected, FastEthernet0/0
C 10.10.200.0 is directly connected, FastEthernet0/1
C 10.10.100.0 is directly connected, FastEthernet0/2
```

Now, the networks (10.10.10.0 and 10.10.1.0) from LAN B and LAN C, respectively, are shown in this table. Router A learns these network routes via its FastEthernet0/1 interface from the IP address 10.10.200.2, which is the FastEthernet0/2 interface of Router B.

Verify the settings in the running-configuration file by using the **sh run** command, as outlined in Table 2-5. Recall that this is the abbreviated command for **show running-configuration**. The configuration list should show that the interfaces have been assigned an IP address and that RIP has been configured.

TABLE 2-5   sh run Command Output

CLI	Comments
RouterA#**sh run**	! 1. sh run command
Building configuration	! 2. assembling the data file
!	! 3. ! is used for spaces or comments
Current configuration:	
!	
version 12.0	! 6. displays the Cisco IOS version
service timestamps debug uptime	
service timestamps log uptime	
no service password-encryption	! 9. the enable (line 14) and vty (line 42) passwords appear as plaintext
!	
hostname RouterA	! 11. the name of the router
!	
enable secret 5 $1$6EWO$kWlakDz89zac.koh/pyG4.	! 13. the encrypted enable secret
enable password Salsa	! 14. the enable password
!	
ip subnet-zero	! 16. enables subnet zero routing
!	
Interface FastEthernet0/0	! 18. FastEthernet0/0 settings
ip address 10.10.20.0 255.255.255.0	
no ip directed-broadcast	
!	
interface FastEthernet0/1	! 22. FastEthernet0/1 settings
ip address 10.10.200.1 255.255.255.0	
no ip directed-broadcast	
no mop enabled	
!	
interface FastEthernet0/2	! 27. FastEthernet0/2 settings
ip address 10.10.100.1 255.255.255.0	
no ip directed-broadcast no mop enabled	
!	
router rip	! 33. enable RIP

CLI	Comments
network 10.0.0.0	! 34. specify a network class address
!	
ip classless	
!	
line con 0	
transport input none	
line aux 0	
line vty 0 4	! 41. virtual terminal settings for telnet
login	! 42. This command enables login
password ConCarne	! 43. telnet password
	login
!	
end	

Lines 18, 22, and 27 list the assigned IP addresses for the interface. Lines 33 and 34 show that RIP has been configured for the router. The **sh run** command displays the router's running configuration. The **copy run start** command must be entered to save the changes to NVRAM.

RIP is among the oldest protocols; it was introduced in 1988. It has a number of limitations that makes it inefficient in handling a lot of newer IP features. Some of its limitations are

- RIP is a classful routing-only protocol. It, therefore, does not support Variable Length Subnet Mask (VLSM) and Classless Inter-Domain Routing (CIDR). This prevents it from being the routing protocol of choice when having to deal with different sized subnets in a network.

- RIP does not support router authentication, which can be exploited as vulnerability.

- RIP has a hop count limit of 15, which means a destination that is 15 hops away is considered to be unreachable.

- RIP uses hop count as a metric. What this means is that RIP determines the best route by counting the number of hops to reach the destination. A lower hop count wins over the higher hop count. This is a disadvantage when dealing with different bandwidth between hops. RIP does not take into consideration whether the higher hop count route might have higher bandwidth. Therefore, the lower bandwidth route could be taken.

The following example demonstrates one of RIP's limitations. In this example, the subnet mask of the LAN C network will be changed to 255.255.255.128. To accomplish this task, the FastEthernet 0/1 interface for Router B needs to be reconfigured as follows:

```
RouterB# conf t
Enter configuration commands, one per line. End with CNTL/Z.
Router(config)#int fa0/1
Router(config-if)#ip address 10.10.1.250 255.255.255.128
```

Because RIP does not support VLSM, what will happen to the newly reconfigured subnet? The answer is the network 10.10.1.0 will not be advertised by RIP. The route for network 10.10.1.0 is not displayed in the routing table of Router A, as shown with the command **sh ip route**:

```
RouterA#sh ip route
Codes: C - connected, S - static, I - IGRP, R - RIP, M - mobile, B -
BGP D - EIGRP, EX - EIGRP external, O - OSPF, IA - OSPF inter area
N1 - OSPF NSSA external type 1, N2 - OSPF NSSA external type 2
E1 - OSPF external type 1, E2 - OSPF external type 2, E - EGP
I - IS-IS, L1 - IS-IS level-1, L2 - IS-IS level-2, * candidate default
U - per-user static route, o - ODR T - traffic engineered route
Gateway of last resort is not set
10.0.0.0/24 is subnetted, 5 subnets
R 10.10.10.0 [120/1] via 10.10.200.2, 00:00:05, FastEthernet0/1
C 10.10.20.0 is directly connected, FastEthernet0/0
C 10.10.200.0 is directly connected, FastEthernet0/1
C 10.10.100.0 is directly connected, FastEthernet0/2
```

To address some of RIP's limitations, the second version of RIP was developed as RIP version 2 (RIPv2) in 1993. The original version of RIP is then called RIP version 1 (RIPv1). RIPv2 is not quite a redesign of RIPv1; it could be thought more of an enhanced version of RIP version 1. RIPv2 works basically just like RIPv1. It introduced new features, such as support for VLSM and CIDR, router authentication, next hop specification, route tag, and the use of multicasting. However, it still cannot resolve some of the limitations found in RIPv1, which are hop count and metric decisions.

Configuring Routes with RIP Version 2

The steps needed to configure RIPv2 are almost exactly the same as configuring RIPv1. The only difference is the version must be specified in the **router rip** configuration. Let's take the RIP configuration that was done earlier in this section, then enter the router's configuration mode [**Router(config)#**], and input the command **router rip** to use the RIP routing protocol. The next step is to configure RIPv2 to be used with the command **version 2**. Without specifying the version, RIPv1 will be used by default. These two steps are shown here:

```
RouterA(config)#router rip
RouterA(config-router)#version 2
```

To verify that RIPv2 is the routing protocol, the command **sh ip protocol** is used. Notice the line **Default version control**. This confirms that RIP version 2 is being sent as well as being received by the RouterA.

```
RouterA#sh ip protocol
Routing Protocol is "rip"
Sending updates every 30 seconds, next due in 17 seconds
Invalid after 180 seconds, hold down 180, flushed after 240
Outgoing update filter list for all interfaces is not set
Incoming update filter list for all interfaces is not set
Redistributing: rip
Default version control: send version 2, receive version 2
Interface          Send  Recv  Triggered RIP  Key-chain
FastEthernet0/0      2     2
FastEthernet0/1      2     2
FastEthernet0/2      2     2
Automatic network summarization is in effect
Maximum path: 4
Routing for Networks:
10.0.0.0
Routing Information Sources:
Gateway         Distance      Last Update
10.10.200.2        120        00:00:20
Distance: (default is 120)
```

Even though, RIPv2 is a classless routing protocol, it still summarizes routes at the class network boundaries by default. Therefore, it may appear as if RIPv2 only advertises classful networks, like RIPv1. To disable the auto summarization function, the command no auto-summary is used. This command instructs the router not to summarize the network routes. The **no auto-summary** command alters this behavior by enabling RIP to advertise the actual networks, not the classful summary. The **no auto-summary** command should be used when a classful network is divided and parts of the same classful network exist in different parts of the network topology.

> **no auto-summary**
> This instructs the router not to summarize the network routes.

```
RouterA(config)#router rip
RouterA(config-router)#no auto-summary
```

Now, let's reexamine the previous demonstration of RIPv1, where the subnet mask for the network 10.10.1.0 was changed to 255.255.255.128. This resulted in the network no longer showing up in the routing table. The same command **version 2** needs to be applied under **router rip** on Router B. With the RIP version 2 enabled, the command **sh ip route** is reissued on Router A. This time, the routing table shows that the LAN C network 10.10.1.128/25 is being displayed, even though it has a different sized subnet than the others:

```
Router#sh ip route
Codes: C - connected, S - static, I - IGRP, R - RIP, M - mobile, B -
BGP D - EIGRP, EX - EIGRP external, O - OSPF, IA - OSPF inter area
N1 - OSPF NSSA external type 1, N2 - OSPF NSSA external type 2
E1 - OSPF external type 1, E2 - OSPF external type 2, E - EGP
```

```
I - IS-IS, L1 - IS-IS level-1, L2 - IS-IS level-2, * candidate default
U - per-user static route, o - ODR T - traffic engineered route
Gateway of last resort is not set
10.0.0.0/24 is subnetted, 5 subnets
R 10.10.10.0 [120/1] via 10.10.200.2, 00:00:05, FastEthernet0/1
C 10.10.20.0 is directly connected, FastEthernet0/0
R 10.10.1.128/25 [120/1] via 10.10.200.2, 00:00:15, FastEthernet0/1
C 10.10.200.0 is directly connected, FastEthernet0/2
C 10.10.100.0 is directly connected, FastEthernet0/1
```

Networking Challenge—RIP

Use the router simulator software included with the text's companion CD-ROM to demonstrate that you can configure RIP for Router A in the campus LAN. (*Note:* The campus LAN is shown in Figure 2-8 and is displayed on the computer screen if the topology button is selected.) Place the CD-ROM in your computer's drive. Open the *Net-Challenge* folder, and click NetChallenge V3-2.exe. When the software is running, click the Select Router Challenge button to open a Select Router Challenge drop-down menu. Select Chapter 2—RIPv2. This opens a checkbox that can be used to verify that you have completed all the tasks:

1. Enter the privileged EXEC mode on the router.

2. Enter the router configuration mode: Router(config).

3. Configure the FastEthernet0/0 interface with the following:

    IP address: 10.10.20.250

    Subnet mask: 255.255.255.0

4. Enable the FA0/0 interface.

5. Configure the FastEthernet0/1 interface with the following:

    IP address: 10.10.200.1

    Subnet mask: 255.255.255.0

6. Enable the FA0/1 interface.

7. Configure the FastEthernet0/2 interface with the following:

    IP address: 10.10.100.1

    Subnet mask: 255.255.255.0

8. Enable the FA0/2 interface.

9. Enable RIP V2.

10. Use the **network** command to specify the class network address to be used by RIP (10.0.0.0).

11. Use the **sh ip int brief** command to check the interface status.

12. Use the **sh ip protocol** command to see whether RIP is running. (*Note:* This requires that Steps 9 and 10 are complete or the response will be "no protocol.")

13. Use the **show ip route** command to verify whether the three FastEthernet ports are connected to the router.

14. Display the contents of the running-configuration file. Verify that RIP is enabled and the proper network address is specified.

15. Copy the router's running-configuration to the startup-configuration.

16. Display the contents of the startup-configuration.

2-4 TFTP—TRIVIAL FILE TRANSFER PROTOCOL

Trivial File Transfer Protocol (TFTP) is a simple File Transfer Protocol often used with routers and switches to save and reload the configuration files to and from a remote server. The files are saved in case of equipment failure, for rebooting, or for upgrading or archiving the configuration files. It is not uncommon for the configuration files to be backed up daily. The backup is typically done automatically. Changes to router and switch configuration files can occur on a daily basis, and an automatic or regularly scheduled backup is a safe way to ensure the configuration files are archived. Isn't it true that the configuration files can be saved to NVRAM? The answer is yes, but if there is a complete equipment failure, the current router or switch configuration will be lost. Saving the configuration files to another machine is a safer way to prevent loss. The TFTP server is also used for updating and saving the Internetwork Operating System (IOS) files stored in flash. Examples of how to save and reload files stored on the TFTP server are demonstrated later in this section.

> **TFTP**
> Trivial File Transfer Protocol.

TFTP uses port 69 to establish the network connection and the User Datagram Protocol (UDP) to transport the files. TFTP has no authentication or encryption capabilities and is not a secure transfer; therefore, it is recommended that file transfers should be limited to private networks or a secure TFTP version should be used.

Configuring TFTP

Before you can save the router or switch configuration files, you must install the TFTP server software on your computer. Many freeware and shareware TFTP software packages are available on the Internet. The available software can be found by searching for "tftp server" using your Internet search engine. (Note: You must have the TFTP software running on your computer for the file transfer to work). Newer versions of the router and switch IOS now support FTP in addition to TFTP for the file transfer. The advantage of FTP is that a secure file transfer can be established using, for example, SSH File Transfer Protocol (SFTP), while TFTP is not secure. Additionally, FTP overcomes the 16-megabyte file transfer limit of some IOS versions. FTP file transfer sizes are not limited.

When you first set up the router or switch, you must make sure it is on the same subnet as the TFTP server because you don't have routing set up yet; therefore, the destination IPs for the router/switch and the TFTP server must be on the same subnet. Figure 2-12 provides an example of this. The IP address for Router C has been configured to 192.168.10.1/28. The TFTP server software has been installed on the computer, D2 and the IP address for computer D2 has been configured to 192.168.10.5/28. This places Router C and computer D2 (TFTP server) on the same subnet in the 192.168.10.0 network. Also note that both Router C and computer D2 are connected to the same switch.

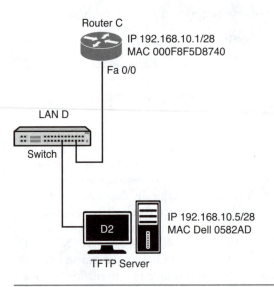

FIGURE 2-12 An example of placing the router and the TFTP server on the same network

The following are the basic commands used to save and load files to and from the TFTP server. (Abbreviated commands that are recognized by the Net-Challenge software are provided in brackets [ ].) Your first requirement is that you place the router in the privileged EXEC mode, as shown:

1. Enter the enable mode on your router.

```
RouterC>enable
Password:
```

The router's running-configuration file can be reloaded using the command demonstrated in the next step.

2. Save to the TFTP server.

```
RouterC#copy running-config tftp [copy run tftp]
Address or name of remote host []?192.168.10.5
Destination filename [running-config]? <enter the filename to be
saved>
!!
872 bytes copied in 5.176 secs (174 bytes/sec)
```

The router's running-configuration file stored on the TFTP server can be reloaded using the command demonstrated in the next step.

3. Load from the TFTP server.

```
RouterC#copy tftp running-config [copy tftp run]
Address or name of remote host [  ]? 192.168.10.5
Source filename [  ]? <enter the saved file name>
Destination filename [running-config]?
Accessing tftp://192.168.10.5/network-name...
Loading network-name from 192.168.10.5 (via Ethernet0): !
[OK - 872/1024 bytes]

872 bytes copied in 4.400 secs (218 bytes/sec)
router#
```

Figures 2-13 to 2-15 are captured data files of the TFTP write process using a network protocol analyzer. Figure 2-13 shows the capture for packet 2. The source is the router with an IP address of 192.168.10.1 and the destination is the TFTP server with an IP address of 192.168.10.5. The middle of Figure 2-13 shows that the User Datagram Protocol (UDP) is being used with a source port of 56401 and a destination port 69 (the Trivial File Transfer port). The bottom of Figure 2-13 shows that a write request has been requested. The filename is config, which is the destination filename. The data is being transferred in the octet mode (also called the binary image transfer mode). In this mode, the data is transferred in one-byte units.

FID	BookMark	Stat...	Elapsed [sec]	Size	Destination	Source	Summary
000000			0.655.510.120	64	000F8F5D8740	000F8F5D8740	LOOPBACK Receipt=0
000001			10.653.683.040	64	000F8F5D8740	000F8F5D8740	LOOPBACK Receipt=0
000002			19.696.837.720	64	192.168.10.5	192.168.10.1	TFTP Write Request File = config
000003			19.704.961.080	64	192.168.10.1	192.168.10.5	TFTP Ack Packet (# 0)
000004			19.707.427.880	562	192.168.10.5	192.168.10.1	TFTP Data Packet (# 1)
000005			19.708.614.640	64	192.168.10.1	192.168.10.5	TFTP Ack Packet (# 1)
000006			19.711.632.880	200	192.168.10.5	192.168.10.1	TFTP Data Packet (# 2)
000007			19.712.675.760	64	192.168.10.1	192.168.10.5	TFTP Ack Packet (# 2)
000008			20.654.757.760	64	000F8F5D8740	000F8F5D8740	LOOPBACK Receipt=0

```
User Datagram Protocol
(UDP)
  Source Port            56401
  Destination Port       69    (Trivial File Transfer)
  Length                 23 bytes
  CheckSum               0x8938   (Correct)
                         [15 bytes of data]
Trivial File Transfer
Protocol
  Packet Opcode          2 (Write Request)
  File Name              config
  Mode                   octet
Data/FCS
```

FIGURE 2-13   A TFTP write request to port 69

Figure 2-14 (packet 3) shows that the TFTP server computer at source port (SP) 1102 replies back to the router (destination port DP 56401). Note that the TFTP server is now using port 1102. Port 69 is used initially to establish the TFTP connection, but the server will select an available port for the data transfer.

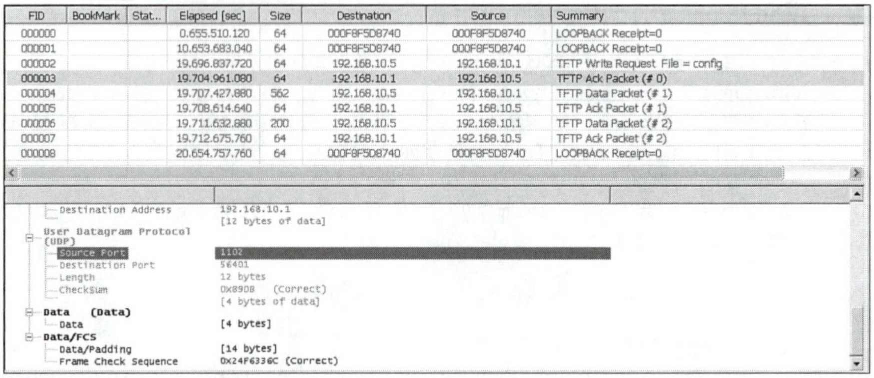

FIGURE 2-14   A TFTP write request—port assignments

The beginning of the data transfer is shown in Figure 2-15 in packet 4 (FID 000004). The source port is 56401 (router) and the destination port is 1102 (TFTP server). The packet size of the initial data transfer is 562 bytes. The actual text of the data transfer is displayed at the bottom of Figure 2-15. Notice that the data transfer text is readable, which introduces security issues if the configuration data is being transferred over a network.

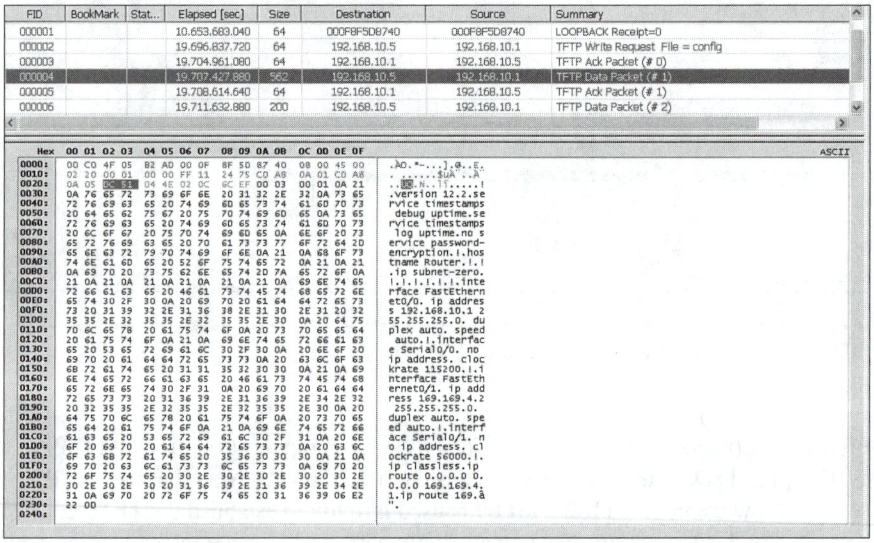

FIGURE 2-15   A TFTP write request—data transfer

SUMMARY

This chapter presented examples of configuring static and the RIP/RIPv2 routing protocols. The network challenge exercises provided the opportunity for the student to test her or his configuration skill prior to actually configuring a real router. The student should also have gained an understanding of advanced routing configuration concepts, such as load balancing and redundancy. Additionally, this chapter introduced the steps for configuring a TFTP server.

QUESTIONS AND PROBLEMS

Section 2-1

1. What is a routing table?

2. What is the most common static route used in a host computer?

3. What command is used to view a PC computer's routing table?

4. What is meant by a 0.0.0.0 network address entry with a subnet mask of 0.0.0.0 in a PC's routing table?

5. What is the 127.0.0.1 IP address, and what is it used for?

6. What is the router command to configure a static route from LAN A to LAN B for the network shown in Figure 2-16?

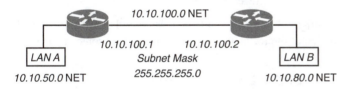

FIGURE 2-16 The network for problem 6

7. What is the difference in a router's running-configuration and startup-configuration?

8. What is the router command that is used to view the routes entered into the router's routing table?

9. What is the router command that is used to configure a static route for a router?

10. List two static routes to route data from LAN A to LAN C. The network is shown in Figure 2-17. Assume a subnet mask of 255.255.255.0.

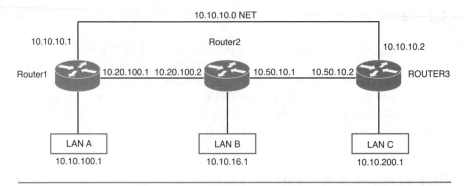

FIGURE 2-17 The network for problems 10 through 13

11. List two static routes to route data from LAN B to LAN C in Figure 2-17. Assume a subnet mask of 255.255.255.0.

12. Which of the following are suitable subnet masks for use in configuring static routes for the network shown in Figure 2-17?

    a. 255.255.0.0.

    b. 255.0.0.0.

    c. 255.255.255.224.

    d. All of these answers are correct.

    e. None of these answers are correct.

13. A static route is configured to route data from LAN A to LAN B on Router 1 in Figure 2-17. Which of the following are appropriate static routes to achieve this goal?

    a. ip route 10.10.16.0 255.255.255.255 10.20.100.2

    b. ip route 10.10.16.0 255.255.255.0 10.20.100.2

    c. ip route 10.10.16.0 255.255.255.255 10.10.10.2

    d. ip route 10.10.16.0 255.255.255.0 10.10.10.2

14. What is the purpose of the gateway of last resort?

15. What is the command for defining the gateway of last resort if the IP address for the next hop is 192.168.45.1?

16. The command **sh ip route** is entered on a router. What does it mean if the following command is displayed?

    ```
    Gateway of last resort is not set
    ```

17. The following information is displayed after entering the **sh ip int brief** command. What is this indicating?

```
RouterA#sh ip int brief
00:22:18: %SYS-5-CONFIG_I: Configured from console
Interface        IP-Address  OK? Method Status    Protocol
FastEthernet0/0  192.168.200.1 YES manual up       down
```

18 What is the command for showing only the static routes? Indicate the command and the router prompt.

19. What is the purpose of the exit interface?

20. Specify the command for setting the exit interface to be FA0/1 if the destination network is 10.10.20.0, the subnet mask is 255.255.255.128, and the next hop address is 10.100.25.1.

21. The **show ip route** command is entered on a router. What information does the following indicate?

```
S 192.168.10.0/24 is directly connected, Null 0
```

22. In regards to Figure 2-17, the network engineer would like to trace a route from Router 1 to 10.10.200.1. What command should be used if the 10.10.200.1 interface is a PC?

23. In regards to problem 22, how many hops will the **traceroute** require?

24. What is load balancing?

Section 2-2

25. What is the difference between a *static* and a *dynamic* routing protocol?

26. What are the four key issues in dynamic routing protocols?

27. Define hop count.

28. Which of the following is *not* a metric used in dynamic routing protocols?

    a. Hop count

    b. Cost

    c. Runs

    d. Ticks

29. A distance vector protocol typically uses what as the metric?

30. Determine the hop count for Router 2 to subnet B in Figure 2-18.

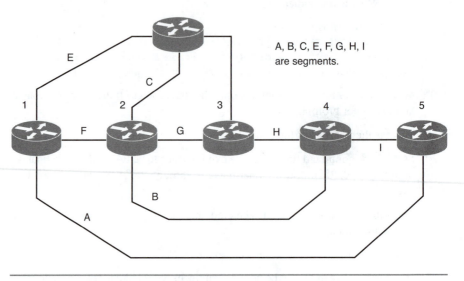

A, B, C, E, F, G, H, I are segments.

FIGURE 2-18 The network for problems 2-30 through 2-32

31. For Figure 2-18, what is the hop count from Router5 to subnet G?

32. For Figure 2-18, what is the hop count from Router3 to subnet A?

33. Link state protocols issue what to update neighbor routers regarding route status?

    a. Hop status

    b. Link state advertisements

    c. "Hello" packets

    d. Adjacencies

34. Which of the following are key issues of link state protocols?

    a. Send updates every 90 seconds

    b. Send update when routing changes

    c. Use link lights to establish adjacencies

    d. Use a hop count metric to determine the best route to a destination

Section 2-3

35. RIP is classified as which of the following?

    a. Distance vector protocol

    b. Dynamic routing protocol

    c. Link state protocol

    d. a and c

    e. a and b

    f. b and c

36. Define routing loops.

37. Which of the following are examples of classful addresses?

    a. 10.10.0.0

    b. 192.168.0.0

    c. 10.1.0.0

    d. 10.0.0.0

38. What is the router command to enable the RIP routing protocol on a router?

    a. **config router RIP**

    b. **router rip**

    c. **rip 10.0.0.0**

    d. **network 10.0.0.0**

39. What does it mean to *advertise* a network?

40. The network shown in Figure 2-19 is an example of which of the following?

10.10.20.0 NET   10.10.100.0 NET

192.168.10.0 NET

FIGURE 2-19 The network for problem 39

    a. Contiguous network

    b. Discontiguous network

    c. Continuous network

    d. Discontinuous network

41. Write the commands to enable RIP for use on a 192.168.10.0 network.

42. The command **show ip protocol** is used on a router to

    a. Display the routing protocol that can run on the router

    b. Display the IP address of the routers running an IP protocol

    c. Display the routing protocols running on the router

    d. None of the above

43. The command **show ip interface brief** is used on a router to

    a. Check the current configuration of the interfaces

    b. Check the assigned IP addresses for the interface

    c. Check the status of the interfaces

    d. All the above

    e. None of the above

44. The command **show ip route** is used on a router to

    a. Set a static route

    b. Configure a static route

    c. Display the configured routes on a router

    d. Display how often routing updates are sent

    e. C and D

    f. B and D

45. The command used to display the router's current running-configuration is

    a. **show run**

    b. **show routing**

    c. **show interface**

    d. **show controller**

46. List four limitations of RIP.

47. What router command is issued to specify that the routing protocol is RIPv2? Specify the prompt and the command.

48. What is the hop count limit in a network using RIP?

49. RIP is specified as the routing protocol on a router. There are two possible routes to a destination. What metric does RIP use to determine which route to take?

50. RIP is configured for a 192.168.25.0 network. The subnet mask on a router interface is configured as follows:

    ```
    Router(config)#int fa0/0
    Router(config-if)#ip address 192.168.25.15  255.255.255.128
    ```

    What happens?

51. The **show ip protocol** command is issued on a router running RIP. What does this part of the message indicate?

```
Default version control: send version 2, receive version 2
```

Section 2-4

52. What port does TFTP use?

53. List the command and prompt used to save a router configuration file to the TFTP server.

54. List the command and prompt used to load a save configuration file from the TFTP server.

Critical Thinking

55. You are configuring a router connection to a remote network. What protocol would you select if there is only one network route to the remote network? Explain why you selected the protocol.

56. You are configuring the routing protocols for a small network. What routing protocol would you select, and why?

57. A router's interface FastEtheret0/1 is configured with the network 172.16.7.0/24. Then, a static route command of **ip route 172.16.7.0 255.255.255.0 10.10.7.254** is entered. What will happen? Discuss and explain your answer.

58. A router's interface FastEtheret0/1 is configured with the network 172.16.7.0/24. Then, a static route command of **ip route 172.16.7.0 255.255.255.128 10.10.7.254** is entered. What will happen? Discuss and explain your answer.

59. The network shown in Figure 2-17 has been configured to run RIP routing. The **sh ip route** command is issued on Router1 and the following information is displayed. Are all of the routes defined for this network? If not, then how many routes should be listed in this network, and list the missing route and interface information.

```
Router1#sh ip route
Codes: C - connected, S - static, I - IGRP, R - RIP, M - mobile,
B - BGP D - EIGRP, EX - EIGRP external, O - OSPF, IA - OSPF inter
area
N1 - OSPF NSSA external type 1, N2 - OSPF NSSA external type 2
E1 - OSPF external type 1, E2 - OSPF external type 2, E - EGP
I - IS-IS, L1 - IS-IS level-1, L2 - IS-IS level-2, * candidate
default
U - per-user static route, o - ODR T - traffic engineered route
Gateway of last resort is not set
10.0.0.0/24 is subnetted, 5 subnets
R 10.10.16.0 [120/1] via 10.20.100.2, 00:00:05, FastEthernet0/2
R 10.50.10.0 [120/1] via 10.20.100.2, 00:00:05, FastEthernet0/2
C 10.10.20.0 is directly connected, FastEthernet0/0
C 10.10.10.0 is directly connected, FastEthernet0/1
C 10.20.100.0 is directly connected, FastEthernet0/2
```

60. Your task is to configure static routes on Router 1 to reach every network in the network diagram shown in Figure 2-17. Be sure to use a route with less hop count as the primary route and designate the other as the backup route if there are multiple routes to the same destination. If the routes have equal cost, then pick either one as the primary. Assume that all networks are using a 255.255.255.0 subnet mask.

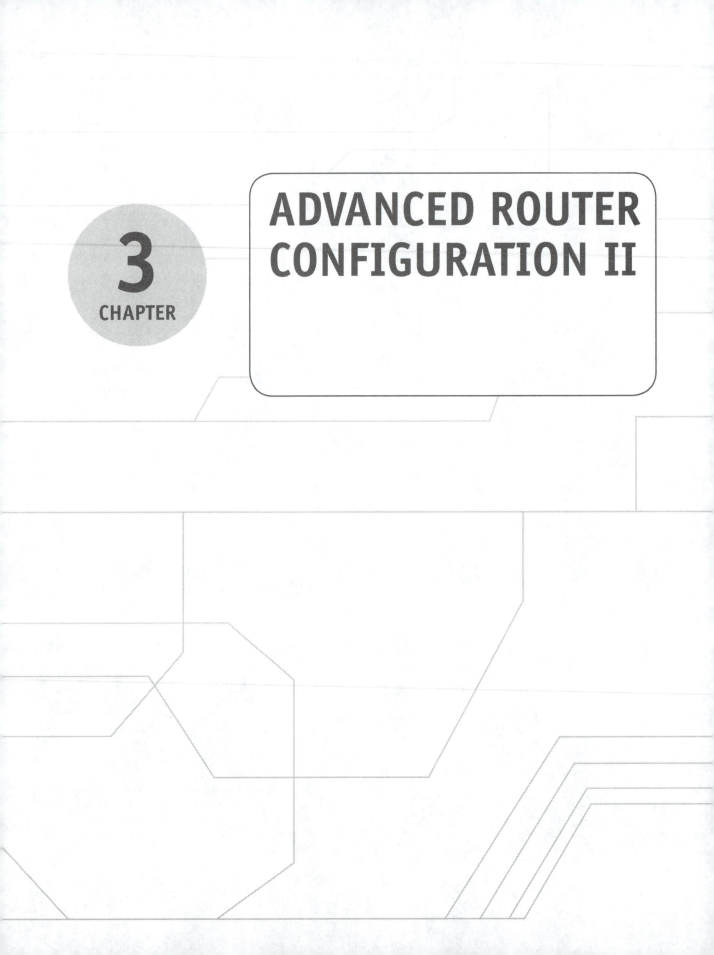

3

CHAPTER

ADVANCED ROUTER CONFIGURATION II

Chapter Outline

Objectives

- Be able to configure a basic setup for OSPF, ISIS, and EIGRP routing protocols
- Be able to configure load balancing and redundancy
- Be able to configure route redistribution
- Understand the relative amount of traffic generated by each protocol
- Describe the purpose of the "Hello" packet

Key Terms

OSPF
IETF
Link State Advertisements
link state protocol
Hello packets
areas
backbone
Variable Length Subnet Masks (VLSM)
route flapping
router ospf process id
network number
wild card bits
Area 0
Neighbor ID
Designated Router (DR)
Backup Designated Router (BDR)
state of FULL
dead time
interface cost
L1 routers
L2 routers

L1/L2 routers
ABR
Connectionless Network Service (CLNS)
integrated IS-IS
NET
area ID
system ID
Network Service Access Point Selector (NSEL)
IS-IS
cnls routing
router isis
ip router isis
show ip route isis (sh ip route isis)
show clns is-neighbors
show clns interface
EIGRP
hybrid routing protocol
show ip eigrp neighbors
uptime
Q Cnt

H
address
interface
hold
SRTT
RTO
Q Cnt
Seq Num
show ip eigrp topology
bandwidth
delay
routing redistribution
redistribute *protocol*
redistribute connected
redistribute static
redistribute ospf *process_id* **metric** *0-16*
redistribute eigrp *AS_number* **metric** *0-16*
redistribute isis *IS-IS Level* **metric** *0-16*
redistribute connected subnets

continues

E2

redistribute eigrp *AS_id*
[**metric** *0-16777214*]

redistribute rip

redistribute isis *IS-IS Level*

EX

redistribute rip metric
*bandwidth delay reliability
load MTU*

default-metric *bandwidth
delay reliability load MTU*

"Hello" packets

network mask

Hello Interval

Router Dead Interval

RID

OSPFIGP

IGP

INTRODUCTION

This chapter examines advanced routing protocols. Configuring the link state protocols Open Shortest Path First (OSPF) and Intermediate System-to-Intermediate System (IS-IS) are examined in Sections 3-1 and 3-2. In link state protocols, updates are only sent when there is a change in the network. There are many similarities between IS-IS and OSPF; however, there is a difference in the way in which the areas are defined for each protocol. Another big difference is that the IS-IS backbone area can be segmented, unlike the backbone area in OSPF.

The steps for configuring the Enhanced Interior Gateway Routing Protocol (EIGRP) are examined in Section 3-3. EIGRP is a Cisco proprietary protocol and is often called a hybrid routing protocol that incorporates the best of the distance vector and link-state algorithms.

Section 3-4 takes a look at advanced route redistribution. This section explores different routing redistribution techniques used to redistribute routes into dynamic routing protocols, such as Routing Information Protocol (RIP), OSPF, IS-IS, and EIGRP. This chapter concludes with a look at the OSPF "Hello" packets that are used by routers to initiate and maintain communication with neighbor routers. The parameters of the "Hello" packet are examined using a network protocol analyzer.

Each routing protocol section in this chapter contains a networking challenge that is included with the Net-Challenge Software. These challenges enable you to configure each routing protocol on a virtual router.

3-1 CONFIGURING LINK STATE PROTOCOLS—OSPF

Open Shortest Path First (OSPF) is a dynamic routing protocol, classified specifically as a link state protocol. It was developed by the Interior Gateway Protocol (IGP) working group for the Internet Engineering Task Force (IETF) specifically for use in TCP/IP networks. OSPF is an open, not proprietary, protocol and is supported by many vendors. The main advantages of OSPF are rapid convergence and the consumption of very little bandwidth. When a network is completely *converged*, all the routers in the network agree on the best routes. After the initial flooding of routes in the form of link state advertisements (LSA), OSPF sends route updates only when there is a change in the network. Every time LSAs are sent, each router must recalculate the routing table.

> **OSPF**
> Open Shortest Path First routing protocol.
>
> **IETF**
> Internet Engineering Task Force.
>
> **Link State Advertisement (LSA)**
> The exchange of updated link state information when routes change.

This is a distinct advantage over RIP. Recall that RIP exchanges the entire routing table at fixed time intervals and RIP updates every 30 seconds. Also, in RIP, the routing table update is propagated through the network at regular timer intervals; therefore, the convergence to final routes is slow. In OSPF, an LSA is sent only when a loss of a route has been detected or when a network comes back online. The loss is immediately reported to neighbor routers, and new routes are calculated much faster than with RIP.

Link State Protocols

Link state protocols establish a relationship with a neighboring router. The routers exchange LSAs to update neighbors regarding route status. The LSAs are sent only if there is a change or loss in the network routes and the link state protocols converge to route selection quickly. This is a distinct advantage over distance vector protocols that exchange updated routing tables at fixed time intervals and are slow to converge. In fact, link state routing protocols are replacing distance vector protocols in most modern networks. Link state protocols are also called *shortest-path first protocols*, based on the algorithm developed by E. W. Dijkstra. Link state protocols use "Hello" packets to verify that communication is still established with neighbor routers. The key issues of link state protocols are summarized as follows:

- Finds neighbors/adjacencies
- Uses route advertisements to build routing table
- Sends "Hello" packets
- Sends updates when routing changes

OSPF sends small **"Hello" packets** at regular time intervals to adjacent routers to verify that the link between two routers is active and the routers are communicating. If a router fails to respond to a Hello it is assumed that the link or possibly the router is down. The OSPF Hello packet captured with a network protocol analyzer is discussed in Section 3-5.

OSPF uses the concept of **areas** to partition a large network into smaller networks. The advantage of this is that the routers have to calculate routes only for their area. If a route goes down in a given area, only the routers in that area have to calculate new routes. Any number between 0 and 4,294,967,295 ($2^{32} - 1$) can be used; however, area 0 is reserved for the root area, which is the **backbone** for the network. The backbone is the primary path for data traffic to and from destinations and sources in the campus network. All areas must connect to area 0, and area 0 cannot be split. The area numbers can also be expressed in IP notation—for example, area 0 could be 0.0.0.0—or you can specify an area as 192.168.25.0 or in subnet notation. Hence, the need for the large upper-area number ($2^{32} - 1$) = 255.255.255.255 when converted to a decimal number.

OSPF allows the use of **variable length subnet masks (VLSM)**, which enable different size subnets in the network to better meet the needs of the network and more efficiently use the network's limited IP address space. For example, point-to-point inter-router links don't need a large block of addresses assigned to them. Figure 3-1 illustrates an example of an inter-router link.

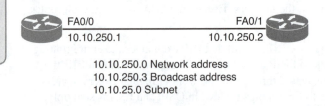

FA0/0   FA0/1
10.10.250.1   10.10.250.2

10.10.250.0 Network address
10.10.250.3 Broadcast address
10.10.25.0 Subnet

FIGURE 3-1 An inter-router link subnetted to provide for two host IP addresses, a network address, and a broadcast address

A subnet of size 4 is sufficient for the inter-router link that includes the IP addresses for the router interfaces, the network address, and the broadcast address. A subnet mask of 255.255.255.252 meets this requirement of a subnet size 4 and is permissible in OSPF. This subnet mask provides for the addressing of the two host addresses (the router interfaces on each end), and the network and broadcast addresses, which provides the total subnet size of 4. This is an important advantage of OSPF because using variable length subnet masks minimizes the waste of IP addresses when interconnecting subnets. Table 3-1 summarizes the advantages and disadvantages of OSPF.

TABLE 3-1   Summary of Advantages and Disadvantages of OSPF

Advantages	Disadvantages
Not proprietary—available for use by all vendors.	Can be complicated to implement.
Link state changes are immediately reported, which enables rapid convergence.	Is process intensive due to routing table calculations.
Consumes little network bandwidth.	Intermittent routes that are going up and down will create excessive LSA updates—this is called route flapping.
Uses VLSM	
Uses areas to partition the network into smaller networks, minimizing the number of route calculations.	

> **Route Flapping**
> Intermittent routes going up and down creating excessive LSA updates.

Configuring Routes with OSPF

This section describes a procedure for configuring OSPF on a router. The first example is for configuring the three routers in the campus LAN shown in Figure 3-2.

The routers will be configured to run OSPF on each of the router's three Ethernet interfaces. The example begins with configuring Router A. Router A must first be placed in the router's configuration mode [Router(config)#], as shown:

```
RouterA#conf t
Enter configuration commands, one per line. End with CNTL/Z.
RouterA(config)#
```

The next step is to enter the information about the IP address for each of the Ethernet interfaces. The IP addresses for Router A are as follows:

FastEthernet0/0: 10.10.20.250
FastEthernet0/1: 10.10.200.1
FastEthernet0/2: 10.10.100.1

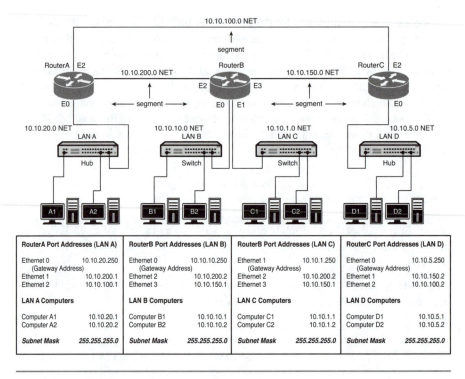

10.10.100.0 NET

↑

segment

RouterA | E2   RouterB   RouterC | E2

10.10.200.0 NET   10.10.150.0 NET

E2   E3

E0   ←— segment —→ E0 E1 ←— segment —→   E0

10.10.20.0 NET   10.10.10.0 NET   10.10.1.0 NET   10.10.5.0 NET
LAN A   LAN B   LAN C   LAN D

Hub   Switch   Switch   Hub

A1   A2   B1   B2   C1   C2   D1   D2

RouterA Port Addresses (LAN A)		RouterB Port Addresses (LAN B)		RouterB Port Addresses (LAN C)		RouterC Port Addresses (LAN D)	
Ethernet 0 (Gateway Address)	10.10.20.250	Ethernet 0 (Gateway Address)	10.10.10.250	Ethernet 1 (Gateway Address)	10.10.1.250	Ethernet 0 (Gateway Address)	10.10.5.250
Ethernet 1	10.10.200.1	Ethernet 2	10.10.200.2	Ethernet 2	10.10.200.2	Ethernet 1	10.10.150.2
Ethernet 2	10.10.100.1	Ethernet 3	10.10.150.1	Ethernet 3	10.10.150.1	Ethernet 2	10.10.100.2
LAN A Computers		**LAN B Computers**		**LAN C Computers**		**LAN D Computers**	
Computer A1	10.10.20.1	Computer B1	10.10.10.1	Computer C1	10.10.1.1	Computer D1	10.10.5.1
Computer A2	10.10.20.2	Computer B2	10.10.10.2	Computer C2	10.10.1.2	Computer D2	10.10.5.2
Subnet Mask	*255.255.255.0*	*Subnet Mask*	*255.255.255.0*	*Subnet Mask*	*255.255.255.0*	*Subnet Mask*	*255.255.255.0*

FIGURE 3-2   The three-router campus LAN

A subnet mask of 255.255.255.0 is assigned to each of the FastEthernet interfaces. After the FastEthernet interfaces are configured, verify the configuration settings using the **sh ip int brief** command, as shown. Make sure that the status for the FastEthernet interfaces are *up*. This indicates that the interfaces are turned on and an Ethernet networking device is connected. The protocol will show *down* until the Ethernet cable is connected and the connecting interface is enabled. In this case, the connecting interfaces to FA0/1 and FA0/2 are not enabled and, therefore, show a status of *down*.

```
RouterA#sh ip int brief
Interface          IP-Address      OK?   Method   Status   Protocol
FastEthernet0/0    10.10.20.250    YES   manual   up       up
FastEthernet0/1    10.10.200.1     YES   manual   up       down
FastEthernet0/2    10.10.100.1     YES   manual   up       down
```

router ospf [*process id*]

The command used to enable OSPF routing.

Next, the command **router ospf** *process id* is used to enable OSPF routing. In this case, the command **router ospf 100** is entered. The 100 is the *process id number*. This number must be the same on each router for OSPF to exchange routes. The process ID number is selected by the network administrator and is not used for routing outside the network. It is customary to use the same process ID throughout the network for ease of management, but it is not required. Entering the **router ospf 100** command places the router in the RouterA(config-router)# prompt:

```
RouterA(config)#router ospf 100
RouterA(config-router)#
```

The next step is to define the network running OSPF by entering the **network** command followed by the IP address of the interface, the OSPF wild card bits, and then an area number. The following text shows each step and lists the results of entering a question mark as the command is entered. When entering the command **network ?**, the router prompts you to enter the IP address of the interface:

```
RouterA(config-router)#network ?
A.B.C.D Network number
```

A.B.C.D is the IP address or network number for the Ethernet interface. Next, entering network 10.10.20.250 ? prompts you to enter the OSPF wild card bits in the form of A.B.C.D. The wild card bits, also called the *inverse mask bits,* are used to match the network IP address (A.B.C.D format) to interface IPs. If there is a match, the subnet on the interface is advertised out OSPF, and OSPF packets are sent out the interface. A 0 wild card bit is used to indicate a "must" match. A 255 is a "don't care," hence the name *inverse mask.*

The last entry when defining an OSPF route is for the area. Remember, areas are used to partition a large network into smaller networks. Area 0 is the root area and is the backbone for the network. All other areas must connect to area 0. Area 0 cannot be split. Other area numbers are specified by the network administrator.

Assume that the router command **network 10.10.20.250 0.0.0.0 area 0** is entered. The wild card bits indicate that any interface with an address of 10.10.20.250 must run OSPF on the interface and will be assigned to area 0 (the network backbone). Assume that the router command network **10.10.20.250 0.255.255.255 area 0** is entered. The wild card bits indicate that any interface with an IP address of 10.x.x.x must run OSPF on the interface and will be assigned to area 0:

```
RouterA(config-router)#network 10.10.20.250 ?
A.B.C.D OSPF wild card bits
RouterA(config-router)#network 10.10.20.250 0.0.0.0 ?
area Set the OSPF area ID
RouterA(config-router)#network 10.10.20.250 0.0.0.0 area 0
```

The following command sequence details the three OSPF network entries needed to configure OSPF routing for Router A:

```
RouterA(config-router)#network 10.10.20.250 0.0.0.0 area 0
RouterA(config-router)#network 10.10.200.1 0.0.0.0 area 0
RouterA(config-router)#network 10.10.100.1 0.0.0.0 area 0
```

Note that the Router A interface to LAN A (10.10.20.250 NET) is listed when configuring OSPF. This is used in OSPF to advertise the LAN to the other routers. Also note that the network has been assigned to area 0 (the backbone). The command **sh ip int brief** is used to check the status of the interfaces. The output **Protocol down** indicates that the cable to the interface is either unplugged or the interface is shut down:

```
RouterA#show int brief
Interface        IP-Address     OK?   Method   Status   Protocol
FastEthernet0/0  10.10.20.250   YES   NVRAM    up       up
FastEthernet0/1  10.10.200.1    YES   manual   up       down
FastEthernet0/2  10.10.100.1    YES   manual   up       down
```

> **Network Number**
> Another name for the IP subnet.
>
> **Wild Card Bits**
> Used to match network IP addresses to interface IPs.
>
> **Area 0**
> In OSPF, this is the root area and is the backbone for the network.

This problem with the **Protocol down** is fixed by reestablishing the physical connection between the routers.

The next step is to configure RouterB. First, configure the four FastEthernet interfaces on RouterB. Next, the OSPF routing protocol for RouterB is set. In this example, one command-line instruction is used to configure RouterB to run OSPF on all four of its interfaces. This is done with a subnet mask or wild card in OSPF. First, enter RouterB's configuration mode using the **conf t** command. The command **router ospf 100** is entered. Note that the same process ID number of 100 is being used. The next step is to enter **network 10.0.0.0 0.255.255.255 area 0**. This command tells the router that any address that starts with a "10" belongs to area 0 on RouterB:

```
RouterB#conf t
Enter configuration commands, one per line. End with CNTL/Z.
RouterB(config)#router ospf 100
RouterB(config-router)#network 10.0.0.0 0.255.255.255 area 0
```

Verify that the interfaces are properly configured using the **sh ip int brief** command, as shown:

```
RouterB#sh ip int brief
Interface         IP-Address       OK?   Method    Status    Protocol
FastEthernet0/0   10.10.10.250     YES   manual    up        up
FastEthernet0/1   10.10.1.250      YES   manual    up        up
FastEthernet0/2   10.10.200.2      YES   manual    up        up
FastEthernet0/3   10.10.150.1      YES   manual    up        down
```

The FastEthernet0/3 interface shows the protocol is **down** because the connecting interface is shut down on RouterC.

The next step is to configure RouterC. The OSPF routing protocol for RouterC is set using the command **router OSPF 100** followed by **network 10.0.0.0 0.255.255.255 area 0**, as shown:

```
RouterC(config)#router ospf 100
RouterC(config-router)#network 10.0.0.0 0.255.255.255 area 0
```

The interfaces on RouterC are checked using the **sh ip int brief** command, as shown:

```
RouterC#sh ip int brief
Interface         IP-Address   OK? Method Status Protocol
FastEthernet0/0   10.10.5.250  YES manual up     up
FastEthernet0/1   10.10.150.2  YES manual up     up
FastEthernet0/2   10.10.100.2  YES manual up     up
```

Notice that the **Protocol** column shows **up** for all interfaces. This is because all interfaces are connected and the interfaces are enabled.

The following is a partial listing of the running-configuration file on Router A that shows the router OSPF network configuration. Similar information will appear on Routers B and C:

```
.
.
router ospf 100
 network 10.10.200.1 0.0.0.0 area 0
 network 10.10.20.250 0.0.0.0 area 0
 network 10.10.100.1 0.0.0.0 area 0
.
.
```

The routing table for Router A can be checked using the command **sh ip route**, as shown. The routing table indicates there are seven subnets in the campus network shown in Figure 3-2. The **O**s indicate the subnets running OSPF, and C indicates the subnets directly connected to the router:

```
RouterA#sh ip route
Codes: C connected, S static, I IGRP, R RIP, M mobile, B BGP D EIGRP,
EX EIGRP external, O OSPF, IA OSPF inter area
N1 OSPF NSSA external type 1, N2 OSPF NSSA external type 2
E1 OSPF external type 1, E2 OSPF external type 2, E EGP
i IS-IS, L1 IS-IS level-1, L2 IS-IS level-2, * candidate default
U per-user static route, o ODR T traffic engineered route
Gateway of last resort is not set
10.0.0.0/24 is subnetted, 7 subnets
O 10.10.5.0 [110/74] via 10.10.100.2, 00:03:28, FastEthernet0/2
O 10.10.10.0 [110/74] via 10.10.200.2, 00:03:28, FastEthernet0/1
O 10.10.1.0 [110/74] via 10.10.200.2, 00:03:28, FastEthernet0/1
C 10.10.20.0 is directly connected, FastEthernet0/0
C 10.10.100.0 is directly connected, FastEthernet0/2
O 10.10.150.0 [110/128] via 10.10.200.2, 00:03:28, FastEthernet0/1
                       [110/128] via 10.10.100.2, 00:03:28,
FastEthernet0/2
C 10.10.200.0 is directly connected, FastEthernet0/1
```

To display only the OSPF routes, you can use the **sh ip route ospf** command. The following are the results for this command from Router A:

```
RouterA#sh ip route ospf
10.0.0.0/24 is subnetted, 6 subnets
O 10.10.5.0 [110/74] via 10.10.100.2, 00:10:03, FastEthernet0/2
O 10.10.10.0 [110/74] via 10.10.200.2, 00:10:03, FastEthernet0/1
O 10.10.150.0 [110/128] via 10.10.200.2, 00:10:03, FastEthernet0/1
                       [110/128] via 10.10.100.2, 00:10:03,
FastEthernet0/2
```

Another command used for displaying protocol information for the router is **sh ip protocol**. The following are the results for entering this command for Router A:

```
RouterA#sh ip protocol
Routing Protocol is "ospf 100" Sending updates every 0 seconds
Invalid after 0 seconds, hold down 0, flushed after 0
Outgoing update filter list for all interfaces is Incoming update
filter list for all interfaces is Redistributing: ospf 100
Routing for Networks:
10.10.20.250/32
10.10.100.1/32
10.10.200.1/32
Routing Information Sources:
Gateway Distance Last Update
10.10.100.1 110 00:06:01
10.10.200.2 110 00:06:01
Distance: (default is 110)
```

To verify the adjacent OSPF neighbors of the router and observe the neighbor state, you can use the **sh ip ospf neighbor** command. This command displays the directly connected neighbors, since the hello packets are exchanged among them. The following are the results for this command from Router A:

```
RouterA#sh ip ospf neighbor
Neighbor ID     Pri   State        Dead Time    Address
Interface
10.10.150.2      1    FULL/BDR     00:00:39     10.10.100.2
FastEthernet0/2
10.10.200.2      1    FULL/DR      00:00:31     10.10.200.2
FastEthernet0/1
```

Neighbor ID

The highest IP address defined by the loopback address of the neighbor router ID.

Designated Router (DR)

The router with the highest priority.

Backup Designated Router (BDR)

The router or routers with lower priority.

State of FULL

Indicates that the routers are fully adjacent to each other.

Dead Time

The Hello time interval an OSPF router will wait before terminating adjacency with a neighbor.

The **show ip ospf neighbor** command shows there are two adjacent neighbors: 10.10.150.2 and 10.10.200.2. The Neighbor ID is the highest IP address defined by the loopback address of the neighbor router ID. In this case, 10.10.150.2 is the highest IP address for Router C, and 10.10.200.2 is the highest IP address of Router B. Refer to Figure 3-2 for the IP assignments for each router. The **Pri** column stands for Priority, which indicates the priority of the neighbor routers. The router with the highest priority becomes the Designated Router (DR), and the router or routers with lower priority will become a Backup Designated Router (BDR). In this case, the priority is the same, so the router with the highest router ID becomes the DR, which is Router B, and Router C becomes the BDR. This process is called a **DR Election**. It happens during the exchange of Hello packets. The main purpose of the DR router is to maintain the OSPF topology table of the network. This way, there is only one source that can send the OSPF routing updates to the routers within the area, thus minimizing the network traffic. Every router also sends its update to the DR and BDR via the multicast address. If the DR should fail, the BDR will assume the role of the designated router. The state of FULL is a good and desired state, which indicates that the routers are fully adjacent to each other. The dead time is the Hello time interval an OSPF router will wait before terminating adjacency with a neighbor. The address is the IP address of its directly connected neighbor and the interface indicates the interface on which the neighbor is connected.

Load Balancing and Redundancy with OSPF

As long as there is an equal cost path, traffic load balancing on a per-packet basis can be configured with OSPF. For example, if there is an additional link of the same type interface and speed between Router A and Router B (refer to Figure 3-2), OSPF will automatically load balance the network traffic to the network 10.10.10.0 NET between the two links because they both have the same OSPF cost. To find out the OSPF cost of an interface, use the **sh ip ospf interface** command. The following example shows the OSPF interface information on FastEthernet0/2, including its interface cost of 1.

```
RouterA#sh ip ospf interface
FastEthernet0/2 is up, line protocol is up
  Internet Address 10.10.100.1/24, Area 0
  Process ID 100, Router ID 10.10.200.1, Network Type BROADCAST, Cost:
1
  Transmit Delay is 1 sec, State DR, Priority 1
  Designated Router (ID) 10.10.200.1, Interface address 10.10.100.1
  Backup Designated router (ID) 10.10.150.2, Interface address
10.10.100.2
              :
              :
```

With the Shortest Path First protocol, OSPF uses the Dijkstra algorithm to calculate the shortest path. The algorithm takes into consideration the topology path and the associated cost and calculates the cumulative cost to reach a destination.

With destinations with multiple paths, OSPF will calculate the best shortest path and install the route into the routing table. For the example network (refer to Figure 3-2), Router A has two paths to reach the 10.10.10.0 network on Router B. One route is via FastEthernet0/1 to Router B and another route is via FastEthernet0/2 to Router C and then to Router B. The output of **show ip route** shows that the Router A has selected the path via its FastEthernet0/1 as the best path and this is confirmed when issuing the command **sh ip route 10.10.10.0**.

```
RouterA#sh ip route 10.10.10.0
Routing entry for 10.10.10.0/24
  Known via "ospf 100", distance 110, metric 2, type intra area
  Last update from 10.10.200.2 on FastEthernet0/1, 00:44:13 ago
  Routing Descriptor Blocks:
  * 10.10.200.2, from 10.10.200.2, 00:44:13 ago, via FastEthernet0/1
      Route metric is 2, traffic share count is 1
```

When the path via the interface FastEthernet0/1 becomes unavailable, the OSPF database gets updated, and another available route via RouterC is automatically selected, as shown here:

```
*Mar  1 01:31:40.399: %LINEPROTO-5-UPDOWN: Line protocol on Interface
FastEthernet0/1, changed state to down
*Mar  1 01:31:41.411: %OSPF-5-ADJCHG: Process 100, Nbr 10.10.200.2 on
FastEthernet0/1 from FULL to DOWN, Neighbor Down: Interface down or
detached
RouterA#sh ip route 10.10.10.0
Routing entry for 10.10.10.0/24
  Known via "ospf 100", distance 110, metric 3, type intra area
  Last update from 10.10.100.2 on FastEthernet1/0, 00:00:16 ago
  Routing Descriptor Blocks:
  * 10.10.100.2, from 10.10.200.2, 00:00:16 ago, via FastEthernet1/0
      Route metric is 3, traffic share count is 1
```

Interface Cost
One of the factors used in calculating the best path.

Because OSPF uses the **interface cost** as one of the factors in calculating the best path, one of the easiest ways to influence the OSPF path selection is by manipulating the interface cost. In our example, there are two equal routes to the network 10.10.150.0 Net, as shown.

```
RouterA#sh ip route 10.10.150.0
Routing entry for 10.10.150.0/24
  Known via "ospf 100", distance 110, metric 2, type intra area
  Last update from 10.10.200.2 on FastEthernet0/1, 00:00:05 ago
  Routing Descriptor Blocks:
  * 10.10.100.2, from 10.10.200.2, 00:00:05 ago, via FastEthernet0/2
      Route metric is 2, traffic share count is 1
    10.10.200.2, from 10.10.200.2, 00:00:05 ago, via FastEthernet0/1
      Route metric is 2, traffic share count is 1
```

If the preferred route to reach the 10.10.150.0 network is via Router B, then the OSPF cost of the interface connected to Router C can be increased. The default OSPF cost of the interface is 1. To change the cost of this interface, issue the **ip ospf cost** command at the interface, as shown:

```
RouterA(config)#int fastEthernet 0/2
RouterA(config-if)#ip ospf cost 5
RouterA#sh ip route 10.10.150.0
Routing entry for 10.10.150.0/24
  Known via "ospf 100", distance 110, metric 2, type intra area
  Last update from 10.10.200.2 on FastEthernet0/1, 00:00:07 ago
  Routing Descriptor Blocks:
  * 10.10.200.2, from 10.10.200.2, 00:00:07 ago, via FastEthernet0/1
      Route metric is 2, traffic share count is 1
```

By increasing the OSPF cost of interface0/2, the route to the network 10.10.150.0 is being preferred via the interface FastEthernet0/1 off Router B. However, changing the OSPF cost could have side effects if you are not careful. In our case, because the interface to Router C now has a higher OSPF cost, what will happen to the LAN

D or 10.10.5.0 network? The following output shows the current routing table after the OSPF cost has changed:

```
RouterA#sh ip route ospf
     10.0.0.0/24 is subnetted, 7 subnets
O        10.10.1.0 [110/2] via 10.10.200.2, 00:09:08, FastEthernet0/1
O        10.10.5.0 [110/3] via 10.10.200.2, 00:09:08, FastEthernet0/1
O        10.10.10.0 [110/2] via 10.10.200.2, 00:09:08, FastEthernet0/1
O        10.10.150.0 [110/2] via 10.10.200.2, 00:09:08, FastEthernet0/1
```

As you can see, the route to LAN D is now preferred through Router B. This means one extra router hop that it must take from Router A to reach LAN D. By increasing the interface cost, it affects everything along its path. This is definitely not the desirable side effect that you want. The network engineer must understand the network topology before adjusting the OSPF cost, Administrative Distance (AD), or any routing protocol metrics. This has to be carefully done and thoroughly verified; otherwise, it can result in a routing abnormality such as this.

Networking Challenge—OSPF

Use the Net-Challenge Simulator Software included with the text's companion CD-ROM to demonstrate that you can configure OSPF for Router A in the campus LAN (the campus LAN is shown in Figure 3-2 and is displayed by clicking the View Topology button when the software is started). Place the Net-Challenge CD-ROM in your computer's drive. Open the Net-Challenge folder and click **NetChallenge V3-2.exe**. When the software is running, click the **Select Router Challenge** button to open a **Select Router Challenge** drop-down menu. Select **Chapter 3—OSPF**. This opens a checkbox that can be used to verify that you have completed all the tasks:

1. Enter the privileged EXEC mode on the router.

2. Enter the router's terminal configuration mode: **Router(config)**.

3. Set the hostname to *Router A*.

4. Configure the FastEthernet0/0 interface with the following:

   IP address: 10.10.20.250

   Subnet mask: 255.255.255.0

5. Enable the FA0/0 interface.

6. Configure the FastEthernet0/1 interface with the following:

   IP address: 10.10.200.1

   Subnet mask: 255.255.255.0

7. Enable the FA0/1 interface.

8. Configure the FastEthernet0/2 interface with the following:

   IP address: 10.10.100.1

   Subnet mask: 255.255.255.0

9. Enable the FA0/2 interface.

10. Enable OSPF with a network number of 100.

11. Use a single command-line instruction to configure Router A to run OSPF on all three of the FastEthernet interfaces (use area 100).

12. Use the **sh ip int brief** command to check the interface status.

13. Use the **sh ip protocol** command to see whether OSPF is running on Router A.

14. Use the **sh ip route** command to verify that the three FastEthernet ports are connected to Router A.

15. Use the **sh run** command to view the running-configuration file on Router A. Verify that OSPF is enabled and the proper network address is specified.

16. The preferred route to reach the 10.10.150.0 network is via Router B. Issue the command to increase the OSPF cost of the interface connected to Router C to 5 using the **ip ospf cost** command.

3-2 CONFIGURING LINK STATE PROTOCOLS—IS-IS

L1 Routers
Analogous to OSPF nonbackbone routers.

L2 Routers
Analogous to OSPF backbone routers.

L1/L2 Routers
Analogous to OSPF area border routers.

ABR
Area border routers.

Connectionless Network Service (CLNS)
IS-IS is designed to work on the same network layer just like IP; therefore, it does not require an IP protocol for it to function.

Integrated IS-IS
Term indicating IS-IS was adapted to work with IP.

NET
Network Entity Title.

Area ID
Analogous to OSPF area number, and it is used by L2 routers.

There are many similarities between IS-IS and OSPF. Both protocols use the link state protocol with the Dijkstra algorithm. Both are classless protocols, which enable the support of VLSM. Both protocols use Hello packets to form and maintain adjacencies and both use the area concept. However, there is a difference in the way in which the areas are defined for each protocol. In IS-IS, there are two hierarchical topology areas: level 1 (Intra-area) and level 2 (Inter-area). A router can either be a level 1 (L1) router, a level 2 (L2) router, or both (L1/L2) routers. **L1 routers** are analogous to OSPF nonbackbone routers, **L2 routers** are analogous to OSPF backbone routers, and **L1/L2 routers** are analogous to OSPF area border routers (**ABR**). Unlike OSPF ABRs, L1/L2 routers do not advertise routes from L2 routers to L1 routers. The packets from different areas can only be routed through the L1/L2 routers. Essentially, L1/L2 routers are default gateways to L1 routers. Another big difference is that the IS-IS backbone area can be segmented. Unlike the backbone area in OSPF, all routers in area 0 must be connected; the IS-IS L2 routers do not need to be connected directly together.

IS-IS was originally designed as part of the Open System Interconnection (OSI) network layer service called **Connectionless Network Service (CLNS)**. This means that IS-IS is designed to work on the same network layer just like IP; therefore, it does not require IP protocol for it to function. Later, it was adapted to work with IP. Hence, it is sometimes referred to as *integrated* IS-IS. In IS-IS, every router uses the Network Entity Title (**NET**) to define its process. The NET address is unique to each router; it is comprised of the following components in hexadecimal format:

- The **area ID** in IS-IS is analogous to OSPF area number, and it is used by L2 routers.

- The **system ID** is analogous to the OSPF router ID, and it is used by L1 routers.
- The **Network Service Access Point Selector (NSEL)** identifies the network service type.

<aside>
System ID
Analogous to the OSPF router ID, and it is used by L1 routers.

Network Service Access Point Selector (NSEL)
Identifies the network service type.

IS-IS
Interior Gateway Routing Protocol.
</aside>

The NET address can look intimidating because of its long hexadecimal format, but it is not as bad as it seems. The way to work with a NET address is to start from right and work left. For example, given a NET address of 49.0001.0014.a909.5201.00, the last 1 byte from the right is NSEL, which is always set to 00 on a router. The next six bytes from the right are separated into three groups of 2 bytes and define the system ID. In this example, the system ID is 0014.a909.5201. The system ID is always unique and is typically represented as the MAC address of the router. The remaining numbers to the left of the System ID define the Area ID, which is 49.0001. The area ID has a variable length, but its first number must be at least 1 byte long.

Configuring Routes with IS-IS

This section demonstrates how to configure the routers to use the IS-IS routing protocol for the three-router campus network shown in Figure 3-3. For this exercise, RouterB has been turned off. This is reflected in the output of the command **show ip int brief**. Notice that the Router A interface FastEtherent0/1, which connects RouterB, is showing Status **down** and Protocol **down**.

```
RouterA#show ip int brief
Interface       IP-Address     OK? Method  Status  Protocol
FastEthernet0/0 10.10.20.250   YES NVRAM   up      up
FastEthernet0/1 10.10.200.1    YES manual  down    down
FastEthernet0/2 10.10.100.1    YES manual  up      up
```

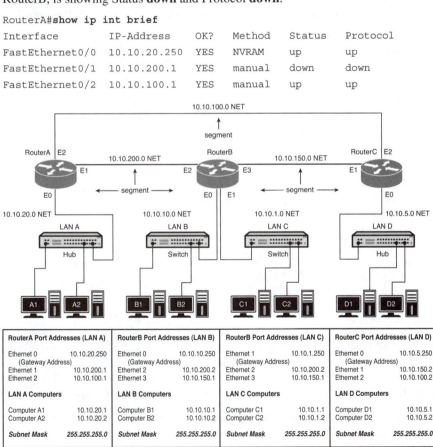

FIGURE 3-3 Routers A, B, and C in the three-router campus network

cnls routing

The global command for IS-IS.

router isis

Starts the IS-IS routing protocol.

ip router isis

Specifies the network that will be using IS-IS for routing.

The first step in configuring Router A to use IS-IS is to enable the protocol globally. As mentioned earlier, IS-IS is a part of CNLS as its network layer routing protocol. When configuring most routing protocols, the global command of **ip routing** must be issued. With IS-IS, the global command of **cnls routing** must be issued. Then, at the *RouterA(config)#* prompt, enter the command **router isis** to start using the IS-IS routing protocol. Next, the NET address will need to be entered to specify the area the router belongs to as well as defining the System ID and the NSEL of 00. Unlike other routing protocols, to specify the network that will be using IS-IS for routing, this will need to be configured at each individual interface with the command **ip router isis**. These steps are as follows:

```
RouterA(config)#cnls routing
RouterA(config)#router isis
RouterA(config-router)# net  49.0001.c202.00e8.0000.00
RouterA(config-router)#interface fastethernet0/0
RouterA(config-router)#ip router isis
RouterA(config-router)#interface fastethernet0/2
RouterA(config-router)#ip router isis
```

On Router A, the interface FastEthernet 0/0 and the interface Fastethernet 0/2 are configured to use IS-IS. The same set of commands is issued on Router B and Router C to route with IS-IS. You can verify that IS-IS is running on Router A by entering the command **sh ip protocol**, as shown at the enable prompt (**RouterA#**):

```
RouterA# sh ip protocol
Routing Protocol is "isis"
  Outgoing update filter list for all interfaces is not set
  Incoming update filter list for all interfaces is not set
  Redistributing: isis
  Address Summarization:
    None
  Maximum path: 4
  Routing for Networks:
    FastEthernet0/0
    FastEthernet0/1
    FastEthernet0/2
  Routing Information Sources:
    Gateway          Distance      Last Update
    10.10.100.2           115        00:02:44
    10.10.150.1           115        00:02:44
  Distance: (default is 115)
```

The text shows that the routing protocol is "isis." The networks it is routing are on the interface FastEthernet0/0, FastEthernet0/1, and FastEthernet0/2. It also shows that it is receiving routing information from the source 10.10.100.2, which is the Router C interface FastEthernet0/2 and 10.10.150.1, which is the Router B interface FastEthernet0/3. The routing information was updated 2 minutes 44 seconds ago.

Next, the command **show ip route** *(sh ip route)* can be used to examine the contents of Router A's routing table to see if any IS-IS routes have been received:

```
RouterA# sh ip route
Codes: C - connected, S - static, R - RIP, M - mobile, B - BGP
       D - EIGRP, EX - EIGRP external, O - OSPF, IA - OSPF inter area
       N1 - OSPF NSSA external type 1, N2 - OSPF NSSA external type 2
       E1 - OSPF external type 1, E2 - OSPF external type 2
       i - IS-IS, su - IS-IS summary, L1 - IS-IS level-1, L2 - IS-IS
level-2
       ia - IS-IS inter area, * - candidate default, U - per-user
static route
       o - ODR, P - periodic downloaded static route

Gateway of last resort is not set

     10.0.0.0/24 is subnetted, 7 subnets
i L1    10.10.1.0 [115/20] via 10.10.200.2, FastEthernet0/1
i L1    10.10.5.0 [115/20] via 10.10.100.2, FastEthernet0/2
i L1    10.10.10.0 [115/20] via 10.10.200.2, FastEthernet0/1
C       10.10.20.0 is directly connected, FastEthernet0/0
C       10.10.100.0 is directly connected, FastEthernet0/2
i L1    10.10.150.0 [115/20] via 10.10.100.2, FastEthernet0/2
                    [115/20] via 10.10.200.2, FastEthernet0/1
C       10.10.200.0 is directly connected, FastEthernet0/1
```

The command **sh ip route** indicates that the network 10.10.5.0 has been received via the IP 10.10.100.2, which is directly connected to the interface FastEthernet0/2. The routes for network 10.10.1.0 and 10.10.10.0 are learned via the IP 10.10.200.2 on interface FastEthernet0/1. The network 10.10.150.0 is learned via both FastEthernet0/1 and FastEthernet0/2. As a matter of fact, the routing table looks similar to the one of OSPF. The "i" before the route indicates IS-IS routes, and "L1" stands for IS-IS level 1. The command show ip route isis can be used to view the routing table just for IS-IS, as shown:

> **show ip route isis (sh ip route isis)** Displays only the IS-IS routes.

```
RouterA#sh ip route isis
10.0.0.0/24 is subnetted, 7 subnets
i L1    10.10.1.0 [115/20] via 10.10.200.2, FastEthernet0/1
i L1    10.10.5.0 [115/20] via 10.10.100.2, FastEthernet0/2
i L1    10.10.10.0 [115/20] via 10.10.200.2, FastEthernet0/1
i L1    10.10.150.0 [115/20] via 10.10.100.2, FastEthernet0/2
                    [115/20] via 10.10.200.2, FastEthernet0/1
```

Similar to an OSPF router, IS-IS establishes its adjacencies with its neighbors and the neighbor information can be found with the command show clns is-neighbors.

> **show clns is-neighbors** Command used in IS-IS to find adjacencies with neighbors.

```
RouterA#sh clns is-neighbors
```

System Id Format	Interface	State	Type	Priority	Circuit Id
RouterB Phase V	Fa0/1	Up	L1L2	64/64	RouterA.02
RouterC Phase V	Fa1/0	Up	L1L2	64/64	RouterA.03

IS-IS is identified by its NET address not the IP address. Therefore, the network administrator will need to remember the NET address. This can be a challenge, especially in a big network but IS-IS does provide dynamic hostname exchange. This allows the ASCII router name to be exchanged among the routers; therefore, it can be used to associate with the system instead of the NET address. An example of the IS-IS dynamic hostname exchange is next shown resulting from the **sh clns is-neighbor** command. Notice that the router names are displayed in the System ID and Circuit ID fields.

One confusing issue regarding IS-IS is when to use the command **isis** or **clns**. The **clns** commands are used when dealing with the protocol at the Layer 2 level. The **isis** commands are used when dealing with IP information. For example, the similar neighbor information can be displayed with command **show isis neighbor**. The differences are the IP address and IS-IS level type information are displayed using **show isis neighbor**.

```
RouterA#sh isis neighbors
System Id  Type  Interface  IP Address   State  Holdtime  Circuit Id
RouterB    L1    Fa0/1      10.10.200.2  UP     28        RouterA.02
RouterB    L2    Fa0/1      10.10.200.2  UP     20        RouterA.02
RouterC    L1    Fa1/0      10.10.100.2  UP     20        RouterA.03
RouterC    L2    Fa1/0      10.10.100.2  UP     22        RouterA.03
```

The final step is to view the running-configuration in each router using the **sh run** command. The running-configuration for Router A is provided. Notice the entries for **router isis** and **net 49.0001.c202.00e8.000.00, and ip router isis** in the running-configuration file.

```
RouterA#sh run
Building configuration...
Current configuration:
!
version 12.0
service timestamps debug uptime service timestamps log uptime no
service password-encryption
!
hostname RouterA
!
enable secret 5 $1$6M4r$dleo7h1WP0AYu0K/cM6M91
enable password Salsa
!
ip subnet-zero
!
interface FastEthernet0/0
 ip address 10.10.20.250 255.255.255.0
 ip router isis
 no ip directed-broadcast
!
interface FastEthernet0/1
 ip address 10.10.200.1 255.255.255.0
 no ip directed-broadcast
```

```
!
interface FastEthernet0/2
 ip address 10.10.100.1 255.255.255.0
 ip router isis
 no ip directed-broadcast
!
router isis
 net 49.0001.c202.00e8.0000.00
!
ip classless
!
line con 0
transport input none line aux 0
line vty 0 4 password chile login
!
end
```

Remember to use the **copy run start** command to save the changes made to NVRAM.

Load Balancing and Redundancy with IS-IS

Because IS-IS is another SPF protocol, its load balancing and redundancy capabilities are almost identical to those used by OSPF. IS-IS can load balance the network traffic over equal cost paths. On the unequal cost paths, only the best path is installed into the routing table and that path becomes the primary route where the network traffic will flow. When the primary link fails, the routes will converge to the secondary link until the primary link is back in operation. All of these examples have been shown within the OSPF section.

These same concepts explored in the OSPF section, as well as the cautions, still apply to IS-IS. The only big differences between the two protocols usually are the command syntax used in configuring some of the functions. In OSPF, an OSPF cost is the value assigned to the interface, and its default value is 1. In IS-IS, it is a metric that is assigned to the interface and its default metric value is 10. The IS-IS metric can be adjusted at the interface level with the following command sequence:

```
RouterA(config)#int fastEthernet 0/2
RouterA(config-if)#isis metric 30
```

By increasing the IS-IS metric on the FastEthernet0/2 on Router A, the same results happen as when increasing the OSPF cost on this very same interface. That is all routes destined to any networks on Router C now prefer the interface FastEthernet0/1 via Router B as their primary route or best path. The result of adjusting the IS-IS metric is shown via command **show ip route isis**:

```
RouterA#sh ip route isis
10.0.0.0/24 is subnetted, 7 subnets
i L1    10.10.1.0 [115/20] via 10.10.200.2, FastEthernet0/1
i L1    10.10.5.0 [115/20] via 10.10.200.2, FastEthernet0/1
i L1    10.10.10.0 [115/20] via 10.10.200.2, FastEthernet0/1
i L1    10.10.150.0 [115/20] via 10.10.200.2, FastEthernet0/1
```

show clns interface
The command used to verify the IS-IS interface metric.

To verify the IS-IS interface metric, issue the **show clns interface** command. The output displays the interface FastEthernet0/2, which now has the level1-metric and level2-metric of 30:

```
RouterA#sh clns  interface
:
FastEthernet0/2 is up, line protocol is up
  Checksums enabled, MTU 1497, Encapsulation SAP
  ERPDUs enabled, min. interval 10 msec.
  RDPDUs enabled, min. interval 100 msec., Addr Mask enabled
  Congestion Experienced bit set at 4 packets
  CLNS fast switching enabled
  CLNS SSE switching disabled
  DEC compatibility mode OFF for this interface
  Next ESH/ISH in 19 seconds
  Routing Protocol: IS-IS
    Circuit Type: level-1-2
    Interface number 0x2, local circuit ID 0x3
    Level-1 Metric: 30, Priority: 64, Circuit ID: RouterA.03
    Level-1 IPv6 Metric: 10
    Number of active level-1 adjacencies: 1
    Level-2 Metric: 30, Priority: 64, Circuit ID: RouterA.03
    Level-2 IPv6 Metric: 10
    Number of active level-2 adjacencies: 1
```

Networking Challenge: IS-IS

Use the Net-Challenge Simulator Software included with the text's companion CD-ROM to demonstrate that you can configure IS-IS for Router A in the campus LAN. (The campus LAN is shown in Figure 3-3 and is displayed on the computer screen after the software is started.) Place the Net-Challenge CD-ROM in your computer's drive. Open the **Net-Challenge** folder, and click **NetChallenge V3-2.exe**. When the software is running, click the **Select Router Challenge** button to open a **Select Router Challenge** drop-down menu. Select **Chapter 3—IS-IS**. This opens a checkbox that can be used to verify that you have completed all the tasks. A check next to a task indicates that the task has been successfully completed:

1. Click the Router A button.

2. Enter the privileged EXEC mode on the router.

3. Enter the router configuration mode, **Router(config)**.

4. Set the hostname to **RouterA**.

5. Configure the FastEthernet0/0 interface with the following:

   IP address: 10.10.20.2

   Subnet mask: 255.255.255.0

6. Enable the FA0/0 interface.

7. Configure the FastEthernet0/1 interface with the following:

   IP address: 10.10.200.1

   Subnet mask: 255.255.255.0

8. Enable the FA0/1 interface.

9. Configure the FastEthernet0/2 interface with the following:

   IP address: 10.10.100.1

   Subnet mask: 255.255.255.0

10. Enable the FA0/2 interface.

11. Enable CNLS routing.

12. Enable IS-IS on Router A.

13. Use the **net** command to specify the NET address to be used by IS-IS.

14. Enable IS-IS on FA0/0 and FA0/2.

15. Use the **sh ip int brief** command to check the interface status.

16. Use the **sh ip protocol** to see whether IS-IS is running.

17. Use the **sh ip route** command to verify that the four FastEthernet ports are connected to the router.

18. Use the **sh run** command to view the running-configuration file. Verify that IGRP is enabled and the proper network address is specified.

19. Copy the running-configuration to the startup-configuration.

20. Display the contents of the startup configuration.

3-3 CONFIGURING HYBRID ROUTING PROTOCOLS—EIGRP

This section introduces techniques for configuring a router's interface to run **EIGRP**, the Enhanced Interior Gateway Routing Protocol. EIGRP is an enhanced version of the Interior Gateway Routing Protocol (IGRP). EIGRP is a Cisco proprietary protocol and is often called a **hybrid routing protocol** that incorporates the best of the distance vector and link-state algorithms.

EIGRP allows the use of variable length subnet masks, which is beneficial when you're trying to conserve the use of IP addresses. EIGRP also uses Hello packets to verify that a link from one router to another is still active. This is similar to the OSPF Hello packet described in Section 3-5. The routing table updates are exchanged when there is a change in the network. In other words, the routers don't exchange unnecessary information unless a route changes. This helps conserve the limited bandwidth of the network data link. When route information is exchanged, EIGRP quickly converges to the new route selection.

EIGRP
Enhanced Interior Gateway Routing Protocol.

Hybrid Routing Protocol
Protocol that incorporates the best of the distance vector and link-state algorithms.

The four components of EIGRP are as follows:

- **Neighbor Discovery Recovery:** Used to learn about other routers on directly attached networks. This is also used to discover whether neighbor routers are unreachable. This discovery is accomplished by periodically sending Hello packets. The Hello packets are used to verify that a neighbor router is functioning.

- **Reliable Transport Protocol:** Used to guarantee delivery of EIGRP packets to neighbor routers. Both unicast and multicast packet transmission are supported.

- **DUAL Finite State Machine:** Used to track all routes advertised by its neighbors and is used for route computation to obtain loop-free routing.

- **Protocol Dependent Modules:** Responsible for handling network layer, protocol-specific requirements. For example, the IP-EIGRP module is responsible for extracting information from the EIGRP packets and passing this information to DUAL. DUAL uses this information to make routing decisions, and IP-EIGRP then redistributes the learned routes.

Configuring Routes with EIGRP

This section describes a procedure for configuring EIGRP on a router. The first example is for configuring Router A in the campus LAN shown in Figure 3-4.

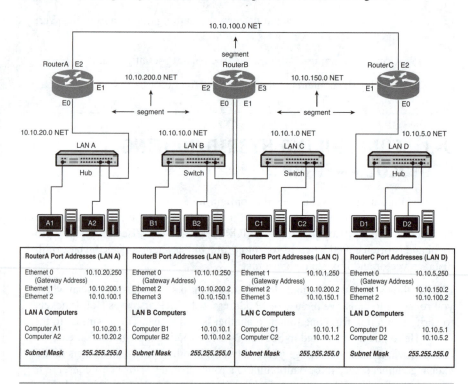

RouterA Port Addresses (LAN A)		RouterB Port Addresses (LAN B)		RouterB Port Addresses (LAN C)		RouterC Port Addresses (LAN D)	
Ethernet 0 (Gateway Address)	10.10.20.250	Ethernet 0 (Gateway Address)	10.10.10.250	Ethernet 1 (Gateway Address)	10.10.1.250	Ethernet 0 (Gateway Address)	10.10.5.250
Ethernet 1	10.10.200.1	Ethernet 2	10.10.200.2	Ethernet 2	10.10.200.2	Ethernet 1	10.10.150.2
Ethernet 2	10.10.100.1	Ethernet 3	10.10.150.1	Ethernet 3	10.10.150.1	Ethernet 2	10.10.100.2
LAN A Computers		**LAN B Computers**		**LAN C Computers**		**LAN D Computers**	
Computer A1	10.10.20.1	Computer B1	10.10.10.1	Computer C1	10.10.1.1	Computer D1	10.10.5.1
Computer A2	10.10.20.2	Computer B2	10.10.10.2	Computer C2	10.10.1.2	Computer D2	10.10.5.2
Subnet Mask	*255.255.255.0*	*Subnet Mask*	*255.255.255.0*	*Subnet Mask*	*255.255.255.0*	*Subnet Mask*	*255.255.255.0*

FIGURE 3-4   The three-router campus LAN

The first step is to configure the interfaces on each of the three routers. Table 3-2 lists the IP addresses and the subnet masks for the router interfaces.

TABLE 3-2 Router Interface IP Addresses and Subnet Masks

Interface	IP Address	Subnet Mask
Router A		
FA0/0	10.10.20.250	255.255.255.0
FA0/1	10.10.200.1	255.255.255.0
FA0/2	10.10.100.1	255.255.255.0
Router B		
FA0/0	10.10.10.250	255.255.255.0
FA0/1	10.10.1.250	255.255.255.0
FA0/2	10.10.200.2	255.255.255.0
FA0/3	10.10.150.1	255.255.255.0
RouterC		
FA0/0	10.10.5.250	255.255.255.0
FA0/1	10.10.150.2	255.255.255.0
FA0/2	10.10.100.2	255.255.255.0

After configuring the router interfaces, the EIGRP routing protocol for Router A will be configured. Use the **conf t** command to enter the router's configuration mode. Next, enter the command **router eigrp** *[AS-number]*. Any AS number can be used. The router uses the AS numbers to determine which routers share routing tables. Only routers with the same AS number will share routing updates. The command **router eigrp 150** is entered as shown. The prompt changes to (config-router) and the next command entered sets the network to run EIGRP. In this example, the command **network 10.0.0.0** is entered. This instructs the router to run EIGRP on any of the router's interfaces that have an IP address that begins with 10. A different network command will be used on Router B to show how the command can be used to specify a limited IP address range.

```
RouterA(config)#router eigrp 150
RouterA(config-router)#network 10.0.0.0
```

Now, the 10.x.x.x interfaces on Router A are configured to run EIGRP. The command **sh ip protocol** is entered to verify that the EIGRP routing protocol is enabled on Router A:

```
RouterA# sh ip protocol
Routing Protocol is "eigrp 150"
Outgoing update filter list for all interfaces is Incoming update
filter list for all interfaces is Default networks flagged in outgoing
updates Default networks accepted from incoming updates EIGRP metric
weight K1 1, K2 0, K3 1, K4 0, K5 0
```

```
EIGRP maximum hopcount 100
EIGRP maximum metric variance 1
Redistributing: eigrp 150
Automatic network summarization is in effect
Routing for Networks:
10.0.0.0
Routing Information Sources:
Gateway Distance Last Update
10.10.200.2 90 00:00:09
Distance: internal 90 external 170
```

The top line states that the routing protocol is "eigrp 150" and indicates that it has been 9 seconds since the last update to the routing table. In EIGRP, updates to the routing table are made when there are changes in the network.

Another useful command is **sh ip route**. The following are the results of entering the command. In this case, the router does not show any EIGRP routes to the subnets in the network, because EIGRP has not been configured on Router B or Router C:

```
RouterA#sh ip route
Codes: C connected, S static, I IGRP, R RIP, M mobile, B BGP D EIGRP,
EX EIGRP external, O OSPF, IA OSPF inter area
N1 OSPF NSSA external type 1, N2 OSPF NSSA external type 2
E1 OSPF external type 1, E2 OSPF external type 2, E EGP
i IS-IS, L1 IS-IS level-1, L2 IS-IS level-2, * candidate default
U per-user static route, o ODR T traffic engineered route
Gateway of last resort is not set
10.0.0.0/24 is subnetted, 3 subnets
C 10.10.20.0 is directly connected, FastEthernet0/0
C 10.10.200.0 is directly connected, FastEthernet0/1
C 10.10.100.0 is directly connected, FastEthernet0/2
```

The command **sh ip int brief** is entered and the status and protocols for the Ethernet interfaces are **up**. These will show **up** as long as there is a network connection to the interfaces:

```
RouterA#sh ip int brief
Interface       IP-Address     OK?  Method  Status  Protocol
FastEthernet0/0 10.10.20.250   YES  NVRAM   up      up
FastEthernet0/1 10.10.200.1    YES  manual  up      up
FastEthernet0/2 10.10.100.1    YES  manual  up      up
```

The **sh run** command is used to view the contents of the router's running-configuration file. The following shows the part of the configuration file that shows the entries for EIGRP. Notice that these entries are the same as the commands entered earlier when configuring EIGRP:

```
!
router eigrp 150
 network 10.0.0.0
!
```

The next step is to configure Router B. The configuration mode (config)# for Router B is entered and the command **router eigrp 150** is entered. Remember, 150 is the AS number, which is the same number used when configuring Router A. The next command is used to set the network that is running EIGRP. In this case, the command **network 10.10.0.0** is entered. This means that interfaces on Router B with a 10.10.x.x address will run the EIGRP protocol. In this case, all interfaces on Router B have a 10.10.x.x address and will run EIGRP:

```
RouterB#conf t
Enter configuration commands, one per line. End with CNTL/Z.
RouterB(config)#router eigrp 150
RouterB(config-router)#network 10.10.0.0
```

The command **sh ip protocol** is used to verify that EIGRP is running on Router B. The text shows that eigrp 150 is running on Router B, and it has been 27 seconds since the last update to the routing table:

```
RouterB#sh ip protocol
Routing Protocol is "eigrp 150"
Outgoing update filter list for all interfaces is Incoming update
filter list for all interfaces is Default networks flagged in outgoing
updates Default networks accepted from incoming updates EIGRP metric
weight K1 1, K2 0, K3 1, K4 0, K5 0
EIGRP maximum hopcount 100
EIGRP maximum metric variance 1
Redistributing: eigrp 150
Automatic network summarization is in effect
Routing for Networks:
10.0.0.0
Routing Information Sources:
Gateway Distance Last Update
10.10.200.1 90 00:00:27
Distance: internal 90 external 170
```

The **sh ip route** command for Router B shows that six routes are on Router B, and there are EIGRP routes to the 10.10.20.0 and 10.10.100.0 subnets. The code for the EIGRP routes is D. Remember, the C code is for the subnets directly connected to the router:

```
RouterB#sh ip route
Codes: C connected, S static, I IGRP, R RIP, M mobile, B BGP D EIGRP,
EX EIGRP external, O OSPF, IA OSPF inter area
N1 OSPF NSSA external type 1, N2 OSPF NSSA external type 2
E1 OSPF external type 1, E2 OSPF external type 2, E EGP
i IS-IS, L1 IS-IS level-1, L2 IS-IS level-2, * candidate default
U per-user static route, o ODR T traffic engineered route
Gateway of last resort is not set
10.0.0.0/24 is subnetted, 6 subnets
C 10.10.10.0 is directly connected, FastEthernet0/0
C 10.10.1.0 is directly connected, FastEthernet0/1
D 10.10.20.0 [90/2195456] via 10.10.200.1, 00:00:09, FastEthernet0/2
D 10.10.100.0 [90/2681856] via 10.10.200.1, 00:00:09, FastEthernet0/2
```

```
C 10.10.150.0 is directly connected, FastEthernet0/3
C 10.10.200.0 is directly connected, FastEthernet0/2
```

A check of the IP routes on Router A also shows that Router A and Router B are exchanging routes with each other. Router A now shows six subnets. Once again, the D indicates the EIGRP routes, and the C indicates the directly connected subnets:

```
RouterA#sh ip route
Codes: C connected, S static, I IGRP, R RIP, M mobile, B BGP D EIGRP,
EX EIGRP external, O OSPF, IA OSPF inter area
N1 OSPF NSSA external type 1, N2 OSPF NSSA external type 2
E1 OSPF external type 1, E2 OSPF external type 2, E EGP
i IS-IS, L1 IS-IS level-1, L2 IS-IS level-2, * candidate default
U per-user static route, o ODR T traffic engineered route
Gateway of last resort is not set
10.0.0.0/24 is subnetted, 6 subnets
D 10.10.10.0 [90/2195456] via 10.10.200.2, 00:00:50, FastEthernet0/1
D 10.10.1.0 [90/2195456] via 10.10.200.2, 00:00:50, FastEthernet0/1
C 10.10.20.0 is directly connected, FastEthernet0/0
C 10.10.100.0 is directly connected, FastEthernet0/2
D 10.10.150.0 [90/2681856] via 10.10.200.2, 00:00:50, FastEthernet0/1
C 10.10.200.0 is directly connected, FastEthernet0/1
```

The last step is to configure EIGRP for Router C using the **router eigrp 150** command. The command **network 10.10.0.0** is used to instruct the router to assign EIGRP to all interfaces that are part of the 10.10.0.0 network. In this case, all interfaces on Router C have a 10.10.x.x address and therefore will run EIGRP:

```
RouterC(config)#router eigrp 150
RouterC(config-router)#network 10.10.0.0
```

The **sh ip route** command is used to display the IP routes for Router C. Router C shows seven subnets. In fact, there are seven subnets in the campus LAN shown in Figure 3-4. This completes the setup for running EIGRP on the campus LAN:

```
RouterC#sh ip route
Codes: C connected, S static, I IGRP, R RIP, M mobile, B BGP D EIGRP,
EX EIGRP external, O OSPF, IA OSPF inter area
E1 OSPF external type 1, E2 OSPF external type 2, E EGP
i IS-IS, L1 IS-IS level-1, L2 IS-IS level-2, * candidate default
Gateway of last resort is not set
10.0.0.0 255.255.255.0 is subnetted, 7 subnets
C 10.10.5.0 is directly connected, FastEthernet0/0
D 10.10.10.0 [90/2195456] via 10.10.150.1, 00:00:01, FastEthernet0/1
D 10.10.1.0 [90/2195456] via 10.10.150.1, 00:00:01, FastEthernet0/1
D 10.10.20.0 [90/2195456] via 10.10.100.1, 00:00:01, FastEthernet0/2
C 10.10.100.0 is directly connected, FastEthernet0/2
C 10.10.150.0 is directly connected, FastEthernet0/1
D 10.10.200.0 [90/2681856] via 10.10.150.1, 00:00:01, FastEthernet0/1
                     [90/2681856] via 10.10.100.1, 00:00:01,
FastEthernet0/2
```

Just like other dynamic routing protocols, one useful command for troubleshooting routing problems is to look at the router's neighbors, because that is how routes are exchanged. The command **show ip eigrp neighbors** will display the EIGRP adjacency neighbor.

```
RouterA#sh ip eigrp neighbors
IP-EIGRP neighbors for process 150
H  Address       Interface  Hold  Uptime     SRTT  RTO  Q    Seq
                            (sec)  (ms)                 Cnt  Num
1  10.10.200.2   Fa0/1      10     00:31:06   152   912  0    30
0  10.10.100.2   Fa0/2      11     00:31:51   86    516  0    37
```

show ip eigrp neighbors
The command used to display the EIGRP adjacency neighbor.

The output result of the **show ip eigrp neighbors** command is simpler comparing to other routing protocol **neighbor** commands. There is no state that one has to decipher. If the neighbor adjacency is established it will be displayed. The important fields that one should pay attention to when troubleshooting EIGRP routing are **Uptime** and **Q Cnt**. The uptime indicates the time the neighbor has last established its adjacency. If the number is much lower than the others, there could be a neighbor or connection issue. The Q Cnt is the number of EIGRP packets being queued to its neighbor. The expected number is 0. If the number is consistently higher, this could mean that there is a link issue or link congestion.

Uptime
Indicates the time the neighbor has last established its adjacency.

Q Cnt
The number of EIGRP packets being queued to its neighbor.

The output of the **show ip eigrp neighbors** command consists of the following fields:

- **H:** The order in which the adjacency is established with the specific neighbor.
- **Address:** The IP address of the neighbor router interface.
- **Interface:** The router interface connected to the neighbor.
- **Hold:** Amount of time EIGRP will wait to hear from its neighbor before declaring it down.
- **Uptime:** The uptime of the adjacent neighbor.
- **SRTT:** Smooth Round Trip Time for sending and receiving EIGRP packet from its neighbor.
- **RTO:** Retransmission Timeout to resend EIGRP packet as calculated by SRTT.
- **Q Cnt:** Queue count is the number of EIGRP packets in the queue waiting to be sent.
- **Seq Num:** Sequence number of the last update sent by its neighbor.

Load Balancing and Redundancy

EIGRP is a popular routing protocol to use on Cisco routers, not because it is Cisco proprietary, but because it is easy to configure and manage. Like other dynamic protocols, EIGRP is capable of load balancing over equal cost paths. By design, EIGRP can use bandwidth, delay, reliability, load, and MTU as values to calculate its composite metric to determine the best path to a destination.

By default, only bandwidth and delay are used by Cisco to calculate the composite metric. Bandwidth is the minimum bandwidth of the entire path. Delay is the total

show ip eigrp topology

Command used to view the composite metric of the current EIGRP topology, the command.

delay of the entire path. To view the composite metric of the current EIGRP topology, issue the **show ip eigrp topology** command. The highlighted numbers are the EIGRP composite metric of each path:

```
RouterA#sh ip eigrp topology
IP-EIGRP Topology Table for AS(150)/ID(10.10.200.1)

Codes: P - Passive, A - Active, U - Update, Q - Query, R - Reply,
       r - reply Status, s - sia Status

P 10.10.1.0/24, 1 successors, FD is 30720
        via 10.10.200.2 (30720/28160), FastEthernet0/1
P 10.10.5.0/24, 1 successors, FD is 30720
        via 10.10.100.2 (30720/28160), FastEthernet0/2
P 10.10.10.0/24, 1 successors, FD is 30720
        via 10.10.200.2 (30720/28160), FastEthernet0/1
P 10.10.20.0/24, 1 successors, FD is 28160
        via Connected, FastEthernet0/0
P 10.10.100.0/24, 1 successors, FD is 28160
        via Connected, FastEthernet1/0
P 10.10.150.0/24, 2 successors, FD is 30720
        via 10.10.100.2 (30720/28160), FastEthernet0/2
        via 10.10.200.2 (30720/28160), FastEthernet0/1
P 10.10.200.0/24, 1 successors, FD is 28160
        via Connected, FastEthernet0/1
```

bandwidth

Command used to adjust the bandwidth value.

It is typically not recommended to manually adjust the EIGRP composite metric. Cisco's recommendation is to leave the EIGRP as it is; however, if this must be done, then the two less destructive ways for setting an EIGRP preferred path is by adjusting the bandwidth value or by adjusting the delay value. To adjust the bandwidth value, this can be done via the **bandwidth** command at the router interface:

```
RouterA(config)#int fastEthernet 0/2
RouterA(config-if)#bandwidth 1000
```

The **bandwidth** command is in kilobits, so **bandwidth 1000** would mean 1,000 Kbits or 1 Mbits as its value. The interface FastEthernet0/2 on Router A is connecting Router C. By reducing the bandwidth value, the composite metric of any route via the interface FastEthernet0/2 has changed as reflected in the recent **show ip eigrp topology** command. The composite metric that used to be 30,720 is now 2,565,120:

```
RouterA#sh ip eigrp topology
IP-EIGRP Topology Table for AS(150)/ID(10.10.200.1)

Codes: P - Passive, A - Active, U - Update, Q - Query, R - Reply,
       r - reply Status, s - sia Status

P 10.10.1.0/24, 1 successors, FD is 30720
        via 10.10.200.2 (30720/28160), FastEthernet0/1
P 10.10.5.0/24, 1 successors, FD is 33280
```

```
           via 10.10.200.2 (33280/30720), FastEthernet0/1
           via 10.10.100.2 (2565120/28160), FastEthernet0/2
P 10.10.10.0/24, 1 successors, FD is 30720
           via 10.10.200.2 (30720/28160), FastEthernet0/1
P 10.10.20.0/24, 1 successors, FD is 28160
           via Connected, FastEthernet0/0
P 10.10.100.0/24, 1 successors, FD is 2562560
           via Connected, FastEthernet1/0
           via 10.10.200.2 (33280/30720), FastEthernet0/1
P 10.10.150.0/24, 1 successors, FD is 30720
           via 10.10.200.2 (30720/28160), FastEthernet0/1
           via 10.10.100.2 (2565120/28160), FastEthernet0/2
P 10.10.200.0/24, 1 successors, FD is 28160
           via Connected, FastEthernet0/1
```

The **show ip route eigrp** also confirms that the path via FastEthernet0/1 to Router
B is now the preferred path for all network routes:

```
RouterA#sh ip route eigrp
      10.0.0.0/24 is subnetted, 7 subnets
D       10.10.1.0 [90/30720] via 10.10.200.2, 00:11:42,
FastEthernet0/1
D       10.10.5.0 [90/33280] via 10.10.200.2, 00:11:42,
FastEthernet0/1
D       10.10.10.0 [90/30720] via 10.10.200.2, 00:11:42,
FastEthernet0/1
D       10.10.150.0 [90/30720] via 10.10.200.2, 00:11:42,
FastEthernet0/1
```

Changing the bandwidth value could have more impact beyond EIGRP routing;
other protocols, like QoS, depend on the bandwidth value to make their decisions.
Between the **bandwidth** *value* and the **delay** *value*, the **delay** *value* command is the
one with the least impact. Therefore, to manipulate the EIGRP composite metric,
adjusting the delay value is preferred over adjusting the bandwidth value. To adjust
the bandwidth value, this can be done by adjusting the **delay** command at the router
interface:

> **delay**
> This command sets the
> delay on the interface.
> The delay value is
> measured in tens of
> microseconds.

```
RouterA(config)#int fastEthernet 0/2
RouterA(config-if)#delay 100
```

The delay value is measured in tens of microseconds. The command **delay 100**
changes the default delay value from 100 microseconds to 1,000 microseconds.
This, in turn, increases the composite metric of the interface FastEthernet0/2 on
Router A connecting to Router C. The composite metric of any route via the interface FastEthernet0/2 has changed as reflected in the recent **show ip eigrp topology**
command. The path composite metric that used to be 30,720 is now 53,760. Again,
the path via FastEthernet0/1 to Router B is now a more preferred path for all network routes.

```
RouterA#sh ip eigrp topology
IP-EIGRP Topology Table for AS(150)/ID(10.10.200.1)
```

```
Codes: P - Passive, A - Active, U - Update, Q - Query, R - Reply,
       r - reply Status, s - sia Status

P 10.10.1.0/24, 1 successors, FD is 30720
        via 10.10.200.2 (30720/28160), FastEthernet0/1
P 10.10.5.0/24, 1 successors, FD is 33280
        via 10.10.200.2 (33280/30720), FastEthernet0/1
        via 10.10.100.2 (53760/28160), FastEthernet0/2
P 10.10.10.0/24, 1 successors, FD is 30720
        via 10.10.200.2 (30720/28160), FastEthernet0/1
P 10.10.20.0/24, 1 successors, FD is 28160
        via Connected, FastEthernet0/0
P 10.10.100.0/24, 1 successors, FD is 51200
        via Connected, FastEthernet1/0
        via 10.10.200.2 (33280/30720), FastEthernet0/1
P 10.10.150.0/24, 1 successors, FD is 30720
        via 10.10.200.2 (30720/28160), FastEthernet0/1
        via 10.10.100.2 (53760/28160), FastEthernet0/2
P 10.10.200.0/24, 1 successors, FD is 28160
        via Connected, FastEthernet0/1
```

Networking Challenge: EIGRP

Use the Net-Challenge Simulator Software included with the text's companion CD-ROM to demonstrate that you can configure EIGRP for Router A in the campus LAN (the campus LAN is shown in Figure 3-2 and is displayed by clicking the View Topology button when the software is started). Place the Net-Challenge CD-ROM in your computer's drive. Open the Net-Challenge folder and click **Net Challenge V3-2.exe**. When the software is running, click the **Select Router Challenge** button to open a **Select Router Challenge** drop-down menu. Select **Chapter 3—EIGRP**. This opens a checkbox that can be used to verify that you have completed all the tasks:

1. Enter the privileged EXEC mode on the router.

2. Enter the router configuration mode: **Router(config)**.

3. Set the hostname to **RouterA.**

4. Configure the FastEthernet0/0 interface with the following:

   IP address: 10.10.20.250

   Subnet mask: 255.255.255.0

5. Enable the FA0/0 interface.

6. Configure the FastEthernet0/1 interface with the following:

   IP address: 10.10.200.1

   Subnet mask: 255.255.255.0

7. Enable the FA0/1 interface.

8. Configure the FastEthernet0/2 interface with the following:

   IP address: 10.10.100.1

   Subnet mask: 255.255.255.0

9. Enable the FA0/2 interface.

10. Enable EIGRP with an AS number of 200.

11. Enter the **network** command that enables EIGRP on the router.

12. Use the **sh ip int brief** command to check the interface status.

13. Use the **sh ip protocol** command to see whether EIGRP is running on Router A.

14. Use the **sh ip route** command to verify that the three FastEthernet ports are connected to RouterA.

15. Use the **sh run** command to view the running-configuration file on Router A.

    Verify that EIGRP is enabled and the proper network address is specified.

16. Use the **ping** command to verify connection to the following interfaces:

    10.10.5.250

    10.10.150.1

    10.10.200.2

    10.10.100.2

3-4 ADVANCED ROUTING REDISTRIBUTION

Routing redistribution is another important practice that a network engineer may have to address when working in a big network environment. Routing redistribution is the technique of injecting routes from one routing protocol into another routing protocol. In general, routes are only exchanged automatically with other routers that are running the same routing protocol (for example, OSPF-OSPF or EIGRP-EIGRP). Each routing protocol speaks its own language and does not automatically communicate with other routing protocols. Additionally, each routing protocol has its own metric or cost associated with it. For example, static routes use administrative distance, OSPF uses cost, IS-IS uses metric, and EIGRP uses a composite metric. Therefore, routes from different routing protocols cannot be exchanged automatically. As will be demonstrated, this process of exchanging routes has to be configured manually.

> **Routing Redistribution**
> The technique of injecting routes from one routing protocol into another routing protocol.

There are several reasons why routing redistribution is necessary:

- **One common reason is to redistribute static routes**: These routes are not learned, but are configured manually. They must be redistributed into a dynamic routing protocol so that they can be advertised.

- **Another reason is when two or more dynamic routing protocols are used on the network**: This scenario happens often when connecting one network to another either for peering purposes or for when companies merge their network infrastructures due to a business acquisition. It is much easier to accept the new routing protocol from another network and distribute the new routes into the existing routing protocol rather than converting both routers to single routing protocol. This saves time and money.

- **Another reason is that certain routing protocols may not be supported by certain network devices**: A prime example of this is the EIGRP, which is a Cisco proprietary protocol and is not supported by other network vendors. If a non-Cisco router connects to a Cisco router that is running EIGRP, then the Cisco router will need to redistribute routes learned from the other routing protocol into EIGRP.

This section explores different routing redistribution techniques to redistribute routes into dynamic routing protocols, such as RIP, OSPF, IS-IS, and EIGRP. Static routing is not a dynamic routing protocol and is not applicable in this case, because static routes must be configured manually. The configuration for this section is based on the network diagram of Figure 3-5. Router A and Router B make up an existing network and both routers are connected and are running the same routing protocol. Router C brings in a new network with a different routing protocol that will need to be redistributed into the existing network. Router B is where the redistribution happens since this is the router that is directly connected to Router C.

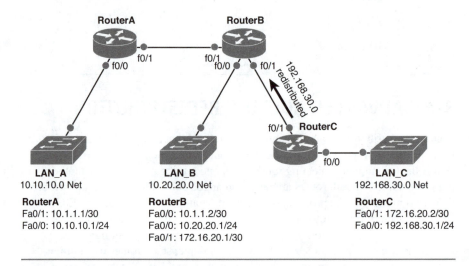

FIGURE 3-5   Route redistribution from LAN C network to LAN A and LAN B

Route Redistribution into RIP

This section examines route redistribution into RIP. First, let's explore the basic RIPv2 configuration required for Router A and Router B. Both routers will have the same routing configuration as shown and will be running a 10.0.0.0 classful network:

```
!
router rip
 version 2
 network 10.0.0.0
!
```

The output from the **show ip route** command displays the expected network routes are being learned via RIPv2. The following is the result from Router A when the command **sh ip route rip** is issued. This result shows that Router A has a RIP route to the 10.20.20.0/24 network via the 10.1.1.2 interface on Router B:

```
RouterA#sh ip route rip
     10.0.0.0/8 is variably subnetted, 3 subnets, 2 masks
R        10.20.20.0/24 [120/1] via 10.1.1.2, 00:00:02, FastEthernet0/1
```

However, Router B has an interface that is connected to Router C that is not part of the network advertised via RIP. This interconnected interface on Router B is FastEthernet0/1 and has an IP address of 172.16.20.1. This interface is not expected to participate in RIP advertisement since Router C is running a different routing protocol. This is why this route it is not included as a network statement in the RIP configuration. Nonetheless, Router A should still learn about this interconnected network, so Router A can reach it over the network.

In order to accomplish this, Router B can redistribute its connected network into RIP. The command to do this is **redistribute** *protocol*. The following is a list of the options of what can be used to redistribute the networks into RIP:

> **redistribute** *protocol*
> The command used to inject routes from one routing protocol into another routing protocol.

```
RouterB(config)#router rip
RouterB(config-router)#redistribute ?
  bgp              Border Gateway Protocol (BGP)
  connected        Connected
  eigrp            Enhanced Interior Gateway Routing Protocol (EIGRP)
  isis        I    SO IS-IS
  iso-igrp         IGRP for OSI networks
  metric           Metric for redistributed routes
  mobile           Mobile routes
  odr              On Demand stub Routes
  ospf             Open Shortest Path First (OSPF)
  rip              Routing Information Protocol (RIP)
  route-map        Route map reference
  static           Static routes
  <CR>
RouterB(config-router)#redistribute connected
```

Therefore, the command **redistribute connected** can be issued to redistribute the connected networks, which, in this case, is the interface between Router B and Router C.

> **redistribute connected**
> The command issued to redistribute the connected networks.

Once the command is issued, you can verify the results on Router A. The **show ip route rip** command now shows that the network 172.16.20.0 is being advertised by RIP:

```
RouterA#sh ip route rip
     172.16.0.0/30 is subnetted, 1 subnets
R        172.16.20.0 [120/1] via 10.1.1.2, 00:00:08, FastEthernet0/1
     10.0.0.0/8 is variably subnetted, 3 subnets, 2 masks
R        10.20.20.0/24 [120/1] via 10.1.1.2, 00:00:08, FastEthernet0/1
```

redistribute static

The command issued to redistribute the static networks.

Now, assume there is a static route on Router B to the LAN C network of 192.168.30.0. This static route is only known by Router B; therefore, it will need to be redistributed into RIP, so that Router A can learn of it as well. Similar to the **redistribute connected** command, you can use the **redistribute static** command on Router B:

```
RouterB(config)#ip route 192.168.30.0 255.255.255.0 172.16.20.2
RouterB(config)#router rip
RouterB(config-router)#redistribute static
```

As a result, the redistributed static route to the 192.168.30.0 network entered in Router B, is now known to Router A and as shown, Router A now learns of the route to the LAN C network via RIP:

```
RouterA#sh ip route rip
R    192.168.30.0/24 [120/1] via 10.1.1.2, 00:00:12, FastEthernet0/1
     172.16.0.0/30 is subnetted, 1 subnets
R       172.16.20.0 [120/1] via 10.1.1.2, 00:00:08, FastEthernet0/1
     10.0.0.0/8 is variably subnetted, 3 subnets, 2 masks
R       10.20.20.0/24 [120/1] via 10.1.1.2, 00:00:08, FastEthernet0/1
```

The other dynamic protocols are distributed into RIP in similar fashion. If Router C runs OSPF as its routing protocol, then Router B will need to run the same in order for the routers to communicate. To do this, both routers will have to agree on the OSPF Process ID. In the following example, the OSPF Process ID will be 200. The OSPF configuration for Router C and Router B are shown.

Router C's OSPF configuration:

```
!
router ospf 200
 log-adjacency-changes
 network 192.168.30.0 0.255.255.255 area 0
 network 172.16.20.0 0.0.0.3 area 0
!
```

Router B's OSPF configuration:

```
!
router ospf 200
 log-adjacency-changes
 network 10.0.0.0 0.255.255.255 area 0
 network 172.16.20.0 0.0.0.3 area 0
!
```

Now, Router B can receive an OSPF route from Router C as shown as the result of issuing the command **show ip route**. Along with it, Router B receives a RIP route from Router A. It is important to verify the routes of the protocol one is trying to redistribute. Note: This important step is often neglected. Remember, the router cannot redistribute what it doesn't know and the route must be there for you to redistribute.

```
RouterB#sh ip route
Codes: C - connected, S - static, R - RIP, M - mobile, B - BGP
       D - EIGRP, EX - EIGRP external, O - OSPF, IA - OSPF inter area
       N1 - OSPF NSSA external type 1, N2 - OSPF NSSA external type 2
       E1 - OSPF external type 1, E2 - OSPF external type 2
       i - IS-IS, su - IS-IS summary, L1 - IS-IS level-1, L2 - IS-IS
level-2
       ia - IS-IS inter area, * - candidate default, U - per-user
static route
       o - ODR, P - periodic downloaded static route

Gateway of last resort is not set

O    192.168.30.0/24 [110/2] via 172.16.20.2, 00:00:09,
FastEthernet0/1
     172.16.0.0/30 is subnetted, 1 subnets
C       172.16.20.0 is directly connected, FastEthernet0/1
     10.0.0.0/8 is variably subnetted, 3 subnets, 2 masks
C       10.20.20.0/24 is directly connected, FastEthernet0/0
R       10.10.10.0/24 [120/1] via 10.1.1.1, 00:00:23, FastEthernet1/0
C       10.1.1.0/30 is directly connected, FastEthernet1/0
```

Router A does not know of the new OSPF route yet, so the route has to be redistributed. On Cisco routers, there is a caveat for redistributing dynamic routing protocols into RIP. That caveat is the metric must be assigned in order for the routes to be redistributed properly. This is not required for static and connected routes since RIP assigns the metric of 1 to each of these by default. Also, recall that the metric value for RIP is hop count and each hop count along the path has the value of 1. The maximum hop count value is 16. The command to redistribute OSPF routes into RIP is **redistribute ospf** *process_id* **metric** *0-16*.

> **redistribute ospf**
> *process_id* metric
> *0-16*
> The command to redistribute OSPF routes into RIP.

```
RouterB(config)#router rip
RouterB(config-router)#redistribute ospf 200 metric 1
```

Now, the RIP routing table on Router A shows the route 192.168.30.0 that is learned from the LAN C network:

```
RouterA#sh ip route rip
R    192.168.30.0/24 [120/1] via 10.1.1.2, 00:00:12, FastEthernet0/1
     172.16.0.0/30 is subnetted, 1 subnets
R       172.16.20.0 [120/1] via 10.1.1.2, 00:00:08, FastEthernet0/1
     10.0.0.0/8 is variably subnetted, 3 subnets, 2 masks
R       10.20.20.0/24 [120/1] via 10.1.1.2, 00:00:08, FastEthernet0/1
```

For EIGRP, the command to redistribute routes into RIP is almost the same as OSPF. The command is **redistribute eigrp** *AS_number* **metric** *0-16*. For IS-IS, the command is **redistribute isis** *IS-IS_Level* **metric** *0-16*. The configuration example is as follows:

> **redistribute eigrp**
> **AS_*number* metric**
> *0-16*
> Command to redistribute EIGRP routes into RIP.
>
> **redistribute isis**
> *IS-IS_Level* metric
> *0-16*
> Command to redistribute IS-IS routes into RIP.

```
RouterB(config)#router rip
RouterB(config-router)#redistribute eigrp 200 metric 1
RouterB(config-router)#redistribute isis level-1-2 metric 1
```

Route Redistribution into OSPF

Next, the steps for route redistribution for OSPF are examined for Router A and Router B in the network shown in Figure 3-5. Both routers have been configured to run OSPF using the following commands:

```
!
router ospf 200
 network 10.0.0.0 0.255.255.255 area 0
!
```

Once the basic configuration for OSPF has been configured, the routers will have the OSPF neighbor adjacency established and the OSPF routes will be exchanged. The result of the **show ip ospf neighbor** and **show ip route ospf** on Router A are shown in the output examples that follow. The results confirm the neighbor adjacency and that the expected network routes are being learned via OSPF:

```
RouterA#sh ip ospf neighbor

Neighbor ID     Pri  State          Dead Time    Address
Interface
172.16.20.1      1   FULL/BDR       00:00:34     10.1.1.2
FastEthernet0/1
RouterA#sh ip route ospf
     10.0.0.0/8 is variably subnetted, 3 subnets, 2 masks
O       10.20.20.0/24 [110/2] via 10.1.1.2, 00:15:38, FastEthernet0/1
```

Router B's connected interface to Router C is not advertised as a network statement in the OSPF configuration. Therefore, its connected network will not be shown in Router A's routing table. This is the same behavior demonstrated for RIP. Just like RIP, connected networks can be redistributed in OSPF by using the **redistribute connected** command. This command is next issued on Router B:

```
RouterB(config)#router ospf 200
RouterB(config-router)#redistribute connected
% Only classful networks will be redistributed
```

However, what we get is the message stating that only classful networks can be redistributed. Because the connected network is 172.16.20.0/30, which is not a classful network, this will not work. Cisco provides a solution to this problem with a slightly different command:

```
RouterB(config-router)#redistribute connected subnets
```

> **redistribute connected subnets**
> Allows the classless network to be distributed.
>
> **E2**
> An OSPF external type 2 route.

This command allows the classless network to be distributed. Once the command is issued, we can then verify the result on Router A. The **show ip route** command now shows the network 172.16.20.0 is being advertised by OSPF. Not only that, the network route is flagged as an **E2** or an OSPF external type 2 route, which is different than other OSPF internal routes. By default, any routes that are being redistributed from another routing protocol into OSPF will appear as OSPF E2 routes that are the least preferred among the OSPF route types.

```
RouterA#sh ip route
Codes: C - connected, S - static, R - RIP, M - mobile, B - BGP
       D - EIGRP, EX - EIGRP external, O - OSPF, IA - OSPF inter area
```

```
        N1 - OSPF NSSA external type 1, N2 - OSPF NSSA external type 2
        E1 - OSPF external type 1, E2 - OSPF external type 2
        i - IS-IS, su - IS-IS summary, L1 - IS-IS level-1, L2 - IS-IS
level-2
        ia - IS-IS inter area, * - candidate default, U - per-user
static route
        o - ODR, P - periodic downloaded static route

Gateway of last resort is not set

     172.16.0.0/30 is subnetted, 1 subnets
O E2    172.16.20.0 [110/20] via 10.1.1.2, 00:01:59, FastEthernet0/1
     10.0.0.0/8 is variably subnetted, 3 subnets, 2 masks
O        10.20.20.0/24 [110/2] via 10.1.1.2, 00:06:49, FastEthernet0/1
C        10.10.10.0/24 is directly connected, FastEthernet0/0
C        10.1.1.0/30 is directly connected, FastEthernet0/1
```

Now, configure a static route on Router B to the LAN C network of 192.168.30.0 and redistribute it into OSPF. This enables Router A to learn the route to 192.168.30.0. To redistribute static routes, issue the command **redistribute static** on Router B:

```
RouterB(config)#ip route 192.168.30.0 255.255.255.0 172.16.20.2
RouterB(config)#router ospf 200
RouterB(config-router)#redistribute static
% Only classful networks will be redistributed
```

The same warning message is shown saying that, "only classful networks will be redistributed." This time, the network 192.168.30.0/24 is a classful network, so the network will be redistributed; otherwise, the command **redistribute static subnets** will need to be used to distribute classless networks similar to what was done for the connected network. As a result of the redistributed static route entered in Router B, Router A now learns of the route to LAN C network via OSPF and the network is shown as an OSPF external type 2 route:

> **redistribute static subnets**
> Allows the static network to be distributed.

```
RouterA#sh ip route ospf
O E2 192.168.30.0/24 [110/20] via 10.1.1.2, 00:03:37, FastEthernet0/1
     172.16.0.0/30 is subnetted, 1 subnets
O E2    172.16.20.0 [110/20] via 10.1.1.2, 00:51:59, FastEthernet0/1
     10.0.0.0/8 is variably subnetted, 3 subnets, 2 masks
O        10.20.20.0/24 [110/2] via 10.1.1.2, 00:42:28, FastEthernet0/1
```

The other dynamic protocols are distributed into OSPF in similar fashion. For example, if Router C runs EIGRP as its routing protocol, then Router B will need to run EIGRP in order for Router B and Router C to communicate. Both routers have to agree on an EIGRP Autonomous system number. In this example, an EIGRP AS number of 200 is selected. The EIGRP routing configuration for Router C and Router B follow.

Router C's EIGRP configuration:

```
!
router eigrp 200
 network 192.168.30.0 0.
 network 172.16.0.0
no auto-summary
!
```

Router B's EIGRP configuration:

```
!
router eigrp 200
 network 10.0.0.0
 network 172.16.0.0
no auto-summary
!
```

Now, verify that Router B is able to receive an EIGRP route from Router C before proceeding with the route redistribution. This can be done using the **sh ip route** command. The routing table for Router B is shown. It shows a network route of 192.168.30.0/24 learned from Router C's interface 172.16.20.2 via EIGRP:

```
RouterB#sh ip route
Codes: C - connected, S - static, R - RIP, M - mobile, B - BGP
       D - EIGRP, EX - EIGRP external, O - OSPF, IA - OSPF inter area
       N1 - OSPF NSSA external type 1, N2 - OSPF NSSA external type 2
       E1 - OSPF external type 1, E2 - OSPF external type 2
       i - IS-IS, su - IS-IS summary, L1 - IS-IS level-1, L2 - IS-IS
level-2
       ia - IS-IS inter area, * - candidate default, U - per-user
static route
       o - ODR, P - periodic downloaded static route

Gateway of last resort is not set

D    192.168.30.0/24 [90/30720] via 172.16.20.2, 00:50:45,
FastEthernet0/1
     172.16.0.0/30 is subnetted, 1 subnets
C        172.16.20.0 is directly connected, FastEthernet0/1
     10.0.0.0/8 is variably subnetted, 3 subnets, 2 masks
C        10.20.20.0/24 is directly connected, FastEthernet0/0
O        10.10.10.0/24 [110/2] via 10.1.1.1, 00:53:18, FastEthernet1/0
C        10.1.1.0/30 is directly connected, FastEthernet1/0
```

The next step is to configure Router B to redistribute a learned EIGRP route into OSPF. Recall that the OSPF cost or metric is derived from the bandwidth of the interface. By default, Cisco routers will assign an OSPF cost/metric of 20 to any redistributed routes with exception for redistributed routes from BGP. If the metric does not need to be set, the command to distribute dynamic routing protocols is all the same for OSPF. The command to redistribute EIGRP routes into OSPF is

redistribute eigrp *AS_id* [**metric** *0-16777214*]. This time, the keyword **subnets** will be used to avoid the warning message of only classful networks will be redistributed:

```
RouterB(config)#router ospf 200
RouterB(config-router)#redistribute eigrp 200 subnets
```

The command **show ip route ospf** on Router A would confirm the result that the network 192.168.30.0/24 is advertised as an OSPF external type 2 route:

```
RouterA#sh ip route ospf
O E2 192.168.30.0/24 [110/20] via 10.1.1.2, 00:03:37, FastEthernet0/1
        172.16.0.0/30 is subnetted, 1 subnets
O E2    172.16.20.0 [110/20] via 10.1.1.2, 00:51:59, FastEthernet0/1
        10.0.0.0/8 is variably subnetted, 3 subnets, 2 masks
O       10.20.20.0/24 [110/2] via 10.1.1.2, 00:42:28, FastEthernet0/1
```

To redistribute RIP into OSPF, the command is **redistribute rip**. For IS-IS, the command is **redistribute isis** *IS-IS_Level*. The configuration example is as follows:

```
RouterB(config)#router ospf 200
RouterB(config-router)#redistribute rip
RouterB(config-router)#redistribute isis level-1-2
```

Route Redistribution into EIGRP

Next, the steps for route redistribution of routers into EIGRP is examined. First, EIGRP is configured for Router A and Router B. Both routers will have the same EIGRP routing configuration, as shown:

```
!
router eigrp 200
 network 10.0.0.0
 no auto-summary
!
```

The EIGRP neighbor adjacency can be verified with the command **show ip eigrp neighbor**, and the EIGRP route is verified with **show ip route eigrp** on Router A. The results confirm that the neighbor adjacency is established and the correct network routes are being exchanged via EIGRP:

```
RouterA#sh ip eigrp neighbors
IP-EIGRP neighbors for process 200
H  Address    Interface  Hold  Uptime    SRTT   RTO   Q    Seq
                               (sec)     (ms)         Cnt  Num
0  10.1.1.2   Fa0/1      11    00:03:39  40     240   0    4

RouterA#show ip route eigrp
      10.0.0.0/8 is variably subnetted, 3 subnets, 2 masks
D       10.20.20.0/24 [90/30720] via 10.1.1.2, 00:03:48,
FastEthernet0/1
```

redistribute eigrp *AS_id* [**metric** *0-16777214*]
The command to redistribute EIGRP routes into RIP.

redistribute rip
The command to redistribute RIP into OSPF.

redistribute isis *IS-IS_Level*
The command to redistribute EIGRP routes into IS-IS.

Router B's connected interface to Router C will need to be redistributed, because it is not included as a network statement in the EIGRP configuration. Router A's routing table does not show a connected network for 172.16.20.0/30. This is expected, because it has not yet been redistributed by Router B, as previously discussed in the RIP and OSPF example. The command **redistribute connected** is issued on Router B to redistribute the connected network:

```
RouterB(config)#router eigrp 200
RouterB(config-router)#redistribute connected
```

EX
External EIGRP type.

Once the command **redistribute connected** is issued, the command **sh ip route** can be issued on Router A to verify that the network 172.16.20.0 is being advertised via EIGRP. The network route is also flagged as an **EX** or an external EIGRP type. The external EIGRP route has an administrative distance (AD) value of 170, which is higher than the internal EIGRP route's AD value of 90:

```
RouterA#sh ip route
Codes: C - connected, S - static, R - RIP, M - mobile, B - BGP
       D - EIGRP, EX - EIGRP external, O - OSPF, IA - OSPF inter area
       N1 - OSPF NSSA external type 1, N2 - OSPF NSSA external type 2
       E1 - OSPF external type 1, E2 - OSPF external type 2
       i - IS-IS, su - IS-IS summary, L1 - IS-IS level-1, L2 - IS-IS
level-2
       ia - IS-IS inter area, * - candidate default, U - per-user
static route
       o - ODR, P - periodic downloaded static route

Gateway of last resort is not set

     172.16.0.0/30 is subnetted, 1 subnets
D EX    172.16.20.0 [170/30720] via 10.1.1.2, 00:23:14,
FastEthernet0/1
     10.0.0.0/8 is variably subnetted, 3 subnets, 2 masks
D       10.20.20.0/24 [90/30720] via 10.1.1.2, 00:37:20,
FastEthernet0/1
C       10.10.10.0/24 is directly connected, FastEthernet0/0
C       10.1.1.0/30 is directly connected, FastEthernet0/1
```

Next, a static route on Router B needs to be configured to the LAN C network of 192.168.30.0. Additionally, the static route must be redistributed into EIGRP. This enables Router A to learn the route as well. To redistribute static routes, the command **redistribute static** is issued on Router B.

```
RouterB(config)#ip route 192.168.30.0 255.255.255.0 172.16.20.2
RouterB(config)#router eigrp 200
RouterB(config-router)#redistribute static
```

As a result, Router A now learns of the route to LAN C network via EIGRP, and the network 192.168.30.0 is displayed as an EIGRP external route, just like the distributed connected route:

```
RouterA#sh ip route eigrp
D EX 192.168.30.0/24 [170/30720] via 10.1.1.2, 00:00:17,
FastEthernet0/1
     172.16.0.0/30 is subnetted, 1 subnets
D EX    172.16.20.0 [170/30720] via 10.1.1.2, 00:33:53,
FastEthernet0/1
     10.0.0.0/8 is variably subnetted, 3 subnets, 2 masks
D       10.20.20.0/24 [90/30720] via 10.1.1.2, 00:47:59,
FastEthernet0/1
```

As we have learned, EIGRP uses a composite metric, which consists of bandwidth, delay, reliability, load, and MTU. To redistribute other dynamic routing protocols, the metric value has to be converted into EIGRP's metric values or new EIGRP metric values must be assigned. Routes will not be redistributed properly without these values. Cisco recommends that every redistributed dynamic routing protocol be assigned with EIGRP metrics. As it turns out, even though only the two EIGRP metric values of bandwidth and delay are used by default, Cisco enforces all the metric values be defined. The parameters defining the EIGRP metric assignments are as follows:

- Bandwidth metric is a value between 1–4294967295 in Kbps.

- Delay metric is a value between 0–4294967295 in ten microseconds.

- Reliability metric is a value between 1–255, where 255 is 100 percent reliable.

- Load metric is a value between 0–255, where 255 is a 100 percent load.

- MTU is a maximum transfer unit value between 1-65,535, where 1,500 is a norm.

The following example demonstrates how to redistribute RIPv2 routes into EIGRP. Router C and Router B are both configured to run RIPv2. The RIPv2 routing configurations for Router C and Router B follow:

Router C's RIPv2 configuration:

```
!
router rip
 version 2
 network 172.16.0.0
 network 192.168.30.0
!
```

Router B's RIPv2 configuration:

```
!
router rip
 version 2
 network 10.0.0.0
 network 172.16.0.0
!
```

Now, you must verify that Router B is able to receive a RIP route from Router C before proceeding with the route redistribution. The routing table of Router B is shown in the output that follows that shows a network route of 192.168.30.0/24, learned from Router C's 172.16.20.2 interface via RIP.

```
RouterB#sh ip route
Codes: C - connected, S - static, R - RIP, M - mobile, B - BGP
       D - EIGRP, EX - EIGRP external, O - OSPF, IA - OSPF inter area
       N1 - OSPF NSSA external type 1, N2 - OSPF NSSA external type 2
       E1 - OSPF external type 1, E2 - OSPF external type 2
       i - IS-IS, su - IS-IS summary, L1 - IS-IS level-1, L2 - IS-IS
level-2
       ia - IS-IS inter area, * - candidate default, U - per-user
static route
       o - ODR, P - periodic downloaded static route

Gateway of last resort is not set

R    192.168.30.0/24 [120/1] via 172.16.20.2, 00:00:20,
FastEthernet0/1
     172.16.0.0/30 is subnetted, 1 subnets
C        172.16.20.0 is directly connected, FastEthernet0/1
     10.0.0.0/8 is variably subnetted, 3 subnets, 2 masks
C        10.20.20.0/24 is directly connected, FastEthernet0/0
D        10.10.10.0/24 [90/30720] via 10.1.1.1, 00:48:39,
FastEthernet1/0
C        10.1.1.0/30 is directly connected, FastEthernet1/0
```

redistribute rip metric *bandwidth delay reliability load MTU*

The command to redistribute RIP routes into EIGRP.

The next step is to configure Router B to redistribute a learned RIP route into EIGRP. As previously discussed, all the EIGRP metric values will need to be assigned to the redistributed routing protocol. The command to redistribute RIP routes into EIGRP is **redistribute rip metric** *bandwidth delay reliability load MTU*, as demonstrated here:

```
RouterB(config)#router eigrp 200
RouterB(config-router)#redistribute rip metric 100000 10 255 1 1500
```

default-metric *bandwidth delay reliability load MTU*

The command for setting the default metric.

Instead of entering the long metric command every time, a default metric can be defined. For every redistribute statement, it will use the default metric. If the **redistribute** statement has metric values assigned, it overrides the default metric. The command for setting the default metric is **default-metric** *bandwidth delay reliability load MTU*. The following is an example of how a default metric is configured:

```
RouterB(config)#router eigrp 200
RouterB(config-router)#default-metric 100000 10 255 1 1500
RouterB(config-router)#redistribute rip
```

This command sets the default metric to the following:

> Bandwidth: 100000 kbps
> Delay: 1000 microseconds
> Reliability: 100 percent reliable
> Load: minimal
> MTU: norm

The command **show ip route eigrp** on Router A confirms the result that the network 192.168.30.0/24 is advertised as an external EIGRP route:

```
RouterA#sh ip route eigrp
D EX 192.168.30.0/24 [170/30720] via 10.1.1.2, 00:00:02,
FastEthernet0/1
        172.16.0.0/30 is subnetted, 1 subnets
D EX     172.16.20.0 [170/30720] via 10.1.1.2, 01:18:33,
FastEthernet0/1
        10.0.0.0/8 is variably subnetted, 3 subnets, 2 masks
D        10.20.20.0/24 [90/30720] via 10.1.1.2, 01:32:39,
FastEthernet0/1
```

Once the default metric is defined in EIGRP, the command **redistribute ospf** can be used to redistribute OSPF into EIGRP. For IS-IS, the command is **redistribute isis** *IS-IS_Level*. The configuration example is as follows:

```
RouterB(config)#router eigrp 200
RouterB(config-router)#redistribute rip
RouterB(config-router)#redistribute isis level-1-2
```

Route Redistribution into IS-IS

Surprisingly, the configuration for route redistribution into IS-IS is simple to apply. First, let's configure Router A and Router B with IS-IS routing and then enable the interfaces that will participate in IS-IS routing. The running configuration files for Router A and Router B are next shown for IS-IS.

Router A's configuration

```
interface FastEthernet0/0
 ip address 10.10.10.1 255.255.255.0
 ip router isis
!
interface FastEthernet0/1
 ip address 10.1.1.1 255.255.255.252
 ip router isis
!
router isis
 net 49.0001.c202.00e8.0001.00
!
```

Router B's configuration:

```
interface FastEthernet0/0
 ip address 10.20.20.1 255.255.255.0
 ip router isis
!
interface FastEthernet1/0
 ip address 10.1.1.2 255.255.255.252
 ip router isis
!
```

```
router isis
 net 49.0001.c202.00e8.0002.00
 !
```

The IS-IS routing is verified with **show ip route isis** on Router A. The result confirms the correct network routes are being exchanged via IS-IS:

```
RouterA#sh ip route isis
      10.0.0.0/8 is variably subnetted, 3 subnets, 2 masks
i L1    10.20.20.0/24 [115/20] via 10.1.1.2, FastEthernet0/1
```

One caveat to know about redistributing routes into IS-IS is that if no metric is assigned, all distributed routes will be automatically assigned a metric value of 0. In IS-IS, the default metric value for each interface is 10. Therefore, redistributed routes could end up with lower metric values than IS-IS learned routes. If there happens to be multiple routes to the same network, one is learned via internal IS-IS routes and another one is learned via redistributed routes. IS-IS would prefer the redistributed routes. It is recommended that at least a metric value of 10 be assigned to redistributed routes. To advertise a connected network of 172.16.20.0/30, the command **redistribute connected** is issued on Router B with a metric of 10:

```
RouterB(config)#router isis
RouterB(config-router)#redistribute connected metric 10
```

Once the command is issued, you can then verify the results on Router A. The **show ip route** command now shows the network 172.16.20.0 is being advertised via IS-IS and the network route is also flagged as an L2 or an IS-IS level-2 type:

```
RouterA#sh ip route
Codes: C - connected, S - static, R - RIP, M - mobile, B - BGP
       D - EIGRP, EX - EIGRP external, O - OSPF, IA - OSPF inter area
       N1 - OSPF NSSA external type 1, N2 - OSPF NSSA external type 2
       E1 - OSPF external type 1, E2 - OSPF external type 2
       i - IS-IS, su - IS-IS summary, L1 - IS-IS level-1, L2 - IS-IS
level-2
       ia - IS-IS inter area, * - candidate default, U - per-user
static route
       o - ODR, P - periodic downloaded static route

Gateway of last resort is not set

      172.16.0.0/30 is subnetted, 1 subnets
i L2    172.16.20.0 [115/20] via 10.1.1.2, FastEthernet0/1
      10.0.0.0/8 is variably subnetted, 3 subnets, 2 masks
i L1    10.20.20.0/24 [115/20] via 10.1.1.2, FastEthernet0/1
C       10.10.10.0/24 is directly connected, FastEthernet0/0
C       10.1.1.0/30 is directly connected, FastEthernet0/1
```

Now, configure a static route on Router B to the LAN C network of 192.168.30.0 and redistribute it into IS-IS. This enables Router A to learn the route as well. To redistribute static routes into IS-IS, the command **redistribute static** is issued on Router B.

```
RouterB(config)#ip route 192.168.30.0 255.255.255.0 172.16.20.2
RouterB(config)#router isis
RouterB(config-router)#redistribute static metric 10
```

As a result, Router A now learns of the route to LAN C network via IS-IS and the network is displayed as an IS-IS level-2 route just like the distributed connected route:

```
RouterA#sh ip route isis
i L2 192.168.30.0/24 [115/20] via 10.1.1.2, FastEthernet0/1
     172.16.0.0/30 is subnetted, 1 subnets
i L2    172.16.20.0 [115/20] via 10.1.1.2, FastEthernet0/1
     10.0.0.0/8 is variably subnetted, 3 subnets, 2 masks
i L1    10.20.20.0/24 [115/20] via 10.1.1.2, FastEthernet0/1
```

To redistribute dynamic routing protocols into IS-IS, the **redistribute** command is configured in the same fashion. The following configurations show how to redistribute RIP, OSPF, and EIGRP into IS-IS respectively:

```
RouterB(config)#router isis
RouterB(config-router)#redistribute rip metric 10
RouterB(config-router)#redistribute ospf 200 metric 10
RouterB(config-router)#redistribute eigrp 200 metric 10
```

As long as those dynamic routing protocols are configured on Router B and Router C correctly and their routes are exchanged, the result of **show ip route isis** on Router A should yield the same result as the one from the static route.

3-5   ANALYZING OSPF "HELLO" PACKETS

Hello packets are periodically sent in OSPF networks to initiate and maintain communications with neighbor routers. The Hello packets contain parameters including specifications for the following:

- **Network Mask:** The mask contains 32 bits in four octets (8-bit groups). The masking is a logical AND operation, and the bits that are set high allow the address data to pass. For example, a network mask of 255.255.255.0 has the first 24 bits set high in the first three octets. The hexadecimal equivalent (base 16) for this network mask is 0xffffff00.
- **Hello Interval:** The time between Hello packets.
- **Router Dead Interval:** The length of time a router neighbor is quiet (no Hello packets) before assuming the neighbor is dead.

OSPF uses a Class D multicast IP address to send out the Hello packets to the neighbors. OSPF networks have been assigned the multicast IP address of 224.0.0.5 for sending Hello packets. Multicast IP addresses for use with multicast protocols are in the range of 224.0.0.0 to 239.255.255.255. This is called the *Class D IP address range*. The IP address range above Class D is called Class E, and addresses

Hello Packets
Periodically sent in link state protocols to initiate and maintain communications with neighbor routers.

Network Mask
A 32-bit value used to divide sections of IP addresses.

Hello Interval
The time between Hello packets.

Router Dead Interval
The length of time a router neighbor is quiet (no Hello packets) before assuming the neighbor is dead.

range from 240.0.0.0 to 254.255.255.255. Class E is called the *IP address experimental range.*

The test network shown in Figure 3-6 was set up so that the transmission of OSPF Hello packets could be viewed. The Wireshark protocol analyzer was installed on computer D1 in LAN D (192.168.1.0 NET). LAN D has been configured to be an OSPF advertised route; therefore, computers in LAN D will receive the OSPF multicasts used to capture the data packets. OSPF broadcasts the LAN address as part of the routed addresses. The multicast is sent to all neighbor OSPF router connections. Figure 3-7 shows the captured data packets for the network. The highlighted line, beginning with the ID of "000001" in the first column, is the first detected occurrence of a data packet on the network. The elapsed time is 5.278.530.840 seconds (column 2). The size of the packet is 82 bytes (column 3). The destination (specified in column 4) is an OSPFIGP_Router multicast. The source IP address is 192.168.1.250, which is the IP address for the router interface. The packet summary (column 6) indicates this is an OSPF Hello from **RID** (router ID) 192.168.200.11.

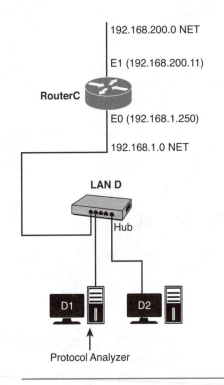

FIGURE 3-6 The test network for capturing the OSPF Hello packets

One of the complex things about OSPF is the assignment of the router ID (RID). The router ID is an IP address chosen from all interfaces on the router. Cisco IOS first examines the loopback address for the router's ID IP address. If a loopback address is not being used, the highest IP address for a router interface is selected as the router ID. In this case, the highest loopback IP address is 192.168.200.11, the IP address for the E1 Ethernet interface. The middle panel in Figure 3-7 shows that the destination address is 224.0.0.5 and defines this as OSPFIGP_Router. **OS-PFIGP** stands for Open Shortest Path First Interior Gateway Protocol, which is a concatenated form of OSPF and IGP. The OSPF protocol is classified as an Interior Gateway Protocol (IGP). **IGP** represents entities under the same autonomous domain (administrative and security policies). Remember, when you specify the OSPF protocol, a process ID number is entered; for example, **router ospf 100**.

OSPFIGP

Open Shortest Path First Interior Gateway Protocol.

IGP

Interior Gateway Protocol.

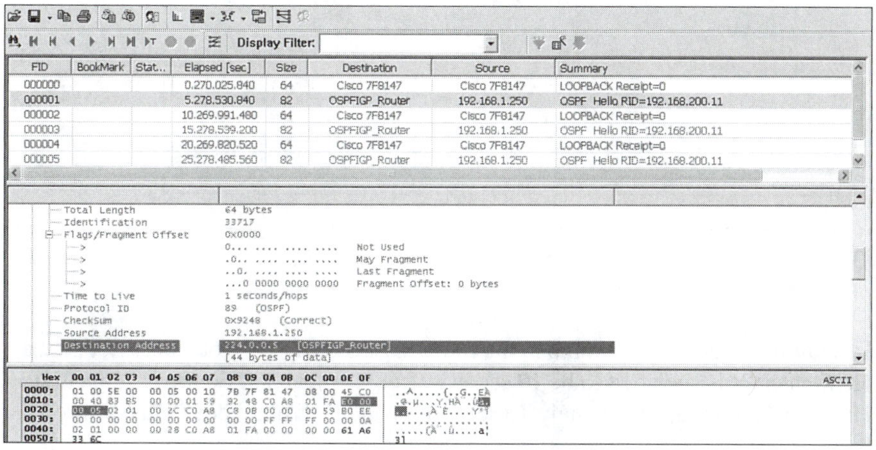

FIGURE 3-7 The captured OSPF multicasts

The bottom panel in Figure 3-7 is the actual data packet displayed in hexadecimal (base 16) code. The highlighted hex code is

E 0 0 0 0 0 0 5

This is the hexadecimal value for 224.0.0.5, the destination IP address of the multicast.

Hexadecimal Value: E 0	0 0	0 0	0 5
Decimal Equivalent: 224	0	0	5

Note

The decimal equivalent of E0 is 14, and $(14 \times 16 + 0) = 224$.

A detailed view of the OSPF packet information is provided in Figure 3-8. This information is available in the Open Shortest Path First (OSPF) window, as shown in Figure 3-8.

```
 Open Shortest Path First
 (OSPF)
   Version                  2
   Type                     1   (Hello)
   Length                   44 bytes
   Router ID                192.168.200.11
   Area ID                  0.0.0.89
   Checksum                 0xB0EE
   AuType                   0   (Null Authentication)
   Authentication           0000000000000000
   Network Mask             255.255.255.0
   Hello Interval           10 seconds
   Optional Capabilities    0x02
     >                      0... ....     Not Used (MBZ)
     >                      .0.. ....     Opaque-LSAs NOT Forwarded
     >                      ..0. ....     Demand Circuit Bit
     >                      ...0 ....     External Attributes Bit
     >                      .... 0...     No NSSA Capability
     >                      .... .0..     No Multicast Capability
     >                      .... ..1.     External Routing Capability
     >                      .... ...0     No Type of Service Routing Capability
   Router Priority          1
   Router Dead Interval     40 seconds
   Designated Router        192.168.1.250
   Backup Designated Router 0.0.0.0
```

FIGURE 3-8 A detailed view of the OSPF packet information

In addition to the version number, the router ID is listed (192.168.200.11), and the
Hello interval is specified to be 10 seconds. Looking again at Figure 3-7, the OSPF
Hello packets are approximately 10 seconds apart. The router dead interval is 40
seconds.

This section has demonstrated how to use the Surveyor Demo Protocol Analyzer to
capture OSPF "Hello" packets. Figures 3-7 and 3-8 and the accompanying text explained how to extract information from the captured packets.

SUMMARY

This chapter presented examples of configuring routing protocols. The network challenge exercises provided the opportunity for the student to test her or his configuration skill prior to actually configuring a real router. The student should be able to configure and verify operation of the following protocols:

Static
RIP/RIPv2
OSPF
ISIS
EIGRP

Additionally, this chapter examined the steps for route redistribution. The last section examined the OSPF Hello packets.

QUESTIONS AND PROBLEMS

Section 3-1

1. OSPF is (select all that apply)

   a. Open Shortest Path First routing protocol

   b. An open protocol

   c. Developed specifically for TCP/IP networks

   d. Developed specifically for IPX networks

   e. A distance vector protocol

   f. A dynamic routing protocol

   g. A link state protocol

   h. A high consumer of bandwidth

2. In OSPF, route updates are sent in the form of

   a. Link state advertisements

   b. Exchanging routing tables every 30 seconds

   c. Exchanging routing tables every 90 seconds

   d. IETF packets

3. The OSPF routing protocol uses these to verify that a link between two routers is active and the routers are communicating

   a. LSAs

   b. Hello packets

   c. ARP messages

   d. Ping

4. Areas in the OSPF protocol are

    a. Not used

    b. Used to partition a large network into small networks

    c. Used to combine small networks into one large network

    d. An inefficient use of bandwidth

5. Variable length subnet masks

    a. Minimize wasted IP address space when interconnecting subnets

    b. Are not recommended in modern computer networks

    c. Reduce the number of bits required in a subnet mask from 32 to 24

    d. Are the same as classful addressing

6. Which is *not* an advantage of OSPF?

    a. Very easy to implement

    b. Uses VLSM

    c. Link state changes are immediately reported

    d. Not a proprietary protocol

7. Define router flapping.

8. The command structure for enabling OSPF routing on a router is

    a. **router ospf**

    b. **router ospf** [*area*]

    c. **routing protocol ospf**

    d. **router ospf** [*number*]

9. Another name for wild card bits is

    a. OSPF pass-through bits

    b. Area 0 selection bits

    c. Inverse mask bits

    d. Route selection bits

10. Area 0 is

    a. Used to hide data packets

    b. Root or backbone for the network

    c. Inverse mask bits

    d. Route selection bits

11. Which of the following is *not* a correct statement for configuring a route to run over OSPF? Assume that the OSPF protocol has been enabled.

   a. network 10.10.20.1 1.1.1.1 area 0

   b. network 10.10.20.1 1.0.0.0 area 0

   c. network 10.0.0.0 1.0.0.0

   d. network 10.10.100.1 0.0.0.0 area 0

12. The command **show ip route ospf** is best characterized by which of the following?

   a. Is not valid in OSPF

   b. Displays only the IP routes

   c. Displays only the OSPF routes

   d. Enables OSPF routing

13. The **sh ip route** command is entered on Router B in the campus LAN shown in Figure 3-2. The LAN has been fully configured to run the OSPF protocol.

   a. How many OSPF subnets are running on the network?

   b. Identify the connected C and OSPF O subnets.

14. The **sh ip route** command is entered on Router C in the campus LAN shown in Figure 3-2. The LAN has been fully configured to run the OSPF protocol.

   a. How many OSPF subnets are running on the network?

   b. Identify the connected C and OSPF O subnets.

Section 3-2

15. What are the two topology areas In IS-IS?

16. L1/L2 routers are analogous to what in OSPF?

17. IS-IS was designed as part of the Open System Interconnection (OSI) network layer service called Connectionless Network Service (CLNS). What is a Connectionless Network Service (CLNS)?

18. What command is used to enter the global configuration command in IS-IS?

19. What command is used to Instruct the router to start6 using the IS-IS routing protocol?

20. To specify the network that will be using IS-IS for routing, which of the following needs to be configured?

    a. The command **clns routing** will need to be configured at each individual interface.

    b. The command **ip router isis** will need to be configured at each individual interface.

    c. The command **ip router isis** will need to be configured globally for the router.

    d. The command **router isis** will need to be configured globally for the router.

    e. None of these answers are correct.

21. What is the command in IS-IS that is used to display adjacencies with its neighbors and the neighbor information?

22. What is the NET address in IS-IS? Also define the area ID, system ID, and NSEL.

23. Identify the NSEL, system ID, and area ID for the IS-IS NET address of 45.0001.0015.b2501.4808.00.

24. Why is the system ID in IS-IS always unique?

25. The command **show ip protocol** is issued on a router as displayed. What is required for routing to take place on the FastEthernet interfaces 0/0 and 0/2?

```
RouterA# sh ip protocol
Routing Protocol is "isis"
  Outgoing update filter list for all interfaces is not set
  Incoming update filter list for all interfaces is not set
  Redistributing: isis
  Address Summarization:
    None
  Maximum path: 4
  Routing for Networks:
    FastEthernet0/0
    FastEthernet0/2
  Routing Information Sources:
    Gateway          Distance       Last Update
    192.168.12.5          115          00:02:44
    192.168.12.65         115          00:02:44
  Distance: (default is 115)
```

26. The command **sh ip route** is issued on a router. What does this information tell you about the 10.20.10.0 network? What does i L1 indicate?

```
Gateway of last resort is not set

     10.0.0.0/24 is subnetted, 7 subnets
i L1    10.20.15.0 [115/20] via 10.20.100.2, FastEthernet0/2
i L1    10.20.10.0 [115/20] via 10.20.200.2, FastEthernet0/1
C       10.20.20.0 is directly connected, FastEthernet0/0
C       10.20.100.0 is directly connected, FastEthernet0/2
```

```
i L1    10.20.150.0 [115/20] via 10.20.100.2, FastEthernet0/2
                    [115/20] via 10.20.200.2, FastEthernet0/1
C       10.20.200.0 is directly connected, FastEthernet0/1
```

27. IS-IS can load balance which of the following?

    a. The network traffic over equal cost paths

    b. On the unequal cost paths

    c. On the unequal cost paths, only the best path is installed into the routing table

    d. All of the above

28. In IS-IS, what is the IS-IS cost value assigned to the interface and its default value?

29. The following sequence of commands is entered on a router running IS-IS for the 3 router campus network shown in Figure 3-3:

    ```
    RouterA(config)#int fastEthernet 0/1
    RouterA(config-if)#isis metric 20
    ```

Section 3-3

30. *EIGRP* stands for

    a. Enhanced Interior Routing Protocol

    b. Enhanced Interior Gateway Routing Protocol

    c. Enhanced Internet Gateway Routing Protocol

    d. None of these answers are correct

31. The command for enabling EIGRP on a router is

    a. **router igrp** [as number]

    b. **router eigrp**

    c. **router eigrp** [as number]

    d. **router eigrp enable**

32. The command **network 10.10.0.0** is entered on a router after EIGRP has been enabled. Define what this means.

33. What router command can be used to verify EIGRP is running on the router?

    a. **show run**

    b. **show ip int brief**

    c. **show history**

    d. **show ip protocol**

34. What router command will show how many subnets are configured?

    a. **show run**

    b. **show ip int brief**

    c. **show list**

    d. **show ip route**

35. What router command will show whether the router is exchanging routes?

    a. **show run**

    b. **show ip int brief**

    c. **show list**

    d. **show ip route**

36. The **sh ip route** command is entered on RouterA in the campus LAN shown in Figure 3-4. The LAN has been fully configured to run the EIGRP protocol.

    a. How many EIGRP subnets are running on the network?

    b. Identify the connected C and EIGRP D subnets.

37. The **sh ip route** command is entered on Router B in the campus LAN shown in Figure 3-4. The LAN has been fully configured to run the EIGRP protocol.

    a. How many EIGRP subnets are running on the network?

    b. Identify the connected C and EIGRP D subnets.

38. EIGRP can use which of the following to determine the best path to a destination?

    a. Bandwidth

    b. Delay, reliability

    c. Load

    d. All of these answers are correct

    e. None of these answers are correct

39. By default, only bandwidth and delay are used by Cisco to calculate the composite metric. Define bandwidth and delay.

40. What is the command to view the composite metric of the current EIGRP topology?

41. What does the command **bandwidth 1000** do?

42. What does the command **delay 1000** do on a router?

Section 3-4

43. Define routing redistribution.

44. List three reasons why routing distribution is necessary.

45. What is the command issued to redistribute the connected networks on a router?

46. Identify the prompt and the command to redistribute a connected network in RIP.

47. Identify the router prompt and the command to redistribute a static route.

48. Identify the router prompt and the command to redistribute an OSPF route into RIP. Use a process ID of 100 and a metric of 2.

49. Identify the router prompt and the command to redistribute an EIGRP route into RIP. Use an AS number of 100 and a metric of 5.

50. Identify the router prompt and the command to redistribute an IS-IS route into RIP. Use a metric of 10.

51. What is the router prompt and the command that is used to distribute classless networks, such as static routes?

52. The following information is displayed when redistributing a static route. What does this mean?

```
RouterB(config-router)#redistribute static
% Only classful networks will be redistributed
```

53. What is the command to redistribute EIGRP routes into RIP? Assume an AS ID of 100 and a hop count metric of 5. Also, include the command that prevents the warning about classful subnets.

54. What is the router prompt and the command to redistribute RIP into OSPF?

55. What is the router prompt and the command to redistribute IS-IS into OSPF?

56. The following command is entered on a router:

```
Router(config-router)#redistribute rip metric 100000 10 255 1
1500
```
What does this command do and what are the values indicating?

57. What does the following command do?

```
RouterB(config-router)#default-metric 100000 10 255 1 1500
```
58. What is the router prompt and the command to redistribute RIP into IS-IS? Use a metric of 5.

59. What is the router prompt and the command to redistribute OSPF into IS-IS? Use a process id of 150 and a metric of 10.

60. What is the router prompt and the command to redistribute EIGRP into IS-IS? Use an AS of 150 and a metric of 10.

Section 3-5

61. The hello interval is

    a. The time between Hello packets

    b. The timing of the Hello header

    c. The timing of the router dead interval

    d. None of these answers are correct

62. OSPF multicasts are sent out as what class of address?

    a. Class A

    b. Class B

    c. Class C

    d. Class D

    e. Class E

63. OSPF Hello packets are sent out every

    a. 30 seconds

    b. 90 seconds

    c. 10 seconds

    d. None of these answers are correct

64. The Router ID (RID) in OSPF Hello packets is chosen from

    a. Loopback addresses

    b. OSPF 16P_Router

    c. Highest IP address on an interface

    d. a and c

    e. b and c

Critical Thinking

65. You are configuring a router connection to a remote network. What protocol would you select if there is only one network route to the remote network? Explain why you selected the protocol.

66. You are configuring the routing protocols for a small network. What routing protocol would you select and why?

67. Router A and Router B are connected and both are running OSPF protocol. The following is a sample configuration from Router A:

```
interface FastEthernet0/0
 ip address 10.10.3.1 255.255.255.252
 duplex auto
 speed auto
!
interface FastEthernet0/1
 ip address 10.100.1.1 255.255.255.0
 duplex auto
 speed auto
!
ip route 172.16.0.0 255.255.0.0 Null 0
!
                           router ospf 200
network 10.0.0.0 0.255.255.255 area 0
```

```
                    redistribute static subnets
        !
The following is a sample configuration from RouterB:
interface FastEthernet0/0
 ip address 10.10.3.2 255.255.255.252
 duplex auto
 speed auto
!
interface FastEthernet0/1
 ip address 172.16.10.1 255.255.255.0
 duplex auto
 speed auto
!
                         router ospf 200
network 10.0.0.0 0.255.255.255 area 0
                 redistribute connected subnets
        !
```

What routes are redistributed from Router A's and Router B's perspectives?
What would be an effect of using the **redistribute connected** instead of **redistribute connected subnets** on Router B?

68. From the **show ip route** output and the configuration of Router A, reconstruct
the rough network diagram from the point of view of Router A. Label the interfaces and draw the connections to other router(s). Specify the network learned
from the connected router(s).

```
###########Configuration File###################
!
version 12.3
service timestamps debug datetime msec
service timestamps log datetime msec
no service password-encryption
!
hostname RouterA
!!
interface FastEthernet0/0
 ip address 192.168.3.1 255.255.255.252
 duplex auto
 speed auto
!
interface Serial0/0
 ip address 192.168.1.1 255.255.255.252
 clock rate 2000000
!
interface FastEthernet0/1
 ip address 10.100.1.1 255.255.255.0
 duplex auto
 speed auto
!
router eigrp 200
 network 10.0.0.0
 network 192.168.0.0 0.0.255.255
 no auto-summary
```

```
!
############IP Route####################

RouterA#sh ip route
Codes: C - connected, S - static, R - RIP, M - mobile, B - BGP
       D - EIGRP, EX - EIGRP external, O - OSPF, IA - OSPF inter
area
       N1 - OSPF NSSA external type 1, N2 - OSPF NSSA external
type 2
       E1 - OSPF external type 1, E2 - OSPF external type 2
       i - IS-IS, su - IS-IS summary, L1 - IS-IS level-1, L2 -
IS-IS level-2
       ia - IS-IS inter area, * - candidate default, U - per-user
static route
       o - ODR, P - periodic downloaded static route

Gateway of last resort is not set

     10.0.0.0/8 is variably subnetted, 4 subnets, 2 masks
D       10.8.8.0/23 [90/2172416] via 192.168.1.2, 00:05:30,
Serial0/0
C       10.100.1.0/24 is directly connected, FastEthernet0/1
D       10.200.1.0/24 [90/30720] via 192.168.3.2, 00:14:04,
FastEthernet0/0
     192.168.1.0/30 is subnetted, 1 subnets
C       192.168.1.0 is directly connected, Serial0/0
        192.168.3.0/30 is subnetted, 1 subnets
C       192.168.3.0 is directly connected, FastEthernet0/0
RouterA#
```

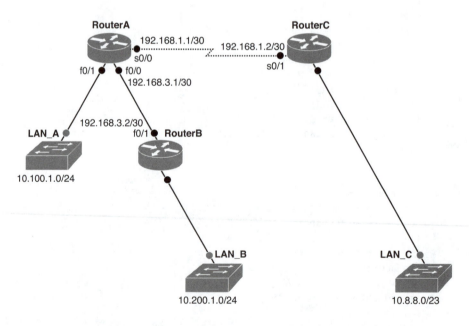

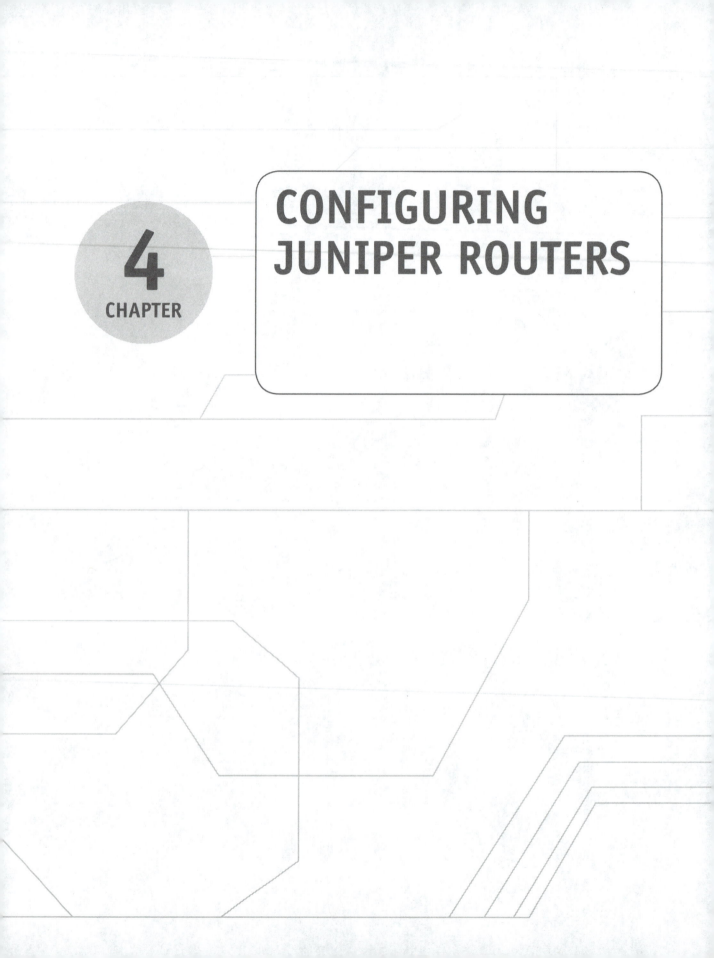

4
CHAPTER

CONFIGURING JUNIPER ROUTERS

Chapter Outline

Objectives

- Understand and identify the difference between the operational and configuration modes
- Understand the basic steps for working in the operational mode
- Understand the steps for configuring the router's interface
- Explain how to configure static, RIP, OSPF, and IS-IS routing
- Understand the steps for route redistribution

Key Terms

JUNOS
{master}
re0 { and re1 { ..
Out of Band Management
PIC
multi-services card
t3/ds3 card
at
oc-3
oc-12
permanent interfaces
Management Ethernet Interface

Internal Ethernet interface
transient interfaces
Inet
preferred
edit routing-options
static
edit protocols rip
show rip neighbor
commit
commit and- quit
show route
show route protocol rip
set protocols ospf area

area **interface** *interface*
hello-interval *seconds*
dead-interval *seconds*
set metric *value*
set protocols isis interface *interface*
show isis adjancency
edit policy-options
set policy-statement
top
export

INTRODUCTION

This chapter examines the steps for basic configuration of a Juniper router. There are distinct differences between the Juniper router configurations compared to Cisco IOS; however, many of the steps and prompts are similar to Cisco router configuration, as you'll learn. The operating system (OS) used by Juniper routers is called JUNOS. The JUNOS software has two different command modes:

- Operational mode
- Configuration mode

JUNOS
The operating system used by Juniper routers.

The basic commands used in the operational mode of the JUNOS command-line interface (CLI) are presented in Section 4-1. In this chapter, you learn about the {master} prompt and the >, indicating you are now in the operational mode. You also learn about the re0 { and re1 { .. notations that are used to identify the system configuration for the routing engines 0 and 1. In Section 4-2, the steps for configuring the router interface are examined. In addition, the commands for displaying the router interface, configuring the hostname, and assigning an IP address to an interface are examined. Section 4-3 introduces route configuration featuring static, RIP, OSPF, and IS-IS. Section 4-4 examines route redistribution. Juniper takes a different approach when it comes to route redistribution. In the JUNOS software, there is no redistribute command. Unlike Cisco where a route distribution is done in a routing process, Juniper uses its routing policy to inject routing protocols.

4-1 OPERATIONAL MODE

The operational mode is the first mode encountered after logging in to the Juniper router. This mode allows for the following:

1. Monitoring network connectivity (for example, using the **ping** command)

2. Troubleshooting the router interface and network connections

3. Entry point for router configuration

The following examples demonstrate the basic commands used in the operational mode of the JUNOS command-line interface (CLI). The connection to the Juniper router demonstrated in this section is being made via an SSH session (secure telnet); however, a console serial connection can also be made directly with the Juniper router, and this connection is used to make the initial router interface configurations.

The first prompt displayed after connecting to the router is the request for a password. After you correctly enter the password, you enter the router's {master} mode and the **router>** prompt is displayed, indicating that you are in the operational mode. The text preceding the **>** lists the name of the user and the router. In this example, the username is **net-admin** and the router name is **noc**. Juniper routers use the {master} prompt to indicate that you are in the master routing engine mode. This prompt appears only when the Juniper router is equipped with two routing engines, and the two engines are running in a graceful switchover redundancy mode.

The following shows an example of the prompts displayed after establishing the router connection. In this example, the connection is made by net-admin, and this user has superuser privileges. A superuser has root access with full access to all configuration modes. Notice that prompt is **>**, indicating you are now in operational mode.

```
Password:

{master}
net-admin@noc>
```

The question mark (**?**) is used for the universal help command in JUNOS (operating system). For example, the **?** can be entered to see what options are available. It is not necessary to press **Enter** after typing the question mark. The following is a list of the available commands available at the **>** prompt:

```
net-admin@noc> ?

Possible completions:
   clear        Clear information in the system
   configure    Manipulate software configuration information
   file         Perform file operations
   help         Provide help information
   mtrace       Trace mtrace packets from source to receiver.
   monitor      Real-time debugging
   ping         Ping a remote target
   quit         Exit the management session
   request      Make system-level requests
   restart      Restart a software process
   set          Set CLI properties, date, time, craft display text
   show         Show information about the system
   ssh          Open a secure shell to another host
   start        Start a software process
   telnet       Telnet to another host
   test         Diagnostic debugging commands
   traceroute   Trace the route to a remote host
net-admin@noc>
```

> **{master}**
> The prompt indicating you are in the master routing engine mode on a Juniper router.

The question mark can also be added after part of a command is entered. For example, the following is a partial listing of the options with the **show ?** command:

```
{master}

net-admin@noc> show ?
Possible completions:
  Accounting      Show accounting profiles and records
  aps             Show Automatic Protection Switching information
  arp                     Show system Address Resolution Protocol table
entries
  as-path         Show table of known autonomous system paths
  bfd             Show Bidirectional Forwarding Detection
information
  bgp             Show Border Gateway Protocol information
  chassis         Show chassis information
  class-of-service Show class-of-service (CoS) information
  cli             Show command-line interface settings
  configuration   Show current configuration
  connections     Show circuit cross-connect connections
      .
      .
      .
```

The JUNOS operating system has another option that enables the user to enter only part of a command. With this feature, the incomplete command will be completed by JUNOS if the user is still in the operational mode, indicated by the > prompt. This means the user doesn't have to remember the full command. JUNOS will fill in the expected text given the information obtained from the entered keystrokes. This is accomplished by entering a partial command and then pressing the spacebar or the tab key. For example, entering **show in <spacebar>** lists the remaining text of a possible matching command, **terfaces**. Press **Enter** to accept the displayed text. The following is an example:

```
net-admin@noc>show in <spacebar>terfaces <Enter>

Physical interface: at-0/1/0, Enabled, Physical link is Up
  Interface index: 11, SNMP ifIndex: 65
  Link-level type: ATM-PVC, MTU: 4482, Clocking: Internal, SONET mode
  Speed: OC12, Loopback: None, Payload scrambler: Enabled
  Device flags   : Present Running
  Link flags     : 0x01
[...Output truncated...]
```

The following shows another example of entering an incomplete command where an ambiguous result can occur. For example, entering **show c <spacebar>** results in an ambiguous result, because there are many possible matching commands. In this case, the user must type more characters for JUNOS to recognize the desired command, or the user must type the complete command:

```
net-admin@noc> show c<Space>
'c' is ambiguous.
```

```
Possible completions:
  chassis               Show chassis information
  class-of-service      Show class-of-service (CoS) information
  cli                       Show command-line interface settings
  configuration         Show current configuration
  connections           Show circuit cross-connect connections
```

The next example demonstrates the results of entering the **show version** at the **>** prompt. This command can be used to show which version of the Juniper software is running on the router, and it also lists all the software suites installed on the router:

```
--- JUNOS 7.6R2.6 built 2006-07-08 09:43:10 UTC

{master}
net-admin@noc> show version

Hostname: noc
Model: m10i
JUNOS Base OS boot [7.6R2.6]
JUNOS Base OS Software Suite [7.6R2.6]
JUNOS Kernel Software Suite [7.6R2.6]
JUNOS Packet Forwarding Engine Support (M7i/M10i) [7.6R2.6]
JUNOS Routing Software Suite [7.6R2.6]
JUNOS Online Documentation [7.6R2.6]
JUNOS Crypto Software Suite [7.6R2.6]
```

In this case, the router is running the Model: m10i software. The Juniper system is based on the UNIX OS platform. It has a Free BSD UNIX-based kernel with different software systems handling different functions. For example, this listing shows that there is a JUNOS routing software suite, a packet forwarding engine, a crypto software suite, and other software. This individual software suite setup allows one feature to be updated (for example, router updates) without having to update the entire router box.

The next example uses the **show configuration** command to display the Juniper router current configuration. This is analogous to entering the **show running-config** command on a Cisco router.

```
{master}
net-admin@noc>show configuration

version 7.6R2.6;
groups {
    re0 {
        system {
            host-name checs-atm-re0;
            backup-router 10.10.20.250 destination 10.10.10.5/24;
        }
        interfaces {
            fxp0 {
```

```
                    description "Out of Band Management interface re0";
                    unit 0 {
                        family inet;
                    }
                }
            }
        }

    re1 {
        system {
        .
        .
        .
```

re0 { and re1 { ...

This identifies the system configuration for the routing engines 0 and 1.

Out of Band Management

Indicates that an additional interface can be used to connect to the router if the main network is down.

PIC

Physical interface card.

Multi-Services Card

Enables expanded services, such as stateful firewall protection and Network Address Translation.

t3/ds3 card

Provides for a 44.736-Mbps data rate connection.

at

Asynchronous Transmission Mode (ATM).

oc-3

155.52 Mbps.

oc-12

622.08 Mbps.

The re0 { and re1 { .. notations identify the system configuration for the routing engines 0 and 1. (The location of the routing engines on a Juniper router is shown in Figure 4-1.) The statement Out of Band Management indicates that the FastEthernet0 (fxp0) interface is an additional interface that can be used to connect to the router if the main network is down. The term *in band* refers to the primary network connection.

The Juniper router, shown in Figure 4-1, shows several types of physical interface cards (PIC). Each interface plus its name are listed. The **ge** interfaces are gigabit Ethernet. The multi-services card enables expanded services, such as stateful firewall protection, Network Address Translation, and other functions. The t3/ds3 card provides for a 44.736-Mbps data rate connection. The **at** is for Asynchronous Transmission Mode (ATM), and this example also shows oc-3 (155.52 Mbps) and oc-12 (622.08 Mbps) connections. This router also has two routing engines; the duplicate engines are for redundancy.

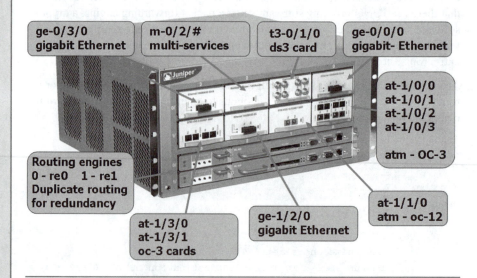

FIGURE 4-1   The physical interfaces on a Juniper router

Network connectivity with other networking devices can be verified with the Juniper router by using the **ping** command, as shown next. This command is being issued in the operational mode, the > prompt.

```
{master}
net-admin@noc> ping 192.168.32.5
{master}
net-admin@noc-atm-re1> ping 172.16.83.3
PING 172.16.83.3 (172.16.83.3): 56 data bytes
64 bytes from 172.16.83.3: icmp_seq=0 ttl=62 time=1.493 ms
64 bytes from 172.16.83.3: icmp_seq=1 ttl=62 time=1.000 ms
64 bytes from 172.16.83.3: icmp_seq=2 ttl=62 time=1.096 ms
64 bytes from 172.16.83.3: icmp_seq=3 ttl=62 time=1.082 ms
64 bytes from 172.16.83.3: icmp_seq=4 ttl=62 time=1.417 ms
64 bytes from 172.16.83.3: icmp_seq=5 ttl=62 time=1.159 ms
^C
--- 172.16.83.3 ping statistics ---
6 packets transmitted, 6 packets received, 0% packet loss
round-trip min/avg/max/stddev = 1.000/1.208/1.493/0.182 ms
```

Table 4-1 provides a summary of the commands and prompts discussed in this section.

TABLE 4-1 Section 4-2 Command/Prompt Summary

Command/Prompt	Description
{master}	Indicates you are in the master routing engine mode on a Juniper router.
>	Prompt for the operational mode.
username@router-name>	Structure preceding the > prompt.
?	Universal help command.
show version	Shows the version of the Juniper software running on the router, and it lists all the software suites installed on the router.
show configuration	Used to display the Juniper router current configuration.
re0 { and re1 { ...	Identifies the system configuration for the routing engines 0 and 1.

4-2 ROUTER CONFIGURATION MODE

There are two types of interfaces for the Juniper routers: permanent and transient. Two types of **permanent interfaces** exist:

- **Management Ethernet Interface:** This interface enables the router to establish both ssh and telnet connections.

- **Internal Ethernet interface:** This interface is the main communications link between the JUNOS software and the router's packet forwarding engines.

Transient interfaces receive and transmit the data packets to and from the network. They are located on the physical interface card and can be inserted and removed at any time. These interfaces must be configured before they can be used.

The Juniper routers also have both a console and auxiliary serial port. The console port is used to establish a serial terminal connection and is used for the initial router configuration. The auxiliary port is used to connect to a modem and for remote access when there is a failure with the regular network connection.

Displaying the Router Interfaces

The command for displaying the router interfaces and their status is **show interfaces brief**. The following shows an example of using this command. Notice that the command is issued at the > operational mode prompt, and the {master} prompt indicates the Juniper router is equipped with two routing engines.

```
{master}
net-admin@noc> show interfaces brief
Physical interface: ge-0/0/0, Enabled, Physical link is Up
  Description: Feed to Network-Backup
  Link-level type: Ethernet, MTU: 1514, Speed: 1000mbps, Loopback:
Disabled,
  Source filtering: Disabled, Flow control: Enabled, Auto-negotiation:
Enabled,
  Remote fault: Online
  Device flags   : Present Running
  Interface flags: SNMP-Traps Internal: 0x4000
  Link flags     : None

  Logical interface ge-0/0/0.0
    Description: Feed to Network-Backup
    Flags: SNMP-Traps Encapsulation: ENET2
    inet   172.16.35.12/30

Physical interface: ge-0/1/0, Enabled, Physical link is Down
  Link-level type: Ethernet, MTU: 1514, Speed: 1000mbps, Loopback:
Disabled,
```

```
  Source filtering: Disabled, Flow control: Enabled, Auto-negotiation:
Enabled,
  Remote fault: Online
  Device flags   : Present Running Down
  Interface flags: Hardware-Down SNMP-Traps Internal: 0x4000
  Link flags     : None

Logical interface ge-0/1/0.0
    Description: Feed to Network-Backup
    Flags: SNMP-Traps Encapsulation: ENET2
    inet  192.168.12.7/30
      .
      .
      .
```

The ge-0/0/0 physical interface shows that it is enabled and the physical link is up. This indicates that the link can pass data packets. The ge-0/1/0 physical interface shows that it is down and the interface is disabled. This listing also shows logical interfaces for ge-0/0/0.0 and 0/1/0.0, which are defined by the IP addresses (**inet**) set for each interface. Notice that each of the two gigabit Ethernet interfaces (ge-0/1/0 and ge-0/0/0) has both a physical and a logical interface setting. The ge-#/#/# notation for the physical interfaces is defined as follows:

> **inet**
> IP address.

- **Media type:** ge (gigabit Ethernet). Other options for media type are Sonet (so), ATM (at), FastEthernet(fxp)
- **Slot number:** 0
- **Slot number on the interface:** 0
- **Port**: 0

The notation for the logical interface lists the media type, slot number, slot number for the interface, and port. It also shows a description, the IP address, and the interface flags. Flags give information like the state or the status of the interface.

Hostname Configuration

The hostname on a Juniper router can be changed by entering the configuration mode. This can be done by entering the **configure** command, which places you in the [edit] mode. Notice that the prompt now has a # after it, indicating that you are in the configuration mode. Next, enter **edit system,** which places you in the [edit system] mode. The hostname of the router is changed by entering the **set hostname** *name* command. The following is an example where the hostname of the router is changed from noc to Juniper. (*Note:* This change will not be implemented until the configuration is saved using the **commit** command.)

> **commit**
> Command used to save changes.

```
net-admin@noc> configure
[edit]
net-admin@noc>#edit system
[edit system]
net-admin@noc># set host-name Juniper
[edit system]
net-admin@noc>#commit
```

```
[edit system]
net-admin@Juniper>#
```

Assigning an IP Address to an Interface

The next example shows how an IP address is assigned to an interface. In this case, the interface is ge-0/0/0. The command **configure** places you in the edit mode. The ge-0/0/0 interface is specified by using the **edit interfaces ge-0/0/0** command. The prompt displays [edit interfaces ge-0/0/0] to indicate that you are configuring the ge-0/0/0 interface. The interface ge-0/0/0 is a physical interface. Next, the logical unit of the physical interface has to be configured. The logical unit 0 is chosen and the command **edit unit 0** is entered.

The notation of the physical interface and the logical unit is ge-0/0/0.0, and this is referred to as logical interface. This is similar to Cisco's way of creating a virtual subinterface. Once this is complete, the IP address can be configured using the **set address** command. In order to configure the IP address, the family protocol will need to be specified. The family inet is a family protocol that supports all the IP traffic. As a matter of fact, inet denotes the IP address in UNIX-based systems. The prompt now changes to [edit interfaces ge-0/0/0 unit 0 family inet]:

```
net-admin@noc> configure
[edit]
net-admin@noc>#edit interfaces ge-0/0/0
[edit interfaces ge-0/0/0]
net-admin@noc>#edit unit 0
[edit interfaces ge-0/0/0 unit 0]
net-admin@noc>#edit family inet
[edit interfaces ge-0/0/0 unit 0 family inet]
net-admin@noc>#set address 192.168.1.1/24
[edit interfaces ge-0/0/0 unit 0 family inet]
net-admin@noc>#
```

preferred
Used after the **ip address** statement to signify the primary IP address.

In the previous chapter, an example of how to configure a secondary IP address on a Cisco router was shown. When the keyword secondary is used after the IP address statement in Cisco, it signifies this is a secondary IP address. On a Juniper router, the same concept exists, but the configuration is done in reverse. The primary IP address is specified with a keyword, but the secondary IP address is not. In this case, we can specify the IP address 192.168.1.1/24 as the primary by issuing the command **set address 192.168.1.1/24 preferred**, then configure the secondary IP addresses without the keyword **preferred**. The following is the configuration of the primary IP address and secondary IP address on a Juniper router:

```
ge-0/0/0 {
    unit 0 {
    family inet {
        address 192.168.1.1/24 {
        preferred;
        }
        address 192.168.2.1/24;
        }
    }
}
```

This section has demonstrated steps for hostname configuration and assigning an IP address to the interface. Although the command sequence is similar to Cisco routers, there are some distinct differences. Table 4-2 provides a summary of the commands and prompts discussed in this section.

TABLE 4-2   Section 4-2 Command/Prompt Summary

username@router-name configure	Command used to enter the configuration mode
{master} [edit]	Places you in the [edit] mode
net-admin@noc> **show interfaces brief**	The command for displaying the router interfaces and their status
username@router-name>#	The # indicates you are in the configuration mode
username@router-name>#**edit system**	Places you in the [edit system] mode
[edit system] net-admin@noc># **set host-name Juniper**	Sets the hostname of the router to Juniper
[edit system] net-admin@noc>#**commit**	Command used to save changes

4-3   CONFIGURING ROUTES ON JUNIPER ROUTERS

This section examines the steps for configuring routes on a Juniper router. The steps for configuring static routes, RIP routing, OSPF, and IS-IS are demonstrated. You might ask what about EIGRP routes? Remember, EIGRP is proprietary to Cisco and is only available on Cisco routers.

Configure STATIC Routes on Juniper Routers

You can configure a static route on a Juniper router by entering the configuration mode. The {master}[edit] prompts should be displayed after you enter this mode, and the # symbol should be displayed. The command **edit routing-options static** places you in the mode to configure the static route. The prompt changes to {master}[edit routing-options static]. The following shows an example:

```
{master}[edit]
net-admin@noc# edit routing-options static

{master}[edit routing-options static]
net-admin@noc#
```

> **edit routing-options static**
> Places you in the mode to configure the static route.

The next step is to configure the static router. This simply requires you to enter the destination IP address / {subnet – CIDR} and next-hop address. The following shows an example:

```
{master}[edit routing-options static]
net-admin@noc# set route 172.16.32.0/24  next-hop 172.16.64.1


{master}[edit routing-options static]
net-admin@noc#
```

To verify the result, the command **show route** is used to display the routing table. To display only the static routes, the command **show route protocol static** is used:

```
net-admin@noc#  show route protocol static

inet.0: 10 destinations, 10 routes (10 active, 0 holddown, 0 hidden)
+ = Active Route, - = Last Active, * = Both
172.16.30.0/24 *[Static/5] 14w1d 22:09:22
                     > to 172.16.65.1 via ge-0/0/0.0
172.16.31.0/24  *[Static/5] 20w3d 15:07:25
                     > to 172.16.64.1 via ge-0/0/1.0
172.16.32.0/24  *[Static/5] 14w1d 22:09:22
                     > to 172.16.64.1 via ge-0/0/1.0
```

The command for adding a default route or default gateway is very similar to adding a normal static route. The following is an example of adding a default route or a default gateway. The command **set route 0.0.0.0/0 next-hop** *IP address* is entered. The all zeroes indicate that the destination and subnet mask are not known and send the packet to the default gateway:

```
{master}[edit routing-options static]
net-admin@noc# set route 0.0.0.0/0  next-hop 172.16.1.1
```

To remove the static route, the command is **del** for delete followed by the route that you want to delete. The following shows an example:

```
{master}[edit routing-options static]
net-admin@noc# del route 172.16.32.0/24  next-hop 172.16.64.1
```

Juniper also offers similar null routes as in Cisco, where packets destined to a matching route will get dropped; however, Juniper provides two different options to drop packets. One is **discard**, which will silently drop any packet that matches a route. Another one is **reject**, which will drop the packet and will generate an ICMP error message "the destination is unreachable" to the source. The following shows an example of using the **reject** and **discard** feature:

```
{master}[edit routing-options static]
net-admin@noc# set route 172.16.0.0/16  reject
net-admin@noc# set route 172.16.0.0/16  discard
```

Configure RIP on Juniper Routers

This section demonstrates how to configure RIP on a Juniper router. The first step is to enter the **configure** command. Notice that this places you in configuration mode, and the # prompt is displayed. Next, enter the command **edit protocols rip**, which places you in the mode to configure RIP routing. Unlike static route configuration, RIP configuration is programmed under the protocols section, not the routing-options section. The prompt changes to {master}[edit protocols rip]. The following shows an example:

edit protocols rip
Places you in the mode to configure RIP routing.

```
{master}[edit]
net-admin@noc# edit protocols rip

{master}[edit protocols rip]
net-admin@noc#
```

The next step is to define a RIP group and place the interfaces that will be participating in RIP routing in the group. These interfaces will be connecting to other RIP devices, and they will be RIP neighbors. The following shows an example of joining the interface ge-0/0/0 to the group rip_group1. The **show** command entered at the prompt displays the configuration under the section. Recall that the protocol family inet is configured at the logical interface level, so the RIP protocol will be configured on the logical interface of ge0/0/0, which is ge-0/0/0.0:

```
{master}[edit protocols rip]
net-admin@noc# # set group rip_group1 neighbor ge-0/0/0.0

{master}[edit protocols rip]
net-admin@noc#show
group rip_group{
      neighbor ge-0/0/0.0;
}
```

When configuring RIP on a Juniper, there is no option to specify the RIP version. This is because JUNOS will automatically configure both versions of RIP. So, it can be connected to either a RIP version 1 device or a RIP version 2 device. The command **show rip neighbor** can be used to display its neighbors.

show rip neighbor
Command used to display RIP neighbors.

```
net-admin@noc# # show rip neighbor
```

Neighbor	State	Source Address	Destination Address	Send Mode	Receive Mode	In Met
ge-0/0/0.0	Up	172.16.10.1	224.0.0.9	mcast	both	1

The result shows that the router the RIP neighbors via the interface ge-0/0/0.0 is up. The destination of RIP updates is a multicast address of 224.0.0.9, which indicates this is using RIPv2. The receive mode is set to receive both RIPv1 and RIPv2. At this point, a Juniper router is equipped with a minimum configuration to receive all RIP routing information from its neighbor. By default, JUNOS does not advertise any RIP routes, unless it is specified in the routing policy. To enable RIP advertisement to its neighbor in a Juniper router, a routing policy to advertise RIP routes has to be created, and then it must be applied to the RIP group. The routing policy is entered under the policy options as follows:

```
{master}[edit policy-options]
net-admin@noc# # set policy-statement advertise_rip term 1 from
protocol rip then accept
```

The **show** command displays the configuration under the policy-options:

```
{master}[edit policy-options]
      net-admin@noc# # show
policy-statement advertise_rip{
     term 1{
             from protocol rip;
             then accept;
     }
}
```

The policy is created, but it is not yet applied. The policy must be applied to the RIP group by the key command **export**. To configure that, we must be out of the policy-options section. The command **top** takes the user out of the current configuration section and back to the top of the configuration mode:

```
net-admin@noc# # top
{master}[edit]
net-admin@noc# # set protocol rip group rip_group1 export advertise_
rip
```

The **commit** command is used to save software configuration changes to the configuration database, and it also activates the configuration on the router. Changes to the configuration are not saved unless you issue the commit command.

```
net-admin@noc# commit
commit complete
```

<table>
<tr><td>

commit and- quit

The command used to save the configuration and exit the configuration mode.

</td><td>

Or you can issue the **commit and –quit** command to commit the configuration and exit the configuration mode:

```
[edit]
net-admin@noc# commit and- quit
```

</td></tr>
<tr><td></td><td>

```
commit complete
exiting configuration mode
net-admin@noc>
```

</td></tr>
<tr><td>

show route

Command used to display all routes.

show route protocol rip

Command used to display only RIP routes.

</td><td>

When the configuration is saved and applied, the routing table information can be verified via the command **show route**, or the command **show route protocol rip** can be used to display only the RIP routes:

```
net-admin@noc# # show route protocol rip
    inet.0: 10 destinations, 10 routes (10 active, 0 holddown, 0
hidden)
```

</td></tr>
</table>

```
+ = Active Route,  - = Last Active,  * = Both
172.16.1.0/24     [RIP/100] 00:03:03, metric 2
                           > via ge-0/0/0.0
172.16.20.0/24    [RIP/100] 00:03:38, metric 2
                           > via ge-0/0/0.0
192.168.2.1/32    [RIP/100] 00:03:19, metric 1
                           > via ge-0/0/0.0
```

Configure OSPF on Juniper Routers

The next example examines configuring the OSPF routing protocol for the Juniper
router using a script. In this case, the current system configuration file is edited with
the required information. The commands in the following OSPF script are set off
with brackets { }. There is an open bracket at the beginning of each command level
and a closing brace at the end for each open brace. The following is an example of
how to configure an OSPF backbone that has two gigabit Ethernet interfaces. You
must be in the [edit] mode, which requires the entry of the **configure** command.
You enter the script after entering the configure mode, which has the [edit] prompt
displayed:

```
net-admin@noc> configure
[edit]
protocols {
    ospf {
        area 0.0.0.0 {
            interface ge-0/0/0.0 {
                hello-interval 5;
                dead-interval 20;
            }
            interface ge-0/0/1.0 {
            hello-interval 5;
            dead-interval 20;
            }
        }
    }
}
```

This configuration is for the backbone (area 0.0.0.0). The two gigabit interfaces are
ge-0/0/0 and ge-0/0/1. The "Hello" interval is being set to 5 seconds and the dead
interval is being set to 20 seconds. The "Hello" interval is how often OSPF "Hello"
packets are sent to other routers in the same area, and the dead interval is how much
time can expire before the other routers in the area assume the router is dead or the
link has failed.

Another way to configure the same information for OSPF is shown next. This
example produces the same result as previously presented for the OSPF routing,
except everything is entered at the command line. The first step is to enter the [edit]
mode using the **configure** command. Next, enter the **set protocols** command followed by the desired settings for the interface. The **set protocols** command and

> **set protocols ospf
> area** *area* **interface**
> *interface* **hello-
> interval** *seconds*
> **dead-interval** *seconds*
> The command for setting
> the protocol to OSPF.

desired settings must be repeated for each interface. Enter the command sequence **commit and- quit** to save the configuration and exit the configuration mode.

```
net-admin@noc> configure
[edit]
user@host# set protocols ospf area 0.0.0.0 interface ge-0/0/0.0 hello-
interval 5 dead-interval 20
[edit]
user@host# set protocols ospf area 0.0.0.0 interface ge-0/0/1.0 hello-
interval 5 dead-interval 20

[edit]
net-admin@noc# commit and- quit

commit complete
exiting configuration mode
net-admin@noc>
```

Similar to Cisco's command **show ip ospf neighbor**, JUNOS has the command **show ospf neighbor**, which displays the following: Interface Address, Interface, State, Router ID, Router Priority, and Dead Timer. An example of using the command is as follows:

```
net-admin@noc> show ospf neighbor

  Address      Interface    State     ID                Pri  Dead
  172.16.64.1  ge-0/0/0.0   Full      10.206.155.171    1    36
  172.16.65.1  ge-0/0/1.0   Full      10.206.155.172    1    32
```

The only information missing from the **show ospf neighbor** command output is the information of the DR (designated router) and BDR (backup designated router). This information can be retrieved from the command **show ospf interface**. Also, the command shows the OSPF area of which the interfaces are connected:

```
net-admin@noc> show ospf interface

Interface   State  Area    DR ID           BDR ID            Nbrs
ge-0/0/0.0  DR     0.0.0.0 10.206.155.171  10.206.155.173    1
ge-0/0/1.0  BDR    0.0.0.0 10.206.155.172  10.206.155.171    1
```

The command to display the OSPF routing table is **show route protocol ospf.** Note the * indicates that the route is active and valid. It is the best route and will be placed in the router's forwarding table. Some of the routes may be in the routing table, but might not be used because they are not the best routes:

```
net-admin@noc> show route protcol ospf
inet.0: 10 destinations, 10 routes (10 active, 0 holddown, 0 hidden)
+ = Active Route, - = Last Active, * = Both
172.16.1.0/24        *[OSPF/30] 9w6d 11:15:25, metric 2
                        > to 172.16.64.1 via ge-0/0/0.0
172.16.20.0/24       *[OSPF/30] 9w6d 11:15:25, metric 2
                        > to 172.16.64.1 via ge-0/0/0.0
```

```
192.168.2.1/32      *[OSPF/30] 9w6d 11:15:25, metric 2
                    > to 172.16.64.1 via ge-0/0/0.0
```

As we learned earlier of how to adjust the OSPF interface cost on a Cisco router, there is also a way on a Juniper router to manually adjust or assign a cost or metric to a particular interface or a path segment to control the flow of the traffic. This is accomplished by way of setting a metric using the **set metric** *value* command, as demonstrated in the following example. In this case, the metric is being set to 5:

> **set metric** *value*
> The command for setting the metric value in OSPF.

```
net-admin@noc> configure
[edit]
net-admin@noc# edit protocols ospf area 0.0.0.0 interface ge-0/0/0.0
[edit protocols ospf area 0.0.0.0 interface ge0/0/0.0]
net-admin@noc# set metric 5
```

The same caution still applies when adjusting the routing metric manually in that one must understand the topology of the network before making any changes. For example, a route could be preferred via a path with hop counts. One must be careful and verify all the routing associated with the change.

Configure IS-IS on Juniper Routers

The next example examines configuring the IS-IS routing protocol for the Juniper router that has two gigabit Ethernet interfaces. You must be in the [edit] mode, so enter the **configure** command. The IS-IS routing is configured under the protocols section.

By default, all interfaces specified as IS-IS interfaces on Juniper routers are both Level 1 and Level 2. To enforce the level, a non-desired level can be disabled on the interface. The following script is an example of configuring the IS-IS routing protocol on interface ge-0/0/0.0 and interface ge-0/0/1.0, where only IS-IS level 1 is enforced. Therefore, IS-IS level 2 is disabled:

```
net-admin@noc> configure
[edit]
protocols {
    isis {
      interface ge-0/0/0.0 {
      }
      interface ge-0/0/1.0 {
            level 2 disable;
      }
    }
}
```

Another way to configure the same information for IS-IS is shown next. This example produces the same result as previously presented, except everything is entered at the command line. Enter the [edit] mode by using the **configure** command. Next, enter the **set protocols isis** *interface* command followed by the desired settings for

> **set protocols isis interface** *interface*
> The command for setting the protocol to IS-IS.

the interface. In this case, the desired settings are isis interface ge-0/0/0.0. The set protocols command and desired settings must be repeated for each interface:

```
net-admin@noc> configure
[edit]
user@host# set protocols isis interface ge-0/0/0.0
[edit]
user@host# set protocols isis interface ge-0/0/1.0 level 2 disable
```

The next step is to enable the ISO protocol family on the physical interfaces. ISO must be enabled on all interfaces that will run IS-IS. This is configured under the section interfaces. The following is the configuration script to enable ISO on the interfaces ge-0/0/0.0 and ge-0/0/1.0:

```
net-admin@noc> configure
[edit]
interfaces {
    ge-0/0/0 {
      unit 0 {
      family iso;
      }
    }
    ge-0/0/1 {
      unit 0 {
      family iso;
      }
    }
}
```

The following is the example of how to enable the ISO protocol family via the CLI interface. This same result can be obtained by entering the following set of commands via the CLI interface:

```
net-admin@noc> configure
[edit]
user@host# set interfaces ge-0/0/0 unit 0 family iso
[edit]
user@host# set interfaces ge-0/0/1 unit 0 family iso
```

The last step is to assign the NET address to one of the router's interfaces. Usually, a loopback interface is used. The NET address is part of the family ISO configuration. The following is the command set that will assign a NET address to the loopback 0 interface. The **show interfaces lo0** command displays the configuration that was entered:

```
net-admin@noc> configure
[edit]
user@host# set interfaces lo0  unit 0 family iso address 49.0001.
c190.00e8.0000.00
[edit]
```

```
user@host# show interfaces lo0
unit 0 {
     family inet {
        address 172.16.0.1/32;
     }
     family iso{
        address 49.0001.c190.00e8.0000.00;
     }
 }
```

The configuration will need to be committed before it takes effect. Enter the command sequence **commit and- quit** to save the configuration and exit the configuration mode:

```
[edit]
net-admin@noc# commit and- quit

commit complete
exiting configuration mode
net-admin@noc>
```

To view the IS-IS adjacency status and its connected IS-IS adjacent routers, use the **show isis adjancency** command. The command shows the adjacent routers via their names and their IS-IS level. This command is analogous to the **show ospf neighbor** in Cisco:

> **show isis adjacency**
> The command used to view the IS-IS adjacency status and its connected IS-IS adjacent routers.

```
net-admin@noc> show isis adjacency
IS-IS adjancency database:
Interface   System      L State      Hold (secs)  SNPA
ge-0/0/0.0  RouterX     2 Up         18           0:a:24:b1:21:11
ge-0/0/1.0  RouterY     1 Up         10           0:a:24:b1:22:11
```

The command to display the IS-IS routing table is **show route protocol isis**:

```
net-admin@noc> show route protcol isis
inet.0: 10 destinations, 10 routes (10 active, 0 holddown, 0 hidden)
+ = Active Route, - = Last Active, * = Both
172.16.1.0/24     *[IS-IS/18] 9w6d 11:15:25, metric 20
                   > to 172.16.64.1 via ge-0/0/0.0
172.16.20.0/24    *[IS-IS/18] 9w6d 11:15:25, metric 20
                   > to 172.16.64.1 via ge-0/0/0.0
192.168.2.1/32   *[IS-IS/18] 9w6d 11:15:25, metric 10
                   > to 172.16.64.1 via ge-0/0/0.0
```

Table 4-3 provides a summary of the commands and prompts discussed in this section.

TABLE 4-3 Section 4-3 Command/Prompt Summary

Command	Description
net-admin@noc# **edit routing-options static**	This command places you in the mode to configure the static route.
net-admin@noc# # **set route 172.16.32.0/24** next-hop 172.16.64.1	This command specifies the destination IP address / {subnet – CIDR} and next-hop address.
net-admin@noc# # **show route protocol** **static**	This command only displays the static routes.
del	The command used to delete a route.
{master}[edit] net-admin@noc# **edit protocols rip**	Places you in the mode to configure RIP.
{master}[edit protocols rip] net-admin@noc# # **set group rip_group1** neighbor ge-0/0/0.0	Defines the RIP group and places the interfaces that will be participating in RIP routing in the group.
net-admin@noc# # **show rip neighbor**	Command used to display RIP neighbors.
{master}[edit policy-options]	The prompt for entering routing policies.
set protocols ospf area *area* **interface** *interface* **hello-interval** *seconds* **dead-interval** *seconds*	Command used to place the router in the mode to configure OSPF.
set protocols isis interface *(interface)*	Command used to place the router in the mode to configure IS-IS.

4-4   CONFIGURING ROUTE REDISTRIBUTION ON JUNIPER ROUTERS

Juniper takes a different approach when it comes to route redistribution. There is no **redistribute** command in the JUNOS software. Unlike Cisco, where a route distribution is done in a routing process, Juniper uses its routing policy to inject routing protocols. This procedure is the same for any of the routing protocols supported by JUNOS. Juniper's routing policy can be used to control or filter routes, and this is a straightforward process.

The first step in this process is to configure a routing policy to accept a routing protocol that will be injected or redistributed. Next, the routing policy is applied to a routing protocol as an export. JUNOS uses these same steps when a Juniper router is configured to advertise RIP routes. To allow static route injection, a routing policy has to be created to advertise static routes.

The following example shows steps on how to configure a routing policy to accept static routes. The first step is to enter the configuration mode and the edit mode on the router. The command **edit policy-options** is entered and the prompt changes to [edit policy-options]. The policy is next entered using the **set policy-statement** command. A policy can have more than one "term." Each term defines a matched condition and an action. This way, a single policy with multiple matched conditions and actions can be implemented. In this case, the policy name is advertise_static, and it contains one term called 1. The term 1 is to accept any network that comes from static protocol. The **show** command lists the values assigned by the **set-policy-statement**. The changes are then saved using the command **commit and- quit**.

edit policy-options
The command used to enter the mode so the set policy statement can be entered.

set policy-statement
The command for setting a routing policy.

```
{master}[edit]
net-admin@noc# configure
Entering configuration mode

{master}[edit]
net-admin@noc# edit policy-options

{master}[edit policy-options]
net-admin@noc# set policy-statement advertise_static term 1 from
protocol then accept


{master}[edit policy-options]
    net-admin@noc# show
policy-statement advertise_static{
    term 1{
            from protocol static;
            then accept;
    }
}
{master}[edit policy-options]
net-admin@noc# commit and- quit

commit complete
exiting configuration mode
```

Now, a routing policy to advertise static routes is ready. The other routing protocols can be configured in a similar manner. Before we proceed, let's look at the routing policies for redistributing other routing protocols. The following are scripts that are used to set the policy statements for ISIS, OSPF, RIP, and static routing. Similar to the advertise_static policy, a policy called **advertise_connected** is created with a single term called **1**. The term is to accept any network that is directly connected. Similarly, a policy called **advertise_isis** is also created with a single term to accept any network learned from IS-IS protocol. With OSPF, a policy is called advertise_ospf. It contains a single term called 1, which is used to accept any network that is learned via the OSPF backbone area 0. The last policy is **advertise_rip**, which was used in the RIP routing section.

```
{master}[edit policy-options]
    net-admin@noc# # show
policy-statement advertise_connected{
```

```
            term 1{
                  from protocol direct;
                  then accept;
            }
      }
      policy-statement advertise_isis{
            term 1{
                  from protocol isis;
                  then accept;
            }
      }
      policy-statement advertise_ospf{
            term 1{RIP
                  from {
                        protocol ospf;
                        area 0.0.0.0;
                  }
                  then accept;
            }
      }
      policy-statement advertise_rip{
            term 1{
                  from protocol rip;
                  then accept;
            }
      }
```

top

Takes the user out of the current configuration section and back to the top of the configuration mode.

export

The command used to apply a policy.

The next step is to apply a routing policy to a routing protocol. The following example demonstrates how to apply the policy statement **advertise_static** to the OSPF routing protocol. The command **top** takes the user out of the current configuration section and back to the top of the configuration mode. The policy is then applied with the command **export** under the protocol ospf section. The command **set ospf export advertise_static** is issued from the configuration mode to apply the policy. The **show** command is used to verify the configuration under the protocol ospf section. Note the entry under ospf{ lists **export advertise_static**.

```
net-admin@noc# # top
{master}[edit]
net-admin@noc# # edit protocol
{master}[edit protocol]
net-admin@noc# # set ospf export advertise_static
{master}[edit protocol]
net-admin@noc# # show
ospf {
    export advertise_static
    area 0.0.0.0 {
          interface ge-0/0/0.0;
          interface ge-0/1/0.0;
      }
    }
```

The following are static routes on Router noc. These are the routes that are injected into OSPF area 0, as shown in the preceding OSPF configuration. Its neighboring OSPF routers will be receiving these routes. In this example, its OSPF neighbor is Router boc:

```
net-admin@noc# # show route protocol static

inet.0: 10 destinations, 10 routes (10 active, 0 holddown, 0 hidden)
+ = Active Route, - = Last Active, * = Both
172.16.30.0/24 *[Static/5] 14w1d 22:09:22
                   > to 172.16.65.1 via ge-0/0/0.0
172.16.31.0/24  *[Static/5] 20w3d 15:07:25
                   > to 172.16.64.1 via ge-0/0/1.0
```

To verify the redistributed static routes, the command **show route 172.16/16** is issued on Router boc to verify all the routes for network CIDR 172.16.0.0/16.

```
net-admin@boc> show route 172.16/16
inet.0: 28 destinations, 30 routes (28 active, 0 holddown, 0 hidden)
+ = Active Route, - = Last Active, * = Both
192.168.30.0/24 *[OSPF /150] 00:01:00, metric 2, tag 0
      > to 10.0.10.2 via ge-0/1/0.0
192.168.31.0/24 *[OSPF/150] 00:01:00, metric 2, tag 0
      > to 10.0.10.2 via ge-0/1/0.0
```

Indeed, these routes are shown in Router boc's routing table as OSPF routes. These routes now have the preference value of 150, which is a value for OSPF external route. Note that there are no special configurations needed at Router boc. It is just another OSPF router in the backbone area 0. All the configurations are done at Router noc, because it is the redistribution point of other routing protocol into the OSPF backbone.

Table 4-4 provides a summary of the commands and prompts discussed in this section.

TABLE 4-4 Section 4-4 Command/Prompt Summary

Command	Description
set policy-statement *parameters*	The command for setting a routing policy.
set ospf export advertise_static	This command is used to apply the policy.
edit policy-options	The command used to enter the mode so the set policy statement can be entered.
set policy-statement	The command for setting a routing policy.
top	Takes the user out of the current configuration section and back to the top of the configuration mode.
export	The command used to apply a policy.

SUMMARY

This chapter presented an overview of using the JUNOS operating system to configure Juniper routers. Although there are some similarities to Cisco routers, there are also distinct differences. The concepts the student should understand include the following:

- Understand and identify the difference between the operational and configuration modes
- Understand the basic steps for working in the operational mode
- Understand the steps for configuring the router's interface
- Explain how to configure static, RIP, OSPF, and IS-IS routing
- Understand the steps for route redistribution

QUESTIONS AND PROBLEMS

Section 4-1

1. What is the first mode encountered after logging in to the Juniper router?

2. What does the **{master}** prompt indicate in JUNOS?

3. What does the net-admin@noc> prompt indicate in JUNOS?

4. What is the help command in JUNOS?

5. What is the command used to display the Juniper router current configuration?

   Show the proper prompt for the command.

6. The following is displayed after entering the show configuration command.

   ```
   {master}
   net-admin@noc>show configuration
   version 7.6R2.6;
   groups {
   re0 {
   system {
   host-name checs-atm-re0;
   backup-router 10.10.20.250 destination 10.10.10.5/24;
   }
   }
   }
   ```

   What does **re0 {** represent?

7. What command displays the router's current configuration?

8. What command lists the software suites installed on a Juniper router?

9. The command **show configuration** is issued on a Juniper router. The following is part of the information displayed.

```
interfaces {
        fxp1 {
            description "Out of Band Management interface
re0";
            unit 0 {
                family inet;
```

What does the statement, "Out of Band Management" indicate?

Section 4-2

10. What is a management Ethernet interface?

11. What is an internal Ethernet interface?

12. What are transient interfaces?

13. What is the command for displaying the router interfaces and their status?

14. What is the command sequence to change the hostname on a Juniper router to Piyasat?

15. Can the following command sequence be used to change the IP address on a Juniper router interface?

```
net-admin@noc> configure
[edit]
net-admin@noc>#edit interfaces ge-0/0/0
[edit interfaces ge-0/0/0]
net-admin@noc>#edit unit 0
[edit interfaces ge-0/0/0 unit 0]
net-admin@noc>#edit family inet
[edit interfaces ge-0/0/0 unit 0 family inet]
net-admin@noc>#set address 192.168.1.1/24
[edit interfaces ge-0/0/0 unit 0 family inet]
net-admin@noc>#
```

16. A Juniper router has been assigned the IP address 192.168.12.1 to its ge-0/0/1 interface. This is to be the preferred IP address. An IP address of 192.168.22.1 is to be the secondary IP address. List the command sequence to configure the preferred route off the ge-0/0/1.

17. The hostname for a Juniper router has been entered. What is the command that is used to save the changes? List the command, the prompt, and the mode.

18. The **show interfaces** command is entered. What does the following mean?

```
 Physical interface: ge-0/0/0, Enabled, Physical link is Up
```

19. What is the meaning of the ge-#/#/# notation for the physical interfaces on a juniper router?

Section 4-3

20. What prompts are displayed after entering the edit mode on a Juniper router?

21. What command places you in the mode to configure the static route?

22. What prompts are displayed after entering the **edit routing-options static** command?

23. You are configuring a static route on a Juniper router. The destination network is 192.168.12.0, the subnet mask is 255.255.255.192, and the next hop address is 10.10.200.2. Specify the command for configuring the static route.

24. What is the command for setting the default gateway to 10.10.200.2?

25. List the command used to delete or remove the static route to the destination network 192.168.12.0, the subnet mask is 255.255.255.192, and the next hop address is 10.10.200.2.

26. The following command is entered:

    ```
    net-admin@noc# # set route 192.168.10.0/24  reject
    ```
    What does this do?

27. List the command used to enter the mode to configure RIP routing. Indicate the mode and prompt along with the command.

28. What is the command that joins the interface ge-0/0/0 to the rip_group1?

29. What is the command for configuring the Juniper router to run RIPv2?

30. List the command used to save the configuration file in JUNOS.

31. List the command used to save the configuration file and quit.

32. The following information is entered on a Juniper router. What does this mean?

33. List the script entry for setting the dead interval for OSPF to 40 seconds.

34. List the command used at the command-line interface for setting OSPF to run on the ge-0.0.1.0 interface.

    Use an area of 0.0.0.0, a hello interval of 10, and a dead interval of 40.

35. List the command and the prompt for displaying the Interface Address, Interface, State, Router ID, Router priority, and Dead Timer in OSPF.

36. What command can be used to display the backup designated router in OSPF? List the command and the prompt.

37. What command can be used to display the designated router in OSPF? List the command and the prompt.

38. What level are interfaces in IS-IS on a Juniper router?

39. List the command-line sequence to enable the IS-IS protocol on the ge-0/0/0 interface.

40. List the command-line sequence to set the NET address to one of the router's interfaces to

    49.0002.d111.00e3.0000.00.

41. List the prompt and the command to display the IS-IS routing table.

42. List the prompt and the command to view the IS-IS adjacency status and its connected IS-IS adjacent routers.

Section 4-4

43. How does Juniper establish route redistribution on a router?

44. What is the purpose of the following command?

```
net-admin@noc# set policy-statement advertise_static term 1 from
protocol then accept
```

45. Create a script that will define a policy that advertises connected with the single-term "2." List the script.

46. What command in JUNOS takes the user out of the current configuration section and back to the top of the configuration mode?

47. A Juniper router is running OSPF. List the command that is used to apply a static policy.

48. What does the following script do?

```
policy-statement advertise_ospf{
    term 1{RIP
        from {
            protocol ospf;
            area 0.0.0.0;
        }
        then accept;
    }
}
```

49. What does the following script do?

```
policy-statement advertise_rip{
    term 1{
        from protocol rip;
        then accept;
    }
}
```

50. What command is used to apply a policy in JUNOS?

Critical Thinking Questions

51. The following information is displayed. What do metric 4, metric 2, and metric 1 mean?

```
net-admin@noc# # show route protocol rip
    inet.0: 10 destinations, 10 routes (10 active, 0 holddown, 0
hidden)
+ = Active Route, - = Last Active, * = Both
172.16.1.0/24    [RIP/100] 00:03:03, metric 2
                    > via ge-0/0/0.0
172.16.20.0/24    [RIP/100] 00:03:38, metric 2
                    > via ge-0/0/0.0
192.168.2.0/24    [RIP/100] 00:04:27, metric 4
                    > via ge-0/0/0.1
224.0.0.9/32    [RIP/100] 00:03:19, metric 1
                    > MultiRecv
```

52. Issue the command to set OSPF to run on the ge-0.0.0.0 interface. Use an area of 0.0.0.0 and a metric of 10. List the command and the prompt.

53. List the script to disable the level 2 interface on the ge-0/0/0.0 interface.

54. The following information is displayed after entering the **show interfaces** command. Describe what information is displayed.

```
net-admin@noc>show interfaces

Physical interface: at-0/1/0, Enabled, Physical link is Up
  Interface index: 11, SNMP ifIndex: 65
  Link-level type: ATM-PVC, MTU: 4482, Clocking: Internal, SONET
mode
  Speed: OC12, Loopback: None, Payload scrambler: Enabled
  Device flags   : Present Running
  Link flags     : 0x01
```

55. Provide the OSPF configuration for RouterJuniper and RouterCisco in order to connect them to the OSPF backbone 0. The following are their interfaces configuration:

```
RouterJuniper:
interfaces {
    ge-0/0/0 {
        description "Connection to RouterCisco";
        unit 0 {
            family inet {
                address 192.168.145.45/30;
            }
        }
    }
    ge-0/1/0 {
        description "Network 10";
        unit 0 {
            family inet {
                address 10.206.0.1/16;
            }
        }
    }
}

RouterCisco:
 !
interface GigabitEthernet0/1/1
 description Connection to RouterJuniper
 ip address 192.168.145.46 255.255.255.252
 negotiation auto
!
 !
interface GigabitEthernet0/1/2
 description Network 172
 ip address 172.16.0.1 255.255.252.0
 negotiation auto
!
```

5

CHAPTER

CONFIGURING AND MANAGING THE NETWORK INFRASTRUCTURE

Chapter Outline

Objectives

- Describe the steps for obtaining a domain name
- Describe the steps for getting IP addresses assigned to your network
- Understand the purpose of the DHCP server
- Describe the use of NAT and PAT and how these technologies differ
- Understand the function of the DNS server
- Describe the purpose of SNMP

Key Terms

IANA
gTLDs
ccTLDs
.int
in-addr.arpa
RIRs
AS
ICANN
ARIN
domain registrars
whois protocol
BOOTP
DHCP
Lease Time
DHCP Discover
DHCP Offer
DHCP Request
DHCP ACK
ipconfig/release
ipconfig /renew
Automatic Private IP addressing (APIPA)
Unicast

ip helper [*ip address of the DHCP server*]
MT Discover
MT Offer
MT Request
MT ACK
ARP broadcast
SOHO
binding
Network Address Translation (NAT)
Port Address Translation (PAT)
local address
global address
static NAT
dynamic NAT
NAT overload
DNS
Forward Domain Name Service
Reverse Domain Name Service
Root Hints file (root.hints)

TLD
Country Domain
Dig (Domain Information Groper)
nslookup
authoritative name server
non-authoritative answer
FQDN
PQDN
RR
SOA
A record (Address record)
PTR record (Pointer record)
CNAME record (Canonical name record)
NS record
MX record
TXT record
SPF
SRV record

INTRODUCTION

This chapter examines the issue of configuring and managing the network infrastructure. Section 5-1 addresses the procedure used to obtain a domain name for your network and the steps required to get IP addresses assigned to your network. After you have an IP address assigned to your network, you will have to manage the IP assignment.

Section 5-2 discusses IP management with DHCP. DHCP simplifies the steps for IP assignment by dynamically assigning IP addresses as they are needed. This section also examines the deployment of the DHCP relay function that is provided by a router.

Public IP addresses are a commodity and the network administrator must be aware of the techniques used to properly manage the existing pool of IP addresses. This is discussed in Section 5-3, which examines the techniques for scaling the network with NAT and PAT. The steps for configuring NAT and PAT on a router are also presented.

Section 5-4 looks at the Domain Name Service (DNS). The purpose of the DNS server is to translate a human readable name to an IP address or an IP address to a domain name. This section also examines the DNS tree hierarchy and the many DNS services currently available.

5-1 DOMAIN NAME AND IP ASSIGNMENT

There are two key elements used by the general population when accessing websites on the Internet. One is the Internet name of the website and the other is its public IP address. These two elements go hand in hand. People generally connect to Internet services via Internet hostnames, (for example, www.example.com), but behind the scenes, the Internet name is translated to a public IP address. Both the IP address assignment and the Internet domain name are governed at the highest level by the Internet Assigned Numbers Authority (**IANA**).

IANA is one of the Internet's oldest organizations and was set up to be in charge of the Internet management authorities or registration authorities. IANA has three primary functions:

1. **Domain name management**: IANA manages the DNS root zone for the generic (g) top-level domains (**gTLDs**), such as .COM, .NET, .ORG, .INFO, and country-code (cc) top-level domains (**ccTLDs**), such as .US, .UK, and .AU. IANA maintains the **.int** (intergovernmental) domain registries, which are exclusive registrations for intergovernmental treaty organizations, such as the United Nations (un.int) and NATO (nato.int), Asnthe.int, .arpa domains, and an IDN practices resource. IANA maintains the .arpa domain registries, which include the in-addr.arpa domain. The **in-addr.arpa** is the reverse DNS lookup for IPv4 addresses on the Internet. IANA also maintains the IDN (Internationalized

---

IANA

Internet Assigned Numbers Authority, which is responsible for the global coordination of the DNS Root, IP addressing, and other Internet Protocol resources.

gTLDs

Generic (g) top-level domains. Includes .com, .net, .org, and .info.

ccTLDs

Country-code (cc) top-level domains. Includes .us, .uk, .ca, and .au.

.int

Intergovernmental domain registries is used for registering organizations established by international treaties between or among national governments.

in-addr.arpa

The reverse DNS lookup for IPv4 addresses on the Internet.

Domain Name) practices repository known as the language table registry. This allows for domain name registration containing international characters (for example, müller.info).

2. **Number resources management**: IANA coordinates the global pool of IP addresses, which include both IPv4 and IPv6. To coordinate the global effort of IP address allocation more effectively, IANA delegates the allocation to the regional Internet registries (**RIR**), each of which is responsible for a different area. The five RIRs accounting for the different regions of the world are as follows:

   - **AfriNIC**: Africa Region
   - **APNIC**: Asia/Pacific Region
   - **ARIN**: North America Region
   - **LACNIC**: Latin America and some Caribbean Islands
   - **RIPE NCC**: Europe, the Middle East, and Central Asia

   IANA is also responsible for the **AS** (Autonomous System) number allocation, which is used in BGP to route Internet traffic. This allocation is delegated to the RIRs the same as the IP address allocation.

3. **Protocol Assignments**: IANA is also responsible for maintaining the registries of protocol names and numbers used in the Internet today. These protocol-numbering systems are managed by IANA in conjunction with standards bodies.

Today, IANA is working under the direct support from the Internet Corporation of Assigned Names and Numbers (**ICANN**); however, these organizations do not directly allocate IP address space nor do they register domain names for the general public. In North America, IP addresses are assigned by the American Registry for Internet Numbers (**ARIN**). The web address for ARIN is http://www.arin.net. ARIN assigns IP address space to Internet service providers (ISP) and end users, but only to those who qualify. To qualify requires that the ISP or end user be large enough to merit a block of addresses.

When ARIN allocates a block of addresses to the ISP, the ISP will then issue addresses to their customers. For example, Telco could be the ISP that has a large block of IP addresses and issues an IP address to a user. It is also possible for a local ISP to be assigned a block of IP addresses from ARIN, but the local ISP must have a large number of users.

ARIN also assigns end users IP addresses. Once again, the end user must qualify to receive a block of addresses from ARIN. This usually means that the end user must be large. For example, many universities and large businesses can receive a block of IP addresses from ARIN; however, most end users will get their IP addresses from an ISP (for example, Telco) or have IP addresses assigned dynamically when they connect to the ISP.

Today, available IPv4 address space is limited. It is predicted that the available IPv4 space will be totally depleted within a few years. As a result, it has become increasingly difficult to acquire IPv4 space from ARIN. In fact, it is next to impossible to acquire Class B IP space nowadays; however, it is possible to buy a pool of IP addresses from the ISP, but the larger the IP range, the more expensive it is. There

RIRs

Regional Internet registries. The RIRs are the organizations that actually allocate IP addresses to ISPs.

AS

Autonomous System. These numbers are used by various routing protocols and are a collection of connected Internet Protocol (IP) routing prefixes.

ICANN

Internet Corporation of Assigned Names and Numbers. This organization coordinates the Domain Name System (DNS), Internet Protocol (IP) addresses, space allocation, protocol identifier assignment, generic (gTLD), country code (ccTLD), top-level domain name system management, and root server system management functions.

ARIN

American Registry for Internet Numbers. Allocates Internet Protocol resources; develops consensus-based policies; and facilitates the advancement of the Internet through information and educational outreach.

is good news, however. There is a big push by the Internet community to transition to IPv6. There are more abundant resources of IPv6 addresses available, and it is much easier to acquire IPv6 address space. This is being used to encourage people to make the transition to IPv6 (which is covered in Chapter 8, "IPv6").

The Internet hostname is a subset of the Internet domain name that people can identify with. For example, **www.example.com** is a web server for the domain example.com. The Internet domain name is the identity of the organization. The first step to obtain an Internet domain name is to find a domain name registrar. The **domain registrar** has control over the granting of domains within certain Top Level Domains (TLD). IANA and ICANN do not directly register domain names for the general public. ICANN delegates the top-level domain (TLD) registry to other companies or organizations. A couple of the most notable TLD registrars are Verisign, which is a company authorized to operate the TLD for .com and .net, and Educause, which is an organization operating the TLD for the .edu domain. The company Verisign, delegates the responsibilities further to other domain registrars like networksolutions.com, godaddy.com, tucows.com, and so on.

An Internet domain can be purchased from any of these registrars. When you get on the registrar's website, you will be able to input a domain name. The registrar will check whether the domain name is available. If the domain name is available, you will be prompted to complete the application for the domain name and enter the DNS servers that are to be used to host the domain. The DNS servers will be assigned an IP address and names. When the network's DNS servers are placed online, the root servers will point to the network's DNS servers. These DNS servers then become the authoritative DNS servers for the domain.

The registration for both the IP address and the Internet domain name can be verified using the **whois protocol** in a Linux environment. The *whois* protocol queries databases that store user registration information of an Internet domain name and IP space. The *whois* information gives the ownership information that includes the point of contact of a resource. There are many *whois* servers that are accessible via the web interface. All of these derive from the simple UNIX line command **whois**, which is still available today. The following example shows the result of the **whois** command entered at a UNIX prompt for the domain "example.com."

```
[admin@noc ~]$ whois  example.com
[Querying whois.verisign-grs.com]
[whois.verisign-grs.com]


Whois Server Version 2.0


Domain names in the .com and .net domains can now be registered with
many different competing registrars. Go to http://www.internic.net for
detailed information.

   Domain Name: EXAMPLE.COM
   Registrar: RESERVED-INTERNET ASSIGNED NUMBERS AUTHORITY
   Whois Server: whois.iana.org
   Referral URL: http://res-dom.iana.org
   Name Server: A.IANA-SERVERS.NET
   Name Server: B.IANA-SERVERS.NET
```

```
       Status: clientDeleteProhibited
       Status: clientTransferProhibited
       Status: clientUpdateProhibited
       Updated Date: 14-aug-2011
       Creation Date: 14-aug-1995
       Expiration Date: 13-aug-2012

>>> Last update of whois database: Tue, 07 Feb 2012 03:55:40 UTC <<<
```

It is surprising that the domain example.com is actually a reserved domain registered by IANA. The domain has two authoritative domain name servers of a.iana-servers.net and b.iana-servers.net. The following example shows the whois result when querying an IP space of 10.0.0.0:

```
[admin@noc ~]$ whois 10.0.0.0
[Querying whois.arin.net]
[whois.arin.net]
#
# Query terms are ambiguous. The query is assumed to be:
#     "n 10.0.0.0"
#
# Use "?" to get help.
#


#
# The following results may also be obtained via:
# http://whois.arin.net/rest/nets;q=10.0.0.0?showDetails=true&showARIN
=false&ext=netref2
#


NetRange:       10.0.0.0 - 10.255.255.255
CIDR:           10.0.0.0/8
OriginAS:
NetName:        PRIVATE-ADDRESS-ABLK-RFC1918-IANA-RESERVED
NetHandle:      NET-10-0-0-0-1
Parent:
NetType:        IANA Special Use
Comment:        This block is used as private address space.
Comment:        Traffic from these addresses does not come from IANA.
Comment:        IANA has simply reserved these numbers in its database
Comment:        and does not use or operate them. We are not the source
Comment:        of activity you may see on logs or in e-mail records.
Comment:        Please refer to  http://www.iana.org/abuse/
Comment:
Comment:        Addresses from this block can be used by
Comment:        anyone without any need to coordinate with
Comment:        IANA or an Internet registry. Addresses from
Comment:        this block are used in multiple, separately
Comment:        operated networks.
Comment:
```

```
Comment:          This block was assigned by the IETF in the
Comment:          Best Current Practice document, RFC 1918
Comment:          which can be found at:
Comment:
Comment:          http://www.rfc-editor.org/rfc/rfc1918.txt
RegDate:
Updated:          2011-04-12
Ref:              http://whois.arin.net/rest/net/NET-10-0-0-0-1
OrgName:          Internet Assigned Numbers Authority
OrgId:            IANA
Address:          4676 Admiralty Way, Suite 330
City:             Marina del Rey
StateProv:        CA
PostalCode:       90292-6695
Country:          US
RegDate:
Updated:          2004-02-24
Ref:              http://whois.arin.net/rest/org/IANA

OrgAbuseHandle: IANA-IP-ARIN
OrgAbuseName:     Internet Corporation for Assigned Names and Number
OrgAbusePhone:  +1-310-301-5820
OrgAbuseEmail:  abuse@iana.org
OrgAbuseRef:      http://whois.arin.net/rest/poc/IANA-IP-ARIN

OrgTechHandle: IANA-IP-ARIN
OrgTechName:      Internet Corporation for Assigned Names and Number
OrgTechPhone:   +1-310-301-5820
OrgTechEmail:   abuse@iana.org
OrgTechRef:       http://whois.arin.net/rest/poc/IANA-IP-ARIN

#
# ARIN WHOIS data and services are subject to the Terms of Use
# available at: https://www.arin.net/whois_tou.html
#
```

The IP space of 10.0.0.0, which is a well-known private IP address range, is registered as a reserved private IP address block by IANA. The information shows the ownership information (IANA), as well as the point of contacts for the IP space. (Note: This is listed under OrgId: and Address:.) Note that the **whois** results for example.com show that the Internet domain name has an expiration date, while the IP address space 10.0.0.0 does not. The expiration date for example.com is listed as **Expiration Date: 13-aug-2012**.

Typically, an Internet domain name is purchased through a domain registrar for one year or multiple years and that sets the expiration date of the domain from the date of purchase. The domain owner can renew the domain name at any time before the expiration date or after the domain expires, as long as it falls within a grace period set by the registrar.

If a user acquires a block of IP addresses from an ISP, the ISP typically imposes a charge of IP space within the contract. If an IP block is acquired through ARIN, there is an annual fee associated with it. Such contractual information is not kept in the *whois* databases.

5-2 IP MANAGEMENT WITH DHCP

This section reviews the hierarchy of DHCP. You will understand how the BOOTP and DHCP processes work, as well as the steps for incorporating DHCP service into a campus network.

An IP address is one of the most basic pieces of information needed for a computer to communicate on a network. An IP address can be configured either manually or it can be assigned dynamically. In the manual process, a network administrator assigns an IP address to a user computer. Then, either the administrator or the user has to configure the computer's network settings with the assigned IP address along with other network parameters, such as the subnet mask, default gateway, domain name, and domain name servers. This can be a tedious process, especially when it involves multiple machines.

This process can be automated to some extent using a program called BOOTP for IP assignment. BOOTP stands for Bootstrap Protocol, and it enables computers to discover their own IP addresses. BOOTP uses UDP as its transport protocol. It utilizes UDP port 67 for BOOTP server (BOOTPS) and UDP port 68 for BOOTP client (BOOTPC). When a client requests an IP address, it is assigned to the Ethernet address (MAC address) based on the BOOTP record. In this case, the IP and MAC addresses have a one-to-one relationship. This means that a MAC address must be preregistered before its static or fixed IP address can be assigned. This makes BOOTP less robust for mobility and less efficient in IP space management.

Dynamic Host Configuration Protocol (DHCP) enhances BOOTP and simplifies the steps for IP assignment even further. DHCP is a superset of BOOTP and runs on the same UDP port numbers. Therefore, it interoperates with BOOTP clients. DHCP's function is to assign a pool of IP addresses to requesting clients. In this process, DHCP requests an IP address from the DHCP server. The DHCP server retrieves an available IP address from a pool of addresses dedicated to the subnet of the requesting client. The IP address is passed to the client, and the server specifies a length of time that the client can hold the address. This is called the lease time. This feature keeps an unused computer from unnecessarily tying up an IP address. DHCP servers will typically grant IP addresses for a limited time and the DHCP clients are responsible for renewing the address before it expires. Along with an IP address, other network settings such as gateway, subnet mask, DNS, Time Server, LDAP server, boot server, and boot filename can be included.

DHCP was originally designed to work on a local physical subnet, where both the DHCP server and the DHCP clients reside in the same LAN. When a computer is configured to obtain an IP address automatically or to use the DHCP option, the typical process of requesting an IP address with DHCP is as follows:

1. The client boots up and broadcasts a DHCP Discover message on its local network. This is a broadcast, meaning that the message is sent to all computers in the LAN.

BOOTP

Bootstrap Protocol. A network protocol used by a network client to obtain an IP address from a configuration server.

DHCP

Dynamic Host Configuration Protocol. The protocol used to assign a pool of IP addresses to requesting clients.

Lease Time

The amount of time that a client can hold an IP address.

DHCP Discover

This is a broadcast, meaning that the message is sent to all computers in the LAN.

---

2. A DHCP server listening on the LAN will take the packet, retrieve an available IP address from the address pool, and send the address to the client in a form of DHCP Offer message. The server sends the IP address and the server will send the lease time and other necessary network parameters, such as subnet mask, default gateway, domain name server, and so on. The DHCP Offer is a unicast message from the server to the client.

3. The client receives the OFFER from the server and agrees to use the lease. It replies back to the server in a form of DHCP Request to formally request and confirm the offered IP with the server. The DHCP Request is a broadcast message.

4. The server receives the REQUEST and sends back a DHCP ACK, which is a unicast packet, back to the client with the same IP information. The client applies the IP address and its network settings to the computer; then, it is ready to make network connections. An example of this process is provided in Figure 5-1.

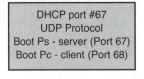

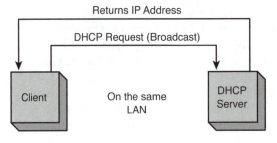

FIGURE 5-1 An example of a DHCP server and client in the same LAN

When a computer boots up, its network software will automatically engage in a DHCP process. However, this process can be invoked by using the command line. In Windows, the command **ipconfig /release** can be used to release the current IP address, then the command **ipconfig /renew** can be used to initiate the DHCP process. A frequently asked question is, "What happens if the DHCP server is not available?"

This scenario happens more often than one would think. A DHCP server could be offline or a broken network path to the server can cause the server to not be available. When this happens, a DHCP client will use a self-assigned IP address known as Automatic Private IP addressing (APIPA). APIPA uses a reserved IP range of 169.254.1.0–169.254.254.255. The client will select a random IP address in that range with a netmask of 255.255.0.0. The client will then send a gratuitous ARP packet asking for that IP address to see if any other machine is using it. If there is an ARP reply by another machine, the client will generate another random IP address and try again. This could be deceiving to a typical user, because it looks as if the machine is getting an IP address; however, the machine will not be able to access the Internet.

DHCP was originally designed to only work in a local network. What if a DHCP server is on the other side of the router (for example, not in the same LAN)? The DHCP Discover and DHCP Request are broadcast messages, and they cannot propagate beyond their broadcast domains. Remember, routers don't pass broadcast addresses, so the DHCP broadcast is not forwarded. This situation requires that a DHCP relay be used, as shown in Figure 5-2. The DHCP relay sits on the same LAN as the client. It listens for DHCP requests and then takes the broadcast packet and issues a **unicast** packet to the network DHCP server. Unicast means that the packet is issued a fixed destination and therefore is no longer a broadcast packet. The DHCP relay puts its LAN address in the DHCP field so the DHCP server knows the subnet the request is coming from and can properly assign an IP address. The DHCP server retrieves an available IP address for the subnet and sends the address to the DHCP relay, which forwards it to the client.

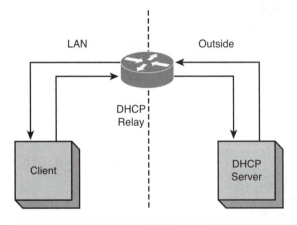

FIGURE 5-2 An example requiring the use of a DHCP relay

Cisco routers have a DHCP relay built in to their operating systems. The router command to enable the DHCP relay is Router(config-if)# **ip helper** [*ip address of the DHCP server*]. Note that this command is issued from the interface that connects to the LAN. In fact, the IP address for the interface is typically the gateway address for the LAN.

It was mentioned earlier that DHCP is a UDP protocol and uses port number 68 for the BOOTP-client and port 67 for the BOOTP-server. (BOOTP and DHCP use the same port numbers.) The BOOTP-client is the user requesting the DHCP service. The BOOTP-server is the DHCP server. The following discussion describes how these services are used in a DHCP request. The DHCP proxy on the router listens for the packets that are going to DHCP or BOOTP port numbers.

DHCP Data Packets

The following is a discussion on the packets transferred during a DHCP request. The network setup is the same as shown in Figure 5-2. The data traffic shown in this example will contain only the data packets seen by the client computer. The Wireshark protocol analyzer was used to capture the data packets. Figure 5-3 provides a portion of the captured data packets. Packet 31 is a DHCP broadcast with a message type discover (**MT Discover**). In Wireshark, this is called the DHCP Discover packet. The destination for the packet is a broadcast, which is identified by the 255.255.255.255 destination IP address. The message source has a MAC address of Apple_f8:e2:dd, and the IP address is 0.0.0.0. The 0.0.0.0 indicates that an IP address has not been assigned to the computer. The source and destination ports are shown in the User Datagram Protocol (UDP) section in Figure 5-3. The source port is 68, which is for the Bootstrap Protocol Client (the computer requesting the IP address). The destination port is 67, the Bootstrap Protocol Server (the DHCP server).

No.	Time	Source	Destination	Protocol	Info
31	15.648973	0.0.0.0	255.255.255.255	DHCP	DHCP Discover - Transaction ID 0x4f4f0a9f
33	15.694065	128.123.3.38	128.123.139.56	ICMP	Echo (ping) request (id=0xa45e, seq(be/le)=0/0, ttl=62)
36	16.796505	128.123.139.1	128.123.139.56	DHCP	DHCP Offer - Transaction ID 0x4f4f0a9f
50	17.797198	0.0.0.0	255.255.255.255	DHCP	DHCP Request - Transaction ID 0x4f4f0a9f
60	17.954954	128.123.139.1	128.123.139.56	DHCP	DHCP ACK - Transaction ID 0x4f4f0a9f
61	17.955472	Apple_f8:e2:dd	Broadcast	ARP	Who has 128.123.139.56? Tell 0.0.0.0
62	18.355727	Apple_f8:e2:dd	Broadcast	ARP	Who has 128.123.139.56? Tell 0.0.0.0
65	18.756145	Apple_f8:e2:dd	Broadcast	ARP	Who has 128.123.139.56? Tell 0.0.0.0
67	19.156603	Apple_f8:e2:dd	Broadcast	ARP	Gratuitous ARP for 128.123.139.56 (Request)
68	19.557224	Apple_f8:e2:dd	Broadcast	ARP	Gratuitous ARP for 128.123.139.56 (Request)
69	19.557823	Apple_f8:e2:dd	Broadcast	ARP	Who has 128.123.139.1? Tell 128.123.139.56

```
Frame 31: 342 bytes on wire (2736 bits), 342 bytes captured (2736 bits)
Ethernet II, Src: Apple_f8:e2:dd (90:27:e4:f8:e2:dd), Dst: Broadcast (ff:ff:ff:ff:ff:ff)
 ▷ Destination: Broadcast (ff:ff:ff:ff:ff:ff)
 ▷ Source: Apple_f8:e2:dd (90:27:e4:f8:e2:dd)
   Type: IP (0x0800)
▽ Internet Protocol, Src: 0.0.0.0 (0.0.0.0), Dst: 255.255.255.255 (255.255.255.255)
   Version: 4
   Header length: 20 bytes
 ▷ Differentiated Services Field: 0x00 (DSCP 0x00: Default; ECN: 0x00)
   Total Length: 328
   Identification: 0x93ec (37868)
 ▷ Flags: 0x00
   Fragment offset: 0
   Time to live: 255
   Protocol: UDP (17)
 ▷ Header checksum: 0x26b9 [correct]
   Source: 0.0.0.0 (0.0.0.0)
   Destination: 255.255.255.255 (255.255.255.255)
 User Datagram Protocol, Src Port: bootpc (68), Dst Port: bootps (67)
   Bootstrap Protocol
```

FIGURE 5-3 The captured DHCP packets

Figure 5-4 shows a reply from the router acting as a relay agent on behalf of the DHCP server. Packet 36 is an offer of the IP address, 128.123.139.56 to the client. This is called the DHCP Offer packet (**MT Offer**). This packet contains the following information, as well as other network information that the client may need to connect to the network:

> Domain name: (nmsu.edu)
> DHCP server: (128.123.3.5)
> Default gateway: (128.123.139.1)
> Leased time: (12 hours)

Packet 50, shown in Figure 5-5, has a message type of **MT Request**, also called the DHCP Request packet. This packet is sent from the client back to the server that has been selected to provide the DHCP service (Note: It is possible for a campus LAN to have more than one DHCP server answering the DHCP request). Even though this packet is destined for the DHCP server as specified by the DHCP Server Identifier (128.123.3.5), the DHCP Request is still a broadcast message to its local network. The packet is picked up by the DHCP relay agent (router) and sent to the DHCP server. This means that the client is accepting the IP address offer.

No.	Time	Source	Destination	Protocol	Info
31	15.648973	0.0.0.0	255.255.255.255	DHCP	DHCP Discover - Transaction ID 0x4f4f0a9f
33	15.694065	128.123.3.38	128.123.139.56	ICMP	Echo (ping) request (id=0xa45e, seq(be/le)=0/0, ttl=62)
36	16.796505	128.123.139.1	128.123.139.56	DHCP	DHCP Offer - Transaction ID 0x4f4f0a9f
50	17.797198	0.0.0.0	255.255.255.255	DHCP	DHCP Request - Transaction ID 0x4f4f0a9f
60	17.954954	128.123.139.1	128.123.139.56	DHCP	DHCP ACK - Transaction ID 0x4f4f0a9f

▷ Frame 36: 342 bytes on wire (2736 bits), 342 bytes captured (2736 bits)
▷ Ethernet II, Src: Cisco_3c:a0:30 (00:00:0c:3c:a0:30), Dst: Apple_f8:e2:dd (90:27:e4:f8:e2:dd)
▷ Internet Protocol, Src: 128.123.139.1   139.1), Dst: 128.123.139.56 (128.123.139.56)
▷ User Datagram Protocol, Src Port: bootps (67), Dst Port: bootpc (68)
▽ Bootstrap Protocol
    Message type: Boot Reply (2)
    Hardware type: Ethernet
    Hardware address length: 6
    Hops: 1
    Transaction ID: 0x4f4f0a9f
    Seconds elapsed: 0
    ▷ Bootp flags: 0x0000 (Unicast)
    Client IP address: 0.0.0.0 (0.0.0.0)
    Your (client) IP address: 128.123.139.56 (128.123.139.56)
    Next server IP address: 0.0.0.0 (0.0.0.0)
    Relay agent IP address: 128.123.139.1 (128.123.139.1)
    Client MAC address: Apple_f8:e2:dd (90:27:e4:f8:e2:dd)
    Client hardware address padding: 00000000000000000000
    Server host name not given
    Boot file name not given
    Magic cookie: DHCP
    ▷ Option: (t=53,l=1) DHCP Message Type = DHCP Offer
    ▷ Option: (t=54,l=4) DHCP Server Identifier = 128.123.8.5
    ▷ Option: (t=51,l=4) IP Address Lease Time = 12 hours
    ▷ Option: (t=1,l=4) Subnet Mask = 255.255.255.0
    ▷ Option: (t=3,l=4) Router = 128.123.139.1
    ▷ Option: (t=6,l=8) Domain Name Server
    ▷ Option: (t=15,l=8) Domain Name = "nmsu.edu"
    ▷ Option: (t=44,l=8) NetBIOS over TCP/IP Name Server
    End Option

FIGURE 5-4 The DHCP offer packet

No.	Time	Source	Destination	Protocol	Info
31	15.648973	0.0.0.0	255.255.255.255	DHCP	DHCP Discover - Transaction ID 0x4f4f0a9f
33	15.694065	128.123.3.38	128.123.139.56	ICMP	Echo (ping) request (id=0xa45e, seq(be/le)=0/0, ttl=62)
36	16.796505	128.123.139.1	128.123.139.56	DHCP	DHCP Offer - Transaction ID 0x4f4f0a9f
50	17.797198	0.0.0.0	255.255.255.255	DHCP	DHCP Request - Transaction ID 0x4f4f0a9f
60	17.954954	128.123.139.1	128.123.139.56	DHCP	DHCP ACK - Transaction ID 0x4f4f0a9f

▷ Frame 50: 342 bytes on wire (2736 bits), 342 bytes captured (2736 bits)
▷ Ethernet II, Src: Apple_f8:e2:dd (90:27:e4:f8:e2:dd), Dst: Broadcast (ff:ff:ff:ff:ff:ff)
▷ Internet Protocol, Src: 0.0.0.0 (0.0.0.0), Dst: 255.255.255.255 (255.255.255.255)
▷ User Datagram Protocol, Src Port: bootpc (68), Dst Port: bootps (67)
▽ Bootstrap Protocol
    Message type: Boot Request (1)
    Hardware type: Ethernet
    Hardware address length: 6
    Hops: 0
    Transaction ID: 0x4f4f0a9f
    Seconds elapsed: 2
    ▷ Bootp flags: 0x0000 (Unicast)
    Client IP address: 0.0.0.0 (0.0.0.0)
    Your (client) IP address: 0.0.0.0 (0.0.0.0)
    Next server IP address: 0.0.0.0 (0.0.0.0)
    Relay agent IP address: 0.0.0.0 (0.0.0.0)
    Client MAC address: Apple_f8:e2:dd (90:27:e4:f8:e2:dd)
    Client hardware address padding: 00000000000000000000
    Server host name not given
    Boot file name not given
    Magic cookie: DHCP
    ▷ Option: (t=53,l=1) DHCP Message Type = DHCP Request
    ▷ Option: (t=55,l=10) Parameter Request List
    ▷ Option: (t=57,l=2) Maximum DHCP Message Size = 1500
    ▷ Option: (t=61,l=7) Client identifier
    ▷ Option: (t=50,l=4) Requested IP Address = 128.123.139.56
    ▷ Option: (t=54,l=4) DHCP Server Identifier = 128.123.3.5
    ▷ Option: (t=12,l=9) Host Name = "Ignorance"
    End Option

FIGURE 5-5 The DHCP Request packet

Packet 60, shown in Figure 5-6, is a message type of **MT ACK** or DHCP ACK. The DHCP server is acknowledging the client's acceptance of the IP address from the DHCP server. The packet is being relayed to the client via the router.

> **MT ACK**
> Message type acknowledgment, a DHCP ACK packet.

No.	Time	Source	Destination	Protocol	Info
31	15.648973	0.0.0.0	255.255.255.255	DHCP	DHCP Discover - Transaction ID 0x4f4f0a9f
33	15.694065	128.123.3.38	128.123.139.56	ICMP	Echo (ping) request (id=0xa45e, seq(be/le)=0/0, ttl=62)
36	16.796505	128.123.139.1	128.123.139.56	DHCP	DHCP Offer - Transaction ID 0x4f4f0a9f
50	17.797198	0.0.0.0	255.255.255.255	DHCP	DHCP Request - Transaction ID 0x4f4f0a9f
60	17.954954	128.123.139.1	128.123.139.56	DHCP	DHCP ACK - Transaction ID 0x4f4f0a9f

▷ Frame 60: 342 bytes on wire (2736 bits), 342 bytes captured (2736 bits)
▷ Ethernet II, Src: Cisco_3c:a0:30 (00:00:0c:3c:a0:30), Dst: Apple_f8:e2:dd (90:27:e4:f8:e2:dd)
▷ Internet Protocol, Src: 128.123.139.1 (128.123.139.1), Dst: 128.123.139.56 (128.123.139.56)
▷ User Datagram Protocol, Src Port: bootps (67), Dst Port: bootpc (68)
▽ Bootstrap Protocol
   Message type: Boot Reply (2)
   Hardware type: Ethernet
   Hardware address length: 6
   Hops: 1
   Transaction ID: 0x4f4f0a9f
   Seconds elapsed: 2
  ▷ Bootp flags: 0x0000 (Unicast)
   Client IP address: 0.0.0.0 (0.0.0.0)
   Your (client) IP address: 128.123.139.56 (128.123.139.56)
   Next server IP address: 0.0.0.0 (0.0.0.0)
   Relay agent IP address: 128.123.139.1 (128.123.139.1)
   Client MAC address: Apple_f8:e2:dd (90:27:e4:f8:e2:dd)
   Client hardware address padding: 00000000000000000000
   Server host name not given
   Boot file name not given
   Magic cookie: DHCP
  ▷ Option: (t=53,l=1) DHCP Message Type = DHCP ACK
  ▷ Option: (t=54,l=4) DHCP Server Identifier = 128.123.3.5
  ▷ Option: (t=51,l=4) IP Address Lease Time = 12 hours
  ▷ Option: (t=1,l=4) Subnet Mask = 255.255.255.0
  ▷ Option: (t=3,l=4) Router = 128.123.139.1
  ▷ Option: (t=6,l=8) Domain Name Server
  ▷ Option: (t=15,l=8) Domain Name = "nmsu.edu"
  ▷ Option: (t=44,l=8) NetBIOS over TCP/IP Name Server
   End Option

FIGURE 5-6 The DHCP ACK packet

ARP Broadcast
Used to inform everyone on the network that it now is the owner of the IP address.

The client computer now has an IP address assigned to it, but before the client can use it, the client will perform an ARP broadcast for the assigned IP address to verify no one else has been assigned this address. This step is shown in Figure 5-7. In this case, the ARP query is asking who has the IP address 128.123.139.56 and reply to 0.0.0.0. If there is no reply, the machine safely assumes that the IP address is good. It then performs a gratuitous ARP broadcast, informing everyone on the network that it now is the owner of the IP address. This is shown in Figure 5-8.

No.	Time	Source	Destination	Protocol	Info
31	15.648973	0.0.0.0	255.255.255.255	DHCP	DHCP Discover - Transaction ID 0x4f4f0a9f
33	15.694065	128.123.3.38	128.123.139.56	ICMP	Echo (ping) request (id=0xa45e, seq(be/le)=0/0, ttl=62)
36	16.796505	128.123.139.1	128.123.139.56	DHCP	DHCP Offer - Transaction ID 0x4f4f0a9f
50	17.797198	0.0.0.0	255.255.255.255	DHCP	DHCP Request - Transaction ID 0x4f4f0a9f
60	17.954954	128.123.139.1	128.123.139.56	DHCP	DHCP ACK - Transaction ID 0x4f4f0a9f
61	17.955472	Apple_f8:e2:dd	Broadcast	ARP	Who has 128.123.139.56? Tell 0.0.0.0
62	18.355727	Apple_f8:e2:dd	Broadcast	ARP	Who has 128.123.139.56? Tell 0.0.0.0
65	18.756145	Apple_f8:e2:dd	Broadcast	ARP	Who has 128.123.139.56? Tell 0.0.0.0
67	19.156603	Apple_f8:e2:dd	Broadcast	ARP	Gratuitous ARP for 128.123.139.56 (Request)
68	19.557224	Apple_f8:e2:dd	Broadcast	ARP	Gratuitous ARP for 128.123.139.56 (Request)

▷ Frame 61: 42 bytes on wire (336 bits), 42 bytes captured (336 bits)
▷ Ethernet II, Src: Apple_f8:e2:dd (90:27:e4:f8:e2:dd), Dst: Broadcast (ff:ff:ff:ff:ff:ff)
▽ Address Resolution Protocol (request)
   Hardware type: Ethernet (0x0001)
   Protocol type: IP (0x0800)
   Hardware size: 6
   Protocol size: 4
   Opcode: request (0x0001)
   [Is gratuitous: False]
   Sender MAC address: Apple_f8:e2:dd (90:27:e4:f8:e2:dd)
   Sender IP address: 0.0.0.0 (0.0.0.0)
   Target MAC address: 00:00:00_00:00:00 (00:00:00:00:00:00)
   Target IP address: 128.123.139.56 (128.123.139.56)

FIGURE 5-7 The ARP query asking who has the IP address 128.123.139.56

No.	Time	Source	Destination	Protocol	Info
31	15.648973	0.0.0.0	255.255.255.255	DHCP	DHCP Discover - Transaction ID 0x4f4f0a9f
33	15.694065	128.123.3.38	128.123.139.56	ICMP	Echo (ping) request (id=0xa45e, seq(be/le)=0/0, ttl=62)
36	16.796505	128.123.139.1	128.123.139.56	DHCP	DHCP Offer - Transaction ID 0x4f4f0a9f
50	17.797198	0.0.0.0	255.255.255.255	DHCP	DHCP Request - Transaction ID 0x4f4f0a9f
60	17.954954	128.123.139.1	128.123.139.56	DHCP	DHCP ACK - Transaction ID 0x4f4f0a9f
61	17.955472	Apple_f8:e2:dd	Broadcast	ARP	who has 128.123.139.56? Tell 0.0.0.0
62	18.355727	Apple_f8:e2:dd	Broadcast	ARP	who has 128.123.139.56? Tell 0.0.0.0
65	18.756145	Apple_f8:e2:dd	Broadcast	ARP	who has 128.123.139.56? Tell 0.0.0.0
67	19.156603	Apple_f8:e2:dd	Broadcast	ARP	Gratuitous ARP for 128.123.139.56 (Request)
68	19.557224	Apple_f8:e2:dd	Broadcast	ARP	Gratuitous ARP for 128.123.139.56 (Request)

```
▷ Frame 67: 42 bytes on wire (336 bits), 42 bytes captured (336 bits)
▷ Ethernet II, Src: Apple_f8:e2:dd (90:27:e4:f8:e2:dd), Dst: Broadcast (ff:ff:ff:ff:ff:ff)
▽ Address Resolution Protocol (request/gratuitous ARP)
    Hardware type: Ethernet (0x0001)
    Protocol type: IP (0x0800)
    Hardware size: 6
    Protocol size: 4
    Opcode: request (0x0001)
    [Is gratuitous: True]
    Sender MAC address: Apple_f8:e2:dd (90:27:e4:f8:e2:dd)
    Sender IP address: 128.123.139.56 (128.123.139.56)
    Target MAC address: 00:00:00_00:00:00 (00:00:00:00:00:00)
    Target IP address: 128.123.139.56 (128.123.139.56)
```

FIGURE 5-8 The gratuitous ARP broadcast for 128.123.139.56

DHCP Deployment

In a small office/home office (SOHO) environment, the network is typically small and only one router is needed. In this kind of network, a router performs simple routing functions, acts as a gateway to the outside world, and manages IP assignment via DHCP. Most network routers are capable of running the DHCP service, so it makes sense and is more cost-effective to deploy DHCP service at the router.

A DHCP configuration on any network device typically will start with defining a scope, a pool, or a range of the IP addresses that will be made available for allocation. Then, the network settings, such as gateway, subnet mask, DNS servers, domain name, leased time, and other information, will need to be assigned to the scope. The following is the example of how to configure a Cisco router to provide DHCP service.

When running DHCP service on a local router, the *ip helper-address* is not needed anymore to relay the DHCP information. This is because the DHCP service is in the same LAN as the client computer. The router must be placed in the router's configuration mode in order to configure the DHCP service. The DHCP pool must be configured with the command **ip dhcp** [*pool_name*]. Then, an IP network must be defined as the IP allocation pool. In this case, the IP addresses from 172.20.224.0–172.20.224.255 have been set aside for the address pool.

```
RouterA#conf t
Enter configuration commands, one per line. End with CNTL/Z.
RouterA(config)#
RouterA(config)# ip dhcp pool dhcp1pool
RouterA(dhcp-config)# network 172.20.224.0 255.255.255.0
```

Now that the basic DHCP pool is set up, it is time to associate other network settings to it. The following steps show how to define the DNS server, domain name,

> **SOHO**
> Small office or home office network.

and gateway to the DHCP pool. The subnet mask is already defined as part of the network.

```
RouterA(dhcp-config)# dns-server 172.20.224.8
RouterA(dhcp-config)# domain-name et477.com
RouterA(dhcp-config)# default-router 172.20.224.1
```

Even though an entire Class C network is being configured for the DHCP network, a portion of it might be reserved for something else, like static IP machines and servers. The command **ip dhcp** *excluded-address* is used to exclude a portion of IP addresses from being allocated to the DHCP devices. In this example, the IP addresses from 172.20.224.0 to 172.20.224.20 are excluded leaving the rest of network addresses available for DHCP allocation use:

```
RouterA(config)# ip dhcp excluded-address 172.20.224.0 172.20.224.20
```

To verify the DHCP pool status and information, the command **show ip dhcp pool** can be used:

```
RouterA#show ip dhcp pool

Pool dhcp1pool :
 Utilization mark (high/low)     : 100 / 0
 Subnet size (first/next)        : 0 / 0
 Total addresses                 : 254
 Leased addresses                : 5
 Pending event                   : none
 1 subnet is currently in the pool :
 Current index    IP address range                 Leased addresses
 172.20.224.132   172.20.224.1 - 172.20.224.254    5
```

> **Binding**
>
> An association of the IP address to the DHCP server.

Also, to see what IP addresses have been allocated by the DHCP server, the command **show ip dhcp binding** can be used. The binding is an association of the IP address to the DHCP server:

```
RouterA#show ip dhcp binding
Bindings from all pools not associated with VRF:
IP address        Client-ID/         Lease expiration        Type
172.20.224.12     0013.2126.9f2d     Feb 12 2012 02:17 PM    Automatic
172.20.224.47     0100.1143.bdda.03  Feb 12 2012 11:17 AM    Automatic
172.20.224.53     0100.0f1f.e82f.45  Feb 12 2012 04:07 AM    Automatic
172.20.224.62     0100.1143.11bb.ed  Feb 12 2012 12:04 PM    Automatic
172.20.224.114    0100.1143.11bc.5d  Feb 12 2012 11:33 AM    Automatic
```

In a larger and more complex environment where there are multiple networks and multiple routers, deploying DHCP service at the routers is not as simple. Having to manage a different DHCP service for each network on multiple routers can be tedious, time-consuming, and inefficient. This is where centralized DHCP service fares better.

This setup offers a centralized management, which scales better and is easier to support. A typical setup is to run a DHCP service program on a centralized server. With centralized DHCP service, the IP address assignment is typically tracked by the network administrator or the network operations center (NOC). The tracking information can include more than the IP and MAC addresses, and the user information can also be included. This information can be kept in a central log file or in the database so that the administrator can troubleshoot network problems. For example, a machine could be causing network problems possibly due to hacked or corrupted software. The NOC needs to be able to track down the network problem(s). The NOC database will have the MAC address, the IP address, and the name of the person who uses the computer.

Also, in a large environment, DCHP pools are usually planned and pre-allocated. IP addresses are assigned by NOC based on where the subnet for the computer is located. The subnet could be in a building, a floor of the building, a department, and so on. The subnets are created by the network administrators based on the expected number of users (hosts) in a subnet. For example, the 192.168.12.0 network, shown in Figure 5-9, has been partitioned into four subnets. The network addresses for each of the subnets are provided in Table 5-1. Any computer in subnet B is assigned one of the 62 IP addresses from the range 192.168.12.65 to 192.168.12.126. Remember that the first IP address in the subnet is reserved for the network address and the last is reserved for the broadcast address.

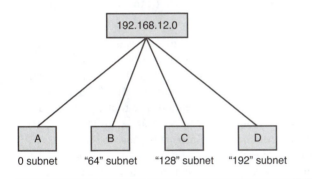

FIGURE 5-9 IP assignment of computers in a network's subnet

TABLE 5-1 Subnet Addresses for the Subnets Shown in Figure 5-9

Subnet	Network Address	Broadcast Address	Subnet Mask
A	192.168.12.0	192.168.12.63	255.255.255.192
B	192.168.12.64	192.168.12.127	255.255.255.192
C	192.168.12.128	192.168.12.191	255.255.252.192
D	192.168.12.192	192.168.12.255	255.255.255.192

5-3 SCALING THE NETWORK WITH NAT AND PAT

It was mentioned in Chapter 1, "Network Infrastructure Design," that public IP addresses are a commodity, and not many institutions have a luxury of using public IP addresses in their network. In most cases, the demand of IP network devices exceeds the number of public IP addresses assigned to them. Most institutions have to use private IP addresses in their network. These private IP addresses must be able to communicate with outside or Internet hosts. This cannot be done because the private IP addresses are not routable on the Internet. These private IP addresses must be translated to public IP addresses using techniques like Network Address Translation (NAT) or Port Address Translation (PAT) for use on the Internet.

Network Address Translation is a technique used to translate an internal private IP address to a public IP address before the packets leave the local network to the public network. NAT is typically implemented and deployed at the router facing the outside network. NAT is a one-to-one translation of a private IP address to a public IP address. This means that, for every connection made to the outside world, there must be a public IP address available. The public IP address is relinquished when it is no longer used or when the NAT timeout occurs. NAT is used not only for a way to communicate to the outside world; it can be used to hide the internal IP infrastructure of the network.

To enhance NAT's limitation, **Port Address Translation (PAT)** was developed. PAT is sometimes referred to as many-to-one NAT and NAT overload, because of its capability to translate many IP addresses with a single public IP address or a handful of public IP addresses. PAT accomplishes this by using the TCP/UDP ports. The PAT process tracks a port number for the connection. The router stores the IP address and port number in a NAT lookup table. The port number differentiates the computer that is establishing a connection to the Internet because the router uses the same public IP address for all computers. This port number is used when a data packet is returned to the home network. The port number identifies the computer that established the Internet connection, and the router can deliver the data packet to the correct computer.

For example, if computer 1 establishes a connection to a website on the Internet, the data packets from the website are sent back to computer 1 using the network's routable public IP address. This first step enables the data packet to be routed back to the home network. Next, the router uses the NAT lookup table and port number to translate the destination for the data packet back to the computer 1 private IP address and original port number, which might be different. Table 5-2 demonstrates an example of a PAT table of a router. The router translates the private IP addresses to the public routable IP address assigned by the ISP. Additionally, the router tracks a port number with the public IP address to identify the computer. For example, the computer with the private IP address of 10.0.0.1 is assigned the public IP address 12.0.0.1:2000, where 2000 is the port number tracked by the router. The term NAT is used more generally than PAT and, most times, it covers PAT.

Network Address Translation (NAT)

A technique used to translate an internal private IP address to a public IP address.

Port Address Translation (PAT)

A technique that uses the port number to identify the computer that established the Internet connection; also called many-to-one NAT and NAT overload.

TABLE 5-2   Example of a Router's PAT Table

Inside IP	Inside Port	Outside IP	Outside Port
10.0.0.1	2000	12.0.0.1	2000
10.0.0.2	3000	12.0.0.1	3000
10.0.0.2	30001	12.0.0.1	4000
10.0.0.3	3000	12.0.0.1	5000
10.0.0.3	20010	12.0.0.1	6000

Configuring NAT

When dealing with NAT on Cisco routers, one must be familiar with the Cisco terminologies. Cisco uses the term *local address* to define any IP address that is on the inside of or internal to the network. The term *global address* is used to define any IP address that is on the outside of or external to the network. The first step of configuring NAT is to define the NAT points on a router's interfaces to designate the inside area and the outside area. Only when a packet passes through from the inside interface to the outside interface, a NAT will occur. The following example demonstrates how to define NAT points. The FastEthernet0/0 will be the inside interface and the FastEthernet0/1 will be the outside interface. This concept is graphically defined in Figure 5-10. To define the NAT area, the command **ip nat inside/outside** is used:

> **Local Address**
> Defines any IP address that is on the inside of or internal to the network.
>
> **Global Address**
> Defines any IP address that is on the outside of or external to the network.

```
RouterA#conf t
Enter configuration commands, one per line. End with CNTL/Z.
RouterA(config)#
RouterA(config)# interface FastEthernet0/0
RouterA(config-if)# ip nat inside
RouterA(config)# interface FastEthernet0/1
RouterA(config-if)# ip nat outside
```

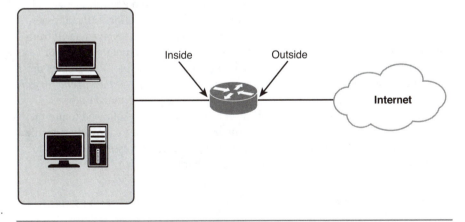

FIGURE 5-10 A graphical depiction of NAT inside and out

After the NAT interfaces are defined, a NAT statement can be configured. There are several types of NAT. One of them is static NAT. A **static NAT** is a fixed one-to-one mapping of an inside IP address to an outside IP address. The static NAT command is **ip nat inside source static** [*local_ip*] [*global_ip*]. The following example demonstrates how to configure a static NAT on a Cisco router:

```
RouterA(config)#
RouterA(config)# ip nat inside source static 10.0.0.5 12.0.0.5
```

The preceding command will entirely map the inside private IP address of 10.0.0.5 to the outside public IP address of 12.0.0.5. There is no port translation when the internal host 10.0.0.5 is making a connection outside. This host appears to the outside world as 12.0.0.5, and it is accessible from the outside via the very same public IP address. In the case where an internal server needs to be reached from the outside, then a static NAT can be used. However, this brings up a security concern of exposing an IP address entirely to the external network, so a static NAT is usually discouraged.

A better approach is to expose only network ports that need to be accessible by the external network. For example, if a web server is on the internal network and it must be made accessible to the external network, there is no need to map an entire IP address to it. Because a web server runs on specific TCP ports, like 80 for HTTP and 443 for HTTPS, these TCP ports can be made available via the static NAT instead. Sometimes, this technique is referred to as static PAT, port mapping, port forwarding, or port redirect. The following example demonstrates how to configure static NAT statements to map TCP port 80 of the inside host to TCP port 80 of the outside public IP address as well as TCP port 443 to cover all web traffic ports:

```
RouterA(config)#
RouterA(config)# ip nat inside source static tcp 10.0.0.5 80 12.0.0.5
80
RouterA(config)# ip nat inside source static tcp 10.0.0.5 443 12.0.0.5
443
```

Another type of NAT configuration is **dynamic NAT**. With dynamic NAT, it is not a fixed one-to-one IP mapping; it is a one-to-one mapping from an available global pool. A router is assigned a pool of IP addresses that contains global IP addresses, and every inside host that tries to access a public network will be given an IP from the global pool. In order to configure dynamic NAT on Cisco routers, a pool of global IP addresses and an access list containing allowable inside IP addresses must be defined. The command **ip nat pool** [*pool_name*] [*start_ip_address*] [*end_ip_address*] **netmask** [*subnet_mask*] is used to create a NAT pool. A standard or extended access list can be used to create a set of networks that is allowed to use the NAT pool. Then, a dynamic NAT statement can be configured to allow the specified IP addresses to be translated using the specified global IP addresses from the pool. The following example shows step-by-step configuration:

```
RouterA(config)#
RouterA(config)# ip nat pool global_ip 12.0.0.6 12.0.0.26 netmask
255.255.255.0
RouterA(config)# access-list 1 permit 10.0.0.0 0.0.0.255
RouterA(config)# ip nat inside source list 1 pool global_ip
```

With dynamic NAT, there is a limitation of the global pool being depleted, because of a limited number of global IP addresses available for the one-to-one IP mapping. Another type of NAT configuration is NAT overload or PAT and is supposed to solve that problem. Similar to dynamic NAT, a pool of global IP addresses and an access list containing allowable inside IP addresses must be defined. (Note: The use of access lists is discussed in Chapter 7, "Network Security"). Then, the PAT statement can be configured just by issuing the keyword **overload**. The following example shows step-by-step configuration. This example presents a slightly different way of doing the access list. Access-list 101 is an extended access list, but it still does the same as the access list 1 from the previous example, which is to allow only the network 10.0.0.0/8.

> **NAT Overload**
> Another name for PAT.

```
RouterA(config)#
RouterA(config)# ip nat pool global_ip 12.0.0.6 12.0.0.26 netmask
255.255.255.0
RouterA(config)# access-list 101 permit ip 10.0.0.0 0.0.0.255 any
RouterA(config)# ip nat inside source list 101 pool global_ip overload
```

If one cannot acquire a pool of global IP addresses from an ISP, then the NAT overload will have to be configured using the router interface facing the public network. This interface will have a public IP address assigned to it. For example, Router's FastEthernet 0/1 is the interface facing the outside public network. It has an IP address of 12.0.0.2. The maximum theoretical number of ports that a single IP can use is about 64,000. Even though the practical limit will not be as high due to a router's hardware limitation, a single public IP address will be more than enough to support a small to medium network's simultaneous connections to the external network. A NAT overload can then be configured to use the interface's IP address as the global address. In this case, the global IP pool is not needed, only an access list is required. The following example shows step-by-step configuration:

```
RouterA(config)#
RouterA(config)# access-list 101 permit ip 10.0.0.0 0.0.0.255 any
RouterA(config)# ip nat inside source list 101 interface
FastEthernet0/1 overload
```

To display active translations, the command **show ip nat translation** is used. The command will show the active NAT table in column format. The column "Pro" is the protocol (TCP, UDP, ICMP) being translated. The "Inside global" is the global IP address used by the inside IP address after the NAT process. The "Inside local" is the inside IP address. The "Outside local" corresponds to the destination IP address of the inside local before the NAT translation. The "Outside global" corresponds to the destination IP address of the inside global after the NAT translation. The following output shows the display of the active NAT translations. The example shows the global IP address of 12.0.0.2, which is an outside interface IP address of Router A:

```
RouterA# show ip nat translation
Pro Inside global      Inside local        Outside local
Outside global
tcp 12.0.0.2:57425   10.10.70.5:57425      74.125.227.20:80
74.125.227.20:80
```

```
tcp 12.0.0.2:57426      10.10.70.5:57426      74.125.227.17:80
74.125.227.17:80

tcp 12.0.0.2:57427      10.10.70.5:57427      173.194.69.94:80
173.194.69.94:80

tcp 12.0.0.2:53222      10.10.70.6:53222      192.65.78.152:80
192.65.78.152:80

tcp 12.0.0.2:53395      10.10.70.6:53395      192.65.78.150:80
192.65.78.150:80

tcp 12.0.0.2:53424      10.10.70.6:53424      216.38.172.205:1935
216.38.172.205:1935

tcp 12.0.0.2:54816      10.10.70.6:54816      74.125.224.175:80
74.125.224.175:80

tcp 12.0.0.2:55932      10.10.70.6:55932      192.65.78.151:80
192.65.78.151:80

tcp 12.0.0.2:57256      10.10.70.7:57256      74.125.224.173:80
74.125.224.173:80

tcp 12.0.0.2:58003      10.10.70.7:58003      66.220.145.45:80
66.220.145.45:80

tcp 12.0.0.2:59108      10.10.70.10:59108     192.65.78.152:80
192.65.78.152:80

tcp 12.0.0.2:59283      10.10.70.10:59283     96.7.191.139:80
96.7.191.139:80

tcp 12.0.0.2:59555      10.10.70.10:59555     96.7.191.139:443
96.7.191.139:443

tcp 12.0.0.2:1153       10.10.70.15:1153      65.55.223.34:40008
65.55.223.34:40008

tcp 12.0.0.2:1312       10.10.70.15:1312      192.65.78.152:80
192.65.78.152:80

tcp 12.0.0.2:1965       10.10.70.15:1965      213.146.189.204:12350
213.146.189.204:12350

tcp 12.0.0.2:1966       10.10.70.15:1966      213.146.189.205:12350
213.146.189.205:12350

udp 12.0.0.2:1882       10.10.70.16:1882      75.178.0.20:9967
75.178.0.20:9967

udp 12.0.0.2:1882       10.10.70.16:1882      85.27.9.65:15268
85.27.9.65:15268

udp 12.0.0.2:1882       10.10.70.16:1882      157.55.235.142:40019
157.55.235.142:40019

udp 12.0.0.2:1882       10.10.70.16:1882      157.56.52.14:40019
157.56.52.14:40019

udp 12.0.0.2:1882       10.10.70.16:1882      173.17.231.210:30850
173.17.231.210:30850

udp 12.0.0.2:1882       10.10.70.16:1882      178.207.64.233:7563
178.207.64.233:7563

udp 12.0.0.2:9001       10.10.70.16:9001      66.151.151.20:5062
66.151.151.20:5062

tcp 12.0.0.2:3593       10.10.70.16:49262     111.221.74.38:40008
111.221.74.38:40008

tcp 12.0.0.2:49307      10.10.70.16:49307     193.120.199.12:12350
193.120.199.12:12350
```

5-4   DOMAIN NAME SERVICE (DNS)

This section examines the Domain Name Service (DNS) services typically available in a campus network. Domain Name Service (DNS) translates a human-readable name to an IP address or an IP address to a domain name. The translation of a name to an IP address is called forward DNS lookup or forward DNS resolution, and translation of an IP address to a domain name is called reverse DNS lookup or reverse DNS resolution. DNS runs on UDP protocol port 53.

The DNS is a tree hierarchy. Everything in DNS starts at the "." servers, or generally called root servers, which are at the top of the hierarchy, as illustrated in Figure 5-10. The root servers are well-known IP addresses that have been programmed into DNS servers. When the DNS is installed on a server, a list of the root server's IP addresses is automatically configured in the DNS. A file containing the list of the most up-to-date root servers is available for the public, and it can be downloaded at the IANA's website. The file is known as the Root Hints file (root.hints). According to IANA, there are currently 13 root servers distributed around the world operated by different independent entities. Each server is typically a cluster of servers spreading throughout different regions or countries. Table 5-3 shows the current list.

> **DNS**
> Domain Name Service.
>
> **Forward DNS**
> Translation of a name to an IP address.
>
> **Reverse DNS**
> Translation of an IP address to a name.
>
> **Root Hints File (root. hints)**
> A file containing the list of the most up-to-date root servers.

TABLE 5-3   **International Root Servers**

Hostname	IP Address	Manager
a.root-servers.net	198.41.0.4	VeriSign, Inc.
b.root-servers.net	192.228.79.201	University of Southern California (ISI)
c.root-servers.net	192.33.4.12	Cogent Communications
d.root-servers.net	128.8.10.90	University of Maryland
e.root-servers.net	192.203.230.10	NASA (Ames Research Center)
f.root-servers.net	192.5.5.241	Internet Systems Consortium, Inc.
g.root-servers.net	192.112.36.4	US Department of Defense (NIC)
h.root-servers.net	128.63.2.53	US Army (Research Lab)
i.root-servers.net	192.36.148.17	Netnod
j.root-servers.net	192.58.128.30	VeriSign, Inc.
k.root-servers.net	193.0.14.129	RIPE NCC
l.root-servers.net	199.7.83.42	ICANN
m.root-servers.net	202.12.27.33	WIDE Project

The next hierarchical level from the root is the top-level domain. As discussed in Section 5-1, the top-level domains (TLD) registries are managed by IANA and ICANN. Examples of generic top-level domains (**TLD**) are as follows: .com, .net, .org, .edu, .mil, .gov, .us, .ca, .info, .biz, and .tv. **Country domains** are usually defined by two letters, such as .us (United States) and .ca (Canada). The primary domain server for that domain has to exist in the same country; for example, the .us primary domain server is located in the United States. Figure 5-11 shows the top-level domains and their relationship to the subdomains and root servers. Examples of country-coded TLDs are as follows: .us, .uk, .au, .ru, .cn, .jp, .de, .ca, and so on.

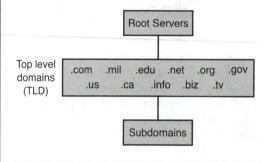

FIGURE 5-11 The domain name service tree hierarchy

DNS Tree Hierarchy

By having a tree hierarchy structure, DNS operates in a delegation mode starting from the root to subtree levels. This way, each level only has to maintain the information of the next level. With this structure, the root servers only know of the TLD servers, to which they can delegate the top level domain queries. The root servers will not know of **www.example.com**. They will delegate the query to a next level authoritative server, which repeats the delegation to the next level until it reaches the final destination that can authoritatively give the answer of **www.example.com**.

The following steps outline the typical name look-up process by a machine on the network (for example, if a machine called C1 wants to know the IP address for the www server at example.com):

1. C1 queries its network or campus domain name server as defined in its network settings for an IP address of the hostname www.example.com.

2. If the DNS server has the IP address of **www.example.com**, then it answers the name lookup query and the process is done. The DNS server could possess the IP address of **www.example.com**, because it is either an authoritative DNS server for the domain example.com or it has the IP information in its DNS cache.

3. If the campus or network DNS server does not have the IP address of **www.example.com**, it will start by querying one of the root servers to find the IP address of **www.example.com**.

4. The root server will return a list of delegated name servers for top level domain ".com" to the campus name server.

5. The campus DNS server will then query one of the .com TLD name servers on the list for the IP address of **www.example.com**.

6. A .com server will return a list of delegated servers for the domain "example.com" to the campus name server.

7. The campus DNS will then query one of the example.com domain name servers for the IP address of **www.example.com**.

8. A domain name server for example.com will return an IP address of **www.example.com** to the campus DNS server. When a domain name server can answer a query for that domain, it is said to be an authoritative DNS server of the domain.

9. The campus DNS server will update its DNS cache, so this multiple-step process of obtaining an IP address does not have to be repeated unnecessarily. Then, it will pass the IP information to the machine C1.

The UNIX program called "dig" will next be used to illustrate the delegation process during the name lookup query. **Dig (Domain Information Groper)** is a DNS lookup utility that is readily available on most UNIX/Linux operating systems. Another widely used DNS lookup utility is **nslookup**, which comes with Windows, Mac, and UNIX/Linux. The command **nslookup** is a very simple command-line program; however, its output is not as detailed as that provided with dig. Throughout this section, we explore how to use both of the DNS utility programs: **dig** and **nslookup**. The following demonstrates the name lookup steps mentioned previously. The command **dig +trace www.example.com** is issued at the UNIX prompt. This command traces every step of the name lookup process.

> **Dig (Domain Information Groper)**
> A DNS lookup utility.
>
> **nslookup**
> A DNS lookup utility.

```
[admin@noc ~]$ dig +trace www.example.com

; <<>> DiG 9.6-ESV-R4-P3 <<>> +trace  www.example.com
;; global options: +cmd
.                   492498    IN    NS    a.root-servers.net.
.                   492498    IN    NS    b.root-servers.net.
.                   492498    IN    NS    c.root-servers.net.
.                   492498    IN    NS    d.root-servers.net.
.                   492498    IN    NS    e.root-servers.net.
.                   492498    IN    NS    f.root-servers.net.
.                   492498    IN    NS    g.root-servers.net.
.                   492498    IN    NS    h.root-servers.net.
.                   492498    IN    NS    i.root-servers.net.
.                   492498    IN    NS    j.root-servers.net.
.                   492498    IN    NS    k.root-servers.net.
.                   492498    IN    NS    l.root-servers.net.
.                   492498    IN    NS    m.root-servers.net.
;; Received 512 bytes from 128.123.3.6#53(128.123.3.6) in 8 ms

com.                172800    IN    NS    d.gtld-servers.net.
com.                172800    IN    NS    c.gtld-servers.net.
com.                172800    IN    NS    l.gtld-servers.net.
com.                172800    IN    NS    b.gtld-servers.net.
```

```
com.              172800    IN    NS    e.gtld-servers.net.
com.              172800    IN    NS    i.gtld-servers.net.
com.              172800    IN    NS    k.gtld-servers.net.
com.              172800    IN    NS    h.gtld-servers.net.
com.              172800    IN    NS    m.gtld-servers.net.
com.              172800    IN    NS    a.gtld-servers.net.
com.              172800    IN    NS    j.gtld-servers.net.
com.              172800    IN    NS    g.gtld-servers.net.
com.              172800    IN    NS    f.gtld-servers.net.
;; Received 493 bytes from 192.228.79.201#53(b.root-servers.net) in 28
ms

example.com.         172800      IN    NS    a.iana-servers.net.
example.com.         172800      IN    NS    b.iana-servers.net.
;; Received 169 bytes from 192.54.112.30#53(h.gtld-servers.net) in 185
ms

www.example.com.     172800      IN    A     192.0.43.10
example.com.         172800      IN    NS    b.iana-servers.net.
example.com.         172800      IN    NS    a.iana-servers.net.
;; Received 97 bytes from 199.43.132.53#53(a.iana-servers.net) in 26
ms
```

The **dig** result shows that the first step for looking up the name **www.example.com**, the campus DNS server, 128.123.3.6, is queried on port 53, even though it is not specified as UDP port 53. The campus DNS server has a list of 13 root servers, as shown as **a – m.root-servers.net**. It queries one of the root servers, which happens to be **b.root-servers.net**. The b.root-servers.net returns a list of the .com TLD name servers, **a – m.gtld-servers.net**.

The **h.gtld-servers.net** is then queried by the campus DNS server for **www. example.com**. It replies back with a list of two name servers for the domain example.com, which are a.iana-servers.net and b.iana-servers.net. The campus DNS server then queries the name **a.iana-servers.net** for **www.example.com**, which it replies back with the IP address of 192.0.43.10.

Authoritative Name Server

A name server that is authorized and configured to answer DNS queries for a particular domain or zone.

The server **a.iana-servers.net** is an authoritative name server for the domain example.com. An authoritative name server is a name server that is authorized and configured to answer DNS queries for a particular domain or zone. So, how does one become an authoritative name server of a domain? The answer is that this is done when a domain is registered. To successfully register an Internet domain name, the authoritative name servers must be specified. So, the authoritative name servers of a domain can be found by using the **whois** command. In Section 5-1, the command **whois example.com** was issued, and it showed the registration information of the domain example.com, which included its name servers: A.IANA-SERVERS.NET and B.IANA-SERVERS.NET. These name servers are the true authoritative domain name servers of the domain example.com.

In the example, the query was done against the campus DNS server, 128.123.3.6. This DNS server is said to be a non-authoritative name server, because it does not contain a copy of the domain example.com; therefore, it is not authorized to answer the query. A non-authoritative name server will always query the authoritative name servers of the domain for the answer. A name lookup answer received by a client via a non-authoritative server is called a **non-authoritative answer**.

The next examples demonstrate the difference when querying the authoritative server and the non-authoritative server. The program **nslookup** is used in this demonstration. During the first case, **nslookp** will query against an authoritative server, such as the example.com domain and b.iana-servers.net. The second time, it will query against a non-authoritative server, such as a campus name server. Both will yield the same IP address result, but the second attempt will show that the answer is a non-authoritative, because it is coming from the campus DNS server.

```
authoritative server
[admin@noc ~]$ nslookup
> server b.iana-servers.net
Default server: b.iana-servers.net
Address: 199.43.133.53#53
> www.example.com
Server:     b.iana-servers.net
Address:    199.43.133.53#53

Name:   www.example.com
Address: 192.0.43.10
>
> server 128.123.3.6
Default server: 128.123.3.6
Address: 128.123.3.6#53
> www.example.com
Server:     128.123.3.6
Address:    128.123.3.6#53
Non-authoritative server:
Name:   www.example.com
Address: 192.0.43.10
>
```

In the preceding examples, the hostname **www.example.com** is said to be a fully qualified domain name (**FQDN**) because it contains a full path of the domain name. Not all DNS queries are done with an FQDN, because of a domain name suffix that is configured as part of the network settings configuration. For example, a domain suffix example.com may be configured as a default domain or a search domain on a host. Therefore, instead of issuing an FQDN of **www.example.com** or web. example.com, partial qualified domain names (**PQDN**) of www or web can be used. PQDNs serve as shorthand, so that users don't have to provide the full name of the host. This is a general practice in a campus network.

DNS Resource Records

As mentioned previously, an authoritative name server is a name server that is authorized and configured to answer DNS queries for a particular domain or zone. The authoritative name server is in charge of managing the information about that zone or domain. The information of the domain and its hosts and services are defined by resource records (RR) and are organized by zones. The terms *domain* and *zone* are often used interchangeably.

When a name server is hosting a single domain with no subdomains, the domain and the zone are the same. However, this creates multiple zones within a domain when there are subdomains involved. For example, the domain example.edu could have subdomains of engineering.example.edu and business.example.edu. This creates three different zones: one for example.edu, one for engineering.example.edu, and one for business.example.edu. Each zone contains resource records that define or describe a domain or subdomain. The following are the common resource records that would accompany a zone.

SOA Resource Records   SOA or Start of Authority is a mandatory RR for each zone. It marks the start of the zone and provides the technical details of the zone, such as zone name, the primary authoritative name server, the email address of the domain administrator, serial number of the domain, TTL (Time to Live) of the domain, refresh, retry, and expire time for the slave name server. The SOA record of the domain can be found by using either the **dig** or **nslookup** command. The following example uses the **nslookup** command to find the SOA record of the domain example.com.

```
C:\nslookup -query=SOA example.com
  Server:   192.168.1.1
  Address:  192.168.1.1#53
```

```
Non-authoritative answer:
example.com
        primary name server = dns1.icann.org
        responsible mail addr = hostmaster.icann.org
        serial  = 2011063168
        refresh = 7200 (2 hours)
        retry   = 3600 (1 hour)
        expire  = 1209600 (14 days)
        default TTL = 3600 (1 hour)
```

This shows that the IP address is 192.168.1.1 using UDP port 53. Notice that this states that this is a non-authoritative answer. Also, the technical details of the zone are listed such as the primary name server and responsible mail address.

A Resource Records   The A record or Address record is the most common record in DNS. It is a hostname mapping to an IP address. For example, the host1 entry in domain network-B.edu is an A record. The A record is used by a DNS server at the parent company for network-B to convert the name host1.network-B.edu to an IP address. By default, both **dig** and **nslookup** command will yield the IP address of the hostname. It is not necessary to specify the option for A record when using dig or nslookup. The following example uses the **nslookp** command to find the A record of the host **www.example.com**.

```
C:\nslookup  www.example.com
   Server:  192.168.1.1
   Address:  192.168.1.1#53
```

```
Non-authoritative answer:
Name: www.example.com
Address: 192.0.43.10
```

This shows that the IP address for **www.example.com** is 192.0.43.10.

PTR Resource Records The PTR record or Pointer record is a reverse of an A record. It is a mapping of an IP address to a hostname. It is sometimes referred to as a reverse record. The following example uses the **nslookp** command to find the PTR record or the reverse record of the IP address given as the result of www.example. com:

PTR Record (Pointer Record)
The reverse of an A record.

```
C:\nslookup -query=PTR 192.0.43.10
   Server:  192.168.1.1
   Address:  192.168.1.1#53
```

```
Non-authoritative answer:
10.43.0.192.in-addr.arpa name = 43-10.any.icann.org.
```

Interestingly, the answer is not the exact reverse hostname that one would expect. One would think that name result would be reciprocal to the previous exercise, which is www.example.com. In this case, the name listed is 43-10.any.icann.org instead. This is common on the Internet. This has to do with how the Internet domain name is registered and how the IP address is acquired. As we have learned, the Internet domain name can come from different sources. An Internet domain name is generally purchased from a domain registrar, and the IP address has to be allocated from ARIN (in North America) or from an ISP. This results in one entity being in charge of the forward DNS zone and another entity being in charge of the reverse DNS zone. The information is not usually synchronized, hence the result above.

CNAME Resource Records CNAME (Canonical name) record is generally called an alias. It allows another name to be defined and points to the real name. CNAME record is mapped to an A record. Similar to an A record query, it is not necessary to specify the option for CNAME record when using dig or nslookup. Both commands yield a canonical name or an alias of a hostname, if it exists. The following example reveals that www.iana.org is actually a name of an A record of ianawww. vip.icann.org:

CNAME (Canonical Name) Record
Generally called an alias of a hostname.

```
C:\nslookup  www.iana.org
   Server:  192.168.1.1
   Address:  192.168.1.1#53
```

```
Non-authoritative answer:
www.iana.org     canonical name = ianawww.vip.icann.org.
```

```
Name:    ianawww.vip.icann.org
Address: 192.0.32.8
```

CNAME is useful in applications like virtual web hosting. Being able to create multiple names and mapping these names to one canonical name that in turn associates to one IP address, allows multiple websites to be served by one server. The effect is seamless to general users. As a matter of fact, this is how most of the virtual services and cloud services are able to provide their services. For example, what if the website www.example.com moved to a cloud service provider by creating a CNAME record and then mapped the website to a specific cloud service provider's server? To general users, the website is still www.example.com, but the destination where the service is hosted is now different.

> **NS Record**
> Specifies the name of the authoritative name server of the domain.

NS Resource Records   NS record or Name Server record is another mandatory RR for a zone. This specifies the name of the authoritative name server of the domain. The record must map to a valid A record, not an IP address or a CNAME. The NS records are associated with the domain, not a particular host. Therefore, one will need to look up the name server information based on the domain. The following example demonstrates the use of the **nslookup** command to lookup the NS records of the domain example.com.

```
C:\nslookup  -query=NS example.com
  Server:   192.168.1.1
  Address:  192.168.1.1#53

Non-authoritative answer:
example.com nameserver = a.iana-servers.net.
example.com nameserver = b.iana-servers.net.
```

In this case, the authoritative name servers are a.iana-servers.net and b.iana-servers.net.

> **MX Record**
> Specifies the email handling server of the domain.

MX Resource Records   The MX record or Mail Exchange record specifies the email handling server of the domain. This is the server where all the incoming emails to the domain will go to. The MX record must also map to a valid A record, not an IP address or a CNAME. The MX record is a crucial piece of information in today's Internet. Without correct MX records, emails to the domain will stop flowing. The following example demonstrates the use of the **nslookup** command to search the MX records information of the domain network-b.edu. The command is issued per entire domain, just like the NS information.

```
C:\nslookup  -query=MX network-b.edu
  Server:   192.168.1.1
  Address:  192.168.1.1#53

  Non-authoritative answer:
network-b.edu  mail exchanger = 20 mx02.cloud.example.com.
network-b.edu  mail exchanger = 30 mx03.cloud.example.com.
network-b.edu  mail exchanger = 10 mx01.cloud.example.com.
```

The MX records yields three email servers for the domain network-b.edu. Each server has a different preference number, where 10 is the preference number of mx01.cloud.example.com server, 20 is the preference number of mx02.cloud.example.com server, and 30 is the preference number of mx03.cloud.example.com server. The preference number is sometimes referred to as the distance or the priority. The lowest preference number signifies the most preferred server. Therefore, the server mx01.cloud.example.com, which has the preference number of 10, is the most preferred mail server of the three. Email service is another popular service offered by many cloud service providers. Many entities do not have resources to manage the amount of emails going to and coming from their domain. Similar to how CNAME records are used to map to the cloud server, the MX records can be used in similar fashion. To move the email service of the domain to the cloud service, the MX will need to be changed to the cloud service provider's email servers. As shown in the preceding example, the domain network-b.edu is using cloud.example.com as their email cloud service.

TXT Resource Records   The TXT record or Text record is used to hold arbitrary text information of the domain. Besides storing arbitrary information or comments for the domain, this record is being used increasingly more to validate the authenticity of the domain. One of its popular applications is to authenticate the email sender domain. SPF or Sender Policy Framework can be entered into a TXT record. This piece of information can be used as a validation of the legitimate sources of email from a domain. Another application is for the cloud service providers to validate the authenticity of the domain ownership. Many cloud service providers will ask for the proof of the domain ownership by providing the domain owner with a token value that needs to be added to the TXT record. The following example shows the TXT record with the specific token value (t=) for a cloud service.

> **TXT Record**
> Used to hold arbitrary text information of the domain.
>
> **SPF**
> Sender Policy Framework.

```
C:\nslookup  -query=TXT network-b.edu
  Server:   192.168.1.1
  Address:  192.168.1.1#53

  Non-authoritative answer:
alumni.nmsu.edu  text = "v=msv1 t=3b6735dd2923c44e99c313ac4adb65"
```

SRV Resource Records   The SRV record or Service record is used to identify a host or hosts that offer a specific type of service. This is sometimes called a service location record. The uniqueness of this type of record is its syntax. The SRV record has a syntax of _service._protocol.name (for example, _ldap._tcp.network-b.edu or _http._tcp.example.com). Not only does the SRV record provide typical host information, it also provides the TCP or UDP port of the service. The SRV record is used all the time with Microsoft Windows, especially in the Active Directory (AD) environment. The following example shows the SRV record of _ldap._tcp.network-b.edu. This service record allows a client to locate a server that is running the LDAP service for the domain network-b.edu.

> **SRV Record**
> Used to identify a host or hosts that offer that specific type of service.

```
C:\nslookup  -query=SRV _ldap._tcp.network-b.edu
  Server:   192.168.1.1
  Address:  192.168.1.1#53

Non-authoritative answer:
```

```
_ldap._tcp.network-b.edu   service = 0 100 389 dc2.network-b.edu.
_ldap._tcp.network-b.edu   service = 0 100 389 dc1.network-b.edu.
```

The output yields two servers that can provide the service. Both of them have priority of 0, which is the highest, and the weight value of 100. Both of them provide the LDAP service on TCP port 389.

Administering the Local DNS Server—A Campus Network Example The primary records are the A records of a campus network and, as previously mentioned, are the most common records in DNS. These records contain the hostname and IP addresses for the computers. For example, network-B.edu has an assigned IP address of 172.16.12.1:

1. When a host pings www.network-B.edu, the host computer first checks its DNS cache; assuming the DNS cache is empty, the host then sends a DNS request to the campus DNS server. Typically, the host will know the IP addresses of the primary and secondary DNS server through either static input or dynamic assignment.

2. The request is sent to the primary DNS server requesting the IP address for www.network-B.edu. The primary DNS server is the authority for network-B. edu and knows the IP address of the hosts in the network.

3. The primary DNS server returns the IP address of www.network-B.edu, and then the ICMP process associated with a ping is started.

You might ask, "How does a PC in the campus network become part of the campus domain?" Specifically, how is an A record entered into the campus domain? Recall that the A record provides a host to IP address translation. Adding the PC to the campus domain is done either manually or dynamically.

The Steps for Manually Adding a Client to the Campus Network The steps for manually updating the DNS A records are graphically shown in Figure 5-12 and are as follows:

1. A client PC updates the A record when an IP address is requested for a computer.

2. The user obtains the PC name and the PC's MAC address.

3. This information is sent to the network administrator or the NOC.

4. The NOC issues an IP address to the client, updates the NOC database of clients on the network, and enters a new A record into the primary DNS. The entry is made only on the primary DNS.

5. The entry will be later replicated on the secondary DNS.

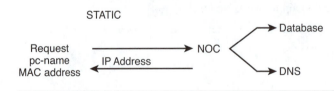

FIGURE 5-12 Manually updating the A record

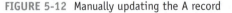

The Steps for Dynamically Adding a Client to the Campus Network   A new A record can be entered dynamically when the client computer obtains an IP address through DHCP registration. This is graphically depicted in Figure 5-13. The DHCP server will issue an IP address to the client and at the same time send an updated A record to the network's primary DNS. This process is called dynamic DNS (DDNS) update. The client name and the IP and MAC addresses are stored in the DHCP database.

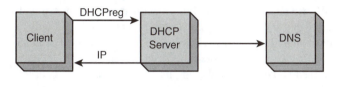

FIGURE 5-13   Dynamic updating of the A record using DHCP

Why obtain the MAC address when entering the information into DNS? This re-cord is used to keep track of all the machines operating on the network. The MAC address is a unique identifier for each machine. The MAC address is also used by BOOTP, which is a predecessor to DHCP. This is where a MAC address is specifi-cally assigned to one IP address in the network.

Reverse DNS returns a hostname for an IP address. This is used for security pur-poses to verify that your domain is allowed to connect to a service. For example, pc-salsa1-1 (10.10.20.1) connects to an FTP server that allows only machines in the salsa domain to make the connection. When the connection is made, the FTP server knows only the IP address of the machine making the connection (10.10.20.1). The server will use the IP address to request the name assigned to that IP. A connection is made to the salsa domain server, and the salsa DNS server returns pc-salsa1-1 as the machine assigned to 10.10.20.1. The FTP server recognizes this is a salsa do-main machine and authorizes the connection.

SUMMARY

This chapter provided a detailed look at configuring and managing the network infrastructure. The concept of the domain name and IP assignment was first examined. The whois protocol was demonstrated and we showed how the databases can be queried to get information of an Internet domain name and an IP space. The issues of IP management with DHCP were also examined and how a name is translated to an IP address. Public IP addresses are a commodity and the steps for using NAT/PAT to translate a private IP address to a public IP address were demonstrated. The benefit is the network can use private IP address assignments inside and only require a limited number of shared public IP addresses for outside access. The DNS services typically available in a campus network have been presented. The DNS Tree Hierarchy was examined and examples of using the **dig** and **nslookup** commands were presented. The concept of an authoritative and non-authoritative name server was presented. A definition of the DNS source records was also presented.

QUESTIONS AND PROBLEMS

Section 5-1

1. What are the two key elements used by the general population when accessing websites on the Internet?

2. What is the purpose of IANA?

3. COM is an example of which of the following?

    a. DNS root zone for a generic (cc) top-level domain

    b. DNS root zone for a generic (d) top-level domain

    c. DNS root zone for a generic (g) top-level domain

    d. DNS root zone for a generic (int) top-level domain

4. gTLD stands for which of the following?

    a. Global top-level domain

    b. Generic top-level domain

    c. Gated top-level domain

    d. None of the above

5. An example of a ccTLD is which of the following? (Select two.)

    a. .net

    b. .uk

    c. .org

    d. .au

6. What is the .int domain registries?

7. What is the purpose of the IDN (Internationalized Domain Name) practices repository?

8. What are the three primary functions of IANA? (Select three.)

    a. Domain Name Management

    b. Portal Assignments

    c. Numbers Resource Management

    d. Protocol Assignments

    e. ASE Number Allocation

9. What organization is responsible for IP address assignment in North America?

10. ARIN's responsibility is to assign IP addresses to which of the following? (Select two.)

    a. Internet service providers

    b. Home networks

    c. Corporate networks

    d. Large end users

11. Which of the following are world Regional Internet Registries?

    a. AfriNIC

    b. AFrNIC

    c. LACNIC

    d. ARIN

    e. AIRN

12. What is the purpose of the in-addr.arpa domain?

13. Who handles the assignment of a domain name?

    a. ICANN

    b. Domain registrar

    c. Network administrator

    d. TLD

14. What protocol is used to query databases that store user registration information of an Internet domain name and IP space?

    a. whois protocol

    b. whereis protocol

    c. whatis protocol

    d. None of the above

15. In regards to campus DHCP service, the IP address assignment is based on what?

16. How are BOOTP and DHCP related?

17. Define lease time.

18. What networking function is required if the DHCP server is not on the same LAN? Why is this networking function required?

19. What command enables a DHCP relay on a Cisco router?

20. What are the port numbers for the DHCP protocol?

21. What command is used to release a current IP address on a computer?

22. What command is used to initiate the DHCP process?

23. What happens if a DHCP server is not available?

    a. The client will issue a global broadcast to search for available DHCP server.

    b. The host computer will issue unicast packets to the 169.254.1.1 address and then obtain an IP address.

    c. A DHCP client will use a self-assigned IP address known as Automatic Private IP addressing (APIPA).

    d. The ipconfig/redo command is automatically issued to establish connectivity.

24. What is the command on the router to enable the DHCP relay function?

25. What information is contained in the MT offer (DHCP Offer) packet? (Select three.)

    a. Default gateway

    b. Leased time

    c. Internet address

    d. IP address of the Domain Name server

    e. Hostname

26. What is a gratuitous ARP broadcast?

27. What is the purpose of the following command?

    ```
    ip dhcp pool address-pool
    ```

28. The following commands are entered into a router. Explain what this does.

    ```
    RouterA(dhcp-config)# dns-server 192.168.10.52
    RouterA(dhcp-config)# domain-name networks.com
    RouterA(dhcp-config)# default-router 192.168.10.1
    ```

29. What information does NOC typically associate with an IP address?

Section 5-3

30. How is IP addressing typically handled in a home network?

31. What is Port Address Translation (PAT)?

32. A router on a home network is assigned an IP address of 128.123.45.67. A computer in the home network is assigned a private IP address of 192.168.10.62. This computer is assigned the public IP address 128.123.45.67:1922. Which IP address is used for routing data packets on the Internet? Is overloading being used?

33. For Cisco routers, what is a local address?

34. For Cisco routers, what is a *global address?*

35. If an interface Fastethernet0/0 is the interface for the internal private LAN and the interface Fastethernet0/1 is the interface facing the public Internet, provide the configuration for the appropriate NAT interfaces.

36. What does the following statement do?

```
RouterA(config)# ip nat inside source static 10.10.20.1
128.123.14.10
```

37. What does the following command do?

```
RouterA(config)# ip nat inside source static tcp 192.168.12.5 443
12.0.0.5 443
```

38. What does the following command do? Does this bring up any security concerns?

```
RouterA(config)# ip nat inside source static 10.10.20.1 15.1.1.2
```

39. The command **show ip nat translation** is entered on a router. The following information is displayed. What is this showing?

```
RouterA# show ip nat translation
Pro Inside global    Inside local      Outside local
Outside global
tcp 15.1.1.2:35425   10.10.20.1:35425  55.105.35.15:80
55.105.35.15:80
```

40. What is the maximum theoretical number of ports that a single IP can use?

41. What is dynamic NAT?

Section 5-4

42. List 11 top-level domains.

43. What is the purpose of a root server in DNS?

44. A new network wants to obtain a domain name. The first step is what?

45. The hostname and IP address for a computer is stored in what for a campus DNS service?

46. How is it possible for the command **ping www.networkB.edu** to find the destination without an IP address?

47. What is the purpose of reverse DNS? Where is it used?

48. What is the purpose of the reverse domain name service?

49. What is the purpose of the root hints file?

50. In regards to the Internet, what is a domain?

51. What is an authoritative name server?

52. Explain how a machine obtains the IP address of a website on the Internet.

53. The following entry is made on a UNIX server. Describe what this is doing.

```
[admin@noc ~]$ dig +trace www.example.com
```
54. What does it mean to be a non-authoritative name server?

55. What is a fully qualified domain name (FQDN)?

56. What is the difference in a domain and a zone?

57. What is the Start of Authority?

58. This record is a mapping of an IP address to a hostname. It is sometime referred to as a reverse record.

59. What is this information showing?

```
www.iana.orgcanonical name = ianawww.vip.icann.org.
```
60. Where is the authoritative name server of the domain listed?

61. What is the purpose of the TXT record?

Critical Thinking

62. Describe the typical process for requesting an IP address using DHCP.

63. How does NAT (Network Address Translation) help protect outsider access to computers in the home network?

64. Why would the pointer record not be the exact reverse of the A record?

65. The following query is submitted. What is this information showing? Which server is the preferred server? What is the cloud being used for?

```
C:\nslookup  -query=MX network-b.edu
    Server:   192.168.1.1
    Address:  192.168.1.1#53

    Non-authoritative answer:
et477.com  mail exchanger = 15 mx02.cloud.sample.com.
et477.com  mail exchanger = 25 mx03.cloud.sample.com.
et477.com  mail exchanger = 5 mx01.cloud.sample.com.
```

6
CHAPTER

ANALYZING NETWORK DATA TRAFFIC

Chapter Outline

Objectives

- Review the TCP/IP suite of protocols
- Introduce the use of netstat for troubleshooting TCP and UDP connections
- Introduce the use of the Wireshark network protocol analyzer
- The use of SNMP for the gathering of the statistical information from network devices
- Introduce the use of NetFlow for acquiring IP traffic operational data
- Introduce filtering techniques for analyzing network data traffic

Key Terms

network forensics
Internet sockets
well-known ports
ICANN
registered ports
transport layer protocols
TCP
connection-oriented protocol
SYN

SYN ACK
ACK
UDP
netstat
ARP
arp –a
show arp
ARP Reply
Echo Request
SNMP (SNMPv1)

management information base (MIB)
snmp community
[*community string*]
SNMPv2
SNMPv3
NetFlow
Jflow
Sflow
collector

INTRODUCTION

This chapter looks at the use of a network protocol analyzer to examine data packets. Section 6-1 introduces the concept of protocol analysis/forensics. This section reviews the TCP/IP suite of protocols, the TCP connection states, and the use of the **netstat** command. Section 6-2 introduces the use of the Wireshark protocol analyzer. This section introduces the techniques for using a protocol analyzer to examine how networking packets are exchanged in a TCP/IP network. Section 6-3 examines analyzing network data traffic. The first part of the chapter examines SNMP (Simple Network Management Protocol). The section concludes with a look at NetFlow, which is used for acquiring IP traffic operational data in order to provide network and security monitoring, traffic analysis, and IP accounting. This chapter concludes with Section 6-4, which looks at filtering the captured data packets. Data capture files can be quite large and it often requires that the network administrator search the capture files to find specific information. This section examines techniques to filter the captured data packets using Wireshark.

6-1 PROTOCOL ANALYSIS/FORENSICS

Network Forensics

The steps required for monitoring and analyzing computer network data traffic.

Internet Sockets

An endpoint across a computer network.

Well-Known Ports

Ports reserved by ICANN.

ICANN

Internet Corporation for Assigned Names and Numbers. ICANN is responsible for IP address space allocation, domain name system management, and root server system management functions.

Registered Ports

Ports registered with ICANN—ports 1024–49151.

This section examines the process of protocol analysis and **network forensics**. Network forensics is basically the steps required for monitoring and analyzing computer network data traffic. A solid foundation in the underlying protocols comprising the TCP/IP suite, namely TCP and UDP, is required to be able to analyze network traffic or to be able to gather information for network forensics or intrusion detection.

TCP/IP applications process requests from/to hosts via specific TCP or UDP ports. These ports are called **Internet sockets**, and each has a unique number. An Internet socket is an endpoint across a computer network. There are 65,536 possible TCP/UDP ports. Ports 1–1023 are called **well-known ports** or *reserved* ports. These ports are reserved by Internet Corporation for Assigned Names and Numbers (**ICANN**), and they represent some well-known network services. Ports 1024–49151 are called **registered ports** and are registered with ICANN. Ports 49152–65535 are called *dynamic* or *private* ports.

Examples of well-known ports include HTTP (TCP port 80) for web service and HTTPS (TCP port 443) for secure web service. Applications use these port numbers when communicating with another application as illustrated in Figure 6-1. Host B is passing to Host A data that is destined for TCP port 80 (HTTP). The HyperText Transfer Protocol (HTTP) is used for transferring non-secure web-based documents to a web browser, such as Internet Explorer or Mozilla Firefox. Host A receives the packet and passes the application up to the port 80 application. Table 6-1 lists some popular applications and their port numbers for TCP/IP. This list includes FTP, SSH, SMTP, DNS, DHCP, HTTP, and HTTPS.

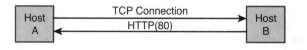

FIGURE 6-1 An example of two hosts connected for a TCP transmission

TABLE 6-1 Common Applications and Their Port Numbers

Transport Protocol	Port Number	Application	Description
TCP	20 (data port) 21 (command/ control port)	FTP	File Transfer Protocol
TCP	22	SSH	Secure Shell
TCP	23	Telnet	Virtual terminal connection
TCP	25	SMTP	Simple Mail Transfer Protocol
UDP	53	DNS	Domain name server
UDP	67, 68	DHCP (BOOTP-Client) (BOOTP-Server)	Dynamic Host Control Protocol
UDP	69	TFTP	Trivial File Transfer Protocol
TCP and UDP	80	HTTP	Hypertext Transfer Protocol
UDP	110	POP3	Post Office Protocol
TCP	143	IMAP	Internet Message Access Protocol
UDP	161	SNMP	Simple Network Management Protocol
TCP	443	HTTPS	Secure HTTP
TCP	445	SMB	Server message block
UDP	1701	L2TP	Layer 2 Tunneling Protocol
TCP	1720	H.323/Q.931	Voice over IP
TCP/UDP	1723	PPTP	Point-to-point Tunneling Protocol
TCP/UDP	3389	RDP	Remote Desktop Protocol

You can find a complete list of ports at http://www.iana.org/assignments/port-numbers.

The transport layer protocols in TCP/IP are important in establishing a network connection, managing the delivery of data between a source and destination host, and terminating the data connection. There are two transport protocols within the TCP/IP transport layer: TCP and UDP. TCP, the Transport Control Protocol, is a connection-oriented protocol, which means it establishes the network connection, manages the data transfer, and terminates the connection. The TCP protocol establishes a set of rules or guidelines for establishing the connection. TCP verifies the delivery of the data packets through the network and includes support for error checking and recovering lost data. TCP then specifies a procedure for terminating the network connection. Figure 6-2 illustrates the TCP datagram. The first two fields are the Internet socket numbers mentioned earlier. The first 16 bits represent the source port and the second 16 bits represent the destination port.

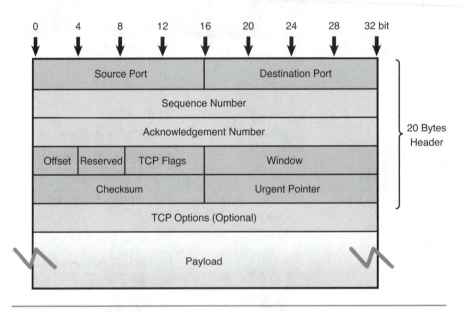

FIGURE 6-2 TCP datagram

Before any TCP connection is made, a TCP three-way handshake must happen to initiate the connection. A TCP three-way handshake is a unique sequence of three data packets exchanged at the beginning of a TCP connection between two hosts, as shown in Figure 6-3. This sequence is as follows:

1. The SYN (Synchronizing) packet
2. The SYN+ACK (Synchronizing Acknowledgment) packet
3. The ACK (Acknowledgment) packet

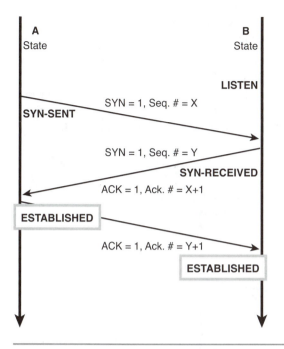

A
State

B
State

LISTEN

SYN = 1, Seq. # = X

SYN-SENT

SYN = 1, Seq. # = Y

SYN-RECEIVED

ACK = 1, Ack. # = X+1

ESTABLISHED

ACK = 1, Ack. # = Y+1

ESTABLISHED

FIGURE 6-3 The TCP three-way handshake

The host initiating the connection will send a synchronizing packet (SYN). The SYN flag is set in the TCP flags field. In this example, Host A issues a SYN packet to initiate the TCP handshake. The SYN will have a sequence number (SEQ) associated with it. In the example shown in Figure 6-3, the sequence number is x. The sequence number is used to keep track of the data packets being transferred from Host A to Host B. The length of the packet being sent by Host A is 0 (LEN 0), which indicates that the packet contains no data. At this point, Host A changes its TCP state to SYN-SENT.

In packet 2, Host B replies with a SYN+ACK packet. Both SYN flag and ACK flag are set in the TCP flags field. The ACK is an acknowledgment that Host B received the packet from Host A. A number is attached to the ACK with a value of $(x + 1)$ that should be the sum of the SEQ# from packet 1 plus the length (LEN) of packet 1. Recall that the length of packet 1 is 0 (LEN 0), but packet 1 counts as one packet; therefore, Host B replies with an acknowledgment of packet 1 sequence number plus 1 $(x + 1)$. This acknowledgment notifies Host A that the packet (packet 1) was received. Packet 2 from Host B will also have a sequence number issued by Host B. In this packet, the sequence number has a value of y. This sequence number is used to keep track of packets transferred by Host B. When this happens, Host B changes its TCP state from LISTEN to SYN-RECEIVED.

In packet 3, Host A acknowledges the reception of Host B's packet. The ACK number is an increment of one higher than the SEQ# sent by Host B in packet 2 $(y + 1)$. Host A also sends an updated SEQ# that is one larger than the SEQ# Host A sent in packet 1 $(x + 1)$. Remember, Host A and Host B each have their own sequence numbers. Host A changes its TCP state to ESTABLISHED and, upon receiving the ACK packet from Host A, Host B changes its TCP state to ESTABLISHED as well.

This completes the three-packet handshake that establishes the TCP connection. This handshake appears at the beginning of all TCP data transfers.

The last part of the TCP connection is terminating the session for each host. A TCP connection can be terminated gracefully or abruptly due to loss of the network. Typically, TCP has a graceful way of terminating its connection. The first thing that happens is when a network application is about to close, it signals a host to send a FIN (finish) packet to the other connected host, as illustrated in Figure 6-4.

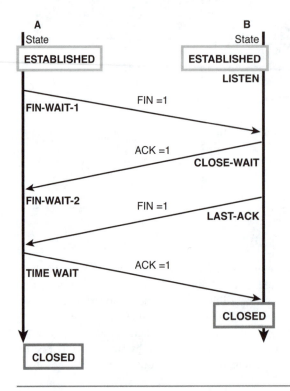

FIGURE 6-4 Terminating the TCP connection

Both Host A and B are in the TCP ESTABLISHED state. Host A sends a FIN packet to Host B indicating the data transmission is complete. This puts Host A in a FIN-WAIT-1 TCP state. Host B responds with an ACK packet acknowledging the reception of the FIN packet. It signals its application to close the connection and put itself in a CLOSE-WAIT state. Host A receives an ACK from Host B and for another FIN packet, and it changes its state to FIN-WAIT-2. Host B then sends Host A a FIN packet when its application is closed, indicating the connection is being terminated. At this point, Host B is in the LAST-ACK state. Host A replies with an ACK packet and changes its state to TIME-WAIT. Upon receiving an ACK, Host B's TCP state becomes CLOSED. Table 6-2 summarizes and briefly explains the TCP connection state.

TABLE 6-2 TCP Connection State

State	Description
LISTEN	The host is listening and ready to accept connections.
SYN-SENT	The first SYN sent to establish the connection indicates active open.
SYN-RECEIVED	The receiving host receives and acknowledges the SYN.
ESTABLISHED	The connection is fully established.
FIN-WAIT-1	The terminating host sends the FIN to terminate the connection indicates active close.
CLOSE-WAIT	The receiving host acknowledges the FIN.
FIN-WAIT-2	The terminating host receives the acknowledgment from the receiving host.
LAST_ACK	The receiving host sends its own FIN to signal the end and wait for the acknowledgment.
TIME-WAIT	The terminating host acknowledges the last FIN and waits for the connection to close.
CLOSED	Connection is closed.

The User Datagram Protocol (**UDP**) is a *connectionless* protocol. This means that UDP packets are transported over the network without a connection being established and without any acknowledgment that the data packets arrived at the destination. UDP is useful in applications such as videoconferencing and audio feeds, where such acknowledgments are not necessary.

Figure 6-5 shows the UDP datagram. It is much simpler than TCP datagram with only 8 Bytes of header. Often times, UDP and TCP co-exist in the same application. Many of these applications use TCP to initiate the connection and then use UDP to deliver connectionless packets. No acknowledgments are sent back from the client. UDP does not have a procedure for terminating the data transfer; either the source stops delivery of the data packets or the client terminates the connection.

> **UDP**
> User Datagram Protocol. A connectionless protocol that transports data packets to a connection being established and without any acknowledgment that the data packets arrived at the destination.

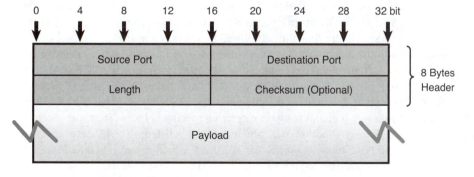

FIGURE 6-5 UPD datagram

Basic TCP/UDP Forensics

A useful tool for troubleshooting TCP and UDP connections is netstat. **netstat** (Network Statistics) is a command-line program readily available in multiple platforms (such as Windows, Mac, and Linux). The **netstat** utility has many options, and it can display information such as network statistics, routing tables, and TCP/UDP connections. Some options might vary depending on the operating system. To view all the network connections of a host, the command **netstat –an** is generally used. The option **–a** is for displaying all connections, including listening ports. The option **–n** is used to display the addresses and ports in numerical format. These options are standard on all OS platforms. Here is the example of the **netstat –an** output on Windows:

```
C:\Users\admin>netstat -an
Active Connections
```

Proto	Local Address	Foreign Address	State
TCP	0.0.0.0:22	0.0.0.0:0	LISTENING
TCP	172.16.101.7:139	0.0.0.0:0	LISTENING
TCP	172.16.101.7:445	0.0.0.0:0	LISTENING
TCP	127.0.0.1:1900	0.0.0.0:0	LISTENING
TCP	172.16.101.7:49188	96.17.159.58:80	ESTABLISHED
TCP	172.16.101.7:49189	173.194.79.95:443	ESTABLISHED
TCP	172.16.101.7:49190	199.7.71.190:80	TIME_WAIT
TCP	172.16.101.7:49191	74.125.224.48:443	ESTABLISHED
TCP	172.16.101.7:49192	199.7.59.72:80	TIME_WAIT
TCP	172.16.101.7:49193	74.125.224.48:443	ESTABLISHED
TCP	172.16.101.7:49195	192.168.3.4:80	ESTABLISHED
TCP	172.16.101.7:49196	192.168.3.4:80	ESTABLISHED
TCP	172.16.101.7:49197	74.125.224.47:443	ESTABLISHED
TCP	172.16.101.7:49198	192.168.3.4:80	ESTABLISHED
TCP	172.16.101.7:49199	192.168.3.4:80	ESTABLISHED
TCP	172.16.101.7:49200	192.168.3.4:80	ESTABLISHED
TCP	172.16.101.7:49201	192.168.3.4:80	ESTABLISHED
TCP	172.16.101.7:49202	74.125.224.36:80	CLOSE_WAIT
UDP	172.16.101.7:139	*:*	
UDP	172.16.101.7:445	*:*	

The preceding output shows all the TCP and UDP connections associated with the host (172.16.101.7). The Proto column is the connection protocol (TCP or UDP). The local address is the IP address followed by the port number of the local host connection immediately following the colon (:) . The Foreign Address is the remote host and its port, of which the connection belongs. The State is the TCP state of the connection as previously discussed in the TCP handshakes. Note that UDP does not have any state. When the connection is in the LISTENING state, the local host is listening on that port and ready to receive connections. In this state, the local address will display either 0.0.0.0, which means it is listening on all network interfaces (second NIC, modem, tunnel), or 127.0.0.1, which means it is only listening for connections from the local host itself, or its IP address (172.16.101.7), which means it is listening for connections from the network.

The output shows that the local host is listening on port 22 (SSH) on all of its interfaces. This is indicated by 0.0.0.0:22. It is also listening on TCP port 139 and 445 on the network. These ports are for Microsoft NetBIOS and Microsoft Directory Service, which are used for file and printer sharing. The last listening port is the TCP 1900 for only the local host itself to connect. For the port 1900, this means that there is some program running or listening on TCP port 1900, and it is only expecting the local host itself to use it. Some programs create a network socket port just for itself to connect. The rest of the TCP connections are made from the host to several IP addresses on TCP port 80 (http) and 443 (https). Judging from those well-known ports, these probably are the web servers on the Internet. Most of these TCP connections to port 80 and 443 are in the ESTABLISHED state. This means that these connections were successfully initiated after the TCP three-way handshake, and they are active. One TCP connection, 74.125.224.36, is in a CLOSE_WAIT state, which means the local host has just acknowledged the FIN packet to terminate the connection from the remote host. A couple of connections are in the TIME_WAIT state, which is the last state before local host closes the TCP connection.

netstat also can provide information about the executable program that created or is involved in the TCP connection. The option **-b** in Windows or the option **–p** in Linux is used to find out what programs are running and what network resources are being used. This is a powerful function that can be used to track down open network ports or exposed network security holes. Sometimes, people do not know what programs are running in the background. They also might not know what programs are communicating over the network, and some of these programs might be unwanted. The ability to associate a program to the network connection and port is extremely useful. The following is the output of the command **netstat -abn** on Windows:

```
C:\Users\admin>netstat -bn

Active Connections

   Proto  Local Address              Foreign Address            State
   TCP    127.0.0.1:49318              127.0.0.1:49320            TIME_
WAIT
   TCP    128.123.101.13:49289     96.17.159.58:80          ESTABLISHED
[jucheck.exe]
   TCP    128.123.101.13:49315     74.125.224.128:80        ESTABLISHED
[chrome.exe]
   TCP    128.123.101.13:49316     74.125.224.143:80        ESTABLISHED
[chrome.exe]
   TCP    128.123.101.13:49317     128.123.128.102:443      CLOSE_WAIT
[asdm-launcher.exe]
   TCP    128.123.101.13:49335     128.123.128.102:443      CLOSE_WAIT
[javaw.exe]
```

ARP and ICMP

ARP and ICMP are two of the most common network layer protocols seen on any network. Along with TCP or UDP, these protocols show up all the time when scanning the network. ARP is used to discover the neighboring devices, and ICMP is used to report back information and errors. These protocols are examined next.

ARP The Address Resolution Protocol (**ARP**) resolves an IP address to a hardware address for final delivery of data packets to the destination. ARP issues a query in a network called an *ARP request*, asking which network interface has this IP address. The host assigned the IP address replies with an *ARP reply*, the protocol that contains the hardware address for the destination host. Figure 6-6 shows the ARP packet. When an ARP is issued, the requester fills out the source hardware address with its MAC address and the source protocol address with its IP address. It also puts the querying IP address in the destination protocol address field. The destination hardware address is left blank to be filled out by the destination host.

> **ARP**
> Address Resolution Protocol, used to map an IP address to its MAC address.

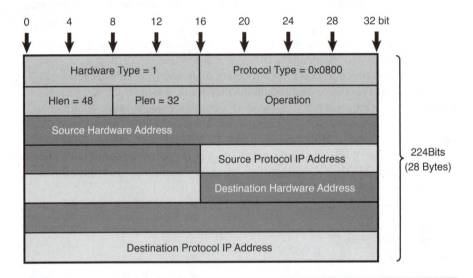

FIGURE 6-6 ARP packet

An ARP request is issued on the LAN as a broadcast, which means this message is being sent to all computers in the local-area network. Additionally, an ARP request is generated for every network device if the MAC address is not known. This is why ARP is one of the most seen protocols on a local network. The destination computer sends an ARP reply back to the source with its MAC address. The ARP request is sent back as a unicast packet. The ARP conversations are illustrated in the next section with the Wireshark protocol analyzer. In typical cases, the owner of the IP address replies to the message, but this is not always the case. Sometimes, another networking device, such as a router, can provide the MAC address information. In that case, the MAC address being returned is for the next networking device in the route to the destination.

To help reduce the amount of ARP broadcast traffic on the network, a network host or device is generally equipped with an ARP cache. When a destination host receives an ARP request packet and when a source host receives an ARP reply packet, it updates its ARP cache with the IP address and the MAC address that it receives. This way, it does not need to generate an ARP broadcast every time it needs to communicate with its neighbors. The ARP cache can be viewed on most computers using the command **arp –a**. This command works on Windows, Mac, and Linux. The output of the **arp –a** command issued on a Linux host is as follows:

```
[root@noc-server ~]# arp -a
? (10.20.101.146) at 0:15:e9:1f:2:c6 on en1 [ethernet]
server1.et477.local (10.10.101.1) at 0:25:b4:cf:57:80 on en0
[ethernet]
server2.et477.local(10.10.101.4) at 0:21:70:5b:f7:ea on en0 [ethernet]
```

The output may contain different information and may display in different formats depending on the operating system. The ARP output previously listed shows the IP addresses and their associated MAC addresses. Along with these, the hostname will be displayed if the IP address has a DNS hostname. The ARP cache can also be viewed on network devices, such as routers and switches. On Cisco routers, the command to display the ARP cache entries is **show ip arp** or **show arp**, as shown here:

```
et477-router#sh arp
Protocol  Address          Age (min)  Hardware Addr   Type  Interface
Internet  192.168.247.10           0  a4ba.db1d.190e  ARPA  Vlan100
Internet  192.168.246.95           3  0018.8b22.9141  ARPA  Vlan100
Internet  192.168.245.135          0  0023.ae8a.0831  ARPA  Vlan100
Internet  192.168.245.246        216  001e.7aa3.0980  ARPA  Vlan30
Internet  192.168.245.242        236  001e.7aa3.0980  ARPA  Vlan30
Internet  192.168.245.226         54  000f.8f5d.86e0  ARPA  Vlan10
Internet  192.168.245.227         96  000f.8f5d.86e0  ARPA  Vlan10
```

Similar to the ARP output from Linux, the ARP output from the router shows the IP address, MAC address, and the interface where an ARP entry is learned. Additional information associated with the **show arp** command is the age of each ARP entry. This information is displayed in minutes under the Age (min) column.

ICMP The Internet Control Message Protocol (ICMP) is used to control the flow of data in the network, to report errors, and to perform diagnostics. Figure 6-7 illustrates the ICMP packet. Depending on the type, each ICMP packet serves different functions. For example, a networking device, such as a router, can send an ICMP *source-quench* packet to a host that requests a slowdown in the data transfer. The ICMP packet then will have the type of 4.

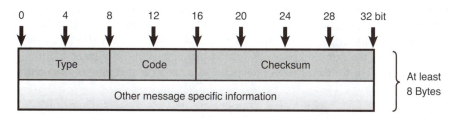

FIGURE 6-7 ICMP packet

An important troubleshooting tool within the ICMP protocol is **ping**, which was named after the "ping" sound the sonar makes. The **ping** command is used to verify connectivity with another host in the network. The destination host could be in a LAN, in a campus LAN, or on the Internet. The **ping** command uses a series of echo requests, and the networking device receiving the echo requests responds with a series of echo replies to test a network connection. The **ping** request is an ICMP type 8 and the **ping** reply is the ICMP type 0. These ICMP types are used to exchange message information. Some other types, like ICMP type 3 and ICMP type 11, are used to report error messages. ICMP type 3 packet reports destination unreachable message to the originating host. ICMP type 11 is the error message for time to live (TTL) exceeded, which indicates that the packet life has expired. Some of the common ICMP messages are as follows:

```
Type    Name                                Reference
----    -------------------------           ---------

  0     Echo Reply                          [RFC792]

  3     Destination Unreachable             [RFC792]

  4     Source Quench                       [RFC792]

  5     Redirect                            [RFC792]

  8     Echo                                [RFC792]

  9     Router Advertisement                [RFC1256]

 10     Router Selection                    [RFC1256]

 11     Time Exceeded                       [RFC792]
```

ping is the most common tool used in troubleshooting connectivity on the network. Ping is available on every operating system and on most network devices by default. A general **ping** command format is **ping** *hostname/ip address*. There are options that can be used with **ping**, and these can vary depending on the OS. For example, there is an option to change the size of the default ICMP packet. This option is **–l** for Windows and is **–s** for the Mac and Linux machines. This option is useful when trying to simulate bigger size packets and test respond time. Another useful option is **–t**, which will allow a continuous ping to the target in a Windows environment. Typically, Windows sends only four ICMP packets whereas Linux and Mac machines will send continuous ICMP packets until it is stopped.

Ping is also available on routers and switches. On Cisco routers, one can get more use of a ping command by using the extended **ping** option. Typically, a router has multiple network interfaces. When a **ping** command is executed, it will use the interface where the packet exits as its source IP address. The extended **ping** on Cisco gives users the option to choose a different source IP address. This comes in handy when testing out connectivity from a different network. Extended **ping** provides more ways to perform advanced check of host reach ability and network connectivity. To do this, simply enter **ping** at the router prompt and press return. By doing this, step-by-step extended options will be provided to users. When the extended **ping** command is used, the source IP address can be changed to any IP address on the router. Also, the extended **ping** command works only at the privileged EXEC command line. The following is an example of how the extended **ping** is executed on a Cisco router:

```
et477-gate#ping
Protocol [ip]:
```

```
Target IP address: 128.123.2.19
Repeat count [5]: 200
Datagram size [100]: 200
Timeout in seconds [2]:
Extended commands [n]: y
Source address or interface: 128.123.247.44      (This features let's
you specify the source address)
Type of service [0]:
Set DF bit in IP header? [no]:
Validate reply data? [no]:
Data pattern [0xABCD]:
Loose, Strict, Record, Timestamp, Verbose[none]:
Sweep range of sizes [n]:
Type escape sequence to abort.
Sending 200, 200-byte ICMP Echos to 128.123.2.19, timeout is 2 sec-
onds:
Packet sent with a source address of 128.123.247.44
!!!!!!!!!!!!!!!!!!!!!!!!!!!!!!!!!!!!!!!!!!!!!!!!!!!!!!!!!!!!!!!!!!!!!!!
!!!!!!!!!!!!!!!!!!!!!!!!!!!!!!!!!!!!!!!!!!!!!!!!!!!!!!!!!!!!!!!!!!!!!!!
!!!!!!!!!!!!!!!!!!!!!!!!!!!!!!!!!!!!!!!!!!!!!!!!!!!!!!!!!!!!
Success rate is 100 percent (200/200), round-trip min/avg/max = 1/1/4
ms
```

6-2   WIRESHARK PROTOCOL ANALYZER

This section introduces the techniques for using a protocol analyzer to examine how networking packets are exchanged in a TCP/IP network. By using a protocol analyzer, such as Wireshark, you will actually be able to develop a better understanding of the protocols being used and how the data packets are being transferred.

The Wireshark software includes many advanced features for packet capture and analysis. The capabilities of this software will help you gain a thorough understanding of packet transfers and networking protocols. In this chapter, you will gain an introductory understanding of the capabilities and techniques for using a sophisticated software protocol analyzer. The protocol analyzer has the capability to capture and decode data packets and allows the user to inspect the packet contents. This enables the user to investigate how information is being transferred in the network. Additionally, the information provided by the protocol analyzer enables the user to detect, identify, and correct network problems. In this section, you are guided through the steps of using the Wireshark Network Analyzer.

The following steps guide you through installing and using the Wireshark software. To download the latest version of the software, visit **www.WireShark.org**. At the WireShark.org home page, select **Download Wireshark**. Once completed, select your corresponding operating system. Click **Run** when the dialog box appears to initiate the download process. At the prompt of the setup wizard, select **Next** and agree to the license agreement. Choose the components you want to install and click **Next** to continue. At the next screen, choose your program shortcuts and click **Next** to continue. Use the default directory paths specified in the setup menu. To complete setup, click **Install** to start the installation process. After installation, you are ready to begin using the software.

In the first exercise, the Wireshark software is used to examine the packets transferred in the process of pinging a computer. This exercise uses the IP and MAC addresses specified in Table 6-1 and the CD provided with this book includes the .cap files used in the following exercises:

1. In Windows, Click **Start** > ALL **Programs** > **WireShark** to start the analyzer program. The procedure for starting the WireShark Network Analyzer is the same for a MAC OS X operating in the dualboot mode with XP.

2. Once WireShark is open, click **File** > **Open**, select your CD-ROM drive, and select the *WireShark* file folder. Double-click the **Ch6-1.cap** file to open the file.

Once you open the Ch6-1.cap capture in WireShark, you should see the captured packets displayed on the detail view screen, as shown in Figure 6-8.

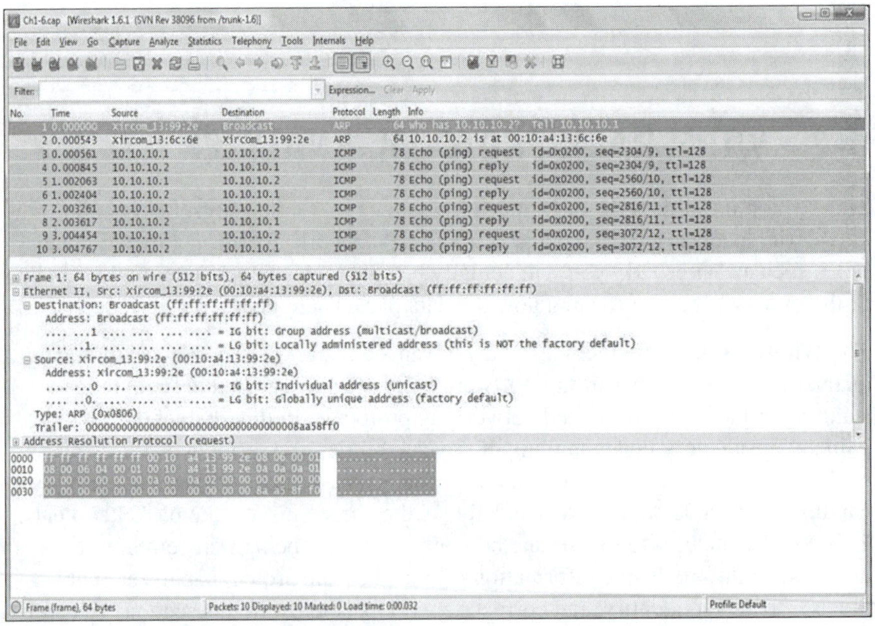

FIGURE 6-8 The captured packets showing the ping from computer 1 to computer 2

In this example, the information on the screen is showing the transfer of packets that occurs when one computer pings another. In this case, computer 1 pinged computer 2. The MAC and IP addresses are listed for your reference in Table 6-3.

TABLE 6-3   The MAC and Assigned IP Addresses for Computer 1 and Computer 2

Name (Hostname)	MAC Address	IP Address
Computer 1	00-10-A4-13-99-2E	10.10.10.1
Computer 2	00-10-A4-13-6C-6E	10.10.10.2

In this example, a **ping** command is issued from computer 1 to computer 2. The structure of the command issued by computer 1 at the command prompt is

`ping 10.10.10.2`

Shown in packet number 1 in Figure 6-8, computer 1 issues an **ARP** request on the LAN. The source of the packet is 00-10-A4-13-99-2E (computer 1). The destination address on the local-area network shown is BROADCAST, which means this message is being sent to all computers on the network. A query (Q) being asked is who has the IP address 1 0.10.10.2 (PA). In Figure 6-8, the wording to the right of ARP says, "Who has 10.10.10.2?"

The highlighted area (Number 2) in Figure 6-9 shows computer 2 replying with its MAC address back to computer 1. This is called an **ARP reply**, which is a protocol where the MAC address is returned. The source of the ARP reply is from 00-10-A4-13-6C-6E (computer 2), which is replying that the MAC address for 10.10.10.2 is 00-10-A4-13-6C-6E (HA). In this case, the owner of the IP address replied to the message.

> **ARP Reply**
> A network protocol where the MAC address is returned.

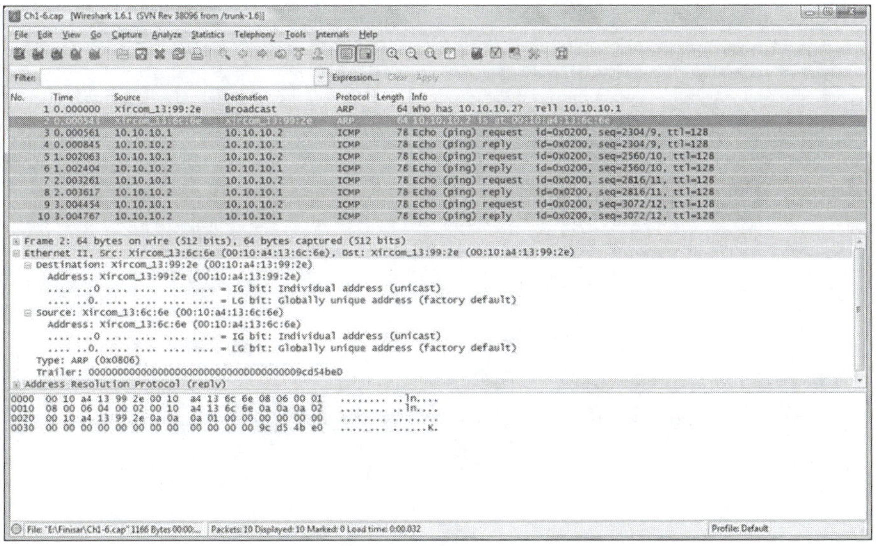

FIGURE 6-9   Computer 2 replying with its MAC address back to computer 1

Figure 6-10 shows computer 1 sending an **echo request** directly to computer 2. An echo request is the part of the ICMP protocol that requests a reply from a computer. Notice in the echo request that the destination address is 00-10-A4-13-6C-6E (computer 2's MAC address), and the source is 00-10-A4-13-99-2E (computer 1's

> **Echo Request**
> Part of the ICMP protocol that requests a reply from a computer.

MAC address). Recall that computer 1 now knows the MAC address for IP address 10.10.10.2, so the **ping** request can be sent directly. In this step, computer 1 uses the ICMP **ping** command to verify network connectivity. The highlighted area in Figure 6-11 (number 4) shows computer 2's echo reply. This series of echo requests and replies repeats three more times for a total of four cycles.

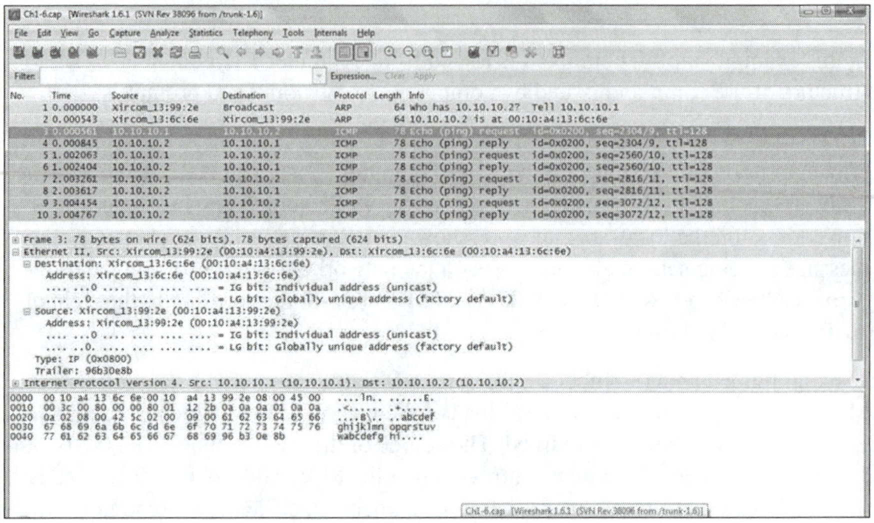

FIGURE 6-10 Computer 1 is sending an echo request to computer 2

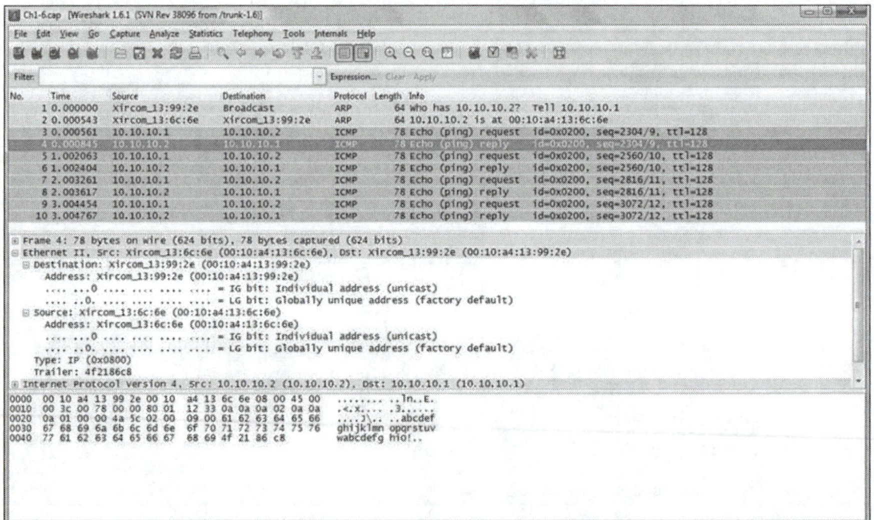

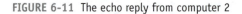

FIGURE 6-11 The echo reply from computer 2

Using Wireshark to Capture Packets

The first exercise with the WireShark software demonstrated how to use the protocol analyzer to inspect captured packets. In most cases, the user will want to capture data packets from their own network. The following steps describe how to use the software to capture packets:

1. In Windows, click **Start** > **Programs** > **WireShark** > and select **WireShark** to start the program.

2. To capture packets on an operating network, you first need to select the interfaces in which you would like to obtain the capture (see Figure 6-12). You can do this by going to **Capture** > **Interfaces**. After selecting your interfaces, click **Start** to start capturing, as shown in Figure 6-13. You can also get to the interface list by clicking on **Interface List** from the WireShark home screen.

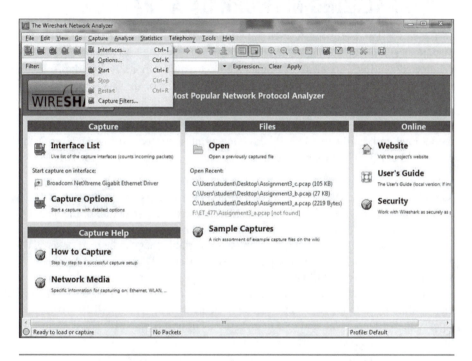

FIGURE 6-12 Initializing Wireshark to capture data packets from your network

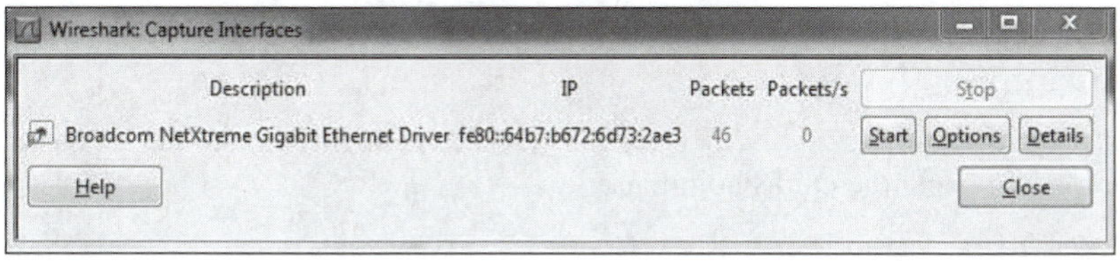

FIGURE 6-13 Starting the capture

3. To examine the packets, stop the simulation by clicking **Capture > Stop**. Remember, there must be some activity on your network for packets to be transferred. You may see little traffic activity if your network is in the lab, and there is limited network activity. You can always use the **ping** command to generate some network data activity, if needed.

To open a saved capture file, click **File > Open** or click **Open** from the Wireshark home screen.

To change capture options, click **Capture > Options** to change the options to your preferred settings.

6-3 ANALYZING NETWORK DATA TRAFFIC

A network of moderate size has a tremendous number of data packets entering and leaving. The number of routers, switches, hubs, servers, and host computers can become staggering. Proper network management requires that all network resources be managed. This requires that proper management tools be in place.

A fundamental network management tool is SNMP (SNMPv1), the Simple Network Management Protocol. SNMPv1, developed in 1988, is widely supported in most modern network hardware. SNMP is a connectionless protocol using the User Datagram Protocol (UDP) for the transmission of data to and from UDP port 161.

SNMP (SNMPv1)
Simple Network Management Protocol.

Management Information Base (MIB)
A collection of standard objects that are used to obtain configuration parameters and performance data on a networking device.

SNMP uses a management information base (MIB), which is a collection of standard objects that are used to obtain configuration parameters and performance data on a networking device, such as a router. MIBs describe the structure of the management data of a device subsystem using a hierarchical namespace that contains object identifiers or OID. Each OID identifies a variable that can be read or set via SNMP. For example, the MIB's object, ifDescr, has an OID of 1.3.6.1.2.1.2.2.1.2. This particular object or OID is used to return a description of the router's interfaces as demonstrated in Figure 6-14. An SNMP software tool was used to collect the interface description information. The IP address of the router is 10.10.10.1, and a get request ifDescr was sent to port 161, the UDP port for SNMP. The descriptions of the interfaces were returned as shown.

Obtaining the SNMP data requires that SNMP be configured on the router. The following discussion demonstrates how to configure SNMP on a Cisco router.

Configuring SNMP

The first step for configuring SNMP on a Cisco router is to enter the router's configuration mode using the **conf t** command:

```
RouterB#conf t
Enter configuration commands, one per line. End with CNTL/Z.
```

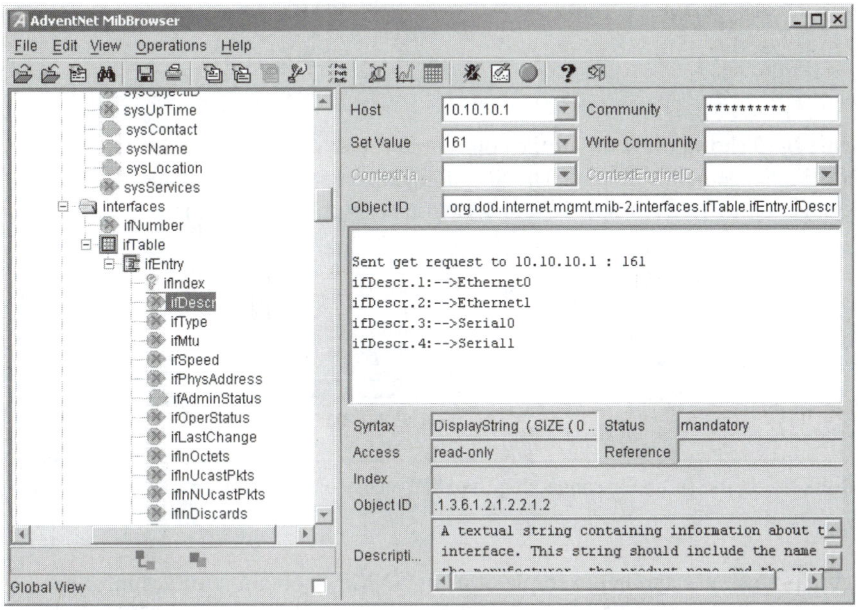

FIGURE 6-14 An example of using an SNMP software management tool to obtain descriptions of a router's interfaces using the MIB (ifDescr)

From the router's (config)# prompt, enter the command **snmp community** [*community string*] [*permissions*]. The community string can be any word. The permissions field is used to establish whether the user can read only (**ro**), or read and write (**rw**). The options for configuring SNMP on the router are shown here:

```
RouterB(config)#snmp community ?
WORD SNMP community string
```

snmp community
[*community string*]
SNMP Community string is a user ID or password that allows access to a network device's statistics.

The router was connected to the computer running the SNMP management software, as shown in Figure 6-15. The router's configuration mode was entered, and the **snmp community public ro** command was issued. The word **public** is used as the community string. The community string is the password used by the SNMP software to access SNMP (port 161) on the router. The **ro** sets the permission to read only:

```
RouterB(config)#snmp community public ro
```

In the next example, the community string password is set to **makesecret**, and the permission is set to read write (**rw**). Once again, the router's (config)# mode is entered and the command **snmp community makesecret rw** is entered:

```
RouterB(config)#snmp community makesecret rw
```

The configuration for SNMP can be verified using the **show run** command from the router's privileged mode prompt. A portion of the configuration file that lists the SNMP configuration for the router is shown here:

```
RouterB#sh run
.
.
.
```

```
snmp-server community makesecret RW
```
.

.

Figure 6-15 shows the setup of the configured router and the computer running the SNMP management software. The SNMP management software issues the SNMP message to the router at port 161, and the router returns the response.

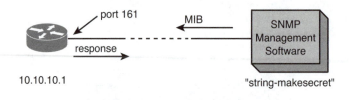

10.10.10.1   "string-makesecret"

FIGURE 6-15 The setup for connecting the SNMP management software tool to the router

Figure 6-16 shows another example of using SNMP to obtain interface information about a router. The SNMP manager was configured with the host IP address of 10.10.10.1, a set value (port #) of 161, and the 10 character community string of **makesecret** shown as * * * * * * * * * *. The MIB's object (ifspeed) was sent to the router and a status for each of the interfaces was provided. The data displayed shows the speed settings for the router's interfaces.

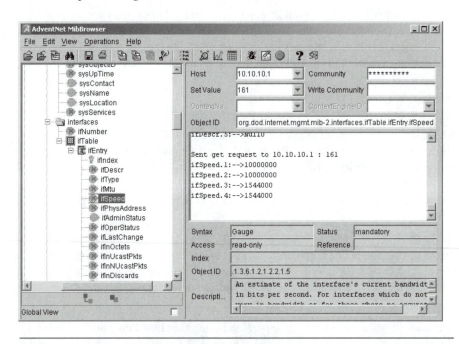

FIGURE 6-16 Using an SNMP software management tool to obtain interface speed settings

Another important application of SNMP is for obtaining traffic data statistics. An example of this is shown in Figure 6-17. The SNMP management program issued an SNMP message with a MIB's object (ifOutOctets), which returns the number of octets of data that have left the router. (The router has a counter that keeps track.) The first result shows ifOutOctets 7002270. The next result display shows that the ifOutOctets returns a value of 7002361.

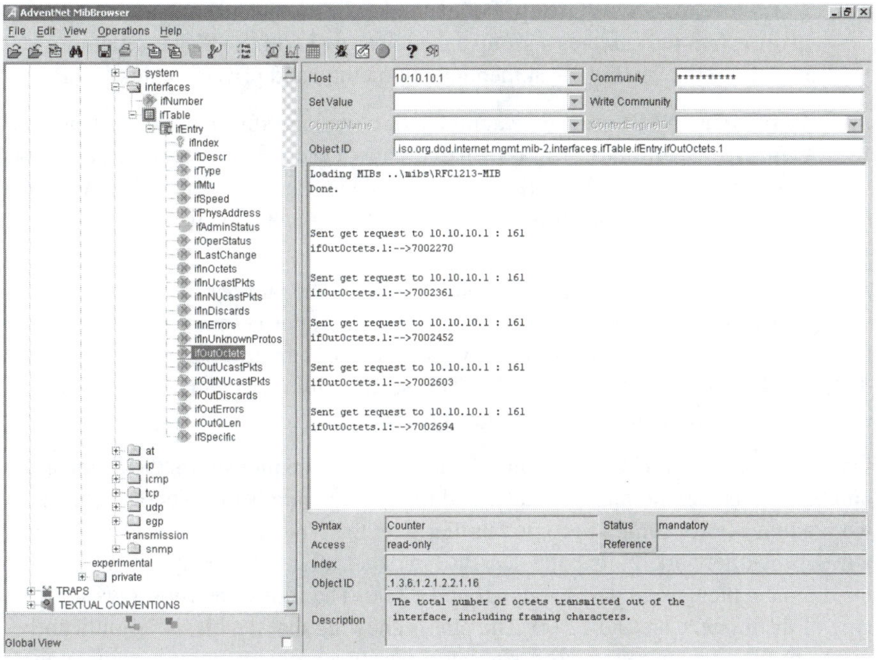

FIGURE 6-17 An example of using SNMP to collect data traffic statistics

The SNMP management program collecting the statistics keeps track of the time interval between measurements and the number of octets that have passed. This information can be used to calculate the average traffic flow by hour, day, week, or month, depending on the information needed. A final note about the router's counter: The counter does not reset unless the router is rebooted.

Two other versions of SNMP have been developed for network management. These versions are SNMPv2 and SNMPv3. SNMPv2 was developed in 1993; however, this version was not directly compatible with SNMPv1. SNMPv2 attempted to address security issues, but this led to the development of many variants and SNMPv2 was never fully accepted by the networking industry. One of the variants called SNMPv2c (Community-based SNMP version 2) was adopted more widely than the others. SNMPv3 was developed in 1998 and achieved the important goal of maintaining compatibility with SNMPv1 and adding security to SNMP. The security features of SNMPv3 include confidentiality, integrity, and authentication. *Confidentiality* means the packets are encrypted to prevent snooping; *integrity* ensures the data being transferred has not been tampered with; and *authentication* means

SNMPv2

Simple Network Management Protocol version 2.

SNMPv3

Simple Network Management Protocol version 3.

the data is from a known source. The steps of how to configure SNMPv3 on Cisco routers are as follows.

```
RouterA(config)#snmp-server group groupv3 v3 priv
RouterA(config)#snmp-server user userv3 groupv3 v3 auth md5 v3password
```

Configuring SNMPv3 on Cisco routers and switches consists of two steps:

1. **Configure an SNMP group**. For example, the command **snmp-server group groupv3 v3 priv** creates a group called **groupv3** with SNMPv3 capability and it will use the version 3's authentication method and privacy (encryption).

2. **Configure SNMP user**. For example, the command **snmp-server user userv3 groupv3 v3 auth md5 v3password** creates a user named **userv3** that belongs to the group **groupv3** created previously. This user will use the HMAC MD5 algorithm for authentication with the password **v3password**.

An example was presented that shows how to obtain the number of octets leaving a router. This type of information can be used in a campus network to monitor the flow of data for many points in the network. Statistics can be obtained for hourly, daily, weekly, and monthly data traffic. This section discusses plots of network router utilization obtained via the router's SNMP port.

Figure 6-18 is a plot of a router's hourly data traffic. The plot shows the average number of bits coming into the router and the average number of bits out. The network administrator should become familiar with the typical hourly data traffic pattern for their network. Notice the decrease in data traffic in the early morning and the dramatic increase in data traffic around 12:00. The traffic clearly shows some type of disturbance around 12:00. The plot is showing that the bit rate significantly increases for a few minutes. This is not necessarily a problem, but it is something that a network administrator will want to watch.

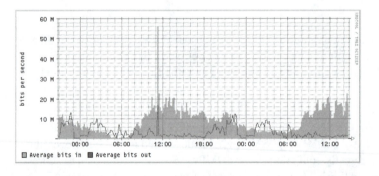

FIGURE 6-18 The hourly plot of a router's data traffic

In this case, the network administrator looked at the daily log of network activity for the same router. This plot is shown in Figure 6-19. The cycle of the data traffic from morning to night is as expected, heavy data traffic about noon and very low data traffic in the mornings. An interesting note is the noon data traffic spikes on the first Wednesday and then repeats the following Wednesday. Whatever is causing the change in traffic appears to happen on Wednesdays. If this sudden change in data traffic turned out to be something of concern, a protocol analyzer could be set up to capture the data traffic on Wednesdays around noon so that the traffic pattern could be explained.

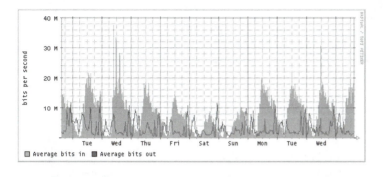

FIGURE 6-19 The daily plot of a router's data traffic

Sometimes, the graph of the network traffic over a longer period of time is needed. Figure 6-20 shows the data traffic through the router over a six-week period. The traffic shows some consistency except for a change from week 11 to week 12. Most likely, this can be explained by examining the network trouble reports and maintenance logs to see if this router was briefly out of service.

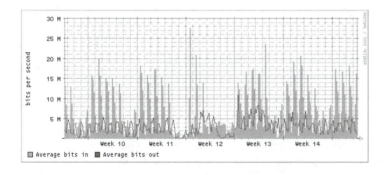

FIGURE 6-20 The weekly plot of a router's data traffic

Justifying the expansion of a network's capability (for example, higher data rate or better core or distribution service) requires showing the manager data traffic statistics. Figure 6-21 is a plot of the router's monthly data traffic. The summer shows a significant decrease in data traffic. The plot also shows that the network was down once in the June–July period and again in January. The manager wants to know if there is justification to increase the data rate of the router to 1 gigabit (1 GB). (The router's current data rate is 100 Mbps.) Is there justification to upgrade the router to 1 GB? Probably not, at least not immediately. The maximum measured average data rate is about 16 Mbps. The router's 100 Mbps data rate does not seem to be causing any traffic congestion problems.

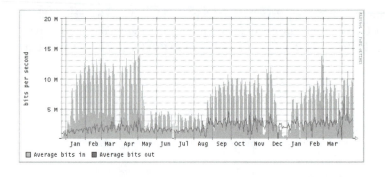

FIGURE 6-21 The monthly plot of a router's data traffic

This section showed how keeping logs of data traffic can be used to spot potential network problems and help plan for possible future expansion of the network.

NetFlow

SNMP allows for the gathering of the statistical information from network devices; however, it does not dive deep into IP information, such as source, destination, or protocol of each data packet. **NetFlow** allows for such data collection. Contrasted to SNMP, NetFlow is a push technology where NetFlow data is pushed from a network device to a collector. NetFlow was created by Cisco in 1996 for acquiring IP traffic operational data in order to provide network and security monitoring, traffic analysis, and IP accounting. Currently, there are 10 versions of NetFlow. NetFlow version 5 is the most common version deployed on many network devices from different vendors. NetFlow version 9 is the first version to support IPv6 and that version is now standardized by the IETF to NetFlow version 10 or Internet Protocol Flow Information Exchange (IPFIX).

Even though NetFlow was developed by Cisco, it is not Cisco proprietary protocol. Many network vendors have adopted NetFlow to collect their IP traffic flow statistics. Nonetheless, there are still variants of the NetFlow protocol available to the public. For example, **Jflow** is Juniper's IP traffic flow technology. It is similar to NetFlow version 5; however, it is a flow sampler technology, which samples the number of packets as defined in the router configuration. Created by InMon, **Sflow** (Sampled Flow) is another traffic flow technology. Similar to Jflow, Sflow is also a sampling technology that is designed to collect a large scale of statistical network information. It has many performance counters that it is collecting, which is different than information collected from NetFlow and Jflow. It can be thought of as SNMP on steroids. Its main deployment is in high-speed switched networks with big support from HP, Extreme, and Alcatel. Sflow is not compatible with NetFlow or Jflow.

There is one thing that all these flow technologies have in common: All the flow information has to be exported or sent to the collector. The **collector** stores and analyzes the flow information. There are many flavors of Flow collector software available. Some of them can even collect all different type of flows (NetFlow, Jflow, and Sflow) and are able to correlate information among them. A final note on any flow technologies is that, because it is a push technology from a network device itself, enabling flow could increase the CPU utilization of the device. This is true especially if the device is a busy router with heavy load of network traffic. One should constantly monitor the CPU health of the device when turning flow on. The following examples demonstrate how to configure NetFlow on Cisco routers.

The first step is to define the version of the NetFlow, the source of the export, and the destination and its listening UDP port where the flows will be exported as follows:

```
RouterA (config)# ip flow-export source Loopback0
RouterA (config)# ip flow-export version 5
RouterA (config)# ip flow-export destination 10.10.101.19 5000
```

The second step is to enable NetFlow on an interface by using the command **ip route-cache flow**. This command enables NetFlow on the physical interface and its associated subinterfaces, if there are any. The command **ip flow ingress** is used to enable NetFlow on particular subinterfaces. In this example, the Gigabit 1/0 interface is enabled with NetFlow monitoring, as shown:

```
RouterA (config)# int GigabitEthernet1/0
RouterA (config-if)# ip route-cache flow
```

The NetFlow information can be verified with a **show** command. The command **show ip flow export** shows the NetFlow configuration and its basic statistics. Note that all the flow information has to be sent to the collector. The collector stores and analyzes the flow information. There are many flavors of Flow collector software available. Some of them can even collect all information.

```
RouterA#sh ip flow export
Flow export v5 is enabled for main cache
  Exporting flows to 10.10.101.19 (5000)
  Exporting using source interface Loopback0
  Version 5 flow records
  4196949232 flows exported in 139898308 udp datagrams
  138 flows failed due to lack of export packet
  178 export packets were sent up to process level
  0 export packets were dropped due to no fib
  0 export packets were dropped due to adjacency issues
  0 export packets were dropped due to fragmentation failures
  0 export packets were dropped due to encapsulation fixup failures
```

6-4   FILTERING

Data capture files can be quite large, and it often requires that the network administrator search the capture files to find specific information. This could require searching for a specific IP address, or possibly the contents of a file transfer, or searching for a network problem. This section examines several filtering techniques that are available with Wireshark, which include the following:

1. Typing in the display filter

2. Apply saved display filters

3. Right-click filtering

4. Apply conversation filters

Typing in the display filter is a technique that allows you to create your own filter syntax that enables more complex filtering. The following in an exercise that demonstrates how to filter out any occurrences of a specified IP address from a saved capture file. This exercise requires that you first open Wireshark. Select the 6.2.cap file that is provided in the Wireshark folder that is provided in the CD that comes with the text. Figure 6-22 provides a screenshot of the 6-2.cap file. In the upper-left corner of the screen, you will see the word filter. This indicates the location of the filter button. Click the filter button, and this will open the saved display filters option box. This is shown in Figure 6-23. This is showing that the display filters box is empty.

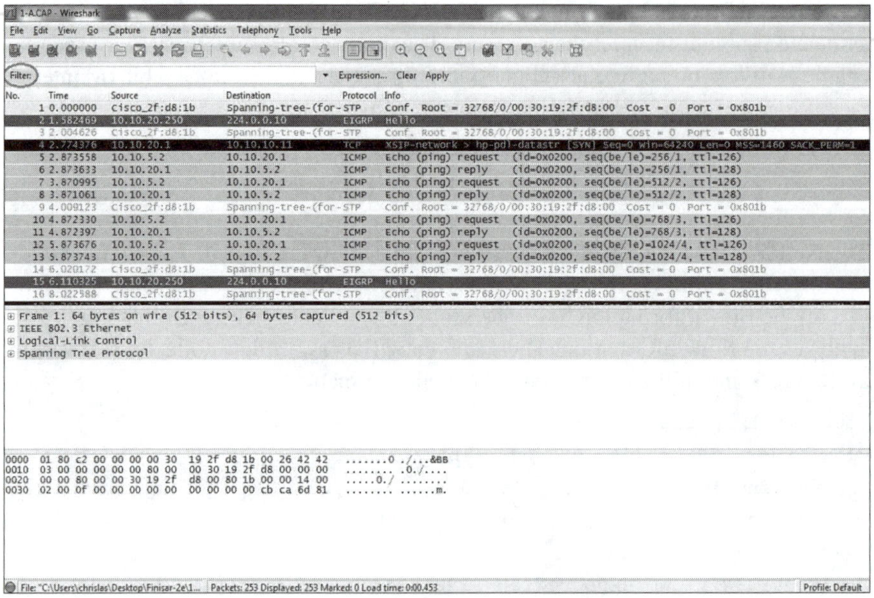

FIGURE 6-22 Screenshot of 6-2.cap file showing the location of the filter button

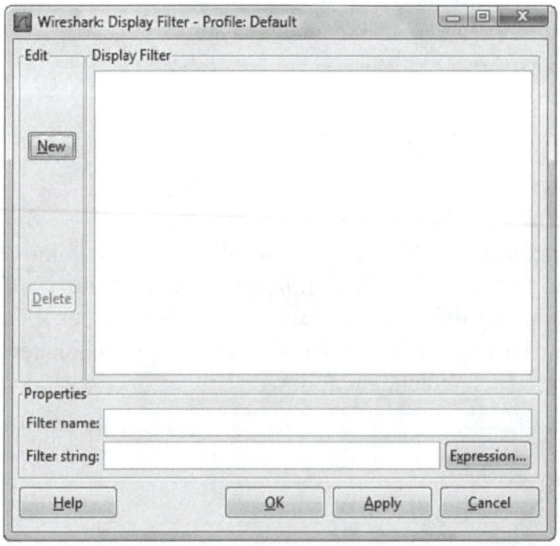

FIGURE 6-23 The Wireshark: Display Filter – Profile menu

In this example, you will first select a filter that only displays IP data packets. To add a filter, click **Expression** at the bottom right of the Wireshark: Display Filter menu. This will open the Wireshark: Filter Expressions – Profile menu. Scroll down until you see IPv4 and click **OK**. You will be returned to the Wireshark: Display Filter menu. The text "ip" is now placed in the Filter String. Next, enter the filter name of **ip only**, as shown in Figure 6-24. Click **New** and the filter for selecting only IP data traffic is entered, as shown in Figure 6-25.

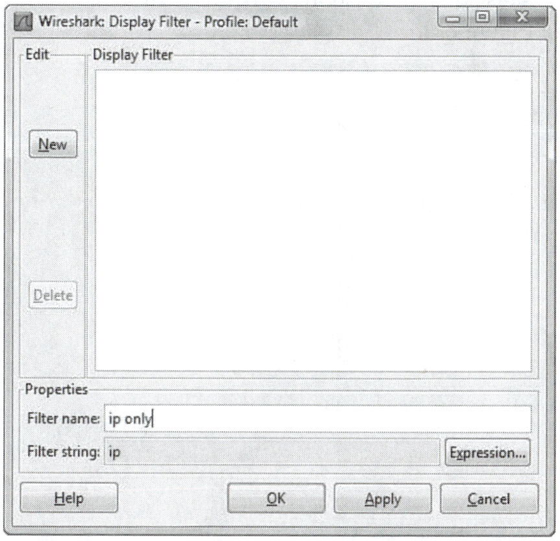

FIGURE 6-24 The creation of the IP only filter

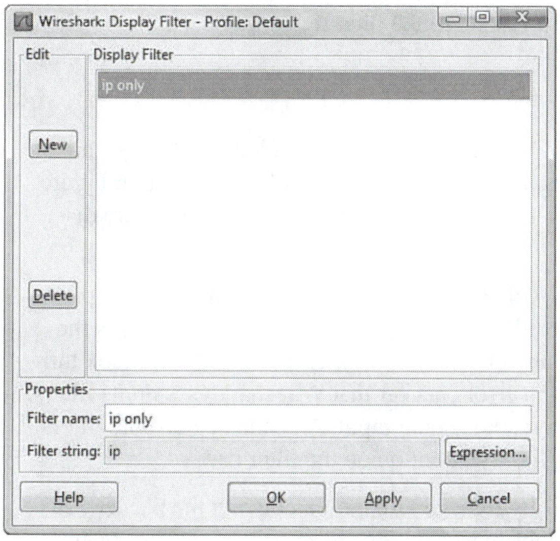

FIGURE 6-25 The addition of the IP only filter to the Wireshark: Display Filter menu

Figure 6-25 shows that the **ip only** filter has been added to the Filter – Profile. Apply this filter by clicking the **OK** button. Notice that the Wireshark screen changes and the non-IP related traffic is filtered out and the Wireshark screen is only displaying Internet Protocol–based traffic. You can also limit this filter down further to show only a specific IP address. For example, search for the IP address 10.10.5.2 by clicking the filter button, which displays the Display Filter – Profile menu.

In the Filter string box, enter **ip == 10.10.5.2**, add the Filter name of **ip address equals 10.10.5.2**, and click **New**. This adds the IP address 10.10.5.2 filter to the Display Filter menu, as shown in Figure 6-26.

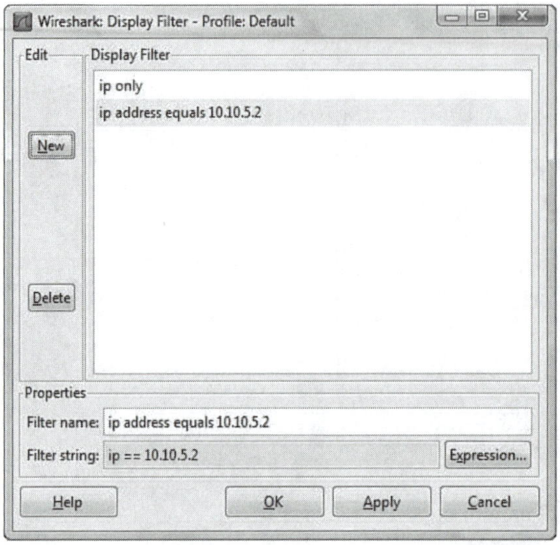

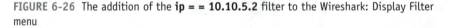

FIGURE 6-26 The addition of the **ip = = 10.10.5.2** filter to the Wireshark: Display Filter menu

Click the **Apply** button and only data packets with the IP address 10.10.5.2 are displayed. The result of applying the **ip.addr = = 10.10.5.2** filter is shown in Figure 6–27. Notice that only data packets containing the IP address 10.10.5.2 are displayed.

Notice that the Filter String box will change color according to the syntax error checker. The text box is highlighted green, meaning that the entered filter is the correct syntax and will produce an output. If an error exists then the text box turns from green to red. This is a built in error checker that Wireshark uses on its filters. The red indicates that incorrect syntax is being input. Any enabled display filters can be cleared at any time using the Clear button on the filter bar.

Another technique for filtering is by right-mouse button clicking the packet you are interested in. For example, right-mouse button click packet 5 from 6-2.cap. Select **Conversation Filter** and **IP**, as shown in Figure 6-28. This produces the same results as generated using the **ip.addr = = 10.10.5.2** filter. The result is the filtered output showing any traffic that is sent in or out of the machine with the IP of 10.10.5.2. This result is shown in Figure 6-29.

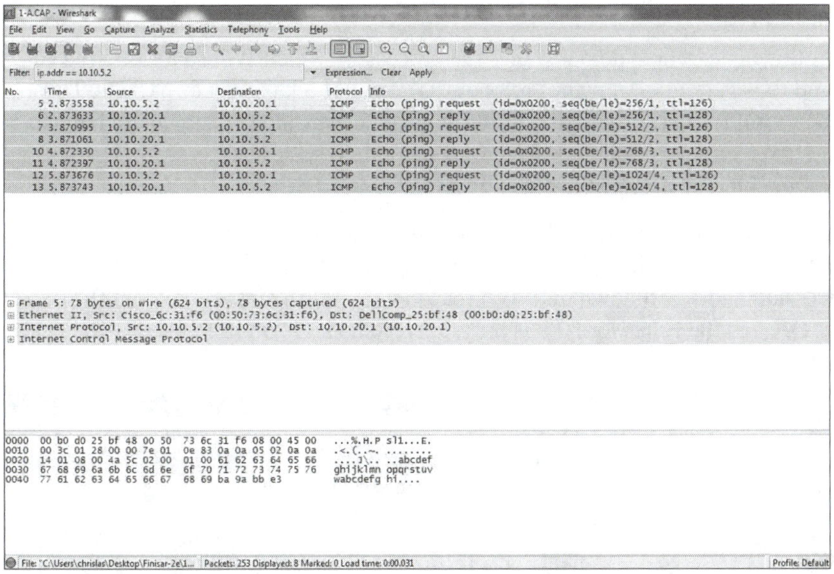

FIGURE 6-27 The results of applying the **ip.addr = = 10.10.5.2** filter

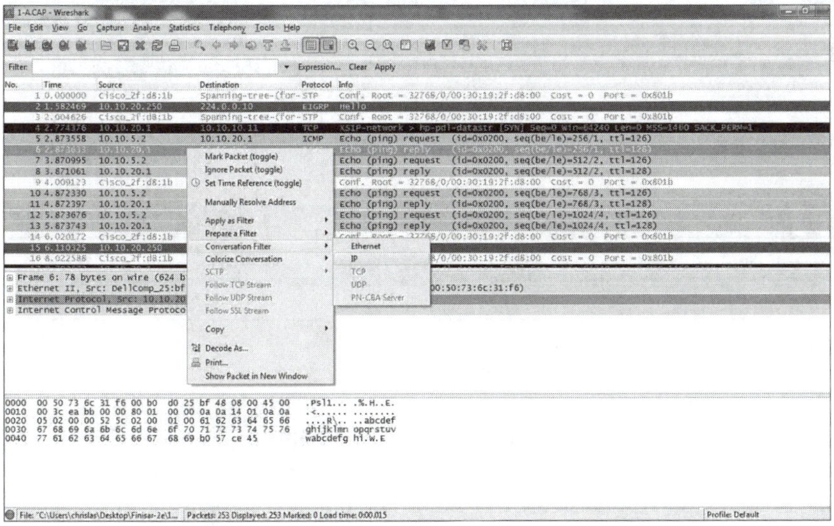

FIGURE 6-28 An example of using the right-mouse button click feature

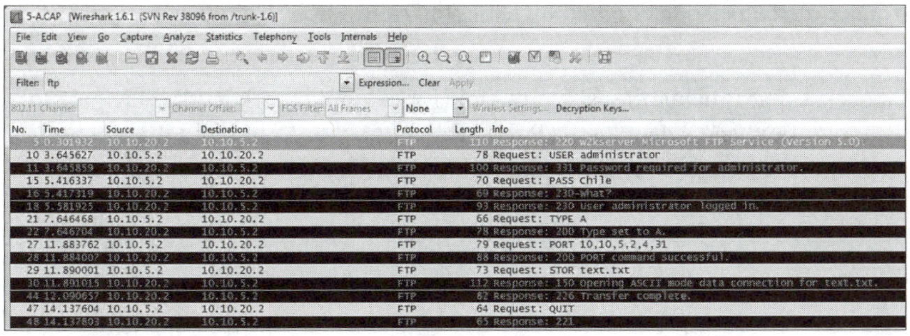

FIGURE 6-29 The result of applying the **ip.addr = = 10.10.5.2** filter

FTP Filtering

The following example demonstrates the process by which Wireshark filtering can be used to isolate File Transfer Protocol (FTP) out of a large list of packets. This can be useful for several reasons. You can use filtering rules to help us find user-names and passwords being used to connect to the FTP servers as well as get an idea of the kind of data that is being transferred.

Start this exercise by opening the capture file 5-A.cap in Wireshark. This is not a huge file, but it's a little difficult to sort through all of it just by looking. Click **Expression** and scroll down until you reach FTP—File Transfer Protocol (FTP). Click **OK** and the Filter for FTP is now displayed, as shown in Figure 6-30.

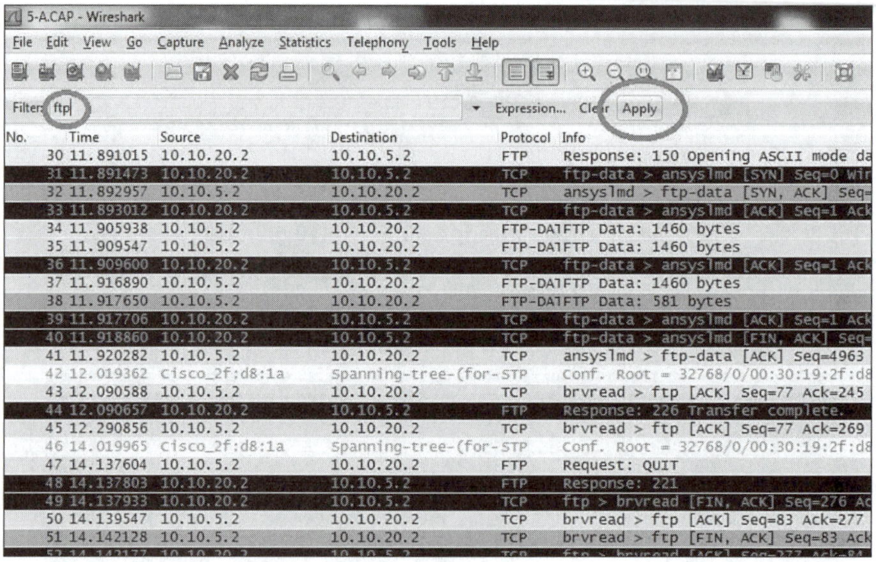

FIGURE 6-30 Adding the FTP filter

Click **Apply**, and the packet list is thinned out to 15 total packets relating to the FTP protocol, as shown in Figure 6-31. From this, we are able to view the username and password used to establish the FTP connection. In this case, the username and passwords are listed in plaintext, as well as the file that was accessed. Most times, a secure version of FTP (SFTP) will be used and this information will be encrypted.

This same rule can also be applied by using the right-click method as previously shown.

Find a packet that is using the FTP protocol (for example, packet 44). Navigate to the datagram field and select the FTP row. Right click -> **Apply as Filter** -> **Selected**. This will generate the same results provided in Figure 6-32 that are used for the FTP filter.

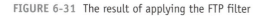

FIGURE 6-31 The result of applying the FTP filter

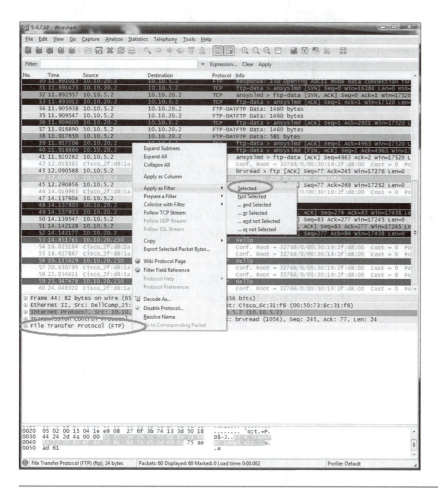

FIGURE 6-32 An example of using the right-mouse button click to filter the FTP data

Another important task is to extract the actual data packets from the capture file. This can be done by using the FTP-DATA protocol filter. To select this filter, click **Expressions** and scroll down to FTP Data. Click **OK** and the FTP Data filter is added to the menu. This filter can be applied by using FTP-DATA in place of FTP. Once filtered, Wireshark can be used to read the plaintext of the file. An example of this is provided in Figure 6-33.

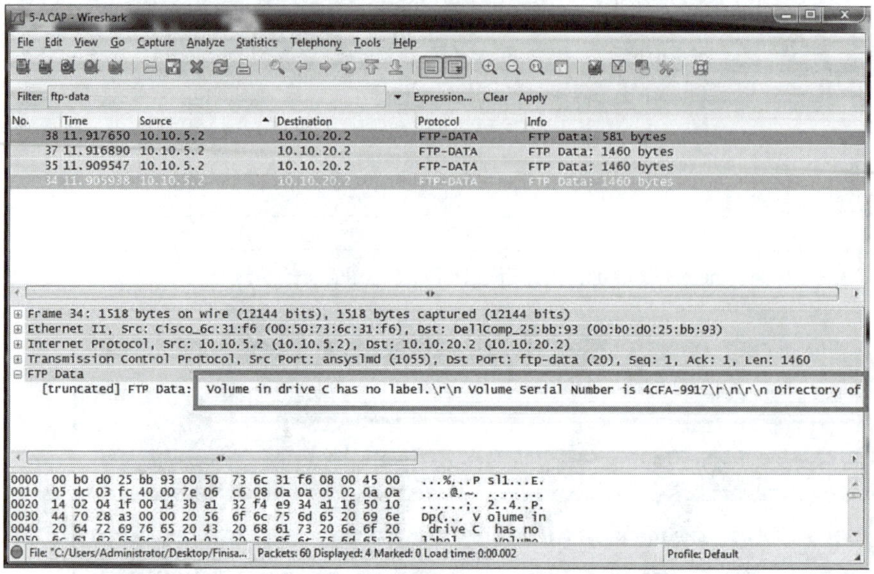

FIGURE 6-33 An example of extracting the data packets from a capture file

Figure 6-33 shows that packet 34 is selected and the FTP data field is expanded. The boxed area shows the first part of the txt file that was transferred. The user can scroll right and read more. Each packet is only 1460 bytes so a text file, even a relatively short one, will be split up in multiple packets. This example text file is only split into four components, but it is a very small text file. When transferring video or audio files over FTP, the files can get large, and there will be many more packets to be examined.

Right-Click Filtering Logic Rules

Within the Apply as Filter and Prepare as Filter menu options are some logical operators. We have already gone over the use of Selected and what it does, but there are other useful operators that can be used. For the purposes of this example, we will also use the Prepare as Filter method. This allows us to verify our filter before applying it. The available logical operators are provided in Figure 6-34.

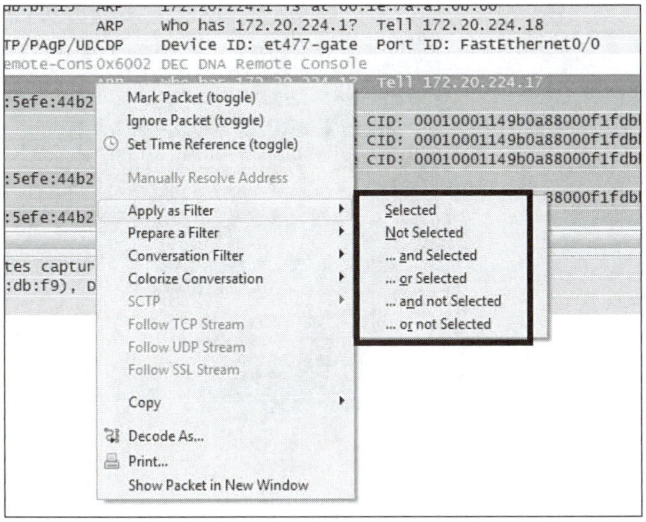

FIGURE 6-34 Available logical operators

In some cases, the network administrator might find it useful to filter out one or more sets of packets at the same time. For this, the **...or Selected** option will be used. In this example, we want to filter the ARP and DHCP data traffic pertaining to releasing and renewing an IP address. To start the exercise, open the 6-DHCP.cap file located in the Chapter 6_Wireshark folder. Both ARP data and the DHCP data will need to be analyzed, so we need to prepare a filter that will show us both of these types of data packets. Begin by selecting an ARP packet and, in the datagram field, right-click **-> Prepare a filter -> ...or Selected**. This puts ARP in the filter string box, but we also need DHCP information. Highlight a DHCP packet and do the same as before. In the datagram field, right-click **-> Prepare a filter -> ...or Selected**. Notice the filter string box now and its inclusion of both sets of filter strings and the newly added or logical operator:

```
(arp) || (dhcpv6)
```

This filter string is used to search for both ARP or DHCPv6 packets. Figure 6-35 shows the newly sorted packet list with only ARP and DHCPv6 Solicit information.

Another possibility is to use the **Not Selected** operator. The objective in this case is to remove protocols one by one that do not pertain to what we need to analyze. For this, you would use the **Not Selected** operator. Start by opening the 6-2.cap file. Next, remove all occurrences of the NBNS protocol. Select an NBNS packet and in the datagram field right-click **-> Prepare a filter -> ...or not Selected**. Next, find and select an EIGRP data packet and in the datagram field and right-click **-> Prepare a filter -> ...and not Selected**. The resulting filter string will list (**!(stp)**) **&& !(eigrp)**. Apply the filter. All occurrences of STP or EIGRP data packets are removed.

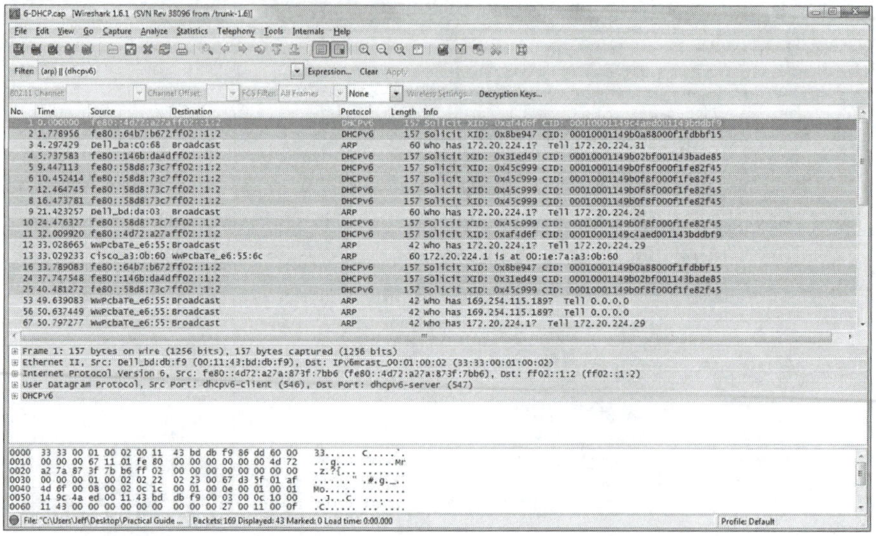

FIGURE 6-35 The results of applying the (arp) || (dhcpv6) filter to the 6-DHCP.cap file

Filtering DHCP

In this exercise, you learn how to filter DHCP packets from a CAP file in Wireshark. You will be using the DHCP.cap file found in the Wireshark folder provided in the companion CD. The filtering method used for this exercise will be typing in the display filter. Open Wireshark and open the DHCP.cap file. As you can see there is a lot of data traffic that was captured in this CAP file. To filter out DHCP, you must type in **bootp** in the filter textbox, as shown in Figure 6-36. (Note: This is case sensitive; do not use BOOTP). The field name for BOOTP can be found by clicking **Expression** and scrolling until you see the **BOOTP/DHCP** filter option.

To apply the **bootp** filter to the DHCP.cap file, click **Apply**. What should be displayed in the packet pane list? You should only see the DHCP protocol data packets displayed, as shown in Figure 6-37.

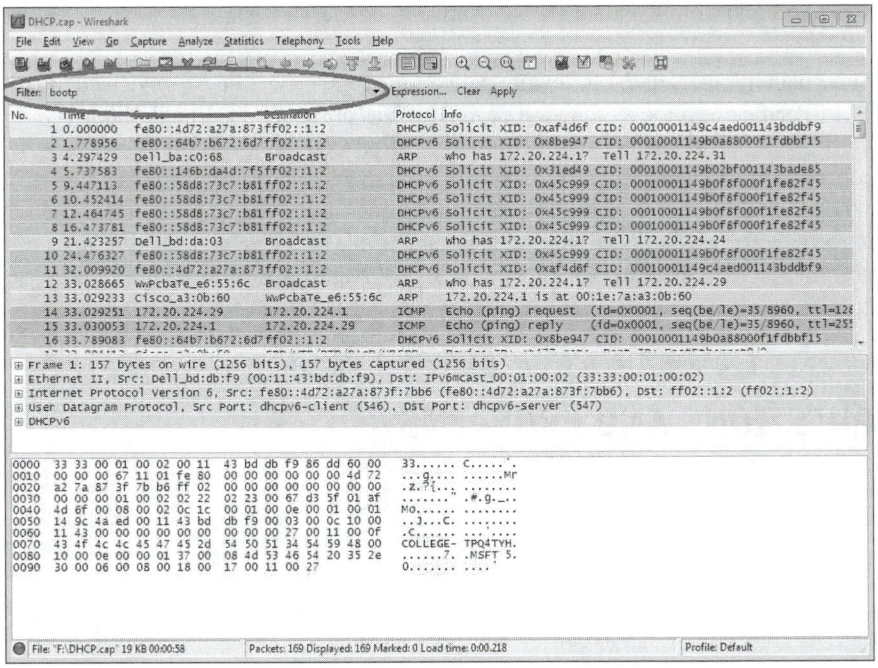

FIGURE 6-36 A screenshot of the DHCP.cap file with "bootp" filter syntax displayed in the filter textbox

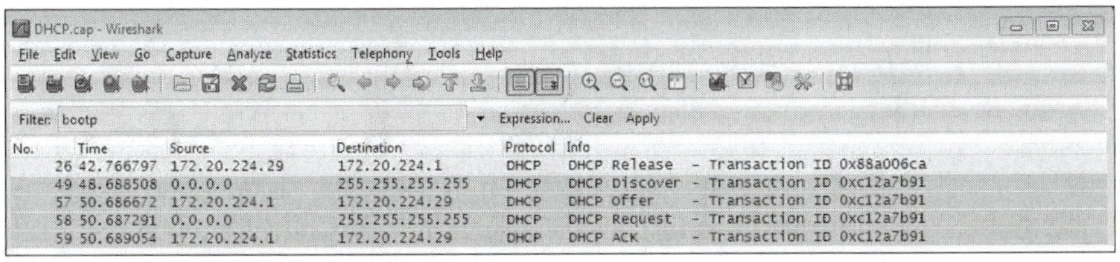

FIGURE 6-37 A screenshot of the DHCP.cap file with the DHCP protocol filtered in the packet list pane

SUMMARY

This chapter looked at the following networking topics. Section 6-1 reviewed the TCP/IP suite of protocols. The use of **netstat** was presented for troubleshooting TCP and UDP connections. Section 6-2 introduced the use of the Wireshark network protocol analyzer. This section is used to get the student started using Wireshark. Section 6-4 introduced filter techniques using Wireshark. Section 6-3 introduced the use of SNMP for the gathering of the statistical information from network devices. Also introduced was the use of NetFlow for acquiring IP traffic operational data.

QUESTIONS AND PROBLEMS

Section 6-1

1. What is an Internet socket?

2. What is network forensics?

3. What are well-known ports?

4. Identify the port numbers for the following applications:

    a. Telnet

    b. HTTP

    c. FTP

    d. DNS

    e. DHCP

5. Define the purpose of a *connection-oriented protocol*. Give an example.

6. What three packets are exchanged between two hosts when establishing a TCP connection?

7. What is the purpose of a sequence number (SEQ=) in TCP data packets?

8. Explain how a host knows whether a data packet was not received.

9. Describe how a TCP connection is terminated.

10. What is a *connectionless protocol*? Give an example.

11. What is the SYN-SENT state?

12. What is the SYN-RECEIVED state?

13. What is the purpose of an ARP request?

14. This state indicates that the three-packet handshake established a TCP connection.

15. What is the FIN-WAIT-1 state, and where is it used?

16. In this state, the terminating host acknowledges the last FIN and waits for the connection to close.

17. In this TCP Connection state, the host is listening and ready to accept connections.

18. In this TCP Connection state, the receiving host acknowledges the FIN.

19. In this TCP Connection State, the terminating host receives the acknowledgment from the receiving host.

20. The **netstat –an** command is issued. What does the following indicate?

    ```
    TCP    0.0.0.0:22              0.0.0.0:0               LISTENING
    ```
21. The **netstat –an** command is issued. What does the following indicate?

    ```
    TCP    172.16.101.7:49192  199.7.59.72:80        TIME_WAIT
    ```
22. What is the purpose of an ARP reply?

23. What command is used to view the ARP cache?

24. What command can be used to display the age of each ARP entry?

25. What important networking-troubleshooting tool is part of ICMP, and how does it test a network connection?

26. What is the purpose of the ICMP message type 0?

27. What ICMP message type is Time Exceeded?

28. What is the purpose of the ICMP message type 8?

Section 6-2

29. Expand the acronym *ARP*.

30. What is the purpose of an ARP request?

31. Expand the acronym *ICMP*.

32. What is an *echo request*?

33. What is the purpose of a protocol analyzer?

    Included on the companion CD-ROM in the Wireshark capture file folder is a network packet capture file called *Packet11a.cap*. Open this file using Wireshark. The following five questions refer to this file.

34. What are the MAC addresses of the computers involved?

35. Which IP addresses correspond to each MAC address?

36. Which packet IDs correspond to ARP requests?

37. Which packet IDs correspond to ARP replies?

38. Which computers are pinging which computers?

39. In terms of computer security, a switch offers better security than a hub. Why is this?

Section 6-3

40. What is the management information base?

41. What port does SNMP use and what transport protocol?

42. The SNMP MIB get request *ifDescr* returns what information from a router?

43. What is the purpose of the MIB?

44. Write the Cisco router command for configuring SNMP on a Cisco router. Assume a community string of networking and set the permissions to read-only. Show the router prompt.

45. The command **show run** is entered on a Cisco router. Describe what the output "SNMP-server test RO" means.

46. What SNMP MIBs were most likely issued to the router discussed in Section 6-4?

Use Figure 6-38 to answer questions 47 to 51.

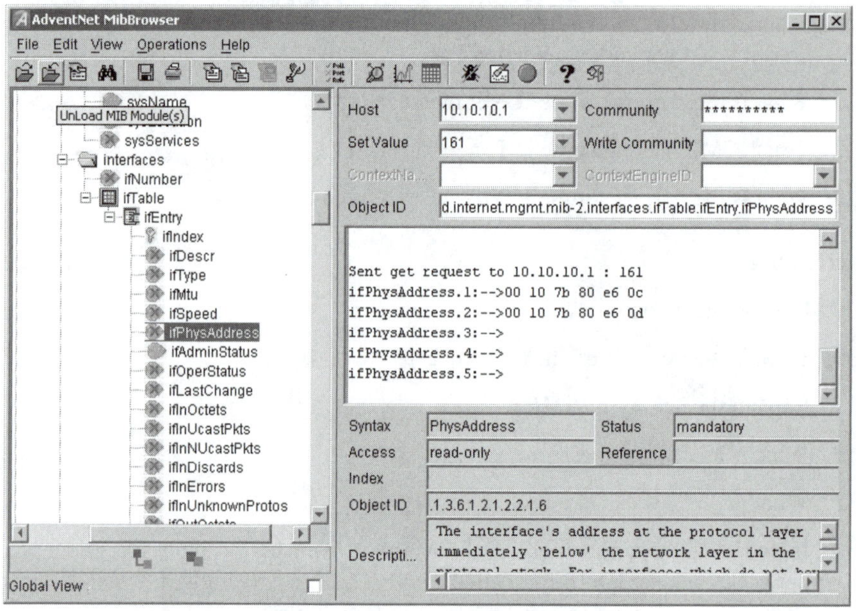

FIGURE 6-38 For problems 47–51

47. What MIB was issued?

48. What information was returned?

49. What port number was used?

50. What protocol is being used? How do you know?

51. Who is the manufacturer of this networking device?

52. What is the advantage of SNMPv3?

53. What security features are provided with SNMPv3?

54. What is confidentiality?

55. What is integrity relative to security?

56. What is authentication relative to security?

57. What is the purpose of NetFlow?

58. What is the purpose of the collector when used with "flow" technologies.

59. What is the following command doing?

    ```
    RouterA (config)# ip flow-export source Loopback0
    ```

60. What is the purpose of the command **ip route-cache flow**?

61. What command is used to display the NetFlow information?

62. What does the following command do?

    ```
    RouterA (config)# ip flow-export version 5
    ```

63. What is the purpose of the following command?

    ```
    RouterA (config)# ip flow-export destination 10.10.101.19 5000
    ```

Section 6-4

64. A filter with the **ip.addr = = 10.10.10.1** filter is applied to captured network data traffic. What happens?

65. What filter could be used to display on data packets containing the IP address 192.168.12.5?

66. What filter could be used to only display data files containing the FTP protocol?

67. What is the purpose of the FTP-DATA filter?

68. What is the purpose of applying the (arp) || (dhcpv6) filter?

69. List a filter to remove all occurrences of STP or EIGRP.

70. List a filter to remove all occurrences of ARP or ICMP.

71. List a filter that can be used to display only data packets containing the IP address 208.76.11.230?

Critical Thinking

72. Use the Wireshark protocol analyzer to capture a file transfer to a TFTP server. Prepare a report on your findings. Identify the port used to establish the TFTP transfer and the source and destination ports used for the TFTP file transfer.

73. Repeat problem 72 for loading a file from a TFTP server.

74. Open the sample **wireless capture.pcap** file provided in the Chapter 6 Wireshark folder in the textbook CD. Search for the 74.125.239.27 IP address. Describe what is happening at this address.

75. When issuing a command **netstat -an** on a server, there are a lot of TCP state of SYN-RECEIVED and ESTABLISHED showing. Should there be any concerns with what netstat is reporting?

7
CHAPTER

NETWORK SECURITY

Chapter Outline

Objectives

- Review denial of service attacks
- Introduce the procedures for configuring access lists
- Examine "best practice" for router security
- Examine "best practices" for switch security
- Examine the issues of wireless security
- Introduce the steps for configuring VPNs

Key Terms

denial of service (DoS)
SYN attack
smurf attack
spoof
directed broadcast
hacked
distributed denial of service (DDoS) attack
firewall
access lists (ACL)
packet filtering
proxy server
stateful firewall
demilitarized zones
access lists
SMB
edge router
permit ip any any
host
filter list
line password
EXEC level password
Type 7
Type 5
AAA
transport input none

crypto key generate rsa
CDP
NTP
switchport port-security
violation action
protected
restrict
shutdown
ERRDISABLE
storm control
pps
rising threshold/falling threshold
STP Portfast
BPDU guard
BPDU filter
STP Root guard
DTP
SSID
Beacon
open authentication
Sharekey Authentication
WEP
WPA
TKIP
AES

CCMP
LEAP
EAP
RADIUS
VPN
IP tunnel
GRE
PPP
PAP
CHAP
EAP
MD5
RADIUS
PPTP
L2F
L2TP
AH
ESP
SHA-1
DES, 3DES
AES
IKE
ISAKMP
Diffee-Hellman

INTRODUCTION

This chapter examines the topics of network security. The concept of denial of service (DoS) is first examined in Section 7-1. This section also examines the SYN attack, smurf attack, and distributed denial of service (DDoS) attacks. Section 7-2 examines firewalls and access lists. Topics included in the section include stateful firewalls, demilitarized zones, and configuring access lists. Sections 7-3 through 7-5 look at "best practices" for setting up security on routers, switches, and wireless networks. This chapter concludes with a look at configuring external access to networks using a VPN in Section 7-6.

7-1 DENIAL OF SERVICE

Denial of Service (DoS)
Means that a service is being denied.

Denial of service (DoS) means that a service is being denied to a computer, network, or network server. DoS attacks can be on individual machines, on the network that connects the machines, or on all machines simultaneously.

You can initiate a DoS attack by exploiting software vulnerabilities. For example, a software vulnerability can permit a buffer overflow, causing the machine to crash. This affects all applications, even secure applications. A database of software vulnerabilities is available online at http://web.nvd.nist.gov/.

The vulnerable software DoS attack attacks the system by making it reboot repeatedly. DoS attacks can also be on routers via the software options that are available for connecting to a router. For example, SNMP management software is marketed by many companies and is supported by many computer platforms. Many of the SNMP packages use a similar core code that could contain the same vulnerability.

SYN Attack
This attack refers to the opening up many TCP sessions to limit access to network services.

Another DoS attack is a **SYN attack**. This refers to the TCP SYN (synchronizing) packet. An attacker sends many TCP SYN packets to a host, opening up many TCP sessions. The host machine has limited memory set aside for open connections. If all the TCP connections are opened by the SYN attack, other users are kept from accessing services from the computer, because the connection buffer is full. Most current operating systems take countermeasures against the SYN attack.

Smurf Attack
A way of generating a large amount of data traffic.

Spoof
Inserting a different IP address in place of an IP packet's source address to make it appear that the packet came from another network.

DoS attacks can affect the network bandwidth and the end points on the network. The classic example is the **smurf attack** (see Figure 7-1), which requires few resources from the attacker.

In the smurf attack shown in Figure 7-1, the attacker sends a small packet and receives many packets in return. The attacker then picks a victim and an intermediate site. Figure 7-1 shows an attacker site, an intermediate site, and a victim site. The intermediate site has subnets of 10.10.1.0 and 10.10.2.0. The victim is at 10.10.1.0. The attackers send a packet to 10.10.1.255, which is a broadcast address for the 10.10.1.0 subnet. The attacker will **spoof** the source address information, making it look as if the packet came from the victim's network. *Spoof* means the attacker doesn't use his IP address but will insert an IP address from the victim's network or another network as the source IP. All the machines on the 10.10.1.0 subnet will send a reply back to the source address. Remember that the attacker has spoofed the source address so the replies will be sent to the victim's network. If this attack were increased to all the subnets in the 10.0.0.0 network, an enormous amount of data packets will be sent to the victim's network. This enables the attacker to generate a lot of data traffic on the victim's network without requiring the attacker to have many resources.

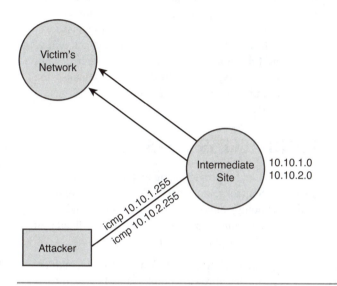

FIGURE 7-1 An example of a smurf attack

This type of attack is not new, and there are some steps that can be taken to stop a network from becoming an intermediate site. Cisco routers have an interface command that blocks broadcast packets to that subnet. This prevents a network from becoming an intermediate site for a network attack such as this. Make sure this command or a similar command is a default or has been enabled on the router's interface:

```
no ip directed-broadcast
```

But aren't Layer 3 devices supposed to stop broadcasts? This is true for general broadcasts (all 32 bits set to 1s or F F F F F F F F or 255.255.255.255). Routers will always stop these broadcasts. The type of broadcast used in a smurf attack is a **directed broadcast**, which is passed through the router. The **no ip directed-broadcast** command enables only the router to reply.

> **Directed Broadcast**
> The broadcast is sent to a specific subnet.

To prevent your network from becoming a host for an attacker, use access lists to allow only specific sources from the network to enter the router's interfaces. For example, network B connects to a router. Only packets sourced from network B are allowed to pass through the router. The downside of this is it does become a maintenance problem: Keeping track of the access lists can be a challenge for the network administrator and processing access lists on the router is processor intensive and can slow the throughput of the packets. Access lists do help eliminate spoofed packets, however. There is a lot of software on the Internet that enables someone to spoof an IP address. To prevent yourself from becoming a victim, well...there isn't a way unless you aren't connected to any network or to any other users.

Distributed Denial of Service Attacks (DDoS)

Hacked

Attacked.

Distributed Denial of Service (DDoS) Attack

An attack that comes from a potentially large number of machines.

The number of packets that can be generated by a single packet as in the smurf attack can be limited on a router; however, attackers now use worms to distribute an attack. The attacker will do a port scan and look for an open port or a software application that is vulnerable to an attack. The machine is *hacked* (attacked) and distributes the malicious software. The attacker will repeat this for many victim machines. Once the software is on the victim machines, the attacker can issue a command or instruction that starts the attack on a specific site. The attack will come from a potentially massive amount of machines that the worm has infected. This is called a **distributed denial of service (DDoS) attack.** To stop DDoS attacks, stop intrusions to the network. The bottom line is **PREVENT INTRUSIONS**.

7-2 FIREWALLS AND ACCESS LISTS

Firewall

Used in computer networks for protecting the network.

Access Lists (ACL)

A basic form of firewall protection.

Firewalls are used in computer networks for protection against the "network elements" (for example, intrusions, DoS attacks, etc.). **Access lists (ACLs)** are the basic form of firewall protection, although an access list is not stateful and is not by itself a firewall. Access lists can be configured on a router, on a true dedicated firewall, or on the host computer. Firewalls are examined first in this section.

Firewalls allow traffic from inside the network to exit but don't allow general traffic from the outside to enter the network. The firewall monitors the data traffic and recognizes where packets are coming from. The firewall will allow packets from the outside to enter the network if they match a request from within the network. The followings are some of the well-known technologies that most firewalls are based on:

- Packet filtering
- Proxy server
- Stateful packet filtering

Packet Filtering

A technique used to determine whether a packet is allowed to enter or exit the network.

Packet filtering is a technique used to determine whether a packet is allowed to enter or exit the network based on its Layer 3 IP header information, such as source IP address and destination IP address, or its Layer 4 header information, such as protocol and port number. A limit is placed on the packets that can enter the network or it can be used to limit information moving from one segment to another. ACLs are used to enable the firewall to accept or deny data packets. The disadvantages of packet filtering are as follows:

- Packets can still enter the network by spoofing or fragmenting the data packets.
- It is difficult to implement complex ACLs.
- Not all network services can be filtered.

Proxy Server

An agent for handling requests from clients seeking resources.

A **proxy server** is used by clients to communicate with secure systems using a proxy. Essentially, the proxy server acts as an agent for handling requests from clients seeking resources, such as access to the network. This step is used to authenticate the user, establish the session, and set policies. The client must connect to the proxy server to connect to resources outside the network. The disadvantages of the proxy server are as follows:

- The proxy server requires processing power.
- Adding services can be difficult.
- There can be a potential problem with network failure if the proxy server fails or is corrupted.

In a stateful firewall, the state of inbound and outbound data packets are tracked and compared to determine if a connection should be allowed. This includes tracking the source and destination port numbers and sequence numbers, as well as the source and destination IP addresses. Stateful packet filtering, sometimes referred to as dynamic packet filtering, monitors the session or state of the connection initiated from the trusted network and allows the return traffic to enter the network. This technique is used to protect the inside of the network from the outside world but still allow traffic to go from the inside to the outside and back. The firewall needs to be stateful to accomplish this.

<aside>
Stateful Firewall
The inbound and outbound data packets are compared to determine if a connection should be allowed.
</aside>

For example, a machine called NVL is on the inside of a network. NVL establishes a connection to the outside at www.network-A.edu. The connection requires the initial TCP handshake sequence and the first SYN packet hits the firewall. The firewall has been configured to allow packets to leave the network. The firewall recognizes that a connection is being established outside the network and the firewall creates a state that includes the source and destination IP address numbers for the connection. The TCP packets arrive at www.network-A.edu (port 80) and the server at networkA.edu returns a SYN-ACK packet back through the firewall. The firewall examines the SYN-ACK packet, and matches the stored source and destination IP addresses with the packet's source/destination IP addresses and port numbers. If the information matches, the IP packets are allowed to pass. This repeats until the connection ends.

What if an attacker tries to spoof the firewall to gain access to the interior of the network?

In this case, a connection already exists between NVL and www.network-A.edu. The attacker spoofs the network-A.edu domain www server's IP address and port 80 (the web server) and tries to use this to gain access to the network. Remember that there is a sequence number associated with the data transfers in the TCP connection. The server recognizes that there is a discrepancy with the sequence and rejects the hacker's connection, preventing the attack.

But, what if the campus network has a web server? How are outside users allowed access?

This requires that holes must be opened in the network that allow data packets to pass through. The three most common traffic types that require holes to be opened are web servers, DNS, and email. The firewall must be modified so that anybody can connect to the web server via port 80. But, what if a vulnerability is discovered on port 80 for the server's operating system? When you open ports, the network administrator must continually upgrade the software so that vulnerabilities are removed. The web server may also need to have its own firewall. Most firewalls can perform deep packet inspection. This may catch some of the protocol vulnerabilities.

A big problem with firewalls is that users assume a firewall catches all possible problems. This is a wrong assumption. The user may be slow to update the patches and fixes to the software. For example, an attacker sends an email message with an attachment to a user. The user opens the attachment and unknowingly loads a Trojan horse on his or her computer that scans all of the machines on the LAN, checking for any possible open ports, compromising the entire LAN. A firewall is not the end-to-end solution.

Network Attack Prevention

Demilitarized Zones

A physical or logical network designed to house the public servers that will have direct exposure from the outside network.

A general rule of thumb is to place the firewall close to the machines you want to protect (for example, the network servers). Do not assume that the clients on the network will never attack your system. Create **demilitarized zones** (DMZ) for the public or outside servers, which mean that they are moved to a segment on the network so that they are separated from the inside or trusted network. The DMZ is a physical or logical network designed to have the contact with and the exposure from the outside or untrusted network. This limits the direct exposure of the inside network from the outside network. If the machines are compromised, the intruder will have limited access to the inside of the network. Keep in mind that firewalls do not protect the network from viruses or malwares. Clients can and will get viruses on their machines. Other countermeasures such as antivirus policies and OS patches must be deployed along with firewall for more effective security.

Firewalls are not the solution for everybody. Open networks, such as a university's, have limited areas where a firewall can be placed. For example, firewalls will be placed close to critical machines, such as academic records. There are so many entities on a university campus network that need connections around the world. The university campus network will have multiple web servers that can't be centrally located. If a firewall was placed on the whole university network, many holes would be required and thus negate the usefulness of the firewall. One solution is to put in server firewalls.

Access Lists

Access Lists

Used to tell a networking device who and what are allowed to enter or exit a network.

Access lists provide basic protection for the network. It is what tells a networking device who and what are allowed to enter or exit a network. The access list compares the source and destination IP address and the source and destination port numbers and sometimes might examine the packet contents above Layer 4 (transport). However, access lists primarily focus on the network (Layer 3) and transport (Layer 4) layers. A router is often placed on the edge of a network to handle data traffic entering and exiting the network, and it is common practice to block some data traffic. The first two steps for applying access lists on a router are

1. Identify the problem.

2. Decide where to place the access list.

There can be many problems encountered on a network that require the application of an access list to a router. For example, the network administrator will block certain types of data packets from entering and exiting a network. For example, the

Microsoft NetBIOS protocol for mapping drives (also called **SMB** [server message block] over TCP) is an intranet protocol and is not intended to be run over the Internet. SMB data packets use ports 137, 138, and 139. SMB packets will be blocked from entering and exiting the network. The next issue is where to place the access list.

In this case, the best place to apply the access list is the network's Internet connection. The following discussion describes the steps for applying an access list to a router. The network management protocol SNMP (port 161) can be blocked to prevent an outside attacker from getting into your router(s). The following is an example of how to configure an **edge router** to block SNMP from entering a specific LAN.

In this case, the term "edge router" is describing the Internet connection to the campus network, and the LAN being protected is LAN B. The network topology is shown in Figure 7-2.

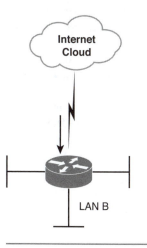

FIGURE 7-2 An example of setting an access list on an edge router to block SNMP data packets

The first step for configuring the access list is to enter the router's configuration mode using the **configure terminal** command, as shown:

```
RouterB# conf t
RouterB(config)#
```

Next, define the access list to be applied to the router interface. Access lists can be specified in two ways: They can be either a standard or extended type. A *standard* access list is used when specifying access for only IP addresses. An *extended* access list allows the addition of port numbers. For example, the access list could be defined to deny SMB data packets to enter or exit the network. In the following example, an extended access list of 100 is being defined with the instructions to deny UDP packets from any source going to any destination equal to port 161 (SNMP). (*Note:* The 100 is just an identifier used to indicate what list is being defined.) The command **access-list 100 deny udp any any eq 161** is entered.

SMB

Server message block. A protocol used by Windows computers to share folders, printers, and serial ports to other computers on the same network.

Edge Router

Describes the Internet connection to network.

This command is used to deny all SNMP data packets from entering or exiting the network. Remember that the first step is to identify the problem. Unauthorized access to the network's router must be prevented, so the access list is being applied. SNMP uses the UDP protocol for transferring data; therefore, it is also a good idea to block UDP packets. The command **access-list 100 deny udp any any eq snmp** is used to instruct the router to deny UDP packets from any source to any destination equal to SNMP. In this example, SNMP is used instead of 161. Cisco routers allow the use of names for well-known port numbers, for example, SNMP (port 161). The entry of these two commands from the router's (config)# prompt is provided:

```
RouterB(config)# access-list 100 deny tcp any any eq 161
RouterB(config)# access-list 100 deny udp any any eq snmp
```

permit ip any any
The instruction added to the last line of an access list to allow all other data packets to enter and exit the router.

These commands form an access list that blocks TCP and UDP data packets from any source going to any destination equal to SNMP (port 161). Even though SNMP uses UDP port 161 as defined by the RFC, it is not uncommon to see network administrators blocking the same port number for both TCP and UDP as a precaution. There is an implicit denial at the end of an access list in Cisco routers, and this statement alone will block all data packets. The access lists must be modified to permit any other data packets to enter and exit the LAN. The command **access-list permit ip any any** must be added to the last line of an access list to allow all other data packets to enter and exit the router. An example is shown here. This instruction is for access-list 100, and it instructs the router to permit IP packets from any source to any destination:

```
RouterB(config)# access-list 100 permit ip any any
```

The content of the access list just created can be checked using the command **show access-list 100**, as demonstrated here:

```
RouterB# sh access-list 100
Extended IP access list 100
deny tcp any any eq 161
deny udp any any eq snmp
permit ip any any
```

The next step is to decide where to place the access list. Specifically, this is asking what router interface is to be used to apply the list. In this case, the access list is to be applied to the Serial0/0 interface and to the inbound data packets (coming from the Internet). The access list can be applied to both in and outbound data packets. The format of the command is

```
Router (config)# int s0/0
Router (config-if)# ip access-group 100 in
```

The **100** matches the number from the access list being applied. This access list is being applied on the *in direction*. This denies any SNMP packets from the outside into the interface serial0/0. If this command was modified to **ip access-group 100 out**, this would deny any SNMP packets coming from inside the network going out. This would prevent users on the network to do SNMP queries on the Internet, but it would allow SNMP queries from the outside to come in. This is obviously the opposite of the intent of the access list. There is a limit on applying access lists to a router's interface, one access list–in per interface and one access list–out per interface. The following example demonstrates the use of an access list.

Example 7-1

Problem: Develop an access list to prevent any port 137 SMB data packets from anywhere or going anywhere to enter or exit the router's Serial0/0 interface.

Solution:

Configure the router to use access list 120:

```
access-list 120 deny tcp any any eq 137
access-list 120 permit ip any any
```

Apply the access list to the Serial0/0 interface:

```
ip access-group 120 in
ip access-group 120 out
```

Extended access lists identifiers are not restricted to numbers. A more convenient way to identify them is to use a name to describe the purpose of the access list. For example, in the previous example, an access list called block-snmp could be used. The network administrator can quickly identify the purpose of the list without having to check each entry. An example is shown:

```
LAN-B(config)#ip access-list extended block-snmp
LAN-B(config-ext-nacl)#deny tcp any any eq 161
LAN-B(config-ext-nacl)#deny udp any any eq snmp
LAN-B(config-ext-nacl)#permit ip any any
LAN-B(config-ext-nacl)# end
LAN-B#sh access-list
Extended IP access list 100
10 deny tcp any any eq 161
20 deny udp any any eq snmp
30 permit ip any any
Extended IP access list block-snmp
10 deny tcp any any eq 161
20 deny udp any any eq snmp
30 permit ip any any
```

Notice the **show access-list** command lists both the 100 and the block-snmp access lists. Both lists actually do the same thing. Next, the block-snmp access list is applied to the router's Serial0/0 interface, as shown:

```
LAN-B(config)#int s0/0
LAN-B(config-if)#ip access-group block-snmp in
```

Example 7-2 demonstrates an application of the named access list.

Example 7-2

Problem: Create an access list to block any UDP packets from the network 10.66.66.0/24 to enter the Serial0/1 interface on a router. Specify an extended access list of block-udp.

Solution:

From the router's (config)# prompt:

```
ip access-list extended block-udp
deny udp 10.66.66.0 0.0.0.255 any
permit ip any any
```

On the serial interface:

```
interface s0/1
ip access-group block-udp in
```

Notice that the access list uses the wild card mask 0.0.0.255 to describe the network 10.66.66.0. The 0 indicates a "must match" and 255 indicates a "don't care." This results in a match for 10.66.66.0. An interesting statistic to look at is how many times an access list has been matched. The command **show access-list** followed by the name or number of the list enables the statistics to be viewed. The **(# matches)** indicates how many times there has been a match to the access list. An example is shown here for the blocksnmp access list:

```
LAN-B#sh access-list block-snmp
Extended IP access list block-snmp
deny tcp any any eq 161
deny udp any any eq snmp
permit ip any any (7 matches)
LAN-B#sh access-list block-snmp
Extended IP access list block-snmp
deny tcp any any eq 161 (6 matches)
deny udp any any eq snmp
permit ip any any (7 matches)
```

The first display for the **show access-list** indicates that no packets have been denied, but there have been seven matches for **permit ip any any**. The second group shows that TCP data packets have been denied six times. This information can be useful for the network administrator when evaluating the effectiveness of an access list. There are times when a host with a specific IP address needs to be denied. For example, an attacker could have gained access to a host computer in the network and configured it to continually ping a server, attempting to generate a denial of service or just to slow down data traffic.

Another possibility is the computer could be on a host external to the network that is continually pinging a server within the network. The network administrator examines the data traffic and determines that the IP address of the attack is from a remote computer (192.168.12.5). The computer is not in the administrator's LAN;

therefore, the data traffic must be stopped in the administrator's network. Configuring an access list to deny any packets from the remote host can do this. Assume that the data traffic is entering the network via the Serial0/0 interface on RouterB, the Internet router, as shown in Figure 7-3.

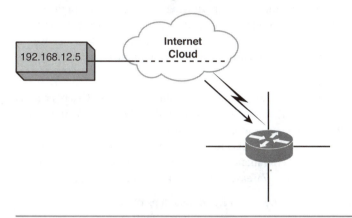

192.168.12.5

Internet
Cloud

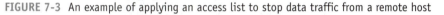

FIGURE 7-3 An example of applying an access list to stop data traffic from a remote host

```
The following demonstrates how the access list could be
configured:LAN-B(config)#ip access-list extended block-badguy
LAN-B(config-ext-nacl)#deny ip host 192.168.12.5 any
LAN-B(config-ext-nacl)#permit ip any any
LAN-B(config-ext-nacl)#int ser0/0
LAN-B(config-if)#ip access-group block-badguy in
```

This example shows that an extended access list called block-badguy was created. The access list denies source packets from the host 192.168.12.5 with any destination. The **host** entry enables a specific IP address to be entered. Next the access list is applied to the router's Serial0 interface in the in direction. The **in** describes that the list is applied to any data packets coming into the interface.

Example 7-3 shows the blocking of a host IP address.

> **Host**
> Enables a specific host IP address to be entered in the access list.

Example 7-3

Problem: Create an access list to block any data traffic from the IP address 192.168.12.5 to anywhere. Specify an extended access list name of border-router. Apply the access list to the router's Serial1 interface. Assume that the router interface is connected to the Internet, and the 192.168.12.5 host is external to the network.

Solution:

```
ip access-list extended border-router
deny ip host 192.168.12.5 any
permit ip any any
int s1
ip access-group border-router in
```

A bad thing about access lists is that they are not stateful. This means they don't keep track of the data packet flow. They only examine the current packet, and they contain no information about the recent history of data traffic on that connection. This makes it hard for access lists to allow connections to be made to the outside world. Access lists try to address this need for allowing a connection from the outside to the inside if an Established connection exists. This requires using a flag in the TCP header, but TCP headers can be falsified; therefore, the access list is useless for verifying an established connection. Someone could fake an acknowledgement flag so his or her packet could enter the network.

Filter List
Juniper's non-stateful packet filter.

Juniper Filter List The Juniper JUNOS has something similar to Cisco's access list called a filter list. Juniper's filter list is a non-stateful packet filter. A filter list is configured in a similar fashion as configuring a routing policy. The programming syntax in most part is the same. Filter lists are defined under the firewall section. Typically, filter lists are used in conjunction with prefix lists, which are groups of networks and IP addresses. This is for ease of programming and organizing.

The example that follows demonstrates configuration steps of how to create a JUNOS filter list. The following is a filter list to allow SNMP access for a trusted network of 192.168.10.0/24 and a trusted host of 10.20.20.32. This filter list will deny all SNMP traffic from everywhere else.

```
net-admin@noc# configure
Entering configuration mode
[edit]
net-admin@noc# set policy-options prefix-list snmp-list
192.168.10.0/24
[edit]
net-admin@noc# set policy-options prefix-list snmp-list 10.20.20.32/32
[edit]
net-admin@noc# edit firewall family inet
[edit firewall family inet]
net-admin@noc# # edit filter protect
[edit firewall family inet filter protect]
net-admin@noc# # edit term allow-snmp
[edit firewall family inet filter protect]
net-admin@noc# set term allow-snmp from source-prefix-list snmp-list
[edit firewall family inet filter protect]
net-admin@noc# set term allow-snmp from protocol udp
[edit firewall family inet filter protect]
net-admin@noc# set term allow-snmp from destination-port 161
[edit firewall family inet filter protect]
net-admin@noc# set term allow-snmp then accept
[edit firewall family inet filter protect]
net-admin@noc# set term block-snmp from protocol udp
[edit firewall family inet filter protect]
net-admin@noc# set term block-snmp from destination-port 161
[edit firewall family inet filter protect]
net-admin@noc# set term block-snmp then reject
[edit firewall family inet filter protect]
net-admin@noc# set term everything-else then accept
[edit firewall family inet filter protect]
```

A prefix list called snmp-list is created and it contains two trusted SNMP sources. A filter called protect has three terms: **allow-snmp**, **block-snmp**, and **everything-else**. The term **allow-snmp** permits the traffic from the prefix list snmp-list to UDP port 161 (SNMP). The term **block-snmp** denies any traffic to UDP port 161 and the term **everything-else** permits the rest of the traffic that neither match the term allow-snmp nor block-snmp to pass through. After the filter list is created, it can be applied as the input filter or the output filter to an interface similar to Cisco access-list. For example, to apply the preceding filter list to the interface ge-0/2/0 of a Juniper router, use the following command:

```
[edit]
net-admin@noc# set interface ge0/2/0 unit 0 family inet filter input
protect
```

You can verify the filter list configuration with the **show firewall** command, which will show any configuration within the firewall section:

```
[edit ]
net-admin@noc# # show firewall
family inet {
      filter protect {
            term allow-snmp {
              from {
              source-prefix-list {
                      snmp-list;
              }
              protocol udp;
              destination-port snmp;
              }
              then accept;
      }
      term block-snmp {
            from {
            protocol udp;
            destination-port snmp;
            }
            then reject;
      }
term everything-else {
      then accept;
      }
}
```

7-3 ROUTER SECURITY

Routers perform essential services for the network. The majority of the routers are deployed at the perimeter of the network. Therefore, they are the first line of defense of the network. Compromise of a router can lead to many issues on the network, such as degrading network performance, denial of network services, exposure of network configuration details and exposure of the sensitive data. A poorly configured router can easily become a compromised router, thereby reducing the overall security of the network and potentially exposing the internal network to scans and attacks. The following section focuses on the "best practice" on how to configure a network router to avoid or prevent very serious security problems.

Physical security is always on top of the list of any best security practice. Routers should be placed in a secure area where it is accessible only to authorized personnel. Recall that the easiest access to a router is via its console port. If someone gains access to the premise, then they have physical control of the router. The router may be secured with a password, but the router's password can be recovered if someone has console access. Even worse, the router can become disabled or damaged and all network services will be halted until the situation is repaired.

The operating system of the router is another crucial component that any network administrator must keep up to date. However, it has been known that the latest version of any IOS is not the greatest. Its reliability is questionable because of its limited exposure of testing. Most network administrators will wait before upgrading to the latest version to make sure that there are no side effects or bugs. Most network administrators will settle for the latest stable release of the IOS, but not the very latest one.

Configuration hardening is needed to limit the exposure of a router. This section focuses on configuration hardening of Cisco routers. The same concepts still apply to other vendor routers; however, the configuration method and commands will be different.

Router Access

Local access and remote access to the router are the common ways of gaining control of a router, and access must be restricted to only authorized personnel. A typical way of securing the local access or remote access is to create a password. There are two types of passwords used on a router: the **line password** and EXEC password. The line password is used to gain access to the router and the privileged EXEC level password that is used to gain access to EXEC commands. The line password is recommended to be used in conjunction with the command **service-password encryption**. This global command will encrypt the password and display it in the encrypted form. It is not a strong encryption, but it can be used to provide low level security. The **EXEC level password** used to be enabled with the **enable password** command, but that command has been replaced by the **enable secret** command. This command provides a stronger password encryption. There are two password protection schemes used in Cisco IOS: Type 7 and Type 5. **Type 7** uses a Cisco encryption algorithm, which is not as strong as **Type 5** protection, which uses MD5 hash. Therefore, it is recommended that you use Type 5 protection whenever possible.

A security step beyond typical password protection is to create a user account for authorized personnel. This provides the capability to track and log each time a system is accessed. A local user account can be created on a router by using the command **username** [*name*] **privilege** [*level*] **password** [*password_string*] as shown:

```
RouterA(config)# username admin privilege 10 password @dm1np@$$wd
```

Cisco provides 16 levels (0–15) of privileges. Each level is pre-assigned with commands that can be run. Level 15 is the highest and is equivalent to privileged EXEC

Line Password
Used to gain access to the router.

EXEC Level Password
Used to gain access to EXEC commands.

Type 7
Uses a Cisco encryption algorithm.

Type 5
Uses MD5 hash for encryption.

mode. The command **username admin privilege 10 password @dm1np@$$wd** creates a local user called admin with privilege level 10. The drawback of creating a local user is that the same user has to be created on every router on the network. This does not provide scalability. Cisco offers Authentication, Authorization, and Accounting (AAA) service as a way to centrally manage and control user access. With AAA, two of the most used access protocols, RADIUS (Remote Authentication Dial In User Service) and TACACS+ (Terminal Access Controller Access-Control System Plus), are supported. This means that Cisco routers can communicate with RADIUS or TACACS+ servers for central authentication. AAA enables authentication based on the router's local user database, enable, line passwords, as well as other access protocols. The following shows an example of how to configure AAA on a Cisco router:

```
RouterA(config)# aaa new-model
RouterA(config)# aaa authentication login default local group tacacs+
RouterA(config)# aaa authorization exec default local group tacacs+
if-authenticated
```

> **AAA**
> Authentication, Authorization, and Accounting.

Once the authentication method is defined, it can be applied to any access entry point whether it is local or remote. The local access can be via the console port or the auxiliary port. The remote access is via VTY or virtual terminal. The following example shows how to configure a console port with security access. It enforces the authentication using the local user database and the timeout of 5 minutes if the user input is not detected. Also, it prevents the remote access to the console port via reverse-telnet with the command **transport input none**:

```
RouterA(config)#line con 0
RouterA(config-line)#login local
RouterA(config-line)#exec-time 5 0
RouterA(config-line)#transport input none
```

> **transport input none**
> This command prevents the remote access to the console port via reverse-telnet with the command.

The remote access to the router can be made via Telnet or SSH. Telnet is a default transport protocol into a router, but its unencrypted traffic is a big security flaw. Therefore, SSH is recommended whenever possible. To enable the SSH transport requires an extra step of generating an RSA key. To generate an RSA key, the hostname and the domain name must be pre-configured on the router as this information will be used as part of the key. To generate the key, the command **crypto key generate** rsa is issued:

> **crypto key generate**
> rsa
> Command used to generate an RSA key.

```
RouterA(config)#crypto key generate rsa
The name for the keys will be: RouterA.et477.local
Choose the size of the key modulus in the range of 360 to 2048 for
your
  General Purpose Keys. Choosing a key modulus greater than 512 may
take a few minutes.
How many bits in the modulus [512]: 1024
% Generating 1024 bit RSA keys, keys will be non-exportable...[OK]
```

After the RSA key is generated, the remote VTY access can be configured with SSH as the transport. The following is an example configuring the VTY remote access with SSH. The configuration uses the default login authentication that was defined in the AAA section. The command **transport input ssh** enforces SSH as the only access method. The access-class 15 defines the access-list of the network that is allowed to connect to the router via SSH. Lastly, the exec-timeout of 5 minutes is configured:

```
RouterB(config)# access-list 15 permit 10.10.20.0 0.0.0.255
RouterB(config)# access-list 15 deny any
RouterA(config)# line vty 0 4
RouterA(config-line)# access-class 15 in
RouterA(config-line)# login authentication default
RouterA(config-line)# transport input ssh
RouterA(config-line)#exec-time 5 0
```

Router Services

A router has many services enabled by default. These services vary from vendor to vendor. Unnecessary services should be disabled and those services deemed necessary should be tightened. The TCP/IP services like echo, discard, daytime, chargen, bootps, finger, identd, and snmp, are enabled automatically on a Cisco router and most of these are not needed. They can be disabled globally as follows:

```
RouterA(config)#no service tcp-small-servers
RouterA(config)#no service udp-small-servers
RouterA(config)#no ip bootp server
RouterA(config)#no service finger
RouterA(config)#no ip identd
```

Services such as echo, discard, daytime, and chargen are considered TCP and UDP small services and can be disabled using **no service tcp-small-servers** and **no service udp-small-servers**. Some services might be needed, such as Simple Network Management Protocol (SNMP) and HTTP. These services will need to be tightened. The SNMP default community string must not be used and the new community string must be difficult to guess. The read-write access should be avoided at all costs and read-only access should be configured. Also, SNMP access should be restricted to certain known SNMP agents. Better yet, SNMP version 3 should be used instead. The topic of SNMP was discussed in Chapter 6, "Analyzing Network Data Traffic." The following is the example of the SNMP configuration on a Cisco router with read-only and with restricted access as defined in the access-list 10:

```
RouterA(config)#snmp-server community M@ke1tD1ff1cuLT ro 10
```

The Cisco IOS supports web-based remote administration, which is easier and more intuitive to use than the CLI mode that is used with telnet or SSH. However, HTTP has no encryption. Therefore, web-based administration via HTTP can reveal the passwords. This should be avoided just like Telnet. More recent Cisco IOS Software versions, starting from release 12.2(15)T, do provide another option of HTTPS that provides end-to-end SSL encryption, as shown:

```
RouterA(config)# no ip http server
RouterA(config)# ip http secure-server
RouterA(config)# ip http access-class 15
RouterA(config)# ip http authentication aaa
```

The configuration shows the normal HTTP service is disabled, and the HTTPS service is enabled instead. The HTTP access is also restricted with the access-list 15, and it will use the AAA authentication.

Besides disabling unnecessary services running on the router, some services or features that Cisco routers utilize should be disabled. It is highly recommended that services such as CDP, remote configuration downloading, and source-routing are disabled, as shown:

```
RouterA(config)#no cdp run
RouterA(config)#no service config
RouterA(config)#no ip source-route
```

Cisco equipment uses Cisco Discovery Protocol (CDP) to identify each other on a LAN segment. This feature is enabled automatically and it allows anyone on the network to collect the information of the network. The remote configuration is disabled by the command **no service config**. This stops the router from loading its configuration from the network, which is not secure. The routers are capable of loading their startup configuration from the local memory and this is more secure. Source-routing can be used in many kinds of attacks. By disabling this feature, the router will disregard the IP packet with source routes information.

> **CDP**
> Cisco Discovery Protocol. Proprietary protocol is used to obtain the platform and the protocol addresses of neighboring devices.

On the interface level, any unused interfaces should be disabled so that they cannot participate in any network activity. Directed broadcasts allow a host on another network segment to initiate a broadcast to a different network segment. This can be used as a denial of service attack like the smurf attack. This feature should be disabled. Newer IOS versions disable the directed broadcast by default.

The router interfaces should not be acting as the intermediary for ARP or ARP proxy. This feature will extend ARP traffic between the two network segments. This is not desirable and should be avoided. Also, the router can be used to relay ICMP messages that can be used by attackers, and the generation of these messages should be disabled on the interface. The common ICMP messages that are commonly exploited are Host unreachable, Redirect, and Mask reply. The following is the example configuration to secure the router interface:

```
RouterA(config)# interface fastethernet0/1
RouterA(config-if)#shutdown
RouterA(config)# interface fastethernet0/2
RouterA(config-if)# no ip directed-broadcast
RouterA(config-if)# no ip proxy-arp
RouterA(config-if)# no ip unreachables
RouterA(config-if)# no ip redirects
RouterA(config-if)# no ip mask-reply
```

Router Logging and Access-List

Logging is a critical part of security. Logging allows the administrator to analyze the events that occur and use the given information to correlate and find the issues. Cisco routers provide a great deal of logging events. They can log system errors, network and interface status, login access, access list matches, routing changes, and many more types of events. Cisco's log messages can be directed to the console, terminal line, memory buffer, and syslog server. There are 8 levels (0–7) of log severity:

Emergencies (0)
Alerts (1)
Critical (2)
Errors (3)
Warnings (4)
Notifications (5)
Informational (6)
Debugging (7)

NTP
Network Time Protocol. A protocol that synchronizes the router's clock with the time server.

It is recommended that for best security, syslog logging and buffered logging in debugging level should be set up. To keep accurate logs, the correct time on a router has to be set up. This tends to be a step that many disregard. Cisco routers support the Network Time Protocol (NTP), which can be set up to synchronize the router's clock with the time server. To correlate the time with the log events, a timestamp service will need to be initiated. The following example shows the log configuration of a Cisco router. It consists of enabling timestamp service for log with the date and time down to millisecond detail. The logging can be enabled with the simple command **logging on**. A memory buffer of 16 Kbytes was reserved for logging with debugging level. In addition, the same debugging level log messages will be sent to a syslog server with the IP address 172.20.20.20:

```
RouterA(config)# service timestamps log datetime msec
RouterA(config)# logging on
RouterA(config)# logging buffered 16000 debugging
RouterA(config)# logging trap debugging
RouterA(config)# logging 172.20.20.20
```

The log information can be verified with the command **show log**, as demonstrated here:

```
RouterA#sh log
Syslog logging: enabled (11 messages dropped, 1 messages rate-limited,
                0 flushes, 0 overruns, xml disabled, filtering
disabled)
    Console logging: disabled
    Monitor logging: disabled
    Buffer logging: level debugging, 1 messages logged, xml disabled,
                filtering disabled
    Logging Exception size (4096 bytes)
    Count and timestamp logging messages: disabled
No active filter modules.
    Trap logging: level debugging, 3882 message lines logged
        Logging to 172.20.20.20(global) (udp port 514, audit disabled,
link up), 5 message lines logged, xml disabled,
                filtering disabled

Log Buffer (16000 bytes):
```

```
*May 20 23:32:37.286: %SYS-5-CONFIG_I: Configured from console by
piyasat on vty1 (192.168.101.121)
```

Another way to use the log is via the access list. The router's access list and log can indeed be used in conjunction. As a matter of fact, it is a best practice to use log in every deny statement in each extended access list. This will provide valuable information of what is being denied, and it is useful as a security detection tool of probes and attacks against the network. The following is an access list statement with a keyword **log**:

```
access-list 101 permit ip 192.168.0.0 0.0.255.255 any
access-list 101 permit tcp any any eq 80
access-list 101 deny ip any any log
```

Typically, access lists vary from place to place depending on each entity's security policy. A type of traffic that is allowed on one network might not be desirable on another; however, there is a basic access list that is recommended for every network. This access list is used to protect against IP address spoofing. The IP address spoof protection concept is simple: Do not allow any inbound IP packets that contain IP source addresses of the internal network or any reserved private IP addresses. The following example shows an access-list 102 that contains an IP address spoofing protection for the internal network of 12.12.12.0/24. This access list will be applied to the outbound interface of the router as **ip access-group 102 in**:

```
access-list 102 deny ip 12.12.12.0 0.0.0.255 any log
access-list 102 deny ip 10.0.0.0 0.255.255.255 any log
access-list 102 deny ip 172.16.0.0 0.15.255.255 any log
access-list 102 deny ip 192.168.0.0 0.0.255.255 any log
access-list 102 permit ip any any
```

7-4 SWITCH SECURITY

Switches are another common network device. Typically, there are more switches than routers on a network. Switches are commonly used in the access layer of the network hierarchy. The access layer connects users who will share the common network resources and bandwidth. Directly interfacing with users can be a security challenge since there is no way to know what will be connecting to the switch access ports. The bottom line is that the better the network will be if more control or policies are enforced at the switch port level.

The previous section had covered the necessary steps to secure the routers. All discussed security steps or best practices, such as physical security, IOS updates, configuration hardening for local and remote access, disabling unnecessary services, logging and access lists apply to the switches as well. This is especially true on Cisco equipment because the IOS configuration is similar, if not the same, on the Cisco routers and switches. The major differences are with the interfaces commands. Some commands are reserved for only the router interface and some commands are reserved only for the switch interface. This section's focus is on manageable Cisco switches. Some of these concepts can apply to other switch vendors as well.

Switch Port Security

Since switch interfaces or ports directly connect users or network equipment, they should be securely configured to prevent malicious attacks or exploitations from end users. The very fundamental security rule is to disable the ports that are not being used. There are definitely more ports on switches than routers. A useful command to use when applying the same command to a group of switch ports is the range command. This will make it easier for the administrator to apply the same security policy on switch ports. The following example shows the commands to shut down a group or a range of interfaces:

```
SwitchA(config)# interface range Gigabitethernet1/1-24
SwitchA(config-if)#shutdown
```

On Cisco switches, you can take advantage of a built-in set of switch port security commands. Switch port security can be configured to restrict a port's ingress traffic by limiting the MAC addresses that are allowed to send traffic into the port. The command to enable the port security is **switchport port-security**, and this command has to be issued at the interface level. A switch port can be configured to restrict access by setting a maximum number of MAC addresses or it can be configured to allow only known MAC addresses to pass traffic.

To configure the maximum number of MAC addresses on a switch port, use the command **switchport port-security maximum** [*number*]. To configure a port to allow certain MAC addresses to pass traffic, use the command **switchport port-security mac-address** [*mac_address*] or **switchport port-security mac-address sticky** [*mac_address*]. The big difference between the first **port-security mac-address** command and the second command with the **sticky** option is that the first command will not get the configured MAC address into the running configuration, while the second command with sticky option will. With the sticky option, the configured MAC address will appear in the running-config of the switch and it can then be saved into the startup-config. This way, when the switch reboots, the configured MAC address remains part of the configuration.

Along with the security configuration, one will need to define a **violation action**. When a violation occurs, one of the selected violation actions will take an effect. These violation actions are protected, restrict, and shutdown. The violation action **protected** will drop packets from the violated MAC address(es). The violation action **restrict** is the same as the protected mode, but it will also send SNMP trap messages to the SNMP server. The violation action **shutdown** is to shutdown the port and put the port in ERRDISABLE state. The following is an example of a port security configuration. The port security command **switchport port-security maximum 2** allows at most only two MAC addresses on this switch port Gigabitethernet 1/10. Not only that, only the specified MAC addresses of 0011.2233.440a and 0011.2233.440b are allowed to pass the traffic. If the violation occurs, the switch port will be shut down:

```
SwitchA(config)# interface Gigabitethernet1/10
SwitchA(config-if)#switchport port-security maximum 2
SwitchA(config-if)#switchport port-security mac-address sticky
0011.2233.440a
SwitchA(config-if)#switchport port-security mac-address sticky
0011.2233.440b
SwitchA(config-if)#switchport port-security violation shutdown
```

When a port is in the ERRDISABLE state, the port is automatically disabled by the switch operating system software because an error condition has been encountered on the port. This requires a manual intervention by the administrator in order to re-enable the port. The administrator will need to issue the command **shutdown** and then **no shutdown** to re-enable the port. Another way of re-enabling a port from ERRDISABLE state is to configure the errdisable recovery feature. The following example shows the errdisable discovery configuration to recover the port from port security violation after 10 minutes (600 seconds):

```
SwitchA(config)# errdisable recovery cause psecure-violation
SwitchA(config-if)#errdisable recovery interval 600
```

> **ERRDISABLE**
>
> In this state, the port is automatically disabled by the switch operating system software because an error condition has been encountered on the port.

Another port security feature that is not part of the **switchport port-security** command is **storm control**. The storm control feature can be used to limit the amount of unicast, multicast, or broadcast packets that each port can receive. When there is an excessive amount of any kind of these packets, it becomes a network storm. A network storm disrupts network services or degrades the network performance. The storm control feature is generally available on other switch vendors; however, their storm control features are limited only to broadcast and multicast. Cisco is one of the only few manufacturers to have unicast storm control. This is proven to be useful to help stopping denial of service attacks where a machine is transmitting an excessive amount of unicast packets.

> **storm-control**
>
> Used to limit the amount of unicast, multicast, or broadcast packets that each port can receive.
>
> **pps**
>
> Packets per second. A measure of the data transfer rate.

The **storm-control** command is applied at the switch port level. The following example shows the options that one could choose for unicast storm control. The storm can be suppressed by defining the bandwidth percentage of the interface or by defining the bps (bits per second) to limit the bandwidth the unicast traffic is allowed to consume. The storm can also be suppressed by defining the **pps** (packet per second) to limit the number of unicast packets a switch port can forward. Note that older Cisco switches might not be equipped with the pps option of the unicast storm:

```
SwitchA(config-if)#storm-control unicast level ?
  <0.00 - 100.00>  Enter rising threshold
  bps              Enter suppression level in bits per second
  pps              Enter suppression level in packets per second
```

The storm-control is configured with a **rising threshold** and a **failing threshold**. When the traffic rises above the rising threshold, the interface drops that specific traffic until the traffic comes down below the failing threshold. The administrator can enforce all types of storm controls as shown in the configuration of interface Gigabit Ethernet 1/0/8 here:

> **rising threshold/ failing threshold**
>
> When the traffic rises above the rising threshold, the interface drops that specific traffic until the traffic comes down below the failing threshold.

```
interface GigabitEthernet1/0/8
 storm-control broadcast level 2 1
 storm-control multicast level bps 50m 10m
 storm-control unicast level pps 6k 2k
 storm-control action trap
```

In this example configuration, the broadcast traffic is discarded if it uses more than 2 percent of the available bandwidth. This is 20 Mbps (2) for a Gigabit interface, and it will resume the broadcast traffic again if the traffic falls below 10 Mbps (1).

The multicast storm is set to use only 50 Mbps (50 m) and its threshold is set at 10 Mbps (10 m). The unicast storm is configured to discard any unicast packets above 6,000 (6 k) packets per second, and the unicast traffic will resume if it falls below the 2,000 (2k) packets per second. The default action for storm-control is to drop packets (trap) when the rising threshold is met. It can also be configured to shut-down an interface or to send SNMP trap messages.

Switch Special Features

The Spanning Tree Protocol (STP) is a common protocol found in every network switch. STP is a Layer 2 protocol designed to prevent loops within switched networks. STP builds its topology based on BPDU (Bridge Protocol Data Unit) messages. A vulnerability associated with STP is that a STP enabled device within the network can actively change the STP topology by sending an unexpected BPDU message. In order to prevent such events, features such as BPDU guard and BPDU filter can be used.

STP Portfast

This speeds up the STP process and transitions the port into a forwarding state bypassing the listen and learn states.

BPDU Guard

Feature used to prevent a STP Portfast to receive any BPDU message to modify the Spanning Tree topology.

On STP enabled switches, a switch port has to go through four STP states (i.e., block, listen, learn, and forward), before it can pass traffic. This process can take between 30 to 50 seconds. To reduce this time, a switch port can be configured to be an **STP Portfast**, which speeds up the STP process, and transitions the port into a forwarding state bypassing the listen and learn state. Typically, a STP Portfast interface is used to directly connect a host device, which does not send BPDU messages. **BPDU guard** is used to prevent a STP Portfast to receive any BPDU message to modify the Spanning Tree topology. Upon receipt of a BPDU, BPDU guard puts the interface configured for STP Portfast into the ERRDISABLE state. By default, BPDU guard is disabled. The following command is used to globally enable BPDU guard on all edge ports of a Cisco switch by default:

```
SwitchA(config)# spanning-tree portfast bpduguard default
```

BPDU guard can also be enabled at the interface level with the following command:

```
SwitchA(config)# interface gigabitethernet 0/1
SwitchA(config-if)# spanning-tree bpduguard enable
```

BPDU Filter

Feature that effectively disables STP on the selected ports by preventing them from sending or receiving any BPDU messages.

STP Root Guard

Feature that allows participation in spanning tree and BPDU messages as long as the attached device does not attempt to become the root bridge.

Another STP feature called **BPDU filter** offers a different flavor when dealing with BPDU. BPDU guard prevents a switch port from receiving any BPDU messages, but it does not prevent it from sending them. The BPDU filter feature effectively disables STP on the selected ports by preventing them from sending or receiving any BPDU messages. The switch port will ignore all BPDUs, and it will send no BPDUs. Similar to BPDU guard, the BPDU filter can be configured globally or on an individual port. The global command is **spanning-tree portfast bpdufilter default**. The command to enable the BPDU filter on the interface level is **spanning-tree bpdufilter enable**.

STP Root guard is another feature that can be used to protect the STP topology. Unlike the BPDU guard, STP Root guard allows participation in spanning tree and BPDU messages as long as the attached device does not attempt to become the root bridge. Essentially, STP Root guard provides a way to enforce the root bridge placement in the network. If an unauthorized device starts sending BPDU messages with a better bridge ID, the Root guard disables the switch port on which those

BPDU messages were received. The switch port will be in the ERRDISABLE state. The STP Root guard feature can only be enabled at the interface level. It is recommended to apply this feature to those switch ports that are not connected to the root bridge. The following is the command used within the interface configuration mode to enable STP Root guard:

```
SwitchA(config-if)# spanning-tree guard root
```

There are a few features that are specific to Cisco switches. It was recommended in the previous section that CDP should be disabled on the routers. This is the same on switches as well. Another Cisco proprietary feature is Virtual Trunking Protocol (VTP), which is a Layer 2 messaging protocol used to automatically add, delete, and rename VLANs on a network-wide basis. Using VTP allows for consistent VLAN configuration across all switches on the network. Cisco switches come with VTP enabled by default and they are enabled as VTP server mode. It is possible for a single switch to overwrite all VLAN assignments. It is recommended that VTP be disabled if it is not being used. The following is the example:

```
SwitchA(config)# no vtp mode
SwitchA(config)# no vtp password
SwitchA(config)# no vtp pruning
```

Another Cisco proprietary switch protocol is Dynamic Trunking Protocol (DTP), which is used to automatically negotiate a switch port to be either an access port or a trunk port. This is convenient, but at the same time, can be exploited to reveal all the VLANs or to gain access to all the VLANs. It is recommended that access ports and trunk ports should all be manually configured without negotiation. Also, it is best practice to control the number of VLANs that are allowed through the trunk port, as shown in the following example where VLANs 2, 3, and 30 are being allowed:

DTP

Dynamic Trunking Protocol. Used to automatically negotiate a switch port to be either an access port or a trunk port.

```
SwitchA(config)# interface gigabitethernet 0/1
SwitchA(config-if)# switchport mode trunk
SwitchA(config-if)# switchport trunk allowed vlan 2,3,30
SwitchA(config-if)# switchport nonnegotiate
```

7-5 WIRELESS SECURITY

This section provides an overview of securing 802.11 wireless LANs. The network administrator must be aware of the security issues when configuring a wireless LAN. The fact is, radio frequencies (RF) will pass through walls, ceilings, and floors of a building even with low signal power. Therefore, the assumption should never be made that the wireless data is confined to only the user's area. The network administrator must assume that the wireless data can be received by an unintended user. In other words, the use of an unsecured wireless LAN is opening a potential threat to network security.

To address this threat to WLAN security, the network administrator must ensure that the WLAN is protected by firewalls and intrusion detection, and most importantly the network administrator must make sure that the wireless security features are

7-5: WIRELESS SECURITY   289

TURNED ON! This might seem to be a bold statement, but surprisingly enough, many WLANs are placed on a network without turning on available wireless security features. Many times, the user in the WLAN assumes that no one would break into their computer because nothing important exists on the system. This may be true, but to an attacker, the user has one very important item—access to the wired network through an unsecured client.

WLANs use an SSID (service set identifier) to authenticate users, but the problem is that the SSID is broadcast in radio link beacons about 10 times per second. In WLAN equipment, the beacons are transmitted so that a wireless user can identify an access point to connect to. The SSID can be turned off so it isn't transmitted with a beacon, but it is still possible for the SSID to be obtained by packet sniffing. As noted previously, packet sniffing is a technique used to scan through unencrypted data packets to extract information. In this case, an attacker uses packet sniffing to extract the SSID from data packets. Disabling SSID broadcasting will make it so that most client devices (such as Windows devices and Mac devices) won't notice that the wireless LAN is present. This at least keeps "casual snoopers" off the network. Enterprise-grade access points implement multiple SSIDs, with each configured SSID having its own VLAN and wireless configuration. This allows the deployment of a common wireless LAN infrastructure that supports multiple levels of security, which is important for some venues such as airports and hospitals (where there are both public and private users).

IEEE 802.11 supports two ways to authenticate clients: open and sharekey. Open authentication basically is a null authentication that can enable any client to authenticate to an AP as long as the client knows the correct SSID. In sharekey authentication, both the client and the access point share a key called a pre-shared key (PSK). The client sends a shared key authentication request and then a packet of text called a challenge text is sent by the access point to the client with the instruction to encrypt the text and return it to the access point. This requires that wired equivalent privacy (WEP) be turned on. WEP is used to encrypt and decrypt wireless data packets. The exchange and the return of the encrypted text verify that the client has the proper WEP key and is authorized to be a member of the wireless network. Note that shared key authentication is extremely vulnerable. As a result, it's standard practice to avoid the use of shared key authentication. Figure 7-4 provides an example of the setting for WEP encryption. In part a of Figure 7-4, the user has the WEP options of disabled (No Privacy), 64-bit WEP (Privacy), and 128-bit WEP (More Privacy). Part b of Figure 7-4 shows the wireless security settings in Windows Vista. There are clearly more options, and these newer wireless security settings are discussed next.

It is well-known that WEP is a weak wireless security system. It doesn't use a strong enough encryption to secure a wireless network. The RC4 algorithm is used for encryption in WEP. A couple of the weaknesses of WEP include that the challenge text in WEP is sent in clear text. Additionally, the WEP initialization vector is only 24-bits in size and is always static. WEP also does not use a key management and its pre-shared key never changes. Because of these factors, it is not too difficult to obtain the pre-shared key. There is published information about WEP vulnerabilities, but even with this, WEP does provide some basic security and is certainly better than operating the network with no security.

SSID

Service set identifier. A 32 alphanumeric character unique identifier that's attached to data packets transmitted over a wireless network (WLAN). The SSID is essentially a password that enables the client to connect to the access point.

Beacon

Used to identify a wireless link.

Open Authentication

A null authentication that can enable any client to authenticate to an AP.

Sharekey Authentication

Both the client and the access point share a key called a pre-shared key (PSK).

WEP

Wired equivalent privacy. WEP provides a secure wireless channel by encrypting the data so that it is protected as it is transmitted from one end point to another.

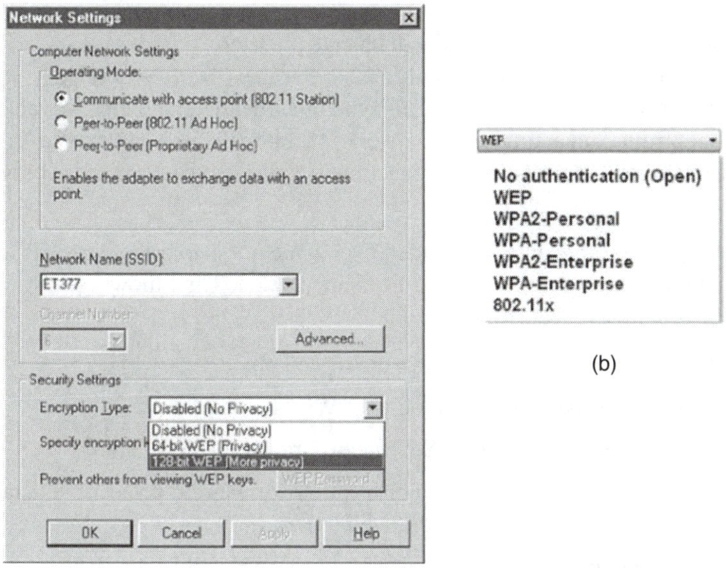

FIGURE 7-4 An example of setting WEP encryption on a wireless client

An improvement with wireless security is provided with WPA and WPA2. WPA stands for Wi-Fi Protected Access, and it supports the user authentication provided by 802.1x and replaces WEP as the primary way for securing wireless transfers. WPA still uses RC4 as the encryption algorithm, but it provides a key management mechanism via Temporal Key Integrity Protocol (TKIP). TKIP basically generates a sequence of WEP keys based on a master pre-shared key and rekeys periodically every 10,000 packets. TKIP also uses an integrity check value to ensure that the packet is not tampered with. If so, WPA will stop using the current key and will re-key. WPA2 is an improved version of WPA. It uses Advance Encryption Standard (AES) as its encryption algorithm and Counter Mode with Cipher Block Chaining Message Authentication Code Protocol (CCMP) as its key management.

The encryption algorithm and key management alone cannot truly secure the wireless connection. The 802.1x standard enhances wireless security by incorporating authentication of the user. Cisco Systems uses an 802.1x authentication system called Lightweight Extensible Authentication Protocol (LEAP). In Cisco LEAP, the user must enter a password to access the network. This means that if the wireless client is being used by an unauthorized user, the password requirement will keep the unauthorized user out of the network.

WPA is considered to be a higher level of security for wireless systems. In the 802.1x system, a user requests access to the wireless network via an access point. The next step is for the user to be authenticated. At this point, the user can only send Extensible Authentication Protocol (EAP) messages. EAP is used in both WPA and WPA2 by the client computer and the access point. The access point sends an EAP message requesting the user's identity. The user (client computer) returns the identity information that is requested by the access point to an authentication

WPA

Wi-Fi Protected Access. Replaces WEP as the primary way for securing wireless transfers and it supports the user authentication provided by 802.1x.

TKIP

Temporal Key Integrity Protocol. Generates a sequence of WEP keys based on a master pre-shared key and rekeys periodically every 10,000 packets.

AES

Advance Encryption Standard. A 128-bit block data encryption technique.

CCMP

Counter Mode with Cipher Block Chaining Message Authentication Code Protocol. An encryption protocol designed for wireless LANs.

LEAP

Lightweight Extensible Authentication Protocol. A wireless security system used by Cisco.

EAP

Extensible Authentication Protocol. A general protocol used for supporting multiple authentication methods.

server. The server will then accept or reject the user's request to join the network. If the client is authorized, the access point will change the user's (client's) state to authorized. A Remote Authentication Dial-In User Service (RADIUS) service is sometimes used to provide authentication. This type of authentication helps prevent unauthorized users from connecting to the network. Additionally, this authentication helps to keep authorized users from connecting to rogue or unauthorized access points.

Another way to further protect data transmitted over a WLAN is to establish a VPN connection. In this way, the data is protected from an attacker. The following are basic guidelines for wireless security:

- Make sure the wireless security features are turned on.
- Use firewalls and intrusion detection on your WLAN.
- Improve authentication of the WLAN by incorporating 802.1x features.
- Consider using third-party end-to-end encryption software to protect the data that might be intercepted by an unauthorized user.
- Whenever possible, use encrypted services such as SSH and Secure FTP.

The bottom line is that the choice of the level of security will be based on multiple factors within the network. For example, what is the cost benefit ratio of increased security? How will incorporating or not incorporating increased wireless security affect users? The network administrator and the overall management will have to make the final decision regarding wireless security before it is installed and the network becomes operational.

7-6 VPN SECURITY

When a network is protected behind the firewall, it is sometimes referred to as a *private* network. Only computers on the same private network are considered to be trusted. Public access to this kind of network can be very limited. Access to a private network requires special permission to be granted on the firewall. Imagine a sales company that has its sales workforce throughout the country. The salespeople need to access the company's servers and databases at its headquarters, which is protected behind a firewall. It would be a network administrator's nightmare to grant individual access through the company's firewall. This idea does not allow for flexibility and mobility. Virtual private network (VPN) offers a solution to this problem. As the name implies, VPN is a concept of extending a private or a trusted network over public infrastructure like the Internet. A VPN accomplishes this by establishing a secure connection between the remote end and the private network, therefore enabling the remote clients to become part of the trusted network.

A secure VPN connection between two endpoints is known as an **IP tunnel**. A tunnel is created by an encapsulation technique, which encapsulates the data inside a known protocol (IP) that is agreed upon by the two end points. A tunnel creates a virtual circuit-like between the two endpoints and makes the connection appear like a dedicated connection even though it spans over the Internet infrastructure. Two types of VPNs are commonly used today:

- **Site-to-site VPN**: Used to create a virtual link from one site to the other. It essentially replaces the traditional WAN-type connection used in connecting typical sites. This type of VPN requires network hardware like a router or a firewall to create and maintain the connection.

- **Remote-access VPN**: Used to facilitate network access for users in remote office networks or for remote users that travel a lot and need access to the network. The client usually initiates this type of VPN connection.

VPN Tunneling Protocols

This section provides a quick overview of the protocols used in the creation of these VPN tunnels. One of the original tunneling protocols is the Generic Routing Encapsulation (**GRE**). GRE was developed by Cisco in 1994 and is still being used today. GRE is commonly used as a site-to-site VPN solution because of its simplicity and versatility. It is the only tunneling protocol that can encapsulate up to 20 types of protocols. In the past, when protocols like AppleTalk, Novell IPX, and NetBEUI roamed the network, GRE was the tunneling protocol of choice to carry these protocols to other remote sites.

Establishing a GRE tunnel through the IP telco cloud to connect Router A with Router C requires that the source and destination addresses of the physical network connection be defined as shown in Figure 7-5; Router A connects to the telco cloud via the router's Serial 0/1 interface. The IP address of 192.168.210.5 with a subnet mask of 255.255.255.0 has been assigned to the Router A Serial1 interface. Router C (the remote router) connects to the telco cloud via its Serial 0/1 interface. The IP address assigned to Router C's Serial1 interface is 192.168.100.3 with a subnet mask of 255.255.255.0. (*Note:* Any interface that connects to the telco cloud can be used to set up the VPN interface.) A tunnel is next established on each of the routers. The tunnel is assigned an IP address that is used in the home network. For example, the home network is a 10.0.0.0 network; therefore, the tunnel between Router A and Router C will have a 10.x.x.x IP address. The tunnel between Router A and Router C is called *tunnel 0* and is assigned IP addresses of 10.10.30.1 and 10.10.30.2. After the tunnel has been created across the IP network, the two routers appear to be on the same 10.10.30.x network.

The tunnel connection makes remote users appear as if they are part of the home network. This is accomplished by encapsulating the IP packet. The first packet uses the IP address that the remote user will use after the connection has been made. The encapsulation is used to transport the data across the networks.

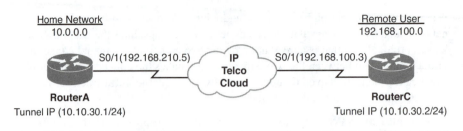

FIGURE 7-5 An example of a GRE tunnel through the IP telco cloud

Figure 7-6 provides an example of tunnel encapsulation. Part a of Figure 7-6 shows the basic IP packet. The source and destination IP address for the packet are listed. The source IP address for the remote tunnel is 10.10.30.2. The IP tunnel address for the home router interface is 10.10.30.1. This is the destination IP address. Part b of Figure 7-6 shows the layer of encapsulation for the VPN tunnel. The source IP address of 192.168.100.3 is for Router C's Serial 0/1 interface. The destination IP address of 192.168.210.5 is for the home network's Router A Serial 0/1 interface.

The 192.168.100.3 and 192.168.210.5 IP addresses are used to deliver the VPN encapsulated data packets over a TCP/IP network. When a packet is delivered to the destination, the encapsulation layer is removed and the data packet will appear as if it came from the home 10.10.30.x network. Remember, the original packet, shown in part a of Figure 7-6, contains the IP addresses for the VPN tunnel, and the encapsulation layer [part b of Figure 7-6] includes the actual physical interface IP addresses for the VPN tunnel.

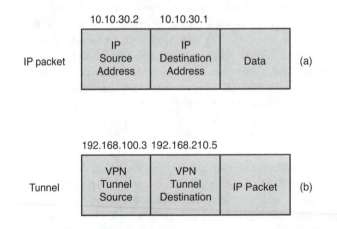

FIGURE 7-6 Data encapsulation for VPN data packets

Configuring a VPN Virtual Interface (Router to Router)

In this example, a VPN virtual interface will be configured on two routers on two separate networks. Figure 7-7 provides an illustration of the VPN. This example simulates a situation in which a VPN virtual interface is to be established between two networks. This requires that a virtual interface be established on the home router, Router A, and the remote user on Router C in Figure 7-7. The tunnels on each router will be called *tunnel 0*. These interfaces each have their own IP addresses. The difference is the tunnels require a source and destination IP address for the tunnel. The source and destination addresses are the physical addresses (IP addresses) for the serial interfaces on each router that connect to the telco cloud.

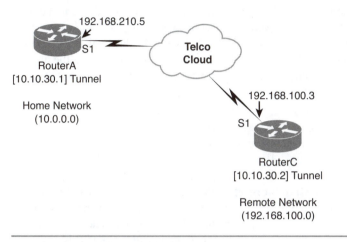

FIGURE 7-7   A virtual private network

Make sure routing has been properly configured for each router in the network, the interfaces have been assigned an IP address, and the destination physical interface from each end can be pinged prior to setting up the VPN interface and the tunnel. For example, Router A can ping the remote network router (Router C) using the command **ping 192.168.100.3**. Remember, the IP address for the serial interface is being pinged, and the virtual interfaces have not yet been configured:

```
RouterA#ping 192.168.100.3
Type escape sequence to abort.
Sending 5 100-byte ICMP Echos to 192.168.100.3, timeout is 2 seconds:
!!!!!
Success rate is 100 percent (5/5), round-trip min/avg/max 52/56/72 ms
```

The successful ping indicates that there is a network connection between Router A on the home network (192.168.210.0) and Router C on the remote network (192.168.100.0). The next step is to configure the tunnel to establish a virtual private network between the two networks.

A tunnel is added to the router from the configuration mode **(config)#**. The command **int tunnel0** is entered to configure the tunnel interface. This places the router in the interface configuration mode—**(config-if)#**. The next step is to configure the virtual IP address to be used by the VPN tunnel. The IP address for the VPN tunnel must be on the same subnet as the home network IP address. For example, the home network is from the 10.0.0.0 network. In this case, the tunnel 0 interface on Router A will be assigned an IP address of 10.10.30.1. The following shows the two steps for configuring the IP tunnel:

```
RouterA(config)#int tunnel0
RouterA(config-if)#ip 10.10.30.1 255.255.255.0
```

The next step is to define the IP destination and source address for the tunnel created on the home network router, Router A. Referring to Figure 7-7, the source IP address for tunnel 0 from Router A is 192.168.210.5 and the destination IP address for the remote interface on Router C is 192.168.100.3. After configuring the tunnel source and destination IP addresses, the router prompts that the "line protocol on Interface Tunnel0" changed state to **up**:

```
RouterA(config-if)#tunnel destination 192.168.100.3
RouterA(config-if)#tunnel source 192.168.210.5
00:31:37: %LINEPROTO-5-UPDOWN: Line protocol on Interface Tunnel0,
changed state to up
```

You can use the command **sh ip int brief** to check the configuration for the tunnel interface as shown. A tunnel will show status **up** and protocol **up** even if it is not actually up. In this case, the other end of the tunnel connection has not yet been configured. The only way to really test the virtual link is with a **ping**. This will be demonstrated after the remote router (Router C) is configured:

```
RouterA#sh ip int brief
Interface         IP-Address      OK?  Method  Status  Protocol
FastEthernet0/0   10.10.20.250    YES  NVRAM   up      up
Serial0/0         10.10.100.10    YES  NVRAM   up      down
Serial0/1         192.168.210.5   YES  NVRAM   up      up
Tunnel0           10.10.30.1      YES  manual  up      up
```

The Serial1 interface shows status **up** and protocol **up**. This is the connection to the communications carrier (telco), and this interface must be up for the tunnel to work. The command **sh int tunnel 0** can be used to check to see whether tunneling has been configured on the router:

```
RouterA#sh int tunnel 0
Tunnel0 is up, line protocol is up
Hardware is Tunnel
Internet address is 10.10.30.1/24
MTU 1514 bytes, BW 9 Kbit, DLY 500000 usec, rely 255/255, load 1/255
Encapsulation TUNNEL, loopback not set, keepalive set (10 sec) Tunnel
source 192.168.210.5, destination 192.168.100.3
Tunnel protocol/transport GRE/IP, key disabled, sequencing disabled
Checksumming of packets disabled, fast tunneling enabled
Last input never, output 00:00:01, output hang never Last clearing of
"show interface" counters never Queueing strategy: fifo
Output queue 0/0, 0 drops; input queue 0/75, 0 drops
5 minute input rate 0 bits/sec, 0 packets/sec
5 minute output rate 0 bits/sec, 0 packets/sec
```

```
0 packets input, 0 bytes, 0 no buffer
Received 0 broadcasts, 0 runts, 0 giants, 0 throttles
0 input errors, 0 CRC, 0 frame, 0 overrun, 0 ignored, 0 abort
20 packets output, 1200 bytes, 0 underruns
0 output errors, 0 collisions, 0 interface resets
0 output buffer failures, 0 output buffers swapped out
```

The following output is a portion of the configuration file displayed using the **show run** command. This output shows that the tunnel has been configured on Router A:

```
RouterA#sh run
.
.
!
!
interface Tunnel0
ip address 10.10.30.1 255.255.255.0
 no ip directed-broadcast tunnel source 192.168.210.5
 tunnel destination 192.168.100.3
!
!
RouterC#conf t
.
```

The next step is to configure the remote user on Router C. First, enter the router's configuration mode using the **conf t** command. Remember, Router C's connection to the telco cloud has already been established and a connection verified using the **ping** command. Recall that the IP address of 192.168.100.3 was pinged from Router A. Next, enter the configuration for the tunnel 0 interface using the **int tunnel 0** command. At the **(config-if)#** prompt, enter the source and destination addresses for tunnel 0 as shown in the following code:

```
Enter configuration commands, one per line. End with CNTL/Z.
RouterC(config)#int tunnel 0
RouterC(config-if)#ip address 10.10.30.2 255.255.255.0
RouterC(config-if)#tunnel destination 192.168.210.5
RouterC(config-if)#tunnel source 192.168.100.3
```

The configuration for the interfaces can be checked using the **sh ip int brief** command as shown in the following code. Note that the tunnel is listed as a separate interface on the router:

```
RouterC#sh ip int brief
Interface       IP-Address      OK? Method Status                 Protocol
FastEthernet0/0 unassigned      YES not set administratively down down
Serial0/0       192.168.100.3 YES manual  up                     up
Serial0/1       unassigned      YES not set administratively down down
Tunnel0         10.10.30.2      YES manual  up                     up
```

The following output is a portion of the configuration file displayed using the **show run** command. This output shows that the tunnel has been configured on Router C:

```
RouterC#sh run
.
.
!
!
interface Tunnel0
ip address 10.10.30.2 255.255.255.0
 no ip directed-broadcast tunnel source 192.168.100.3
 tunnel destination 192.168.210.5
!
!
.
.
```

Each end of the VPN has now been configured. The next step is to check the link using the **ping** command. The VPN tunnel virtual address of 10.10.30.2 is pinged from computer A, as shown next:

```
RouterA#ping 10.10.30.2
Type escape sequence to abort.
Sending 5 100-byte ICMP Echos to 10.10.30.2, timeout is 2 seconds:
!!!!!
Success rate is 100 percent (5/5), round-trip min/avg/max 80/80/84 ms
```

The **ping** shows that a virtual connection has been established between the remote user and the home network router. An interesting test of the network is to compare the results of running a **traceroute** from the home network to the remote user using the IP address for the remote user's router interface [192.168.100.3] and then running a traceroute from the home network to the remote user's VPN tunnel address [10.10.30.2]. The results of the test are shown here:

Traceroute to the physical interface IP address:

```
RouterA#trace 192.168.100.3
Type escape sequence to abort. Tracing the route to 192.168.100.3
1 192.168.210.5 16 msec 16 msec 16 msec
2 192.168.100.3 32 msec 32 msec *
```

Traceroute to the VPN tunnel IP address:

```
RouterA#trace 10.10.30.2
Type escape sequence to abort.
Tracing the route to 10.10.30.2
1 10.10.30.2 48 msec 48 msec *
```

The results of the first trace show that it takes two hops to reach the destination. In fact, a **traceroute** to the physical IP address will typically show multiple router hops. The test on the VPN tunnel shows that the trace took only one hop because the remote end of the VPN tunnel is configured to be directly connected to the home 10 network. The **traceroute** on a VPN tunnel from a home router to the remote user will show only one hop.

This section has described how to configure a VPN tunnel link. The commands for configuring and verifying the link have been discussed. The following describes steps for troubleshooting a VPN tunnel link if problems should occur.

Troubleshooting the VPN Tunnel Link

The following steps are used to verify that the VPN tunnel is properly configured:

1. Confirm connection to the physical interface's IP address using a **ping**.

2. Check the source and destination IP addresses of the tunnel configured on the router.

3. Make sure the IP addresses on the ends of the tunnel are in the same subnet.

4. **Ping** the destination from the source.

5. Use **show run** to make sure the source and destinations are properly configured.

This example has shown how a VPN tunnel can be established using two routers. This situation is appropriate for establishing a permanent VPN connection to a remote user, such as a remote office for a company. However, a remote user who travels will have to establish a VPN connection directly from his or her PC, through an ISP and the VPN server in the home network. The tunneling protocols commonly used in remote access VPNs are mentioned throughout the rest of this section. To better understand remote-access VPN, you should at least understand the importance of Point to Point Protocol (PPP). In the days when modems and dial-ups were kings, PPP was the key to the remote access solution; it was the de facto protocol of the dial-up networking. In those days, people would make a dial-up connection to their ISP and establish a PPP session to the Internet. Even though authentication is optional for PPP, most implementations of PPP provide user authentication using protocols like Password Authentication Protocol (PAP) or Challenge Handshake Authentication Protocol (CHAP). PAP is a simple, clear-text (unencrypted) authentication method, which is superseded by CHAP, an encrypted authentication method that uses the MD5 hashing algorithm. Later, Extensible Authentication Protocol (EAP) was introduced as another PPP authentication method. During the PPP authentication phase, the ISP dial-up server collects the user authentication data and validates it against an authentication server like a RADIUS server. RADIUS stands for Remote Authentication Dial-In User Service. RADIUS is an IETF standard protocol that is widely used for authenticating remote users and authorizing user access. The RADIUS server supports many methods of user authentication including PAP, CHAP, and EAP. Even though PPP dial-up is not as prevalent today, the concepts of central authentication still lend themselves to many technologies and applications.

Point-to-Point Tunneling Protocol (PPTP) was developed jointly by Microsoft, 3Com, and Alcatel-Lucent in 1996. It has never been ratified as a standard. Microsoft was a big advocate of PPTP and made PPTP available as part of Microsoft Windows Dial-up Networking. A PPTP server was included in Microsoft NT 4.0 server, and PPTP was widely used as a remote access solution. PPTP was designed

PPP
Point to Point Protocol. The de facto protocol of the dial-up networking.

PAP
Password Authentication Protocol. A simple, clear-text (unencrypted) authentication method.

CHAP
Challenge Handshake Authentication Protocol. An encrypted authentication method that uses the MD5 hashing algorithm.

MD5
Message Digest 5. A cryptographic hash function that produces a 128-bit (16-byte) hash value.

EAP
Extensible Authentication Protocol. Introduced as another PPP authentication method.

RADIUS
Remote Authentication Dial-In User Service. Widely used for authenticating remote users and authorizing user access.

PPTP
Point to Point Tunneling Protocol. Designed to work in conjunction with a standard PPP.

to work in conjunction with a standard PPP. PPTP client software would establish a PPP connection to an ISP, and once the connection is established, it would then make the PPTP tunnel over the Internet to the PPTP server. The PPTP tunnel uses a modified GRE tunnel to carry its encapsulated packet for IP transmission. The diagram of typical PPTP connection and other tunneling protocols is represented in Figure 7-8. PPTP does not have any authentication mechanism, so it relies heavily on the underlying PPP authentication.

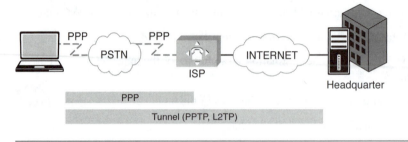

FIGURE 7-8 Tunneling diagram of PPTP and L2TP

Layer 2 Forwarding Protocol (**L2F**) was developed by Cisco around the same time as PPTP. L2F was not used widely in the consumer market due to its requirement of L2F hardware. Unlike PPTP, where the VPN client software is installed and initiated from the client, L2F does not require any VPN client software. An L2F connection is intended to be done by L2F hardware. This hardware is designed to be at the ISP. A client would make a typical PPP connection to the ISP. The ISP will then initiate the L2F tunnel connection on UDP port 1701 to the L2F server at the corporate headquarters. This requires coordination between the ISP and the corporate network. L2F relies on the PPP authentication to be passed on to the corporate authentication server.

Layer 2 Tunneling Protocol (**L2TP**) was developed by the Internet Engineering Task Force (IETF) in 1999. L2TP was created with the intention of merging two incompatibles proprietary tunneling protocols, PPTP and L2F. L2TP is considered to be an enhancement of the two previous protocols. L2TP does not require a specific hardware. It can be initiated directly from the client. L2TP Tunnel encapsulation is done on UDP port 1701. L2TP allows for tunnel authentication, so it does not have to rely heavily on the underlying PPP. If L2TP is used over an IP network where PPP is not used, the tunnel can be created with its own authentication mechanism.

All of the previously mentioned tunneling protocols are lacking one important security feature—encryption. Encryption can guarantee data confidentiality in the tunnel. IPsec offers encryption features that the others lack. IPsec was designed for the purpose of providing a secure end-to-end connection. The VPN can take advantage of IPsec to provide network layer encryption and authentication techniques. IPsec is versatile in that it can be implemented easily as a remote access VPN or as a site-to-site VPN. For IPv6, IPsec becomes an even more integral part as it is embedded within the IPv6 packets. There are two primary security protocols used by IPsec: Authentication Header (**AH**) and Encapsulating Security Payload (**ESP**). AH guarantees the authenticity of the IP packets. It uses a one-way hash algorithm, like

Message Digest 5 (MD5) or Secure Hash Algorithm 1 (SHA-1), to ensure the data integrity of the IP packets. ESP provides confidentiality to the data messages (payloads) by way of encryption. It uses symmetrical encryption algorithms like Data Encryption Standard (DES), Triple Data Encryption Standard (3DES), and Advanced Encryption Standard (AES).

Before an IPsec tunnel can be established, quite a few security parameters have to be negotiated and agreed upon by both ends. IPsec uses the Internet Key Exchange (IKE) protocol to manage such a process. IKE is a hybrid protocol that encompasses several key management protocols, most notably Internet Security Association and Key Management Protocol (ISAKMP). Many times, the term IKE and ISAKMP are mentioned alongside each other. There are two negotiation phases that the two network nodes must perform before the IPsec tunnel is complete. The IKE Phase 1 is a phase where both network nodes authenticate each other and set up an IKE SA (Security Association). In phase 1, the Diffee-Hellman key exchange algorithm is used to generate a shared session secret key to encrypt the key exchange communications. This phase is essentially to set up a secure channel to protect further negotiations in phase 2. The following is an example configuration of the IKE Phase 1 or the IKE policy on Cisco routers.

```
crypto isakmp policy 1
 encr 3des
 hash md5
 authentication pre-share
crypto isakmp key PJtcF7yF2w address 172.16.117.14
```

IKE Phase 2 uses the secure channel established in phase 1 to negotiate the unidirectional IPsec SAs—inbound and outbound—to set up the IPsec tunnel. This is where the algorithm parameters for AH and ESP would be negotiated. The following is an example configuration of the IKE Phase 2 or the Crypto map policy on Cisco routers. Both the AH and ESP will be using SHA with HMAC variant as the authentication algorithm protocol. To encrypt the payload, the ESP uses 3DES as the encryption algorithm. These parameters are entered as the transform-set called "AH-and-ESP" and will be applied to the IPsec to tunnel. The IPsec tunnel configuration itself consists of the IP address of its peer or the other end of the tunnel, the transform-set and the access-list allowing only certain networks to transverse through the secured tunnel:

```
crypto ipsec transform-set AH-and-ESP ah-sha-hmac esp-3des esp-sha-
hmac
!
crypto map IPSec_Phase2 1 ipsec-isakmp
 description Tunnel to 172.16.117.14
 set peer 172.16.117.14
 set transform-set AH-and-ESP
 match address 104
!
```

SHA-1
Secure Hash Algorithm. It is used to ensure the data integrity of the IP packets.

DES, 3DES
Data Encryption Standard, Triple Data Encryption Standard. A symmetrical encryption algorithm.

AES
Advanced Encryption Standard. A symmetrical encryption algorithm.

IKE
Internet Key Exchange. A hybrid protocol that encompasses several key management protocols, most notably Internet Security Association and Key Management Protocol.

ISAKMP
Internet Security Association and Key Management Protocol. A protocol for establishing Security Associations (SA) and cryptographic keys in an Internet environment.

Diffee-Hellman
Key generation algorithm. Used to generate a shared session secret key to encrypt the key exchange communications.

SUMMARY

This chapter examined the topics of network security. The concept of denial of service (DoS) was examined in Section 7-1. This section also examined the SYN attack, smurf attack, and Distributed Denial of Service (DDoS) attack. Section 7-2 examined firewalls and access lists. Topics included in the section included stateful firewalls, demilitarized zones, and configuring access lists. Sections 7-3 through 7-6 provided a look at "best practices" for setting up security on routers, switches, and wireless networks. This chapter concluded with a look at configuring external access to networks using a VPN.

QUESTIONS AND PROBLEMS

Section 7-1

1. What is a denial of service attack?

2. Describe a SYN attack.

3. Cisco routers use what command to block broadcasts to a subnet?

4. Define a directed broadcast.

5. What is the best way to keep from contributing to DDoS attacks?

6. What is a smurf attack?

Section 7-2

7. What is the purpose of a firewall?

8. Why is a stateful firewall important?

9. What is the router command for setting an access list 100 to block SNMP UDP packets from any source to any destination?

10. What command should be added to the end of an access list 150 to allow other data packets to enter and exit the router?

11. An extended IP access list 130 is to be applied to a router's Serial0 interface. The list is to be applied to inbound data packets. What command should be entered from the router's (config-if)# prompt?

12. Modify the command for problem 11 so that the access list is applied to outbound data packets.

13. What command is used to view the number of times an access list has been matched?

14. It has been determined that a computer with an IP address of 192.168.8.4 is flooding the network with ICMP packets. Create an extended access list to stop the flood.

15. Apply the access list created in problem 14 to the inbound data traffic on the router's Serial1 interface.

16. What is the purpose of the demilitarized zone and why is this used?

17. What are first two steps for applying access lists on a router?

18. What is the purpose of the following command in JUNOS?

    `net-admin@noc#` **`set term block-snmp from destination-port 161`**

19. What is the purpose of the following command in JUNOS?

    `net-admin@noc#` **`set term allow-snmp from protocol`** `udp`

20. What is a prefix list in JUNOS?

21. What command is used in JUNOS to verify the filter list? List the prompt and the command.

Section 7-3

22. What is always on top of the list of any "best security" practice, and why is this important?

23. Why is it important to keep the operating system of a router up to date?

24. What are the two types of passwords on a router?

25. What does the following command do?

    `RouterA(config)# username admin privilege 10 password @dm1np@$$wd`

    What is level 10?

26. What is the purpose of configuring AAA on a router?

27. What does the following command do?

    `RouterA(config)#`**`crypto key generate rsa`**

28. What does the command **transport input ssh** do?

29. What commands can be used to disable services like echo, discard, daytime, and chargen? List the prompt and the command used for this.

30. What does the following command do?

    `RouterA(config)#`**`snmp-server community M@ke1tD1ff1cuLT ro 15`**

31. What is the purpose of the following commands, and why is it important to use these?

    `RouterA(config)#`**`no cdp run`**
    `RouterA(config)#`**`no service config`**
    `RouterA(config)#`**`no ip source-route`**

32. What command is used to enable logging on a router?

33. What is the purpose of the network time protocol?

34. Prepare an access-list 102 that can be used to prevent spoofing.

Section 7-4

35. What single command can be used to shut down multiple switch ports? Assume that there are 24 ports. List the command and the prompt.

36. What command is used to enable port security on a switch? List the command and the prompt.

37. What does the following command do?

    ```
    SwitchA(config-if)#switchport port-security maximum 2
    ```

38. What command can be used on a switch to limit the amount of unicast packets that each port can receive if the rising threshold is 15 MBps and the Falling threshold is 5 MBps.

39. What does the following command do?

    ```
    storm-control unicast level pps 7k 3k
    ```

40. What are the four states an STP enabled switch goes through before it can pass data traffic?

41. What does the command **spanning-tree bpdufilter enable** do on a switch?

42. What command is used to enable STP Root guard. List the command and the prompt.

43. What does the following command do?

    ```
    SwitchA(config-if)# switchport trunk allowed vlan 5,7,18,20
    ```

Section 7-5

44. What is the most important thing to do if using a wireless network?

45. What is the purpose of wireless beacons?

46. What information can be obtained from a wireless beacon?

47. What is the purpose of WEP?

48. List five guidelines for wireless security.

49. Describe the steps used by WPA2 to authenticate a user.

50. What is a RADIUS server?

Section 7-6

51. What is the goal of a VPN tunnel?

52. Draw a sketch of the encapsulation of a VPN data packet. Show the IP source and destination address and the VPN tunnel source and destination address encapsulated with the IP packet.

53. Explain the expected difference when running a traceroute from the home network to the remote user using the IP address for the remote user's router interface, and then running a traceroute from the home network to the remote user's VPN tunnel address.

54. List five steps for troubleshooting the VPN tunnel link.

55. Identify two tunneling protocols that can be used to configure a remote user's PC.

56. What does encryption guarantee?

57. What are the two primary security protocols used by IPsec?

58. What is IKE?

59. List the command and the router prompt for configuring an IP tunnel 0 to 172.16.25.1 using a subnet mask of 255.2555.255.0.

60. What does the following command do?

```
RouterA(config-if)#tunnel destination 192.168.200.5
```

Critical Thinking

61. Your network is experiencing an excessive amount of pings to your network server. The pings are from outside the network. Someone suggests that you set an access list to block ICMP packets coming into the network. How would you respond?

62. Your supervisor informs you that a user on the network has requested a VPN connection. Prepare a response to the supervisor discussing what is needed to provide the connection.

63. Provide an example of configuring AAA on a Cisco router. Can authentication be applied locally, remotely, or both?

64. Your task is to configure VTY remote access with SSH. The configuration uses the default login authentication that was defined by AAA. Issue the command to enforce that SSH is the only access method. Use access-class of 12 that defines the access-list of the network that is allowed to connect to the router via SSH. Lastly, the exec-timeout of 10 minutes is configured. List the commands and corresponding prompt to accomplish this.

65. A memory buffer of 16 Kbytes is reserved for logging with debugging level. In addition, the same debugging level log messages will be sent to a syslog server with the IP address of 192168.10.10. List the commands used to enable this feature.

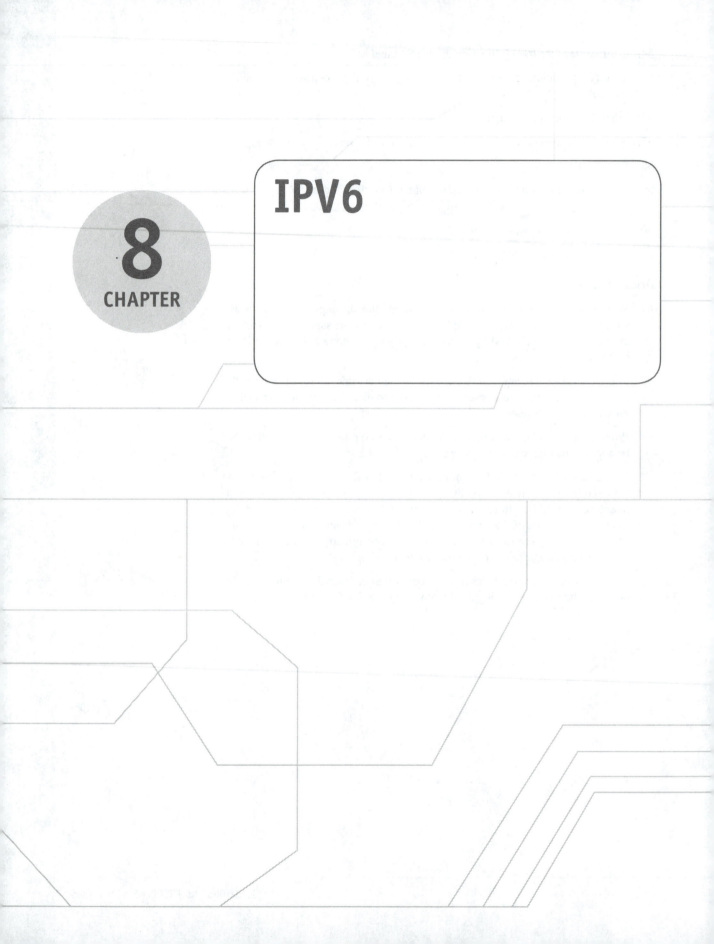

8
CHAPTER

IPV6

Chapter Outline

Objectives

- Develop an understanding of the fundamentals of IPv6
- Define the structure of IPv6
- Understand the IPv6 addressing and its prefix
- Be able to represent the IPv6 with correct notation

- Be able to configure basic IPv6 on computers
- Be able to configure basic IPv6 on routers
- Recognize the IPv6 stateless autoconfiguration settings
- Be able to provide basic IPv6 troubleshooting

Key Terms

IPv6
IPng
datagram
IPsec
stateless address autoconfiguration (SLAAC)
full IPv6 address
double-colon notation
network prefix
prefix length
interface identifier
unicast address
global unicast address
multicast address
anycast address
6to4 prefix
FP

TLA ID (0x2002)
V4ADDR
SLA ID
Interface ID
IPv6 stateless autoconfiguration
link-local address
FE80::/64
Neighbor Solicitation
Duplicate Address Detection (DAD)
Privacy Extensions for Stateless Address Autoconfiguration
MLD (Multicast Listener Discovery)
ipv6 unicast-routing

ipv6 enable
show ipv6 interface
ipv6 address *ipv6 interface address*
eui-64
ND protocol
RA messages
router solicitation messages
2001:DB8::/32 Prefix
RIPng
rip_tag
OSPFv3
ping6
traceroute6/tracert6

INTRODUCTION

This chapter looks at IPv6, the IP addressing system that has been developed to replace IPv4. IP version 4 (IPv4) is the current TCP/IP addressing technique being used on the Internet. The address space for IPv4 is running out, even though there is a theoretical limit of approximately 4.3 billion unique IPv4 addresses. However, not all the IPv4 addresses can be used, because there are IPv4 address blocks reserved for special purposes, such as multicast, unspecified future use, local identification, loopback, and private use. These special purpose reserved addresses account for around 600 million unique addresses.

Address space for IPv4 is quickly running out due to the rapid growth of the Internet and the development of new Internet-compatible mobile technologies. Examples of this include the IP addressable telephone, wireless personal digital assistants (PDAs), cell phones, game consoles, and home-networking systems. There have been many predictions of when the IPv4 address pool will be exhausted. The answer to this question is not clear. Techniques such as Network Address Translation/Port Address Translation (NAT/PAT), Dynamic Host Control Protocol (DHCP), and Classless Inter-Domain Routing (CIDR) have been implemented to prolong the life of IPv4. These techniques reuse the existing IPv4 address space and handle the address space allocation more efficiently.

IPv6
IP version 6.

IPng
Next generation IP.

A solution to the limited number of available IPv4 addresses is to migrate to IPv6. IP version 6 (**IPv6**) is the solution proposed by the Internet Engineering Task Force (IETF) for expanding the possible number of IP addresses to accommodate the growing users on the Internet. IPv6, introduced in 1999, is also called **IPng**.

This chapter provides a comparison of IPv6 and IPv4 in Section 8-1. The structure of the IPv6 address is examined in Section 8-2. Concepts such as the network prefix and the prefix length are examined. IPv6 network settings are examined in Section 8-3. Steps for configuring IPv6 in both the Windows and Mac OS X environments are examined. The steps for configuring a router to run IPv6 are examined in section 8-4. This chapter concludes with a look at troubleshooting the IPv6 connection in Section 8-5.

8-1 COMPARISON OF IPV6 AND IPV4

IPv4 and IPv6 are not compatible technologies, and they cannot communicate directly with each other. So, before migrating to an IPv6 environment, the network devices and network equipment need to be IPv6 compatible or enabled. Most likely new network hardware and software will have to be acquired to make the network IPv6 ready. A good migration plan has to be developed to prepare for IPv6. The investment of time, money, and training is required for a successful adoption of IPv6.

The size of the IPv6 address is increased to 128 bits, which is four times larger than the 32-bit address space IPv4 is using. This significantly increases the number of available IP addresses. By doing this, the theoretical number of unique addresses increases from 4.3x109 (IPv4) to 3.4x1038 in IPv6. This is a staggering number considering the world population is 7x109 people.

Increasing the number of bits for the address also results in changing the IP header size. The IPv4 **datagram** is shown in Figure 8-1. A datagram is a self-contained entity that carries sufficient information to be routed from source to destination without relying on previous data exchanges between the source and destination computers or the transporting network.

The IPv4 header size is comprised of the information detailed in Figure 8-1. A total of 64 bits are used to define the source and destination IP addresses. Note that both the source and destination addresses are 32 bits in length. The combination of the two gives 64 bits. The total length of the IPv4 header is 160 bits; therefore, this means 160 – 64 = 96 bits are used to make up the remaining fields.

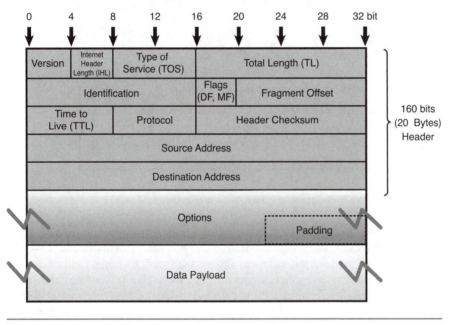

FIGURE 8-1   The IPv4 Datagram (160 bits-96 bits for header fields)

Figure 8-2 shows the IPv6 datagram. The IPv6 header size is 320 bits; however, 256 bits are used to define the source and destination IPv6 addresses. This means that 64 bits are used to define the remaining field as compared to 96 bits for IPv4.

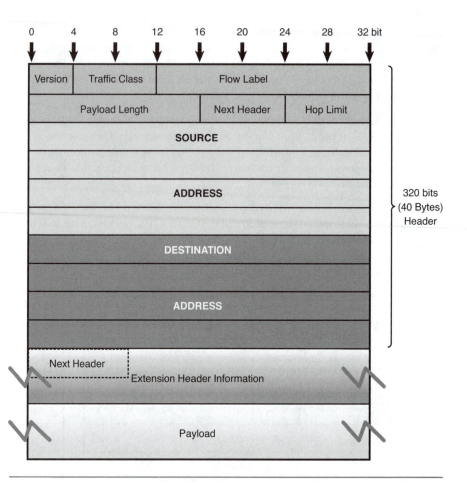

FIGURE 8-2 The IPv6 Datagram (320 bits-64 bits for header fileds)

The IPv6 header has been simplified resulting in less header fields than in IPv4. This is designed to make packet processing more efficient by routers and other network equipments. One noticeably missing header field in IPv6 is the checksum field. This means there is no checksum calculation done by the routers in the path. This increases the routing performance and efficiency. The error detection is now done at the link layer and transport layer. In IPv4, the TCP transport layer is required to check the integrity of the packet by doing a checksum calculation. The same cannot be said for the UDP transport layer because the checksum is optional. Now, the checksums are required for both transport layers in IPv6.

One new feature that is built in with IPv6 is the IP security (IPsec). **IPsec** is the IETF standard for securing the IP communications between the network nodes by authenticating and encrypting the session. When using IPv4, a secure network IP communication link generally has to be initiated to provide security similar to an IPSec application. In IPv6, every node is enabled with the IPSec feature. This makes creating end-to-end IPSec sessions much easier to establish. In addition, IPSec feature is a part of the extension headers. In IPv6, there is a mandatory IPv6 main header and then there could be an extension header or extension headers. All options and special purposed fields can be provisioned into extension headers when needed. IPSec is one of the special options. This is how IPv6 simplifies its header fields.

Another giant step forward taken by IPv6 is the elimination of the broadcast. Broadcasts can cause many problems in computer networks. When a broadcast happens, every computer on the network is interrupted, even if only two computers are involved. The worst case situation is a broadcast storm. When this happens, the performance on a network is severely degraded, and it can bring down an entire network. IPv6 does not use broadcasts. It uses multicasts instead. A multicast is used in the core of many functions in IPv6. The multicast addresses are allocated from the multicast block. Any address starting with "1111 1111" in binary or "FF" in colon hexadecimal notation is an IPv6 multicast address. The concept of colon hexadecimal notation is discussed in Section 8-2. Even though there is no such thing as broadcast, there is a multicast address to the all-host multicast group.

Stateless address autoconfiguration (SLAAC) is another important feature of IPv6. This feature allows for a server-less basic network configuration of the IPv6 computers. With IPv4, a computer generally obtains its network settings from a DHCP server. With IPv6, a computer can automatically configure its network settings without a DHCP server by sending a solicitation message to its IPv6 router. The router then sends back its advertisement message, which contains the prefix information that the computer can use to create its own IPv6 address. This feature significantly helps simplify the deployment of the IPv6 devices, especially in the transient environments such as airports, train stations, stadiums, hotspots, and so on.

> **Stateless Address Autoconfiguration (SLAAC)**
> Allows a server-less basic network configuration of the IPv6 computers.

8-2 IPV6 ADDRESSING

It was previously mentioned that IPv6 uses a 128-bit address technique, as compared to IPv4's 32-bit address structure. There is also a difference in the way the IP addresses are listed. IPv6 numbers are written in hexadecimal rather than dotted decimal, as with IPv4. For example, the following is an IPv6 address represented with 32 hexadecimal digits Note: 32 hex digits with 4 bits/hex digit = 128 bits):

6789:ABCD:1234:EF98:7654:321F:EDCB:AF21

This is classified as a full IPv6 address. The *full* means that all 32 hexadecimal positions contain a value other than 0.

> **Full IPv6 Address**
> All 32 hexadecimal positions contain a value other than 0.

Why doesn't IPv6 use the "dotted decimal" format of IPv4? The answer is it would take many decimal numbers to represent the IPv6 address. Each decimal number takes at least seven binary bits in ASCII (American Standard Code for Information Interchange) code. For example, the decimal equivalent of the first eight hexadecimal characters in the previous full IPv6 address is

6789:ABCD = 103.137.171.205

The completed decimal equivalent number for the full IPv6 address is

103.137.171.205.18.52.239.152.118.84.50.31.237.203.175.33

The equivalent decimal number is 42 characters in length. In fact, the decimal equivalent number could be 48 decimal numbers long.

In terms of bits, one 4 hex bit group requires 4 x 4 = 16 bits. Assuming that 8 bits are used to represent the decimal numbers, it will take 12 x 8 = 72 bits to express one hex bit group in a decimal format. There is a significant bit savings obtained by expressing the IPv6 address in a hexadecimal format.

Double-Colon Notation

A technique used by IPv6 to remove 0s from the address.

IPv6 uses seven colons (:) as separators to group the 32 hex characters into 8 groups of four. Some IPv6 numbers will have a 0 within the address. In this case, IPv6 allows the number to be compressed to make it easier to write the number. The technique for doing this is called **double-colon notation**. For example, assume that an IPv6 number is as follows:

6789:0000:0000:EF98:7654:321F:EDCB:AF21

Consecutive 0s can be dropped and a double-colon notation can be used as shown:

6789::EF98:7654:321F:EDCB:AF21

Recovering the compressed number in double-colon notation simply requires that all numbers left of the double notation be entered beginning with the leftmost slot of the IPv6 address. Next, start with the numbers to the right of the double colon.

Begin with the rightmost slot of the IPv6 address slots and enter the numbers from right to left until the double colon is reached. Zeros are entered into any empty slots:

6789 :0 :0 :EF98 :7654 :321F :EDCB :AF21

IPv4 numbers can be written in the new IPv6 form by writing the IPv4 number in hexadecimal and placing the number to the right of a double colon. Example 8-1 demonstrates how a dotted-decimal IP number can be converted to IPv6 hexadecimal.

Example 8-1   Convert the IPv4 address of 192.168.5.20 to an IPv6 hexadecimal address

Solution:

First convert each dotted-decimal number to hexadecimal.

Decimal	Hex
192	C0
168	A8
5	05
20	14

(Hint: Use a calculator or a lookup table to convert the decimal numbers to hexadecimal.) The IPv6 address will have many leading 0s; therefore, the IPv6 hex address can be written in double-colon notation as

    :: C0A8:0514.

IPv4 addresses can also be written in IPv6 form by writing the IPv4 number in dotted-decimal format, as shown. Note that the number is preceded by 24 hexadecimal 0s:

    0000: 0000: 0000: 0000: 0000: 0000:192.168.5.20

This number can be reduced as follows:

    ::192.168.5.20

Similar to IPv4 classless addresses, IPv6 addresses are fundamentally divided into a network portion followed by a host portion. The network portion is called the **network prefix** and the number of bits used is the **prefix length**. The prefix is represented with a slash followed by the prefix length. This is the same notation used to designate the CIDR in IPv4. For example, the IPv6 address of 2001:DB8:FEED:BEEF::12 has a 64-bits network prefix. It then can be represented as 2001:DB8:FEED:BEEF::12/64. However, the concept of a CIDR is not relevant in IPv6, because there is enough IP address space for everyone. So, in IPv6, the host portion of the address or what is called the **interface identifier** is always 64-bits in length. This automatically leaves 64 bits as the network prefix. In a typical IPv6 customer site, a network of /48 is usually allocated by IANA. This provides the site with 65,536 subnets, which is more than sufficient. This means that when a site is assigned a /48, the site is capable of having up to 65536 subnets and each subnet is capable of hosting more than 1.8×10^{19} IPv6 addresses.

There are three types of IPv6 addresses: unicast, multicast, and anycast. The **unicast** IPv6 address is used to identify a single network interface address and data packets are sent directly to the computer with the specified IPv6 address. There are several types of unicast addresses, including link-local addresses, **global unicast addresses**, and unique local addresses. Link-local addresses are designed to be used for and are limited to communications on the local link. Every IPv6 interface will have one link-local address.

Per RFC 4291, "IP Version6 Addressing Architecture," the network prefix of link-local addresses, is defined as FE80::/10. Unique local unicast addresses are addresses for local use only, and they are similar to the private IP addresses used in IPv4. Unique local unicast addresses use the prefix of FD00::/8 and were designed to replace site-local addresses, which are being deprecated.

Global unicast addresses are equivalent to the public ip addresses in IPv4. They have unlimited scope, and they are routable on the Internet. IANA is responsible for allocating the IPv6 global unicast address space. Currently, the range of allocated IPv6 addresses starts from prefix 2000::/3.

Network Prefix
The network portion of the IPv6 address.

Prefix Length
Number of bits used to make up the network prefix.

Interface Identifier
The host portion of the IPv6 address.

Unicast Address
Used to identify a single network interface address, and data packets are sent directly to the computer with the specified IPv6 address.

Global Unicast Addresses
These are equivalent to the public IP addresses in IPv4.

IPv6 multicast addresses are defined for a group of networking devices. Data packets sent to a multicast address are sent to the entire group of networking devices such as a group of routers running the same routing protocol. Multicast addresses all start with the prefix FF00::/8. The next group of characters in the IPv6 multicast address (the second octet) are called the scope. The scope bits are used to identify which ISP should carry the data traffic.

The anycast IPv6 addresses might seem like a new type of address, but the concept was not new. Anycast addresses can be thought of as a cross between unicast and multicast addresses. While the unicast traffic sends information to one address and the multicast traffic sends information to every address in the group, the anycast traffic sends information to any one address of the group. The trick is which address of the group to send information to. The most logical and efficient answer is the nearest or the closet address. Similar to multicast where the nodes will join the multicast group, the anycast nodes share the same anycast address. The data will be sent to a node within the anycast group. This node is the nearest to the sender.

Actually, the anycast concept is used in the IPv4 environment today with the root DNS servers. There are 13 DNS root servers in the world, but the DNS query is only sent to one of those servers.

IPv6 addressing is being used in a limited number of network sites (e.g., the federal government); however, the Internet is still running IPv4 and will be for some time. But, there are transition strategies in place to help with the IPv4 to IPv6 transition.

One possible transition to IPv6 is called the 6to4 Prefix, which is essentially a technique that enables IPv6 sites to communicate over the IPv4 Internet. This requires the use of a 6to4 enabled router, which means that 6to4 tunneling has been enabled. This also requires the use of a 6to4 Relay router that forwards 6to4 data traffic to other 6to4 routers on the Internet.

Figure 8-3 illustrates the structure of the 6to4 prefix for hosts. The 32 bits of the IPv4 address fit into the first 48 bits of the IPv6 address.

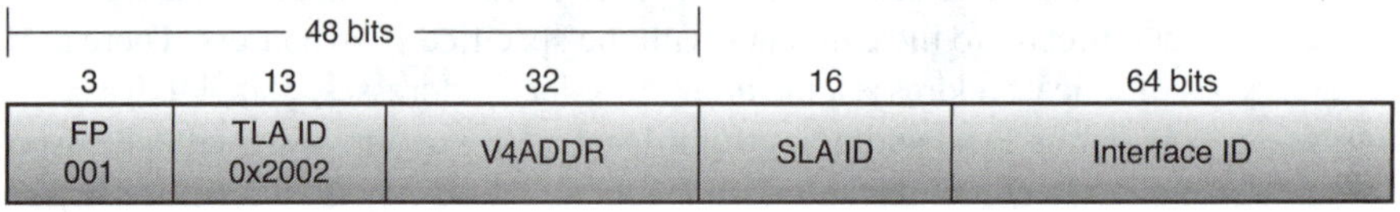

48 bits				
3	13	32	16	64 bits
FP 001	TLA ID 0x2002	V4ADDR	SLA ID	Interface ID

FIGURE 8-3   The 6to4 prefix format

Note the following shown in Figure 8-3:

- FP is the Format Prefix, which is made up of the higher order bits. The **001** indicates that this is a global unicast address. The current list of the IPv6 address allocation can be viewed at www.iana.org/assignments/ipv6-unicast-address-assignments. Currently, IANA allocates 2000::/3 as an IPv6 global pool. 2000 can be written in binary as **001**0 0000 0000 0000. 001 is the 3 highest order bits, which correspond to the FP.

- TLA ID (0x2002) are the top-level identifiers that are issued to local Internet registries. These IDs are administered by IANA (**http://www.iana.org/**). The

TLA is used to identify the highest level in the routing hierarchy. The TLA ID is 13 bits long.

- **V4ADDR** is the IPv4 address of the 6to4 endpoint and is 32 bits long.

- **SLA ID** is the Site Level Aggregation Identifier that is used by individual organizations to identify subnets within their site. The SLA ID is 16 bits long.

- **Interface ID** is the Link Level Host Identifier and is used to indicate an interface on a specific subnet. The interface ID is equivalent to the host IP address in IPv4.

The 6to4 prefix format enables IPv6 domains to communicate with each other even if they don't have an IPv6 ISP. Additionally, IPv6 can be used within the intranet, but access to the Internet is still available. The 6to4 provides unicast IPv6 connectivity between IPv6 host and via the IPv4 Internet.

8-3 IPV6 NETWORK SETTINGS

Almost all the modern computer operating systems being used today are IPv6 capable. On most operating systems, the IPv6 configuration settings can be found at the same location where the TCP/IP settings for IPv4 reside. This is provided in the Local Area Connections Properties window for both Windows XP and Windows 7. The Local Area Connections Properties window for Windows XP is provided in Figure 8-4. The Local Area Connections Properties window for Windows 7 is provided in Figure 8-5.

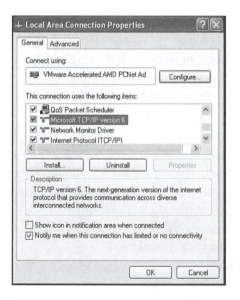

FIGURE 8-4   The Local Area Connections Properties window for Windows XP

There is an option available to obtain the IPv6 configuration automatically as well as an option for manual configuration. This option is available in the Internet Protocol Version 6 (TCP/IPv6) Properties window, as shown in Figure 8-6. This same feature is available with IPv4. However, Windows XP is one of the exceptions where there is no manual configuration mode for assigning the IPv6 address. The majority of the operating systems enable IPv6 with the automatic configuration mode by default. The following is a summary of the configuration options provided in the TCP/IPv6 Properties window:

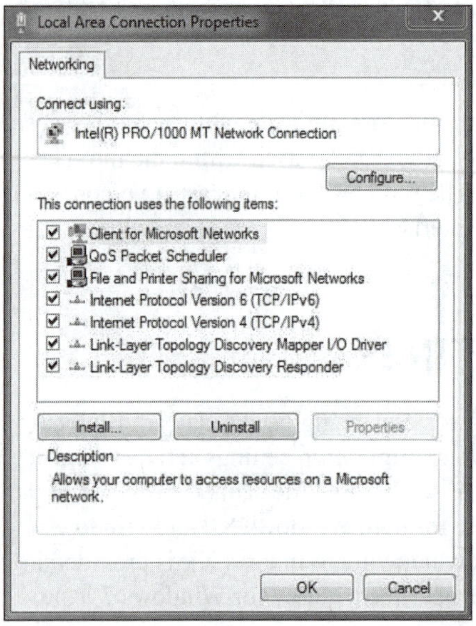

FIGURE 8-5   The Local Area Connections Properties window for Windows 7

- **Obtain an IPv6 address automatically**: In this option, the IPv6 address is automatically configured for this network connection.

- **Use the following IPv6 address**: Specifies the IPv6 address and default gateway are manually configured:

    - **IPv6 address**: This space is used to type in an IPv6 unicast address.

    - **Subnet prefix length**: This space is used to specify the subnet prefix length for the IPv6 address. For unicast addresses, the default value is 64.

    - **Default gateway**: This space is used to enter the IPv6 address for the default gateway.

- **Obtain DNS server address automatically**: This selection indicates the IPv6 addresses for the DNS servers are automatically configured.

- **Use the following DNS server addresses:** This space is used to specify IPv6 addresses of the preferred and alternate DNS servers for this network connection:

    - **Preferred DNS server**: This space is used to input the IPv6 unicast address for the preferred DNS server.

    - **Alternate DNS server**: This space is used to enter the IPv6 unicast address of the alternate DNS server.

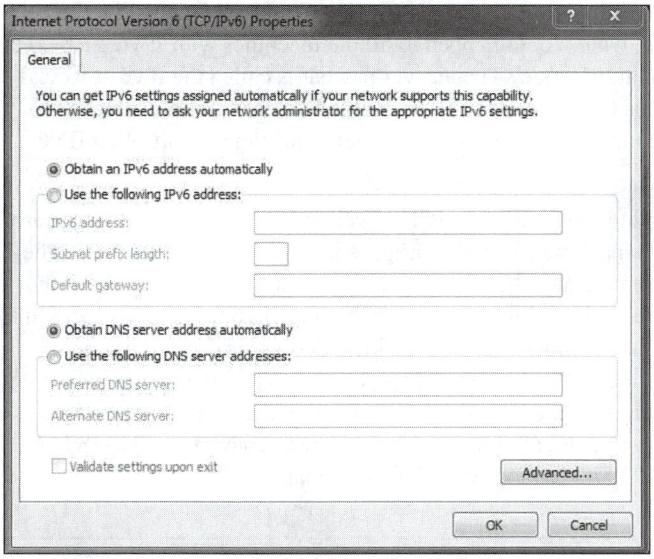

FIGURE 8-6   Internet Protocol Version 6 (TCP/IPv6) Properties window for Windows 7

IPv6 configuration settings are also available for the Mac OS X operating system in the TCP/IP window, as shown in Figure 8-7. The user has the option to configure the IPv6 address automatically or manually. The option for automatically configuring the IPv6 address is selected in Figure 8-7.

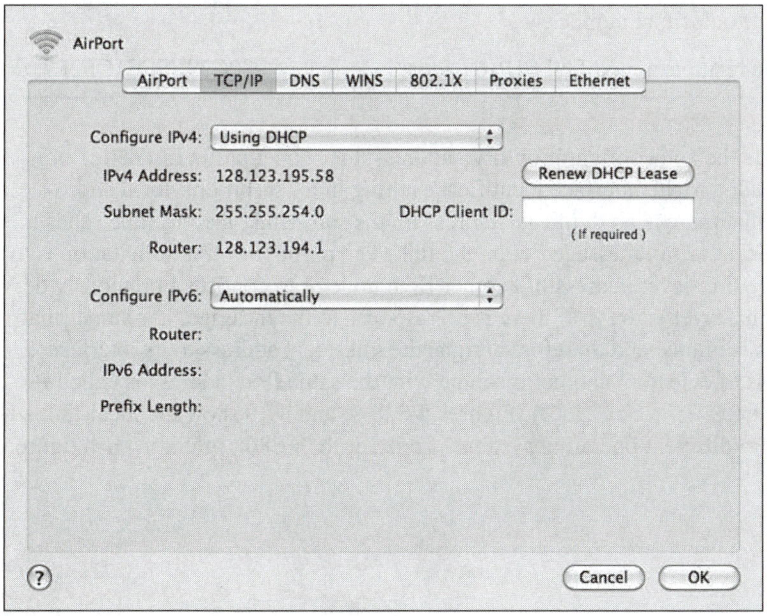

FIGURE 8-7   Mac OS X IPv6 configuration

In typical places, such as homes and businesses, IPv6 is not yet enabled on the network environment. So, what would happen to all the machines with IPv6 enabled in the automatic configuration mode? The answer is what is called the **IPv6 stateless autoconfiguration**. This feature enables IPv6-enabled devices that are attached to the IPv6 network to connect to the network without requiring support of an IPv6 DHCP server.

This means that, even though an IPv6 DHCP server and an IPv6 enabled router are not involved, any IPv6 machine can self-configure its own **link-local address**. The term link-local address indicates the IP address is self-configured. This means that any IPv6 host should be able to communicate with other IPv6 hosts on its local link or network. The interface identifier of the link-local address is derived by transforming the 48 bits of the EUI-48 MAC address to 64 bits for EUI-64. This EUI-48 to EUI-64 transform algorithm is also used to derive the interface identifier for the global unicast address. Example 8-2 demonstrates how to convert an EUI-48 MAC address of 000C291CF2F7 to a modified EUI-64 format.

Example 8-2

1. Expanding the 48-bit MAC address to a 64-bit format by inserting "FFFE" in the middle of the 48 bits.

   000C29 **FFFE** 1CF2F7.

2. Change the seventh bit starting with the leftmost bit of the address from 0 to 1. This seventh bit is referred to as the U/L bit or universal/local bit. 000C29 is 0000 0000 0000 1100 0010 1001 in binary format. When its seventh bit is changed to 1, it becomes 0000 0010 0000 1100 0010 1001, which is 020C29 in hexadecimal number.

3. The result is a modified EUI-64 address format of 020C29FFFE1CF2F7.

To complete the autoconfiguration IPv6 address, the subnet prefix of **FE80::/64** is then prepended to the interface identifier resulting in a 128-bit link-local address. To ensure that there is no duplicate address on the same link, the machine sends a **Neighbor Solicitation** message out on the link. The purpose of this solicitation is to discover the link-layer address of another IPv6 node or to confirm a previously determined link-layer address. If there is no response to the message, it assumes that the address is unique and therefore assigns the link-local address to its interface. The process of detecting another machine with the same IPv6 address is called **Duplicate Address Detection (DAD)**. Figures 8-8, 8-9, and 8-10 show the local-link addresses from different operating systems. Look for the FE80:: prefix in each figure.

```
Ethernet adapter Local Area Connection:

        Connection-specific DNS Suffix  . : nmsu.edu
        Description . . . . . . . . . . . : VMware Accelerated AMD PCNet Adapter
        Physical Address. . . . . . . . . : 00-0C-29-1C-F2-F7
        Dhcp Enabled. . . . . . . . . . . : Yes
        Autoconfiguration Enabled . . . . : Yes
        IP Address. . . . . . . . . . . . : 128.123.195.42
        Subnet Mask . . . . . . . . . . . : 255.255.254.0
        IP Address. . . . . . . . . . . . : fe80::20c:29ff:fe1c:f2f7%4
        Default Gateway . . . . . . . . . : 128.123.194.1
        DHCP Server . . . . . . . . . . . : 128.123.3.5
        DNS Servers . . . . . . . . . . . : 128.123.3.5
                                            128.123.2.19
                                            fec0:0:0:ffff::1%1
                                            fec0:0:0:ffff::2%1
                                            fec0:0:0:ffff::3%1
        Primary WINS Server . . . . . . . : 128.123.2.20
        Secondary WINS Server . . . . . . : 128.123.2.30
        Lease Obtained. . . . . . . . . . : Wednesday, November 10, 2010 3:23:25 PM
        Lease Expires . . . . . . . . . . : Thursday, November 11, 2010 3:23:25 AM
```

FIGURE 8-8   Windows XP—**ipconfig** result with a link-local address

```
Ethernet adapter Local Area Connection:

        Connection-specific DNS Suffix  . : nmsu.edu
        Description . . . . . . . . . . . : Intel(R) PRO/1000 MT Network Connection
        Physical Address. . . . . . . . . : 00-0C-29-02-E5-7E
        DHCP Enabled. . . . . . . . . . . : Yes
        Autoconfiguration Enabled . . . . : Yes
        Link-local IPv6 Address . . . . . : fe80::a1b4:6c3d:b953:6e5%11(Preferred)
        IPv4 Address. . . . . . . . . . . : 128.123.194.226(Preferred)
        Subnet Mask . . . . . . . . . . . : 255.255.254.0
        Lease Obtained. . . . . . . . . . : Wednesday, November 10, 2010 4:30:06 PM
        Lease Expires . . . . . . . . . . : Thursday, November 11, 2010 4:30:06 AM
        Default Gateway . . . . . . . . . : 128.123.194.1
        DHCP Server . . . . . . . . . . . : 128.123.3.5
        DHCPv6 IAID . . . . . . . . . . . : 234884137
        DHCPv6 Client DUID. . . . . . . . : 00-01-00-01-12-26-27-57-00-0C-29-AE-67-F2

        DNS Servers . . . . . . . . . . . : 128.123.3.5
                                            128.123.2.19
        Primary WINS Server . . . . . . . : 128.123.2.20
        Secondary WINS Server . . . . . . : 128.123.2.30
        NetBIOS over Tcpip. . . . . . . . : Enabled
```

FIGURE 8-9   Windows 7—**ipconfig** result with a link-local address

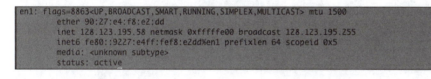
```
en1: flags=8863<UP,BROADCAST,SMART,RUNNING,SIMPLEX,MULTICAST> mtu 1500
        ether 90:27:e4:f8:e2:dd
        inet 128.123.195.58 netmask 0xfffffe00 broadcast 128.123.195.255
        inet6 fe80::9227:e4ff:fef8:e2dd%en1 prefixlen 64 scopeid 0x5
        media: <unknown subtype>
        status: active
```

FIGURE 8-10   Mac OS X—**ifconfig** result with a link-local address

The derivation of the IPv6 interface identifier from the MAC address generates some concerns regarding privacy issues. The concern is that the MAC address can be tracked throughout the Internet. A MAC address always attaches to the device v, and the interface identifier does not change no matter where it is physically located. The danger of this is that the movement or location of the device can be traced using the MAC address. To remedy these concerns, the IETF created RFC 4941 "Privacy Extensions for Stateless Address Autoconfiguration in IPv6." This RFC allows the generation of a random identifier with a limited lifetime to replace the machine's MAC address. An address like this will be difficult to trace because it regularly changes. Figure 8-9 shows the link-local address of a Windows 7 machine, which has been randomly generated. Therefore, this IPv6 address does not appear to be anything resembling its MAC address. The link-local address shown in Figure 8-9 is

fe80::a1b4:6c3d:b953:6e5%11

> **Privacy Extensions for Stateless Address Autoconfiguration**
> Allows the generation of a random identifier with a limited lifetime.

where %11 is the interface index or scope ID designated by Windows 7. IPv6 enables a socket application to specify an interface to use for sending data by specifying an interface index. It is possible for a computer to have more than one network interface card (NIC) and as a result to have multiple link-local addresses. Additionally, each link-local address can have a different scope. The purpose of the scope ID is to indicate which address it is used for.

The MAC or physical address is 000C2902E57E.

8-4 CONFIGURING A ROUTER FOR IPV6

Multicast Listener Discovery (MLD)

Enables the switches to listen to MLD packets to determine how to efficiently forward multicast packets to specific listeners on specific ports.

ipv6 unicast-routing

This command activates the IPv6 forwarding mechanism on the routers.

Not every piece of networking equipment is IPv6-capable, and this must be verified before implementing IPv6. IPv6-capable equipment can operate in the IPv4 and IPv6 environment. IPv6 relies heavily on multicast messages for enabling a lot of functions; therefore, the network switches must be able to support IPv6 multicast functions as well. In IPv4, IGMP (Internet Group Management Protocol) is used for determining which computers should join a multicast group. However, IGMP is no longer used in IPv6. For multicast group management, IPv6 uses Multicast Listener Discovery (MLD) instead. Similar to IGMP in IPv6, MLD snooping enables the switches to listen to MLD packets to determine how to efficiently forward multicast packets to specific listeners on specific ports.

Today, most routers are IPv6-capable. Those that are not might just require a software upgrade. On Cisco routers, IPv6 is not enabled automatically. To enable IPv6 unicast packet forwarding on Cisco routers, the global command **ipv6 unicast-routing** is entered. The following is the sequence of commands required to enable IPv6 unicast-routing:

```
Router# conf t
Router(config)#
Router(config)# ipv6 unicast-routing
```

ipv6 enable

Enables IPv6 on a specific interface.

The **ipv6 unicast-routing** command only activates the IPv6 forwarding mechanism on the routers. However, IPv6 is still not yet enabled on a specific interface. To enable IPv6 on a specific interface, you must enter the **ipv6 enable** command. The following example shows how to enable IPv6 on a gigabitethernet 3/1 interface. This step requires that the interface must first be selected. In this case, the command **int Gig3/1** is entered from the (config)# prompt. The prompt changes to (config-if)# and the command **ipv6 enable** is entered:

```
int Gig3/1
Router(config)# int Gig3/1
Router(config-if)# ipv6 enable
```

For Cisco routers, enabling IPv6 on the interface automatically configures the link-local address for that interface. The link-local address can only communicate with the IPv6 devices on the same network link.

The command **show running-config** is used to verify the IPv6 configuration. The use of this command is next demonstrated and a portion of the running configuration for interface GigabitEthernet 3/1 is provided:

```
Router#show running-config
.
.
!
interface GigabitEthernet3/1
 no ip address
 ipv6 enable
!
```

Also, the command **show ipv6 interface** can be used to show the state of the IPv6 configuration on the interface. This command shows the IPv6 of the interface. In the following example, it shows that IPv6 is enabled on the interface gigabitEtheret3/1. It shows the interface has a link-local address, but not the global address. Along with that the IPv6 network discovery protocol information is shown:

show ipv6 interface
Used to show the state of the IPv6 configuration on the interface.

```
Router#show ipv6 interface gigabitEthernet 3/1
GigabitEthernet3/1 is up, line protocol is up
  IPv6 is enabled, link-local address is FE80::217:DFFF:FEF5:1000
  No global unicast address is configured
  Joined group address(es):
    FF02::1
    FF02::2
    FF02::1:FFF5:1000
  MTU is 1500 bytes
  ICMP error messages limited to one every 100 milliseconds
  ICMP redirects are enabled
  Output features: HW Shortcut Installation
  ND DAD is enabled, number of DAD attempts: 1
  ND reachable time is 30000 milliseconds
  ND advertised reachable time is 0 milliseconds
  ND advertised retransmit interval is 0 milliseconds
  ND router advertisements are sent every 200 seconds
  ND router advertisements live for 1800 seconds
  ND advertised default router preference is Medium
  Hosts use stateless autoconfig for addresses.
```

The IPv6 global address can be configured on the interface by using the command **ipv6 address** *ipv6 interface address* issued from the (config-if)# prompt. There are two ways to program the IPv6 interface address. One is to specify the entire 128-bit IPv6 address followed by the prefix length. Another way is to specify a 64-bit prefix and to use the **eui-64** option. Using the option **eui-64** allows the router to choose its own host identifier (right most 64-bits) from the EUI-64 (Extended Universal Identifier-64) of the interface. The following example uses the IPv6 address of 2001:DB88:FEED:BEEF::1 on the router interface. This has a 64-bit network prefix of 2001:DB88:FEED:BEEF.

ipv6 address *ipv6 interface address*
The command used to configure the IPv6 address on an interface.

eui-64
Allows the router to choose its own host identifier.

```
Router(config)# int Gig3/1
Router(config-if)# ipv6 address 2001:DB88:FEED:BEEF::1/64
```

Next, the command **show ipv6 interface gigabitEthernet 3/1** is used to display the configuration of the Gig3/1 interface. This time the command shows that the interface gigabitEthernet 3/1 now has an IPv6 global address assigned to it, which is 2001:DB8:FEED:BEEF::1:

```
Router#show ipv6 interface gigabitEthernet 3/1
GigabitEthernet3/1 is up, line protocol is up
  IPv6 is enabled, link-local address is FE80::217:DFFF:FEF5:1000
  Global unicast address(es):
  2001:DB8:FEED:BEEF::1, subnet is 2001:DB8:FEED:BEEF::/64
  Joined group address(es):
    FF02::1
    FF02::2
    FF02::1:FF00:1
    FF02::1:FFF5:1000
  MTU is 1500 bytes
  ICMP error messages limited to one every 100 milliseconds
  ICMP redirects are enabled
  Output features: HW Shortcut Installation
  ND DAD is enabled, number of DAD attempts: 1
  ND reachable time is 30000 milliseconds
  ND advertised reachable time is 0 milliseconds
  ND advertised retransmit interval is 0 milliseconds
  ND router advertisements are sent every 200 seconds
  ND router advertisements live for 1800 seconds
  ND advertised default router preference is Medium
  Hosts use stateless autoconfig for addresses.
```

ND Protocol

Network Discovery Protocol. ICMPv6 messages of the type Router Advertisement (RA).

RA Messages

Router advertisement. This is a response to a link-local router solicitation message.

Router Solicitation Messages

These messages are sent to ask routers to send an immediate RA message on the local link so the host can receive the autoconfiguration information.

Now that IPv6 is enabled on the router, the router can begin to participate in the IPv6 functions. The router plays a key role in the stateless autoconfiguration of an IPv6 network. An IPv6 router uses the neighbor discovery (ND) protocol to periodically advertise information messages on the links to which they are connected. These are ICMPv6 messages of the type Router Advertisement (RA). One parameter of the router advertisements is the IPv6 network prefix for the link that can be used for host autoconfiguration. Upon receiving RA messages, an unconfigured host can build its global unicast address by prepending the advertised network prefix to its generated unique identifier just like in the link-local address case.

Another way for a host to autoconfigure itself is by sending router solicitation messages to the connected routers. These messages are sent to ask routers to send an immediate RA message on the local link, so the host can receive the autoconfiguration information without having to wait for the next schedule RA. Note: The time interval between RA messages is configurable. By default, router advertisements are sent every 200 seconds in Cisco routers.

As a result, the global unicast address of every machine on this network is the combination of the network prefix of 2001:DB8:FEED:BEEF and the self-generated interface identifier for that machine. Both Figure 8-11 and Figure 8-12 show two IPv6 addresses with the 2001:DB8:FEED:BEEF prefix. There are two IPv6 addresses. One is a global unicast address and another is a random generated identifier as part of the privacy identifier. This was discussed earlier in this section (see Privacy Extensions for Stateless Autoconfiguration). Microsoft calls this random identifier IPv6 a "temporary IPv6 address." This is shown to be a temporary address in Windows 7.

```
    IP Address. . . . . . . . . . . . : 2001:db8:feed:beef:460:45ab:3d6e:56e3
    IP Address. . . . . . . . . . . . : 2001:db8:feed:beef:20c:29ff:fe1c:f2f7
    IP Address. . . . . . . . . . . . : fe80::20c:29ff:fe1c:f2f7%4
    Default Gateway . . . . . . . . . : 128.123.7.1
                                        fe80::217:dfff:fef5:1000%4
```

FIGURE 8-11   Windows XP—**ipconfig** result with an IPv6 global unicast address

```
IPv6 Address . . . . . . . . . : 2001:db8:feed:beefa1b4:6c3d:b953: 6e5 (Preferred)
Temporary IPv6 Address . . . . . : 2001:db8:feed:beef:44ab:2c4d:f3d0:6674 (Preferred)
Link-local IPv6 Address . . . . . :fe80:a1b4:3c3d:b953:6e5%11 (Preferred)
IPv4 Address · · · · · · · · · : 128.123.7.207 (Preferred)
Subnet Mask · · · · · · · · · · : 255.255.255.0
Lease Obtained · · · · · · · · · : Friday, November 12, 2012 4:49:33 PM
Lease Expires · · · · · · · · · : Saturday, November 13, 2012 4:49:33 AM
Default Gateway · · · · · · · · : fe80::217:dffffef5:1000%11
```

FIGURE 8-12   Windows 7—**ipconfig** result with an IPv6 global unicast address

In Windows XP, both of these are presented as IP addresses. Of course, we can tell that one is a modified EUI-64 format, and the other one is randomly generated. An IPv6 address with ff:fe in the middle indicates the EUI-48 to EUI-64 transform. On Mac OS X, no random identifier is used. The global unicast address is the product of the modified EUI-64 format, as shown in Figure 8-13.

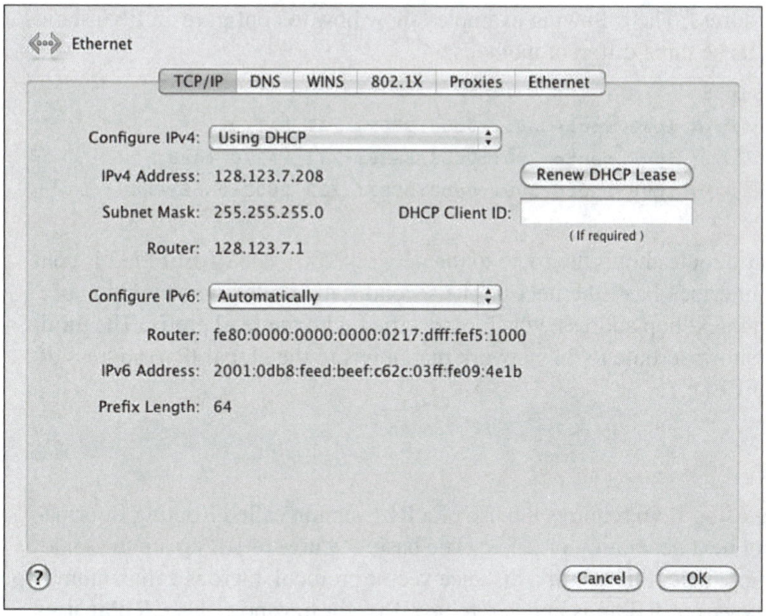

FIGURE 8-13   Mac OS X—**ipconfig** result with an IPv6 global unicast address

Throughout this chapter, the IPv6 prefix used is **2001:DB8::/32**. This is a special range designated by the IANA to be used for any testing or documentation. This IPv6 prefix cannot be used nor can it be routed on the Internet.

With the global unicast address, the machine is now reachable from anywhere on the IPv6 network. However, it is a daunting task to remember the IPv6 global unicast address. It is not practical to use the long 128-bits address. This required a DNS server that can translate a host name to an IPv6 address. The DNS record for IPv6 is called AAAA (Quad A) record.

8-5 IPV6 ROUTING

When interconnecting IPv6 networks together, a routing protocol is required. IPv6 supports static, RIP, OSPF, EIGRP, and IS-IS routing. Most of these protocols had to be revised to be able to deal with IPv6 addresses. However, the routing protocols for IPv6 work the same way as they do with IPv4. In fact, they still maintain the same routing principles. The following material demonstrates how to configure IPv6 routing for static, RIP, OSPF, EIGRP, and ISIS.

IPv6: Static

Configuring a static route for IPv6 is almost the same as it is in IPv4. In IPv4, one can specify the next hop IP address or/and the exit interface. In IPv6, there is an extra feature. The next hop IP address in IPv6 can either be the link local address or the global address. The following examples show how to configure an IPv6 static route using these three different methods:

```
Router# conf t
Router(config)# ipv6 route 2001:0db8:BEEF::/32 FA1/0
Router(config)# ipv6 route 2001:0db8:BEEF::/32 FA1/0 fe80::2
Router(config)# ipv6 route 2001:0db8:BEEF::/32 2001:0db8:FEED::1
```

The first static route shows the route to the network 2001:0db8:BEEF::/32 is configured via interface FastEthernet1/0. The second static route gives an option of the link-local next hop address, which is specified with the fe80 prefix. The third static entry shows a route to the network that points to the global IPv6 address of 2001:0db8:FEED::1.

IPv6: RIP

RIP routing using IPv6 requires the use of a RIP version called Routing Information Protocol next generation or **RIPng**. The basic features of RIPng are the same as RIPv2. For example, this is still a distance vector protocol, there is a maximum hop limitation; however, RIPng is updated to use IPv6 for transport. Also, RIPng uses the IPv6 multicast address of FF02::9 for all RIP updates.

Configuring RIPng on Cisco routers is simple. The biggest difference between configuring RIPv2 and RIPng on Cisco routers is now RIPng must be configured on a per network link or per-interface basis rather than per-network basis as in RIPv2.

The following examples demonstrate how to enable RIPng and how to configure RIPng on a Cisco router interface:

```
Router# conf t
Router(config)#
Router(config)# ipv6  router rip RIP100
Router(config)#
Router(config)# int Gig3/1
Router(config-if)# ipv6 rip RIP100 enable
```

The command **ipv6 router rip** *rip_tag* is used to enable RIPng on Cisco routers. The *rip_tag* is a tag to identify the RIP process. The RIPng is enabled on the Gigabit interface 3/1 with the command **ipv6 rip** *rip_tag* **enable**. The same command will be used to enable other RIP interfaces. This is different than configuring RIPv2 where the network statement needs to be issued for every RIP network.

rip_tag
Used to identify the RIP process.

IPv6: OSPF

The current OSPF version used in IPv4 is OSPFv2. Most of OSPF information relies heavily on the IP number (for example the router ID <area ID> and the link-state ID). To support IPv6, the OSPF routing protocol has been significantly re-vamped. The new OSPF version for IPv6 is OSPFv3. The basic foundation of OSPF still remains intact—for example, OSPFv3 is still a link state routing protocol. However, OSPFv3 uses the IPv6 link-local multicast addresses of FF02::5 for all OSPF routers and FF02::6 for OSPF designated routers.

OSPFv3
The OSPF version that supports IPv6.

OSPFv3 is now enabled on a per-link basis, not on a per-network basis on Cisco routers. This is similar to the changes in RIPng. OSPFv3 indentifies which networks are attached to the link and propagates them into the OSPF area. The following example demonstrates how to enable OSPFv3 and how to configure OSPFv3 on a Cisco router interface:

```
Router# conf t
Router(config)#
Router(config)# ipv6  router ospf 99
Router(config)#
Router(config)# int Gig3/1
Router(config-if)# ipv6 ospf 99 area 0.0.0.0
```

The command **ipv6 router ospf** *process_id* is used to enable OSPFv3 on Cisco routers. OSPFv3 is enabled on the Gigabit interface 3/1 with the command **ipv6 ospf** *process_id* **area** *area_id*. The same command is used to enable other OSPF interfaces. The router in this example is configured to be area 0 which is the backbone (area 0.0.0.0).

IPv6: EIGRP

EIGRP is inherently a multiprotocol routing protocol. It was designed to support non-IP protocols, such as IPX and Appletalk, and it supports the IP protocols IPv4 and now IPv6. IPv6 EIGRP uses the IPv6 link-local multicast addresses of FF02::A for all EIGRP Hello packets and updates.

IPv6 EIGRP is now configured over a network link, so there is no need to configure a network statement as in IPv4 EIGRP. The following example demonstrates how to enable IPv6 EIGRP and how to configure it on a Cisco router interface:

```
Router# conf t
Router(config)#
Router(config)# ipv6  router eigrp 999
Router(config-rtr)# no shut
Router(config)# int Gig3/1
Router(config-if)# ipv6 eigrp 999
```

The command **ipv6 router eigrp** *as_number* is used to enable EIGRP on Cisco routers. The IPv6 EIGRP protocol is created in a shutdown mode by default. The **no shutdown** is issued to ensure that the protocol is enabled. Next, the IPv6 EIGRP is enabled on the Gigabit interface 3/1 with the command **ipv6 eigrp** *as_number*. The network link is now part of the EIGRP routing network.

IPv6: IS-IS

As mentioned in Chapter 3, IS-IS is designed to work on the same network layer just like IP. Therefore, it does not require an IP protocol for it to function. Later, IS-IS was adapted to work with IP. Because of its IP independence, IS-IS is much easier than most protocols to incorporate with IPv6. Only a few adjustments to IS-IS have been made to better support IPv6.

Configuring IPv6 IS-IS is very similar to the method used in IPv4. In IPv6, IS-IS is always enabled on a per network link basis. This is the same for the IPv4 configuration. The same global command (**clns routing**) is used to enable the IS-IS routing protocol. The same NET address is used in the IPv6 configuration as in the IPv4 configuration. The only big difference is the use of keyword **ipv6** when enabling the IPv6 IS-IS interface. The following example demonstrates how to enable IPv6 IS-IS and how to configure it on an interface of a Cisco router:

```
Router# conf t
Router(config)# clns routing
Router(config)# router isis
Router(config-rtr)# net 49.0001.c202.00e8.0202.00
Router(config)#
Router(config)# int Gig3/1
Router(config-if)# ipv6 router isis
```

The command **clns routing** is used to enable the connectionless network service. The command **router isis** will allow the IS-IS protocol to be configured. The **net** *NET Address* assigns the NET address to IS-IS. Then, the IPv6 IS-IS is enabled on the Gigabit interface 3/1 with the command **ipv6 router isis**.

This section demonstrated the steps for configuring IPv6 routing for static, RIP, OSPF, EIGRP, and IS-IS. As was demonstrated, the steps are similar to configuring routing for IPv4; however, there are some distinct differences required to enable an IPv6 interface.

8-6 TROUBLESHOOTING IPV6 CONNECTION

One big question that needs to be answered before troubleshooting IPv6 connectivity is: Does the network environment support IPv6? If the answer is yes, the same network troubleshooting techniques and approaches still apply on IPv6 as on IPv4. Remember what has changed is only the network layer on the OSI model. Other layers are still intact and stay the same. You will still need to troubleshoot the physical connections to make sure the physical layer is working properly. The data link layer still needs to be inspected to see if the packets are being forwarded, MAC addresses are still being seen, and hosts are still in the correct VLANs.

The commands such as **ipconfig** in Windows and **ifconfig** for Linux or Mac OS X can be used to view the TCP/IP configuration information of a host. This is always a good start in network troubleshooting. First, you have to see what is configured and whether it is configured correctly before you can move on to the next step. The examples of these commands are shown throughout this chapter.

Many basic network tools that are available in IPv4 are available in IPv6 as well. Ping is one of the most commonly used tools to test the connectivity between two hosts. Ping is implemented using ICMP echo and Echo reply for a very simple hello network test. In IPv6, the ICMP version 6 is being used instead; therefore the tool has changed slightly to accommodate the change in the ICMP protocol fields. The command **ping6** can be used to explicitly specify the IPv6 address, even though most operating systems have modified the **ping** command to understand both the IPv4 and IPv6 addresses. An issue of using the **ping** command in IPv6 is the lengthy address and the time required for entering the destination address. For example, the following is an example. The first part shows the IPv6 address that is assigned to the router's R1 interface.

> **ping6**
> Command used to explicitly specify the IPv6 address.

```
R2(config-if)# ipv6 address 2001:C16C:0000:0001:0000:0000:0000:0001/64
```

The IPv6 address can be simplified using double colon notation, as shown:

```
R2# ping ipv6 2001:C16C:0:1::1
```

The IPv6 address is still complicated even with the reduced address length. A solution to this is to assign a hostname to the specified IPv6 address. In this case, the hostname R1-WAN will be assigned to the specified IPv6 address using the command **ipv6 host R1-WAN 2001:C16C:0:1::1/64**, as shown:

```
R2(config)# ipv6 host R1-WAN 2001:C16C:0:1::1
```

Now, the **ping** command, using the newly assigned hostnames for R1 and R2, can be used. An example is provided:

```
R2(config)# ipv6 host R1-WAN 2001:C16C:0:1::1
R2# ping R1-WAN
Type escape sequence to abort.
Sending 5, 100-byte ICMP Echos to 2001:C16C:0:1::1, timeout is 2
seconds:
!!!!!
Success rate is 100 percent (5/5), round-trip min/avg/max = 0/0/4 ms
R2#
```

Another useful network tool is **traceroute** or **tracert** in Windows world. This tool enables the user to see the routing information between the two hosts. The IPv6 version of this tool is **traceroute6** or **tracert6** in Windows. Like **ping**, the IPv6 version of traceroute has to understand the ICMP version 6 messages as well. The structure for the **traceroute6** command is shown. The Host name and web addresses assume the DNS entries have been made:

```
traceroute6 <destination address, Host name, or web address>
```

For example, the following could be entered to run a traceroute:

```
traceroute6 2001:C16C:0:2::2
traceroute6 www.6bone.net
traceroute6 R1-WAN
```

When will the Internet switch to IPv6? The answer is not clear, but the networking community recognizes that something must be done to address the limited availability of current IP address space. Manufacturers have already incorporated IPv6 capabilities in their routers and operating systems. What about IPv4? The bottom line is that the switch to IPv6 will not come without providing some way for IPv4 networks to still function. Additionally, techniques such as NAT have made it possible for intranets to use the private address space and still be able to connect to the Internet. This has significantly reduced the number of IPv4 addresses required for each network and have delayed the need to immediately switch to IPv6.

SUMMARY

This chapter presented an overview of the fundamentals of the IP version 6. IPv6 is proposed to replace IPv4 to carry the data traffic over the Internet. The student should understand the following:

- The basic differences between IPv6 and IPv4
- The basic structure of a 128-bit IPv6 hexadecimal address
- The addresses that IPv6 uses
- How to setup IPv6 on the computers
- The purpose of link-local addresses
- How to setup IPv6 on the routers

QUESTIONS AND PROBLEMS

Section 8-1

1. What is the size of the IPv6 address?

2. What is a datagram?

3. How many bits are used to define the IPv4 source and destination address?

4. How many bits are used to define the IPv6 source and destination address?

5. Why is IPv6 faster than IPv4 for transferring packets?

6. At what layer is error detection performed in IPv6?

7. What is IPsec?

8. How is IPsec enabled with IPv6?

9. How are broadcasts handled in IPv6?

10. Why is DHCP not required in IPv6?

Section 8-2

11. How many bits are in an IPv6 address?

12. IPv6 numbers are written in what format?

13. Express the following IPv6 numbers using double-colon notation:

    a. 5355:4821:0000:0000:0000:1234:5678:FEDC

    b. 0000:0000:0000:1234:5678:FEDC:BA98:7654

    c. 1234:5678:ABCD:EF12:0000:0000:1122:3344

14. Express the IPv4 IP address 192.168.12.5 in IPv6 form using dotted decimal.

15. Recover the following IPv6 address from the following double-colon notation:

    1234:5678::AFBC

16. Define the structure of the 6to4 prefix.

17. What is the purpose of the 6to4 relay router?

18. What does it mean to have a full IPv6 address?

19. What is the network prefix for the following IPv6 address and how big is the network prefix?

    2001:1234:ABCD:5678::10/64

20. What is the length of the interface identifier in IPv6?

21. These types of addresses started with FF00::/8:

    a. Anycast

    b. Multicast

    c. Global unicast

    d. Link-local

    e. None of these answers are correct

22. This address is only deliverable to the nearest node.

    a. Anycast

    b. Multicast

    c. Global unicast

    d. Link-local

    e. None of these answers are correct

23. The range of these addresses starts with 2000::/3.

    a. Anycast

    b. Multicast

    c. Global unicast

    d. Link-local

    e. None of these answers are correct

24. The network prefix for this address is FE80::/10.

    a. Anycast

    b. Multicast

    c. Global unicast

    d. Link-local

    e. None of these answers are correct

25. The IPv6 addresses are equivalent to public addresses in IPv4.

    a. Anycast

    b. Multicast

    c. Global unicast

    d. Link-local

    e. None of these answers are correct

26. This type of address can be thought of as a cross between unicast and multicast addresses.

    a. Anycast

    b. Multicast

    c. Global unicast

    d. Link-local

    e. None of these answers are correct

27. Every IPv6 interface will have at least one of these addresses.

    a. Anycast

    b. Multicast

    c. Global unicast

    d. Link-local

    e. None of these answers are correct

28. These types of IPv6 addresses can be thought of as private addresses in IPv4.

    a. Anycast

    b. Multicast

    c. Global unicast

    d. Link-local

    e. None of these answers are correct

29. The 001 of this address indicates it is what type of address?

    a. Anycast

    b. Multicast

    c. Global unicast

    d. Link-local

    e. None of these answers are correct

30. These types of IDs are administered by IANA.

    a. FP ID

    b. SLA ID

    c. TLA ID

    d. Interface ID

    e. None of these answers are correct

31. This type of ID is used to indicate an interface on a specific subnet.

    a. FP ID

    b. SLA ID

    c. TLA ID

    d. Interface ID

    e. None of these answers are correct

32. This ID is used to identify subnet within the site.

    a. FP ID

    b. SLA ID

    c. TLA ID

    d. Interface ID

    e. None of these answers are correct

Section 8-3

33. This type of operating system has no manual configuration mode for assigning the IPv6 address.

34. In regard to subnet address length in IPv6, the default value for unicast addresses is

    a. 32

    b. 64

    c. 128

    d. None of these answers are correct

35. All the machines in a network are running IPv6 enabled in the automatic configuration mode. What mode is this, and what does this mean?

36. Which of the following types of IPv6 address is self-configured?

    a. Anycast

    b. Multicast

    c. Global unicast

    d. Link-local

    e. None of these answers are correct

37. How many DNS root servers are there in the world?

38. Why does a computer issue a neighbor solicitation message?

    a. To discover the unicast address of another IPv6 node

    b. To discover the anycast address of another IPv6 node

    c. To discover the link-layer address of another IPv6 node

    d. To discover the global unicast address of another IPv6 node

39. The process of detecting another machine with the same IPv6 address is called which of the following?

    a. Duplicate Address Detection

    b. Redundant Address Detection

    c. Stateless Address Detection

    d. Global Address Detection

40. What is the benefit of the "Privacy Extensions for Stateless Address Autoconfiguration in IPv6?"

Section 8-4

41. For multicast group management, IPv6 uses which of the following?

    a. Unicast Listener Discovery

    b. Stateless Listener Discovery

    c. Unicast Listener Discovery

    d. Multicast Listener Discovery

42. What global command is used to enable IPv6 unicast packet forwarding on Cisco routers?

43. To enable IPv6 on an interface, which of the following commands must be entered?

    a. **ipv6 enable**

    b. **ipv6 configure**

    c. **ipv6 interface**

    d. **ipv6 routing**

44. The following information is displayed after entering the **show running-config** command:

```
!
interface GigabitEthernet1/1
 no ip address
 ipv6 enable
```

This information verifies which of the following? (Select all that apply.)

   a. IPv4 is configured.

   b. Interface ge1/1 is configured.

   c. IPv6 is enabled.

   d. Interface status is ip.

45. The **show ipv6 interface gigabitEthernet 3/1** command is entered on a router. The address GigabitEthernet3/1 FE80::217:DFFF:FEF5:1000 is listed. What type of address is this?

46. The command **ipv6 address 2001:DC21:2244:3311::1/64** is entered on a router. What is the network prefix of this address and what is its length? What is the command doing?

47. What is the EUI option?

48. What is the purpose of the network discovery protocol in IPv6?

49. What is the purpose of the router solicitation message in IPv6?

Section 8-5

50. What is the following command showing?

```
Router(config)# ipv6 route 2001:0db8:ABCD::/32 FA0/0
```

51. List the command to create a static route for 2001:0db8:1234::/32 that points to the global network 2001:0db8:ABCD::1.

52. Create a static route for 2001:0db8:1234::/32 off the FA0/0 interface that gives the link-local next hop address, which is specified with the fe80::1 prefix.

53. What is RIPng and what is it used for?

54. What is the multicast address for RIPng?

55. List the command that is used to enable RIPng on Cisco routers.

56. What is the purpose of the rip tag?

57. What version of OSPF is used with IPv6?

58. What are the IPv6 link-local multicast addresses for routers and the link-local addresses for designated routers?

59. What command is used to configure OSPF routing for IPv6, using a process ID of 50?

60. What does the following command do?

```
Router(config-if)# ipv6 ospf 50 area 0.0.0.0
```

61. What is the IPv6 link-local multicast addresses for EIGRP? What is the link-local address used for in IPv6?

62. What is the command for enabling EIGRP for IPv6 with a specified AS of 100?

63. List the configuration for enabling ISIS for IPv6. List the router prompts and all commands required for enabling IS-IS on the Gig1/1 interface. Use a net address of 49.0002.b123.a456.0012.00.

Section 8-6

64. What command is used to view the /TCP/IP setting in Windows?

65. What command is used to view the /TCP/IP setting in Linux?

66. What is the purpose of the **ping6** command?

67. What is the purpose of the **traceroute6** or **tracert6** command in IPv6?

68. List three things that should be answered before troubleshooting IPv6 connectivity?

Critical Thinking

69. Your boss read about IPv6 and wants to know if the network you oversee is ready for the transition. Prepare a response based on the networking and computer operating systems used in your facility.

70. The **show ipv6 interface** command is issued to examine a router's R1 interface. The interface has been configured with an IPv6 address. Where is the MAC address of the interface found?

```
R1# sh ipv6 interface
Serial0/0/0 is up, line protocol is up
IPv6 is enabled, link-local address is
FE80::213:19FF:FE7B:1101/64
No Virtual link-local address(es):
Global unicast address(es):
2001:C16C:0:1::1, subnet is 2001:C16C:0:1::/64
Joined group address(es):
FF02::1
FF02::2
FF02::0001:FF00:0001
MTU is 1500 bytes
ICMP error messages limited to one every 100 milliseconds
ICMP redirects are enabled
ICMP unreachables are sent
ND DAD is enabled, number of DAD attempts: 1
ND reachable time is 30000 milliseconds
Hosts use stateless autoconfig for addresses.
```

71. What is the purpose of the command **ipv6 address 2001:C16C:0:2:213:19FF :FE7B:1101/64 eui-64**?

72. Answer the following for the given IPv6 address: 2001:C15C:0000:0001:0000 :0000:0000:0001/64

   a. Write this address using double colon notation

   b. Identify the network prefixs

9 CHAPTER

LINUX NETWORKING

Chapter Outline

Objectives

- Demonstrate the logon/logoff process for Linux

- Examine how to add user accounts

- Develop an understanding of the Linux file structure and related file commands

- Understand how to use key Linux administration commands

- Explore the procedures for adding applications to the Linux system

- Demonstrate the use of Linux networking commands

- Investigate how to use Linux tools to troubleshoot Linux systems and networks

Key Terms

root access	chgrp	net mask
command line	man	lo
ls	ps	ifdown, ifup
ls -l	PID	network stop
hidden files	kill [PID], kill -9 [PID]	network start
ls -la	su	route add default gw
bash	mount	openssh
more	fstab	ncftp
cat	umount	resolv.conf
cd	shutdown -h now	dmesg
pwd	up arrow	reboot
mkdir	history	last
rmdir	telnet	who
rm	yum provides [*filename*]	w
mv	httpd	nmap
cp	Firefox	chkconfig
chmod	httpd.conf	netstat -ap
executable (x) permission	eth0, eth1, eth2, …	system-config- <tool-name>
chown	ifconfig	ls system-config-*

INTRODUCTION

This chapter provides an overview of Linux networking from the point of view of an entry-level network administrator. This chapter guides you through many of the administrative procedures in Linux that the successful administrator must understand.

Section 9-1 discusses the process of logging on to Linux and adding a user account using a Linux user manager. The issues of setting up accounts, establishing a home directory, specifying a user ID, and creating private groups are addressed. Section 9-2 examines the Linux file structure and the basic file commands needed to successfully navigate the system. Examples of file commands are presented. The Linux administration commands, in particular, the operating details of the Red Hat Package Manager, are examined in Section 9-3. Key issues examined are how to kill processes, shutting down the system, and mounting external drives. Section 9-4 examines the steps for installing applications, such as SSH and the Apache web server. Section 9-5 presents an overview of Linux networking. This section demonstrates the use of the commands **ifconfig**, **net mask**, **ifup**, **ifdown**, and **route**, and the steps for starting and stopping network processes. Section 9-6 presents the techniques for troubleshooting Linux systems. This chapter concludes with an overview of the Fedora Linux management tools in Section 9-7. This section introduces the various GUIs that can be used to manage and configure the system.

Most of the examples presented in this chapter examine the use of Linux commands as entered from the terminal emulation mode (command line). Many of the commands presented are also available to the user via the Linux GUI (graphical user interface); however, most network administrators prefer using the command line.

The question often arises: What are the differences between Linux and UNIX? The two systems have many similarities, but they are also quite different. There are many variants of UNIX, and even though they are similar, many of the tasks performed on the system, such as the installation of applications and devices and handling backups, are unique to that version of UNIX. This means that many administrators often have to specialize with a particular brand of UNIX.

Linux, on the other hand, is a standardized operating system and is receiving considerable vendor support. The Linux GUI has many improvements over standard UNIX systems, and in fact, the Linux approach is becoming the standard. Although the Linux and UNIX operating systems are unique, the commands and file structure are very similar. This means that the basic commands presented in this chapter are transportable to UNIX machines. Note that the examples presented in this chapter are based on the Fedora distribution. Other distributions of Linux have many similarities, but they will also have a different set of administrative tools.

9-1   LOGGING ON TO LINUX

This section demonstrates how to log on to Linux, add a new user account, and log out. This section assumes that Linux has already been installed on the user's computer, and the user has root privileges. (*Note:* Many of the examples presented in this chapter require **root access**. Root access is the administrator mode for Linux—the *root user* has the rights to make changes to operating and user parameters.)

The first example demonstrates how to log in to the system. The Linux computer is first powered up, the system initializes, and the system logon screen is displayed. This screen prompts for the username and password. If this is a new installation of Linux, log on as *root* and complete the following steps to create a user account.

A window will open for user login when Linux is running in a GUI (the default installation). This screen is where you enter the user account name and password. (If a user account has not been established, the administrator would log in as *root* to establish the user account name.) Linux will prompt for the password or the default password if the system is just being set up:

```
user account: root password: *******
```

Once logged into Linux (using the GUI interface), you will get a window similar to that shown in Figure 9-1. This is just one of the many possible Linux screens that can be displayed. The screens vary for each distribution for Linux. (*Note:* The root account should only be used for administration duties, such as installing software, establishing user accounts, installing drivers, and so on. Major changes to the Linux machine system are possible with the root account access.)

FIGURE 9-1   The main Linux GUI window

Adding a User Account

The easiest way to add a user to the Linux operating system is from the Linux main GUI. This is accomplished by clicking **Applications > Other** and then selecting the **Users and Groups**, as shown in Figure 9-2. This opens the Fedora User Manager window shown in Figure 9-3. This window is used to add and delete users as well as modify user properties. The window shows there are no current users on the system. Click the **Add User** icon, which opens the Create New User window, as shown in Figure 9-4.

FIGURE 9-2 Selecting the Fedora User Manager

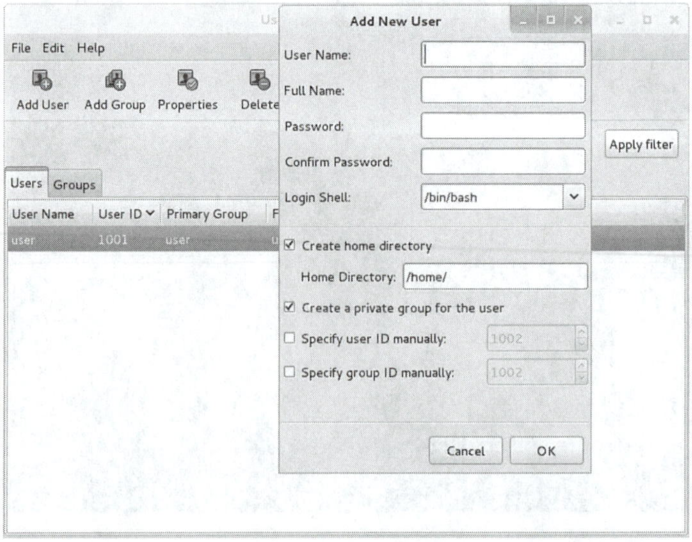

FIGURE 9-3 The Fedora User Manager window

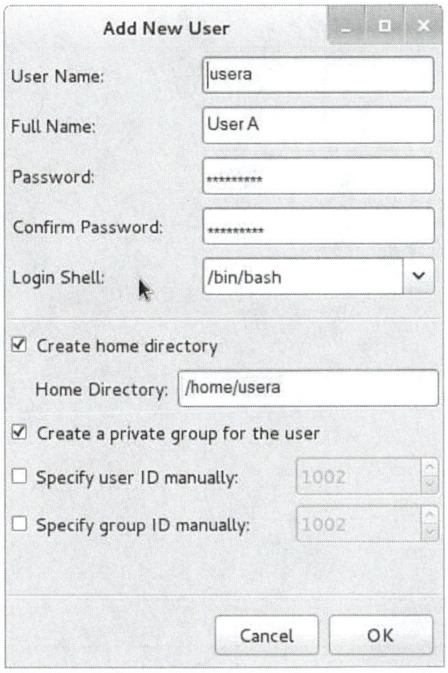

FIGURE 9-4   The Create New User window

A new user called *usera* will be created in this step, with the username being entered on the first line (refer to Figure 9-4). The username must be one continuous text entry containing no spaces. The full name is next entered followed by the password. The full name is used to map the username to a person. For example, *usera* doesn't identify the name of the user on the account. The full name provides this information. The password entered is displayed with asterisks (*). This protects the privacy of the password. The next field requires that the password be reentered, to confirm that the password was correctly entered. The fifth line is for the login shell. The entry */bin/bash* is pointing to the default Linux login shell. The *login shell* is used to set up the user's initial operating environment.

The check on **Create home directory** means that a home directory called */home/usera* is being established, and this is where *usera* will be placed after logging in. The line **Create a private group for the user** is also checked. Any user being added to the Linux system can belong to an existing group, or a new group can be created. In this case, a new group (*usera*) is being created. The next line is used to **Specify user ID manually**. If this option is not checked, the system will select the next available user ID number. The concept of a *user ID* is explained in Section 9-2. Click **OK** to complete this step and close the Create New User menu.

The user account for *usera* has now been established, as shown in the Fedora User Manager window (see Figure 9-5). Notice the entries for the User ID (1002), the Primary Group (User A), the Login Shell (*/bin/bash*), and the Home Directory (*/home/usera*). The next step is to log out as *root* and log in as *usera*. You can log out by clicking **Desktop > Log Out** in the Linux GUI screen, as shown in Figure 9-6. Once logged out, the login screen for Linux is displayed, except this time, the user can log on as *usera*. The user can also log out by entering the **exit** command from the command line.

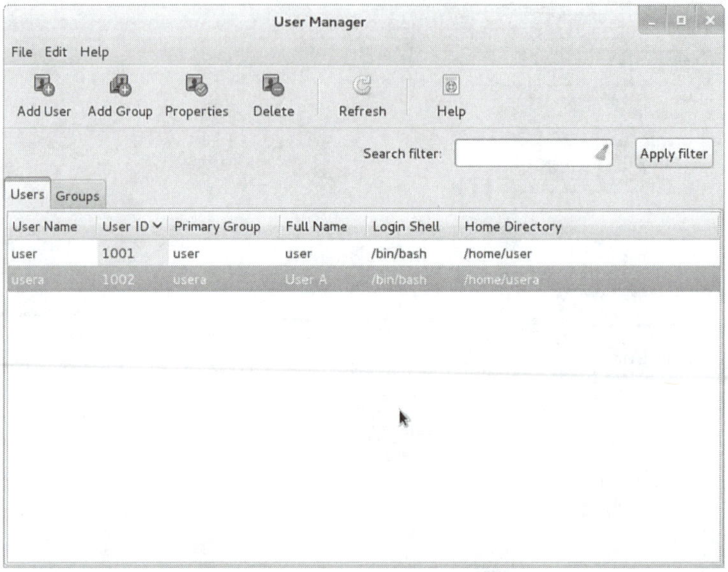

FIGURE 9-5 The addition of the usera account displayed by the Fedora User Manager

FIGURE 9-6   Selecting the Log Out option for Linux

Network and system administrators typically use the command line for entering most Linux commands. The command line is a text-entry level for commands and is accessed from the main GUI window by clicking the **Terminal emulation program** icon shown in Figure 9-7. This places you in the Linux command line, as shown in Figure 9-8. The hostname of the Linux machine is usera@bookfedora.

Command Line
A text entry level for commands.

FIGURE 9-7   Selecting the Terminal emulation program from the Linux GUI

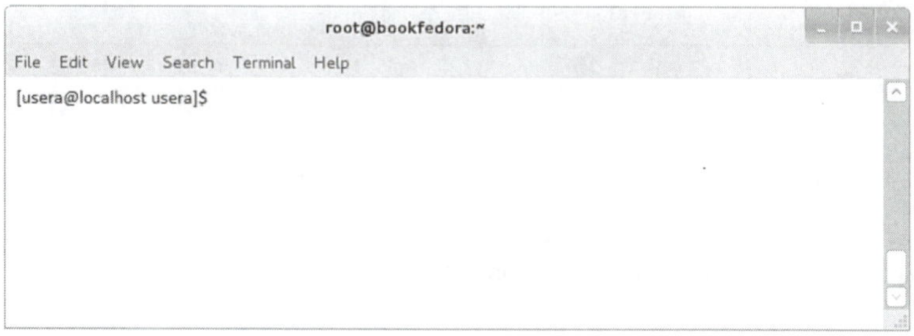

FIGURE 9-8   The Linux command line showing the hostname of usera@bookfedora

9-2   LINUX FILE STRUCTURE AND FILE COMMANDS

The objective of this section is for you to learn both the Linux file structure and how to use Linux commands to view files, file contents, and directory contents. The following Linux commands are presented in this section:

>   Listing Files: **ls**, **ls -l**, **ls -la**
>   Displaying File Contents: **more**, **cat**
>   Directory Operations: **cd**, **pwd**, **mkdir**, **rmdir**
>   File Operations: **rm**, **mv**, **cp**
>   Permissions and Ownership: **chmod**, **chown**, **chgrp**

The file structure in Linux is fairly complex, especially for users who are used to a Windows GUI. You should avoid doing this, because not all Linux GUIs are the same, and the command-line operations are much faster and more flexible. This section demonstrates how to successfully navigate the Linux file structure and to use the commands listed.

Listing Files

The ls Command   The\ first command examined is **ls**. This command is used to display the basic files in the directory and is executed from the command line, as shown in Figure 9-9. In this example, the user is *root*, and the files examined are located in *root*'s home directory.

> **ls**
> Linux command that lists the basic files in the directory.

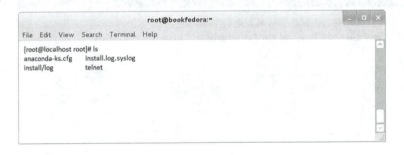

FIGURE 9-9   The results of inputting the **ls** command from the command line

The ls -l Command   The next file command examined is **ls -l**. This command is called a *long listing* and lists file attributes, as shown in Figure 9-10. The second file listed in Figure 9-10 is *install.log*. On the far left of the *install.log* line are the

> **ls -l**
> Linux command that lists file attributes.

permissions for the file listed in 10 character spaces. The first space is reserved for indicating if this is a directory (d), character (c), or block (b), or no entry specified ( ). In this case, no entry is specified for the *install.log* file ( ).

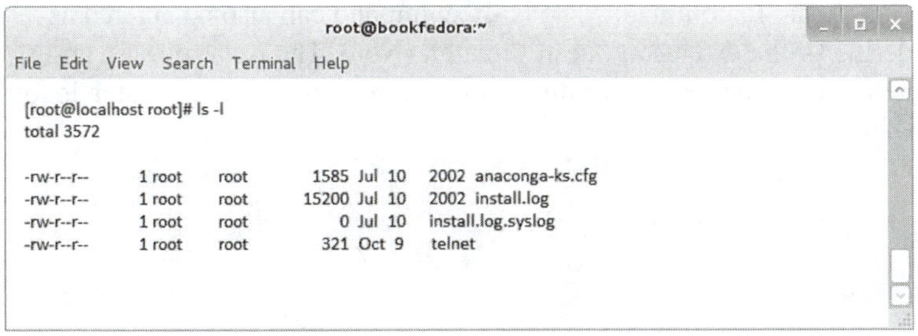

FIGURE 9-10 The results of inputting the **ls -l** command

The remaining nine character positions define three groups: the owner, the group, and everybody. Each group has three attribute settings: read, write, and executable. The attributes are turned on by setting the place value to 1. The concept of *file attributes* is further explained under the **chmod** command later in this section. Table 9-1 lists the attributes for the *install.log* file shown in Figure 9-10, and Table 9-2 provides a summary of the file attributes.

TABLE 9-1 File Attributes for the install.log File (Starting From the Left)

First character	(-)	Means no attribute specified
Characters 2–4	Owner (rw-)	The owner has read/write privileges
Characters 5–7	Group (r--)	The group has read privileges only
Characters 8–10	Everyone else (r--)	Everyone has read privileges only
Owner of the file is *root*		
The group is *root*		
File size = 15,200 bytes		
File created July 10, 2012		

TABLE 9-2 Summary of the Attribute Abbreviations Used in the File Permissions Block

d	Directory	c	Character
b	Block	r	Read
w	Write	x	Executable
-	Not defined		

The ls -la Command   The long listing command **ls -l** can be modified to allow hidden files to be viewed by entering **ls -la**. The *a* extension instructs Linux to display all hidden files. Hidden files start with a period, such as . (home directory) and . (parent directory) and .bash_history and .bash_logout. Figure 9-11 shows the result of entering the **ls -la** command. The **ls -la** command can also be entered as **ls -al**. The ordering of the extension doesn't matter. (Note: The bash files are applied to the shell that defines the environment the user works under. Bash stands for Bourne again shell.)

```
                                    root@bookfedora:~                    _  □  x

 File  Edit  View  Search  Terminal  Help

 [root@localhost root]# ls -la
 total 3720
 drwxr-x---   20   root      root       4096  Jan 15   12:24
 drwxr-xr-x   19   root      root       4096  Jan 13   12:18
 -rw-r--r--    1   root      root       1585  Jul 10    2002   anaconda-ks.cfg
 -rw-------    1   root      root       6472  Jan 15   12:18   .bash_history
 -rw-r--r--    1   root      root         24  Jun 10    2000   .bash_logout
 -rw-r--r--    1   root      root        234  Jul  5    2001   .bash_profile
 -rw-r--r--    1   root      root        176  Aug 23    1995   .bashrc
 drwx------    2   root      root       4096  Oct 25   14:48
 -rw-r--r--    1   root      root        210  Jun 10    2000   .cshrc
 -rw-r--r--    1   root      root      15200  Jul 10    2002   install.log
 -rw-r--r--    1   root      root          0  Jul 10    2002   install.log.sys/log
 -rw-r--r--    1   root      root        321  Oct  9   16:34   telnet
```

FIGURE 9-11   The results of entering the **ls -la** command

Displaying File Contents

The more Command   The next file command demonstrated is **more**. This command is used in Linux to display the contents of a text file at a pace the user controls using the spacebar. Figure 9-12 provides an example of using the **more** command. This example uses the command to display the contents of the *install.log* file. If the information in the file exceeds one screen, a prompt is displayed indicating how much of the file contents has been displayed. In this example (see Figure 9-12), 5 percent of the file contents has been displayed. Pressing the spacebar will display the next page of contents of the *install.log* file contents, and the prompt at the bottom of the screen will display the new percentage that has been viewed. Press the spacebar to keep displaying the file contents until they have all been displayed or press **Ctrl + C** to exit the **more** command.

The cat Command   The next file command used to display file contents is **cat**, which stands for concatenate. This command is used to print the file text to the screen and works fine, as long as the contents of the file will fit on one screen. If the file is larger than one screen, the text will quickly scroll by. In the case of a large file, it is probably best to use the **more** command so that the contents of each page can be viewed. The advantage of **cat** is that it can be tied to other programs. This will be demonstrated later in the chapter.

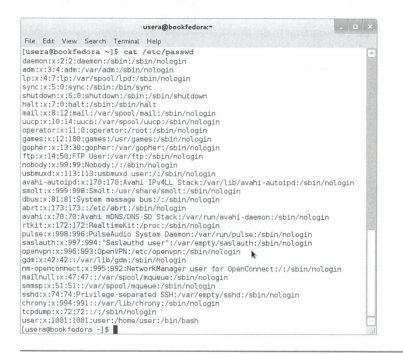

```
                        root@bookfedora:~                      _  □  x
File  Edit  View  Search  Terminal  Help
[root@localhost root]# more install.log
Installing 510 packages

Installing glibc-common-2.2.5-34.
Installing hwdata-0.14-1.
Installing indexhtml-7.3-3.
Installing mailcap-2.1.9-2.
Installing redhat-logos-1.1.3-1.
Installing setup-2.5.12-1.
Installing filesystem-2.1.6-2.
Installing basesystem-7.0-2.
Installing glibc-2.2.5-34.
Installing ldflush-1.5-17.
Installing bzip2-libs-1.0.2-2.
Installing chkconfig-1.3.5-3.
Installing cracklib-2.7-15.
Installing db1-1.85-8.
Installing db2-2.4.14-10.
Installing db3-3.3.11-6.
Installing dosfstools-2.8-1.
Installing e2fsprohs-1.27-3.
--More--(5%)
```

FIGURE 9-12   An example of using the **more** command

Figure 9-13 provides an example of using the **cat** command. In this example, *cat* is being used to view the contents of the password file in the */etc* directory.

The command **cat /etc/passwd** is being used, as shown in Figure 9-13. Notice that the command prompt is displayed at both the top and the bottom of the screen, indicating that the entire contents of the password file are displayed.

```
                        usera@bookfedora:~                      _  □  x
File  Edit  View  Search  Terminal  Help
[usera@bookfedora ~]$ cat /etc/passwd
daemon:x:2:2:daemon:/sbin:/sbin/nologin
adm:x:3:4:adm:/var/adm:/sbin/nologin
lp:x:4:7:lp:/var/spool/lpd:/sbin/nologin
sync:x:5:0:sync:/sbin:/bin/sync
shutdown:x:6:0:shutdown:/sbin:/sbin/shutdown
halt:x:7:0:halt:/sbin:/sbin/halt
mail:x:8:12:mail:/var/spool/mail:/sbin/nologin
uucp:x:10:14:uucp:/var/spool/uucp:/sbin/nologin
operator:x:11:0:operator:/root:/sbin/nologin
games:x:12:100:games:/usr/games:/sbin/nologin
gopher:x:13:30:gopher:/var/gopher:/sbin/nologin
ftp:x:14:50:FTP User:/var/ftp:/sbin/nologin
nobody:x:99:99:Nobody:/:/sbin/nologin
usbmuxd:x:113:113:usbmuxd user:/:/sbin/nologin
avahi-autoipd:x:170:170:Avahi IPv4LL Stack:/var/lib/avahi-autoipd:/sbin/nologin
smolt:x:999:998:Smolt:/usr/share/smolt:/sbin/nologin
dbus:x:81:81:System message bus:/:/sbin/nologin
abrt:x:173:173::/etc/abrt:/sbin/nologin
avahi:x:70:70:Avahi mDNS/DNS-SD Stack:/var/run/avahi-daemon:/sbin/nologin
rtkit:x:172:172:RealtimeKit:/proc:/sbin/nologin
pulse:x:998:996:PulseAudio System Daemon:/var/run/pulse:/sbin/nologin
saslauth:x:997:994:"Saslauthd user":/var/empty/saslauth:/sbin/nologin
openvpn:x:996:993:OpenVPN:/etc/openvpn:/sbin/nologin
gdm:x:42:42::/var/lib/gdm:/sbin/nologin
nm-openconnect:x:995:992:NetworkManager user for OpenConnect:/:/sbin/nologin
mailnull:x:47:47::/var/spool/mqueue:/sbin/nologin
smmsp:x:51:51::/var/spool/mqueue:/sbin/nologin
sshd:x:74:74:Privilege-separated SSH:/var/empty/sshd:/sbin/nologin
chrony:x:994:991:::/var/lib/chrony:/sbin/nologin
tcpdump:x:72:72::/:/sbin/nologin
user:x:1001:1001:user:/home/user:/bin/bash
[usera@bookfedora ~]$
```

FIGURE 9-13   An example of using the **cat** command

The password file contains the accounts of users and processes that can log on to the Linux operating system. The contents of each entry in the password file are divided into seven fields, and each file is divided by a colon (:). For example, the first line displayed is *root:x:0:0:root:/root:/bin/bash*. The first field specifies that the account is *root*. The root user can delete, modify, or do anything with the file. This entry is followed by an *x*. The encrypted passwords have been moved for security purposes to a file called **shadow**. During installation, the option to shadow passwords is normally presented. After *x* comes a colon followed by a zero. The zero is the user ID. This is a unique ID assigned to each account. This identifier is used throughout the Linux operating system to identify users and their files. Another zero follows the user ID. This is the group ID. Notice at the bottom of Figure 9-13 that the entry in the field for the *usera* user ID is *1001*. Refer to Figure 9-5 to see where this ID was assigned. The *root* account belongs to the zero ID. Any user that belongs to the zero group belongs to the same group as *root*. After the second zero is *:root*. This *root* is the account description for the account. After this field is *:/root*, which is the home directory for the account. The user is placed into this account when logged on to the system. The last field is *:/bin/bash*. This defines the executable program that is used during user logon. In this case, **bash** is the command shell that will run.

Directory Operations

The cd Command   The command to change directories in Linux is **cd**. The structure for the **cd** command is **cd *[destination-directory]***. The command **cd** was used to change to the root directory **/**, as shown in Figure 9-14. At that point, the command **ls -l** was entered. This produces the results shown in Figure 9-14. This provides a long listing of the components of the root directory. The following are the directories normally encountered in the Linux file system that will always be there:

> **cd**
> Linux command for changing directories.

```
                              usera@bookfedora:/                       _  □  ×

 File  Edit  View  Search  Terminal  Help
[usera@bookfedora /]$ ls -l
total 90
dr-xr-xr-x.    2 root root  4096 Feb 21 17:20 bin
dr-xr-xr-x.    6 root root  1024 Feb 20 14:25 boot
drwxr-xr-x.   18 root root  3440 Feb 20 05:47 dev
drwxr-xr-x.  117 root root 12288 Feb 21 18:12 etc
drwxr-xr-x.    4 root root  4096 Feb 21 18:07 home
dr-xr-xr-x.   20 root root 12288 Feb 21 17:20 lib
drwx------.    2 root root 16384 Nov  2 20:26 lost+found
drwxr-xr-x.    2 root root    40 Feb 21 17:17 media
drwxr-xr-x.    3 root root  4096 Feb 20 14:24 mnt
drwxr-xr-x.    2 root root  4096 Jul 29  2011 opt
dr-xr-xr-x.  143 root root     0 Feb 20 05:47 proc
dr-xr-x---.    6 root root  4096 Feb 21 18:24 root
drwxr-xr-x.   33 root root  1100 Feb 21 18:36 run
dr-xr-xr-x.    2 root root 12288 Feb 21 17:20 sbin
drwxr-xr-x.    2 root root  4096 Jul 29  2011 srv
drwxr-xr-x.   12 root root     0 Feb 20 05:47 sys
drwxrwxrwt.   22 root root  4096 Feb 21 18:38 tmp
drwxr-xr-x.   12 root root  4096 Nov  2 20:28 usr
drwxr-xr-x.   17 root root  4096 Nov  2 20:31 var
[usera@bookfedora /]$
```

FIGURE 9-14   The long listing of the components in the root directory

- **/bin**: Contains all the binary programs and executables.

- **/boot**: Where the Linux kernel resides. A *kernel* is the actual operating system image that boots up when the computer is turned on. If the kernel is not there, Linux does not boot.

- **/dev**: Where the device files reside. Examples of device files are drivers for the monitor, keyboard, modem, and hard drive.

- **/etc**: Where Linux holds the majority of its configuration files. For example, a program running under Linux will have its configuration files located in */etc*.

- **/home**: The directory where all user directories are located. Home directories for new user accounts are placed in this directory.

- **/lib**: The location for libraries that Linux uses, such as static and shared libraries.

- **/lost+found**: This directory is used to place files that have lost their identity, possibly due to hard drive errors.

- **/mnt**: The location where mounted directories are located. For example, an external drive will be mounted through this directory. *Mount* means that a file system has been made available to the user.

- **/opt**: This is where 'optional' software is typically installed.

- **/proc**: The status of the operating system is kept in this directory—for memory, hard drive, device drivers, memory usage, uptime (how long the computer has been running), and user IDs.

- **/root**: This is the root user ID home directory and is where the root user is placed at login.

- **/run**: The new directory is designed to allow applications to store the data they require in order to operate.

- **/sbin**: The system binary directory, the location where Linux keeps its system and executable program files.

- **/srv**: The directory where server working directories reside.

- **/tmp**: This directory is used as a temporary holding area for applications. This directory is available to all users logged onto the machine. The */tmp* directory gets cleared out when the machine boots up.

- **/usr**: This is the location for the user files that are related to the user programs.

- **/var**: The files in this directory change over time. For example, system log files and mail folders appear here. From time to time, the system administrator will delete files in */var* to clean up the drive.

The pwd Command   The next command examined is **pwd** (print working directory). The Linux directory path is complicated, and this command is available for the user to find where he or she is currently located. This is useful when files are being moved or deleted. The user uses the **pwd** command to verify the current working directory, as demonstrated in Figure 9-15.

> **pwd**
> Linux command to print the working (current) directory.

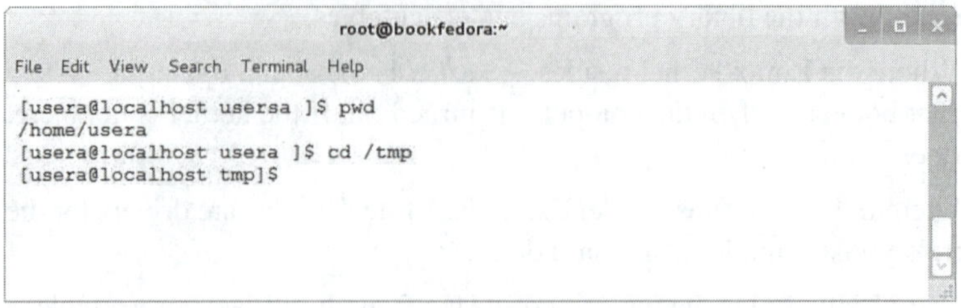

```
                            root@bookfedora:~                    _  □  X
File  Edit  View  Search  Terminal  Help

[usera@localhost usersa ]$ pwd
/home/usera
[usera@localhost usera ]$ cd /tmp
[usera@localhost tmp]$
```

FIGURE 9-15   An example of the text displayed when entering the **pwd** command

In this example, **pwd** returns */home/usera/,* indicating we are in *usera*'s directory. The following information is returned by the **pwd** command:

> *usera:* Account name
>
> *@localhost:* Name of the Linux machine
>
> *usera:* Name of the current directory

The second part of Figure 9-15 demonstrates that the name of the current directory changes if the directory changes. The third line shows that the command **cd tmp** (change directory tmp) is used to change the working directory to *tmp*. The prompt now displays **[usera@localhost tmp]**, indicating that the current directory is *tmp*.

The mkdir and rmdir Commands   This section demonstrates the Linux command for creating or making a directory. The command is **mkdir**, for *make directory.* The structure for the command is **mkdir *[directory-name].*** In the example shown in Figure 9-16, **mkdir files** is used to create a directory called *files.* The command *ls* is used to display the *usera* home directory contents and *files* is listed. The long listing of the directory using the **ls -la** command shows that *files* is indeed a directory, indicated by a *d* in the leftmost field of the attributes. The command to remove a directory is **rmdir**. The structure for the command is **rmdir *[directory-name].*** This command requires that the directory being removed is empty.

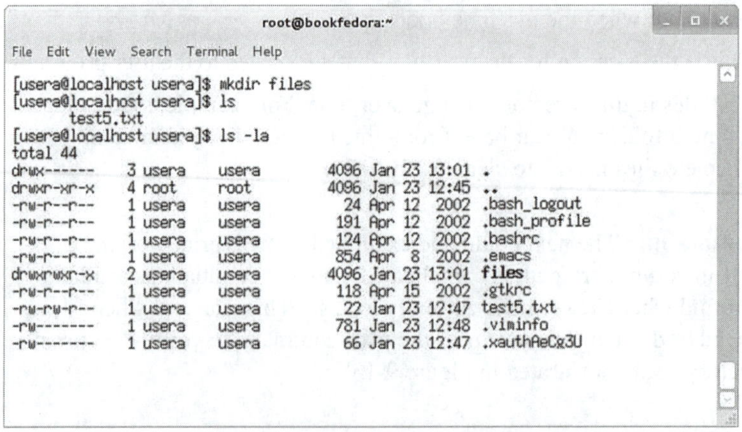

mkdir
Linux command to make a directory.

rmdir
Linux command to remove a directory.

```
                            root@bookfedora:~                    _  □  X
File  Edit  View  Search  Terminal  Help

[usera@localhost usera]$ mkdir files
[usera@localhost usera]$ ls
       test5.txt
[usera@localhost usera]$ ls -la
total 44
drwx------   3 usera    usera         4096 Jan 23 13:01 .
drwxr-xr-x   4 root     root          4096 Jan 23 12:45 ..
-rw-r--r--   1 usera    usera           24 Apr 12  2002 .bash_logout
-rw-r--r--   1 usera    usera          191 Apr 12  2002 .bash_profile
-rw-r--r--   1 usera    usera          124 Apr 12  2002 .bashrc
-rw-r--r--   1 usera    usera          854 Apr  8  2002 .emacs
drwxrwxr-x   2 usera    usera         4096 Jan 23 13:01 files
-rw-r--r--   1 usera    usera          118 Apr 15  2002 .gtkrc
-rw-rw-r--   1 usera    usera           22 Jan 23 12:47 test5.txt
-rw-------   1 usera    usera          781 Jan 23 12:48 .viminfo
-rw-------   1 usera    usera           66 Jan 23 12:47 .xauthAeCg3U
```

FIGURE 9-16   An example of creating a directory using the **mkdir** command

File Operations

The rm Command   The purpose of a basic operating system is to create, modify, and delete files. The next example shows how to delete files in Linux. The command to delete a file is **rm**, short for *remove*. The command structure is **rm *[file-name]*.** The command **ls -al** has been entered to display a long listing of files and hidden files in the directory, as demonstrated in Figure 9-17.

> **rm**
> Linux command to delete a file.

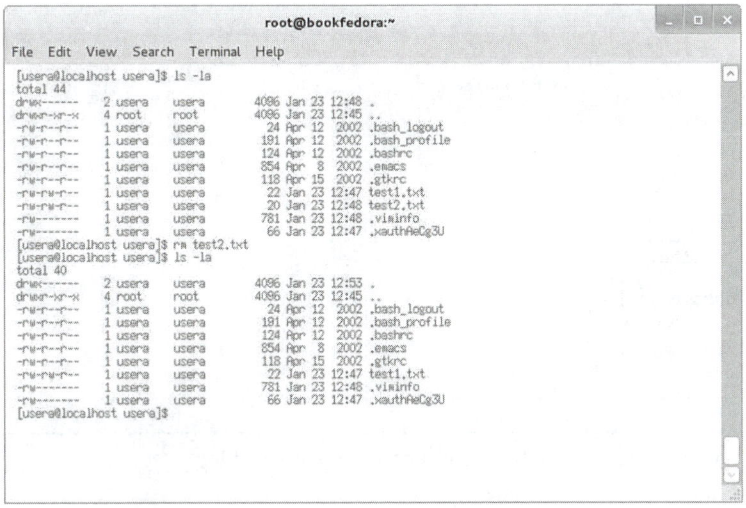

FIGURE 9-17   Using the **rm** command to remove a file in Linux

Notice that the directory contains two text files: *test1.txt* and *test2.txt.* The attributes for these files are listed on the left. These are read/write (rw) for the user, read/write (rw) for the group, and read only (r) for others. This means that any user in the group usera can also change the *usera* file. The owner of the file is *usera,* and the group is also *usera.* The next number is the file size, followed by the date and time the file was created and, lastly, the file name.

In this example, the file *test2.txt* will be removed using the command **rm test2.txt**, as shown in Figure 9-17. The *test2.txt* file is shown in the top of the screen. The command **rm test2.txt** is entered, and the files are redisplayed using **ls -la**, and the *text2.txt* file is no longer listed. The file has been deleted. Note that, in the Linux file system, there is *not* an undo option. This means that once a file is deleted, it is gone. What about a trash bin? Linux does not provide a trash bin to temporarily hold deleted files, but certain Linux GUIs do apply this concept.

The mv Command   The next example demonstrates how to move a file in Linux. The command to move a file is **mv**, short for *move*. The **mv** command serves two purposes:

> **mv**
> Linux command for moving or renaming a file.

- To rename a file
- To move the file to a different directory.

The command structure is **mv** *[filename]* *[new-filename]*.

In this example, the **mv** command is used to rename the file *text1.txt* to *text5.txt,* as demonstrated in Figure 9-18. In this example, the **cat** command is used to display the contents of the *test1.txt* file. This is being done so that the contents of the files can be compared after the move. The **mv** command is next used to rename *text1.txt* to *test5.txt.* The contents of the *test5.txt* file are displayed using the **cat** command, showing that the contents of *test1.txt* and *test5.txt* are the same and only the file-name has changed.

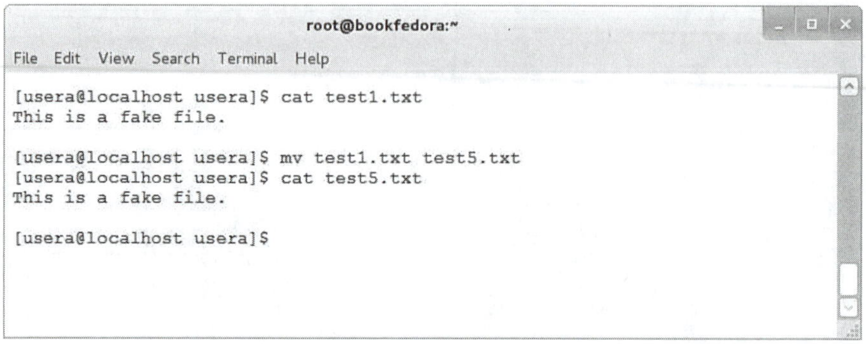

```
                            root@bookfedora:~                          _ □ ×

 File  Edit  View  Search  Terminal  Help

 [usera@localhost usera]$ cat test1.txt
 This is a fake file.

 [usera@localhost usera]$ mv test1.txt test5.txt
 [usera@localhost usera]$ cat test5.txt
 This is a fake file.

 [usera@localhost usera]$
```

FIGURE 9-18   An example of using the **mv** command to rename a file

The next step is to show that files can be moved from one directory to another using the **mv** command. In this case, the *test5.txt* file will be moved from the *usera* direc-tory to the *usera/files* subdirectory. The command for doing this is **mv test5.txt files/,** as shown in Figure 9-19. This specifies that the *test5.txt* file is to be moved to the *files* directory using the directory path *files/.* A logical next step is to verify that the file was moved to the *files* directory. The command **cd files** is entered, changing the working directory to *files,* as shown in Figure 9-19. The prompt now displays [usera@localhost files]. The command **pwd** (print working directory) also shows that the working directory is now */home/usera/files.* The information for the prompt and for print working directory is slightly different, but both indicate that the work-ing directory is *files.* The **ls** command shows that the *test5.txt* file has indeed been moved to the *files* directory. The long listing **ls -la** shows that the file properties have not changed. The owner of the file and group assignment have not changed.

The cp Command   The command to copy files in Linux is **cp**. The structure of the command is **cp** *[source filename] [destination filename].* In this example, a file called *test5.txt* will be copied to a new file called *test6.txt.* The **ls** command is first used to display the files in the *usera@localhost* files directory, as shown in Figure 9-20. The only file listed is *test5.txt.* The **cp** command is next used to copy the file to *test6.txt,* as shown in Figure 9-20. The **ls** command is used again to display the directory contents, and both files *test5.txt* and *test6.txt* are now displayed. The file was successfully copied.

> **cp**
> Linux command to copy files.

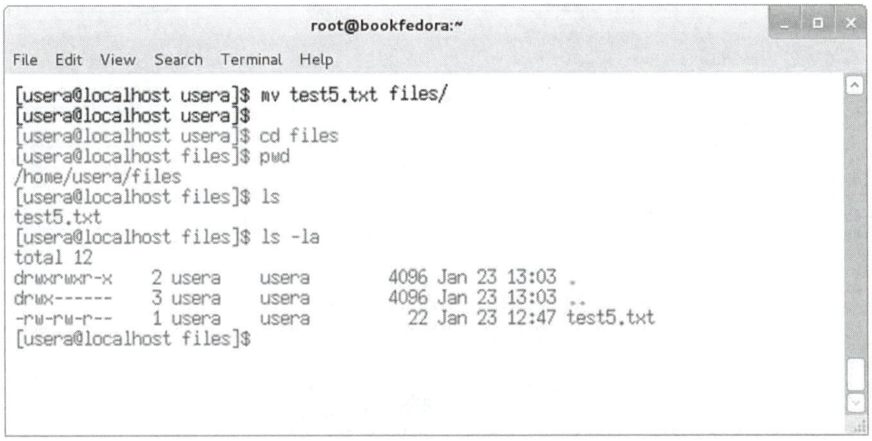

FIGURE 9-19 An example of moving a file using the **mv** command

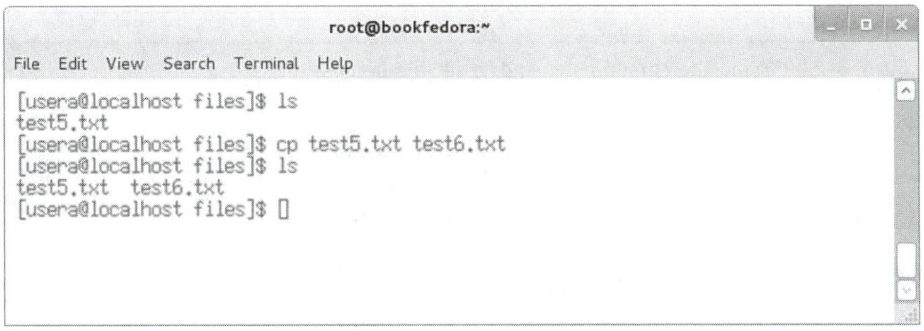

FIGURE 9-20 An example of using the **cp** command

Permissions and Ownership

The chmod Command The **chmod** command is used in Linux to change permissions on files and directories. The structure of the command is **chmod** *[permissions setting] [filename]*. For example, this command lets you specify if the file is readable (r), writable (w), or executable (x). A long list of the files in the *usera* account shows that the file *test5.txt* has *rw* in the attributes in the owner's space, as shown in Figure 9-21. File *test6.txt* shows that the user has read (r)/write (w) privileges, the group has read (r)/write (w) privileges, and the outside world has read (r) privileges (-rw-rw-r--).

chmod uses a value to turn a privilege on or off. The value is specified for the owner, the group, and others. Table 9-3 shows how the place values are established for the owner, group, and outside user. For example, a value of 4 0 0 turns on bit position 2, the read attribute for the owner (-r). A value of 6 0 0 turns on bit positions 2 and 3, read and write for the owner (-rw); and a value of 7 0 0 turns on bits 2, 3, and 4, setting read, write, and executable permissions for the owner (-rwx). A value of 6 4 0 turns on bits 2, 3, and 5, setting read and write permissions for the owner and read permission for the group (-rw -r- ---).

> **chmod**
> Command used in Linux to change permissions on files and directories.

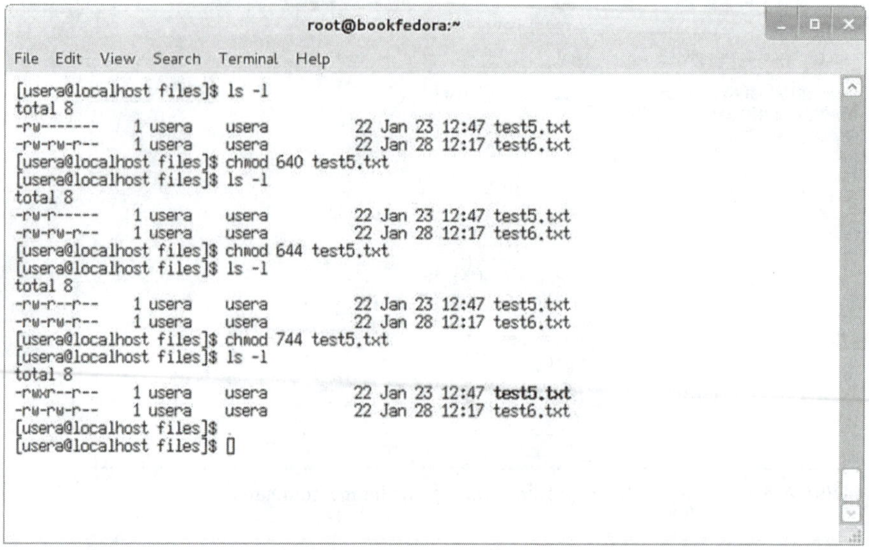

```
                          root@bookfedora:~                          [_][□][X]
 File  Edit  View  Search  Terminal  Help
 [usera@localhost files]$ ls -l
 total 8
 -rw-------    1 usera    usera           22 Jan 23 12:47 test5.txt
 -rw-rw-r--    1 usera    usera           22 Jan 28 12:17 test6.txt
 [usera@localhost files]$ chmod 640 test5.txt
 [usera@localhost files]$ ls -l
 total 8
 -rw-r-----    1 usera    usera           22 Jan 23 12:47 test5.txt
 -rw-rw-r--    1 usera    usera           22 Jan 28 12:17 test6.txt
 [usera@localhost files]$ chmod 644 test5.txt
 [usera@localhost files]$ ls -l
 total 8
 -rw-r--r--    1 usera    usera           22 Jan 23 12:47 test5.txt
 -rw-rw-r--    1 usera    usera           22 Jan 28 12:17 test6.txt
 [usera@localhost files]$ chmod 744 test5.txt
 [usera@localhost files]$ ls -l
 total 8
 -rwxr--r--    1 usera    usera           22 Jan 23 12:47 test5.txt
 -rw-rw-r--    1 usera    usera           22 Jan 28 12:17 test6.txt
 [usera@localhost files]$
 [usera@localhost files]$ []
```

FIGURE 9-21   Using the **chmod** command to set file permissions

TABLE 9-3   **Attribute Settings for File Permissions**

Bit Position	1	2	3	4	5	6	7	8	9	10
	Directory	Owner			Group			Others		
Bit Values		4	2	1	4	2	1	4	2	1
	*	r	w	x	r	w	x	r	w	x

The directory bit can display the following attributes: d—directory; b—block; c—character; —no entry specified

Another way to determine the permission settings for each permission field (owner, group, others) is to assign the following values to each permission:

> read: 4
>
> write: 2
>
> executable: 1

To turn on the read permission for the owner simply requires that a four (4) be placed in the first permission field. For example, **chmod 4 0 0** *[filename]* sets read only permissions for the owner.

Turning on more than one permission requires that the sum of the permission values be entered. For example, turning on read/write privileges for the owner requires entering a six (6) in the proper permission field. The value is determined as follows:

Read: 4
write: 2
executable: <u>0</u>
            6

The zero is assigned to the executable because this permission is not desired. The command to enable read/write privileges for the owner is **chmod 6 0 0 *[filename]*.**

The same steps can be applied to assigning permissions to all fields. For example, assume that the following permissions are specified:

owner: read, write, executable
group: read, executable
everyone: read, executable

The numeric entry for each permission field in the ***chmod*** command can be determined as follows:

	owner	group	others
read	4	4	4
write	2	0	0
executable	<u>1</u>	<u>1</u>	<u>1</u>
	7	5	5

Therefore, the command **chmod 7 5 5 *[filename]*** is used to set the permissions for the owner, group, and others.

In the example shown in Figure 9-21, read permission is to be given to the group for the *test5.txt* file. The command **chmod 640 test5.txt** is entered. The **6** sets the read/write privilege for the owner, the **4** sets the permission to read for the group, and the **0** clears any attributes for others. The **ls** command is next used to provide a long listing of the files in the *usera* account. The attributes for the *test5.txt* file have changed to (r w - r - - - - -), indicating that group now has read privileges.

In the next step, the world will be given the privilege to read the *test5.txt* file. The command **chmod 644 test5.txt** is entered. Again, the **6** sets the read/write privilege for the owner, the *4* sets the permission to read for the group, and the next **4** sets the permission for others to read the file. The attributes for the *test5.txt* file have now changed to (r w - r - - r - -), indicating that outside users have read privileges.

The last example using **chmod** shows how to set the executable (x) permission for a file. An executable permission allows the program or script to run. The command **chmod 744 test5.txt** is entered. This instruction gives the owner read/write and executable privileges on the file and grants the group and everyone else read permission. The **ls** command is used to display a long listing. The attributes for the file

> **executable (x) permission**
> Allows the program or script to run.

test5.txt now show (r w x r - - r - -). This confirms that the permissions have been properly set. The result is shown in Figure 9-21.

The executable setting is used by Linux to distinguish files that can be executed (run) on the system. Files that do not have an *x* attribute are considered to be data files, libraries, and so on. The *x* is also used by Linux when the system searches for executable files on the hard drive.

The chown Command The next Linux command examined is **chown**, which is used to change the ownership of the file. The structure of the command is **chown *[new owner] [filename]*.** This command can only be applied to files the user owns. The exception to this is *root* (the superuser), who can change permissions on any files. In this example, the ownership of the *test5.txt* file is going to be changed to a user called *network*. (*Note:* The new owner will be *network,* a user on this same Linux machine. In fact, changing ownership can only be done using existing users.) The long list of *usera's* files directory shows two files: *test5.txt* and *test6.txt* (see Figure 9-22). The owner of *test5.txt* is *usera*. The objective of this exercise is to change ownership of the *test5.txt* file to *network*. The command **chown network text5.txt** is entered. A long list of the directory now shows that the ownership of *test5.txt* now resides with *network*. The steps for changing file ownership are shown in Figure 9-22.

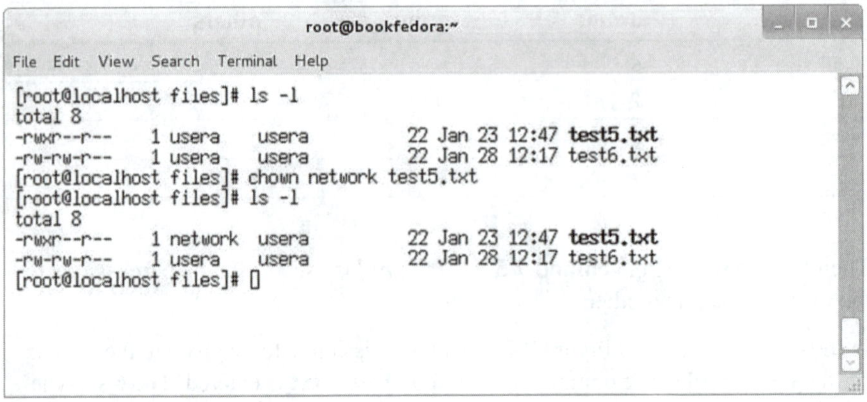

```
                              root@bookfedora:~                        _  □  ×

File  Edit  View  Search  Terminal  Help
[root@localhost files]# ls -l
total 8
-rwxr--r--    1 usera    usera          22 Jan 23 12:47 test5.txt
-rw-rw-r--    1 usera    usera          22 Jan 28 12:17 test6.txt
[root@localhost files]# chown network test5.txt
[root@localhost files]# ls -l
total 8
-rwxr--r--    1 network  usera          22 Jan 23 12:47 test5.txt
-rw-rw-r--    1 usera    usera          22 Jan 28 12:17 test6.txt
[root@localhost files]# []
```

FIGURE 9-22 An example of using the **chown** command to change file ownership

The file is still in *usera*'s directory, but the ownership has changed to *network*. The group attributes (permissions) will now have to be set by *network* if *usera* is to have permission to read, write, or execute this file, even though *usera* was the past owner and the file is in *usera*'s space. In fact, if *usera* tries to change permission on this file (*test5.txt*), Linux will prompt *usera* with the message *changing permissions of 'test5.txt': Operation not permitted.* This is shown in Figure 9-23.

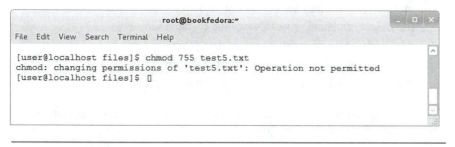

```
                         root@bookfedora:~                    _  □  ×

File  Edit  View  Search  Terminal  Help

[user@localhost files]$ chmod 755 test5.txt
chmod: changing permissions of 'test5.txt': Operation not permitted
[user@localhost files]$ []
```

FIGURE 9-23 The prompt displayed when an unauthorized user attempts to change file permissions

The chgrp Command The Linux command **chgrp** is used to change group ownership of files. The structure of the command is **chgrp** *[new group] [filename]*. This example demonstrates how to change the group ownership of a file. In this example, the group for file *test5.txt* will be changed. Figure 9-24 shows the steps for this operation. A long listing of the *usera* files directory shows that the group associated with *test5.txt* is *usera*. The command **chgrp mail test5.txt** is next used to change group ownership of the file to *mail*. The long listing command is used again to list the file in the *usera* files directory. The screen shows that the owner is *network* and the group ownership of *test5.txt* has changed from *usera* to *mail*. This means that any members of the group *mail* now have read (r -) privileges.

> **chgrp**
> Linux command used to change group ownership of a file.

```
                         root@bookfedora:~                    _  □  ×

File  Edit  View  Search  Terminal  Help

[root@localhost files]# ls -l
total 8
-rwxr--r--   1 network  usera        22 Jan 23 12:47 test5.txt
-rw-rw-r--   1 usera    usera        22 Jan 28 12:17 test6.txt
[root@localhost files]# chgrp mail test5.txt
[root@localhost files]# ls -l
total 8
-rwxr--r--   1 network  mail         22 Jan 23 12:47 test5.txt
-rw-rw-r--   1 usera    usera        22 Jan 28 12:17 test6.txt
[root@localhost files]# []
```

FIGURE 9-24 An example of changing the group ownership of a file

9-3   LINUX ADMINISTRATION COMMANDS

The objective of this section is for you to gain an understanding of the key Linux administration commands. The commands presented focus on those most often used by the network administrator:

man: Used to display the online text manual

ps: Used to examine processes running on the machine

su: Used to become another user on the system

mount: Used in Linux to mount an external drive

shutdown: Used to shut the Linux system down gracefully

This section concludes with an overview of some basic Linux shortcuts that will help simplify the administrator's job.

The *man* (manual) Command

The first command examined is **man**, used to display the online text manual for Linux. Manual pages for most Linux commands and features are available by simply entering the command **man** followed by the name of the option. For example, if you want to know how to use the **ps** command, entering **man ps** (see Figure 9-25) will display the contents of the manual lists for **ps** (see Figure 9-26).

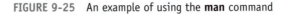

```
                          root@bookfedora:~                    _  □  ×

  File  Edit  View  Search  Terminal  Help

  [root@localhost root]# man ps
  [root@localhost root]#
```

FIGURE 9-25   An example of using the **man** command

```
                          root@bookfedora:~                    _  □  ×

  File  Edit  View  Search  Terminal  Help

  PS(1)                    Linux User's Manual                 PS(1)

  '
  NAME
        ps - report process status

  SYNOPSIS
        ps [options]

  DESCRIPTION
        ps  gives  a snapshot of the current processes. If you want a repetitive
        update of this status, use top. This man page documents the  /proc-based
        version of ps, or tries to.

  COMMAND-LINE OPTIONS
        This version of ps accepts several kinds of options.
              Unix98 options may be grouped and must be preceeded by a dash.
              BSD options may be grouped and must not be used with a dash.
              GNU long options are preceeded by two dashes.
        Options of different types may be freely mixed.

        Set the I_WANT_A_BROKEN_PS environment variable to force BSD syntax even
        when options are preceeded by a  dash.  The  PS_PERSONALITY  environment
        variable  (described  below) provides more detailed control of ps behav-
        ior.

        SIMPLE PROCESS SELECTION
           Switch      Description
           ()                                                         ()
```

FIGURE 9-26   The manual pages displayed by entering the command **man ps**

The manual pages provide extensive information about how to invoke the command, what options are available, what the fields mean that are displayed by the command—basically everything you need to know about the *ps* command.

There are many *man* pages on the Linux system, for utility programs, programming files, networking commands, and others. Adding the **-k** extension to the **man** command (for example, **man -k network**) instructs Linux to list all of the *man* pages that mention the specified topic. An example is provided (see Figure 9-27) that demonstrates how to use the **man -k** command to view all network-related *man* pages.

```
root@bookfedora:~

File   Edit   View   Search   Terminal   Help

[root@localhost root]# man -k network
Net::Cmd            (3pm)  - Network Command class (as used by FTP, SMTP etc)
Net::Time           (3pm)  - time and daytime network client interface
X                   (7x)   - a portable, network-transparent window system
endhostent [gethostbyname] (3)  - get network host entry
getaddrinfo         (3)    - network address and service translation
gethostbyaddr [gethostbyname] (3)  - get network host entry
gethostbyname       (3)    - get network host entry
herror [gethostbyname] (3)  - get network host entry
hstrerror [gethostbyname] (3)  - get network host entry
htonl [byteorder]   (3)    - convert values between host and network byte order
htons [byteorder]   (3)    - convert values between host and network byte order
ifconfig            (8)    - configure a network interface
inet_network [inet] (3)    - Internet address manipulation routines
inet_ntop           (3)    - Parse network address structures
inet_pton           (3)    - Create a network address structure
nameif              (8)    - name network interfaces based on MAC addresses
netdevice           (7)    - Low level access to Linux network devices
netreport           (1)    - request notification of network interface changes
netstat             (8)    - Print network connections, routing tables, interface statist
ics, masquerade connections, and multicast memberships
nhfsstone           (8)    - Network File System benchmark program
nkf                 (1)    - Network Kanji code conversion Filter v1.9
nmap                (1)    - Network exploration tool and security scanner
ntohl [byteorder]   (3)    - convert values between host and network byte order
ntohs [byteorder]   (3)    - convert values between host and network byte order
perlfaq9            (1)    - Networking ($Revision: 1.26 $, $Date: 1999/05/23 16:08:30 $)
ping                (8)    - send ICMP ECHO_REQUEST to network hosts
ping6 [ping]        (8)    - send ICMP ECHO_REQUEST to network hosts
png                 (5)    - Portable Network Graphics (PNG) format
```

FIGURE 9-27   Using the **man** command to display all pages related to *network*

The *ps* (processes) Command

The **ps** command lists the processes (or programs) running on the machine. The command **ps ux** lists all the processes running, as shown in Figure 9-28. Each of the fields returned by the **ps** command is listed from left to right in Table 9-4.

> **ps**
> Linux command used to list processes running on the machine.

```
                              root@bookfedora:~                        _  □  ×
File  Edit  View  Search  Terminal  Help

[root@localhost root]# ps ux
USER       PID %CPU %MEM   VSZ   RSS TTY      STAT START   TIME COMMAND
root         1  0.0  0.1  1368   476 ?        S    Jan18   0:04 init
root         2  0.0  0.0     0     0 ?        SW   Jan18   0:00 [keventd]
root         3  0.0  0.0     0     0 ?        SW   Jan18   0:00 [kapmd]
root         4  0.0  0.0     0     0 ?        SWN  Jan18   0:00 [ksoftirqd_CPU0]
root         5  0.0  0.0     0     0 ?        SW   Jan18   0:00 [kswapd]
root         6  0.0  0.0     0     0 ?        SW   Jan18   0:00 [bdflush]
root         7  0.0  0.0     0     0 ?        SW   Jan18   0:00 [kupdated]
root         8  0.0  0.0     0     0 ?        SW   Jan18   0:00 [mdrecoveryd]
root        12  0.0  0.0     0     0 ?        SW   Jan18   0:01 [kjournald]
root        91  0.0  0.0     0     0 ?        SW   Jan18   0:00 [khubd]
root       196  0.0  0.0     0     0 ?        SW   Jan18   0:00 [kjournald]
root       749  0.0  0.2  1428   560 ?        S    Jan18   0:00 syslogd -m 0
root       754  0.0  0.1  1364   444 ?        S    Jan18   0:00 klogd -x
root       915  0.0  0.1  1360   480 ?        S    Jan18   0:00 /usr/sbin/apmd -p 10 -w 5
root       982  0.0  0.3  2200   948 ?        S    Jan18   0:00 xinetd -stayalive -reuse
root      1023  0.0  0.7  4600  1816 ?        S    Jan18   0:00 sendmail: accepting conne
root      1042  0.0  0.1  1400   452 ?        S    Jan18   0:00 gpm -t ps/2 -m /dev/mouse
root      1060  0.0  0.2  1536   616 ?        S    Jan18   0:00 crond
root      1177  0.0  0.1  1344   400 tty1     S    Jan18   0:00 /sbin/mingetty tty1
root      1178  0.0  0.1  1344   400 tty2     S    Jan18   0:00 /sbin/mingetty tty2
root      1179  0.0  0.1  1344   400 tty3     S    Jan18   0:00 /sbin/mingetty tty3
root      1180  0.0  0.1  1344   400 tty4     S    Jan18   0:00 /sbin/mingetty tty4
root      1181  0.0  0.1  1344   400 tty5     S    Jan18   0:00 /sbin/mingetty tty5
root      1182  0.0  0.1  1344   400 tty6     S    Jan18   0:00 /sbin/mingetty tty6
root      1183  0.0  0.6  6144  1668 ?        S    Jan18   0:00 /usr/bin/gdm -nodaemon
root      1389  0.0  0.1  1716   460 ?        S    Jan18   0:00 esd -terminate -nobeeps -
root     16493  0.0  0.8  6668  2124 ?        S    Jan27   0:00 /usr/bin/gdm -nodaemon
root     16494  0.0  3.6 20120  9440 ?        S    Jan27   0:12 /usr/bin/X11/X :0 -auth /
root     16865  0.0  1.5  7300  4056 ?        S    12:13   0:01 /usr/bin/gnome-session
```

FIGURE 9-28 An example of using the **ps** command to list the processes currently running on a Linux machine

TABLE 9-4 Fields Returned by Inputting the ps Command

Field	Description
User	Identifies the owner of the process.
PID	Identifies the process ID, which is a number assigned to a process when it starts. For example, if PID1, then this is the first process started on the machine.
%CPU	Shows the % utilization of the CPU for that process.
%MEM	Specifies the % of memory being used by that process.
VSZ	The virtual size of the program.
RSS	Shows how much of the program (resident set size) is in memory.
TTY	Indicates if the process is interfacing with a terminal or a serial port.
STAT	The STAT (state field) indicates the status of the process:
	r—running
	z—zombie
	s—sleeping
	t—stopped

PID
Process ID

Field	Description
START	Indicates when the process started. This could list a time of minutes, hours, and/or days. It is not uncommon to have a process running for an extended period on Linux.
Time	Indicates the time the process has actually spent running.
Command	Lists the actual command that was invoked to start the process.

The reason to examine running processes is to determine what processes are using the most machine resources. If a machine is running slowly, the **ps** command can be used to determine what process is using the majority of the CPU time. In some cases, it becomes necessary to *terminate* (shut down) a process to free up the machine's resources. The following are steps that should be followed to shut down a process:

1. Use the **ps** command to identify the process using the computer's resources (CPU and memory). Determine the PID for the process. For example, it has been determined that a process with a PID of 1023 must be shut down.

2. The network administrator should next contact the user of the process and inform him or her to shut down (kill) the process.

3. The command for killing the process is **kill** *[PID]*. An example is shown in Figure 9-29 for killing the process 1023. This command notifies the process to terminate. The process then begins closing files and libraries and shuts down immediately. Some processes are difficult to kill, so the command **kill -9** *[PID]* can be used. An example is shown in Figure 9-29. This is the last-resort step for killing a process. The **kill -9** command is somewhat messy in that the process is stopped without properly closing any open files, libraries, and so on.

> **kill [*PID*], kill -9 [*PID*]**
> Linux commands used to kill a process.

```
                        root@bookfedora:~                       _  □  ×

File  Edit  View  Search  Terminal  Help

root    16987  0.0  0.7   6104 1932 ?    S   12:13  0:00 gnome-smproxy --sm-config
root    17003  0.1  1.3   5888 3564 ?    S   12:14  0:02 sawfish --sm-client-id 11
root    17018  0.1  3.8  31428 9792 ?    S   12:14  0:01 nautilus --sm-client-id 1
root    17020  0.0  2.1   8788 5504 ?    S   12:14  0:01 panel --sm-client-id 117f
root    17022  0.0  1.1   7024 3040 ?    S   12:14  0:00 magicdev --sm-client-id 1
root    17024  0.0  0.6   3144 1588 ?    S   12:14  0:00 /usr/bin/gconfd-1 10
root    17026  0.0  0.4   3076 1180 ?    S   12:14  0:00 gnome-name-service
root    17028  0.0  1.5   7500 3876 ?    S   12:14  0:00 deskguide_applet --activa
[root@localhost root]# kill 1023
[root@localhost root]# kill -9 1023
[root@localhost root]# []
```

FIGURE 9-29   An example of using the **kill** and **kill -9** commands

The *su* (substitute user) Command

The **su** (substitute user) command is used to become another user on the system. This command assumes that the user has a valid account on the system and the password is known. The command structure is **su** *[username]*. Figure 9-30 shows an example of using this command. In this example, *root* is using the **su** command to log in as *usera*. This command is useful for administration. The administrator can be logged in as *root* to make some changes to the system that affect *usera,* such as checking FTP options or web access. The administrator can then use the **su** command to become *usera* and check to see if the changes worked. In fact, root user can use the **su** command and become any user on the system without knowing that user's password. Any authorized user can use the **su** command as long as another valid user account and password are known.

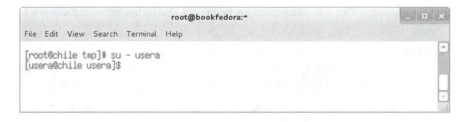

FIGURE 9-30   An example of using the **su** command to become another user

The *mount* Command

The next command examined is **mount**, which is used to join an external file system, such as that found on a CD-ROM or floppy, to the Linux file system to allow the files to be accessed. The external drives (for example, USB and CD-ROM) don't mount automatically unless the system has been previously configured to mount these drives. This means that a directory has to be provided to the Linux file system for the external device to mount to.

Linux lists files in the **fstab** file (*/etc* directory) that contain the arguments used when the mount command for a specific drive is requested. Figure 9-31 shows a listing of the *fstab* file in the */etc* directory.

The contents of the *fstab* file shows the filesystems that will be available (mounted) at boot time. Linux now uses logical volume management to manage hard drives and their partitions, which adds another level of abstraction between the filesystem and the physical hard drive partitions. In this image, one logical volume handles the entire operating system and the other is designated for swap space.

The **mount** command enables a drive, file, and so on, to be mounted (refer to the *man* page for the mount options). There are two ways to mount a drive. In this case, the command will be issued to mount the computer's CD-ROM.

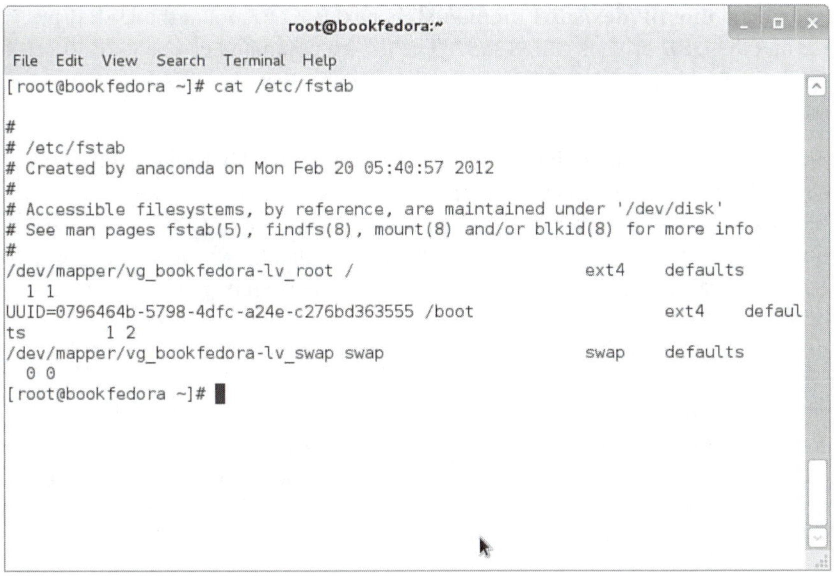

```
[root@bookfedora ~]# cat /etc/fstab

#
# /etc/fstab
# Created by anaconda on Mon Feb 20 05:40:57 2012
#
# Accessible filesystems, by reference, are maintained under '/dev/disk'
# See man pages fstab(5), findfs(8), mount(8) and/or blkid(8) for more info
#
/dev/mapper/vg_bookfedora-lv_root /                       ext4    defaults
  1 1
UUID=0796464b-5798-4dfc-a24e-c276bd363555 /boot           ext4    defaul
ts        1 2
/dev/mapper/vg_bookfedora-lv_swap swap                    swap    defaults
  0 0
[root@bookfedora ~]#
```

FIGURE 9-31 Listing of contents for the fstab file

Newly mounted files will overlay existing files in the *mount* directory; however, this is a virtual mount. No files are actually being written onto the *mount* file directory. The command **df -kh** will display the devices mounted on the system. The **df** command provides a breakdown of the file systems that have been mounted on the operating system. The **-kh** extension instructs the command to display the listing in **k**—kilobytes and **h**—human readable form. Figure 9-32 provides an example of using the **mount** command.

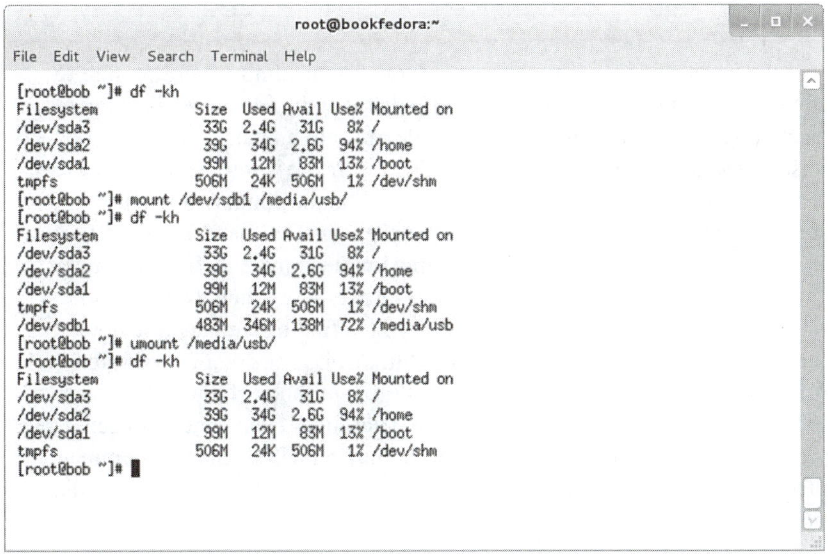

```
[root@bob ~]# df -kh
Filesystem            Size  Used Avail Use% Mounted on
/dev/sda3              33G  2.4G   31G   8% /
/dev/sda2              39G   34G  2.6G  94% /home
/dev/sda1              99M   12M   83M  13% /boot
tmpfs                 506M   24K  506M   1% /dev/shm
[root@bob ~]# mount /dev/sdb1 /media/usb/
[root@bob ~]# df -kh
Filesystem            Size  Used Avail Use% Mounted on
/dev/sda3              33G  2.4G   31G   8% /
/dev/sda2              39G   34G  2.6G  94% /home
/dev/sda1              99M   12M   83M  13% /boot
tmpfs                 506M   24K  506M   1% /dev/shm
/dev/sdb1             483M  346M  138M  72% /media/usb
[root@bob ~]# umount /media/usb/
[root@bob ~]# df -kh
Filesystem            Size  Used Avail Use% Mounted on
/dev/sda3              33G  2.4G   31G   8% /
/dev/sda2              39G   34G  2.6G  94% /home
/dev/sda1              99M   12M   83M  13% /boot
tmpfs                 506M   24K  506M   1% /dev/shm
[root@bob ~]#
```

FIGURE 9-32 An example of using the **mount** and **umount** commands to mount and umount a USB drive

The command **mount /dev/sdb1 media/usb** is next used to mount the USB drive. Notice that the USB drive is called *sdb1*. The **df -kh** command can be used to verify the drive has been mounted. The listing now shows that the USB drive has been mounted.

It is important to understand that a drive must be unmounted before the media can be removed. The USB drive can be unmounted by using the command **umount /media/usb**, as shown in Figure 9-32. Note that you cannot unmount a device that has open files or directories. Entering the **df -kh** command now shows that the USB drive is no longer mounted. At this point, the USB drive can be removed.

The *shutdown* Command

The **shutdown** command is used to shut the Linux system down gracefully. This means that all open files and libraries are closed before the system turns off. The command in Linux to gracefully shut the system down is **shutdown -h now**. This command immediately shuts down the operating system effective. Figure 9-33 shows an example of using this command.

```
                              root@bookfedora:~                    _  □  ×

 File  Edit  View  Search  Terminal  Help

 [root@localhost root]# shutdown -h now
```

FIGURE 9-33   An example of using the **shutdown -h now** command

Linux Tips

Many of the tasks performed by the network or system administrator require repeated use of the same commands or require that lengthy file names be entered. This section presents some shortcuts available in Linux that help speed up the administrator's job. The first shortcut examined is the **up arrow**. The up arrow can be used to display the previous command entered on the command line in Linux. Pressing the up arrow again displays the next previous command. This is a useful way to recall the history of commands entered on the command line. When you find the command that you need, simply press **Enter** to execute the command. Repeatedly pressing the up arrow will allow you to find a command previously executed. The **history** command can be used to display the commands stored in the Linux system buffer. The history buffer can store thousands of entered commands. (*Note:* The history buffer can also be used to determine if someone has been using your computer. Simply entering the **history** command will display all commands executed on the system. You will be able to identify the commands that you did not execute.)

Another shortcut is the Tab key. This can be used to complete entries on the command line. For example, **cd ho[tab]** displays *cd home*. Linux searches for options that begin with *ho* to complete the entry. This is useful when long or complicated entries are used. In the case where there are multiple entries that satisfy the entry, the Tab key can be used to step through the options. Entering **f [tab]** will generate multiple possibilities. Pressing the Tab key will cycle you through each option. Pressing the Tab key twice will display all available Linux commands.

9-4 ADDING APPLICATIONS TO LINUX

The objective of this section is to demonstrate the use of the Yellowdog Updater, Modified (YUM) to install and uninstall applications and to query the system's database. YUM uses a database to keep track of the software installed on the system. This database is updated anytime new software is installed or software is removed. YUM keeps track of the name of the application, the version installed, and any associated files. The term *YUM* describes the entire package application and management system used in Fedora Linux. It is also the command to start the package manager: You obtain the manual listing for YUM by entering the command **man yum**. The text shown in Figure 9-34 will be displayed. The *man* page shows that there are many options for the command. YUM has been adopted by many other Linux distributions as an easy and efficient way to manage applications.

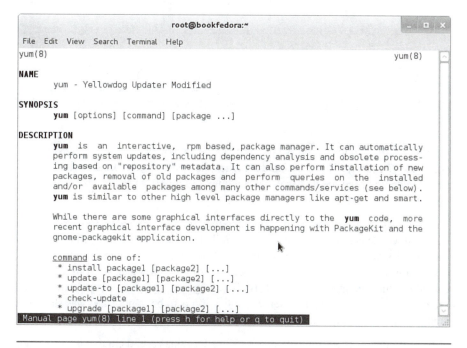

FIGURE 9-34 The man page for YUM

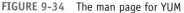

The first example of using YUM is a query all. When entered, the command **yum list** displays all the applications installed on the system. The **yum list** command is often used to search for an application on the Linux system. In this example, the command will be used to search for telnet. This can be done by using the **yum list**

Telnet
Terminal emulation application for TCP/IP networks.

application command, as shown in Figure 9-35. The command for doing this is **yum list telnet**. In this case, telnet (a terminal emulation application for TCP/IP networks) is on the system, and in fact, there is a *telnet-server.i686 1:0.17-51.fc16* and a *telnet 1:0.17-51.fc16,* which is the client.

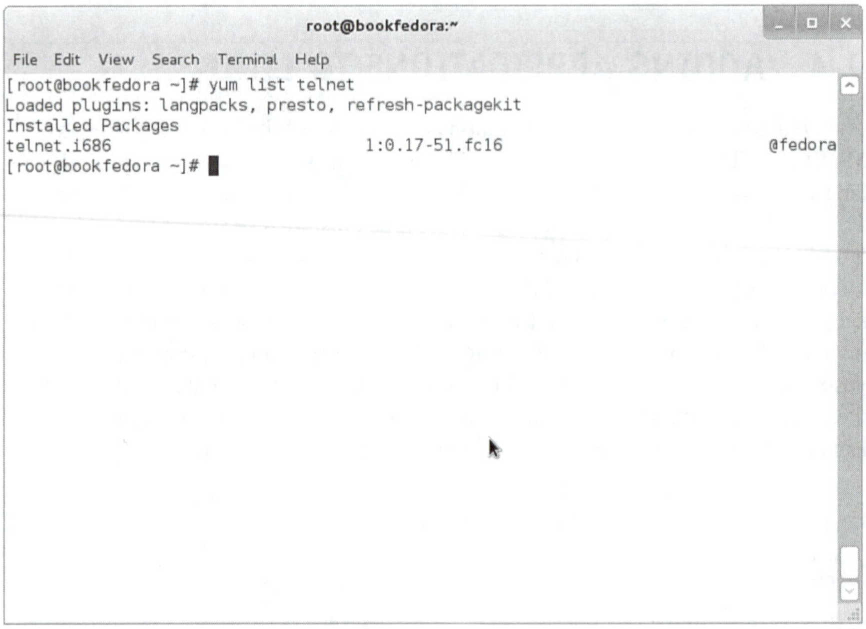

```
                          root@bookfedora:~                          _ □ ×

 File  Edit  View  Search  Terminal  Help
[root@bookfedora ~]# yum list telnet                                        ^
Loaded plugins: langpacks, presto, refresh-packagekit
Installed Packages
telnet.i686                        1:0.17-51.fc16                      @fedora
[root@bookfedora ~]# █
```

FIGURE 9-35   Using the **yum list telnet** command to search for files in the Linux system

yum provides
[filename]
Searches the yum database and returns the name of the file that matches the query.

Another useful tool to find out where a file came from is the command **yum provides** *[filename]*. This command searches the system's *yum* database and returns the name of the file that matches the query. Figure 9-36 shows an example of using this command.

The command **yum provides zdiff** was entered, and the name *gzip-1.4-3.fc15.i686* was returned. This indicates that the file *zdiff* belongs to the *gzip-1.4-3.fc15.i686* package. The next section demonstrates how to uninstall a package from the database. Uninstalling removes all files associated with that package. A prompt is displayed if a file is being removed that is also being used by another application. For example, assume that the telnet-server application is to be removed. It was shown in Figure 9-35 that the command **yum list telnet** command is used to search for telnet.

Every instance of telnet in the database is listed. In this case, the name *telnet-server.i686 1:0.17-51.fc16* and *telnet-0.17-20* (client) are listed.

An example is shown uninstalling both telnet applications in Figure 9-37. The telnet-server application is uninstalled using the command **yum remove telnet-server**. The telnet-client application is removed using the command **yum remove telnet**. The **yum list installed** command can be used to check if the application is still in the database.

FIGURE 9-36 An example of using the **yum provides** [*filename*] command

FIGURE 9-37 The steps for uninstalling the telnet-server and telnet-client applications and verifying that the applications are no longer in the database

An expected task performed by network and system administrators is to add web service to the network. This section presents the steps for adding the Apache web service to the Linux operating system. Apache is the standard web service for Linux, similar to MIIS for Microsoft Windows.

The command for installing the Apache web service is **yum install httpd**, as shown in Figure 9-38. On occasion, a prompt will be displayed that a certain application is missing. In this case, the missing software packages can be found on the Internet. The command to start the web server is */etc/init.d/httpd start,* as shown in Figure 9-39. This file was installed when the **yum command** was issued to install Apache. The screen displays the statement *Starting* httpd: [OK], which indicates that the service was successfully started.

```
                         root@bookfedora:/etc                          _ □ x

 File  Edit  View  Search  Terminal  Help
[root@bookfedora etc]# yum install httpd
Loaded plugins: langpacks, presto, refresh-packagekit
Setting up Install Process
Resolving Dependencies
--> Running transaction check
---> Package httpd.i686 0:2.2.22-1.fc16 will be installed
--> Processing Dependency: httpd-tools = 2.2.22-1.fc16 for package: httpd-2.2.22-1.fc
16.i686
--> Processing Dependency: libaprutil-1.so.0 for package: httpd-2.2.22-1.fc16.i686
--> Processing Dependency: libapr-1.so.0 for package: httpd-2.2.22-1.fc16.i686
--> Processing Dependency: apr-util-ldap for package: httpd-2.2.22-1.fc16.i686
--> Running transaction check
---> Package apr.i686 0:1.4.5-1.fc16 will be installed
---> Package apr-util.i686 0:1.3.12-1.fc16 will be installed
---> Package apr-util-ldap.i686 0:1.3.12-1.fc16 will be installed
---> Package httpd-tools.i686 0:2.2.22-1.fc16 will be installed
--> Finished Dependency Resolution

Dependencies Resolved

================================================================================
 Package              Arch          Version             Repository        Size
================================================================================
Installing:
 httpd                i686          2.2.22-1.fc16       updates          812 k
Installing for dependencies:
 apr                  i686          1.4.5-1.fc16        fedora           103 k
 apr-util             i686          1.3.12-1.fc16       fedora            82 k
 apr-util-ldap        i686          1.3.12-1.fc16       fedora            16 k
 httpd-tools          i686          2.2.22-1.fc16       updates           73 k
```

FIGURE 9-38   The steps for installing the Apache web service

Linux uses **Firefox** for an Internet web browser. The command for starting Firefox is **firefox**. The URL can be changed to the Linux machine simply by entering **http://localhost/**. Remember, the default name for the Linux machine is *localhost*. If the web service is working properly, the test page shown in Figure 9-40 should be displayed. This test page provides the administrator with information about the configuration files. Linux provides this as a default page for setting the web service.

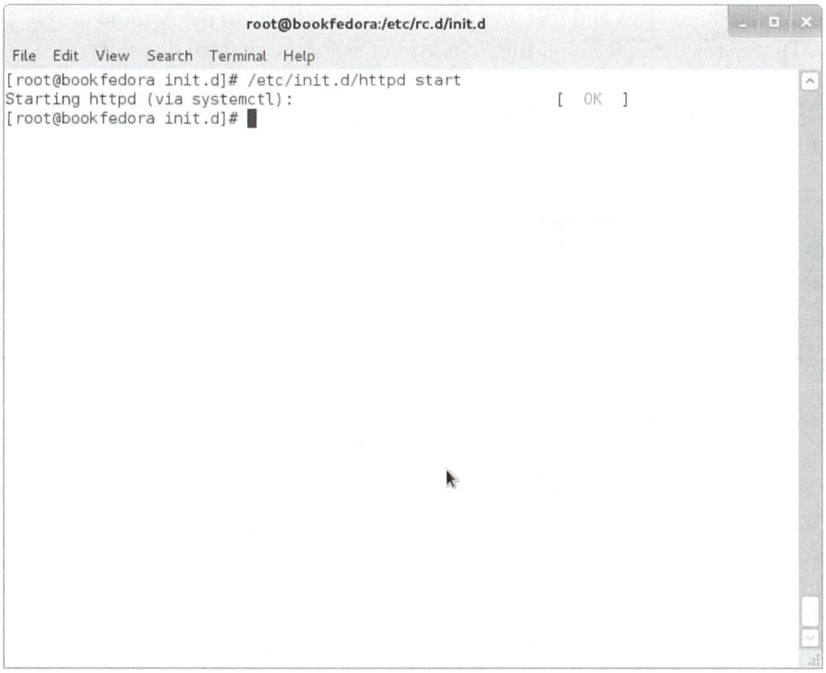

```
root@bookfedora:/etc/rc.d/init.d                            _ □ ×

File  Edit  View  Search  Terminal  Help

[root@bookfedora init.d]# /etc/init.d/httpd start
Starting httpd (via systemctl):                    [  OK  ]
[root@bookfedora init.d]# █
```

FIGURE 9-39   The steps for starting the Apache web service

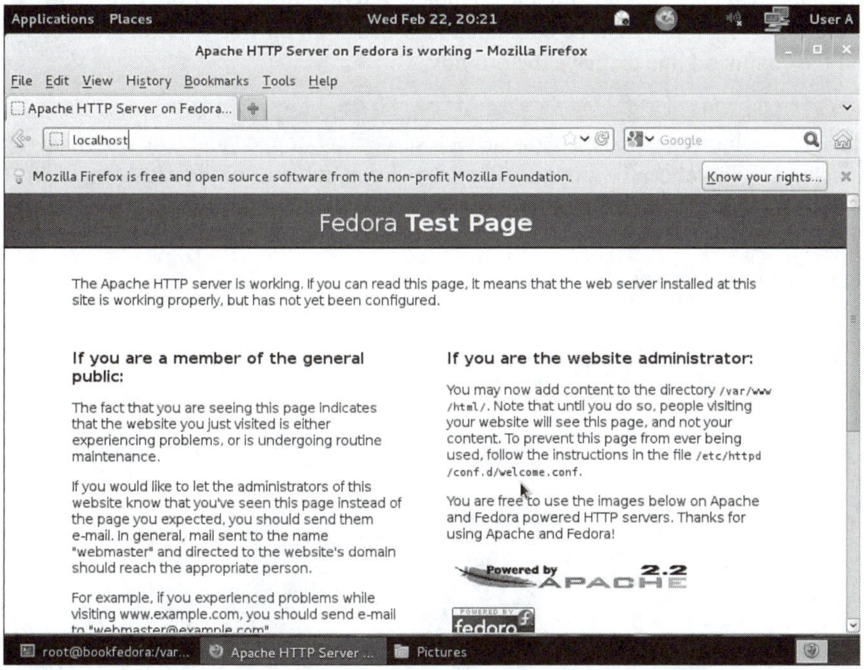

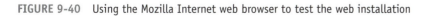

FIGURE 9-40   Using the Mozilla Internet web browser to test the web installation

There are two directories and files that are important relative to the Apache installation. The first is the *index.html* file, located in the */var/www/html* directory, as shown in Figure 9-41. This is the root directory for the web service. The test page actually resides in *index.html.* Users can build their web pages off this file and linked files.

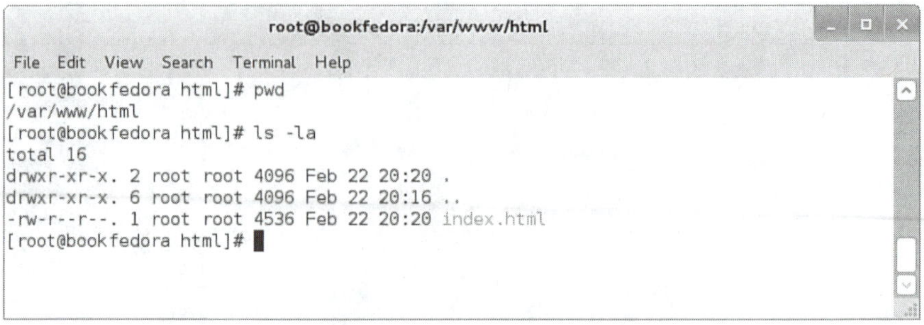

FIGURE 9-41 The location of the *index.html* file

httpd.conf
The configuration file for the Apache web server.

The second important directory and file is the ***httpd.conf*** file located in the */etc/httpd/conf* directory. This is shown in Figure 9-42. This is the configuration file for the Apache web server that is read every time the service is started. The *httpd.conf* file is a text file and can be edited; however, the Apache server must be restarted for the changes to take effect, using the command **/etc/init.d/httpd restart**, as shown in Figure 9-43. Notice that the command is issued from the */etc/rc.d/init.d* directory, and the command line displays the prompt:

```
Stopping httpd: [ OK ] Starting httpd: [ OK ]
```

This prompt indicates that the Apache web server has stopped and restarted. The Apache web server can be stopped using the command **/etc/init.d/httpd stop**. This provides an orderly (scripted) shutdown. The following output will be displayed on the terminal screen:

```
Stopping httpd: [ OK ]
```

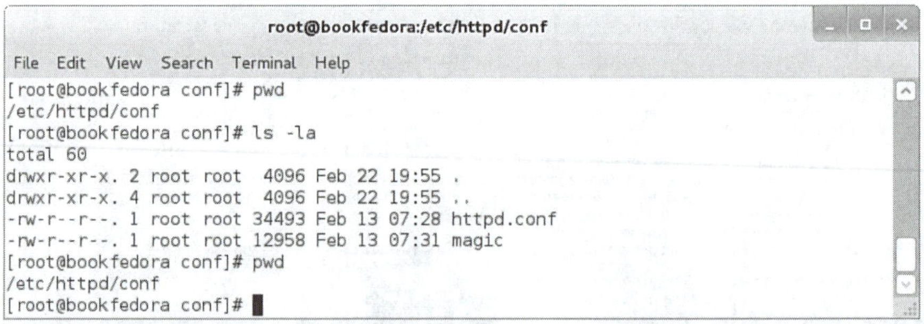

FIGURE 9-42 The location of configuration file (*httpd.conf*) for the Apache web server

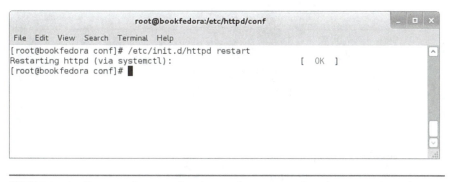

root@bookfedora:/etc/httpd/conf

```
File  Edit  View  Search  Terminal  Help
[root@bookfedora conf]# /etc/init.d/httpd restart
Restarting httpd (via systemctl):                    [  OK  ]
[root@bookfedora conf]#
```

FIGURE 9-43   The steps for restarting the Apache server so that changes made to the *httpd.conf* configuration file can take effect

9-5   LINUX NETWORKING

The objective of this section is to demonstrate how to configure a Linux machine to run on the network. This section assumes that the Linux machine already has a network interface card (NIC) installed. Fedora Linux 16.0 is good at detecting all major brands of network interface cards and contains drivers for the NICs. Linux will automatically detect the card and may prompt you for the IP address, net mask, and gateway address during the installation of the operating system. Hardware installed after the initial system installation will still be detected by the autodetect feature running in Linux.

Ethernet cards in Linux are identified as eth0, eth1, eth2, and so on. The command **ifconfig** is used to report all the network devices recognized and running on the system. This command lists all the interfaces and the configurations for each interface. The configurations include the IP address, the net mask (subnet mask), the broadcast address, and the gateway. The **ifconfig** command also reports back on the status of the loopback (lo), as shown in Figure 9-44.

The **ifconfig** command can also be used in Linux to change the IP address configuration for the network interface. The following examples will demonstrate configuring eth0, the default interface device on most Linux machines. The command **ifconfig** displayed the eth0 and lo, as shown in Figure 9-44. The IP address for the machine is currently 192.168.12.1. This example demonstrates how to change the IP address of the eth0 interface. The command **ifconfig eth0 192.168.20.5** is entered on the command line, and the **ifconfig** command is used to display the interface settings (as shown in Figure 9-45). This applies the IP address to the network interface. The default values for the broadcast and subnet masks are used if no value is specified. In this case, the Bcast (broadcast) address is automatically updated to 192.168.20.255, the broadcast address for this class of network. The Mask (subnet mask) entry is automatically updated to the Class C subnet mask 255.255.255.0.

A different subnet mask can be applied to the network interface by appending the subnet mask value to the **ifconfig** command. An example of this is shown at the bottom of Figure 9-45 using the command **ifconfig Eth0 192.168.20.5 netmask 255.255.0.0.**

eth0, eth1, eth2, ...
The way Linux identifies the Ethernet interface cards.

ifconfig
Command that reports all the network devices recognized and running on the system, listing all the interfaces and the configuration for each.

Net Mask
Linux name for the subnet mask.

lo
The Linux symbol representing the loopback.

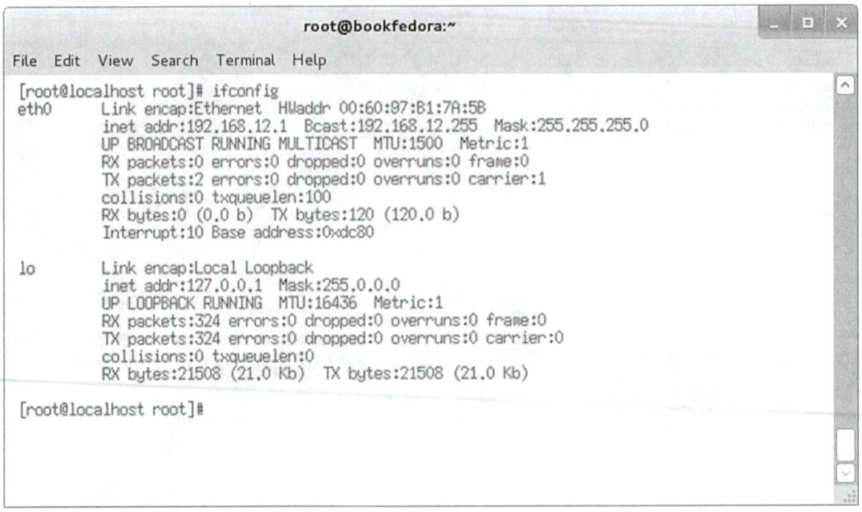

```
                          root@bookfedora:~                          _ □ ×

  File  Edit  View  Search  Terminal  Help

  [root@localhost root]# ifconfig
  eth0      Link encap:Ethernet  HWaddr 00:60:97:B1:7A:5B
            inet addr:192.168.12.1  Bcast:192.168.12.255  Mask:255.255.255.0
            UP BROADCAST RUNNING MULTICAST  MTU:1500  Metric:1
            RX packets:0 errors:0 dropped:0 overruns:0 frame:0
            TX packets:2 errors:0 dropped:0 overruns:0 carrier:1
            collisions:0 txqueuelen:100
            RX bytes:0 (0.0 b)  TX bytes:120 (120.0 b)
            Interrupt:10 Base address:0xdc80

  lo        Link encap:Local Loopback
            inet addr:127.0.0.1  Mask:255.0.0.0
            UP LOOPBACK RUNNING  MTU:16436  Metric:1
            RX packets:324 errors:0 dropped:0 overruns:0 frame:0
            TX packets:324 errors:0 dropped:0 overruns:0 carrier:0
            collisions:0 txqueuelen:0
            RX bytes:21508 (21.0 Kb)  TX bytes:21508 (21.0 Kb)

  [root@localhost root]#
```

FIGURE 9-44   An example of using the **ifconfig** command to display the network interfaces and their configuration

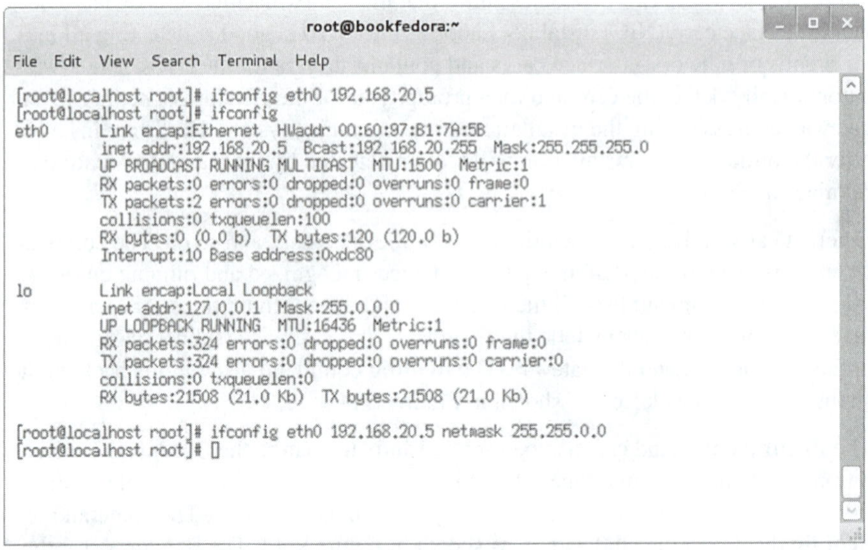

```
                          root@bookfedora:~                          _ □ ×

  File  Edit  View  Search  Terminal  Help

  [root@localhost root]# ifconfig eth0 192.168.20.5
  [root@localhost root]# ifconfig
  eth0      Link encap:Ethernet  HWaddr 00:60:97:B1:7A:5B
            inet addr:192.168.20.5  Bcast:192.168.20.255  Mask:255.255.255.0
            UP BROADCAST RUNNING MULTICAST  MTU:1500  Metric:1
            RX packets:0 errors:0 dropped:0 overruns:0 frame:0
            TX packets:2 errors:0 dropped:0 overruns:0 carrier:1
            collisions:0 txqueuelen:100
            RX bytes:0 (0.0 b)  TX bytes:120 (120.0 b)
            Interrupt:10 Base address:0xdc80

  lo        Link encap:Local Loopback
            inet addr:127.0.0.1  Mask:255.0.0.0
            UP LOOPBACK RUNNING  MTU:16436  Metric:1
            RX packets:324 errors:0 dropped:0 overruns:0 frame:0
            TX packets:324 errors:0 dropped:0 overruns:0 carrier:0
            collisions:0 txqueuelen:0
            RX bytes:21508 (21.0 Kb)  TX bytes:21508 (21.0 Kb)

  [root@localhost root]# ifconfig eth0 192.168.20.5 netmask 255.255.0.0
  [root@localhost root]# []
```

FIGURE 9-45   Using the **ifconfig** command to change the network interface IP address

ifdown, ifup
Linux commands used to shut down and bring back up the network interface.

Another set of commands used for controlling the network interfaces are **ifdown** *[interface]* and **ifup** *[interface]*. These commands enable the administrator to shut down and bring back up the network interface. This is useful when a machine is being subjected to a network attack and the network connection needs to be shut down quickly. The **ifdown eth0** command brings down the Ethernet0 interface. The **ifconfig** command no longer displays the eth0 interface. The interface can be brought back online by issuing the **ifup eth0** command. The **ifconfig** command now shows that the eth0 interface is available. The steps for shutting down and bringing up a network interface are shown in Figure 9-46.

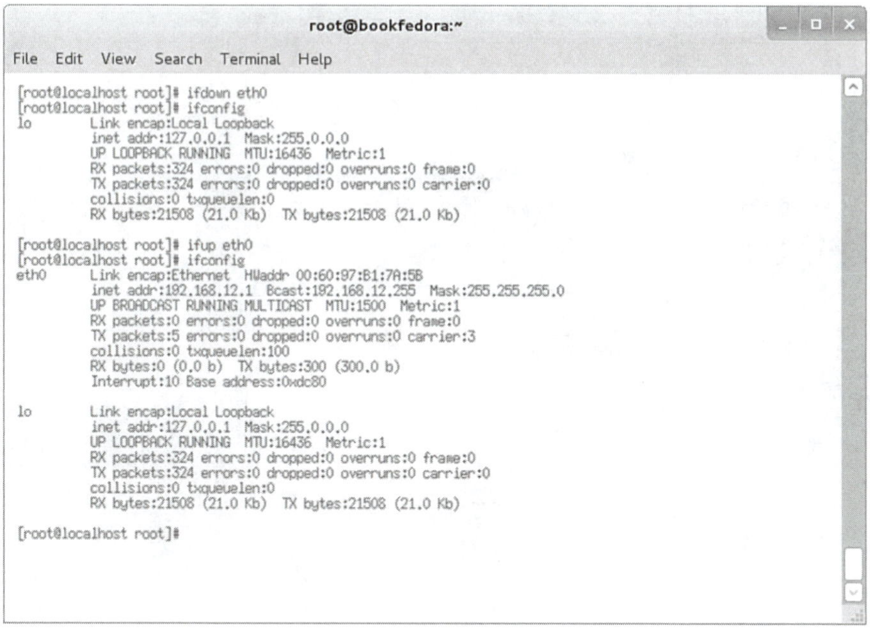

FIGURE 9-46 Examples of using the **ifdown** and **ifup** commands

In some cases, it is necessary to shut down all network interfaces. The command for doing this is **network stop**. Linux will echo a response of the interfaces that are shutting down. Entering the **ifconfig** command will now display that no network interfaces are active. Part a of Figure 9-47 shows an example of stopping the network on Linux. The command for starting the network is **network start**, as shown in part b of Figure 9-47. Linux prompts that it is bringing up interfaces. Issuing the **ifconfig** command now displays that eth0 and lo are both available.

The next step is to provide a gateway address for the Linux network interface. This is accomplished using the **route add default gw** *[ip address]* command. Entering the *route* command without any arguments displays the different routes. This is shown in part a of Figure 9-48. The display shows that the default gateway is 192.168.12.254. This can be changed to 192.168.12.1 by issuing the command **route add default gw 192.168.12.1**, as shown in part b of Figure 9-48. Linux prompts you if an unreachable gateway address has been specified, as shown in part c of Figure 9-48. Linux displays this message if a gateway address outside the network address is specified. For example, the entry **route add default gw 192.168.20.5** displays that the address is unreachable. This is because 192.168.20.0 is a different Class C network.

> **network stop**
> Shuts down all network interfaces.
>
> **network start**
> Brings up the network interfaces.
>
> **route add default gw**
> Linux command used to specify the gateway address.

(a)

```
                          root@bookfedora:~
File  Edit  View  Search  Terminal  Help
[root@localhost root]# /etc/rc.d/init.d/network stop
Shutting down interface eth0:                    [  OK  ]
Shutting down loopback interface:                [  OK  ]
[root@localhost root]# ifconfig
```

(b)

```
                          root@bookfedora:~
File  Edit  View  Search  Terminal  Help
[root@localhost root]# /etc/rc.d/init.d/network start
Setting network parameters:                      [  OK  ]
Bringing up loopback interface:                  [  OK  ]
Bringing up interface eth0:  ^[[A                [  OK  ]
[root@localhost root]# ifconfig
eth0      Link encap:Ethernet  HWaddr 00:60:97:B1:7A:5B
          inet addr:192.168.12.1  Bcast:192.168.12.255  Mask:255.255.255.0
          UP BROADCAST RUNNING MULTICAST  MTU:1500  Metric:1
          RX packets:0 errors:0 dropped:0 overruns:0 frame:0
          TX packets:8 errors:0 dropped:0 overruns:0 carrier:5
          collisions:0 txqueuelen:100
          RX bytes:0 (0.0 b)  TX bytes:480 (480.0 b)
          Interrupt:10 Base address:0xdc80

lo        Link encap:Local Loopback
          inet addr:127.0.0.1  Mask:255.0.0.0
          UP LOOPBACK RUNNING  MTU:16436  Metric:1
          RX packets:328 errors:0 dropped:0 overruns:0 frame:0
          TX packets:328 errors:0 dropped:0 overruns:0 carrier:0
          collisions:0 txqueuelen:0
          RX bytes:21848 (21.3 Kb)  TX bytes:21848 (21.3 Kb)

[root@localhost root]#
```

FIGURE 9-47   (a) Using the command **network stop** for shutting down all network interfaces; (b) using the command **network start** for bringing up all network interfaces

```
                          root@bookfedora:~
File  Edit  View  Search  Terminal  Help
       (a)
[root@localhost root]# route
Kernel IP routing table
Destination     Gateway         Genmask         Flags Metric Ref    Use Iface
192.168.12.0    *               255.255.255.0   U     0      0        0 eth0
127.0.0.0       *               255.0.0.0       U     0      0        0 lo
default         192.168.12.254  0.0.0.0         UG    0      0        0 eth0

       (b)
[root@localhost root]# route add default gw 192.168.12.1
[root@localhost root]# route
Kernel IP routing table
Destination     Gateway         Genmask         Flags Metric Ref    Use Iface
192.168.12.0    *               255.255.255.0   U     0      0        0 eth0
127.0.0.0       *               255.0.0.0       U     0      0        0 lo
default         192.168.12.1    0.0.0.0         UG    0      0        0 eth0

       (c)
[root@localhost root]# route add default gw 192.168.20.5
SIOCADDRT: Network is unreachable
[root@localhost root]#
```

FIGURE 9-48   (a) Using the **route** command to display the network routes available on the machine; (b) changing the network's default gateway address; (c) the Linux prompt for an unreachable gateway address

The Linux network programs take their cue from a set of scripts in the *etc/sysconfig/network-scripts* directory. These scripts contain the values assigned to all network devices in the Linux operating system. This example looks at the contents of the *ifcfg-eth0* script, which is the file associated with the Ethernet0 network interface. The **cat** command is used to display the file, as shown in Figure 9-49. These contents identify how eth0 will be configured when booting or when the network is started. The root user can modify this file as needed.

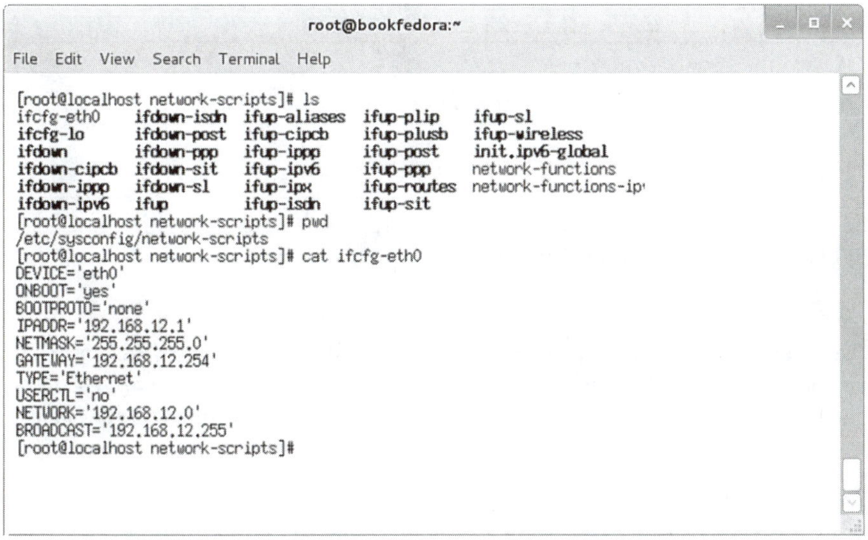

```
root@bookfedora:~
File  Edit  View  Search  Terminal  Help
[root@localhost network-scripts]# ls
ifcfg-eth0    ifdown-isdn   ifup-aliases  ifup-plip    ifup-sl
ifcfg-lo      ifdown-post   ifup-cipcb    ifup-plusb   ifup-wireless
ifdown        ifdown-ppp    ifup-ippp     ifup-post    init.ipv6-global
ifdown-cipcb  ifdown-sit    ifup-ipv6     ifup-ppp     network-functions
ifdown-ippp   ifdown-sl     ifup-ipx      ifup-routes  network-functions-ip'
ifdown-ipv6   ifup         ifup-isdn     ifup-sit
[root@localhost network-scripts]# pwd
/etc/sysconfig/network-scripts
[root@localhost network-scripts]# cat ifcfg-eth0
DEVICE='eth0'
ONBOOT='yes'
BOOTPROTO='none'
IPADDR='192.168.12.1'
NETMASK='255.255.255.0'
GATEWAY='192.168.12.254'
TYPE='Ethernet'
USERCTL='no'
NETWORK='192.168.12.0'
BROADCAST='192.168.12.255'
[root@localhost network-scripts]#
```

FIGURE 9-49   The steps for examining the contents of the ifcfg-eth0 script

Installing SSH

This section demonstrates how to install SSH (the secure shell), which is similar to telnet except SSH encrypts the data traffic between the two hosts. SSH is a better tool for remote administration or remote work. The **openssh**-clients and openssh-server are provided with the Fedora distribution of Linux. Installing the openssh-client application is straightforward using Yum, as shown in Figure 9-50.

> **openssh**
> The secure shell application for Linux.

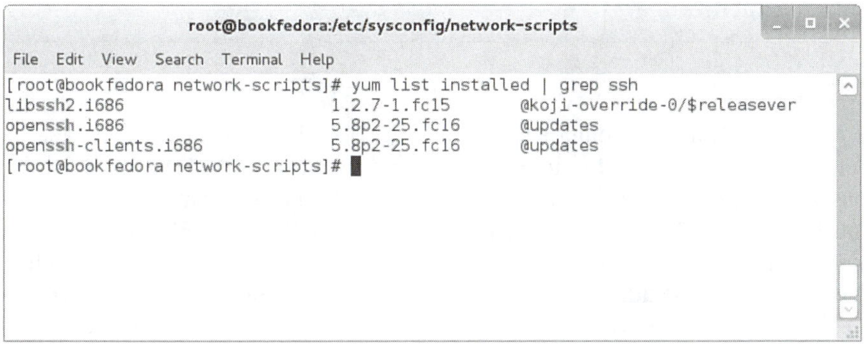

```
root@bookfedora:/etc/sysconfig/network-scripts
File  Edit  View  Search  Terminal  Help
[root@bookfedora network-scripts]# yum list installed | grep ssh
libssh2.i686                 1.2.7-1.fc15          @koji-override-0/$releasever
openssh.i686                 5.8p2-25.fc16         @updates
openssh-clients.i686         5.8p2-25.fc16         @updates
[root@bookfedora network-scripts]# █
```

FIGURE 9-50   The listing of the openssh using Yum

The openssh client is installed on the Linux machine by entering the command **yum install openssh-clients**. The database can be queried using the command **yum list installed | grep openssh**. The openssh files installed are then listed as shown in Figure 9-50.

The command **ssh** *[destination]* can be used to establish an SSH connection. This assumes that the destination has an SSH server running. In this case, the destination is user@machine.edu. An example is shown in Figure 9-51.

```
                          root@bookfedora:~                         _ □ x
 File  Edit  View  Search  Terminal  Help
 [root@localhost RPMS]# ssh user@machinename.edu
```

FIGURE 9-51 Establishing an SSH connection

The installation of the SSH server is similar to the installation of the SSH client. The command **yum install openssh-server** is used to install the openssh-server. The installation can be verified in the same way that the installation was verified for the client.

The FTP Client

> **ncftp**
> An FTP application for Linux.

There are many FTP client applications for Linux. This section demonstrates the use of the FTP application called **ncftp**. This application is popular with network administrators because of its ease with putting files on and getting files from the command line. The command used to start the application is **ncftp** *[server-name],* as demonstrated in Figure 9-52. An FTP server session with 192.168.12.2 is being requested. The screen prompts that a connection is being established, and then the prompt **salsa Microsoft FTP service (Version 5.0)** is displayed. (*Note: salsa* is our example Windows 2003 server machine.) The screen next prompts **Logging in. . . | Anonymous user logged in**. The anonymous login is listed because a user was not specified with the **ncftp** command. The command **ncftp -u** *[server-name]* can be used to instruct the FTP server to prompt you for the user's password. (See the *man* page for **ncftp** for more instructions.) The Linux box then replies **Logged in to 192.168.12.2**, indicating that a connection has been established. The prompt on the Linux machine now shows **ncftp / >**.

DNS Service on Linu

> **resolv.conf**
> Contains the list of DNS servers for the Linux machine.

DNS is used for name resolution (see Chapter 5, "Configuring and Managing the Network Infrastructure"). In Linux, the list of information for the DNS service is found in a file in the */etc* directory called **resolv.conf**. This is shown in Figure 9-53. This file contains the list of the IP addresses for the DNS servers. The contents of an example *resolv.conf* file are listed in Figure 9-54. Two entries are shown for this file. The first is **search localdomain**, and the second entry is **nameserver 192.168.12.1**. This listing shows the search sequence for resolving names to an IP address. Multiple name services can appear in this list, but remember, this is a search order. Linux will not perform any name resolution if this file is empty.

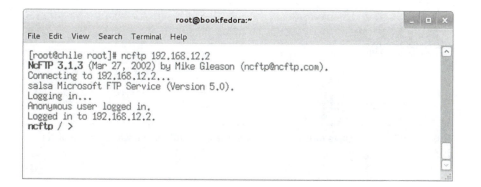

FIGURE 9-52 Using **ncftp** to start an application

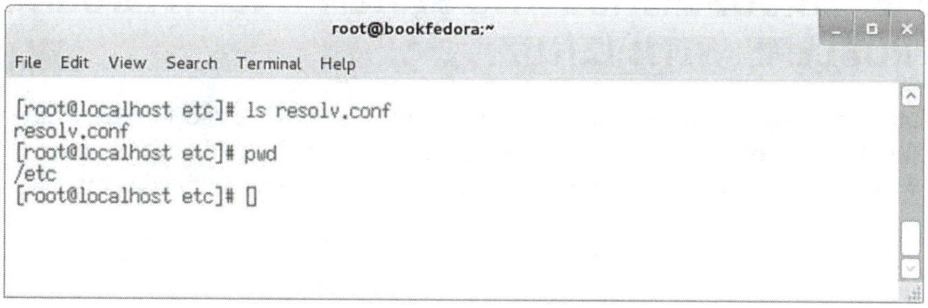

```
root@bookfedora:~
File  Edit  View  Search  Terminal  Help
[root@localhost etc]# ls resolv.conf
resolv.conf
[root@localhost etc]# pwd
/etc
[root@localhost etc]# []
```

FIGURE 9-53 The location of the DNS resolv.conf file in Linux

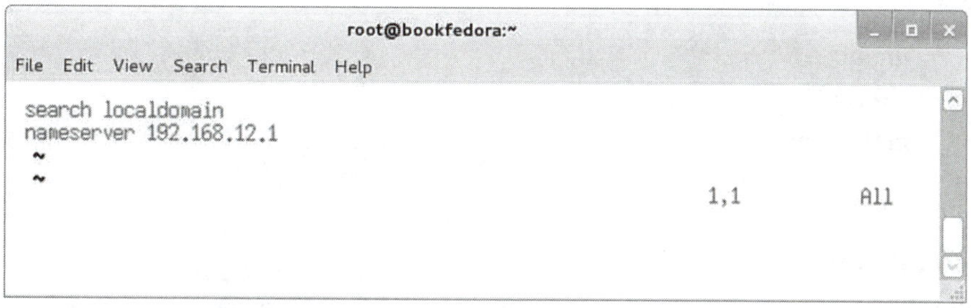

```
root@bookfedora:~
File  Edit  View  Search  Terminal  Help
search localdomain
nameserver 192.168.12.1
~
~
                                          1,1          All
```

FIGURE 9-54 The contents of the example resolv.conf file

Changing the Hostname

This section demonstrates how to change the hostname of a Linux machine. The name of the Linux machine is located in the */etc/sysconfig/network* file. The root user can be changed using the command **hostname *[name]***. In this case, the example is showing that the hostname is being changed to *chile-one* as shown in Figure 9-55. You must log off and back on for the change to take place.

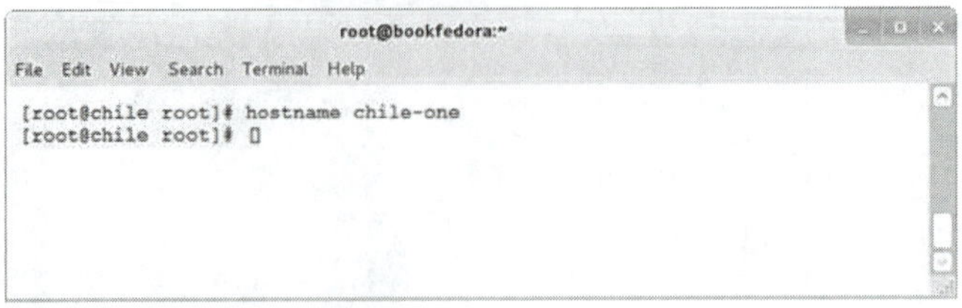

FIGURE 9-55 An example of using the **hostname** command to change the name of the Linux machine

9-6 TROUBLESHOOTING SYSTEM AND NETWORK PROBLEMS WITH LINUX

Linux has many options available for troubleshooting hardware and software problems. This section presents some of the options available to the administrator and the user. The following Linux troubleshooting commands are presented in this section:

> **dmesg**
>
> **reboot**
>
> **last**
>
> **who**
>
> **w**
>
> **nmap**
>
> **chkconfig**
>
> **netstat -ap**

Troubleshooting Boot Processes

The dmesg Command   The first command examined is **dmesg**, which is used to display the boot process for Linux. This command is useful if a certain application fails to be recognized or boot properly. This file will display errors that can be used to better understand why a process failed. This command is available to any user on the system, but remember: Only *root* will be able to fix the problems. This file can contain a large amount of text, so the command can be piped to more using the command **dmesg | more**, as shown in Figure 9-56. This screen shows the text from the last Linux boot process. This provides information on the system devices detected, how memory is configured, hard drive information, and any errors coming from the software.

> **dmesg**
> Command used to display the boot processes for Linux, used to identify why certain processes failed.

```
root@bookfedora:~
File  Edit  View  Search  Terminal  Help
[root@localhost root]# dmesg | more
Linux version 2.4.18-3 (bhcompile@daffy.perf.redhat.com) (gcc version 2.96 20000
731 (Red Hat Linux 7.3 2.96-110)) #1 Thu Apr 18 07:37:53 EDT 2002
BIOS-provided physical RAM map:
 BIOS-e820: 0000000000000000 - 00000000000a0000 (usable)
 BIOS-e820: 00000000000f0000 - 0000000000100000 (reserved)
 BIOS-e820: 0000000000100000 - 0000000010000000 (usable)
 BIOS-e820: 00000000ffe00000 - 0000000100000000 (reserved)
On node 0 totalpages: 65536
zone(0): 4096 pages.
zone(1): 61440 pages.
zone(2): 0 pages.
Kernel command line: ro root=/dev/hda3
Initializing CPU#0
Detected 498.758 MHz processor.
Console: colour VGA+ 80x25
Calibrating delay loop... 996.14 BogoMIPS
Memory: 255508k/262144k available (1119k kernel code, 6252k reserved, 775k data,
 280k init, 0k highmem)
Dentry cache hash table entries: 32768 (order: 6, 262144 bytes)
Inode cache hash table entries: 16384 (order: 5, 131072 bytes)
Mount-cache hash table entries: 4096 (order: 3, 32768 bytes)
Buffer cache hash table entries: 16384 (order: 4, 65536 bytes)
--More--
```

FIGURE 9-56 An example of using the **dmesg** command piped to more

The reboot Command A useful Linux command to use when the system is not operating correctly due to either hardware or software problems is **reboot**. This command gracefully shuts down the system so that it is properly configured on reboot. If a Linux machine needs to be rebooted, use the **reboot** command; *do not press the Reset button on the PC.* Figure 9-57 shows the **reboot** command. The best directory to look for troubleshooting information is the */var/log* directory. Figure 9-58 provides a listing of the */var/log* directory. Many of the files have a .1, .2, .3, and so on following the filename and represent older log files, respectively. For example:

> **reboot**
> Command used to gracefully shut down the Linux machine and reboot.

boot.log
boot.log.1
boot.log.2
boot.log.3

```
root@bookfedora:~
File  Edit  View  Search  Terminal  Help
[root@localhost root]# reboot
```

FIGURE 9-57 Entering the **reboot** command

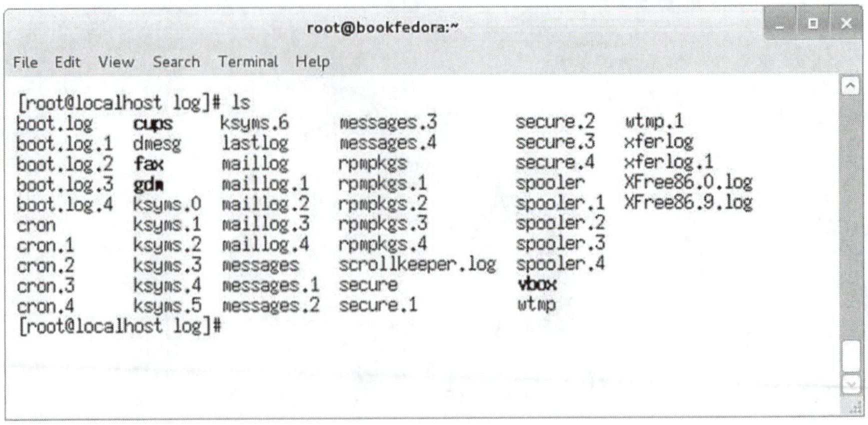

FIGURE 9-58 The listing of the /var/log directory

These files are renamed at regular intervals (hence the .1, .2, .3, … extensions) and are kept in storage. It is important to understand that these are rolling log files. The 1 becomes 2, pushing 2 to 3, 3 to 4, and so on. Eventually, the file is deleted and replaced. A summary of the useful troubleshooting files in the *var/log* directory follows:

- *boot.log*: Keeps track of the boot processes.
- *lastlog*: Keeps track of user login; requires the use of the **last** command to display its contents.
- *maillog*: Keeps a log of mail activity.
- *messages*: Contains most of the system messages that report any software or hardware errors. This is an important troubleshooting file.
- *secure*: Keeps track of any users entering or exiting the system and keeps track of security violations, such as unauthorized users attempting login.
- *spooler*: File for mail management.

Listing Users on the System

last
Command used to display logins to the Linux system.

The last Command   The **last** command is extremely useful in security. This command accesses the login file and reports of logins to the Linux system. Figure 9-59 provides an example of using the **last** command. This command lists all users that have logged on to the system since the last reboot or for the past month. The login information displayed includes the account name, day, date, and time. This command is useful if the administrator suspects that someone has gained unauthorized access to the Linux machine. The information displayed by the **last** command shows that there are two users on the system. The first listed is *usera,* who logged in from *localhost* on Feb. 11 at 12:48 and is still logged in. The other account, *root,* is currently logged in and has logged into and out of the system many times.

```
                        root@bookfedora:~                        _ □ ×

File  Edit  View  Search  Terminal  Help

[root@localhost log]# last
usera      pts/2      localhost      Tue Feb 11 12:48   still logged in
root       pts/3      :0             Tue Feb 11 12:47 - 12:48  (00:00)
root       pts/1      :0             Tue Feb 11 12:46   still logged in
root       pts/1      :0             Tue Feb 11 12:46 - 12:46  (00:00)
root       pts/1      :0             Tue Feb 11 12:46 - 12:46  (00:00)
root       pts/0      :0             Tue Feb 11 12:33   still logged in
root       :0                        Tue Feb 11 12:32   gone - no logout
reboot     system boot 2.4.18-3      Tue Feb 11 12:31          (00:17)
root       pts/0      :0             Tue Feb 11 12:20 - down   (00:09)
root       pts/1      :0             Thu Feb  6 12:58 - 12:58  (00:00)
root       pts/1      :0             Thu Feb  6 12:58 - 12:58  (00:00)
root       pts/0      :0             Thu Feb  6 12:58 - 13:17  (00:19)
root       tty1                      Thu Feb  6 12:57 - down   (4+23:32)
root       pts/0      :0             Thu Feb  6 12:18 - 12:57  (00:39)
root       pts/0      :0             Tue Feb  4 12:15 - 13:15  (00:59)

wtmp begins Tue Feb  4 12:15:26 2003
[root@localhost log]#
```

FIGURE 9-59   Using the **last** command to display the Linux login activity

The who or w Command   Two other ways to check for users on the system are to enter either the command **who** or **w**. The **who** command displays the names of the users presently logged into the system. The **w** command provides similar information and provides additional details on each user, such as the following:

- **from**: Specifies the domain where the user is logging in from
- **login time**: Indicates when the user logged in
- **idle**: Indicates if the user has been busy on the system
- **what**: Displays the last command entered by the user

Figure 9-60 provides examples of the text displayed by using **w** and **who** commands.

> **who**
> Linux command that displays the names of the users presently logged into the system.
>
> **w**
> Linux command that displays the names of the users presently logged into the system plus additional details on each user.

```
                        root@bookfedora:~                        _ □ ×

File  Edit  View  Search  Terminal  Help

[root@localhost log]# w
 12:50pm  up 19 min,  3 users,  load average: 0.27, 0.13, 0.10
USER     TTY      FROM           LOGIN@   IDLE   JCPU   PCPU  WHAT
usera    pts/2    localhost      12:48pm  1:57   0.05s  0.05s -bash
root     pts/0    :0             12:33pm  0.00s  0.20s  0.03s w
root     pts/1    :0             12:46pm  1:57   0.08s  0.02s telnet localhos
[root@localhost log]# who
usera    pts/2    Feb 11 12:48 (localhost)
root     pts/0    Feb 11 12:33 (:0)
root     pts/1    Feb 11 12:46 (:0)
[root@localhost log]#
```

FIGURE 9-60   Examples of the text displayed by the **w** and **who** commands

Network Security

> **nmap**
> A Linux port scanner.

The nmap Command An excellent security tool that runs on Linux is **nmap**. The application can be installed using the command **yum install nmap**, if not already installed. This is a port scanner that is used by the network administrator to scan a local computer or other computers internal to the network to determine what network ports and services are being made available to users. For example, the command **nmap localhost** was entered to scan the Linux machine named *localhost.* Figure 9-61 shows the results of the scan. The scan shows that the ftp, telnet, smtp (email server), sunrpc (network file server), and X11 (the GUI for Linux) are all available. Notice that each service has a port number assigned to it. (The concept of port number was presented in Chapter 5.) For example, FTP is on port 21 and is running TCP. Telnet is running on port 23 and is also running TCP. The network administrator may decide that the FTP or non-secure telnet service is a security threat and that it needs to be disabled. Note that this command can also be used to scan machines outside your network by simply substituting an IP address for the machine name. For example, **nmap 192.168.12.5** can be used to scan the machine at IP address 192.168.12.5. (*Note:* You should only use the **nmap** port scanning utility on your own machines!)

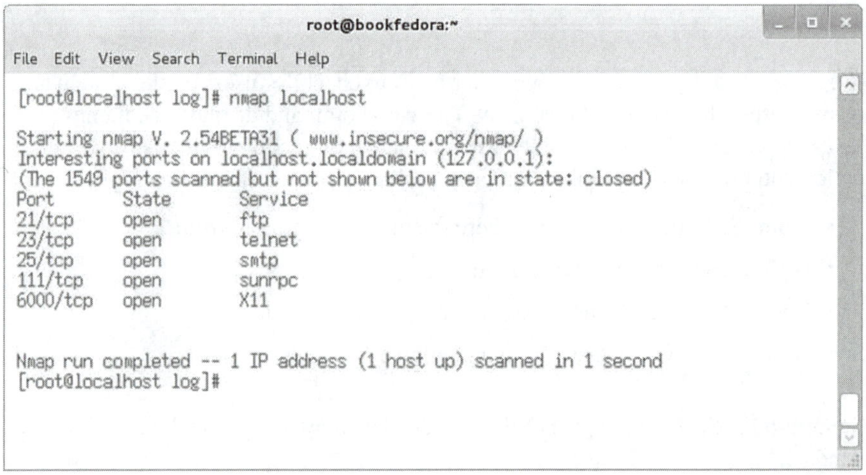
root@bookfedora:~
File Edit View Search Terminal Help
[root@localhost log]# nmap localhost
Starting nmap V. 2.54BETA31 (www.insecure.org/nmap/)
Interesting ports on localhost.localdomain (127.0.0.1):
(The 1549 ports scanned but not shown below are in state: closed)
Port State Service
21/tcp open ftp
23/tcp open telnet
25/tcp open smtp
111/tcp open sunrpc
6000/tcp open X11
Nmap run completed -- 1 IP address (1 host up) scanned in 1 second
[root@localhost log]#

FIGURE 9-61 The results of using the **nmap** command to scan the Linux machine named *localhost*

Enabling and Disabling Boot Services

> **chkconfig**
> Command used by administrators to enable and disable services at boot time.

The chkconfig Command The next command examined is **chkconfig**, which allows the administrator to enable and disable services at boot time. Figure 9-62 shows the options for the **chkconfig** command.

```
                              root@bookfedora:~                    _  □  X

File  Edit  View  Search  Terminal  Help

[root@localhost log]# chkconfig
chkconfig version 1.3.5 - Copyright (C) 1997-2000 Red Hat, Inc.
This may be freely redistributed under the terms of the GNU Public License.

usage:   chkconfig --list [name]
         chkconfig --add <name>
         chkconfig --del <name>
         chkconfig [--level <levels>] <name> <on|off|reset>
[root@localhost log]# chkconfig --list
```

FIGURE 9-62   The options for the **chkconfig** command

The administrator used the **nmap** command to check to see what network services
were running. It was found that the FTP service was running (see Figure 9-61). The
network administrator decided to disable the FTP service. The network administrator can use the **chkconfig --list** command to view the services running on the system. The command is shown at the bottom of Figure 9-62. The results of entering
the **chkconfig --list** command are provided in Figure 9-63. The last line displayed
shows **wu-ftpd: on**. This indicates that the FTP server is on. The FTP service can
be disabled by using the command **chkconfig wu-ftpd off**, as shown in Figure
9-64. The **chkconfig --list** command can be used again to verify the service is off.
The verification that **wu-ftpd** is off is provided in Figure 9-65.

```
                              root@bookfedora:~                    _  □  X

File  Edit  View  Search  Terminal  Help

nfs             0:off   1:off   2:off   3:off   4:off   5:off   6:off
nfslock         0:off   1:off   2:off   3:on    4:on    5:on    6:off
identd          0:off   1:off   2:off   3:off   4:off   5:off   6:off
radvd           0:off   1:off   2:off   3:off   4:off   5:off   6:off
snmpd           0:off   1:off   2:off   3:off   4:off   5:off   6:off
snmptrapd       0:off   1:off   2:off   3:off   4:off   5:off   6:off
isdn            0:off   1:off   2:on    3:on    4:on    5:on    6:off
wine            0:off   1:off   2:on    3:on    4:on    5:on    6:off
xinetd based services:
        chargen-udp:    off
        chargen:        off
        daytime-udp:    off
        daytime:        off
        echo-udp:       off
        echo:   off
        services:       off
        servers:        off
        time-udp:       off
        time:   off
        sgi_fam:        on
        rsync:  off
        telnet: on
        wu-ftpd:        on
[root@localhost log]#
```

FIGURE 9-63   The results of entering the **chkconfig --list** command

FIGURE 9-64 Using the **chkconfig wu-ftpd off** command to disable the ftp service

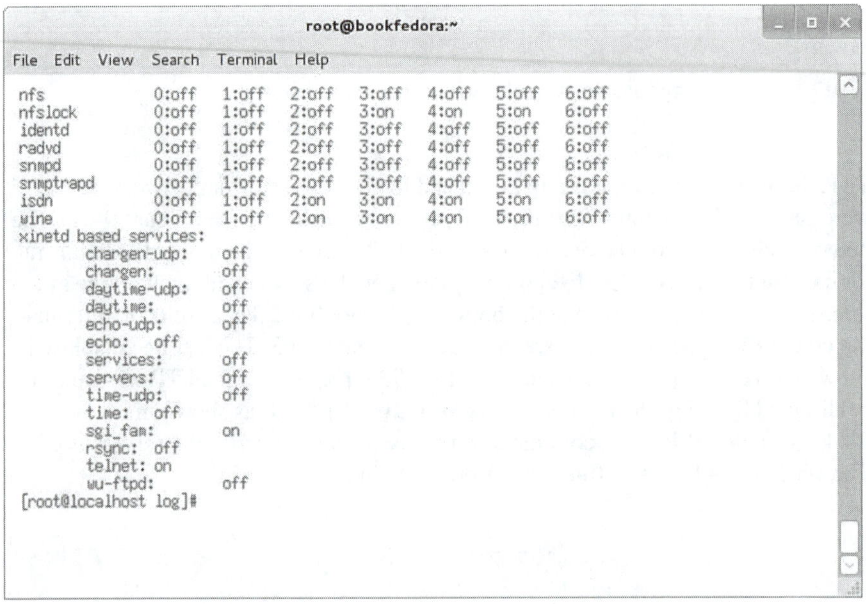

FIGURE 9-65 Using the **chkconfig --list** command to verify the service has been disabled

netstat -ap

Provides information about the network connections.

The netstat -ap Command   Another command used by the network administrator is **netstat -ap**. This command provides information about the network connections that exist on the system. This includes internal programs and connections to the outside world. This command is very useful when the network administrator wants to determine if a machine is being used by unauthorized users, for example, as a music server for the Internet. The **netstat** command will list the connection, and it will list the name of the program that is allowing the connection to be made. Figure 9-66 provides an example of using this command. In this example, the **netstat -ap | more** command is used. This pipes the file contents to *more* to make it easier to view the entire contents. The far right side of Figure 9-66 shows whether the connection is in the listen or established mode. *Listen* means that the program is waiting for a connection to be started. *Established* means that a connection has already been made. For example, a TCP connection is established at port 3102, and the name of the program is *in.telnetd,* which is the telnet-server.

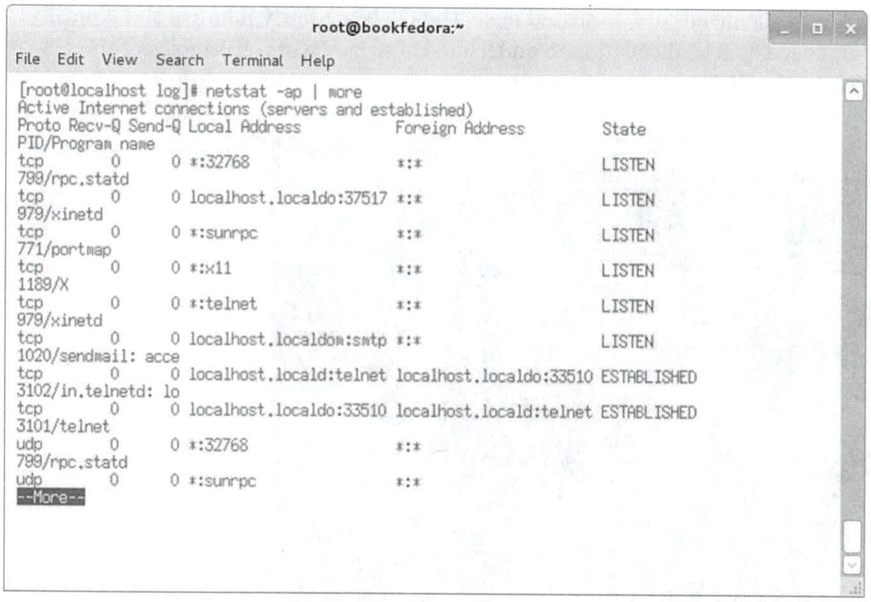

FIGURE 9-66 An example of using the **netstat -ap** command to view the network connections running on the machine

9-7 MANAGING THE LINUX SYSTEM

This section examines some of the management tools available with the Fedora 16 distribution. The previous sections in this chapter examined the Linux command structure as input from the command line interface. Although it is true that the network and system administrators insist that any member of the network management staff fully understand Linux operation from the command line, they also understand the benefits of using the well-developed GUIs available for Linux, such as those available with the Fedora 16.0 distribution. The obvious benefits of using the GUI management tools are time savings and the dependencies for any software installation/deletion are automatically checked for you.

In Fedora 16, the **System Config** tools, which are the system administration tools, are all prefixed with **system-config** followed by the name of the tool. To get to the tools, log in as *root* and, at the command line, enter **system-config- tool-name**. The menu for the tool being requested will be displayed.

The list of system configuration tools can be displayed by changing the directory to /usr/bin and entering the following command from the prompt **[root@bob bin] ls system-config-***. The list generated by this command is provided in Figure 9-67. There are many configuration options available for the user and the administrator.

system-config- *tool-name*
Linux command for displaying the system configuration GUI for a specified tool.

ls system-config- *
Linux command for listing the system configuration tools.

A few of the menus are discussed next. The GUIs are fairly intuitive and typically don't need a lot of discussion to understand how they work. Examples of the system-config GUIs are provided next.

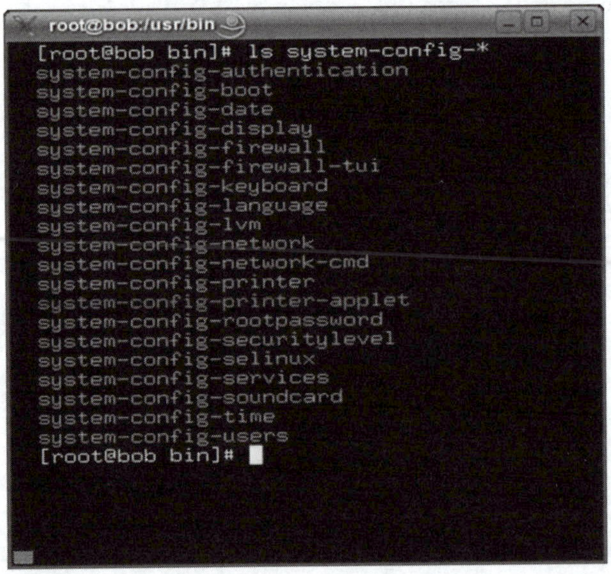

FIGURE 9-67 The list of the system-config- files

For example, **system-config-date** is the GUI that allows you to change the time and date for the computer. Entering the command **system-config-date** will display the menu shown in Figure 9-68. This menu also allows you to set the time zone and also enables you to point this menu (via an IP address) to a time server for obtaining the current time for your location.

The next GUI menu displayed (see Figure 9-69) is for the firewall. The firewall menu settings can be displayed by entering **system-config-firewall** at the command line. You can disable a firewall, configure additional settings, or modify the firewall configurations. This allows you to open ports and block ports, and all the settings are GUI based, which simplifies the tasks. For example, if you want to block port 80 (HTTP), simply click the check box for **WWW (HTTP)** and click **Disable**. On the left side of the menu are other options, such as selecting other ports that are not defined on the main menu screen. You also have settings for trusted services, masquerading (network address translation), and a place for setting custom rules for your firewall.

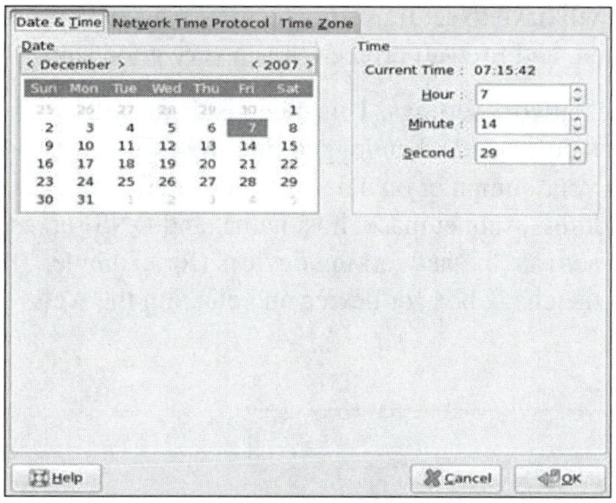

FIGURE 9-68   The system-config-date menu

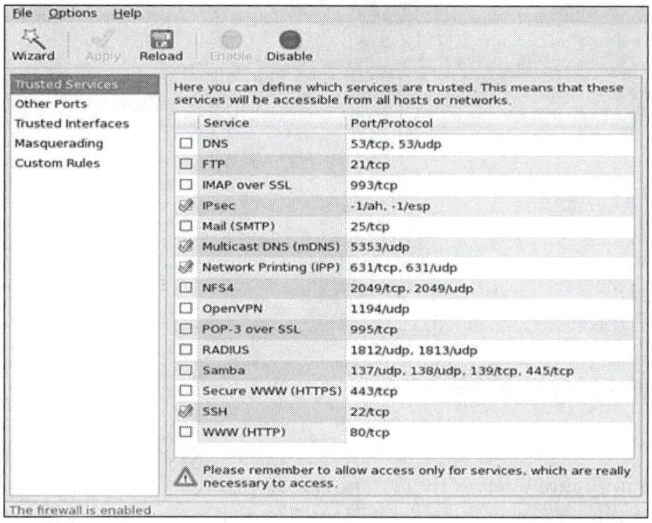

FIGURE 9-69   The system-config-firewall menu

There are many important issues that the network/system administrator faces, but security should be the top concern. When you first go out to install a new service or are maintaining existing systems, the most important issue is the system security and preventing outside threats. You want to fully understand the implications of installing the software and how the installation can possibly affect the overall network. The following is a list of some of the questions that should be asked:

- Who will be the users of the software, and what applications are they going to be running?
- Will they need special permissions?
- Will the software being installed require a firewall?
- Does the software introduce any security threats?

Regardless of the installation, you will have to set limits for security reasons. You don't want your system to get hacked, and firewall protection is a very good start.

Figure 9-70 shows the menu for the network settings. This menu is displayed by entering the **system-config-network** command when logged in as root. This is a good place to start when setting up your computer on a network for the first time. This tool allows you to set the IP address, subnet mask, host name, and DNS server address. You can also activate or deactivate the networking devices (for example, NICs) from this menu by selecting the check box for device and clicking the **Activate** or **Deactivate** button.

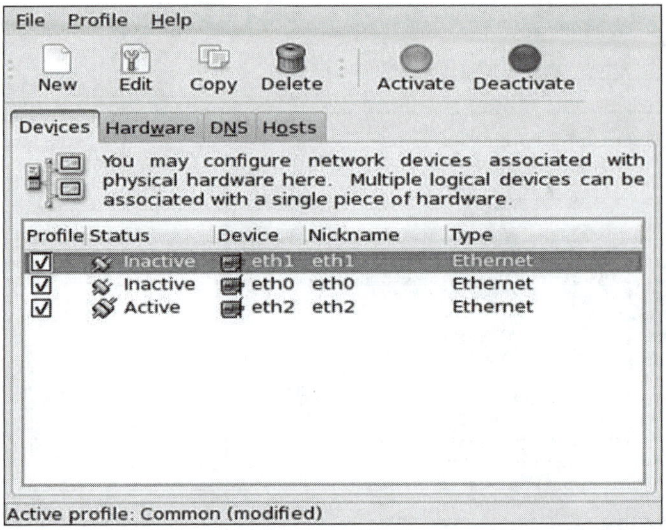

FIGURE 9-70   The system-config-network menu

The next menu, shown in Figure 9-71, is for *system-config-printer.* This menu is used for adding various types of printers to the system. The Fedora software will have most of the commonly used printer drivers installed with the software; however, not all drivers will be there. In the case of a missing printer driver, the system administrator will have to download the driver from a CD or from the Internet. The best locations to locate a printer driver are the manufacturer's website. In some cases, you might have to do an Internet search for the driver, but make sure you download the driver from a trusted site.

The next menu is for *system-config-users.* This menu (see Figure 9-72) is used for the management of the users. You can add/modify/delete users and groups from this menu. Examples of users with their Username, User ID, Primary Group, Full Name, Login Shell, and Home Directory are displayed.

FIGURE 9-71   The system-config-printer menu

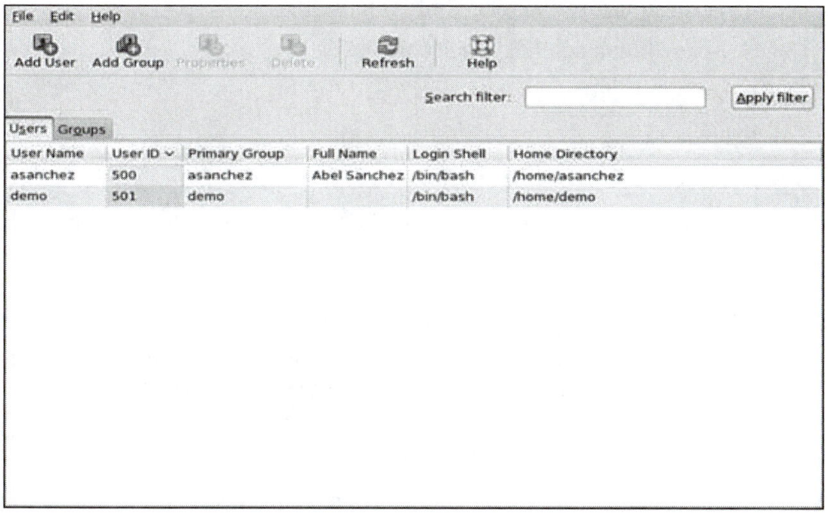

User Name	User ID ∨	Primary Group	Full Name	Login Shell	Home Directory
asanchez	500	asanchez	Abel Sanchez	/bin/bash	/home/asanchez
demo	501	demo		/bin/bash	/home/demo

FIGURE 9-72   The system-config-users menu

SUMMARY

This chapter presented numerous examples of using commands to administer the Linux operating system. You should appreciate the complexity of configuring the Linux network server and the fact that administering a computer network requires the input of personnel with varied skills. You should also understand that this has only been an introduction to the Linux operating system. The chapter demonstrated how to use many commands, one of the most important of which is how to read the online text *man* pages. There is a wealth of information about Linux on the Internet. The online distributions for Linux can be found at www.biblio.org. The Linux concepts that you should understand from this chapter include the following:

- The logon/logoff procedures for Linux
- The steps for adding users to a Linux machine
- The Linux file structure and related file commands
- The use of key Linux administration commands
- How to add applications to Linux
- How to place a Linux machine on the network
- How to configure web services for Linux
- The procedures and tools for using Linux to troubleshoot Linux systems and networks

The following are sites where you can download a bootable version of Linux running off one CD. This means you don't have to create dual-boot partitions on your computer or set up a separate machine running Linux. These bootable versions are available from both Fedora and Knoppix. The latest "live" version from Fedora is available at http://fedoraproject.org (698 MB) and will fit on one CD.

Knoppix is available from http://knoppix.net or from a mirror site, such as http://cs.wisc.edu/pub/mirrors/linux/knoppix/. As of this writing, Knoppix is at version 6.7.1. The file size is approximately 698 MB and will fit on a CD.

The files for Fedora "Live" and Knoppix are ISO images, and the ISO image is a disk image of an ISO 9660 file system. The file needs to be converted into a functional file system before using. This is done when the file is written to a CD using software capable of writing ISOs to CD and making the CD bootable. Most CD burning software for Windows, Mac OS, and Linux will have this capability. Once you write the ISO file to CD, the CD can be used to boot the computer, and you will have Linux running on your computer after the boot process is complete.

QUESTIONS AND PROBLEMS

Section 9-1

1. What are the steps for entering the menu to add a user in Linux?

2. What is the purpose of the Linux login shell?

3. How can Linux be closed from the Linux GUI?

4. How is the command line accessed in Linux?

Section 9-2

5. What is the Linux command to only list files?

6. What Linux command provides a long file listing that includes file attributes?

7. What Linux command lists hidden files and file attributes?

8. What two Linux commands can be used to display file contents?

9. How do the **more** and **cat** commands differ?

10. What is the user ID for *root*?

11. What directory are the binary process and executables located in Linux?

12. What is typically placed in the */etc* directory?

13. Match the following directories to their content:

    1. */boot* a) location of all user directories

    2. */dev* b) system log files, email folders

    3. */home* c) location of user files related to user programs

    4. */mnt* d) location of the Linux kernel

    5. */root* e) drivers for monitors

    6. */tmp* f) the home directory for *root*

    7. */usr* g) temporary holding area for applications

    8. */var* h) the location of mounted directories

14. What is the Linux command for displaying a working directory?

15. What is the Linux command for creating a directory named *chile*?

16. List the command for removing a file named *aaron.*

17. List the command to rename a file named *aaron.txt* to *bueno.txt.*

18. The command **chmod 411 drb.txt** is entered. What does this do?

19. The command **chmod 644 djb.txt** is entered. What does this do?

20. The command **chmod 755 krcb.txt** is entered. What does this do?

21. The permissions for the file *hbmbb.txt* need to be set so that only the owner has permission to read and write the file. List the command that does this.

22. List the command to set the permissions on the text file *dapab.txt* to the following:

    Owner: read/write

    Group: read

    Outside: no access

23. List the commands for setting the permissions on *bc.txt* to the following:

    Owner: read/write/executable

    Group: read/write

    Outside: read

24. The new owner of the file *CQ.txt* is *dd*. Enter the command to change ownership.

25. The new group for the *jc.txt* is *heaven*. Enter the command to change ownership.

Section 9-3

26. What command displays the online text manual for Linux?

27. List the command that returns all *man* pages that mention the topic *Apache*.

28. Why is the **ps -a** command used?

29. How is a program with a PID of 1020 shut down?

30. What command can be used as a last resort to kill a process?

31. *Root* is logged onto a Linux machine and needs to become another user to verify the changes made to the user's account. What command is used for *root* to become the user?

32. *Usera* is logged into Linux and wants to become *userb*. What is the command, and what are the steps required to make this happen?

33. What information is contained in the *fstab* file?

34. What is *kudzu*?

35. List the command for mounting a USB drive.

36. List the Linux command that is used to verify a drive has been mounted.

37. What command must be entered before the media can be removed from a drive that has been mounted?

38. List the command to gracefully shut down the Linux system.

39. The last command entered from the command line in Linux can be repeated by pressing what key?

40. What command can be entered in Linux to display previously entered commands?

41. What is the keystroke that can be used to complete entries on the command line?

Section 9-4

42. List the command to search for installed applications on Linux. Use the **pipe** command to display only results with *wu-ftpd* in them.

43. What command is used to find out where a file comes from?

44. What is the Linux command to uninstall an application?

45. What is the Linux command for installing an application?

46. How is a service controlled by *xinetd* enabled after installation?

47. What command starts the Apache web server?

48. The script for starting the Apache web server is found in what directory?

49. The *index.html* file is found in what directory in Linux?

50. The *httpd.conf* file is located in what directory in Linux?

51. The Apache web server can be restarted using what command?

Section 9-5

52. What is the Linux command for listing all network interfaces running on the system?

53. What is the subnet mask called in Linux?

54. How is the Ethernet1 network interface card identified in Linux?

55. The **ifconfig** command is entered and lo is displayed. What is this?

56. List the command to change the IP address of the Ethernet0 network interface to 10.10.20.5 with a subnet mask of 255.255.255.0.

57. List the command to shut down the Ethernet1 network interface.

58. What command can be used to verify that a network interface is down?

59. What is the command to bring a network interface back online?

60. What command shuts down all network interfaces?

61. List the Linux command for starting the network interfaces.

62. What command can be used to verify that the network has started?

63. List the command for adding a gateway address for the Linux network interface.

64. The Linux network programs use a set of scripts found in what directory?

65. What is the command to install the openssh-server in Linux?

66. FTP is being used to connect to another machine. List the command that instructs the FTP server to prompt for a user's password.

67. The Washington University FTP server is to be installed on a Linux machine. Provide the command and steps required to install the server and make the services available.

68. The list of information for the DNS service is found in what directory in Linux?

69. List the command for changing the hostname of the Linux machine to *chip*.

Section 9-6

70. Why is the **dmesg** command used?

71. What is the Linux command to reboot?

72. Match the following Linux troubleshooting files with their content:

    1. *boot.log* a) keeps track of user login

    2. *lastlog* b) log of mail activity

    3. *maillog* c) keeps track of the boot process

    4. *messages* d) tracks users entering or exiting the system

    5. *secure* e) report on hardware or software errors

    6. *spooler* f) mail management

73. List two commands to check for users that have logged onto the system since the last reboot.

74. Which command lists all users that have logged onto the system since the last reboot?

75. What is the command to scan a computer to determine what network ports and services are being made available to users?

76. List the command used to enable and disable services at boot time.

77. The services running on a Linux machine can be listed by entering what command?

78. Write the command to disable the wu-ftpd service.

79. Identify the command that provides information about network connections that exist on the system.

Section 9-7

80. In Fedora 16, the **System Config** tools, (system administration tools), are all prefixed how?

81. How can the system tools be displayed in Linux? Specify the directory and the command used to list all tools.

82. What is the purpose of the system-config-date tool?

83. What is the purpose of the system-config-firewall tool?

84. What questions should the network administrator ask when setting the security for a new computer installation?

85. What tool is used for the network settings? What options are available through this tool?

Critical Thinking

86. You suspect that someone has broken into a computer. Discuss the steps you might take to correct the problem.

87. You are attempting to install the Apache web server, and a prompt is displayed that states a certain application is missing. Describe how this problem can be corrected.

88. What questions should you ask when installing new software on any machines attached to your network?

89. What steps can you take to find a printer driver that isn't included with a Linux distribution?

10 CHAPTER

INTERNET ROUTING

Chapter Outline

Objectives

- Understand the concept and purpose of the AS number (**ASN**)
- Understand the concept of the stubby areas
- Examine Internet routing using BGP
- Understand the steps for configuring BGP on a router
- Examine the purpose of the BGP Best Path Selection Algorithm
- Examine the issues of running IPv6 over the Internet using BGP4+
- Understand the issues of configuring BGP on a Juniper router

Key Terms

stubby areas
totally stubby areas
BGP
multi-homed
AS
ASN
EGP
peering
iBGP
eBGP
description *description*
router bgp AS

neighbor [*ip-address*]
remote [*AS-number*]
sh ip bgp sum
BGP Best Path Selection Algorithm
show ip bgp
BGP4+
no bgp default ipv4-unicast
neighbor *IPv6_address* **remote as** *AS_Number*
neighbor *IPv6_address* **activate**
network IPv6_network

address-family ipv6
show bgp ipv6 unicast summary
autonomous-system [*AS_Number*]
set router-id [*ip_address*]
set group [*BGP_group_name*] **neighbor** [*next_hop_address*]
set group [*BGP_group_name*] **type** [**external/internal**]
family inet6

INTRODUCTION

This chapter introduces the issues of wide-area networks and configuring Border Gateway Protocol (BGP) for Internet routing. The issues of wide-area networks (WAN) are first examined in Section 10-1. The concepts of **stubby areas** and **totally stubby areas** are examined. Connections to WANs and the Internet are similar and examined in this section; however, the routing protocols typically differ. WANs typically use static routes, Open Shortest Path First (OSPF), and Enhanced Interior Gateway Routing Protocol (EIGRP), but Internet routing uses BGP. Section 10-2 introduces the steps for configuring routers to run BGP. This includes the commands to establish and verify that a BGP connection has been established. The section concludes with an opportunity to verify your understanding of configuring BGP using the Net-Challenge Software.

Section 10-3 introduces BGP. It is amazing when you think about all of the possible paths a data packet can take when traveling from a source to a destination on the Internet. BGP addresses this challenge using the Best Path Selection Algorithm to compare the possible routes and select the best route to reach a destination. Section 10-4 looks at running IPv6 over the Internet. BGP4+ is the primary routing protocol for the Internet, and this is examined in this section. This chapter concludes with the steps required for configuring a Juniper router to run BGP.

10-1   INTERNET ROUTING—BGP

This section examines the routing issues for wide-area network (WAN) and Internet routing. WAN connections typically link remote sites and branch offices to the main network. These links usually have slower connection speeds than LAN connections and usually incorporate smaller and less powerful routers. It is critical that the network administrator be aware of these limited resources when choosing a routing protocol for a link to a WAN.

Configuring a WAN Connection

The easiest routing to configure for WAN links is the *static route*. This requires that the main site will need to configure a static route to each subnet at the remote end, as shown in Figure 10-1. At each remote site, you also need to configure a default static route. Each remote site router will have a static route attached to the network's WAN router that goes back to the main network. No routing updates are passed across the link, and the routing table is small and takes up little memory in the router. Static routing works well for single connections to the remote sites, as shown in Figure 10-1. For multiple connections over a WAN connection, you should use a dynamic routing protocol such as OSPF or EIGRP.

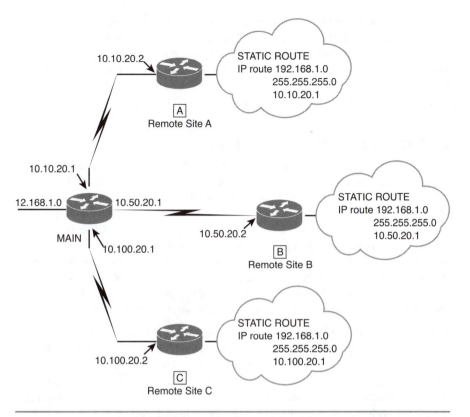

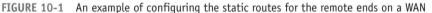

FIGURE 10-1 An example of configuring the static routes for the remote ends on a WAN

When choosing the routing protocol, be cautious about the amount of routing up-dates traversing the link. Remember that distance vector protocols send the entire routing table at set intervals. Routing Information Protocol (RIP) typically sends routing table updates every 30 seconds. This is an issue when large routing tables are exchanged. In some cases, the exchange of the routing table traffic could con-sume more than an acceptable amount of data bandwidth. OSPF and EIGRP are more desirable protocols for WAN routing, because they send updates only when routing changes occur.

The size of the router at the remote site will also play a part in the routing protocols you implement. The amount of memory in the remote routers is usually smaller than in the LAN routers. Therefore, the size of the routing table that can be passed to the remote site might need to be smaller than the routing table at the LAN site. Access lists can be used to filter out routes passed to the remote sites. Route filters or access lists are implemented in most modern routers, including Cisco routers. Chapter 7, "Network Security," examined the procedures for configuring access

Stubby Areas

Stubby areas accept routes from the Internet.

Totally Stubby Areas

Use only a default route to reach destinations external to the autonomous system.

BGP

Border Gateway Protocol.

lists. Some routing protocols, such as OSPF, have built-in functions to filter out routes. These are called **stubby areas** and **totally stubby areas**. Stubby areas give only inter-area routes and do not accept routes from the external network (that is, routes from the Internet). Totally stubby areas use a default route to reach destinations external to the autonomous system (AS). For a more detailed discussion of route filters and OSPF routing, you should seek out a routing reference book.

Configuring an Internet Connection

Configuring an Internet connection is similar to configuring a WAN connection. The Internet connection can use the same type of link. For example, the link to the Internet could be made using a T1 connection or a high-speed link, such as a DS-3 (44.7 Mbps), OC-3 (155 Mbps), or even MetroEthernet. WAN connections typically connect sites that belong to the same organization, such as a branch office of a business. Internet connections are usually between an Internet service provider (ISP) and its customers. Typically, the ISP and its customers do not use routing protocols, such as OSPF, for the Internet connection because these protocols do not scale well to this type of implementation. Instead, the two main routing protocol options that are available for making the Internet connection to the ISP are static routes and **BGP**.

Multi-Homed

This means the customer has more than one network connection.

Static routes are implemented in the same fashion as in the WAN routing section. The procedure for configuring static routes was presented in Chapter 2, "Advanced Router Configuration I." Static routes are used only when the customer has a single Internet connection. If the customer is **multi-homed**, meaning the customer has more than one Internet connection, BGP is used. The most current version of BGP is version 4. Figure 10-2 provides an example of a single and multi-homed customer.

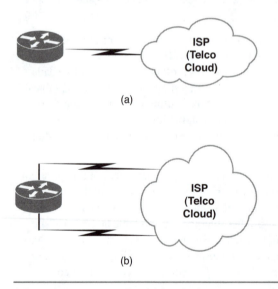

(a)

(b)

FIGURE 10-2 An example of (a) a single Internet connection and (b) a customer that is multi-homed

BGP is considered to be an external routing protocol. This protocol is designed for routing between separate organizational networks. The BGP term for these networks is *autonomous systems* (AS). An AS is assigned an AS number (ASN) by the same organization that assigns North American IP addresses, ARIN. The ASN has a different use than the ASN used in such IGP protocols, such as EIGRP. The routing protocols RIP, OSPF, IS-IS, and EIGRP are considered IGPs (Interior Gateway Protocols), while BGP is considered an Exterior Gateway Protocol (EGP). The ASN in BGP is used to distinguish separate networks and prevent routing loops. Each router participating in BGP must manually make a peering with its BGP neighbor. Peering is an agreement made for the exchange of data traffic between large and small ISPs or, as in this case, between a router and its neighbor router. The agreement on peering is how different networks are joined to form the Internet.

BGP uses TCP as its transport protocol to establish peering and to exchange messages and routes. The network administrator configuring the Internet connection must know the remote IP address and ASN to make this peering. An AS path is created when a network is connected. This is demonstrated in the next subsection.

NOTE

If BGP routers in the same AS peer with each other, that is, have the same ASN, this is called iBGP, or internal BGP, whereas the BGP between separate ASs is called eBGP, or external BGP. The protocols are collectively referred to as BGP.

ASNs have a set of numbers reserved for private use. These numbers are 64512 through 65535 are not to be propagated to the eBGP world (the Internet). It is the ISP's best practice to remove all private ASs before advertising the BGP routes. The public AS numbers are within the range of 1 to 64511. For this chapter, the configurations presented will use the private ASN numbers.

10-2 CONFIGURING BGP

The objective of this section is to examine the issues associated with configuring an Internet connection. This includes the steps for configuring the router for BGP. The section concludes with the Net-Challenge exercise for configuring a BGP connection to the Internet service provider.

Configuring BGP

This section demonstrates how to configure a router to run BGP for connecting to an ISP. Figure 10-3 illustrates the example network for this section. This is typical of the customer's connection to the ISP. In this example, the steps for configuring both the ISP router (Router-ISP) and the customer's router (Router B) will be shown. In practice, however, the ISP router (Router-ISP) will be configured by the networking personnel with the ISP. This exercise begins with configuring the ISP's router (Router-ISP).

AS
Autonomous systems separate organizational networks.

ASN
Autonomous systems number is used to distinguish separate networks and to prevent routing loops.

EGP
Exterior Gateway Protocol is a routing protocol that's used to exchange routing information between hosts in a network of autonomous systems.

Peering
How an agreement is made for the exchange of data traffic between large and small ISPs or between a router and its neighbor router.

iBGP
Internal Border Gateway Protocol—BGP between the same ASN.

eBGP
External Border Gateway Protocol—BGP between separate ASNs.

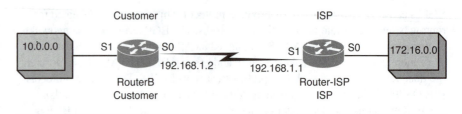

Customer   ISP

RouterB   Router-ISP
Customer   ISP

FIGURE 10-3 A BGP connection to an ISP

The ISP has assigned an IP address of 192.168.1.1 to the interface that connects to the customer. The customer is assigned an IP address of 192.168.1.2. The first step is to enter the configuration mode on Router-ISP using the **conf t** command. This command is issued from the privilege EXEC prompt, as shown. Next, enter the configuration mode for the router's serial interface that connects to the customer. In this example, serial interface 1/0 (S1/0) on the ISP's router is being used for the connection; therefore, enter the command **interface serial 1/0** [*int serial 1/0*]:

```
Router-ISP# conf t
Router-ISP(config)# int serial 1/0
```

Next, enter the IP address for the connection to the customer with a subnet mask of 255.255.255.252. Recall from Chapter 1, "Network Infrastructure Design," that a subnet mask of 255.255.255.252 provides for two usable host IP addresses in the subnet. This is adequate for the connection to the customer. The command **ip address** *[ip address] [subnet mask]* is used to configure the Serial1/0 interface with the specified IP address and subnet mask. The ISP will typically have multiple customer connections; therefore, it is a good idea to document the IP address entry using the command **description**. This command is used to enter a comment in the router's configuration file about an interface configuration. For example, the serial1/0 interface is being configured for the connection to customer B. The router has been placed in the *(config-if)#* mode. The entry **description Customer A** is entered so that the network administrator of the ISP knows what the serial1/0 interface is being used for. (*Note*: Documentation of the router's configuration file is extremely important.)

```
Router-ISP(config-if)#ip address 192.168.1.1 255.255.255.252
Router-ISP(config-if)#description Customer A
```

The next step is to configure the router to run BGP. The ISP has been assigned the AS number of 65000. (*Note:* This is actually a private AS number. In practice the ISP is assigned a public AS number.) The AS number is used when entering the command for BGP. In this example, the command **router bgp 65000** is entered. The command **network 10.20.20.0 mask 255.255.255.0** follows, which instructs the router to advertise the 10.20.20.0/24 network to its BGP peers. The next command is for specifying the IP address of the BGP neighbor. This is the IP address of the serial0/0 interface on the customer's router (Router B). The format for the command is **neighbor** *[ip address]* **remote-as number** *[neighbor's AS number]*. The last command is for entering a description of the entries. The comment **neighbor 192.168.1.2 description Customer BGP** is used to document the router configuration for the neighbor IP address for the customer and that the routing protocol is BGP:

```
Router-ISP(config)#router bgp 65000
Router-ISP(config-router)#network 10.20.20.0 mask 255.255.255.0
Router-ISP(config-router)#neighbor 192.168.1.2 remote-as 65001
Router-ISP(config-router)#neighbor 192.168.1.2 description Customer A
BGP
```

The command **sh ip int brief** can be used to check the configuration for the interface. This shows that the ISP's router serial1/0 interface has been configured and is connected:

```
Router-ISP#sh ip int brief
Interface       IP-Address   OK?  Method  Status           Protocol
FastEthernet0/0 unassigned   YES  unset   administratively
                                          down             down
Serial1/0       192.168.1.1  YES  manual  up               up
```

The next example demonstrates the steps for configuring the customer's router (Router B). The customer receives an IP address and subnet mask from the ISP when the connection is requested. This information is used to configure the serial interface that connects to the ISP.

The first step is to enter the router's configuration mode using the **conf t** command from the privilege EXEC prompt, as shown. Next, enter the configuration mode for the router's serial interface that connects to the ISP. In this example, serial interface 0/0 is being used for the connection; therefore, enter the command **int ser 0/0**:

```
RouterB# conf t
Enter configuration commands, one per line. End with CNTL/Z.
RouterB(config)#int ser 0/0
```

Next, configure the serial interface's IP address and subnet mask. In this case, the ISP assigned an IP address of 192.168.1.2 with a subnet mask of 255.255.255.252. (*Note:* It is a good idea to document your entries into the router's configuration by using the command **description** *(descr)*.) The entries for the IP address and the description are shown:

```
RouterB(config-if)#ip address 192.168.1.2 255.255.255.252
RouterB(config-if)#descr ISP Connection
```

The customer has been assigned the AS number of 65001. (*Note:* This is actually a private AS number. In practice, the customer is assigned a public AS number.) The AS number is used when entering the command for configuring the BGP routing protocol. In this example, the command **router bgp 65001** is entered. The 10.10.10.0/24 network is a network for Customer A. The command **network 10.10.10.0 mask 255.255.255.0** follows, which instructs the router to advertise the Border Gateway Protocol (BGP) over any interfaces with an IP address in the 10.10.10.0/24 network. The next command is for specifying the IP address of the BGP neighbor. This is the IP address of the Serial1/0 interface on the ISP's router. The format for the command is **neighbor** *[ip-address]* **remote-as number** *[neighbor's AS number]*. The last command is for entering a description of the entries.

> **neighbor** [*ip address*] **remote-as number**
> The next command is for specifying the IP address of the BGP neighbor.

The comment **neighbor 192.168.1.1 descr ISP BGP** is used to document the router configuration. The description identifies the neighbor IP address (the ISP) and comments that the routing protocol is BGP:

```
RouterB(config)#router bgp 65001
RouterB(config-router)#network 10.10.10.0 mask 255.255.255.0
RouterB(config-router)#neighbor ?
A.B.C.D  Neighbor  address
WORD     Neighbor  tag
RouterB(config-router)#neighbor 192.168.1.1 remote-as ?
<1-65535> AS of remote neighbor
RouterB(config-router)#neighbor 192.168.1.1 remote-as 65000
RouterB(config-router)#neighbor 192.168.1.1 descr ISP BGP
```

After completing the router configuration, the next step is for the customer to ping the ISP using the IP address provided by the ISP. In this example, the ISP's IP address is 192.168.1.1:

```
RouterB#ping 192.168.1.1
Type escape sequence to abort.
Sending 5 100-byte ICMP Echos to 192.168.1.1, timeout is 2 seconds:
!!!!!
Success rate is 100 percent (5/5), round-trip min/avg/max 32/35/36 ms
```

sh ip bgp sum

The command used to see whether the routers are exchanging BGP routes.

This test verifies that the routers are connected. The command **sh ip bgp sum** can be used to see whether the routers are exchanging routes.

```
RouterB#sh ip bgp sum
BGP router identifier 192.168.1.2, local AS number 65001
BGP table version is 1, main routing table version 1
1 network entries using 101 bytes of memory
1 path entries using 48 bytes of memory
1 BGP path attribute entries using 60 bytes of memory
0 BGP route-map cache entries using 0 bytes of memory
0 BGP filter-list cache entries using 0 bytes of memory
BGP using 209 total bytes of memory
BGP activity 17/16 prefixes, 17/16 paths, scan interval 60 secs


Neighbor      V  AS     MsgRcvd MsgSent TblVer InQ OutQ Up/Down  State/
PfxRcd
192.168.1.1   4  65000 41      34      0      0   0    00:00:14   Idle
```

```
RouterB#sh ip bgp sum
BGP router identifier 192.168.1.2, local AS number 65001
BGP table version is 1, main routing table version 1
1 network entries using 101 bytes of memory
1 path entries using 48 bytes of memory
1 BGP path attribute entries using 60 bytes of memory
0 BGP route-map cache entries using 0 bytes of memory
0 BGP filter-list cache entries using 0 bytes of memory
```

```
BGP using 209 total bytes of memory
BGP activity 17/16 prefixes, 17/16 paths, scan interval 60 secs


Neighbor     V  AS     MsgRcvd MsgSent TblVer InQ OutQ Up/Down  State/
PfxRcd
192.168.1.1  4  65000 41       34      0      0   0    00:00:21
Active
```

The first screen shows a status of **Idle**. The second screen shows a status of **Active**. The screens indicate a local AS number of 65002 and a neighbor IP address of 192.168.1.1. The idle and active indicates the BGP adjacency states of the connection. These states are officially known as a BGP finite state machine (FSM) in RFC 1771, Border Gateway Protocol 4. The BGP FSM consists of six states:

1. Idle state is the initial state where the resources are being initialized and a BGP router is initiating a TCP connection with its BGP peer.

2. Connect state is the next state after the initialization is done. A BGP router waits for a successful TCP connection with its BGP peer.

3. Active state is when the TCP connection between BGP peers cannot be established. The term active is misleading in this case, because it does not imply a positive or successful operation. While in this state, it will continue to try to establish a TCP connection with its peer. If it is still unsuccessful, the state will be reset to idle.

4. Opensent state indicates a successful TCP connection between the BGP peers. At this point, the BGP peers exchange the open message to establish the peering and check the validity of the peering setup information.

5. Openconfirm state is the state where the BGP router is waiting for a BGP keepalive message from its peer. The keepalive message is the indicator the open message is being accepted by its peer.

6. Established state is the final state indicating the BGP peering is established and the routing can be exchanged.

Entering the command **sh ip bgp sum** now shows a *1* in the place where **Idle** and **Active** were present. This indicates the router is exchanging routes. The router is now in the established state and one network route is being received from its BGP peer.

```
RouterB#sh ip bgp sum
BGP router identifier 192.168.1.2, local AS number 65001
BGP table version is 5, main routing table version 5
4 network entries using 404 bytes of memory
4 path entries using 192 bytes of memory
4 BGP path attribute entries using 240 bytes of memory
3 BGP AS-PATH entries using 72 bytes of memory
0 BGP route-map cache entries using 0 bytes of memory
0 BGP filter-list cache entries using 0 bytes of memory
BGP using 908 total bytes of memory
BGP activity 16/12 prefixes, 16/12 paths, scan interval 60 secs
```

```
Neighbor       V  AS    MsgRcvd  MsgSent TblVer InQ OutQ Up/Down
State/PfxRcd
192.168.1.1  4  65000  38       31       5      0   0    00:04:00
1
```

show ip bgp neighbor

This command displays BGP neighbor relationship with its peer.

Another good command used to examine the peering information is **show ip bgp neighbor**. This command displays a BGP neighbor relationship with its peer with more details. This command is generally used to troubleshoot a BGP peering issue. An example of using this command is provided. Notice the amount of detail provided with this command.

```
RouterB# sh ip bgp neighbors
BGP neighbor is 192.168.1.1,  remote AS 65000, external link
  BGP version 4, remote router ID 192.168.1.1
  BGP state = Established, up for 00:00:11
  Last read 00:00:11, hold time is 180, keepalive interval is 60
seconds
  Neighbor capabilities:
    Route refresh: advertised and received(old & new)
    Address family IPv4 Unicast: advertised and received
  Message statistics:
    InQ depth is 0
    OutQ depth is 0
                      Sent        Rcvd
    Opens:             6           6
    Notifications:     0           0
    Updates:           6           16
    Keepalives:        49          49
    Route Refresh:     0           0
    Total:             61          71
  Default minimum time between advertisement runs is 30 seconds

 For address family: IPv4 Unicast
  BGP table version 3, neighbor version 3
  Index 2, Offset 0, Mask 0x4
                         Sent        Rcvd
  Prefix activity:       ----        ----
    Prefixes Current:     1           1 (Consumes 48 bytes)
    Prefixes Total:       1           1
    Implicit Withdraw:    0           0
    Explicit Withdraw:    0           0
    Used as bestpath:     n/a         1
    Used as multipath:    n/a         0

                          Outbound    Inbound
  Local Policy Denied Prefixes:    --------    -------
    Bestpath from this peer:        1           n/a
    Total:                          1           0
  Number of NLRIs in the update sent: max 1, min 0

  Connections established 6; dropped 5
```

```
   Last reset 00:00:51, due to User reset
Connection state is ESTAB, I/O status: 1, unread input bytes: 0
Local host: 192.168.1.2, Local port: 38195
Foreign host: 192.168.1.1, Foreign port: 179

Enqueued packets for retransmit: 0, input: 0  mis-ordered: 0 (0 bytes)

Event Timers (current time is 0x2A88F4):
Timer          Starts    Wakeups           Next
Retrans             4         0             0x0
TimeWait            0         0             0x0
AckHold             2         0             0x0
SendWnd             0         0             0x0
KeepAlive           0         0             0x0
GiveUp              0         0             0x0
PmtuAger            0         0             0x0
DeadWait            0         0             0x0

iss:  950556929  snduna:   950557084  sndnxt:   950557084      sndwnd:
16230
irs: 3579589441  rcvnxt: 3579589596  rcvwnd:        16230  delrcvwnd:
154

SRTT: 124 ms, RTTO: 1405 ms, RTV: 1281 ms, KRTT: 0 ms
minRTT: 16 ms, maxRTT: 300 ms, ACK hold: 200 ms
Flags: higher precedence, nagle

Datagrams (max data segment is 1460 bytes):
Rcvd: 4 (out of order: 0), with data: 2, total data bytes: 154
Sent: 5 (retransmit: 0, fastretransmit: 0), with data: 3, total data
bytes: 154
```

There is a lot of information provided by the **show ip bgp neighbor** command. The first section of the output provides the BGP neighbor relation. Specifically, it provides the following:

- The router ID of the neighbor, which can be different than the next hop ip address (router ID of 192.168.1.1 is shown)
- The BGP state (Established state is shown)
- The BGP messages (opens, notifications, updates, keepalives, and route refreshes) being sent and received between the two BGP peers

The second section gives a more in-depth look into the following;

- How many BGP routes or prefixed are being exchanged between the two BGP peers (one prefix was sent and one prefix was received)
- How many BGP routes are considered best paths (one best path was show)

The last section of the output provides TCP connection status and statistics of the two peers. Information provided includes the following:

- How many times the TCP connection is established and drooped (six times since the connection was established and five times since the connection was dropped).
- The reason of the last peering reset (the reason of user reset was shown).
- The information of the TCP port being used for the BGP connection is identified as TCP port 179.
- The rest of this section displays the TCP packet statistics information for the BGP connection.

The command **sh ip route** can be used to examine the customer's routing table, as shown. The table shows that the Border Gateway Protocol (B) is advertising the 10.10.10.0 network via 192.168.1.1. The 192.168.1.0 network is directly attached to the ISP's router. BGP(B) is also running on the customer's 10.20.20.0 network:

```
RouterB#sh ip route
Codes: C  connected, S  static, I  IGRP, R  RIP, M  mobile, B  BGP D
EIGRP, EX  EIGRP external, O  OSPF, IA  OSPF inter area
N1  OSPF NSSA external type 1, N2  OSPF NSSA external type 2
E1  OSPF external type 1, E2  OSPF external type 2, E  EGP
i  IS-IS, L1  IS-IS level-1, L2  IS-IS level-2, *  candidate default
U  per-user static route, o  ODR T  traffic engineered route
Gateway of last resort is not set
10.0.0.0/24 is subnetted, 2 subnets
B       10.20.20.0 [20/0] via 192.168.1.1, 00:03:56
C       10.10.10.0 is directly connected, FastEthernet0/0
     192.168.1.0/30 is subnetted, 1 subnets
C       192.168.1.0 is directly connected, serial0/1
```

The **show running-configuration (sh run)** command can be used to examine the changes made to the router's configuration file. A partial example of the customer's running-configuration file is shown in the following code. Also, don't forget to save the file to NVRAM after the changes have been verified:

```
RouterB# sh run
.

.
interface Serial0/1
 description ISP Connection
ip address 192.168.1.2 255.255.255.0
 no ip directed-broadcast
!
.

.
router eigrp 100
network 10.10.10.0
!
router bgp 65001
```

```
network 10.10.10.0 mask 255.255.255.0
neighbor 192.168.1.1 remote-as 65000
neighbor 192.168.1.1 description ISP BGP
!
.
.
```

When it comes to BGP routing, you must remember an important concept: BGP can only advertise network routes that are installed in the IGP routing table. The network statement seen above under the router BGP section will not mean anything if the network 10.0.0.0 is not in the IGP routing table of the router. So, one must always check the router's IGP table when troubleshooting BGP. As long as IGP routing protocols, such as RIP, OSPF, EIGRP, IS-IS, or even static are used to advertise the network, BGP will synchronize with the IGP routes and advertise them out. In this case, the network 10.10.10.0 is already in the IGP routing table, because it is being advertised via the EIGRP routing protocol.

Networking Challenge: BGP

Use the Net-Challenge Simulator Software included with the text's companion CD-ROM to demonstrate that you can configure BGP for a router connection to an Internet service provider. The network connection is displayed on the screen when the BGP challenge is started. Place the companion CD-ROM in your computer's drive. Open the *Net-Challenge* folder, and click *Net Challenge V3-2.exe*. When the software is running, click the **Select Challenge** button to open a Select Router Challenge drop-down menu. Select *Chapter 10—BGP*. This opens a checkbox that can be used to verify that you have completed all the tasks. This task assumes that a connection to the Internet cloud has already been established:

1. Enter the privileged EXEC mode on the router.

2. Enter the router configuration mode [the **Router(config)#** prompt].

3. Set the hostname to **Border-Router**.

4. Configure the Fast Ethernet 0/0 interface on Border-Router with the following:

   IP address: 10.10.1.2

   Subnet mask: 255.255.255.0

5. Enable the router's Fast Ethernet 0/0 interface.

6. Configure the Serial0/0 interface with the following:

   IP address: 192.168.1.2

   Subnet mask: 255.255.255.0.

7. Enable the router's Serial0/0 interface.

8. Use the router's **description** command (**descr**) to indicate that this interface is the ISP connection. (*Note:* The text ISP Connection is case-sensitive.)

9. Enable BGP on the router with an AS number of 65002.

10. Configure Border-Router's BGP neighbor with a remote AS of 65001.

11. Configure a BGP route to the 10.0.0.0 network.

12. Use the **show ip route** command to verify that the route from Border-Router to the ISP is configured.

13. Use the **ping** command to verify that the 192.168.1.1 interface is connected.

14. Use the **sh run** command to view the running-configuration file on Border-Router. Verify that BGP is enabled, the description **ISP Connection** has been entered, and the proper network address is specified for the ISP connection.

15. Use the **sh ip int brief** command to check the interface status.

10-3   BGP BEST PATH SELECTION

It is amazing when you think about all the possible paths a data packet can take when traveling from a source to a destination on the Internet. It is equally amazing that the path to a destination can be quickly determined. Selecting the best path to reach a destination is an incredible challenge. This is the challenge addressed by BGP.

BGP Best Path Selection Algorithm
Used to compare the possible routes and to select the best route.

The BGP routing protocol enables computers to connect to other computers in millisecond time to any location around the world. BGP does this by establishing neighbor connections. Once this is done, each neighbor router shares it routes. It has been estimated that there are upward of 400,000 possible routes on the Internet. BGP works differently than IGPs because it does not make routing decisions based on best path metrics. Instead, BGP is a path vector routing protocol, which makes routing decisions based on path attributes that are added to routing information. BGP uses these attributes to make a routing decision and select the best path. It allows an AS to control traffic flow using multiple BGP attributes. More often than not, BGP routers learn multiple paths or routes to the same destination. The **BGP Best Path Selection Algorithm** is used to compare the possible routes and to select the best route. BGP will assign the first valid path as the best path. It will then compare this path with the next path until it reaches the end of the valid paths.

The following list provides the rules in the order of how the path selection is made. These rules are more Cisco-centric, but they generally apply to most of the BGP routers of other vendors:

1. **Weight**: This is a Cisco's proprietary attribute that is assigned locally to your router. This attribute only applies to Cisco routers. This attribute only affects the local router. In situations where there are multiple routes, BGP will select the route with the highest weight.

2. **Local Preference**: This indicates which path to the AS has local preference. The local preference is shared among the iBGP routers within the same AS. Local preferences are widely used to influence the route or path selection as it

propagates throughout the AS. The highest preference is preferred. The default is 100.

3. **Self-Originated**: The routes that are locally originated by BGP running on this router would always be preferred over routes learned from other routers or other BGP networks.

4. **Shortest AS_PATH**: This selection is made based on which route has the shortest AS path. Every route records every AS it has to go through. This makes up an AS path. Every BGP router examines the path of autonomous systems the route has to take before reaching the BGP router. The shortest AS path is preferred. This is used by BGP only when there is a "tie" when comparing weight, local preference, and locally originated vs. aggregate addresses.

5. **Lowest origin type**: The origin attribute that defines the origin of the path. If the path is originated from protocols such as Interior Gateway Protocol (IGP), then it has lower preference to the Exterior Gateway Protocol (EGP).

6. **Lowest multi-exit discriminator (MED)**: This is an external metric of a route. The metric with a lower MED value is preferred over a higher value. The MED value is another widely used attribute to manipulate route selection. Unlike local preference that influences the routing decision within the local AS, the MED value is used to influence the routing decision of an adjacent AS.

7. **eBGP over iBGP**: This simply states that the paths learned via eBGP is preferred over the paths learned via iBGP, which is a way to prevent the loop.

8. **Lowest IGP metric**: The path with the lowest IGP metric is preferred for the BGP next hop.

9. **Multiple paths**: This is used to determine if multiple paths require installation in the routing table.

10. **External paths**: If two paths are external, then BGP prefers the path that was received first.

11. **Lowest router ID**: The route that comes from the BGP router with the lowest router ID (highest IP address on the router) is preferred.

12. **Minimum cluster list**: If the router ID or originator is the same for multiple paths, the path with the minimum cluster list length is preferred.

13. **Lowest neighbor address**: The path that comes from the lowest neighbor address is preferred.

A command that is very useful in examining BGP routes and their attributes is **show ip bgp**. This command by itself displays the summary contents of the BGP routing table. Some of the BGP attributes are also displayed. The following example shows the output of the **show ip bgp** command on Customer's Router B:

> **show ip bgp**
> Displays the summary contents of the BGP routing table.

```
RouterB#sh ip bgp
BGP table version is 5, local router ID is 192.168.1.2
Status codes: s suppressed, d damped, h history, * valid, > best, i -
internal,
          r RIB-failure, S Stale
```

```
Origin codes: i - IGP, e - EGP, ? - incomplete

   Network           Next Hop              Metric  LocPrf  Weight Path
*> 10.20.20.0/24     192.168.1.1              0
0 65000 i
*> 192.168.30.0      192.168.1.1              0
0 65000 65002 i
*> 192.168.200.0     192.168.1.1              0
0 65000 65002 65111 i
```

This time, Router B is receiving more BGP routes from its peer, 192.168.1.1. There are three BGP routes. The * and > indicate that these BGP routes are valid and their paths are the best path to reach these networks. The Next Hop column shows the BGP next hop or peer. The Metric column shows MED value, if it exists. The LocPrf column displays the BGP local preference value, if it is manually configured. The default value is 100. Weight is the Cisco's BGP weight attribute. The result shows that the network 10.20.20.0/24 is from AS 65000. The network 192.168.30.0 was originated from an IGP within the AS 65002 and then it went through AS 65000 before it reaches Router A. The network 192.168.200.0 has the longest AS path of them all. It has to go through three ASs before reaching Router A. The command **sh ip bgp** can be used to display more specific BGP information, such as a specific network prefix or route, as demonstrated in the following example:

```
RouterB#sh ip bgp 192.168.200.0
BGP routing table entry for 192.168.200.0/24, version 5
Paths: (1 available, best #1, table Default-IP-Routing-Table)
  Not advertised to any peer
  65000 65002 65111
    192.168.1.1 from 192.168.1.1 (192.168.1.1)
      Origin IGP, localpref 100, valid, external, best
```

The **sh ip bgp 192.168.200.0** command examines a specific prefix. Instead of having to interpret this route from the output of **sh ip bgp**, this gives a more explanatory version of the route.

10-4   IPV6 OVER THE INTERNET

This section addresses the issue of running IPv6 over the Internet. This section also covers BGP4+, which allows BGP to run IPv6 over the Internet. An example on how to configure a Cisco router for running BGP over the Internet is also presented. Troubleshooting IPv6 and BGP are also presented.

BGP4+
The version of BGP for running IPv6.

The Internet routing is dominated by the BGP routing protocol. This is true for both IPv4 and IPv6 routing over the Internet. The current version of BGP that is used by IPv4 is BGP4. The multiprotocol BGP extensions or **BGP4+** allows BGP4 to be used for IPv6. BGP4+ for IPv6 supports the same features and functionality as IPv4

BGP as well as the additional support for the IPv6 address family and the IPv6 address for the BGP next hop.

The steps to configure IPv6 BGP on Cisco routers are similar to the steps used in IPv4. The first step is to configure the interface on the router that will run IPv6. This requires that the next hop IPv6 address or its IPv6 BGP peer must be reachable by the router. The router BGP process must be configured by issuing the command **router bgp** *AS_Number*. This is not required if a BGP process already exists for IPv4, since the same BGP process will be used.

The **no bgp default ipv4-unicast** command is used to allow protocols other than IPv4 to be activated within the multiprotocol BGP (BGP4+). By default, only the IPv4 unicast is enabled. Next, an IPv6 peer is specified using the command **neighbor** *IPv6_address* **remote as** *AS_Number*. Within the multiprotocol BGP, a protocol must be specified using the command **address-family**. This command is used to specify that IPv6 is selected. Specifically, for IPv6, the command **address-family ipv6** is used.

Within the address family group, the BGP peering with the neighbor can be established using the command **neighbor** *IPv6_address* **activate**. Also, inside the same group, one must specify the IPv6 networks that will be advertised to its peer with the command **network** *IPv6_network*. The following example demonstrates a sample configuration of an IPv6 section of a Cisco router.

```
                    !
router bgp 65203
 no bgp default ipv4-unicast
 neighbor 2001:DB8:1:128::2 remote-as 65200
 neighbor 2001:DB8:1:128::2 description ISP
!
 address-family ipv6
  neighbor 2001:DB8:1:128::2 activate
  neighbor 2001:DB8:1:128::2 soft-reconfiguration inbound
  network 2001:D00::/32
 exit-address-family
!
```

The concepts for troubleshooting IPv6 BGP are still the same as in IPv4 BGP. The peering relationship with the BGP neighbor has to be established before any IPv6 routes can be exchanged. In IPv4 BGP, commands like **sh ip bgp sum** and **sh ip bgp neighbor** were used. However, the IPv6 BGP commands are different in Cisco routers. The IPv6 BGP commands start with the syntax **show bgp ipv6** [**unicast/multicast**]. The type **unicast** or **multicast** must be specified when using the command. The following is the command to view the summary status of the IPv6 BGP neighbor using the command **show bgp ipv6 unicast summary**. This is analogous to the command **show ip bgp summary** in IPv4 that was used to show the summary status of the BGP peering. The output displays almost the same information as what would be in the IPv4 command with the exception of the neighbor IP address, which is shown in IPv6 format:

```
RouterA#sh bgp ipv6 unicast summary
BGP router identifier 10.100.100.100, local AS number 65203
```

no bgp default ipv4-unicast
Used to allow protocols other than IPv4 to be activated within the multiprotocol BGP (BGP4+).

neighbor *IPv6_address* **remote as** *AS_Number*
Used to specify a BGP peer.

address-family ipv6
The command used to specify that IPv6 is specified.

neighbor *IPv6_address* **activate**
Used to establish BGP peering with the neighbor.

network *IPv6_network*
Used to specify the IPv6 networks that will be advertised to its peer.

show bgp ipv6 unicast summary
Command to view the summary status of the IPv6 BGP neighbor.

```
BGP table version is 1843311, main routing table version 1843311
8356 network entries using 1178196 bytes of memory
8356 path entries using 635056 bytes of memory
5835/5831 BGP path/bestpath attribute entries using 933600 bytes of
memory
5649 BGP AS-PATH entries using 232282 bytes of memory
0 BGP route-map cache entries using 0 bytes of memory
0 BGP filter-list cache entries using 0 bytes of memory
BGP using 2979134 total bytes of memory
BGP activity 202608/194251 prefixes, 242511/234155 paths, scan
interval 60 secs


Neighbor            V        AS MsgRcvd MsgSent   TblVer  InQ OutQ
Up/Down  State/PfxRcd
2001:DB8:1:128::2 4     65200 1773365  219989      1843311    0    0
3d13h          8355
```

The IPv6 routes can be examined after the IPv6 BGP peering is successfully established. The same rules for the BGP path algorithm still apply for IPv6. The following is a sample of the IPv6 BGP routes received by Router B from its BGP neighbor: 2001:DB8:1:128::2. The command used to accomplish this task is **sh bgp ipv6 unicast**:

```
RouterB#sh bgp ipv6 unicast
BGP table version is 1843542, local router ID is 10.100.100.100
Status codes: s suppressed, d damped, h history, * valid, > best, i -
internal,
              r RIB-failure, S Stale
Origin codes: i - IGP, e - EGP, ? - incomplete


   Network              Next Hop          Metric LocPrf Weight
Path
*> ::/0                 2001:DB8:1:128::2        0 65200 i
*> 2001::/32            2001:DB8:1:128::2        0 65200 65152
65164 65939 i
*> 2001:200::/32        2001:DB8:1:128::2        0 65200 65152
65153 65388 65660 65500 i
*> 2001:200:900::/40    2001:DB8:1:128::2        0 65200 65152
65153 65537 65660 65660 65660 i
*> 2001:200:C00::/40    2001:DB8:1:128::2        0 65200 65152
651164 65725 65607 65530 i
*> 2001:200:C000::/35   2001:DB8:1:128::2        0 65200 65152
65153 65388 65660 65500 65634 i
*> 2001:200:E000::/35   2001:DB8:1:128::2        0 65200 65152
65153 65388 65660 i
*> 2001:208::/32        2001:DB8:1:128::2        0 65200 65401
65610 65472 i
*> 2001:208:1:1::/64    2001:DB8:1:128::2        0 65200 65401
65610 65472 i
```

The command **sh bgp ipv6 unicast ?** can be used to list more options for looking at more BGP-specific information, such as prefixes or neighbors. The following shows the specific options that can be specified:

```
ict-gate#sh bgp ipv6 unicast ?
  X:X:X:X::X/<0-128>   IPv6 prefix <network>/<length>
  community            Display routes matching the communities
  community-list       Display routes matching the community-list
  dampening            Display detailed information about dampening
  extcommunity-list    Display routes matching the extcommunity-list
  filter-list          Display routes conforming to the filter-list
  inconsistent-as      Display only routes with inconsistent origin
ASs
  injected-paths       Display all injected paths
  labels               Display BGP labels for prefixes
  neighbors            Detailed information on TCP and BGP neighbor
connections
  paths                Path information
  peer-group           Display information on peer-groups
  pending-prefixes     Display prefixes pending deletion
  prefix-list          Display routes matching the prefix-list
  quote-regexp         Display routes matching the AS path "regular
expression"
  regexp               Display routes matching the AS path regular
expression
  replication          Display replication status of update-group(s)
  rib-failure          Display bgp routes that failed to install in
the routing table (RIB)
  route-map            Display routes matching the route-map
  summary              Summary of BGP neighbor status
  update-group         Display information on update-groups
  |                    Output modifiers
  <cr>
```

10-5 CONFIGURE BGP ON JUNIPER ROUTERS

So far, the examples shown in this chapter are for Cisco routers. However, the BGP concepts discussed so far can also be applied to any type of router. BGP is a universal Internet Protocol, and most of the BGP Internet routers comply with the same standard for optimum interoperability. The steps to configure BGP on Juniper routers are similar to Cisco's implementation. First and foremost, the network interface between the router and its BGP neighbor must be configured. This requires that the interface connection has to be up and operational. After the interface connection is established, the BGP configuration can begin.

The first step of the BGP configuration is to define the BGP AS of the router. On Cisco routers, this is accomplished with the command **router** *bgp AS_Number*. On

Juniper routers, the BGP AS is defined within the **routing-options** section. The following section demonstrates the configuration steps:

```
net-admin@j-router> configure
[edit]
admin@j-router# edit routing-options
[edit routing-options]
admin@j-router# set autonomous-system 65555
[edit routing-options]
admin@j-router# set router-id 172.20.1.1
```

The command set **autonomous-system** *[AS_Number]* is used to define the BGP AS for the router. The command **set router-id** *[ip_address]* is used to define the BGP router BGP identifier. This command is optional, just like with Cisco routers. If this command is not specified, the router will use the highest IP address of the loopback addresses or the highest IP address of the interface addresses as the router ID.

The next step of BGP configuration is to define the BGP neighbor or peer. This is configured under the protocol section rather than the routing-options section. The following section demonstrates the configuration steps:

```
[edit]
admin@j-router# edit protocols bgp
[edit protocols bgp]
admin@j-router# set group myISP neighbor 10.200.200.2
[edit protocols bgp]
admin@j-router# set group myISP neighbor 10.200.200.2 description
"Connection to my ISP"
[edit protocols bgp]
admin@j-router# set group myISP neighbor 10.200.200.2 peer-as 65000
[edit protocols bgp]
admin@j-router# set group myISP  type external
[edit protocols bgp]
admin@j-router# show
group myISP {
  type external;
  neighbor 10.200.200.10 {
    description "Connection to my ISP";
    peer-as 65000;
  }
}
```

> **autonomous-system**
> *[AS_Number]*
> This command is used in JUNOS to define the BGP AS for the router.
>
> **set router-id**
> *[ip_address]*
> This command is used in JUNOS to define the BGP router BGP identifier.

> **set group** [*BGP_group_name*]
> **neighbor** [*next_hop_address*]
> Used to define the BGP neighbor on a Juniper router.

In JUNOS, the BGP neighbors are placed within a group, and a group can contain one or multiple BGP neighbors. The routing policy or BGP configuration can be applied to a group of BGP neighbors. The command **set group** [*BGP_group_name*] **neighbor** [*next_hop_address*] is used to define the BGP neighbor. The command can be extended with keywords such as **peer-as** to specify the AS number of the neighbor and **description** to provide short descriptive information. In JUNOS, one must specify the type of BGP (external or internal); therefore, the command **set group** *[BGP_group_name]* **type** *[external/internal]* is used. To verify the BGP configuration, the **show** command displays the configuration under the protocol bgp section.

At this point, the Juniper router is ready to establish external BGP peering with its ISP neighbor router. If the BGP peering is established successfully, it will receive BGP routes from its neighbor. However, no network prefixes will be advertised from this router yet. On Cisco routers, one must issue a network statement command to specify a network prefix that is to be advertised over BGP. This is also required on Juniper routers; however, this will not be a one-line command as in Cisco IOS. In JUNOS, this is done via a routing policy. The routing policy must be defined to include the network prefixes to be advertised over BGP. Then, it must be applied within the BGP configuration with an export statement. The following is a sample configuration of a routing policy to define network prefixes:

```
policy-options {
    prefix-list network-for-BGP {
        192.168.100.0/24;
        192.168.200.0/24;
        172.16.100.0/24;
    }
    policy-statement Export-BGP {
        term local-prefixes {
            from {
                prefix-list network-for-BGP;
            }
            then {
                accept;
            }
        }
        then reject;
    }
}
```

Then, the routing policy must be applied within the BGP configuration with an export statement. The following example shows the routing policy **Export-BGP** being applied to the BGP group **myISP**. This enables the network prefixes of 192.168.100.0/24, 192.168.200.0/24, and 172.16.100.0/24 to be advertised over BGP:

```
[edit]
admin@j-router# edit protocols bgp
[edit protocols bgp]
admin@j-router# set group myISP export Export-BGP
```

This completes the basic BGP configuration for Juniper routers. On Cisco routers, one would use a command like **show ip bgp sum** to verify the summary status of its BGP neighbors after the BGP configuration is complete. A similar command exists in JUNOS as well. The command is **show bgp sum** and its output is shown here:

```
admin@j-router> show bgp summary
Groups: 1 Peers: 1 Down peers: 0
Table    Tot Paths  Act Paths Suppressed  History Damp State   Pending
inet.0         10        10          0          0    0     0         0
Peer              AS    InPkt    OutPkt  OutQ  Flaps Last  Up/Dwn
State|#Active/Received/Damped...
10.200.200.10  65000    53138     53122     0      3       2w4d10h
4/4/0                  10/10/0
```

The output shows that the connection with the BGP neighbor of 10.200.200.10 of the AS number 65000 is established. There are ten prefixes received and active from its peer. The command **show bgp neighbor** can be used for an in-depth view of the neighbor status and statistics similar to the command **show ip bgp neighbor** in Cisco IOS. Another useful command for BGP troubleshooting is **show route protocol bgp**. This command shows the BGP routing table. These are the routes received via BGP and their BGP attributes. This is equivalent to the command **show ip bgp** in Cisco IOS. The following is sample output from the **show route protocol bgp** command:

```
admin@j-router> show route protocol bgp

inet.0: 378081 destinations, 378141 routes (378071 active, 8 holddown,
2 hidden)
+ = Active Route, - = Last Active, * = Both

0.0.0.0/0          *[BGP/10] 1d 11:29:00, MED 0, localpref 100
                      AS path: 65000 I
                    > to 172.20.1.1 via ge-0/0/0.0
10.10.4.0/22        *[BGP/170] 2d 06:12:12, MED 0, localpref 90, from
10.200.200.10
                      AS path: 65000 65215 65164 65323 65545 65620 I
                    > to 172.20.1.1 via ge-0/0/0.0
10.10.16.0/23       *[BGP/170] 1w4d 07:58:48, MED 0, localpref 90,
from 10.200.200.10
                      AS path: 65000 65215 65516 65519 I
                    > to 172.20.1.1 via ge-0/0/0.0
10.10.18.0/23       *[BGP/170] 1w4d 07:58:48, MED 0, localpref 90,
from 10.200.200.10
                      AS path: 65000 65215 65516 65519 I
                    > to 172.20.1.1 via ge-0/0/0.0
10.10.20.0/23       *[BGP/170] 1w4d 07:58:48, MED 0, localpref 90,
from 10.200.200.10
                      AS path: 65000 65215 65516 65519 I
                    > to 172.20.1.1 via ge-0/0/0.0
10.10.22.0/23       *[BGP/170] 1w4d 07:58:48, MED 0, localpref 90,
from 10.200.200.10
                      AS path: 65000 65215 65516 65519 I
                    > to 172.20.1.1 via ge-0/0/0.0
```

```
10.10.25.0/24          *[BGP/170] 1w4d 07:58:48, MED 0, localpref 90,
from 10.200.200.10
                        AS path: 65000 65215 65516 65519 I
                       > to 172.20.1.1 via ge-0/0/0.0
10.10.26.0/23          *[BGP/170] 1w4d 07:58:48, MED 0, localpref 90,
from 10.200.200.10
                        AS path: 65000 65215 65516 65519 I
                       > to 172.20.1.1 via ge-0/0/0.0
10.10.28.0/22          *[BGP/170] 1w4d 07:58:48, MED 0, localpref 90,
from 10.200.200.10
                        AS path: 65000 65215 65516 65519 I
                       > to 172.20.1.1 via ge-0/0/0.0
10.10.64.0/18          *[BGP/170] 1w4d 07:59:01, MED 0, localpref 90,
from 10.200.200.10
                        AS path: 65000 65215 65164 65725 65670 65144 I
                       > to 172.20.1.1 via ge-0/0/0.0
```

The * before the BGP information indicates that the path is the best BGP path.
This command displays the BGP attributes such as AS_path, BGP local preference
value, and the Multi-Exit Discriminator value.

Configuring IPv6 BGP on Juniper routers is not complicated. The following is an
example IPv6 BGP configuration. It is similar to how IPv4 BGP is configured. The
configuration is placed inside a BGP group. The type of BGP is defined as external.
The big differences are the use of IPv6 as the BGP neighbor next-hop address and
the addition of **family inet6**. The **family inet6** enables the IPv6 family address.
Within the **family inet6**, there is an option for **unicast**, **multicast**, or any (both).
In this example, the option specifies support for both **unicast IPv6** and **multicast
IPv6**.

> **family inet6**
> JUNOS command to
> enable the IPv6 family
> address.

```
protocols {
    bgp {
        group myISP6 {
            type external;
            export Export-BGP6;
            family inet6 {
                any;
            }
            neighbor 2001:db8:feed:beef::1 {
                description "Connection to my ISP";
                peer-as 65000;
            }
        }
    }
}
```

Also, you must keep in mind that the routing policy applied to this BGP group, Ex-
port-BGP6, must be written to include IPv6 prefixes instead of IPv4 prefixes. The
example policy statement, Export-BGP6, is slightly different than the one shown
in the IPv4 example because it is using a route-filter statement not prefix-list. Both
will accomplish the same goal, which is to advertise the prefixes into BGP. This

example shows the route-filter is used to filter prefixes of 2001:db8:11::/48 and 2001:db8:22::/48. Only these prefixes will be exported into BGP routing:

```
policy-options {
    policy-statement Export-BGP6 {
        term local-prefixes {
            from {
                route-filter 2001:db8:11::0/48 exact;
                route-filter 2001:db8:22::0/48 exact;
            }
            then {
                accept;
            }
        }
        then reject;
    }
}
```

On Juniper routers, the same BGP troubleshooting commands, such as **show bgp summary**, **show bgp neighbor**, or **show route protocol bgp**, can be used for both IPv4 and IPv6.

SUMMARY

This chapter presented the fundamentals of wide-area networking. The student should understand and appreciate the role that the PSTN (public switched telephone network—telco) plays in wide-area networking. This chapter only introduced a fraction of the technologies and issues needed to be understood by the network administrator. However, this chapter addressed the fundamental or base knowledge needed for a networking administrator to start working in this field.

The student should understand the following:

1. The concept and purpose of the AS number (**ASN**)

2. The concept of the stubby areas

3. Internet routing using BGP

4. The steps for configuring BGP on a router

5. The purpose of the BGP Best Path Selection Algorithm

6. The issues of running IPv6 over the Internet using BGP4+

7. The issues of configuring BGP on a Juniper router

QUESTIONS AND PROBLEMS

Section 10-1

1. What is the purpose of a wide-area network connection?

2. What is the easiest routing protocol to use for WAN links? What if there are multiple connections to the remote sites?

3. Define the following:

    a. Stubby areas

    b. Totally stubby areas

4. A multi-homed customer has

    a. A single Internet connection

    b. More than one Internet connection

    c. Static routes

    d. None of these answers are correct

5. BGP is considered to be

    a. An external routing protocol

    b. Used for routing between the same networks

    c. Outdated

6. Each router participating in BGP manually does what?

    a. Makes an AS path

    b. Makes a peering with its BGP neighbor

    c. Sets the remote router's IP address

    d. Sets the remote router's ASN

7. The network administrator must know this when configuring the Internet connection.

    a. The local address and the ASN

    b. The loopback address and the ASN

    c. The remote-as and the ASN

    d. The remote IP address and ASN

Section 10-2

8. The router command used for entering a description is

    a. Comment

    b. !

    c. *

    d. Description

9. What does the router command **router bgp 65003** mean?

10. Write the router command for specifying the IP address of the BGP neighbor.

Also, show the router prompt.

11. How many IP addresses are provided on each subnet with a 255.255.255.252 subnet mask?

12. List the command that can be used to enter a description that identifies the 10.10.200.2 interface as the connection to the ISP. List the command and the router prompt.

13. The following command is entered on the router:

```
Router-ISP#sh ip int brief
Interface         IP-Address   OK?  Method  Status     Protocol
FastEthernet0/0   unassigned   YES  unset   administratively down
down
```

What does it mean for the protocol to be down?

    a. The routing protocol has not been configured.

    b. BGP routing is not enabled.

    c. The interface is not communicating with another networking device.

    d. All of these answers are correct.

14. What is the purpose of the **sh ip bgp sum** command*?*

15. Which of the following is the code for BGP routes if the command **show ip route** is entered?

    a. O

    b. B

    c. C

    d. D

16. The command **show ip route** is entered on a router. Describe what the following information provides:

```
Gateway of last resort is not set
B 192.10.20.0/24 [20/0] via 192.168.10.1, 00:03:25
172.16.0.0/16 is subnetted, 1 subnets
D 172.16.0.0 is directly connected, Serial1
C 192.168.10.0/24 is directly connected, Serial0
```

17. The following information is displayed after entering the **show running-config** command:

```
router bgp 65020
network 192.168.20.0
neighbor 10.10.100.1 remote-as 65010
neighbor 10.10.100.1 description ISP BGP
```

    What is the AS for the neighbor?

    What network(s) is(are) running BGP?

18. BGP can only advertise network routes that are installed where on a router?

19. List the six states of the BGP finite state machine in the order of their operation?

20. Match the term with the correct BGP state.

    While in this state, the router will continue trying to establish a TCP connection.

    a. Idle State

    b. Active State

    c. Established State

    d. Connect State

21. Match the term with the correct BGP state.

    This state indicates a successful TCP connection between the BGP peers.

    a. Idle State

    b. Active State

    c. Opensent State

    d. Openconfirm State

22. Match the term with the correct BGP state.

This state is where a BGP router is initiating a TCP connection with its BGP peer.

    a. Idle State

    b. Active State

    c. Openconfirm State

    d. Connect State

23. Match the term with the correct BGP state.

This state indicates the BGP peering is established.

    a. Idle State

    b. Active State

    c. Established State

    d. Connect State

24. Match the term with the correct BGP state.

In this state the router is waiting for the keepalive message.

    a. Idle State

    b. Active State

    c. Opensent State

    d. Openconfirm State

25. Match the term with the correct BGP state.

This is the next state after the initialization is done:

    a. Idle State

    b. Active State

    c. Openconfirm State

    d. Connect State

26. The **sh ip bgp sum** command is issued and a 1 shows in the place where Idle and Active were displayed. What does this indicate?

27. What command is generally used to troubleshoot a BGP peering issue?

Section 10-3

28. What is the purpose of the best path selection algorithm?

29. What does BGP use to make routing decisions?

30. What path attributes does the BGP Best Path Algorithm use to make its route selection?

31. In regards to the Cisco rules that are used to select the best path, match the term to the definition.

1. Shortest AS_PATH	a. This indicates which path to the AS has local preference.
2. Lowest Origin Type	b. This is used by BGP only when there is a "tie."
3. Local Preference	c. This is the first rule for selecting the best path.
4. Weight	d. That the BGP AS Path prefers eBGP over iBGP.
5. eBGP over iBGP	e. Protocols, such as Interior Gateway Protocol (IGP), have lower preference to the Exterior Gateway Protocol (EGP).

32. BGP is a path vector routing protocol. What does this mean?

33. What command is used to examine BGP routes and their attributes?

34. How do you know if BGP routes are valid?

35. How do you know if BGP routes are the best path to reach a network?

36. The **sh ip bgp** command shows that following routes to multiple networks:

```
*> 192.20.20.0/24    192.168.10.1                    0
0 65000 i
*> 10.20.30.0      192.168.10.1
0 65000 65002 i
*> 10.10.20.0      192.168.10.1
0 65000 65002 65111 i
```

How can you modify the **sh ip bgp** command so that only the information for the 10.20.30.0 network is displayed?

37. The **sh ip bgp** command is issued. Where is the BGP peer information displayed?

Section 10-4

38. What version of BGP is used to run IPv6 over the Internet?

39. What is the command for configuring the BGP process for IPv6 on a router?

40. What command is issued to allow protocols other than IPv4 to be activated within the multiprotocol BGP.

41. What is the purpose of the neighbor IPv6_address remote as AS_Number command?

42. How is a protocol specified in the multiprotocol BGP?

43. How is IPv6 specified in BGP?

44. What information does the following command display?

```
RouterA#sh bgp ipv6 unicast summary
```
45. List the command that is used to establish BGP peering.

46. What is the purpose of the command **network IPv6_network**?

Section 10-5

47. How is the BGP AS configured on a Juniper router? List the required configuration steps. Assume an AS of 65000 and a router ID of 192.168.20.10.

48. What happens if the **set router-id** command is not issued on a Juniper router?

49. What is this information showing?

```
admin@j-router# set group myISP neighbor 10.200.200.2 peer-as
65000
```

50. How is a network prefix advertised on a Juniper router?

51. What is this information showing on a Juniper router?

```
policy-options {
    prefix-list network-for-BGP {
        172.16.100.0/24;
        192.168.100.0/24;
    }
```

52. What does the following command do on a Juniper router?

```
admin@j-router# set group myISP export Export-BGP
```

53. The command **is show bgp sum** is issued on a Juniper router and its output is shown here. Is a connection to AS 65300 established? How do you know?

```
admin@j-router> show bgp summary
Groups: 1 Peers: 1 Down peers: 0
Table       Tot Paths  Act Paths Suppressed    History Damp State     Pending
inet.0        10          10          0           0         0          0
Peer               AS     InPkt    OutPkt     OutQ    Flaps Last Up/Dwn
State|     #Active/Received/Damped...
192.100.10.10      65300   45138    45122       0       3      2w4d10h
4/4/0              8/8/0
```

54. How is external or internal BGP specified in JUNOS?

55. How is a BGP neighbor defined in JUNOS?

56. What command is used in Juniper to display the BGP routing table?

57. What does the * mean for the following information?

```
10.10.4.0/22          *[BGP/170] 2d 06:12:12, MED 0, localpref 90,
from 10.200.200.10
```

58. What command is used to specify support for both unicast IPv6 and multicast IPv6?

Critical Thinking

59. Answer the following questions for the following information:

```
RouterA#sh ip bgp
BGP table version is 5, local router ID is 192.168.1.2
Status codes: s suppressed, d damped, h history, * valid, > best,
i - internal,
          r RIB-failure, S Stale
Origin codes: i - IGP, e - EGP, ? - incomplete
```

```
    Network                Next Hop            Metric  LocPrf
Weight Path
*> 192.20.20.0/24    192.168.10.1              0           0
65100 i
*> 10.20.30.0              192.168.10.1        0       65100
65102 i
*> 10.10.20.0              192.168.10.1        0       65100
65102 65111   i
```

    a. Is the route to the 10.10.20.0 network valid? How do you know?

    b. What AS is network 192.20.20.0 from?

    c. What network did 10.20.30.0 originate from?

    d. Which network has the longest path? How many ASs does it go through? Identify the ASs.

60. What is the following information showing?

```
router bgp 65203
 no bgp default ipv4-unicast
 neighbor 2001:DB8:1:128::2 remote-as 65200
 neighbor 2001:DB8:1:128::2 description ISP
```

61. What command is used to verify that BGP is exchanging routes? How does this change for IPv6?

62. What is a *cloud*?

63. The running configuration for a router shows the following information. What does this indicate? What is soft-reconfiguration inbound?

```
neighbor 2001:DB8:1:128::2 soft-reconfiguration inbound
```

64. What type of IPv6 address is this and how do you know? What is the purpose of the double colon (::)?

2001:DB8:1:128::2

65. The following information is displayed on Cisco router. What information is being displayed for the IPv6 settings?

```
address-family ipv6
  neighbor 2001:DB8:1:128::2 activate
  neighbor 2001:DB8:1:128::2 soft-reconfiguration inbound
  network 2001:D00::/32
 exit-address-family
```

VOICE OVER IP

Chapter Outline

Objectives

- Examine the technologies used in the generation, management, and transport of Voice over IP calls

- Investigate the ways Voice over IP telephony can be incorporated into a network

- Develop an understanding of the key quality of service issues associated with Voice over IP telephony

- Examine the data packets generated in a Voice over IP call

Key Terms

VoIP

PBX

PSTN

signaling

SS7

H.323

SIP

SSIP

CODEC

RTP

RTCP

packet sequence number

timestamp

tie line

TDM

VoIP gateway

VoIP relay

QoS

jitter

buffer

network latency

weighted random early discard (WRED)

queuing

first queued

FIFO

weighted fair queuing (WFQ)

CBWFQ

PQ

CQ

spit

class map

policy map

DSCP (Differentiated Services Code Point)

EF

AF33

E911

Secure Real Time Protocol (SRTP)

INTRODUCTION

Voice over IP (**VoIP**), or IP telephony, is the transport of phone conversations over packet networks. Many companies and individuals are taking advantage of the development of new technologies that support the convergence of voice and data over their existing packet networks. The network administrator can also see an additional benefit with the cost savings using a converge voice/data network. This has created a new role for the network administrator: telecommunications manager. The network administrator must not only be aware of the issues of data transport within and external to the network, but also the issues of incorporating voice data traffic into the network.

This chapter examines the basics of building Voice over IP (VoIP) networks. The technologies, the data transport, and the quality of service issues are examined. The mechanics of transporting voice data traffic over an IP network are presented in Section 11-1. This includes encoding the voice signal, transporting the digitized voice data, and interfacing the data via a gateway to another IP network. Section 11-2 presents an overview of assembling Voice over IP networks. This section examines three different techniques for incorporating an IP telephony solution.

Many quality of service (QoS) issues arise with the deployment of a Voice over IP network. For example, the packet arrival time is not guaranteed in an IP network; therefore, a noise problem called *jitter* is introduced. This and other QoS issues are examined in Section 11-3. Voice over IP data packets are examined in Section 11-4. This section examines the data packets generated when an IP call is placed and how codes are used to identify the different types of data packets being transported.

VoIP

Voice over IP telephony. Protocol used to pass digitized voice over packet networks.

11-1 THE BASICS OF VOICE OVER IP

This section presents an overview of the technologies used in the generation, management, and transport of Voice over IP (VoIP) calls. The basic VoIP system begins with a telephone. IP telephones are available as standalone units or as software running on a PC. The PC requires a microphone and a speaker to support the telephone call.

Standard telephones can also be used in IP telephony if the telephones connect to a private branch exchange (**PBX**) that supports IP telephony. The PBX is a user's own telephone system. It manages the internal switching of telephone calls and also interfaces the user's phone to the **PSTN** (public switched telephone network—the telephone company [telco]). The interface of the IP telephone system to the PSTN is called a *gateway*.

The gateway's function is to provide an interface for IP telephony calls to the PSTN or to interface one IP telephone system with another. This requires that the voice data be packaged for transport over the IP network or the PSTN. The gateway also makes sure that the proper **signaling** is included for the voice data packet transport.

PBX

Private branch exchange. The user's own telephone system.

PSTN

Public switched telephone network—the telephone company.

Signaling

Used to establish and terminate telephone calls.

Signaling is used to establish and terminate telephone calls and to manage many of the advanced features available with telephones.

The PSTN uses a signaling technique called SS7 that provides enhanced features:

- Toll-free services
- Worldwide telecommunications
- Enhanced call features (for example, call forwarding and three-way calling)
- Local number portability

SS7
Signaling technique used by the PSTN.

IP telephony uses different signaling techniques. The most common of these are H.323 and SIP. H.323 is a suite of protocols that define how voice and video are transported over IP networks. H.323 works with delay-sensitive traffic (for example, voice and video) to help establish a priority for timely packet delivery, critical for real-time applications. The bottom line is that the packets must arrive in a timely manner to ensure quality reproduction of the voice or video.

H.323
Suite of protocols that defines how voice and video are transported over IP networks.

SIP
Session Initiation Protocol. Used to manage multimedia packet transfers over IP networks.

SSIP
Secure Session Initiation Protocol. Provides for end-to-end secure communications by requiring user authentication.

The Session Initiation Protocol (SIP) was developed by the Internet Engineering Task Force (IETF) to manage multimedia packet transfers over IP networks. SIP runs in the application layer of the OSI model and uses the connectionless protocol UDP for packet transport. SIP is responsible for establishing and terminating IP telephony calls and is responsible for transferring the call. A secure version of SIP has been developed called Secure Session Initiation Protocol (SSIP). SSIP provides for end-to-end secure communications by requiring user authentication.

The next part of this section addresses the issues of transporting voice (telephone call) over an IP network. It was previously mentioned that VoIP telephone calls can be made from phone to phone, PC to phone, and PC to PC, as shown in Figure 11-1. The telephones connect to the VoIP gateway, and the computers connect directly to the IP network (intranet or Internet). A popular choice for Internet telephony is Skype. This service offers free global telephony service via the Internet to another Skype user.

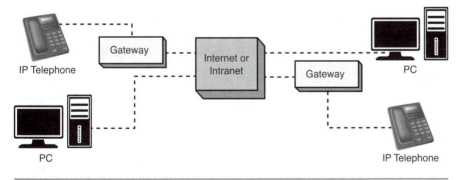

FIGURE 11-1 The various ways of placing VoIP telephone calls

The first step for preparing the VoIP signal for transport is to digitize the analog voice to a PCM (pulse code modulation) digital signal (the PCM data stream). This conversion is taken care of inside the digital telephone, computer, or PBX.

Processors are used to examine the PCM data stream to remove any silent spaces. Transporting data packets that contain no information (that is, silence) is a waste of bandwidth; therefore, any digitized silence is removed. The remaining PCM data is then sent to a CODEC.

The purpose of the coder/decoder (**CODEC**) is to structure the PCM data for inputting into frames. This involves encoding, compressing, and decoding the data.

The frames are then placed into one packet. A Real Time Protocol (**RTP**) header is added to each frame. The RTP header provides the following:

- Packet sequence number
- Timestamp

A companion protocol to RTP is the Real Time Control Protocol (**RTCP**). The purpose of RTCP is to manage packet synchronization and identification and the transport of the data.

The **packet sequence number** is used to keep track of the order of the data packets and to detect any lost packets. RTP uses UDP for transporting the data. There is always a chance that packets could be lost in a congested network or the packets could arrive out of order. The RTP packet sequence number enables a processor to reassemble the data packets. Lost digital voice data packets will cause annoying pops and clicks when converted back to analog at the receiver. One technique is to fill in the blanks with a previously received data packet, as demonstrated in Figure 11-2. This technique helps minimize annoying pops and clicks. The substituted data packets are sometimes played back at a reduced volume to help smooth the transition.

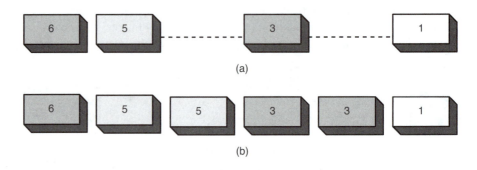

FIGURE 11-2   Reconstructing the data stream at the receiver if packets are missing: (a) the received data stream with missing packets; (b) the reconstructed data stream

Timestamps are assigned to the voice packets by RTP to provide the correct time intervals for a packet. The receivers use the timestamps to reproduce the playback of the voice packets in the same time interval sequence as recorded.

This section examined the fundamental issues of VoIP telephony, including the technologies needed for transporting voice calls. The next section examines the steps for assembling a VoIP network.

11-2 VOICE OVER IP NETWORKS

The advantages of converging voice traffic with existing data traffic are obvious. A company can have a considerable investment in routing data traffic both internally and externally to the home network. Internally, the company will have a substantial investment in installed twisted-pair cable and wall plates for computer networks. Externally, a company might have network connections to remote sites via leased communication lines. It is a reasonable next step for the company to investigate combining voice traffic with the existing data traffic for connecting to external sites; however, best practices dictate that voice and data traffic should remain separated within the LAN. This can be accomplished by establishing VLANs to support the voice traffic.

This section examines three ways a company can implement VoIP telephony into its network:

1. Replace an existing PBX voice tie line (for example, a T1 circuit) with a VoIP gateway.

2. Upgrade the company's existing PBX to support IP telephony.

3. Switch the company over to a complete IP telephone system.

Replacing an Existing PBX Tie Line

It is common practice for companies to use a PBX tie line to interconnect phone systems at different locations. The location of the PBXs could be across town from each other, or across the country or the world. The same company could also have leased data lines to interconnect the same facilities. This is shown in part a of Figure 11-3. The PBXs at each site are interconnected with a T1 tie line for the purpose of transporting telephone calls between sites. In part b of Figure 11-3, the networks are configured as a wide area data network. The company must examine the following issues:

- The company has to lease separate lines for voice (phone) and data.

- There are times when the telephone traffic is minimal and the data traffic movement could be improved if more bandwidth was occasionally available.

A standard solution for combining voice and data networks is to multiplex the voice and data traffic over the same **tie line** (for example, a T1 connection), as demonstrated in Figure 11-4. In this example, a technique called time division multiplexing (**TDM**) is used to divide the available bandwidth of the line interconnecting the two networks to carry both data and voice. The problem with this is the voice bandwidth is reserved for a required number of phone calls even if the calls are not being made. Combining the two networks simplifies the transport, but it doesn't necessarily improve the overall network performance.

> **Tie Line**
> Line used to interconnect PBXs.
>
> **TDM**
> Time division multiplexing.

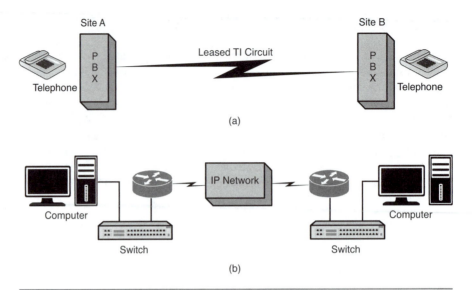

FIGURE 11-3 (a) The traditional interconnection of PBXs between sites; (b) the interconnection of data networks between sites

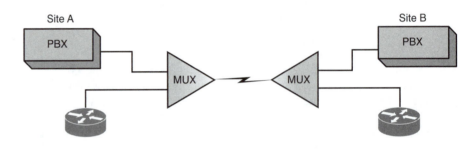

FIGURE 11-4 The use of multiplexing to combine the voice and data traffic for transport over a common T1 line

VoIP Gateway

Provides the proper signaling of digitized voice data for transport over the IP network.

VoIP Relay

Another name for a VoIP gateway.

A VoIP solution addresses the limitations of the traditional TDM arrangement. Figure 11-5 shows the modified network. The PBXs are now connected to a **VoIP gateway** (also called a **VoIP relay**). The VoIP gateway is responsible for providing the proper signaling of the digitized voice data and encapsulating the data packets for transport over the IP network. The advantage of this arrangement is the networks can more efficiently use the available bandwidth.

Note that each site (see Figure 11-5) has a telephone connection to the local telephone company via the public switched telephone network (PSTN). This connection is necessary so that the phone traffic can reach users outside the network. It is also important to note that this connection serves as a backup if the Internet connection goes down.

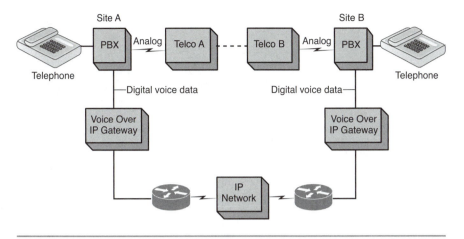

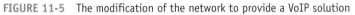

FIGURE 11-5   The modification of the network to provide a VoIP solution

The advantages of this arrangement are as follows:

- The voice and data traffic are combined for more efficient use of the network's available bandwidth.

- The sites can still use the existing PBX, telephones, and connections to the local PSTN.

The potential disadvantage is that growth in data or voice bandwidth requirements can impact the telephone (voice) quality of service. Few companies will be willing to sacrifice *any* quality associated with telephone calls just to implement a VoIP solution. (Note: QoS issues are examined in Section 11-3.)

Upgrading Existing PBXs to Support IP Telephony

A company might decide that IP telephony should be used, but gradual steps should be taken toward IP telephony deployment. A solution would be for the company to upgrade its existing PBXs to support IP telephony. This enables the existing telephones to act like IP telephones and enable the IP telephones to place calls over the PSTN. Figure 11-6 illustrates an example of this Voice over IP solution.

Figure 11-6 shows that the company's PBX has been replaced or upgraded to a PBX capable of supporting IP telephony. In this example, the company is running both conventional and IP telephones. Either of these phones can place telephone calls over the IP network or via the PSTN. The conventional telephones connect to the PBX in the traditional manner. The IP telephones connect to the PBX via a network switch. The PBX will have an IP call manager for placing and receiving calls. The gateway enables both IP and conventional phone calls to exit or enter the IP network. The PBX will have a connection to the PSTN to support traditional call traffic from conventional telephones. Table 11-1 outlines the advantages and disadvantages of upgrading the PBX.

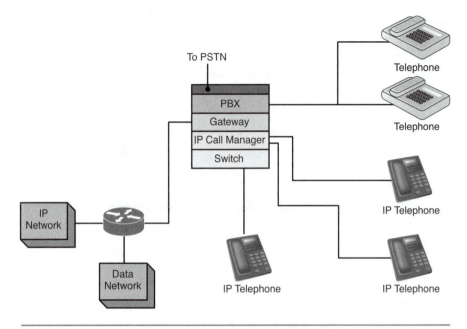

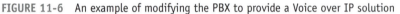

FIGURE 11-6 An example of modifying the PBX to provide a Voice over IP solution

TABLE 11-1 Advantages and Disadvantages of Upgrading the PBX

Advantages	Disadvantages
Conventional telephones will now work with telephony, so existing telephone hardware doesn't need to be replaced.	The cost of upgrading the PBX must justify the potential benefit.
Both PSTN and IP network voice traffic are supported.	QoS issues still exist.
Data traffic is easily integrated with the telephone system.	
The IP telephones can use existing computer network twisted-pair cable and RJ-45 wall plates to connect the new IP telephones.	

Switching to a Complete IP Telephony Solution

A company also has the option of switching completely to an IP telephone system. This requires the company to replace all its conventional telephones with IP telephones and/or PC telephones. The company's PBX is replaced with an IP-based PBX, and a gateway is required for connecting the IP-PBX to the PSTN. Figure 11-7 shows this IP solution.

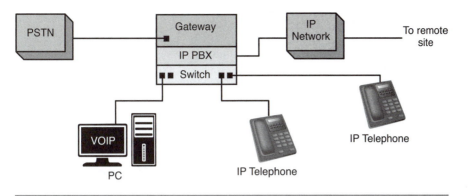

FIGURE 11-7   A complete IP telephony solution

Figure 11-7 shows the IP telephones connecting to the IP-PBX in much the same way computers connect to a switch in computer networking. The company's IP-PBX connects to the remote site's IP telephone network. The IP-PBX also contains a gateway that connects the IP-PBX to the PSTN.

The advantage of a complete IP telephony solution is that the company can use the IP network for delivery of telephone calls within the company and to any remote site connected to the Internet or that supports VoIP.

The disadvantages of a complete IP telephony solution are as follows:

- There is a startup cost of replacing old telephones with IP hardware and/or software-based telephones.
- QoS issues still exist.
- The addition of new IP phones means there are new networked devices to manage, meaning more work for the network administrator.

In today's environment, we are seeing more and more complete IP telephony solutions. New businesses will usually start with the complete VoIP system, because it is more cost effective. In addition, one network infrastructure will be able to support both data and voice. This way there is no need to worry about a separate data infrastructure and phone infrastructure. Both networks can be run on the same copper environment (CAT5 or CAT6), on the same network switches, and on the same network router.

There have been many advancements made toward the support of IP telephony, namely with network routers. Many routers now have integrated service modules that can support Voice over IP directly. Many functions that used to require separate pieces of equipment, for example, gateways or call managers, now can be done using one router. This is a much more effective solution for small to medium sized telephony environments.

11-3 QUALITY OF SERVICE

QoS

Quality of service. Refers to the guaranteed data throughput.

An important issue in the delivery of real-time data over a network (for example, VoIP) is quality of service (QoS). The following are QoS issues for a VoIP network:

- Jitter
- Network latency and packet loss
- Queuing

This section examines each of these issues and how each affects the quality of real-time voice data delivery.

Jitter

Jitter

Produces a poorly reconstructed signal at the receiver due to variability in data packet arrival.

Digitized voice data requires a fixed time interval between data packets for the signal to be properly converted back to an audible analog signal. However, there is a delay problem with transported voice data over a packet network. Variability in data packet arrival introduces jitter in the signal, which produces a poorly reconstructed signal at the receiver. For example, assume that a 1,000-Hz tone is sent over a VoIP network. The tone is digitized at regular time intervals, assembled into frames and packets, and sent out as an RTP packet. Random delays in the packets' travel to the destination result in their arriving at irregular time intervals. The reproduced 1,000-Hz analog tone will contain jitter because the arrival times for each data packet will vary.

Part a of Figure 11-8 shows an accurately reconstructed sine wave, and part b of Figure 11-8 shows an unstable sine wave. This signal will contain significant distortion and may not even sound like a 1000-Hz tone at all. (*Note*: The bandwidth of a typical telephone call is 300–3,000 Hz. The 1,000-Hz tone was selected because it falls in the typical bandwidth for voice.)

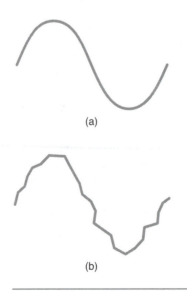

(a)

(b)

FIGURE 11-8   An example of (a) an accurately reproduced sine wave and (b) a sine wave with jitter

Buffering the data packets long enough for the next data packet to arrive can minimize the effects of jitter. A buffer is temporary storage for holding data packets until it is time for them to be sent. The buffer enables the data packets to be output at regular time intervals, thereby removing most of the jitter problem. Buffering works as long as the arrival time of the next packet is not too long. If the arrival time is too late, the data packet might have to be considered "lost" because the real-time data packets can't wait too long for the buffered packet without affecting the quality of the reconstructed signal. Another issue is that the buffering stage introduces delay, and having to wait additional time only introduces more delay.

Network Latency

It takes time for a data packet to travel from the source to the destination. This is called network latency, and it becomes an important issue in VoIP data traffic. Telephones (both traditional and IP) feed a portion of the user's voice into the earpiece. If the round-trip delay of the voice data is too lengthy (> 50 ms), the user will begin to hear an annoying echo in the earpiece.

Delay issues can be minimized by making sure the network routers and switches are optimized for VoIP data traffic. The VoIP network can be configured so that high-priority data packets (for example, voice packets) are transported first over the IP network. Nonsensitive data packets are given a low-priority status and are transmitted only after the high-priority packets are sent.

Another source of packet delay is network congestion. This can have a negative effect on any type of data traffic but is very disruptive to VoIP telephony. The network administrator must make sure that congestion problems are avoided or at least minimized and could have the option of configuring the routers to optimize routes for IP telephony.

One technique used to minimize congestion problems is to configure the network routers and switches to intelligently discard lower-priority packets. This technique is called weighted random early discard (WRED). This is done to maintain acceptable data traffic performance of an integrated data and VoIP network. A dropped TCP/IP data packet will typically cause the TCP data packet flow to slow down. Recall from Chapter 5, "Configuring and Managing the Network Infrastructure," that TCP issues a window size value to the number of data packets that the receiver can accept without acknowledgment. If a packet is lost, the window size decreases until an acceptable window size is obtained that doesn't produce lost data packets. As a result, the intentionally dropped data results in a slowdown in data traffic and a less congested network.

Queuing

Queuing is another technique the network administrator can use to improve the quality of service of data traffic by controlling the transfer of data packets. The administrator must identify the data traffic that must be given priority for transport. The queuing decision is made when the data packet arrives, is first queued, and placed in a buffer. There are many types of queuing arrangements, with the most basic being FIFO (first in, first out). In this case, the data packets are placed in the queue on arrival and transmitted when the channel is available.

Weighted Fair Queuing (WFQ)

Used to determine what data traffic gets priority for transmission.

CBWFQ

Class-based weighted fair queuing. Enables the network administrator to define the amount of data traffic allocated to a class of data traffic.

PQ

Priority queuing. Used to make sure the important data traffic gets handled first.

CQ

Custom queuing. Reserves a portion of the channel bandwidth for selected data traffic.

Spit

Spam over Internet telephony. A situation where the VoIP network can be saturated with unsolicited bulk messages broadcast over the VoIP network.

class map

Defines a group or a selection of IP telephony endpoints.

policy map

Used to specify a series of actions to be performed on each criteria match of the class map.

A technique called **weighted fair queuing (WFQ)** is available on many routers and is used to determine what data traffic gets priority for transmission. This technique applies only if the buffer is full, and a decision must be made as to which data packet goes first. WFQ can be modified to provide a class-based weighted fair queuing (**CBWFQ**). This improvement enables the network administrator to define the amount of data traffic allocated to a class of data traffic (for example, VoIP).

Other queuing techniques are PQ and CQ. Priority queuing (**PQ**) is used to make sure the important data traffic gets handled first. Custom queuing (**CQ**) reserves a portion of the channel bandwidth for selected data traffic (for example, VoIP traffic). This is a decision made by the network administrator based on experience with the network. The problem with CQ is that it doesn't make allowances for other traffic management when the channel is full; therefore, queuing techniques, such as WFQ or WRED, can't be used to manage the data flow. The queuing techniques available to the network administrator are as follows:

- **FIFO** (first in, first out)
- **WFQ** (weighted fair queuing)
- **CBWFW** (class-based weighted fair queuing)
- **PQ** (priority queuing)
- **CQ** (custom queuing)

Two additional areas for consideration in regards to QoS for VoIP are incorporating the use of VLANs within your network to separate voice and data traffic and securing your voice traffic:

- **VLANs for VoIP**: When deploying VoIP on LANs, it is recommended that a separate VLAN be created on your network for IP telephony. The advantage of this is the voice and data networks are kept separate. Network slowdowns or security threats to the data network will not affect the VoIP network or are at least kept to a minimum.
- **Securing the VoIP network**: The traditional PBX used in telephony is not typically vulnerable to the security threats that occur on data networks. However, VoIP networks are vulnerable to similar security threats. The most serious threat to VoIP traffic is denial of service (DoS) attacks. DoS attacks work by flooding the network with server requests or excessive data traffic. The result is a severe degradation in the QoS available for VoIP telephony. Another threat to the quality of service is **spam over Internet telephony** (**spit**). In this case, the VoIP network can be saturated with unsolicited bulk messages broadcast over the VoIP network.

QOS Configuration Example

A minimum typical QOS configuration consists of a class map, and a policy-map. A **class map** defines a group or a selection of IP telephony endpoints. A class map can be configured to match based on Layer 3, Layer 4, or even Layer 7 classifications. A **policy map** is used to specify a series of actions to be performed on each criteria match of the class map:

```
class-map match-any Voice
 match access-group 101
 match ip dscp ef
class-map match-any Signaling
 match access-group 102
 match ip dscp af33
!
!
policy-map WAN
 class Voice
    priority percent 30
 class Signaling
    bandwidth percent 5
  class class-default
    fair-queue
!
access-list 101 remark  _____
access-list 101 remark  ACL for QoS class-map Voice for VoIP
access-list 101 remark  ----------------------------------------
access-list 101 permit udp 10.99.55.0 0.0.0.255 any range 16384 32767
access-list 102 remark  _____
access-list 102 remark  ACL for QoS class-map Signaling for VoIP
access-list 102 remark  ----------------------------------------
access-list 102 permit tcp any any range 2000 2002
access-list 102 permit tcp any any range 5060 5061
```

The example shows two class maps: one is called Voice and another is called Signaling. The class map, Voice, is created by matching either the traffic as specified by access list 101 or the DSCP value. The access list 101 defines traffic from the network 10.99.55.0/24 to any UDP port in the range of 16,384 to 32,767. VoIP uses the UDP traffic within the range to voice packet transmission. If a match is not found, the class map will match the packet based on the DSCP value. **DSCP** (Differentiated Services Code Point) is the six most significant bits of the Diffserv Field in the IP header. DSCP is used to specify a QoS value of an IP endpoint. The class map specifies that the value of DSCP field in the IP header must be set to **EF** (Expedited Forwarding), which has a binary value of 101110. Another class map, Signaling, is created to ensure the VoIP signaling or handshake. This class map matches either the traffic specified by access list 102 or the DSCP value. The first statement in the access list 102 defines any TCP traffic to port 2000, 2001, and 2002 and the second statement defines any TCP traffic to port 5060 and 5061. Another match used by the class map is the DSCP value of **AF33** (Assured Forwarding class 3), which has a binary value of 011110. Once a class map is defined, a policy map called WAN is then created to associate the class maps to the QoS actions. In this case, the class map Voice will be guaranteed 30 percent of the bandwidth of the interface to which it is applied. The class map will be guaranteed 5 percent of the bandwidth of the interface to which it is applied. The rest of the bandwidth will be given to the default class, which is the traffic that is not defined by the class maps.

An important QoS and safety issue is the ability to place emergency 911 calls using your phone system. The traditional phones that connect to the PSTN can be traced to your location. However, VoIP calls are a transfer between IP addresses and, with VoIP,

DSCP (Differentiated Services Code Point)
Six most significant bits of the Diffserv Field in the IP header.

EF
A class map that specifies that the value of DSCP field in the IP header is set to Expedited Forwarding.

AF33
Assured Forwarding class 3. Created to ensure the VoIP signaling or handshake.

there currently isn't a way to determine the physical location of the caller. However, the FCC has developed the Enhanced 911 (E911) feature to address this problem. The E911 standard requires all VoIP service providers to pass the name and the address information to the nearest Public Safety Access Point (PSAP) when 911 is dialed. It is important that you verify that your VoIP service provider supports E911.

Another important QoS issue is the potential loss of service due to power outage. Traditional phones that are operated by the PSTN maintain operation during power outages because they operate on stand-by power. Of course, the VoIP system can be designed to operate with a battery backup system, but this can be a substantial investment. A possible solution is to keep a regular telephone as a backup, but this will add to your overall operational cost.

This section has presented the key quality of service issues in the delivery of real-time data (VoIP). The network administrator must be aware of these techniques and how each can be used to improve the VoIP QoS. The administrator must also be aware of the tradeoff that optimizing an IP network for VoIP traffic can have on the data network.

11-4   ANALYZING VOIP DATA PACKETS

This section examines the packets exchanged during VoIP calls using both voice over Ethernet and Voice over IP. The VoIP data collected for the voice over Ethernet discussion were generated from an IP telephone network that contained two IP telephones and a call processor. Figure 11-9 shows a block diagram of the setup for the circuit. The communications used for these phones is running at Layer 2, the data link layer. The IP phones and the call processor were configured with IP addresses, but the phones are in the same LAN, and IP routing was not necessary. This setup is similar to the phone setup in an office or a small business. The MAC addresses for the networking equipment are listed in Table 11-2.

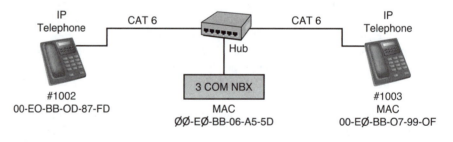

FIGURE 11-9   The setup used to collect the VoIP telephone call data packets

TABLE 11-2   MAC Addresses for Networking Equipment Used When Gathering VoIP Data Packets

Networking Device	MAC Address
Phone (#1002)	00-E0-BB-0D-87-FD
Phone (#1003)	00-E0-BB-07-99-0F
Call processor	00-E0-BB-06-A5-5D

There are some basic codes used by this particular call processor to identify the packet running over the Ethernet network. These codes identify the type of message that is being issued, such as voice data packets, request packets, and acknowledgments. These codes, listed and described in Table 11-3, will be used when analyzing the VoIP data traffic.

TABLE 11-3   IP Telephone Call Packet Codes for the Call Processor

Code	Letter	Description
0x41	A	Voice data packets
0x48	H	Acknowledgment
0x52	R	Request packet, issued when a button is pressed
0x55	U	Update

The following discussion is for a set of voice call data packets obtained using the setup shown in Figure 11-9. The first packet examined is number 7. This packet is from the call processor (MAC 00-E0-BB-06-A5-5D). It is acknowledging that the #1003 phone has been picked up. Phone #1003 has a MAC address of 00-E0-BB-07-99-0F. The data in Figure 11-10 indicates Extension:1003 has been picked up. The code for the call is the hexadecimal numbers (0x48 52). The code is shown boxed in Figure 11-10. This code indicates that the packet includes an acknowledgment (48) and a request (52). In the next data sequence, the #1003 phone begins to dial #1002. The following data packets show the call processor's acknowledgment (code 48) of the buttons as they are pushed. Only the contents of the data packet will be displayed. The sequence is provided in Figure 11-11 (a–d).

The next sequence first shows the call processor notifying phone #1003 that it is dialing #1002 in Figure 11-12. Figure 11-13 shows phone #1002 acknowledging the call from the call processor, basically coming online. The codes (48 48) are acknowledgments that the request was received.

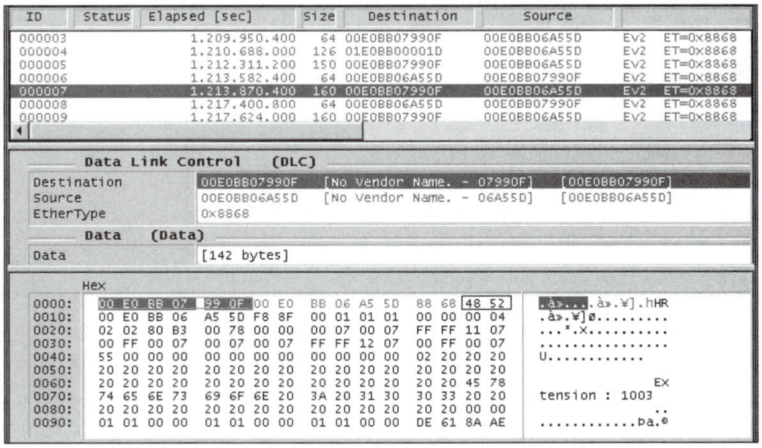

FIGURE 11-10   The acknowledgment that phone #1003 has been picked up

Figure 11-11 (a)

```
     Hex
0000:  00 E0 BB 07  99 0F 00 E0  BB 06 A5 5D  88 68 48 52    .à»....à».¥].hHR
0010:  00 E0 BB 06  A5 5D F8 91  00 01 01 01  00 00 00 04    .à».¥]ø.........
0020:  02 02 80 B3  00 78 00 00  00 07 00 07  FF FF 11 07    ...ª.X..........
0030:  00 FF 00 07  00 17 00 17  FF FF 12 07  00 FF 00 07    ................
0040:  55 00 00 03  00 00 00 03  00 00 00 00  02 20 20 20    U...........
0050:  20 20 20 20  20 20 20 20  20 20 20 20  20 20 20 20
0060:  20 20 20 20  20 20 20 20  20 20 20 20  20 20 31 20                 1
0070:  20 20 20 20  20 20 20 20  20 20 20 20  20 20 20 20
0080:  20 20 20 20  20 20 20 20  20 20 20 20  20 20 00 00                 ..
0090:  01 01 00 00  01 01 00 00  01 01 00 00  C1 10 63 1F    ..........Á.c.
00A0:
```

(a)

Figure 11-11 (b)

```
     Hex
0000:  00 E0 BB 07  99 0F 00 E0  BB 06 A5 5D  88 68 48 52    .à»....à».¥].hHR
0010:  00 E0 BB 06  A5 5D F8 93  00 01 01 01  00 00 00 04    .à».¥]ø.........
0020:  02 02 80 B3  00 78 00 00  00 07 00 07  FF FF 11 07    ...ª.X..........
0030:  00 FF 00 07  00 17 00 07  FF FF 12 07  00 FF 00 07    ................
0040:  55 00 00 03  00 00 00 03  00 00 00 00  02 20 20 20    U...........
0050:  20 20 20 20  20 20 20 20  20 20 20 20  20 20 20 20
0060:  20 20 20 20  20 20 20 20  20 20 20 20  20 20 31 30                10
0070:  20 20 20 20  20 20 20 20  20 20 20 20  20 20 20 20
0080:  20 20 20 20  20 20 20 20  20 20 20 20  20 20 00 00                 ..
0090:  01 01 00 00  01 01 00 00  01 01 00 00  0E 77 B1 9C    ...........w±.
00A0:
```

(b)

Figure 11-11 (c)

```
     Hex
0000:  00 E0 BB 07  99 0F 00 E0  BB 06 A5 5D  88 68 48 52    .à»....à».¥].hHR
0010:  00 E0 BB 06  A5 5D F8 96  00 01 01 01  00 00 00 04    .à».¥]ø.........
0020:  02 02 80 B3  00 78 00 00  00 07 00 07  FF FF 11 07    ...ª.X..........
0030:  00 FF 00 07  00 17 00 07  FF FF 12 07  00 FF 00 07    ................
0040:  55 00 00 03  00 00 00 03  00 00 00 00  02 20 20 20    U...........
0050:  20 20 20 20  20 20 20 20  20 20 20 20  20 20 20 20
0060:  20 20 20 20  20 20 20 20  20 20 20 20  20 20 31 30               100
0070:  30 20 20 20  20 20 20 20  20 20 20 20  20 20 20 20
0080:  20 20 20 20  20 20 20 20  20 20 20 20  20 20 00 00                 ..
0090:  01 01 00 00  01 01 00 00  01 01 00 00  8B 5A 42 39    ...........ZB9
00A0:
```

(c)

Figure 11-11 (d)

```
     Hex
0000:  00 E0 BB 07  99 0F 00 E0  BB 06 A5 5D  88 68 48 52    .à»....à».¥].hHR
0010:  00 E0 BB 06  A5 5D F8 97  00 01 01 01  00 00 00 04    .à».¥]ø.........
0020:  02 02 80 B3  00 78 00 00  00 07 00 07  FF FF 11 07    ...ª.X..........
0030:  00 FF 00 07  00 17 00 07  FF FF 12 07  00 FF 00 07    ................
0040:  55 00 00 03  00 00 00 03  00 00 00 00  02 20 20 20    U...........
0050:  20 20 20 20  20 20 20 20  20 20 20 20  20 20 20 20
0060:  20 20 20 20  20 20 20 20  20 20 20 20  20 20 31 30              1002
0070:  30 32 20 20  20 20 20 20  20 20 20 20  20 20 20 20
0080:  20 20 20 20  20 20 20 20  20 20 20 20  20 20 00 00                 ..
0090:  01 01 00 00  01 01 00 00  01 01 00 00  55 B8 B6 00    ...........U.¶.
00A0:
```

(d)

FIGURE 11-11   (a) The acknowledgment that phone #1003 has pressed number "1"; (b) the acknowledgment that phone #1003 has pressed number "1 0"; (c) the acknowledgment that phone #1003 has pressed number "1 0 0"; (d) the acknowledgment that phone #1003 has pressed number "1 0 0 2"

```
     Hex
0000:  00 E0 BB 07  99 0F 00 E0  BB 06 A5 5D  88 68 48 52    .à»....à».¥].hHR
0010:  00 E0 BB 06  A5 5D F8 99  00 01 01 01  00 00 00 04    .à».¥]ø.........
0020:  02 02 80 B3  00 78 00 00  00 07 00 07  FF FF 11 07    ...ª.X..........
0030:  00 FF 00 07  00 27 03 27  FF FF 12 07  00 FF 00 07    .....'.'........
0040:  55 00 00 03  00 00 00 03  00 00 00 00  02 20 44 69    U............Di
0050:  61 6C 69 6E  67 20 20 20  20 20 20 20  20 20 20 20    aling
0060:  20 20 20 20  20 20 20 20  20 20 20 20  20 20 31 30                10
0070:  30 32 3A 4E  65 77 20 55  73 65 72 20  20 20 20 20    02:New User
0080:  20 20 20 20  20 20 20 20  20 20 20 20  20 20 00 00                 ..
0090:  01 01 00 00  01 01 00 00  01 01 00 00  25 85 43 47    ...........%.CG
00A0:
```

FIGURE 11-12   The message from the call processor that it is dialing #1002

```
     Hex
0000:  00 E0 BB 06  A5 5D 00 E0  BB 00 87 FD  88 68 48 48    .à».¥].à»..ý.hHH
0010:  00 E0 BB 0D  87 FD F5 44  00 01 01 01  00 03 00 00    .à».ýõD.........
0020:  00 00 00 00  00 00 00 00  00 00 00 00  00 00 00 00    ................
0030:  00 00 00 00  00 00 00 00  00 00 00 00  82 04 04 2E    ................
0040:  40 22 1F 7B                                           @".{
```

FIGURE 11-13   The acknowledgment of the call from phone #1002 back to the call processor

Phone #1002 has acknowledged the call, and now the call processor will go through multiple management steps to complete the call. This is shown in Figure 11-14. Notice in Figure 11-14 that the UDP data packets are being used with a source IP address of 192.168.12.6. This is the IP address of the call processor. The destination IP address for the highlighted data packet is 224.0.1.59. This is a multicast address used by the call processor to manage the call setup and functions. This is used only for call setup. Once the call is set up, the IP phones will begin transferring the voice data. This is shown in Figure 11-15. The code for the data packets has changed to (41), which is for "voice" data packets. Notice that the source and destination MAC addresses are alternating during the conversation. The IP phones are communicating directly without further need of the call processor. The data shown at the bottom of Figure 11-15 is the PCM voice data.

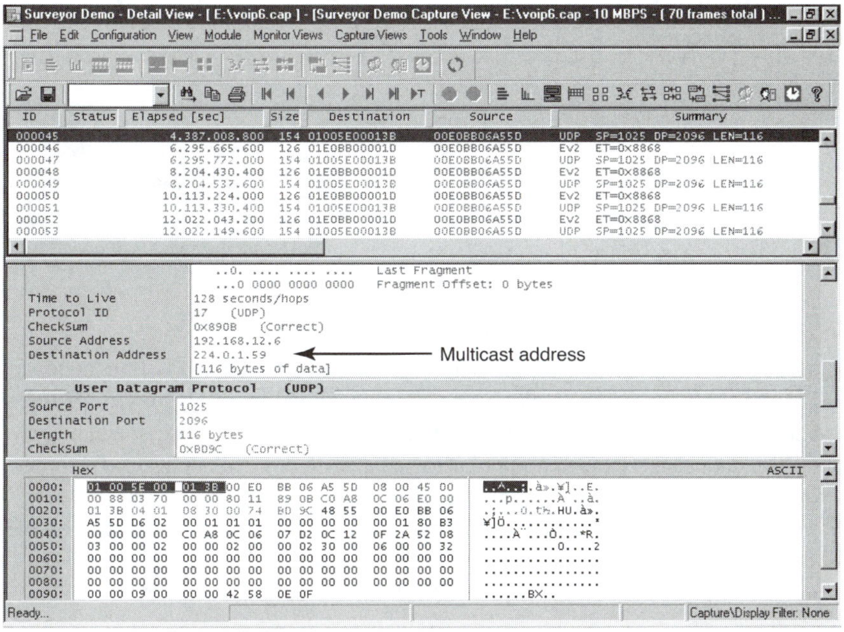

FIGURE 11-14 The call processor's management steps to set up the phones so that voice data transfer can begin

This section has demonstrated the call setup and signaling for establishing an IP telephone call within a local area network. The transfer of the voice data packets between IP phones has also been shown. The reader should understand how the basic call was established and how to identify the type of message using the call codes (see Table 11-3). The reader should also understand that the call processor uses multicast addresses to set up the call before handing it over to the IP phones.

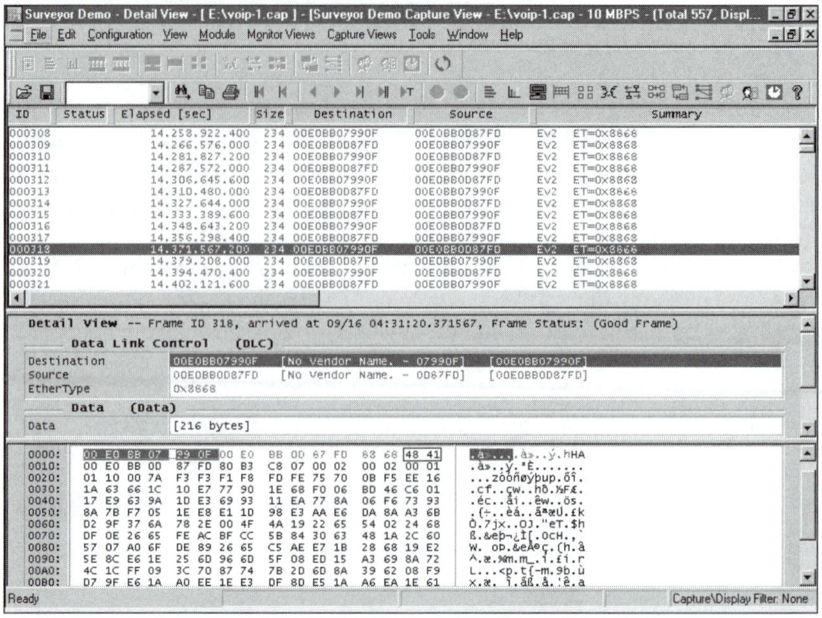

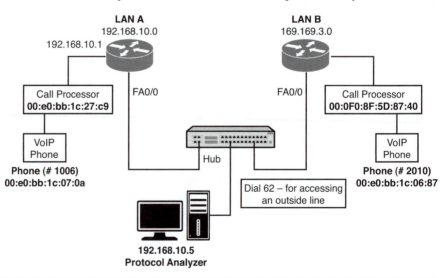

The screenshot shows a Surveyor Demo protocol analyzer capture view with frame details.

FIGURE 11-15 The exchange of voice packets (code 41) between the two IP phones

Analyzing VoIP Telephone Call Data Packets

This section examines the data packets that are being exchanged in a VoIP telephone call. The test setup for the VoIP telephone call is shown in Figure 11-16. This picture shows that the network consists of two VoIP telephones, two call processors, and two routers. The data packets were captured using a network protocol analyzer. The computer running the protocol analyzer and the two call processors were connected to a networking hub so that each share the Ethernet data link. This was done so that all the VoIP data packets being exchanged between the telephones, the call processors, and the routers could be captured at the same time with one protocol analyzer.

FIGURE 11-16 The test setup for the VoIP telephone call

In the following example, a telephone call is being placed from extension 1006 to the 62-2010 extension. The first packet examined is number 5, shown in Figure 11-17. This packet source is from the LANA call processor with the MAC address of 00:E0:BB:1C:27:C9. The HR text (indicated by the arrow) is an acknowledgment that extension 1006 (00:e0:bb:1c:07:0a) was picked up to dial the call. The call packet codes for the call processor are listed in Table 11-3. H (0x48) is an acknowledgment, and R (0x52) is a request packet that is issued when a button is pushed.

Packet number 19 (see Figure 11-18) shows the call processor (00:E0:BB:1C:27:C9) acknowledging back to extension 1006 (00:e0:bb:1c:07:0a) dialing the number 62 to go outside the network (LAN A) to talk to the destination phone in LANB. The 62 is the number used by the call processor to get an outside telephone line. This is defined in the call processors call plan. Once again, the HR code is listed at the beginning of the data packet. The HR codes will repeat throughout the call setup, Figure 11-19 (a–d).

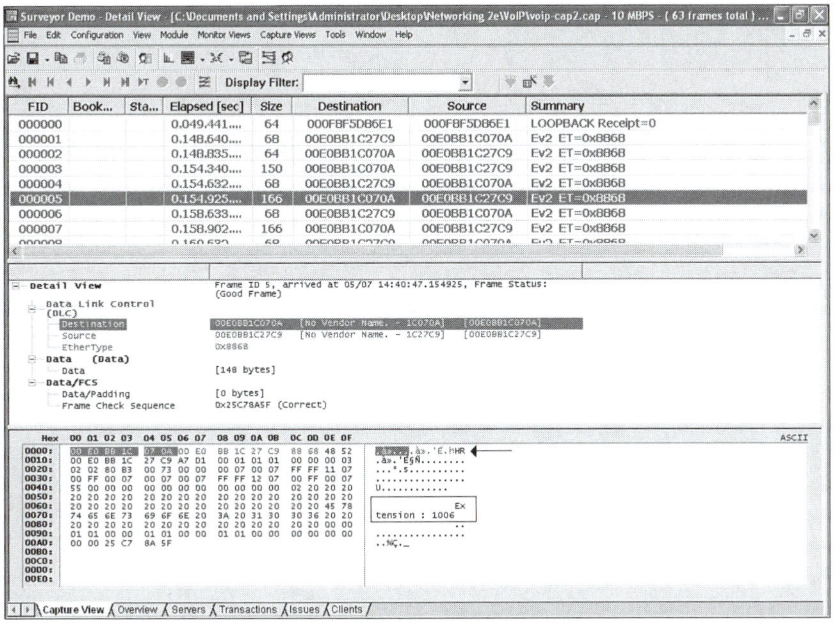

FIGURE 11-17 The acknowledgment that extension 1006 was picked up

- Packet number 23 (see Figure 11-19 [a]) is showing ext. 1006 dialing the first number "2" in the corresponding phone number on LAN B.

- Packet number 27 (see Figure 11-19 [b]) is showing ext. 1006 dialing the second number in the corresponding phone number on LAN B.

- Packet number 33 (see Figure 11-19 [c]) is showing ext. 1006 dialing the third number in the corresponding phone number on LAN B.

- Packet number 39 (see Figure 11-19 [d]) is showing ext. 1006 dialing the forth number in the corresponding phone number on LAN B.

- Packets 41–52 (see Figure 11-19) are showing the handshaking between the two networks. Notice that the source and destination have changed to the IP addresses for the VoIP telephone call.

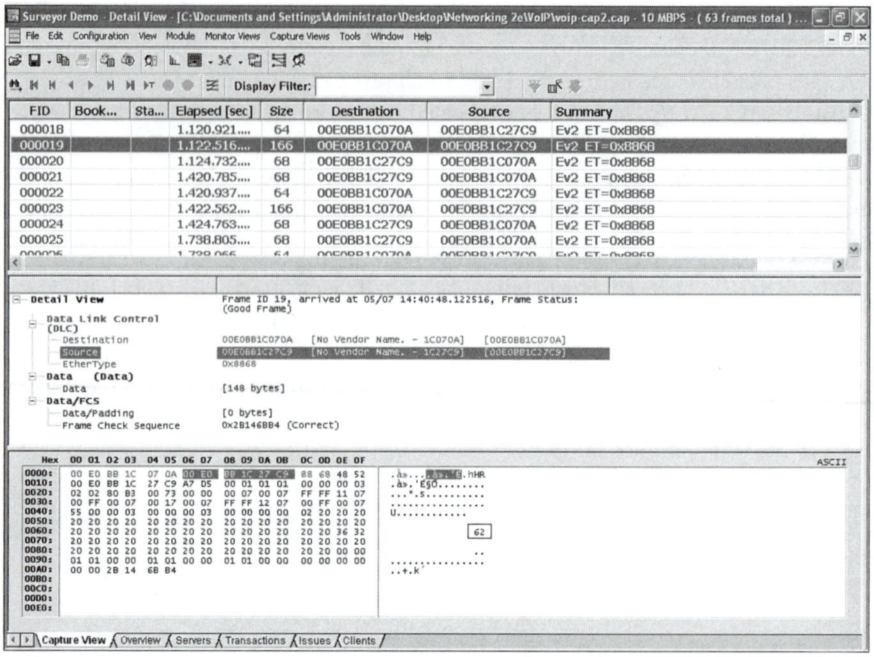

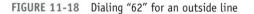

FIGURE 11-18   Dialing "62" for an outside line

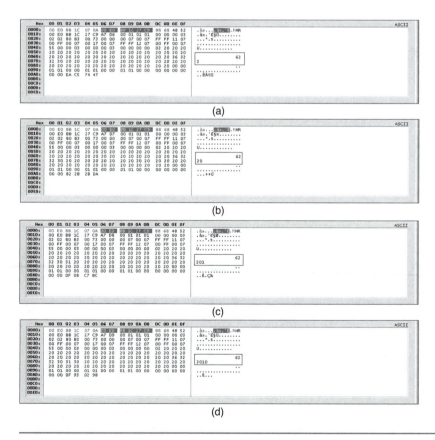

(a)

(b)

(c)

(d)

FIGURE 11-19   Dialing the outside line at 62–2010

Finally, Figure 11-20 shows the packets exchanged between the two IP phones.

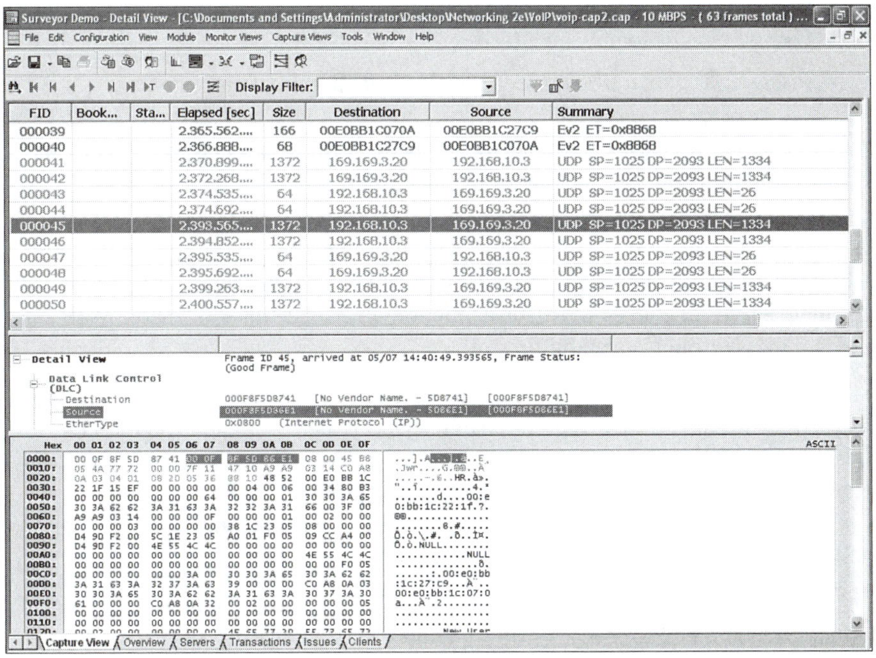

FIGURE 11-20   The handshaking between the two IP networks and the start of the VoIP telephone call

This section demonstrated the call setup and signaling for establishing a VoIP telephone call within two networks. The student should understand how the basic call was established (same as voice over Ethernet) and that dialing "62" was required to get an access line.

11-5   VOIP SECURITY

A question you might ask is if there are security issues with VoIP data traffic? It was shown in this chapter that the network set up and data traffic for VoIP are similar to the expected data traffic in any network. Therefore, similar security concerns exist. For example, the VoIP network can be attacked, so there is a potential for packet sniffing, eavesdropping, and denial of service (DoS). The threat of eavesdropping presents the potential problem that the VoIP data packets can be intercepted. If the packets are intercepted, then it is possible that the audio portion of a phone conversation can be replayed using free software that converts the VoIP data packets to .wav or .au files.

What steps does the network administrator need to take to protect and secure a VoIP network? Possible security steps include the following:

- Encrypting the VoIP data traffic
- Using firewalls to prevent attacks
- Route VoIP data traffic on separate LANs than normal data traffic

Techniques for encrypting VoIP data traffic include IPsec and the Transport Layer Security (TLS). IPsec is a suite of protocols used for securing network connections. This is applied to the call set up and the conversation data packets. The TLS protocol enables network devices (including VoIP devices) to securely communicate across a network. Once a connection is established, both members of the network negotiate a stateful connection. This is important because this will enable VoIP data traffic to pass through a stateful firewall.

> **Secure Real Time Protocol (SRTP)**
> This protocol provides confidentiality, message authentication, and replay protection of VoIP data.

Many VoIP systems use RTP (Real Time Transport Protocol [refer to Section 11-1]) for the transmission of real-time Internet telephony. The problem is RTP is considered to be insecure and the possibility exists of someone eavesdropping on conversations. A solution to this problem is the use of the **Secure Real Time Protocol (SRTP)**. This protocol provides confidentiality, message authentication, and replay protection of VoIP data.

There are many possible threats to VoIP networks. The most common categories of threats include the following:

- **Availability:** Phone systems are intended to be operation 24x7. This means that any threat to availability is a concern. Threats of this type can include interruption of service, call flooding, and call hijacking.

- **Confidentiality:** Ensures that information is not accessed by unauthorized persons.

- **Integrity:** A concern is the verification that the message has not been intercepted and altered. The attacker can potentially alter the message.

- **Social Context:** This concern addresses the issue where an attacker misrepresents himself to the victim thereby creating trust that enables the attacker to be a trusted member of the network.

Firewalls allow traffic from inside the network to exit but don't allow general traffic from the outside to enter the network. The firewall monitors the data traffic and recognizes where packets are coming from. The firewall will allow packets from the outside to enter the network if they match a request from within the network.

In a *stateful firewall,* the inbound and outbound data packets are compared to determine if a connection should be allowed. This includes tracking the source and destination port numbers and sequence numbers as well as the source and destination IP addresses. This technique is used to protect the inside of the network from the outside world but still allow traffic to go from the inside to the outside and back. The firewall needs to be stateful to accomplish this.

As stated in Section 11-3, a good rule is to route VoIP data traffic on separate LANs from traditional data traffic. This will help protect both networks from possible intrusions and viruses. At least if one network is compromised then the other network will remain unaffected.

Another issue to be aware of is that adding security to a VoIP network has the potential of affecting quality of service issues (refer to Section 11-3). The three potential issues that can be affected include

- Latency
- Jitter
- Packet loss

Latency is the time for a data packet to travel from the source to the destination. This is called *network latency*, and it becomes an important issue in VoIP data traffic. Telephones (both traditional and IP) feed a portion of the user's voice into the earpiece. If the round-trip delay of the voice data is too lengthy (> 50 ms), then the user will begin to hear an annoying echo in the earpiece. Variability in data packet arrival introduces *jitter* in the signal, which produces a poorly reconstructed signal at the receiver. The same is also true for packet loss which results in a poorly reconstructed signal.

Is it easy for the attacker to intercept VoIP calls? It actually takes someone who is technically sophisticated to intercept VoIP telephone calls. VoIP systems have two possible types of vulnerabilities. The first is the level of network security that is running the VoIP data traffic. Threats of intrusion and denial of service for VoIP networks are the same that exist in a traditional data network. A well-protected infrastructure will help to better secure the network.

The second issue consists of the security issues associated with the VoIP protocols and the many pieces of VoIP hardware required to setup the network. There are many pieces required to put together a VoIP network and with it are the introduction of many security threats. The VoIP network will never be 100 percent secure, but adding a suite of security tools, including hardware and software, will make the network fairly secure.

SUMMARY

This chapter presented an introduction to Voice over IP telephony. The network administrator must be aware of the impact of integrating VoIP into the network. Advancements in technology are making the integration of voice and data easier, but along with the simplification comes the requirement that the network administrator fully comprehend the capabilities and limitations of the technologies. The student should understand the following concepts:

- How IP telephony interfaces with the PSTN
- The signaling techniques used by IP telephony
- The steps for preparing the VoIP signal for transport
- How VoIP can be integrated into a company's network
- The quality of service (QoS) issues for VoIP
- The importance of using VLANs for VoIP traffic within the LAN
- The potential security threats for VoIP
- The types of data packets issued when setting up a VoIP call

QUESTIONS AND PROBLEMS

Section 11-1

1. Define *PBX*.

2. Define *PSTN*.

3. What is the purpose of a *gateway*?

4. List four enhanced features of SS7.

5. What are the signaling techniques used in IP telephony?

6. What are RTP and RTCP used for in VoIP?

7. What does a processor in a VoIP receiver do if a voice data packet is lost?

8. How is the timestamp on VoIP data packets used?

Section 11-2

9. What are three ways a company can implement VoIP into their network?

10. What is a standard solution for combining voice and data traffic?

11. What is the purpose of a VoIP gateway?

12. What is another term for a VoIP gateway?

13. What are two advantages of replacing an existing PBX tie line with a VoIP/data network?

14. What is the disadvantage of replacing an existing PBX tie line with a VoIP network?

15. List two advantages of upgrading the PBX to support VoIP.

16. What does it mean for a company to switch to a complete IP solution?

Section 11-3

17. What are three QoS issues for a VoIP network?

18. What causes jitter in the received signal?

19. How can the effects of jitter be minimized?

20. When does buffering the received data packets not work in VoIP?

21. What is network latency?

22. What causes network data traffic congestion?

23. What is *WRED*, and what is its purpose?

24. What is the basic form of queuing?

25. What is *WFQ*, and what is its purpose?

26. What is the purpose of priority queuing?

27. Which queuing technique reserves channel bandwidth for selected data traffic?

28. What is the purpose of a class map?

29. What is the purpose of a policy map?

30. What is the purpose of the E911 standard for VoIP service.

31. Why is loss of power a more important issue for VoIP systems?

Section 11-4

32. What is the purpose of the basic codes used by the NBX call processor?

33. Which code identifies voice data packets?

34. What does the code 0x52 identify?

35. What is the purpose of multicasting in IP telephony?

Section 11-5

36. What three steps should be taken to protect and secure the VoIP network?

37. What is the purpose of the TLS protocol?

38. How does SRTP protect and secure a VoIP network?

39. What is the most common category of possible threats to a VoIP network? List each category and a brief definition.

40. What is stateful firewall, and why is it required for VoIP systems?

41. Why is eavesdropping a potential problem in VoIP networks?

Critical Thinking

42. Prepare a technical memo to your supervisor that explains how VoIP can be implemented on your local network.

43. Use the Internet to find out what queuing systems are currently recommended for data traffic.

44. The following is a sample QoS configuration on a Cisco router. Answer the following questions based on this configuration:

```
class-map match-any Voice
 match access-group 110
 match ip dscp ef
class-map match-any Signaling
 match access-group 120
 match ip dscp af33
 !
 !
policy-map WAN
 class Call
    priority percent 25
 class Ringing
    bandwidth percent10
  class class-default
    fair-queue
 !
access-list 110 remark _____
access-list 110 remark  ACL for QoS class-map Call for VoIP
access-list 110 remark -----------------------------------------
access-list 110 permit udp  192.168.10.0  0.0.0.255 any range
16384 32767
access-list 120remark _____
access-list 120 remark  ACL for QoS class-map Ringing for VoIP
access-list 120remark -----------------------------------------
access-list 120 permit tcp any any range 2000 2002
access-list 120 permit tcp any any range 5060 5061
```

a. What does access list 110 define?

b. What does the access list 129 define?

c. What is the purpose of the policy-map WAN?

d. How much of the interface bandwidth is guaranteed for the class map Call?

e. How much of the interface bandwidth is guaranteed for the class map Ringing?

f. How much of the interface bandwidth is guaranteed for the class map default?

KEY TERMS GLOSSARY

6to4 Prefix A technique that enables IPv6 hosts to communicate over the IPv4 Internet.

802.1Q This standard defines a system of VLAN tagging for Ethernet frames.

2001:DB8::/32 Prefix This IPv6 address prefix is reserved for documentation. This is recommended by RFC3849 to reduce the likelihood of conflict and confusion when using the IPv6 address in examples, books, documentation, or even in test environments.

.int Intergovernmental domain registries is used for registering organizations established by international treaties between or among national governments.

{master} The prompt indicating you are in the master routing engine mode on a Juniper router.

A Record (Address Record) This maps a hostname to an IP address.

AAA Authentication, Authorization, and Accounting.

ABR Area border routers.

Access Layer Where the networking devices in a LAN connect together.

Access Lists (ACL) A basic form of firewall protection used to tell a networking device who and what are allowed to enter or exit a network.

ACK Acknowledgment packet.

address-family ipv6 The command used to specify that IPv6 is specified.

Administrative Distance (AD) A number assigned to a protocol or route to declare its reliability.

Advertise The sharing of route information.

AES Advance Encryption Standard. A 128-bit block data encryption technique.

AF33 Assured Forwarding class 3. Created to ensure the VoIP signaling or handshake.

AH Authentication Header. A security protocol used by IPsec that guarantees the authenticity of the IP packets.

AMI Alternate mark inversion. A fundamental line coding scheme developed for transmission over T1 circuits.

Anycast Address Obtained from a list of addresses.

Area 0 In OSPF, this is the root area and is the backbone for the network.

Area ID Analogous to OSPF area number, and it is used by L2 routers.

Areas The partition of a large OSPF network into smaller OSPF networks.

ARIN American Registry for Internet Numbers. Allocates Internet Protocol resources, develops consensus-based policies, and facilitates the advancement of the Internet through information and educational outreach.

ARP Address Resolution Protocol, used to map an IP address to its MAC address.

arp -a The command used to view the ARP cache.

ARP Broadcast Used to inform everyone on the network that it now is the owner of the IP address.

ARP Reply A network protocol where the MAC address is returned.

AS Autonomous System. These numbers are used by various routing protocols and are a collection of connected Internet Protocol (IP) routing prefixes. Autonomous systems separate organizational networks.

ASN Autonomous systems number is used to distinguish separate networks and to prevent routing loops.

at Asynchronous Transmission Mode (ATM) connection for a Juniper router.

ATM Asynchronous transfer mode.

Authoritative Name Server A name server that is authorized and configured to answer DNS queries for a particular domain or zone.

Automatic Private IP Addressing (APIPA) A self-assigned IP address in the range of 169.254.1.0–169.254.254.255.

autonomous-system [AS_Number] This command is used in JUNOS to define the BGP AS for the router.

B8ZS Bipolar 8 zero substitution. A data encoding format developed to improve data transmission over T1 circuits.

Backbone The primary path for data traffic to and from destinations and sources in the campus network.

Backup Designated Router (BDR) The router or routers with lower priority.

Bandwidth Having to do with the data capacity of the networking link; a Fast-Ethernet 100 Mbps link has greater data capacity than a 10 Mbps Ethernet link.

`bandwidth` Command used to adjust the bandwidth value.

Bash Bourne again shell.

Beacon Used to identify a wireless link.

BGP Border Gateway Protocol.

BGP Best Path Selection Algorithm Used to compare the possible routes and to select the best route.

BGP4+ The version of BGP for running IPv6.

Binding An association of the IP address to the DHCP server.

BOOTP Bootstrap Protocol. A network protocol used by a network client to obtain an IP address from a configuration server.

BPDU Filter Feature that effectively disables STP on the selected ports by preventing them from sending or receiving any BPDU messages.

BPDU Guard Feature used to prevent a STP Portfast to receive any BPDU message to modify the Spanning Tree topology.

Broadcast Domain Any broadcast sent out on the network is seen by all hosts in this domain.

Buffer Temporary storage for holding data packets until it is time for them to be sent.

`cat` Linux command used to print the file text to the screen.

CBWFQ Class-based weighted fair queuing. Enables the network administrator to define the amount of data traffic allocated to a class of data traffic.

CCMP Counter Mode with Cipher Block Chaining Message Authentication Code Protocol. An encryption protocol designed for wireless LANs.

ccTLDs Country-code (cc) top-level domains. Includes .us, .uk, .ca, and .au.

`cd` Linux command for changing directories.

CDP Cisco Discovery Protocol. Proprietary protocol is used to obtain the platform and the protocol addresses of neighboring devices.

CHAP Challenge Handshake Authentication Protocol. An encrypted authentication method that uses the MD5 hashing algorithm.

`chgrp` Linux command used to change group ownership of a file.

`chkconfig` Command used by administrators to enable and disable services at boot time.

`chmod` Command used in Linux to change permissions on files and directories.

`chown` Linux command used to change ownership of a file.

CIDR Classless Interdomain Routing.

class map Defines a group or a selection of IP telephony endpoints.

Class Network Address The network portion of the IP address based on the class of the network.

Classful Addressing The network portion of a particular network address.

CNAME (Canonical Name) Record Generally called an alias of a hostname.

`cnls routing` The global command for IS-IS.

CODEC Encodes, compresses, and decodes the data.

Collector Stores and analyzes the flow information.

command line A text entry level for commands.

`commit` JUNOS command used to save changes to the configuration file.

`commit and- quit` JUNOS command used to save the configuration and exit the configuration mode.

Connectionless Network Service (CLNS) IS-IS is designed to work on the same network layer just like IP; therefore, it does not require an IP protocol for it to function.

Connection-Oriented Protocol Establishes a network connection, manages the delivery of data, and terminates the connection.

Convergence This happens when a router obtains a clear view of the routes in a network. The time it takes for the router to obtain a clear view is called the convergence time.

copy run start The command for copying the running-configuration to the startup-configuration.

Core The Backbone of the Network.

Cost A value typically assigned by the network administrator that takes into account bandwidth and expense.

Cost Paths A cost it takes to route traffic along the path from the source to the destination.

Country Domain Usually, two letters, such as United States (.us) or Canada (.ca), that define the location of the domain server for that country.

cp Linux command to copy files.

CQ Custom queuing. Reserves a portion of the channel bandwidth for selected data traffic.

crypto key generate rsa Command used to generate an RSA key.

CSU/DSU Channel service unit/data service unit.

Datagram A self-contained entity that carries sufficient information to be routed from source to destination without relying on previous data exchanges between the source and destination computers or the transporting network. Also known as a data packet.

Dead Time The Hello time interval an OSPF router will wait before terminating adjacency with a neighbor.

default-metric *bandwidth delay reliability load MTU* The command for setting the default metric.

Delay The time it takes for a data packet to travel from source to destination.

delay This command sets the delay on the interface. The delay value is measured in tens of microseconds.

Demilitarized Zones A physical or logical network designed to house the public servers that will have direct exposure from the outside network.

Denial of Service (DoS) Means that a service is being denied.

DES, 3DES Data Encryption Standard, Triple Data Encryption Standard. A symmetrical encryption algorithm.

description The command to enter a description.

Designated Router (DR) The router with the highest priority.

destination unreachable This error is displayed indicating that the destination node received the packet and discarded it because it could not deliver the packet.

DHCP Dynamic Host Configuration Protocol. The protocol used to assign a pool of IP addresses to requesting clients.

DHCP ACK A unicast packet sent back to the client with the same IP information.

DHCP Discover This is a broadcast, meaning that the message is sent to all computers in the LAN.

DHCP Offer The DHCP server listening on the LAN will take the packet, retrieve an available IP address from the address pool, and send the address to the client.

DHCP Request Formally request and confirm the offered IP with the server.

Diffee-Hellman Key generation algorithm. Used to generate a shared session secret key to encrypt the key exchange communications.

Dig (Domain Information Groper) A DNS lookup utility.

Directed Broadcast The broadcast is sent to a specific subnet.

Distance Vector Protocol A routing algorithm that periodically sends the entire routing table to its neighboring or adjacent router.

Distributed Denial of Service (DDoS) Attack An attack that comes from a potentially large number of machines.

Distribution Layer Point where the individual LANs connect together.

dmesg Command used to display the boot processes for Linux, used to identify why certain processes failed.

DNS Domain Name Service.

domain registrars Has control over the granting of domains within certain top-level domains.

Double-Colon Notation A technique used by IPv6 to remove 0s from the address.

DS Digital signal.

DSCP (Differentiated Services Code Point) Six most significant bits of the Diffserv Field in the IP header.

DTP Dynamic Trunking Protocol. Used to automatically negotiate a switch port to be either an access port or a trunk port.

Duplicate Address Detection (DAD) Process of detecting another machine with the same IPv6 address.

Dynamic NAT A one-to-one mapping from an available global pool.

Dynamic Routing Protocols The routing table is dynamically updated to account for loss or changes in routes or changes in data traffic.

Dynamic VLAN Ports are assigned to a VLAN based on either the computer's MAC address or the username of the client logged onto the computer.

E2 An OSPF external type 2 route.

E911 Enhanced 911. Requires all VoIP service providers to pass the name and the address information to the nearest Public Safety Access Point (PSAP) when 911 is dialed.

EAP Extensible Authentication Protocol. A general protocol used for supporting multiple authentication methods.

eBGP External Border Gateway Protocol—BGP between separate ASNs.

Echo Request Part of the ICMP protocol that requests a reply from a computer.

Edge Router Describes the Internet connection to network.

edit policy-options JUNOS command used to enter the mode so the set policy statement can be entered.

edit protocols rip JUNOS command that places you in the mode to configure RIP routing.

edit routing-options static JUNOS command that places you in the mode to configure the static route.

EF A class map that specifies that the value of DSCP field in the IP header is set to Expedited Forwarding.

EGP Exterior Gateway Protocol is a routing protocol that's used to exchange routing information between hosts in a network of autonomous systems.

EIGRP Enhanced Interior Gateway Routing Protocol.

Equal-Cost Load Balancing A way to distribute traffic equally among multiple paths.

ERRDISABLE In this state, the port is automatically disabled by the switch operating system software because an error condition has been encountered on the port.

ESP Encapsulating Security Protocol. A security protocol used by IPsec that provides confidentiality to the data messages (payloads) by ways of encryption.

eth0, eth1, eth2, ... The way Linux identifies the Ethernet interface cards.

eui-64 Command option that allows the router to choose its own host identifier.

EX External EIGRP type.

EXEC Level Password Used to gain access to EXEC commands.

executable (x) permission Allows the program or script to run.

exit interface A router interface will be specified as the outgoing interface that is used to forward packets to the destination network.

export JUNOS command used to apply a policy.

family inet6 JUNOS command to enable the IPv6 family address.

FE80::/64 The prefix for a link-local address.

FIFO First in, first out. The data packets are placed in the queue on arrival and transmitted when the channel is available.

Filter List Juniper's non-stateful packet filter.

Firefox The Linux web browser.

Firewall Used in computer networks for protecting the network.

First Queued Describing when the data packet arrives.

Flat Network A network where the LANs share the same broadcast domain.

floating static route Static backup route.

Forward DNS Translation of a name to an IP address.

FP The Format Prefix that is made up of the higher order bits. The 001 indicates that this is a global unicast address. The current list of the IPv6 address allocation can be viewed at http://www.iana.org/assignments/ipv6-unicast-address-assignments. Currently, IANA allocates 2000::/3 as an IPv6 global pool. 2000 can be written in binary as 0010 0000 0000 0000. 001 is the 3 highest order bits, which correspond to the FP.

FQDN Fully qualified domain name.

fstab The file that contains the arguments used when the Linux mount command for a drive has been requested.

Full IPv6 Address All 32 hexadecimal positions contain a value other than 0.

Gateway Describes the networking device that enables hosts in a LAN to connect to networks (and hosts) outside the LAN.

Gateway of Last Resort The IP address of the router in your network where data packets with unknown routes should be forwarded.

Global Address Defines any IP address that is on the outside of or external to the network.

Global Unicast Addresses These are equivalent to the public IP addresses in IPv4.

GRE Generic Routing Encapsulation. A simple IP packet encapsulation protocol developed by Cisco System, commonly used as a site-to-site VPN solution because of its simplicity and versatility.

gTLDs Generic (g) top-level domains. Includes .com, .net, .org, and .info.

H.323 Suite of protocols that defines how voice and video are transported over IP networks.

Hacked Attacked.

HDLC High-level data link control, a synchronous proprietary protocol.

Hello Interval The time between Hello packets.

Hello Packets Periodically sent in link state protocols (typically associated with OSPF) to initiate and maintain communications with neighbor routers.

Hidden Files Files that start with a period and that can only be viewed with the **ls -la** or **ls -al** command.

history Command that displays the commands entered on the command line in Linux.

Hop count The number of routers the data packet must pass through to reach the destination network.

Host Enables a specific host IP address to be entered in the access list.

httpd The script that starts the web server.

httpd.conf The configuration file for the Apache web server.

Hybrid Routing Protocol Protocol that incorporates the best of the distance vector and link-state algorithms.

IANA Internet Assigned Numbers Authority that is responsible for the global coordination of the DNS Root, IP addressing, and other Internet Protocol resources.

iBGP Internal Border Gateway Protocol—BGP between the same ASN.

ICANN Internet Corporation of Assigned Names and Numbers. This organization coordinates the Domain Name System (DNS), Internet Protocol (IP) addresses, space allocation, protocol identifier assignment, generic (gTLD), country code (ccTLD), top-level domain name system management, and root server system management functions.

IETF Internet Engineering Task Force.

ifconfig Command that reports all the network devices recognized and running on the system, listing all the interfaces and the configuration for each.

ifdown, ifup Linux commands used to shut down and bring back up the network interface.

IGP Interior Gateway Protocol.

IKE Internet Key Exchange. A hybrid protocol that encompasses several key management protocols, most notably Internet Security Association and Key Management Protocol.

in-addr.arpa The reverse DNS lookup for IPv4 addresses on the Internet.

inet Output from the JUNOS show interfaces brief command indicating an IP address.

Integrated IS-IS Term indicating IS-IS was adapted to work with IP.

Interface Cost One of the factors used in calculating the best path.

Interface ID The Link Level Host Identifier is used to indicate an interface on a specific subnet. The interface ID is equivalent to the host IP address in IPv4.

Interface Identifier The host portion of the IPv6 address.

interface VLAN 1 The default VLAN for the switch.

Internal Ethernet Interfaces The main communications link between the JUNOS software and the router's packet forwarding engines.

Internet Sockets An endpoint across a computer network.

Inter-Switch Link (ISL) The Cisco proprietary VLAN tagging protocol.

InterVLAN routing Enables communications among VLANs.

Intranets Internetwork that provides file and resource sharing.

ip helper [*ip address of the DHCP server*] The router command used to enable the router's DHCP relay function.

ip route The router configuration command for manually setting the next hop IP address.

ip router isis Command that specifies the network that will be using IS-IS for routing.

IP Tunnel An IP packet encapsulated in another IP packet.

ipconfig/release Command used to release the current IP address.

ipconfig/renew Command used to initiate the DHCP process.

IPng Next generation IP.

IPsec The IETF standard for securing the IP communications between the network nodes by authenticating and encrypting the session.

IPv6 IP version 6.

ipv6 address *ipv6 interface address* The command used to configure the IPv6 address on an interface.

ipv6 enable Command that enables IPv6 on a specific interface.

IPv6 Stateless Autoconfiguration Enables IPv6-enabled devices that are attached to the IPv6 network to connect to the network without requiring support of an IPv6 DHCP server.

ipv6 unicast-routing This command activates the IPv6 forwarding mechanism on the routers.

ISAKMP Internet Security Association and Key Management Protocol. A protocol for establishing Security Associations (SA) and cryptographic keys in an Internet environment.

IS-IS Interior Gateway Routing Protocol.

ISP Internet service provider: An organization that provides Internet access for the public.

Jflow Juniper's IP traffic flow technology.

Jitter Produces a poorly reconstructed signal at the receiver due to variability in data packet arrival.

JUNOS The operating system used by Juniper routers.

kill [*PID*], **kill -9 [*PID*]** Linux commands used to kill a process.

L1 Routers Analogous to OSPF nonbackbone routers.

L1/L2 Routers Analogous to OSPF area border routers.

L2 Routers Analogous to OSPF backbone routers.

L2F Layer 2 Forwarding.

L2TP Layer 2 Tunneling Protocol.

last Command used to display logins to the Linux system.

Layer 3 Network Another name for a routed network.

LEAP Lightweight Extensible Authentication Protocol. A wireless security system used by Cisco.

Lease Time The amount of time that a client can hold an IP address.

Line Password Used to gain access to the router.

Link State Advertisement (LSA) The exchange of updated link state information when routes change.

Link State Protocol Establishes a relationship with a neighboring router and uses route advertisements to build routing tables.

Link-Local Address Indicates the IP address was self-configured.

lo The Linux symbol representing the loopback.

Load Having to do with the network activity on a link or router.

Load Balancing A procedure in the protocol that enables routers to use any of the multiple data paths available from multiple routers to reach the destination in order to equally distribute data traffic on a per-packet basis.

Local Address Defines any IP address that is on the inside of or internal to the network.

Logical Address This describes the IP address location of the network and the address location of the host in the network.

Loopback The data is routed directly back to the source.

ls Linux command that lists the basic files in the directory.

ls -l Linux command that lists file attributes.

ls -la Linux command that allows you to see hidden files in addition to the file attributes.

ls system-config- * Linux command for listing the system configuration tools.

man Command used to display the online text manual for Linux.

Management Ethernet Interfaces Enable the router to establish both SSH and Telnet connections.

Management Information Base (MIB) A collection of standard objects that are used to obtain configuration parameters and performance data on a networking device.

MD5 Message Digest 5. A cryptographic hash function that produces a 128-bit (16-byte) hash value.

Metric A numeric measure assigned to routes for ranking the routes best to worst; the smaller the number, the better.

Minimum Ones Density A pulse is intentionally sent in the data stream even if the data being transmitted is a series of all 0s.

mkdir Linux command to make a directory.

more Linux command used to display the contents of a text file.

mount Linux command used to access external drives.

MT ACK Message type acknowledgment, a DHCP ACK packet.

MT Discover Message type discover, a DHCP Discover packet.

MT Offer Message type offer, a DHCP offer packet.

MT Request Message type request, a DHCP request packet.

Multicast Address Data packets sent to a multicast address are sent to the entire group of networking devices such as a group of routers running the same routing protocol.

Multicast Listener Discovery (MLD) Enables the switches to listen to MLD packets to determine how to efficiently forward multicast packets to specific listeners on specific ports.

Multi-Homed This means the customer has more than one network connection.

Multilayer Switch (MLS) Operates at Layer 2, but functions at the higher layers.

Multi-Services Card Enables expanded services, such as stateful firewall protection and Network Address Translation.

mv Linux command for moving or renaming a file.

MX Record Specifies the email handling server of the domain.

NAT Network Address Translation. A technique used to translate an internal private IP address to a public IP address.

NAT Overload Another name for PAT.

ncftp An FTP application for Linux.

ND Protocol Network Discovery Protocol. Used by an IPv6 router to periodically advertise ICMPv6 messages of the type Router Advertisement (RA) on the links to which it is connected.

Neighbor ID The highest IP address defined by the loopback address of the neighbor router ID.

neighbor [*ip address*] remote-*as number* The next command is for specifying the IP address of the BGP neighbor.

neighbor *IPv6_address* activate Command used to establish BGP peering with the neighbor.

neighbor *IPv6_address* remote as *AS_Number* Command used to specify a BGP peer.

Neighbor Solicitation Purpose of this solicitation is to discover the link-layer address of another IPv6 node or to confirm a previously determined link-layer address.

NET Network Entity Title.

Net Mask Linux name for the subnet mask.

NetFlow Used to acquire IP traffic operational data in order to provide network and security monitoring, traffic analysis, and IP accounting.

netstat Utility used to display information such as network statistics, routing table, and TCP/UDP connections.

netstat -ap Provides information about the network connections.

netstat -r The command used to obtain the routing table for a host PC computer.

Network Address Another name for the Layer 3 address.

Network Address Translation (NAT) A technique used to translate an internal private IP address to a public IP address.

Network Forensics The steps required for monitoring and analyzing computer network data traffic.

network *IPv6_network* Command used to specify the IPv6 networks that will be advertised to its peer.

Network Latency The time it takes for data packets to travel from source to destination.

Network Mask A 32-bit value used to divide sections of IP addresses.

Network Number Another name for the IP subnet.

Network Prefix The network portion of the IPv6 address.

Network Service Access Point Selector (NSEL) Identifies the network service type.

network start Brings up the network interfaces.

network stop Shuts down all network interfaces.

nmap A Linux port scanner.

no auto-summary This instructs the router not to summarize the network routes.

no bgp default ipv4-unicast Command used to allow protocols other than IPv4 to be activated within the multiprotocol BGP (BGP4+).

no switchport Cisco command to convert the native switch port to a router port.

Non-Authoritative Answer A name lookup answer received by a client via a non-authoritative server.

NS Record Specifies the name of the authoritative name server of the domain.

nslookup A DNS lookup utility.

NTP Network Time Protocol. A protocol that synchronizes the router's clock with the time server.

null0 interface A virtual bit-bucket interface where every packet gets discarded.

oc-3 155.52-Mbps connection.

oc-12 622.08-Mbps connection.

Open Authentication A null authentication that can enable any client to authenticate to an AP.

openssh The secure shell application for Linux.

OSPF Open Shortest Path First routing protocol.

OSPFIGP Open Shortest Path First Interior Gateway Protocol.

Out of Band Management Indicates that an additional interface can be used to connect to the router if the main network is down.

Overloading Where NAT translates the home network's private IP addresses to a single public IP address.

Packet Filtering A technique used to determine whether a packet is allowed to enter or exit the network.

Packet Sequence Number Used to keep track of the order of the data packets.

PAP Password Authentication Protocol. A simple, clear-text (unencrypted) authentication method.

Path Determination A procedure in the protocol that is used to determine the best route.

PBX Private branch exchange. The user's own telephone system.

Peering How an agreement is made for the exchange of data traffic between large and small ISPs or between a router and its neighbor router.

Permanent Interfaces Defined to be either Management or Internal Ethernet interfaces.

permit ip any any The instruction added to the last line of an access list to allow all other data packets to enter and exit the router.

PIC Physical interface card.

PID Process ID.

ping6 Command used to explicitly specify the IPv6 address.

policy map Used to specify a series of actions to be performed on each criteria match of the class map.

Port Address Translation (PAT) Port Address Translation. A port number is tracked with the client computer's private address when translating to a public address. A technique that uses the port number to identify the computer that established the Internet connection; also called many-to-one NAT and NAT overload.

Port-Based VLAN Host computers connected to specific ports on a switch are assigned to a specific VLAN.

PPP Point-to-Point Protocol. A full duplex protocol used for serial interface connections such as that provided by modems.

pps Packets per second. A measure of the data transfer rate.

PPTP Point to Point Tunneling Protocol. Designed to work in conjunction with a standard PPP.

PQ Priority queuing. Used to make sure the important data traffic gets handled first.

PQDN Partial qualified domain name.

preferred Used after the JUNOS `ip address` statement to signify the primary IP address.

Prefix Length Number of bits used to make up the network prefix.

Privacy Extensions for Stateless Address Autoconfiguration Allows the generation of a random identifier with a limited lifetime.

protected Drops packets from the violated MAC address(es).

Protocol-Based VLAN Connection to ports is based on the protocol being used.

Proxy Server An agent for handling requests from clients seeking resources.

ps Linux command used to list processes running on the machine.

PSTN Public switched telephone network—the telephone company.

PTR Record (Pointer Record) The reverse of an A record.

pwd Linux command to print the working (current) directory.

Q Cnt The number of EIGRP packets being queued to its neighbor.

QoS Quality of service. Refers to the guaranteed data throughput.

Queuing Provides control of the data packet transfer.

RA Messages Router advertisement. This is a response to a link-local router solicitation message.

RADIUS Remote Authentication Dial-In User Service. Widely used for authenticating remote users and authorizing user access.

re0 { and re1 { ... Identifies the system configuration for the routing engines 0 and 1 on a Juniper router.

`reboot` Command used to gracefully shut down the Linux machine and reboot.

`redistribute connected` The command issued to redistribute the connected networks.

`redistribute connected subnets` Allows the classless network to be distributed.

`redistribute eigrp` *AS_id* [`metric` *0-16777214*] The command to redistribute EIGRP routes into RIP.

`redistribute eigrp` *AS_number* `metric` *0-16* Command in to redistribute EIGRP routes into RIP.

`redistribute isis` *IS-IS_Level* The command to redistribute EIGRP routes into IS-IS.

`redistribute isis` *IS-IS_Level* `metric` *0-16* Command in to redistribute IS-IS routes into RIP.

`redistribute ospf` *process_id* `metric` *0-16* The command to redistribute OSPF routes into RIP.

`redistribute` *protocol* The command used to injecting routes from one routing protocol into another routing protocol.

`redistribute rip` The command to redistribute RIP into OSPF.

`redistribute rip metric` *bandwidth delay reliability load MTU* The command to redistribute RIP routes into EIGRP.

`redistribute static` The command issued to redistribute the static networks.

`redistribute static subnets` Command that allows the static network to be distributed.

Reliability A measure of the reliability of the link, typically in terms of the amount of errors.

resolv.conf Contains the list of DNS servers for the Linux machine.

`restrict` The same as the protected mode, but it will also send SNMP trap messages to the SNMP server.

Reverse DNS Translation of an IP address to a name.

RID Router ID.

RIP Routing Information Protocol.

rip_tag `ipv6 router rip` Command option used to identify the RIP process.

RIPng Routing Information Protocol next generation, which is required to support IPv6 routing.

RIRs Regional Internet registries. The RIRs are the organizations that actually allocate IP addresses to ISPs.

rising threshold/failing threshold When the traffic rises above the rising threshold, the interface drops that specific traffic until the traffic comes down below the failing threshold.

`rm` Linux command to delete a file.

`rmdir` Linux command to remove a directory.

Root Access The user has the rights to make changes to operating and user parameters.

`route add default gw` Linux command used to specify the gateway address.

Route Flapping Intermittent routes going up and down creating excessive LSA updates.

`route print` Command that produces same displayed result as **netstat -r**.

Routed Network Uses Layer 3 addressing for selecting routes to forward data packets.

`router bgp` *AS* The command entered to run BGP.

Router Dead Interval The length of time a router neighbor is quiet (no Hello packets) before assuming the neighbor is dead.

Router Interface The physical connection where the router connects to the network.

`router isis` Command that starts the IS-IS routing protocol.

router on a stick Eliminates connecting a link from each VLAN to a router port by utilizing a trunk or 802.1Q port.

Router Solicitation Messages These messages are sent to ask routers to send an immediate RA message on the local link so the host can receive the autoconfiguration information.

Routing Loop Data is forwarded back to the router that sent the data packets.

Routing Protocols Provide a standardized format for route management.

Routing Redistribution The technique of injecting routes from one routing protocol into another routing protocol.

Routing Table Keeps track of the routes to use for forwarding data to its destination.

routing table code C The router code for specifying a directly connected network.

routing table code S The router code for a static route.

RR Resource record.

RTCP Real Time Control Protocol. Used to manage packet synchronization and identification and the transport of the data.

RTP Real Time Protocol.

Secondary IP Address Allows multiple Layer 3 networks to reside on the same physical link.

Secure Real Time Protocol (SRTP) This protocol provides confidentiality, message authentication, and replay protection of VoIP data.

`service-module t1` The router command for configuring T1 framing, line coding, and the clock source.

`set group [`*BGP_group_name*`] neighbor [`*next_hop_address*`]` Command used to define the BGP neighbor on a Juniper router.

`set group [`*BGP_group_name*`] type [external/internal]` Command used in JUNOS to specify the type of BGP (external or internal).

`set metric` *value* JUNOS command for setting the metric value in OSPF.

`set policy-statement` JUNOS command for setting a routing policy.

`set protocols isis interface` *interface* JUNOS command for setting the protocol to IS-IS.

`set protocols ospf area` *area* `interface` *interface* `hello-interval` *seconds* `dead-interval` *seconds* JUNOS command for setting the protocol to OSPF.

set router-id [_ip_address_**]** This command is used in JUNOS to define the BGP router BGP identifier.

Sflow A traffic flow technology developed by InMon.

sh ip bgp sum The command used to see whether the routers are exchanging BGP routes.

SHA-1 Secure Hash Algorithm. It is used to ensure the data integrity of the IP packets.

Sharekey Authentication Both the client and the access point share a key called a pre-shared key (PSK).

`show arp` The command to view the ARP cache on Cisco switches and routers.

`show bgp ipv6 unicast summary` Command to view the summary status of the IPv6 BGP neighbor.

`show clns interface` The command used to verify the IS-IS interface metric.

`show clns is-neighbors` Command used in IS-IS to find adjacencies with neighbors.

`show controller T1` *slot/port* Cisco command to verify the status of the T1 interface.

`show interface status` Cisco command used to verify the status of a switchport.

`show interfaces trunk` Cisco command used to verify the 802.1Q configuration.

`show ip bgp` Command that displays the summary contents of the BGP routing table.

`show ip bgp neighbor` This command displays BGP neighbor relationship with its peer.

`show ip eigrp neighbors` The command used to display the EIGRP adjacency neighbor.

`show ip eigrp topology` Command used to view the composite metric of the current EIGRP topology, the command.

`show ip interface brief (sh ip int brief)` Cisco command to verify the status of the router interfaces.

`show ip protocol (sh ip protocol)` Command that displays the routing protocol running on the router.

`show ip route (sh ip route)` The command that displays the routes and the routing address entry into the routing table.

`show ip route isis (sh ip route isis)` Command that displays only the IS-IS routes.

`show ip route static (sh ip route static)` Command that limits the routes displayed to only static.

`show ipv6 interface` Command used to show the state of the IPv6 configuration on the interface.

`show isis adjacency` JUNOS command used to view the IS-IS adjacency status and its connected IS-IS adjacent routers.

`show rip neighbor` JUNOS command used to display RIP neighbors.

`show route` JUNOS command used to display all routes.

`show route protocol rip` JUNOS command used to display only RIP routes.

`show running-config (sh run)` The command that displays the router's running-configuration.

`show startup-config (sh start)` The command that displays the router's startup-configuration.

`show vlan` Cisco command used to verify what ports have been defined for the switch.

`show vlan name` *vlan-name* Cisco command to look specifically at only one of the VLANs.

`shutdown` This shuts down the port and puts the port in ERRDISABLE state.

`shutdown -h now` Command used to gracefully shut down Linux.

Signaling Used to establish and terminate telephone calls.

SIP Session Initiation Protocol. Used to manage multimedia packet transfers over IP networks.

SLA ID The Site Level Aggregation Identifier that is used by individual organizations to identify subnets within their site. The SLA ID is 16 bits long.

SMB Server message block. A protocol used by Windows computers to share folders, printers, and serial ports to other computers on the same network.

Smurf Attack A way of generating a large amount of data traffic.

SNMP (SNMPv1) Simple Network Management Protocol.

`snmp community [`*community string*`]` SNMP Community string is a user ID or password that allows access to a network device's statistics.

SNMPv2 Simple Network Management Protocol version 2.

SNMPv3 Simple Network Management Protocol version 3.

SOA Start of Authority.

SOHO Small office or home office network.

SPF Sender Policy Framework.

Spit Spam over Internet telephony. A situation where the VoIP network can be saturated with unsolicited bulk messages broadcast over the VoIP network.

Spoof Inserting a different IP address in place of an IP packet's source address to make it appear that the packet came from another network.

SRV Record Used to identify a host or hosts that offer that specific type of service.

SS7 Signaling technique used by the PSTN.

SSID Service set identifier. A 32 alphanumeric character unique identifier that's attached to data packets transmitted over a wireless network (WLAN). The SSID is essentially a password that enables the client to connect to the access point.

SSIP Secure Session Initiation Protocol. Provides for end-to-end secure communications by requiring user authentication.

State of FULL Indicates that the routers are fully adjacent to each other.

Stateful Firewall The inbound and outbound data packets are compared to determine if a connection should be allowed.

Stateless Address Autoconfiguration (SLAAC) Allows a server-less basic network configuration of the IPv6 computers.

Static NAT A fixed one-to-one mapping of an inside IP address to an outside IP address.

Static Route A data traffic route that has been manually entered into either a router's or a computer's routing table.

Static VLAN Basically, a port-based VLAN.

storm-control Used to limit the amount of unicast, multicast, or broadcast packets that each port can receive.

STP Portfast This speeds up the STP process and transitions the port into a forwarding state bypassing the listen and learn states.

STP Root Guard Feature that allows participation in spanning tree and BPDU messages as long as the attached device does not attempt to become the root bridge.

Stubby Areas Do not accept routes from the Internet.

su Linux command used to become another user on the system.

Subnet, NET Other terms for the segment.

Supernet Two or more classful contiguous networks are grouped together.

SVI Switched virtual interfaces.

Switched Virtual Circuit (SVC) A dynamic virtual circuit that is established on demand by end devices through the Network-Network Interface signaling method.

switchport mode trunk Cisco command to turn on trunking.

switchport port-security The command to enable the port security.

switchport trunk allowed vlan *vlan-id* Cisco command used to limit the VLANs that can be carried across the link.

switchport trunk encapsulation dot1q Cisco command that defines that 802.1Q tagging protocol is being used.

switchport trunk encapsulation isl Cisco command that defines that the tagging protocol is ISL.

SYN Synchronizing packet.

SYN ACK Synchronizing Acknowledgment packet.

SYN Attack This attack refers to the opening up of many TCP sessions to limit access to network services.

Synchronous Optical Network (SONET) Used to interconnect the router and the network to other WANs.

System ID Analogous to the OSPF router ID, and it is used by L1 routers.

system-config- *tool-name* Linux command for displaying the system configuration GUI for a specified tool.

t3/ds3 card Provides for a 44.736-Mbps data rate connection.

Tagged-Based VLAN Used VLAN ID based on 802.1Q.

TCP Transport Control Protocol.

TDM Time division multiplexing.

Telnet Terminal emulation application for TCP/IP networks.

terminal monitor (*term mon***)** Cisco command to display log messages on the remote terminal.

terminal no monitor (*term no mon***)** Cisco command to disable the logging to the terminal.

TFTP Trivial File Transfer Protocol.

Ticks The measured delay time in terms of clock ticks, where each tick is approximately 55 milliseconds (1/18 second).

Tie Line Line used to interconnect PBXs.

Timestamp Reproduces playback of the voice packets with the same time interval as they were recorded.

TKIP Temporal Key Integrity Protocol. Generates a sequence of WEP keys based on a master pre-shared key and rekeys periodically every 10,000 packets.

TLA ID (0x2002) The Top Level Identifiers are issued to local Internet registries. These IDs are administered by IANA (http://www.iana.org/). The TLA is used to identify the highest level in the routing hierarchy. The TLA ID is 13 bits long.

TLD Top-level domain.

`top` JUNOS command that takes the user out of the current configuration section and back to the top of the configuration mode.

Totally Stubby Areas Use only a default route to reach destinations external to the autonomous system.

`traceroute` *destination-ip-address* Command used to discover the routes the data packets actually take when traveling from the source to the destination.

`traceroute6` The router tool that enables the user to see the routing information between the two hosts.

`tracert` *destination-ip-address* The command used to trace packets on a PC.

`tracert6` The Windows tool that enables the user to see the routing information between the two hosts.

Transient Interfaces These interfaces both receive and transmit data to/from the network.

`transport input none` This command prevents the remote access to the console port via reverse-telnet with the command.

Transport Layer Protocols Define the type of connection established between hosts and how acknowledgements are sent.

Trunk Port A switch interface or port configured to carry multiple VLANs.

TXT Record Used to hold arbitrary text information of the domain.

Type 5 Uses MD5 hash for encryption.

Type 7 Uses a Cisco encryption algorithm.

UDP User Datagram Protocol. A connectionless protocol that transports data packets being established and without any acknowledgment that the data packets arrived at the destination.

`umount` Linux command used to unmount a drive.

Unicast The packet has a fixed destination.

Unicast Address Used to identify a single network interface address, and data packets are sent directly to the computer with the specified IPv6 address.

Up Arrow Used to display the previously entered commands stored in the Linux history buffer.

Uptime Indicates the time the neighbor has last established its adjacency.

V4ADDR The IPv4 address of the 6to4 endpoint and is 32 bits long.

Variable Length Subnet Masks (VLSM) Allows the use of subnet masks to better fit the needs of the network, thereby minimizing the waste of IP addresses when interconnecting subnets.

VCI Virtual channel identifier.

Violation Action Defines the action taken if a switchport is violated.

Virtual Channel Connection (VCC) Carries the ATM cell from user to user.

Virtual Path Connection (VPC) Used to connect the end users.

VLAN (Virtual LAN) A group of host computers and servers that are configured as if they are in the same LAN, even if they reside across routers in separate LANs.

`vlan` [*vlan_id*] The IOS global command used to create VLAN ID.

`vlan database` The command used on older Cisco switches to enter the VLAN database.

VLAN ID Used to identify that a frame belongs to a specific VLAN.

VoIP Voice over IP telephony. Protocol used to pass digitized voice over packet networks.

VoIP Gateway Provides the proper signaling of digitized voice data for transport over the IP network.

VoIP Relay Another name for a VoIP gateway.

VPI Virtual path identifier.

VPN Virtual private network. Enables the remote clients to become part of the trusted network by establishing a secure connection between the remote end and the private network.

VWIC Voice/WAN interface cards.

w Linux command that displays the names of the users presently logged into the system plus additional details on each user.

WAN Wide-area network.

Weighted Fair Queuing (WFQ) Used to determine what data traffic gets priority for transmission.

Weighted Random Early Discard (WRED) Network routers and switches are configured to intelligently discard lower priority packets.

Well-Known Ports Ports reserved by ICANN.

WEP Wired equivalent privacy. WEP provides a secure wireless channel by encrypting the data so that it is protected as it is transmitted from one end point to another.

who Linux command that displays the names of the users presently logged into the system.

whois protocol Queries databases that store user registration information of an Internet domain name and an IP space.

WIC WAN interface cards.

Wild Card Bits Used to match network IP addresses to interface IPs.

Wire Speed Routing Data packets are processed as fast as they arrive.

WPA Wi-Fi Protected Access. Replaces WEP as the primary way for securing wireless transfers, and it supports the user authentication provided by 802.1x.

write memory (wr m) The command that saves your configuration changes to memory.

yum provides [*filename*] Linux command that searches the yum database and returns the name of the file that matches the query.

INDEX

Numbers

Symbols

A